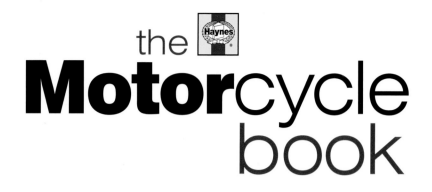

the
Motorcycle
book

First published in September 2002

A catalogue record for this book is available from the British Library

ISBN 1 85960 868 X

Library of Congress catalog card no. 2001099295

Published by Haynes Publishing, Sparkford, Yeovil, Somerset BA22 7JJ, England

Tel: 01963 442030 Fax: 01963 440001
Int. tel: +44 1963 442030 Int. Fax: +44 1963 440001
E-mail: sales@haynes-manuals.co.uk
Website: www.haynes.co.uk

Haynes North America, Inc.,
861 Lawrence Drive, Newbury Park,
California 91320, USA

Printed and bound in England by
J. H. Haynes & Co. Ltd, Sparkford

Designed by Simon Larkin

the Motorcycle book

Everything you need to know about owning, enjoying and maintaining your bike

Which motorcycle?

Training

Clothing

Insurance

Security

Luggage

Tyres

Wheels

Brakes

Suspension

Frames

Engines

Tuning

Exhausts

Accessories

Electrics

MoTs

Storage

Maintenance

Trouble-shooting

Alan Seeley

1

Which motorcycle?

2

Getting on the road

3

Know your motorcycle

4

Looking after your motorcycle

1

Which motorcycle?

Sportsbikes

Sportsbikes represent the pinnacle of motorcycle evolution for fast road riding. Racing, they say, improves the breed, and the influence of competition development can be seen in the lines of many of today's superbikes.

The manufacturers' relentless pursuit of more power from increasingly lighter and compact engines has put blistering performance in the hands of ordinary riders at affordable prices.

Two capacity groups dominate the sportsbike sector – 600cc and the litre class. With about 100bhp on tap and top speeds in the 160mph bracket, it's easy to see the appeal of the 600s – especially if your age, experience or driving record make insurance premiums for larger capacity sportsbikes prohibitively expensive. Fans of the class argue that there's no need for any more performance on the road, further justifying their stance by pointing to the lithe handling of these comparative lightweights.

Honda CBR900RR in-line 4-cylinder 954cc, 130bhp, 168kg   *Aprilia RSVR* 60° V-twin-cylinder 999cc, 113bhp, 165kg

Suzuki GSX-R1000 in-line 4-cylinder 988cc, 161bhp, 170kg

Some 600s are less compromising than others, making them ideal choices for riders who want to explore the outer limits of their bike's performance on track as well as on road. Of the supersports 600s currently available, the Yamaha R6 and, to an only slightly lesser extent, Suzuki's GSX-R600 are the most single-minded. But their ultra-sharp handling and committed riding positions can be a bit much for riders who favour straight-line stability and comfort. Their first choices would be Kawasaki's incredibly capable ZX-6R, up to 636cc from 2002, or the bike that firmly established the class and dominated it for nearly a decade, Honda's venerable CBR600, now available in even sportier F-S form with revised motor and chassis and optional race kit parts.

An outside contender in the class is Triumph's TT600, a capable handler but lacking the power and refined delivery of its classmates.

If in-line four-cylinder 600cc power isn't to your tastes, then Ducati's 748 provides a V-twin alternative with comparable power and peerless race-bred handling.

The litre division is seen by manufacturers and riders alike as the blue riband class of sportsbiking. The benchmark was set by Honda's now near-ubiquitous FireBlade, and the Blade dominated the sector for most of the 1990s, eventually

being outperformed by Yamaha's R1, introduced in 1998. The current crop of 1000cc superbikes offers a winning combination of big-bore behemoth power from compact engines in sparse, nimble chassis. For 2001 Suzuki launched the GSX-R1000, a compelling package that sent bike designers from the other manufacturers scurrying back to their drawing boards. Meanwhile, Kawasaki's ZX-9R and Triumph's 955i founder in the competition's wake, worthy and capable though they are. If you want to go V-twin exotic, then look at Ducati's 996, Aprilia's RSV Mille or Honda's WSB-winning SP1.

If cubes are your ultimate pursuit then consider Suzuki's Hayabusa, a 1300cc monster that can nudge 200mph yet still take you comfortably to work and even touring, or the Kawasaki ZX-12R. Both bikes were built to take the Honda Blackbird's fastest road bike crown, and despite their size they can be surprisingly nimble.

To fulfil a dream of a 750cc sportsbike, there's only one real contender. Suzuki's GSX-R750 almost defies capacity classification and is a cult in its own right. If you fancy a stable and capable, if heavy, 750, then plump for the Kawasaki ZX-7R.

Whichever sportsbike you opt for, don't worry if its performance is a little beyond you on road or track – you'll be able to make good use of your bike's figures in bar room banter.

Suzuki's GSX-R1000 topped the superbike list when it was launched for 2001, but who knows what Honda, Yamaha and Kawasaki have up their sleeves? Sportsbikes are in a constant state of evolution.

They might sound a contradiction in terms, but today's sports-tourers really do offer a decent all-round package. They're the first choice for the rider who demands comfort for serious mile-munching in a bike that can still cut it on a Sunday blast in the twisties.

Sports-tourers

Kawasaki ZZ-R1200 in-line four, 16-valve, 1164cc, 160bhp (claimed), 236kg (dry)

Honda VFR800 Fi V4 16-valve, 781cc, 104.6bhp (claimed), 210kg (dry)

Ducati ST4s V-twin, 8-valve, 996cc, 117bhp (claimed), 212kg (dry)

Sports-tourer bikes have really come into their own in recent years. Not so long ago, manufacturers used to apply the tag to sports models that had been superseded by their own latest, highly advanced offerings, rounding their harder edges and repackaging them as fast but friendly and comfortable all-rounders.

Nowadays, the manufacturers are wise to the needs of intrepid travellers who want the performance to take them where they want to go quickly, and the handling to let them exploit the most exciting route there. Of course there's nothing to stop you touring on a regular sportsbike, but if you're planning to take a pillion, they're going to be pretty uncomfortable even before the first fuel stop, which will come round a lot quicker than on a sports-tourer with its (usually) greater tank range.

The bike that defined the sports-tourer class is Honda's VFR800, a V4 that now features the company's VTEC variable valve system to make the legendary motor even more flexible than its deserved reputation. Optional anti-lock braking makes for an even more refined package.

Where Honda led, others followed, even overtaking the VFR in some areas of performance. A good example is Triumph's Sprint ST, which features the 955cc motor from the sporty T595 Daytona retuned for more of the mid-range beloved of sports-tourer pilots. Kawasaki set out a new marker in the class with its 2002 ZZ-R1200. With an engine based on that from the legendary ZZ-R1100 Rocketship, the new bike claims 160bhp at the crank to make it the most powerful bike in the sport-tourer class. The ZZ-R12 also boasts levels of comfort on a par with some full-blown tourers.

By definition, any sports-tourer is something of a compromise – there are better sportsbikes and there are better tourers. But no sports-tourer blurs the distinction between 'sports' and 'tourer' better than Ducati's ST4s. The Italian firm has taken the V-twin engine from the mighty 996, skimmed some power off the top and fattened up the mid-range to create a bike that satisfies the sportiest of sports-tourists. With its upside-down Showa forks and trademark Ducati trellis frame, the ST4s is basically a sportsbike with a comfortable dual seat and a decent tank range.

If European twins are your thing, you might also like to look at Aprilia's Falco and Futura litre V-twins and BMW's R1100S shaft-drive boxer.

Because their performance is a little down on their full-on sports brethren's and insurers perceive them as tending to attract more 'sensible' riders, sports-tourers fall into similar insurance groups as 600cc sportsbikes, although they frequently cost a bit more to buy. But if you weigh up the price of buying close to big-bore sportsbike performance against lower premiums, sports-tourers start to look like very good value indeed.

Tourers

In theory you can tour on any bike you like, just as, in theory, you can cross the Atlantic in a canoe. But if your aspirations are more club class than leaky coracle, you'll be wanting a full-blown tourer for your high-mileage excursions.

BMW K1200LT in-line 4-cylinder 16-valve, 1171cc, 98bhp (claimed), 378kg (dry)

Honda's Gold Wing represents the pinnacle of grand touring. In its current incarnation, the Wing boasts a huge 1832cc, flat six-cylinder, fuel-injected motor, pumping out a claimed 123ft-lb of torque at a lowly 4000rpm – more than enough to push along its 363kg. A massive 25-litre fuel tank allows you to cover the length of small countries between fuel stops. Just activate the cruise control, sit back and enjoy the ride. An optional six-CD autochanger provides the entertainment on the more boring stretches, or you can talk to your pillion in their armchair-like seat over the intercom. Feeling the windblast? Simply adjust the screen or combat the chill by opening the heater vents, which divert warm air from the engine towards the rider.

There's plenty of room in the lockable panniers – nearly 150 litres – to stash holiday souvenirs and the duty-frees.

The Wing's bulk makes it difficult to carve through traffic like you can on other bikes, but it's otherwise surprisingly nimble for its size. There's even a reverse gear, should you find the need.

Looking at the Wing now, it's hard to believe that it was originally conceived as a sportsbike. But that was back in the late 1970s, when big-cubed motors were seen as the only way to go for performance. Honda soon wised up and the Wing went down another evolutionary path.

If the Wing's opulence seems a little over the top, then smaller tourers are available, but some are almost as well appointed, such as BMW's K1200LT.

Sportsbike purists may scoff at the big tourers, arguing that they have all the disadvantages of a car with none of the advantages of a bike. But with excellent weather protection and superior comfort, maybe the tourists are having the last laugh. In any case, they can't hear you above their CD players.

Taking a peek under the skin of Honda's mighty GL1800 Gold Wing. Big everything. Luxurious seating (bottom left), note speakers and intercom jack. 'What does this button do, dad?' (centre). Should just about hold the duty-free haul (bottom right). Be sure to check for stowaways.

Roadsters occupy motorcycling's middle ground, for price and performance – and not forgetting insurance classification.

Middleweight
Roadsters

Ducati Monster 750 air-cooled V-twin, 4-valve, 748cc, 66bhp (claimed), 183kg (dry)

Suzuki GSF600 Bandit in-line 4-cylinder 16-valve, 599cc, 78.9bhp (claimed), 196kg (dry)

Bikes such as the Yamaha Fazer, Honda Hornet and Suzuki Bandit 600 are ideal first choices for riders who have recently passed their tests. Their user-friendly riding positions and power delivery make for a package that won't intimidate less experienced riders, or rush them headlong into trouble.

Bikes in this class make great all-rounders, even if they don't excel at anything in particular – apart from providing relatively cheap fun.

They lack sportsbike levels of ground clearance, so crazy lean angles are out. But there's enough there for you to cut your trackday teeth on, should you choose. Bikes such as the Fazer and Hornet 600s have detuned engines from earlier Yamaha and Honda sportsbikes. They might lack the top-end of the original sportsbike incarnations but the engines have plenty of mid-range for punchy acceleration. Wind and weather protection is minimal on roadsters since they are usually unfaired – although some have nose cones or half fairings – so they wouldn't be first choice for touring.

Roadsters are built using conventional components, and this is reflected in their cost. Frames are usually cheap tubular steel, not the aluminium alloy spars of sportsbikes. Suspension is usually functional, but budget and non-adjustable. But, pound for pound, roadsters represent great fun.

At the less sparkling end of the performance spectrum lie bikes such as the Honda CB500 and Kawasaki ER5 twins. Honda's CB750 and Kawasaki's ZR-7 still provide an option in the 750 four-cylinder roadster class. The Fazer 600 and Hornet 600 offer performance close to sportsbikes. If you want something different, go for the Italian Cagiva Raptor 650 or the Suzuki SV650, both of which use a 645cc V-twin engine from the Japanese company. And there are Ducati's 650 and 750cc air-cooled V-twin Monsters.

So even if a roadster can't give you a total sportsbike buzz, the money you'll save on insurance, servicing and consumables provides plenty of compensation.

Honda Hornet 600
In-line 4-cylinder 16-valve, 599cc, 96bhp (claimed), 176kg (dry)

Kawasaki ER-5 parallel twin-cylinder 8-valve, 498cc, 50bhp (claimed), 174kg (dry)

Suzuki SV650 liquid-cooled V-twin-cylinder 8-valve, 645cc, 70bhp (claimed), 165kg (dry)

Retros
& Musclebikes

One of the broadest categories of motorcycles. Retros cover everything from bikes that look like 1960s throwbacks with roughly similar performance to the machines that give them their styling cues, to big-bore unfaired musclebikes that don't really deserve the tag at all.

Kawasaki's W650 and Triumph's Bonneville twins faithfully evoke the spirit of a bygone age. For riders who fancy the look, but not the intensive maintenance, of an older bike, they're ideal choices, although you'll need to keep the polishing rag handy for all that chrome. They're not huge on horses – the W650 claims slightly less than 50bhp while the 790cc Triumph claims just over 60. The real back wheel figures will be close to those of the 1960s bikes they mimic. Overhead camshafts and electric starters with be unfamiliar to those who remember pushrod engines and kickstarts, twin-shock rear suspension lives on in a world where the monoshock is the standard. Same goes for the air rather than liquid cooling of the engines. And, of course, owners of these modern classics can enjoy the image with the reassurance that their bikes have 21st century brakes and reliability.

At the other end of the scale sit big-bore naked bikes such as Yamaha's XJR1300 and Suzuki's GSX1400, whose commanding presence makes them look meaner than they really are.

Another Suzuki, the 1200 Bandit, is a cult in its own right, with a motor derived from the company's legendary, bullet-proof GSX-R1100. For many years the Bandit 12 was the naked hooligan weapon of choice, but now it has some serious competition.

Yamaha's Fazer 1000 has a detuned motor from the R1 sportsbike – less top-end but loads in the middle. And where it beats its contemporaries, apart from performance, is in its handling. Where other bikes in the class tend to offer big motors in budget chassis, the Yam skimps in neither department – but that is reflected in the list price.

Honda followed the big Fazer into the fray with the Hornet 900. Its chassis is less well appointed than the Yam's, but it is cheaper and uses an engine from an earlier FireBlade, again detuned to take some off the top and boost the middle.

If you want a V-twin in the big naked class look at Cagiva's Suzuki TL1000-engined Raptors. Ducati's 900 Monsters are rightly popular too.

Retros, nakeds – call them what you will – are huge fun. They're cheaper to insure than the latest cutting-edge sportsbikes, but give you at least as much to grin about.

Suzuki GSX1400 in-line 4-cylinder 16-valve, 1402cc, 104bhp (claimed), 228kg (dry)

Yamaha FZS1000 Fazer in-line 4-cylinder 20-valve, 998cc, 143bhp (claimed), 208kg (dry)

Kawasaki W650 parallel twin-cylinder 8-valve, 676cc, 49.6bhp (claimed), 195kg (dry)

Kawasaki ZRX1200R in-line 4-cylinder 16-valve, 1164cc, 120bhp (claimed), 223kg (dry)

Cruisers

For more show than go, a cruiser is the perfect choice of bike. The classic cruiser configuration is a V-twin motor slung in a long, low frame with a huge wheelbase and low-slung footpegs that mean lairy cornering is firmly off the agenda. Those low footpegs combine with low, comfortable seats and wide bars to give a lazy riding position ideal for cruising at modest speeds.

Suzuki VL1500LC Intruder V-twin 6-valve, 1462cc, 66bhp (claimed), 292kg (dry)

Yamaha XVS250 Dragstar V-twin 4-valve,
249cc, 21bhp (claimed), 147kg (dry)

Kawasaki VN1500 Mean Streak V-twin 8-valve,
1470cc, 72bhp (claimed), 304kg (dry)

*Love 'em or loathe 'em,
there is no class of bike
more likely to provoke
extreme devotion or extreme
derision than cruisers. So
just sit back and enjoy the
scenery and the easy
riding of motorcycling's
showiest showboats.*

Harley-Davidsons epitomise the cruiser style, and for many purists anything else is a feeble imitation. But these days most manufacturers offer a cruiser based on the famous Harley lines. Most feature V-twin motors in a lowly state of tune, designed to deliver optimum torque from minimal revs. They come in all sizes, from Honda's 125cc Shadow and Yamaha's XVS125 Drag Star to big-bore monsters like that same company's 1600cc Wild Star. Despite its massive displacement, the Wild Star manages to pump out only 61.7bhp at an 'is-it-running?' 4000rpm, while making a massive 96.97ft-lb of torque at 2250rpm. See what we mean about massive torque and low power?

One exception to the V-twin cruiser rule is Honda's F6C, which has an outrageous 1520cc flat six-cylinder motor that used to live in the Gold Wing. Again, torque is the thing, with a claimed 95.9ft-lb.

Moto Guzzi has various V-twin cruiser alternatives, but this time the cylinders are arranged across the frame rather than in line with it.

Most cruisers boast enough chrome to keep even the most avid of polishers happy, and if your bike of choice doesn't have quite enough shiny bits for you, there is an endless array of aftermarket bolt-ons to let you customise your steed. If that still doesn't make it sufficiently eye-catching, you can always fit some slash-cut straight-through pipes to herald your arrival.

You get plenty of metal for your money with cruisers, and most are as heavy as their performance is ponderous.

Harley lookalikes became popular because they were often more refined than the Milwaukee vibrators from which they unashamedly stole their looks. Liquid-cooled engines, overhead camshafts and shaft drive were niceties not to be found on the more traditional Harleys, whose harder edges play a big part in their appeal to devotees. But maybe things have come full circle with the Harley V-Rod, a liquid-cooled, double overhead cam, eight-valve V-twin that can haul its 279kg self up the standing quarter mile in 11.5 seconds. Purists will be pleased to hear that the long wheelbase, low seat, wide bars and forward pegs are still present and correct. But what to call the thing. A sports cruiser?

Trail bikes are the 4x4s of the motorcycling world – go-anywhere machines that open up whole new biking vistas. Most trail bikes make reasonably usable road bikes, with dual purpose tyres available to replace dirt knobblies, but some have more off-road purpose than others.

Trail bikes

Suzuki DRZ400 single-cylinder 4-valve, 398cc, 39bhp (claimed), 132kg (dry)

Trail riders largely prefer the light weight and simplicity of a two-stroke – Kawasaki's KMX125 and KDX series spring to mind in this category. Four-strokes are heavier but tend to offer more longevity than a stroker – Honda's XLR125 and Suzuki's DR125 are top choices here.

Going up a bit in capacity, Suzuki's DR-Z400S four-stroke has proved popular since its introduction in 2000. It replaced the DR350, a favourite of clubman enduro event off-road riders, and packs a torquey 398cc motor in a compact, motocross-style chassis. An ideal choice for the trails.

Specialist manufacturers such as Beta, Husqvarna and KTM bring years of off-road market experience to bear on their dirtbikes.

Beta is renowned for its trials competition (as distinct from trail bikes), and its Alp 125 and 200 are four-stroke bikes that draw on that trials heritage while offering more general purpose.

The Husqvarna WRE125 is a gorgeous little two-stroke that also happens to be learner-legal. And the company's TE410 and 610 are big four-stroke thumpers for dedicated trail riders.

KTM has an excellent choice of off-roaders for the trail rider, from 250cc two-strokes to 625cc four-strokes, but they're more for the dirt than the tarmac.

Trail riding is an excellent way to discover old byways that have escaped the scourge of tarmac, but bridleways and footpaths are off-limits in the UK. Because the trails are legally highways, your bike must be road-legal, including MoT and insurance. Show other trail users such as walkers and horse riders courtesy and respect the countryside. That way, trail riding will continue to be one of the great outdoor pursuits.

Honda's XR650 (facing page) gives plenty of four-stroke grunt and torque without imposing too big a weight penalty on the trail rider. Still, looks like this bloke's having fun, and that's what trail riding's all about. As dirty as you can get with your clothes on.

Kawasaki KDX125 single-cylinder 2-stroke, 124cc, 12/24bhp (claimed, restricted/derestricted), 107kg (dry)

Honda XLR125R single-cylinder 2-valve, 124.1cc, 11.4bhp (claimed), 119kg (dry)

Honda XL1000V Varadero V-twin 8-valve, 999cc, 95bhp (claimed), 220kg (dry)

Honda XL650V Transalp V-twin 6-valve, 647cc, 54.3bhp (claimed), 191kg (dry)

Monster trailies

They might take their styling cues from off-roaders, but monster trailies aren't really for the rough stuff unless you have the strength and abilities of a Paris-Dakar desert racing hero.

BMW R1150GS flat twin 8-valve, 1130cc, 85bhp (claimed), 219kg (dry)

Suzuki V-Strom V-twin 8-valve, 996cc, 98bhp (claimed), 211kg (dry)

Aprilia Capo Nord V-twin 8-valve, 997.6cc, 98bhp (claimed), 215kg (dry)

Monster trailies are imposing machines. You can make an aggressive Paris–Dakar statement on the road, even if your off-road ambitions extend no further than bumping on to the pavement outside the cafe.

Despite their looks, monster trailies excel best on the road, especially in town. High riding position and wide bars make for a great view of the road and easy steering. Big-bore engines display a huge appetite for munching the miles. And huge fuel tanks extend the range between filling stations. But while the soft suspension delivers a comfortable ride, it also means cornering potential isn't in the sportsbike league, and that upright riding position puts you right in the windblast. Still, if sportsbikes aren't your bag, a big trailie might be the thing.

Aprilia's Capo Nord is a good example of a monster trailie. With a 997cc V-twin engine taken from Aprilia's sportier big twins (detuned to make less than 100bhp) the Capo Nord is a big softie that also has a harder edge when you turn it up a bit. A tall screen takes away the worst of the wind.

Cagiva's Navigator offers a similar package, its V-twin engine taken from Suzuki's TL1000.

BMW's flat twin R1150GS is the largest and latest of two decades' worth of big Bee-Em trailies. GS stands for Gelande/Strasse, which translates roughly into English as off-road/road, so you can see where the regular Paris–Dakar winning firm is coming from.

Other options include Honda's Varadero, powered by the one-litre V-twin lump from the Firestorm sportsbike. Triumph's 955cc Tiger triple is popular too, as is Yamaha's TDM twin, which was taken from 850 to 900cc for 2002.

If the trail bike style is your thing but you need less than a litre in the engine department, look at bikes such as the 33bhp, 498cc Cagiva Canyon four-stroke single, which is ideal for riders on a restricted licence, or the BMW F650GS single – a 50bhp four-stroke. Honda's Transalp and Africa Twin are 650 and 750cc V-twin alternatives.

Big trailies are extremely popular in continental Europe, and make sound sense as capable all-rounders. Best to stick to the black stuff, though.

Supermotos

Supermotos are the new kids on the biking block and have enjoyed a huge upsurge in interest over the past decade. Supermoto racing is huge in continental Europe and is fast gaining a foothold in the UK, although its origins can be traced back to the 1970s in the States.

KTM Duke single-cylinder, 4-valve, 625cc, 55bhp (claimed), 145kg (dry)

CCM 604e Supermoto single-cylinder, 598cc air-cooled, 53bhp (claimed), 138kg (dry).
CCM were moving to Suzuki power as the first edition of the Motorcycle Book went to press.

When you buy most supermotos, you essentially get a race bike with the legal niceties of lights, indicators and a speedo tacked on. Usually big four-stroke singles, supermotos are being marketed to road riders as fun alternatives to sportsbikes for those riders who don't trust themselves to stick to licence-conserving speeds. And there's something in that. Big, torquey motors and low gearing make them a blast off the line, and if wheelies light your fire, a supermoto will more than happily oblige. Dynamite brakes and light weight make stoppies a breeze too. And top speeds rarely exceed 100mph, keeping licences safe. On the other hand, high riding positions and big, thumping single cylinders aren't much fun on long straights, and small fuel tanks limit mileage between refills.

However, invest in a spare set of wheels for off-road tyres and you have two bikes for the price of one (plus a set of wheels, of course). Most supermotos come with trick, high-quality, off-road suspension, which is more than adequate on road.

European companies dominate the supermoto market. British firm CCM has recently switched from Rotax power to Suzuki single engines. It builds stripped-down competition derived machines, as well as slightly more refined offerings with larger fuel

tanks for more road-going versatility.

Austrian firm KTM is another big name in supermotos, thanks to plenty of competition success. The KTM 640 Duke is a 625cc four-stroke single and production is limited to 1500 bikes per year. There's also the LC4 Supermoto, which boasts the same engine but more basic off-road styling.

Italian firm Husqvarna (formed originally in Sweden) has the 576cc four-stroke 610 SM, introduced as the supermoto version of its TE610 enduro bike. Husky also offers the SMR570 – more refined styling, but even taller than the 610, which like all supermotos has a very high seat.

Supermotos are plenty of fun. Putting a big off-roader on 17-inch road wheels with sticky rubber is a surefire recipe for loads of laughs. Just stay away from the straights.

By the time you read the first edition of this book, British city centres should be reverberating to the sound of supermotos, as they thunder and backslide through purpose-built circuits for a major televised race series. Even if that prediction proves wrong, supermotos are sure to find a foothold in the inner cities as carve-up merchants look for something with more presence, punch and cred than a scooter to haul them to work and back.

Supermotos started as a cult that is now gaining huge momentum. Mainly the pressure of specialist manufacturers, it won't take long for the large bike companies to move in on the action.

Commuters

Any motorcycle can be used as a commuter bike, but some are more suited than others. Riding a sportsbike, say, through the cut and thrust of an urban rush hour can be a regal pain in the neck and wrists, apart from the fact that those bikes are geared for far longer-legged riding. A scooter is a great choice provided your ride to work is over mainly low-speed roads. But lightweights and middleweights are the best overall.

Honda CB500 parallel twin 8-valve, 499cc, 57bhp (claimed), 175kg (dry)

Honda Hornet 600FS in-line 4-cylinder 16-valve, 599cc, 96bhp (claimed), 179kg (dry)

Two simple reasons make an unfaired lightweight or middleweight – rather than a scooter – the top choice of commuter bike. Firstly, they're less likely to attract the attention of thieves when parked up outside work all day. And secondly, if you do come a cropper in the free-for-all that is modern town riding, the bike is likely to sustain minimal damage. Even the lightest tumble on a faired sportsbike is likely to result in a hefty bill because of the costly panels that make up the fairing.

The best alternatives to a bus pass or train season ticket are capable middleweights such as the Kawasaki ER-5 and Honda CB500. Yamaha Fazer and Honda Hornet 600s make good choices too, although they're a little more conspicuous than their blander brethren.

The Kawasaki GT550 is a commuter staple that seems to have been around forever. This bike comes with a bullet-proof shaft drive (hence low maintenance) and a four-stroke four-cylinder that was the mount of choice of many dispatch riders for years (the GT550 first appeared in 1983 and has barely changed since). So there's a recommendation of everyday reliability.

The bottom line is that there are plenty of bikes capable of playing the commuter role, offering an undemanding ride and low maintenance. Just as important, they provide an economic alternative to other means of commuting. And that has to be reason enough to rip up your rail card and extend your motorcycling enjoyment to the everyday task of getting to work and back.

Look at this. BMW's F650 uses a dummy tank to make it the largest capacity, ride-to-work handbag on the planet. Add to that a belt final drive and it has to be a top choice for commuters who prefer to keep bike maintenance to a minimum.

Suzuki GS500E parallel twin, 487cc, 51.3bhp (claimed), 173kg (dry)

Kawasaki ER-5 parallel twin 8-valve, 498cc, 50bhp (claimed), 179kg (dry)

Learner bikes

Unless you're going for a moped licence, at least some of your training will be done on a 125cc bike. And unless you're doing Direct or Accelerated Access (see page 39), you'll probably take your test on a 125 too.

Aprilia RS125R two-stroke single,
124.6cc, 12bhp (restricted), 115kg (dry)

Honda CLR125 City Fly single-cylinder 4-valve,
124.7cc, 15bhp (claimed),145kg (dry)

Honda CG125 single-cylinder 4-valve, 124cc, 10.8bhp (claimed), 137kg (dry)

Honda's CG125 has established itself as a training school staple, and it's easy to see why. The bulletproof little four-stroke single can take as much punishment as even the most novice learner can throw at it, and being a 125 it's economical too. Sure, it isn't exactly the most attractive bike on the planet, but it's more than capable enough for learning on and makes a useful commuter bike once you've passed your test. The front drum brake is a dated touch and not as powerful as a disc, but it's enough to pull up the CG.

You can, of course, learn on a school bike, but if you want your own and the CG125 lacks the street-cred you desire, there are loads of other 125s that mimic the styles of various bigger bikes. Honda offers a 125 custom (VT125 Shadow); the trail-style CLR125 City Fly; a proper trailie in the form of the XLR125; the sporty NSR125 two-stroke; and a baby monster trailie, the V-twin 125 Varadero.

Yamaha has the two-stroke DT125R trailie, the oddball balloon-tyred TW125, the semi-custom SR125 and the XVS125 Dragstar cruiser.

Suzuki options extend to the four-stroke DR125SE trailie and the GZ125 custom-styled roadster.

Kawasaki provides the custom EL125 Eliminator, but its two-stroke KMX125 trailie excites 125 buyers more.

Off-road specialist Husqvarna offers a couple of 125s – the road-wheeled SM125S and knobbly tyred WRE125, but peaky power delivery and uncompromising off-road competition suspension make them perhaps not the best choice for novices.

Fancy a 125cc sportsbike? Aprilia's RS125R is a gorgeous two-stroke racer replica that looks and performs the part. Cagiva's Mito 125 looks like a baby Ducati 996, with a chassis capable of outhandling its two-stroke motor in restricted form. The company also offers the Planet 125, basically a restyled naked Mito.

There's plenty of choice in the 125 market and, just as important, something to suit most budgets.

Reflect your post-test bike aspirations in your choice of 125 for your learner days. Sports, custom, cruiser, trailie or roadster – they're all there in the eighth-of-a-litre class.

Suzuki GZ125 single cylinder, 2-valve, 124cc, 12bhp (claimed), 125kg (dry)

Kawasaki KMX125 two-stroke single, 124cc, 12/24bhp (claimed, restricted/derestricted), 99kg (dry)

Yamaha SR125 single-cylinder 2-valve, 124cc, 12bhp (claimed), 104kg (dry)

Classic bikes

If the latest tackle doesn't light your wick, what about a classic? People are drawn to classics for different reasons. Some older riders choose the bikes they either owned in their youth or couldn't afford back then. Other people just want to own and ride a legendary make or model. The simple satisfaction of keeping an old machine on the road can be a draw, too. And then there are the restorers, who buy machines to return them to original factory condition – known as concours – to show or to ride.

Given that bikes have been around for more than a century, there's plenty of choice. A pre-First World War single with a leather drive belt and only one gear might not make the best choice of ride-to-work bike in the 21st century. So if you plan to use your classic bike fairly frequently, go for something more recent – especially if you're looking at your first classic. It will be easier to source spares, particularly if your classic was a popular model because many of these, spares are being remanu-factured, often improving on the original components.

By going for a classic, you're turning your back on at least two decades of machine development. For regular use, choose a classic with enough performance to keep pace with modern traffic, and remember that braking and reliability will not be as good as with modern machinery. Even so, there are a number of specialists supplying conversions to uprate brakes, replace points with electronic ignition, and generally make classics perform better and more reliably.

A huge network of classic enthusiasts and owners clubs exists to help keep older machinery on the road, so join a club relevant to your classic. Clubs are an indispensable source of advice and many run spares schemes, even going as far as remanufacturing parts if enough owners commit to buying them. They also organise runs and rallies, and many have regular local meetings, which are excellent opportunities to socialise with like-minded enthusiasts.

For many classic fans, the challenge of keeping their bikes on the road and the extra maintenance they tend to demand is all part of the fun – and most older bikes are far easier to work on than modern bikes, which is probably just as well.

As an added incentive, insurance for classics (normally defined as a bike older than 15 years) is extremely cheap, but you'll have to hunt around for cover if you're under 25. And bikes built before 1 January 1973 are exempt from UK road tax. So you'll have a bit more cash for spare parts and consumables.

There are endless classics to choose from, but ideal selections for those new to the joys of older machines of character are the more common recent bikes for ease of spares availability and, in the case of bigger bikes, usable performance.

1973 Norton 850 Commando
parallel twin OHV, 829cc, 185kg (dry approx)

1981 Laverda Formula Mirage
inline triple DOHC, 1116cc, 232kg (dry)

Late Sixties Triumph Bonneville
parallel twin OHV, 649cc, 175kg (dry approx)

Scooters

The scooter market has been motorcycling's biggest boom area in the past few years, but it's more than a passing fad. Scooters offer a cheap and convenient alternative to a car – or even a bus pass. Fashion has played its part in the scooter's rise, but low running costs and cheap insurance are the real clinchers. Small, light and easy to park, scooters are the ultimate solution for battling through the urban jungle. Add in fuel consumption that redefines 'frugal' – 65mpg is the average, and some will happily do close to 100mpg – and scooters are a compelling option.

Aprilia Scarabeo
single-cylinder two stroke,
100/125cc, 92/140kg (dry)

Scooters are a tempting option for many reasons, including their ease of riding. Many are fully automatic – just twist the throttle and go. Most have enough storage space under the seat to store your helmet when you park up, and accommodate a generous load of shopping for the ride home.

It's fitting that scooters are again finding their place transporting urban commuters and riders, because that's how they originally came into being. After the Second World War, there was a huge need for cheap transport in Italy. Aeroplane factories were banned from making planes, but they still had the steel pressing machinery and a surplus of small wheels from making fighters. Out of this adversity, the original Vespa ('wasp') was born, and Italy got on the road again.

Many of today's most desirable scooters are Italian – Piaggio, Vespa, Aprilia. The French are big players too, in the form of Peugeot. And, of course, the Japanese manufacturers would never miss a market. So there's plenty of choice in this very competitive arena.

Suzuki, Yamaha and Honda have been particularly active in creating a new class of superscooter and the Italians are getting in on the act too. These machines combine scooter levels of comfort and weather protection with top speeds (about 100mph) that allow them to keep up with motorway traffic.

But are these scooters or are they bikes? Honda has its 582cc SilverWing, Piaggio the X9 500, Suzuki the Burgman 400 and Yamaha the 500 TMax. There comes a point when the slimline attributes of the smaller scooters are compromised by the manufacturers' desire to be all things to all people.

Italjet Dragster single-cylinder two-stroke, 50/125/180cc, 85/107/109kg (dry)

Honda @125 single-cylinder four-stroke, 13bhp (claimed), 120kg (dry)

Suzuki Burgman single-cylinder 4-valve, 385cc, 32bhp (claimed), 174kg (dry)

Italjet Torpedo (above)
Scooter manufacturers are more than happy to tilt their hats to their heritage with swoopy lines and classic styling, while incorporating modern niceties such as disc brakes and indicators.

Mopeds

Not so long ago it was every 16-year-old's dream to own a moped, and the little fifties introduced many riders to a lifetime of motorcycling. Now the scooter boom has revived interest in motorcycling's mini marvels.

Honda SH50 City Express single cylinder two-stroke, 49cc, 3.8bhp (claimed), 68kg (dry)

Light weight and ease of operation characterise mopeds. At 16 years old, they're your only powered two-wheeled option. Enjoy. More speed and power is only a year's riding away.

A moped is still the only way for anyone under 17 to use a powered machine on the road legally, and opens up a whole new world of freedom. Okay, there are limits. Top speed is limited to 30mph, maximum weight is 250kg (easy for a small two-wheeler to comply with) and maximum engine size is 50cc.

But while they might not be big on speed and power, they don't have to be small on style. The fashionable sixteener these days has plenty of choice.

Top scooter-style options include Aprilia's SR50LC sports moped and the Rally LC trail-style scooter moped. Scooters are huge in Italy and other Italian companies such as Benelli, Beta, Gilera, Italjet, Malaguti, MBK, Piaggio and, of course, Vespa have some stylish scooter-mopeds too – as do Spanish firm Derbi. France isn't known as a big producer of bikes, but Peugeot's 50cc Speedfight has been a soaraway sales success largely because of its styling and handling.

The Japanese ignore few markets, and scooter-mopeds are no exception. Honda, Suzuki and Yamaha all offer scooter-style fifties.

If you're limited to moped performance but demand sportsbike looks, consider Aprilia's RS50, the Moto-Roma RX50 or the more powerful Derbi GPR50R – and head straight to the top of the school bikeshed style charts.

There are plenty of trail-style mopeds to choose from. Take your pick from the Aprilia RX50, Derbi Senda R, Gilera H@K and Suzuki TS50X among others. If you aspire to a supermoto, there are the Gilera GSM, Derbi Supermotard and Beta Supermoto, to name but three.

Mopeds are fun and economical, if lacking in power. A lot of mopeds are restricted, so the potential for more power is there. However, this can put the bike outside the scope of your licence – assuming the powers that be find out – and affect warranties and insurance cover. Many are twist-and-go automatics, particularly the scooter-type, while others feature big-bike controls. Either way, they're a great introduction to the joys of biking.

Aprilia SR50 Di Tech Racing
single-cylinder two-stroke, 50cc, 89kg (dry)

Suzuki AP50W single-cylinder two-stroke, 49cc, 2.9bhp (claimed), 59kg (dry)

Aprilia Enjoy Racing electric bicycle, 31kg

2

Getting on the road

Which
test
option?

Having decided you want to go motorcycling, you need to sort out a licence before taking to the road. Current UK legislation provides a tiered route to motorcycle licences. Which path you take depends on your age and the type of bikes you want your licence to cover – any bike, a 125cc machine for commuting or a moped.

Cut your riding teeth on a blue funky moped . . .

. . . then move up to the giddy power of a CG125

MOPEDS

Aspring riders aged 16 and older can apply for a moped licence. A moped is defined as a bike with a maximum design speed not exceeding 30mph, a weight of less than 250kg, an engine of 50cc or less, and capable of being propelled by pedals if it was first used before 1 September 1977. Hardly a heady mix, but the only option for 16 year-olds – and better than the bus. You'll have to apply for a provisional licence and take Compulsory Basic Training (see page 40) before being able to ride on the road with L-plates. Next, you'll have to pass the theory test (page 42) before taking the moped test. Pass that and you can rip up the L-plates, then get out on the road, carrying a pillion if you wish.

Holders of full car licences first issued before 1 February 2001 can ride a moped without L-plates and without the need to take CBT. If you passed your car test after that date and want to ride a moped, you will need to do CBT.

MOTORCYCLES

Would-be motorcycle riders over 17 will first require provisional bike entitlement. Car licence holders automatically have provisional bike entitlement, but if you have no licence at all, you'll need to apply for a provisional bike licence. These expire after two years if you haven't passed your test, and you'll have to apply all over again.

A provisional motorcycle licence entitles you to ride bikes under 125cc with a power output of no more than 14.6bhp, with L-plates, once you've passed your Compulsory Basic Training (page 40). You can't carry a pillion at this stage.

With CBT under your belt, it's time to take the theory test (page 42). As with provisional licences, your CBT certificate and your theory test pass are valid for two years only and you'll have to retake both if you don't pass your full licence inside that time.

There are three types of motorcycle licence:
1 A1
2 Restricted Licence (A Licence)
3 Direct/Accelerated Access.

If your motorcycling ambition extends no further than a little 125 to get around on, then you'll want to go for an A1 licence. The route for this is the same as for a normal licence, but you'll take your test on a bike of 75–125cc and thereafter be restricted to bikes under 125cc with a power output of no more than 14.6bhp.

The 'restricted' part of the Restricted Licence is the power of the bike you'll be allowed to ride for the two years after you've passed your test – no more than 33bhp or with a power-to-weight ratio under 0.21bhp/kg. Your training school will be able to provide you with a list of bikes that meet these criteria. It is also possible to have a more powerful machine modified to bring its power output in line with the law. In the meantime, you'll be learning on a bike with an engine of 120–125cc, a power output of 14.6bhp and capable of at least 100kmh (62mph in the old money). Training for a Restricted Licence obviously goes beyond the rudimentary skills you learned for the CBT. Riders of any age who want to start out on less powerful machines can opt for a Restricted Licence, but under-21s have no choice.

Younger riders can opt for Accelerated Access if they reach the age of 21 within the two-year restricted period after passing their test. This allows riders to move up to bikes of unlimited power by passing a further test on a bike of 46.6bhp or more. But while you are learning on the larger machine, it's back to L-plates accompanied by an instructor on the road – it's okay, he doesn't sit on the bike with you, he rides his own – but you're still free to ride your sub-33bhp bike unaccompanied.

Anyone over 21 years old can opt for Direct Access. This is the quickest route to a full bike licence, entitling the holder to ride a bike of any power. You'll take your CBT either on a learner bike or larger machine. Once you've passed that, you are allowed to ride a learner bike on the road with L-plates, but an instructor will have to accompany you on the larger bike, which must have a minimum output of 46.6bhp. Kawasaki ER-5s and Honda CB500s are popular choices of training schools.

Whichever training route you choose or are restricted to, you will be able to train and pass your test on bikes hired from your riding school. Many loan riding gear too. This means you can make the financial commitment to a bike and kit once you've passed your test and are sure that biking's for you. But if you want to practice in the meantime, you'll need your own kit and learner bike.

Aspiring riders line up to take the first steps to two-wheel freedom at a riding school (opposite). Everyone has to reach the same basic standard before passing their test.

Compulsory **B**asic **T**raining

Compulsory Basic Training means just what it says, but what does it involve? Its main purpose is to provide you with the fundamental skills for your own road safety as you embark on your biking career. CBT was devised to reduce the accident rate among young and novice riders, and statistics seem to show it's had a positive effect.

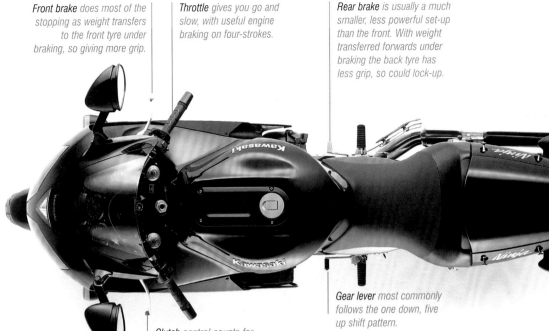

Front brake does most of the stopping as weight transfers to the front tyre under braking, so giving more grip.

Throttle gives you go and slow, with useful engine braking on four-strokes.

Rear brake is usually a much smaller, less powerful set-up than the front. With weight transferred forwards under braking the back tyre has less grip, so could lock-up.

Gear lever most commonly follows the one down, five up shift pattern.

Clutch control counts for a lot, and the CBT features lots of excercises to get it right.

You can take CBT on your own learner bike or moped, or else hire one from your training school (look in *Yellow Pages* for your local training organisations). If you don't have your own riding kit, then gloves, helmets and waterproofs can be hired or borrowed from most schools. Wear sturdy boots, a jacket (leather is best) and jeans in the absence of proper riding kit. The whole ensemble will be topped off by a fetching fluorescent bib provided by the school.

Remember to take your licence with you. The instructor will want to check it before training begins. The next formality is the eye test, where you'll be expected to read an ordinary car numberplate from 20.5 metres. If you usually wear glasses, you must wear them for this part of your CBT as well as the training and the eventual test.

By now, you'll be itching to get on with the business of riding, but first the classroom beckons for a look at what CBT involves and a chat about clothing and riding equipment. Then it's on to the training ground, where you'll be talked through the basics of what the bike's controls do, and practice getting the bike off and on its main stand.

At last it's time to get down to the riding itself. You'll master starting the bike, clutch control, pulling away, controlled braking and emergency stops, turning and U-turns. All this is done in the safe confines of the training ground, which is usually a piece of hard standing a bit like a car park, marked out with cones and white lines for the various exercises. Your instructor will ensure that you get all the tuition you need to grasp the various manoeuvres. Don't panic if things don't seem to be coming easily, because your instructor will give

you all the time and advice you need to crack it.

Just when you're bursting to get out on the road to practise your new-found skills, it's back to class for more instruction. This time you'll find out about riding and the law, the Highway Code, riding in traffic and anticipating other road users. You'll also learn that the need to take account of weather and road conditions is even more acute on a bike than it is in a car. It's all relevant stuff, even to learner riders who have been driving cars for years.

Next you'll put all the classroom theory and the hands-on work on the training ground into practice, with an accompanied road ride that lasts for at least two hours. You'll be equipped with a radio, on which you'll be told what to do by the instructor from his bike. You'll be working on road speed and positioning as you negotiate various junctions and roundabouts, observations (in front and behind), signalling, manoeuvring and more emergency stops. The route you ride is designed to take in most everyday hazards and situations you'll encounter out on the road.

Back at the training centre, provided the instructor's satisfied you've cracked it, you'll be issued with form DL196, your CBT pass. Now you're on the way to your full bike licence and are free to take to the road unaccompanied on a 125cc bike or moped with L-plates, depending on which licence you're aiming for.

CBT takes most riders a day, but don't be downhearted if it takes you longer. Everyone learns at different rates and, remember, your instructor wants to be sure that you're safe. A CBT certificate lasts for two years. If you don't pass your main test in that time, you'll have to take it again.

This learner is getting to grips with the basics of machine control. If he's doing Direct Access he could be on a bike like the 178bhp Kawasaki ZX-12R at the top of the page quite soon.

The **theory** test

With CBT under your belt, the next thing you'll need to pass is your theory test – and that includes holders of car licences too. The only learners exempt from this are moped riders, who obtained their licences by doing a two-part test.

To pass the theory test you'll need to provide 30 correct answers to 35 questions taken from a list of about 300. The questions relate to the meanings of road signs, and the techniques and theory of road safety. Various books containing sample questions have been published and the Driving Standards Agency publishes an official volume called *The Official Theory Test for Motorcyclists*. The whole process has been brought into the computer age too, with a CD-ROM available to help you learn your stuff.

You need to pass your theory test before proceeding to the main test, so do it as soon as you can. Remember that, like the CBT, a theory test pass expires after two years if you haven't passed your main test. If that happens, you'll have to resit it.

The **main** test

Now you're ready for the big one. Time to put everything you've learned in your training under the scrutiny of a DSA examiner in a test lasting up to 40 minutes. Restricted licence candidates will take the test on a 125, but if you're going for a direct or accelerated licence you'll be doing it on a bike of over 46.6bhp.

Your instructor will have to accompany you to the test centre if you're sitting the test on the larger bike. Provided everything goes to plan, he won't be legally required to accompany you on the way back!

The examiner will want to check your documents – licence, CBT and theory test passes – and you'll need to have a signed photo ID with you. This last item is required to discourage candidates from sending someone else along to sit the test for them. You'll be asked to do the same eye test as in CBT (reading a car numberplate from 20.5 metres).

With the formalities out of the way, it's time to take to the road. You'll be kitted out with a two-way radio, like those used by the training school, so the examiner can give you instructions.

The examiner's looking for you to ride safely, sensibly and confidently, and there are certain things the test must cover, regardless of whether it lasts for the whole 40 minutes. You'll have practised all of these at training level. There'll be a separate hill start if the route doesn't feature a junction or set of lights on a hill, where you'd have to perform a hill start in the ordinary course of events. You'll also have to set off safely at an angle from behind a parked vehicle. There'll be an emergency stop, controlled and without locking up any wheels. You'll also have to do a U-turn and a slow ride with the examiner walking alongside, you matching his pace, to make sure your slow-machine control is up to scratch.

Provided you manage to do the set elements of the test competently, and don't make any dangerous or potentially dangerous mistakes on the rest of the ride, you'll pass and be able to rip up those L-plates. Congratulations.

You aren't allowed to take a passenger just yet, though. You have to wait until you've sent off your pass certificate and received your full licence.

Don't let your new-found two-wheel freedom go to your head. If you rack up six or more penalty points in your first two years of riding, you'll lose your licence and have to go through the theory and main tests again. As much as you've enjoyed learning to ride, you don't really want to do it all over again, do you?

Advanced
training

Advanced training has something to offer everyone – whether you've just passed your test, have been riding for years, or are returning to motorcycling after a break from it.

If the ink is barely dry on your bike licence, you might be wondering why you should want to have even more tuition. After all, you've just successfully taken on a whole load of new knowledge and shown the authorities that you know what you're doing, thank you very much. But steep though the learning curve was from wobbly-wheeled novice at CBT to confident, competent rider in the main test, there's always more to learn beyond the bare basics of control that you had to show the examiner. You can accelerate the process and become a faster and safer rider at the same time by taking some advanced training.

Or if you're coming back into motorcycling after a few years away, you can gain an instant boost to your confidence on today's faster bikes and busier road systems by signing up for extra tuition. Even riders who've been at it for years can benefit.

There are a huge number of advanced training organisations springing up, and there's a course to suit you whatever level of skills you currently have. At the moment, there is little formal regulation of advanced training organisations. That's not to say that every other school is a cowboy outfit, but be guided by the recommendations of other riders, bike magazines and dealers.

Many schools are run by ex-police riders and instructors, most of whom will be offering training based around the techniques in 'Roadcraft', the police riding manual. That doesn't mean they make their pupils bimble around in fluorescent jackets – you'll be making what they describe as 'good progress' outside 30, 40 and 50mph zones. But be assured you'll be making that 'good progress' at a rate you're comfortable with. A good instructor will be sensitive to the pace you want to learn and ride at, and will help you concentrate on the areas you most want to improve on. If the pupil-to-instructor ratio is more than one-to-one, a good school will also ensure that pupils of similar ability work with each instructor. That way, no one will be left behind by the rest of the group, and no one will feel held back by the group.

Central to advanced training is observation, and learning to make the most appropriate 'progress' you can in any set of circumstances. You'll hone your machine control techniques to corner and overtake faster and safer, and make the optimum use of your brakes. And the more all this stuff becomes second nature to you, the more fun you'll have on a bike.

Apart from the independent operators, the Institute of Advanced Motorcyclists offers economical advanced training in various parts of the country, as does the British Motorcyclists Federation. Your local police force may offer training too.

With proper instruction, you can learn techniques in a day or two, which otherwise might take years for you to develop on your own. And once you've learned advanced techniques you'll use them every time you ride. View every ride as an opportunity to hone your skills and technique.

Advanced training on the road (above) involves accompanied rides where experienced instructors assess your riding. The California Superbike School (left) holds track-based training in the UK too, where the emphasis is on developing machine control.

A student of the California Superbike School puts the theory into practice, developing skills on the track that will improve his road riding too. The right mix of road and track advanced training makes for more rounded and safer riders.

Think you're fast? Explore the limits of your bike and your riding ability by going on a trackday, or guarantee improved skills by signing up for a race school. And you'll be able to go out on challenging and famous circuits without making the huge commitments of time and cash demanded by racing.

Trackdays

Brands Hatch   *Castle Combe*   *Cadwell Park*

Helmet *Most circuits will expect you to wear a lid with an ACU Gold Seal (below).*

Gloves *Choose race-style for adequate protection and good feel.*

Leathers *A good one-piece is best, a zip-together two-piece is the next choice.*

Knee sliders *Trackday heroics can be measured in how many pairs of sliders you get through. Most circuits frown on sparkies.*

Boots *Good race boots are best for protection and feel.*

Oulton Park

Snetterton

The popularity of trackdays has led to a burgeoning industry that offers events countrywide pretty much all year round.

Apart from yourself and your bike, you'll need one-piece or good quality zip-together two-piece leathers (see page 50), a helmet with a gold ACU stamp (page 48), gloves (page 54) and boots (page 56). You may be required to tape up lights, indicators and mirrors. Most trackday organisers require you to show your driving licence when you sign on at an event, to prove that you've at least some idea of how to ride a bike. This is a condition imposed on them by their insurers. You'll be asked to fill out an indemnity form to limit the liability of the organisers, stating that you understand the nature of the event and that you're fit to take part. Don't forget to check with your own insurers that your policy extends to trackdays. If it doesn't, arrange additional cover, just in case the worst happens.

At most trackdays, riders are divided into groups depending on ability, ranging from novice (slow) to advanced (close to race pace). Choose the group you reckon you'll be most comfortable in. If you find yourself running rings round everyone in the slow group, then have the organisers move you up. It's better that way than starting out in too quick a group, being unsettled by faster riders rattling past you and having to haul yourself and your dented confidence down a class.

Before the track time begins, you'll be given a briefing to explain where the track goes and what the different marshalls flags mean. Start each session slowly and give your tyres time to warm up. Most accidents happen on cold tyres, where the rider gets a bit giddy at the start of a session. Use the day's early sessions to learn where the track goes and the best lines through the turns.

Groups usually go out for 15 to 20 minutes at a time. Doesn't sound like long, but it's long enough when you're concentrating and exerting plenty of physical energy. The hardest part is waiting until it's the turn of your group to go out again. Trackdays can be draining, so keep fluid levels up by drinking plenty of water and eat little and often – high-energy foods such as snack bars are ideal.

If you want to accelerate the learning curve, think about going to a race school. Structures vary, but most assign an instructor (usually a professional racer) to groups of roughly the same ability (typically no more than five riders, and sometimes one-to-one). A race school is the best way to work towards quick results on specific aspects of your riding, and you may not even need to use your own bike since some schools provide the machines.

Approached properly, trackdays and race schools will improve your machine control, which can only add to your riding skills and enjoyment. Check the bike press and the internet or ask your local bike dealer for details of events. And be warned: trackdays are addictive...

Helmets

A helmet is the single most important piece of motorcycle clothing you will buy – and not just because they're a legal requirement. The right lid, fitted correctly, could save your life in an accident. If you ever have to put a helmet properly to the test – and we hope you never do – you'll be glad you're wearing a good one.

ECE mark is replacing old BS tag. ACU Gold Seal

There's no need to spend a fortune to get a helmet that will provide an adequate level of protection. All helmets sold in the UK have to comply to a baseline standard to be legal for road use. More expensive helmets meet exactly the same standards as cheaper ones, the differences being in more complex construction, increased comfort and the quality and complexity of finish, visor mechanism, vents, liner material, removable liners and so on.

After the strap that holds your helmet on (usually a seatbelt-type or a pair of D-rings through which the strap passes), the next most important components are the outer shell and inner liner. Outer shells are usually injection-moulded polycarbonate (normally, but not always, used at the lower end of the market) or a laminate of glass fibre, carbon fibre and Kevlar. The outer shell is there to resist abrasion and penetration of objects in an impact.

The inner is moulded polystyrene designed to deform on impact, absorbing the force of a blow. For this reason, helmets that have sustained an impact should be replaced, or at least inspected – they're designed to take only one hefty hit. Inside the inner is a foam-backed cloth liner. This has no protective value but is there for comfort only. The helmet must fit your head evenly without excessive pressure at any point. If there is pressure, try another size or make.

Many helmets have vents to allow cool air in and warm air out, which is intended to reduce visor misting. There are anti-mist preparations and laminates available to help minimise this almost inevitable problem of full-face helmets. Laminates provide longer-term protection than sprays which have to be regularly applied.

Never let your helmet roll around on the floor; stand it with the head aperture to the ground. Use only very mild detergents and polish on lids, since solvents can attack shells and visors. Never buy a second-hand helmet – you don't know its history and it could have been dropped. Some helmets are quieter than others, but none are so quiet as to prevent hearing damage from wind noise – so always wear ear plugs.

The current British Standard for helmets (BS6658) is currently being phased out in favour of the European ECE22-05. The BS sticker will continue to appear on the back of lids for the next few years. The EC standard is denoted on a label on the chin strap, although some manufacturers are also declaring it on the outside of the shell. Gold ACU stickers show that a helmet has been approved for competition use (the tag is silver for off-road lids).

Reckon to replace your helmet every four to five years, regardless of how well you've looked after it, because the materials that make up your lid degrade over time. And always replace scratched visors as soon as possible.

Full-face helmets provide the most protection.

Motocross lids make for urban cool on the road.

Scooter, retro and classic riders often favour open-face.

Many excellent, high-tech man-made materials are now being used in motorcycle clothing. But when it comes to crash protection, particularly from abrasion, there's still nothing to top good old-fashioned leather – especially when those leathers have state-of-the-art armour built in. Back in 1995, EC legislation called the Personal Protective Equipment (PPE) Directive was introduced, and this is your guarantee that your leathers will do what you hope they'll do. Leathers cannot be sold as protective clothing – as opposed to merely fashion items – in Britain and the rest of Europe, unless their design and construction have passed a British or European Standard or similar approved test. They must also have passed an EC examination. Manufacturers must have EC-approved quality control processes in place too. Only then can leathers carry a CE tag to show they're up to scratch.

Leathers

All the colours, all the shapes, this Spyke suit's top level kit.

While leather is very good for sliding along in, it doesn't have much in-built impact protection. That's why it pays to have decent armour at likely impact points – shoulders, elbows, back, hips and knees. Some cheap leathers (and indeed some more expensive ones) have foam padding in these areas. That isn't going to help much in a crash. Proper armour, designed to absorb some of the energy of an impact, will.

Armour is usually made of two or more materials – a harder outer layer made of dense foam or plastic, and a softer inner. The outer layer spreads the load across the inner, which cushions the impact. Decent armour finds the middle ground between too hard – which only serves to deflect the shock of impact directly to your body, and too soft, which will do the same.

As with the leathers that carry the armour, there are EC standards for armour sold as protective equipment, so the CE tag offers some guarantee of the protective potential. For more detail on armour, see page 62.

With the object of getting decent leathers in mind, there's only one choice left – one-piece or two-piece? A one-piece gives instant racer chic, but unlike a two-piece you can't just slip the jacket off when you reach your destination. Two-piece suits usually zip together, and the further round your waist that zip extends, the better it will hold together in the event of a tumble.

One-piece suits are widely viewed as offering superior protection. That is not always the case – there are good and bad suits in each category. Look for good quality hide, double layers (panels should be sewn on rather than sewn in) and armour on impact points.

If your leathers get wet, let them dry out naturally, otherwise the material and stitching can weaken. Should they become dirty, clean them with a very mild detergent solution and, again, allow them to dry naturally. There are many leather treatments on the market, but some of them are better suited to horse saddles than bike suits. Use sparingly and don't soak stitching with them, at the risk of weakening it. And don't be tempted to use waterproofing solutions on leather for the same reasons. Carry waterproofs (page 58) to wear on top when the clouds open, which given our uncertain weather, they almost certainly will.

Good leathers cost but, just like a decent helmet, they're more than worth it. Looked after properly they will last and, more importantly, protect you for years. Only the colours and styling go out of date.

Another two-piece. This time there are zips right round the waist.

Man-made fabric
jackets &
trousers

Leather might provide the ultimate in crash protection, but other than wind protection, it struggles to keep out the other elements. That's where fabric jackets and trousers come into their own. What's more, modern materials and armour mean they can run leathers a close second when things go pear-shaped.

A fabric jacket can be as stylish as leathers.

There's a huge array of fabric clothing available, at all prices. What the clothing costs isn't always an indication of how water/wind/crash-proof it'll be, but features such as armour, thermal and waterproof linings made of space-age materials and features like pockets and vents all tend to drive prices up.

Fit is all important. Jacket sleeves must be long enough so they don't ride up with arms outstretched; likewise the back and trouser legs when you're crouched in riding position. If you expect to wear the jacket over winter layers or one-piece leathers, it has to be roomy, but ideally not so baggy as to flap around with the thermal liner removed on warmer days. Trousers and jackets that zip together are preferable to those which don't, not only for warmth, but also to prevent them parting company and exposing your flesh in a crash. Adjustable straps on the collar, waist, wrists, elbows and ankles help ensure the best fit. Flaps over zips help keep wind and water out, and check that the poppers nearest the waist and crotch are rubber-covered to prevent damage to tank paintwork.

Armour, preferably CE-approved, is fitted in many fabric jackets and trousers, and is usually removable to allow the garments to be worn over leathers containing armour of their own. When you try on a jacket or trousers, make sure that the armour isn't too free to move around. It needs to stay close to the areas it is designed to protect or else it won't be much use in a crash.

As with leathers, double stitching and layers are definite bonuses on impact points like elbows and posterior. Fabrics lack the durability of leather, so it's pretty much a foregone conclusion that you'll knock holes in them even in low-speed spills.

Most modern jackets and trousers have a waterproof membrane under the outer – look for Gore-Tex and Sympatex labels. These fabrics keep moisture out while allowing sweat to escape.

So while decent fabric clothing should keep you warm and dry, it won't provide ultimate crash protection. But it's certainly better than simple nylon waterproofs, which are very much a second line of defence on top of proper protective clothing.

Here's the basic set-up. Look for decent armour, an effective neck closure, and straps at key points to make the suit fit you. Outer pockets need double closures to keep rain out, and your possessions in.

Waist belt keeps wind from upper body. Good neck closure too.

Plenty of armour and upper-arm straps. Good.

Lots of armour again. And a pocket for the mobile phone.

Here's a test you can conduct in the comparative safety of your own home. Stick an obstacle in the middle of the floor – a kitchen or dining chair should do it – and launch yourself at it in a comedy tumble-down style. In the ensuing melée, one thing will almost certainly happen. Your hands will make contact with the floor before any other part of your body does. This is a reaction that goes back to the dawn of basic survivalism.

Gloves

Consider that your hands shoot out first in a fall, and be assured that gloveless, T-shirted, shorts-wearing, trainer-shoed casual summer riders are cruising for much more than a bruising. It isn't called protective clothing for nothing, and after a decent helmet, proper gloves are the next most essential line of defence.

At their most basic, gloves must let you still feel the controls through their protective layers. Leather is great for this. It breaks in nicely and moulds to the shape of your hands and their movement. Double layer leather and stitched-in protection should be there at impact points – specifically, palms and knuckles. As with most bike clothing, hi-tech materials are being used more extensively, such as Kevlar, Cordura and Thinsulate for, variously, protection, weatherproofing and insulation. Many modern gloves are a combination of leather and these hi-tech fabrics. Some are made wholly from non-leather materials.

Look for velcro wrist straps and do them up tight enough for the gloves to stay on your hands in the event of a tumble.

When buying gloves, it's a good idea to take along your leathers or jacket to check for fit over or under the cuffs.

As the seasons change, so will your glove requirements. In their better made (and usually more expensive) forms, race and summer gloves offer optimal feel of controls and great crash protection but poor insulation from rain and cold weather. Waterproof and windproof but breathable gloves are now available for all-weather riding, and insulated gloves keep out the chill on the coldest days.

If your leather gloves do get wet, let them dry naturally rather than putting them on top of a radiator or in the airing cupboard.

Basic race-style glove, note knuckle protection and long wrist.

Shorty race glove. Good hand protection, elasticated wrist.

Lots of carbon and kevlar in these Spidis. Fine leather for good feel, but no wrist staps.

Double layers, over-and-under the wrist staps, loads of protective inserts. Plenty of protection for even the most paranoid.

Boots

Decent bike boots are an important part of your protective clothing wardrobe. As well as your foot, they should also protect the ankle and lower leg, which are particularly vulnerable.

Leather is still the most common material used in bike boots but, as with clothing, many hi-tech fabrics are being used – and not just for the linings.

Race-style boots usually have impact protection in the shin, ankle, calf and heel areas. Foam is the minimum to look for and additional armour, made from high-impact plastic for example, is a definite bonus. To prevent them flexing in a tumble, soles are often reinforced with metal or plastic inserts, which still allow the sole to give when the wearer is walking. Zip closures are normally concealed behind a Velcro flap to reduce the chances of their opening in an impact and the boot flying off.

Full-on race boots come with toe and calf sliders and most flex sufficiently to make walking around in them reasonably easy. However, there's a rule of thumb that says the more protective a boot, the less comfortable it is off the bike. Not always true, but you certainly wouldn't want to go on a nature ramble in motocross boots.

Touring-style boots offer more of a compromise. Many give good levels of protection with the added bonus of a degree of waterproofing, although some sports boots are now also available with this. Touring boots are usually pretty comfortable off the bike.

Winter boots go even further, offering insulation too. As with gloves, this is important for winter riding. Most of your body's heat is lost through the extremities. Apart from being uncomfortable, coldness can result in reduced concentration or worse, especially when the wind-chill factor is taken into consideration.

Most riders wind up with several pairs of boots to suit the seasons or the type of riding they're doing.

When choosing boots, take your riding suit or trousers with you to ensure they zip up okay over your leathers or under your oversuit. Like gloves, boots should always be allowed to dry naturally to preserve the leather.

Above and below, the simple, clean lines of touring boots can conceal a multitude of weatherproof fabrics.

Motocross boots; very protective, but very stiff for everyday use.

Race boots provide optimum support for least weight.

Back in the bad old days, waterproof clothing meant waxed cotton. And it did a reasonable enough job for the speeds of the day, but it also required continual reproofing and was an absolute dirt magnet. It's still available, but unless you're on some kind of retro trip, you may like to consider something a bit more up-to-date.

Waterproofs

Then there were PVC oversuits. Waterproof all right (until they ripped along their welded seams), but the build-up of sweat on the inside, even on mild days, could make you as sodden as the rain you were trying to keep out.

Nylon is a popular material for waterproofs and has the advantage of folding down small so they can be carried easily, often in an integral bum bag.

Nowadays, though, modern synthetics allow oversuits to pull off that neat trick of being waterproof and breathable at the same time. A real bonus on warm days or when riding any distance. Many suits are lined for additional protection from the cold. Some feature reflective material to boost your visibility at night.

Check that seams are taped on the inside to stop water seeping through. Zips should also have Velcro flaps to prevent water getting in through the closures. And these closures should open sufficiently wide to allow you to get into the suit at the side of the road once the heavens have opened. Choose a suit large enough to go over your usual riding gear, and make sure it's big enough not to restrict your riding position when it's on, but not so big as to flap around like a gigantic sail on the move. Velcro ankle, wrist and neck closures help to fit the suit snugly to your body and prevent water entering through these key areas.

Waterproof overboots and gloves are also available and are worth it if you think you're going to get caught out by the weather while wearing your summer gear. They fold down so small that they take up next to no space under your bike's seat.

Waterproof suits can carry armour too and boast many features of their less rain-stopping equivalents. As with any bike clothing, look for good fit.

Handy nylon one-piece can be carried in integral bum-bag 'til needed.

Thermals

Cold can be one of the rider's biggest enemies. Once you get chilly, your concentration starts to wander and accidents can happen. Even when the weather's just above zero degrees, wind chill can take the temperature you're enduring well down into the negative numbers. Apart from all that, it's just downright miserable, and biking's meant to be fun. But with the right gear, year-round riding needn't be a freezing chore.

Face and neck protector.

Tabard to cover neck and chest.

Fingers get cold first without thermal gloves.

Balaclava extends to upper body.

Just make sure you take this beauty off before going into the bank.

Thermal fleece is something you'll be grateful for.

Thermal trousers – forget style, it's keeping warm that counts. Thermals make a huge difference in cold weather.

You could raid grandad's underwear drawer for a pair of long johns and long-sleeved vest, because they'll serve you pretty well. Thermal underwear is available in most high street clothing chain stores at reasonable prices. More specialised thermals can be had from skiing and outdoor shops too.

Natural materials work well until they get wet, either from sweat or rain, when they tend to hold on to the moisture and take an age to dry out. That's when cold can set in again. Silk is lighter and thinner than cotton or wool, so it tends to work better in this respect. Full synthetics tend to let body heat build up and up, which can be pretty uncomfortable too. One other problem is that synthetics often cause worse abrasions than natural fabrics in the event of a tumble.

Bike clothing manufacturers are wise to the problems and offer a variety of solutions, some of which combine natural and synthetic materials. These allow you to keep warm or cool as required, wicking sweat away from the body in the process.

A thermal neck warmer is a real boon on colder days, filling the vulnerable gap between jacket collar and helmet. A thin thermal balaclava under your helmet is a great help too. As for the other extremities most prone to heat loss, thermal socks and inner gloves are indispensable.

Thermal clothing might just seem like another layer of protection to struggle in and out of, but on long cold rides, you'll be glad you bothered.

Armour

Leathers and man-made fabric suits provide varying degrees of abrasion protection, but neither offers the rider much impact protection. That's where armour comes into play. It can make the difference between serious injury and walking away from a tumble.

Highly protective Knox back protector covering shoulder, spine and kidney areas. Straps go over shoulders and protector is further secured by velcro waist belt.

Simple foam padding provides little if any protection. The most it does is to make suits more comfortable. Armour proper varies in hardness. Too unforgiving, and it transfers the shock of impact directly to the body. Too soft and the same thing happens. Good armour lies between these extremes and often has harder (outer) and softer (inner) elements, because it needs to take the initial impact, then deform to soften the blow as much as it can. It's very similar to what happens with a crash helmet (see page 48), where the hard outer takes the initial whack and prevents penetration of objects, and the soft, deformable inner cushions the impact. In theory, then, the inside of the lid quickly slows the rider's head to a stop, rather than the sudden contact with the ground.

Armour sold as protective equipment must comply to CE tests and carry a label accordingly, just as with leathers. Look for the label and then at least you'll know your money is being invested in something that meets certain base standards. Good armour is designed to pass as little as 30 per cent of the force of an impact. As with helmets, replace any armour that's taken a significant whack in a crash. That's fairly simple on most riding suits, since it's held in Velcro-fastened pockets in the lining.

Check that armour is in the right place on any suit you're thinking of buying – not just where it's located (knees, hips, elbows, shoulders and back), but also how it fits to your body.

Many riders use a separate back protector to give extra peace of mind. For comfort, you'll need to remove the one in your suit, if it has one. First developed for the race track, back protectors have saved many riders from severe injury.

State-of-the-art armour inserts

Above and right, motocross armour

Insurance

Any bike used or kept on the road has to be insured, not least because you need to show a current insurance policy to purchase a tax disc. And even if you're keeping your bike off the road, perhaps for winter, you'll probably want theft cover at least.

There are three main types of insurance cover: third party only; third party, fire and theft; and comprehensive. Cost rises in line with level of cover.

Third party only is the basic legal minimum required to get you on the road. In the event of your causing an accident, it covers injury to other people and damage to their vehicles. It doesn't cover injury or damage to you or your bike and, obviously, fire and theft are excluded.

Third party, fire and theft provides broader cover. Apart from third party liabilities being taken care of, if your bike is destroyed by fire (not that they often combust, spontaneously or otherwise) your insurers will pay out. More importantly, you're covered against theft of your bike, provided you meet the security conditions set out in your policy. But you are not covered for any damage caused to the bike and/or your helmet and leathers through an accident where you're at fault. For that, you'll need comprehensive insurance, but even this doesn't go so far as to cover personal injury claims or loss of earnings where the accident is down to you.

Insurance companies look at a variety of factors in calculating your premium, or even to decide if they want to cover you at all. Your age, how long you've held a full licence, occupation, address, any motoring convictions, previous claims, where the bike will be kept and, of course, the type of bike – all these factors have a bearing on how much your insurance cover will cost.

The cost of insurance tends to drop at the ages of 21, 25 and 35. A 19-year-old pop musician with a Suzuki GSX-R1000, no garage, a dangerous driving conviction, who has held a full licence for only one year and lives in an inner city, is unlikely to find an insurer willing to cover them. Even if an insurer will, the premium is likely to be prohibitively expensive. At the other extreme, a 55-year-old parish priest in a rural outpost, with a commuter bike, a garage and a clean licence for 35 years, is likely to have an easier time of it.

Most riders fall between these extremes of course, and there is much you can do to reduce your premium so it pays to shop around. Insurance policies, apart from third party only, have an 'excess', an initial amount of any claim you agree to pay yourself. If you agree to pay a higher excess, your insurer will reduce the premium. Similarly, you can reduce your premium by garaging your bike, fitting an approved alarm or immobiliser, and using additional locks and data tagging. It's worth taking all the anti-theft precautions that you can. Insurers often refuse theft cover to people who've had machines stolen when they eventually get their replacement bikes.

No-claims discount can make a huge difference to your premium – up to 50 per cent if you can maintain a clean insurance record for five years.

Above all, remember to play it straight with your insurer. If you make any major modifications to your bike, you must tell them or they could refuse to pay out on a claim. And they do keep a register of claims and investigate any dubious claims vigorously.

Most important of all, make sure you can get insurance cover for the bike you want *before* committing to buying it. If you can't, all's not lost. Go for a bike in a lower insurance group that you can get cover for (bikes are graded according to type, performance and how attractive they are to thieves) and do your best to build a good insurance record.

Both ends of the risk scale as perceived by the insurance companies. Of course the truth lies somewhere between...

Bad: young, inner city, big bike, expensive to insure.

Good: old, small bike, more no-claims than nostril hairs!

Security

Bike theft statistics make pretty depressing reading. In the UK alone, 30,000 bikes are stolen every year – that's one every 20 minutes or so. Precious few are ever recovered. Physical security of machines is not high on bike manufacturers' list of priorities. The best you can expect as standard on most bikes is a steering lock on the ignition barrel incapable of withstanding anything more than a half-hearted attempt with a screwdriver. A sharp tug on the bars is enough to pop some. So that's the bad news. But take heart – there's still plenty you can do to reduce the chances of becoming part of the statistics.

U-locks and cables can often be stored under the seat.

If you're able to park your bike where you can see it while you go about your business, so much the better. This is rarely practical, though, so you'll need additional protection.

Always use a lock of some sort, no matter how short a time you're leaving your bike unattended. A disc lock is easy to carry and provides some amount of visible deterrent, hopefully enough to put off casual joyriders while you nip into the shop for a newspaper. But it won't stop more determined thieves lifting your bike into a van.

A U-lock is bulkier and less easy to carry, but provides a similar level of security by passing through the brake discs at the fork legs to prevent the bike being wheeled away. Some are large enough, or come with a cable, to secure the bike to another machine or an immovable object, such as a lamp post. Many modern bikes have a space under the seat for a U-lock, or there are carrying brackets that mount behind the numberplate or on the frame.

The next step up is a high-quality lock and chain that will allow you secure the bike to an immovable object. But while they provide a higher level of security, the larger they are, the more difficult they are to carry. They can be strapped in a bag on the pillion seat or carried in a tank bag or panniers, but for safety's sake don't be tempted to carry a lock and chain around your waist or over your shoulder.

When locking up, take care not to thread the chain through a part of the bike that can be easily removed, such as a footrest hanger, otherwise you might come back to the bike to find yourself with no

more than a solidly secured brake pedal. And if locking one of the wheels to the immovable object, be sure to wrap the chain round the rim rather than one of the spokes. Don't leave so much slack in the chain that its links (or the lock itself) can reach the ground, where they'll be all the easier for a thief to attack with a hammer.

While an alarm should be enough to put off a casual thief, it can't stop your bike being lifted into a van. Neither can an immobiliser, but it can stop it being ridden away. Many insurance companies insist you fit one of these electronic security devices as a condition of your insurance cover. Even where their fitment is not a pre-condition, insurers usually offer a discount if you fit one that's on their approved list of alarms and immobilisers. And as they usually self-arm when you park the bike up, they're one part of your security routine you won't forget. Sadly, though, most people ignore the screeches and bleeps of vehicle alarms these days, so you'll need to employ some form of physical security too.

Where you park is as important as what you do once you've parked. Busy, well-lit areas are best – even the most brazen thieves prefer a little privacy.

Be aware that thieves often follow their targets to see where they're going to park or where they live. Don't get paranoid. But if you suspect you're being tailed, there's no harm in going round the block one more time just to be sure.

When you're parking at work, try to arrange for you and a colleague to lock your bikes together. If

Getting heavy duty with big gauge chain and lock.

enough of you ride to work, your employers might agree to let you use part of a warehouse to park in, or fit ground anchors in the car park for your bikes. And make the security guys aware of your bike, then at least they'll know if the person taking an interest in the machine isn't you.

Some local authorities have fitted anchors in bike bays. Use them whenever possible.

If your only option is to park outside, you might want to consider using a bike cover, which at least hides the bike from casual prying eyes. The more weathered and knackered the cover looks, the better. There could be any old junk under there.

All the advice on parking when you're out also applies at home, if you don't have the luxury of a shed or garage. If you have a back garden, park your bike there in preference to out front.

The safest place to store your bike is a secure shed or garage, and it may be a condition of your insurance that it's locked up at night. It's best to put your bike away as soon as you get home, and don't spend ages warming it up outside your house before you go out. Maintenance and cleaning are best done out of view too, or done quickly. And don't advertise the fact that you're a bike fan by plastering your garage or shed doors with bike stickers.

Fit a ground anchor in your shed or garage. Position it so it's difficult for a thief to access when the bike's parked up and thread the chain through the frame or swingarm and back wheel rather than through the front. Again, make sure the chain is taut enough to be clear of the floor and the lock is positioned so that it can't be pulled to the ground and smacked with a hammer.

Make your garage or shed doors secure too. The popular up-and-over metal garage doors are as easy to pop open as a can of beer. Fit extra deadlocks, but not to the extent of advertising the fact that there's something worth nicking in there. Additional locks are best fitted on the inside of the door, where possible.

If your garage is adjacent to the house, and you have a domestic alarm system, consider extending it to the garage. Should your garage or shed have electricity on the same ring as the house, you could use a cheap baby monitor for extra peace of mind.

No one likes talking about bike theft, but security is as essential to the motorcyclist as decent riding kit. Just ask anyone who's been unfortunate enough to lose a bike to theft.

Remember, the biggest threat of theft comes not from the casual thief or joyrider, but the professional thief, many of whom steal to order. Do what you can to put both classes of scum out of business.

As almost three-quarters of stolen bikes are broken up to be sold on as spares, there's one

more security precaution that might put potential thieves off – marking systems such as Datatag. Tagging makes the rightful owner of stolen parts easier to trace. It uses marking numbers, microdots or microchip tags stamped on or fitted to various of the bike's components. These codes are unique to each owner, which allows the owner's name and address to be traced through a database when the stolen parts are found by the police. Police forces are equipped with scanners to read microchip tags, and tagging can provide the law with the evidence to convict bike thieves.

This is one area of security where many manufacturers are beginning to do more for the purchasers of their bikes, even if these companies are still woefully lax on physical security. Many new bikes come with Datatag or similar as standard. Honda is using a marking system called Smart Water. The company has also introduced a concept called HISS (Honda Ignition Security System), a type of immobiliser that will only allow the bike to be started with the correct key.

If your bike doesn't have tagging, buy a kit from your dealer and mark key components yourself, placing the sticker that comes with the kit on the screen or top of the tank to advertise that you've done it. If you've bought a Datatagged bike second-hand, the previous owner should be able to give you the documentation to register yourself with the company as the new owner.

Don't become a paranoid obsessive about bike security, but be wary. Take as many steps as you reasonably can to protect your bike. Above all, use the best quality gear (look for the Sold Secure and *RiDE* magazine recommended tags on new products, or ask the advice of your local police vehicle security unit and/or insurance company). With a little care and common sense, you can put bike theft lower down your list of worries.

One last thing: we can all do our bit to stop theft by not buying bikes or parts we suspect to be stolen. Take away the demand and the supply will dwindle.

Keep your garage secure, but do it with discreet, internal locks like these (above) so as not to advertise what you've got.

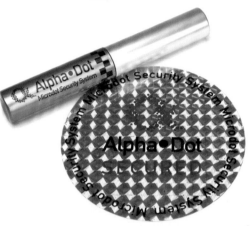

Security is getting smarter, but so are thieves.

Fit an alarm/imobiliser as a first-line deterrent.

Luggage

When you're riding long distances, luggage storage is particularly valuable. There are two types available – hard and soft.

Tank bag mounts either by magnets or straps or a combination of both. Some have a holder which can be left mounted on the tank.

Ventura Bike Pac can be used as a rucksack off the bike. This is better than a conventional rucksack as you don't have to carry weight on your back while riding.

B-Bag mounts over the pillion seat. Design means some weight can be carried lower down.

Frank Thomas Cargo hard luggage is favoured by some for its robustness. Less easy to store off the bike, however.

Hard luggage is available as an option from some bike manufacturers and there is a healthy aftermarket making hard-shelled panniers and top boxes. Some is available colour-matched to your bike's paint scheme. The units are mounted on frames bolted to the bike and can be removed when you arrive at your destination. Most are lockable for limited security when you stop en route.

Soft luggage offers a degree more flexibility than hard luggage, in that it can be easily moved from bike to bike and doesn't need bolted on framework, which can look unsightly when hard boxes are removed.

There are various types of soft luggage. Tank bags have magnetic bases to attach them to the fuel tank, with straps for additional security or for using on plastic tanks. Some are expandable by means of a concertina system of fabric and zips. Others have straps and double up as rucksacks. Clear panels on top allow you to refer to maps or directions.

Throwover panniers attach over the seat by a system of straps and laces. Some are shaped to accomodate the kicked-up silencers of sportsbikes. There are tail packs too, which bungy on to the pillion pad. Others mount on racks at the back of the bike. Panniers and tail packs are often expandable. The better soft luggage comes with rain covers that look like gigantic shower caps.

There are two main things to remember with luggage. The first is to ensure that it's securely mounted and doesn't hamper operation of the bike. Your trip will come to an unscheduled and unpleasant stop if soft panniers, for example, find their way into the back wheel. It's also surprising how much heat silencers generate, enough to set panniers and their contents smouldering nicely.

The second thing to remember is that you shouldn't overload luggage. Too much weight wrongly distributed will upset the handling of your bike. Your owner's manual will tell you how much can be safely carried. At a more basic level, cram too much into the bags and there's a chance they'll burst open. But if you don't mind airing your dirty linen on the M25, then that's up to you.

Throw-over soft panniers
These are from Triumph. Straps and bungees hold them on. Note how they're shaped so as not to touch the kicked-up silencers.

Useful
Gadgets

We're not talking here about simple customising. Instead, we're interested in more handy accessories than Live-to-Ride bolt-ons, tinted headlamp covers, anodised bolts and myriad other tat that gets in between the useful pages of so many accessory catalogues. The engine and chassis sections of this book look at the key items you might consider in those departments, so over the next couple of pages we'll turn our attentions to those items which will improve your biking life in more general and useful ways.

Paddock stands/benches
Few bikes come with centre stands these days. They're options on some and almost a religious no-no on others, particularly sportsbikes. Centre stands make work on a bike easy where wheel removal is required (albeit with the assistance of bottle jacks and arbitrary bits of wood for the front), but in their absence, paddock stands make sense.
Rear paddock stands raise

the back wheel off the floor by holding the swing arm or rear wheel spindle, while front stands raise the forks to bring the front wheel clear. Others, meanwhile, sit under the bottom yoke to hold the bike up in the absence of the front end.
Other stands are available to go under the engine and lift the whole bike up. Going the whole distance, you can buy a hydraulic bench to lift your bike close to eye level for intensive maintenance.

Intercoms *'Hello, hello, are you there? Go ahead London. Did you see that guy? Are we there yet? Slow down. Speed up. Scream if you want to go faster.' Yes, intercoms are endless fun and make riding more sociable. And when the novelty pales, you can always unplug them.*

Tank protectors
These handy little items don't cost much, but spare your tank's finish from the worst your jacket or leathers have to inflict. Depending on the tolerance of your taste, you can choose clear or self-coloured to something with silicone breasts on. But they all work the same.

Battery chargers
If your bike's going to be laid up for any length of time, and there's power in your shed, buy a trickle charger to keep your battery up to power. Otherwise it'll be dead and useless come springtime.

Fasteners
By all means use aftermarket ally fasteners where they don't compromise structural integrity or come under extreme pressure – for example, holding on brake calipers. They save weight, look trick and corrode more slowly than some badly plated original equipment stuff.

Aftermarket bodywork, mirrors, indicators, levers
The first parts to take the flak in a tumble are also highly expensive. If you aren't a stickler for originality, a healthy aftermarket provides more affordable options. Bodywork, mirrors, indicators and levers are all available in varying quality, but almost always at lower prices than original parts from a dealer. Track bike addicts have no qualms about fitting this kit, because it mostly works. Hugger (above) is a useful bolt-on that stops road dirt and water being flung at the rear shock by the back wheel.

Tyre pressure gauges
As anyone who's struggled with garage forecourt air lines and gauges will attest (see Tyres), they were designed by an anti-biking devil who laughs diabolically as your 20p or token runs out. A foot pump and a decent analogue or digital gauge are much better bets to keep pressures spot-on.

3

Know your motorcycle

Tyres

You aren't going anywhere without tyres, and they're arguably the most important parts of a motorcycle, with some of the toughest jobs to do. The rear transmits the power to the ground, while both have a huge part to play in the handling of the bike, offering grip in the turns as well as in a straight line. This grip is also vital for efficient braking.

Fit the correct tyres for your bike and type of the riding you do – and don't be tempted to mix and match brands or types.

Tyres do plenty for us and ask for little in return. Don't take them for granted. Check every week that they're at your bike manufacturer's recommended pressures. Do this when they're cold. Your machine manual will tell you the correct pressures for solo, pillion and riding with luggage.

Under-inflation accelerates wear, ruins handling, raises fuel consumption and lowers top speed. Over-inflation makes the ride less comfortable and reduces the size of the patch of tyre in contact with the road, upsetting handling. It can also lead to premature wear. So it pays to get tyre pressures right, although anyone who's ever struggled to inflate their bike tyres with a garage forecourt air line will understand why people neglect them. Best to get a footpump and a decent tyre pressure gauge – and don't trust the cheap plastic item on top of most footpumps.

Remember to replace the valve caps. At higher speeds, centrifugal forces can have the same effect on a valve stem as putting your finger on it. The only thing stopping the air escaping is the valve cap. Metal ones with rubber seals inside are best for motorcycle applications.

Wear indicators – little raised ridges across and in the bottom of the tread grooves – show when your tyres have reached the end of the manufacturer's recommended safe wear limit. Little arrows or the letters TWI (tread wear indicator) at the 'shoulder' or top of the tyre wall indicate the grooves they're in.

Occasionally, other damage such as punctures or tears might mean they need to be changed before they wear out. It's a good idea before every ride to check for punctures and tears, or any foreign objects such as glass or nails stuck in the tread. There is another thing that might lead to early replacement, especially if your regular riding doesn't feature many corners. That's when the tyres 'square off' – the tyres lose their semi-circular profile at the centre of the tread.

Fit the correct type of tyres to your bike, look after them and they'll look after you.

Tyre types

There are three main tyre types – crossply, bias-belted and radial. These days crossplies are mainly found on lighter, slower bikes, although they are available with up to a 130mph-plus rating for some bikes. Bias-belts were developed for the emerging class of superbikes in the 1970s and are still fairly popular. But radials are the most modern construction. As well as being the most modern, radial construction is fast becoming the most popular tyre type – you'll find nothing else on sportsbikes. Radials almost always run without inner tubes.

In a crossply, the plies that make up the carcass cross the circumference at around 25–35° and are layered to criss-cross each other. A bias-belted tyre has additional plies under the crown (the treaded rubber bit) to prevent centrifugal expansion under load and slow wear.

The plies in a radial tyre run at 90° across the circumference, with what are called crown plies running at more oblique angles to maintain the profile, a bit like the older bias belts do.

Apart from the carcass, there are elements common to all tyres. The bead or tringle is made from wire and holds the tyre to the rim. The bead filler is a rubber insert that helps strengthen the sidewall – the area between the bead and the crown, which is the treaded rubber section. The shoulder is where the sidewall meets the crown.

Tyres come in different compounds of rubber that are invariably a compromise between grip and longevity. Tourer riders will want longevity over ultra-grippiness, while the sportsbike rider seeking to make the most of the bike's handling will want grip above anything else. Some tyres even have multiple compounds on the crown – hard and long-wearing in the middle, softer on the edges for the turns.

Although it's important, compound is not the single most vital aspect of a tyre. It's the carcass that's the busiest part of the tyre. A mix of various synthetic fibres and steel wires, it controls the shape of the tyre, how it deflects and flexes and the temperature it runs at.

A modern radial tyre. Michelin use special Delta construction for stability.

Typical road construction. Tread pattern is optimised for water clearance, ensuring grip in wet and dry conditions

A radial tyre showing the different plies.

Bias belted tyre.

Buying, choosing & fitting

Rear tyres usually wear out before fronts because that's where all the power is transmitted. Don't be tempted to mix and match tyre types or use one from a different manufacturer, though. They're designed and tested in pairs. If your tyres are tubed, fit a new inner tube too. Some radials can be fitted with tubes, but check with the manufacturer's recommendations. And always fit tyres of the correct load and speed ratings for your bike.

Don't buy oversize (that's wider) tyres for your bike thinking they'll give more grip. They won't, and there could be clearance problems with the swingarm or other chassis components, which will upset the handling. Likewise, an undersize tyre will have too flat a profile when fitted.

The Haynes workshop manual for your bike gives instructions on changing tyres, but if you don't feel up to the job, or your tyres are tubeless and you don't have access to a compressed air line, you might want to entrust the job to a tyre fitter. Tyres are directional, and the direction of rotation is indicated by an arrow on the sidewall. They must be fitted the right way round.

It's a good idea to have new valves fitted to the rims when having new tubeless tyres fitted, since the rubber bodies can harden and perish. Short valve stems minimise the problems of centrifugal force described in the first part of this chapter.

Some makes of tyres have coloured dots to indicate the lightest part of the tyre and the fitter must position this adjacent to the valve.

Tyre mounting lubricant or soapy water is used to clean the bead and help it seal. With the stem core of the valve removed, the tyre is inflated to about 50psi until the bead seats. The core is then refitted and the tyre inflated to operating pressure. Control lines concentric with the bead show if the tyre is evenly seated to the bead. If not, the tyre is deflated and the process repeated.

The wheel is then balanced, stick-on weights being put opposite the point the tyre always stops at until the wheel stops randomly when spun. Unbalanced wheels upset handling and tyre wear is accelerated.

Puncture repair with mushroom type plugs is possible on some tubeless tyres, depending on the severity of the hole. Puncture repair is not possible when the damage is on the sidewall rather than the tread. Different countries have different regulations, and manufacturers make their own recommendations. For safety reasons, these are best adhered to. Don't be tempted to patch punctured tubes – use new ones instead. Tubed tyre punctures, where fixable, should be repaired by vulcanisation to prevent moisture from attacking the carcass.

New tyres should be run-in for the first 100 miles or so. The tread of new tyres is smooth and therefore slippy. Running-in takes that top layer off. So no heavy braking, hard acceleration or cornering until the tyres are broken in.

If in doubt, hammer it out, or in. Tyre changer puts the rear spindle back in.

Wheel balancing is essential, especially for the front tyre. A good fitter will use a dynamic machine to do this for you.

Engine **types**

There are plenty of engine configurations in current production, but they all work in one of two ways – as two-strokes and four-strokes. The strokes refer to the number of times the piston moves up and down the bore in each combustion cycle. And that tells you a lot about the characteristics of the engine and its mechanical make-up.

The four-stroke process in four easy steps; suck, squeeze, bang, blow. Also known as the Otto cycle. It's powered most bikes of the last 100 years.

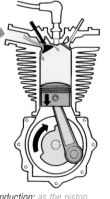

Induction: as the piston descends the inlet valve opens, allowing the fuel/air mixture to be drawn directly into the combustion chamber.

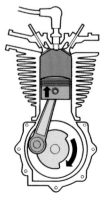

Compression: the piston starts to ascend and the inlet valve closes. The mixture is compressed as the piston rises.

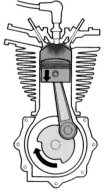

Ignition: the spark plug ignites the compressed mixture, forcing the piston down the bore.

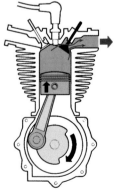

Exhaust: the exhaust valve opens to allow the burnt gases to be expelled through the exhaust port as the piston rises.

A combustion cycle consists of induction (air and fuel in), compression (squeezing the mixture), ignition (setting it alight) and exhaust (getting the spent gases out). This is the same no matter how many strokes an engine is. Helpfully, the stages are pretty self-explanatory.

Air and fuel are drawn into the combustion chamber during induction, squashed in compression, ignited and burnt during ignition (sometimes called power) and removed from the combustion chamber during exhaust. That's the process the engine has to go through in order to covert the chemical energy in petrol into something we can use to make our bike move.

There are several differences between two and four-stroke engines, but the most apparent is how they control the flow of gas in and out of the combustion chamber.

A four-stroke

The four-stroke gets its name because it takes four strokes to complete one combustion cycle. At the start of the cycle, the piston is at TDC (top dead centre – as far up the bore as it can travel), and the valves are shut. As the crankshaft turns, the piston drops down the bore and the inlet valve opens allowing fresh fuel and air mixture into the cylinder.

As the piston reaches BDC (bottom dead centre – as far down the bore as possible), the inlet valve closes, trapping the mixture in the cylinder. That is the induction stroke finished with.

As the crankshaft continues to rotate, it now starts to push the piston back up the bore towards TDC. Since all the valves are shut, sealing the cylinder, the air/fuel mixture has nowhere to go and gets compressed more and more until the piston is again at TDC. The piston has now done two strokes, one down the bore and one back up, and the crankshaft has turned through one revolution.

With the mixture squashed in the small space above the piston, it's ready to ignite – so the spark plug sparks and starts a fire in the mixture, causing it to expand rapidly and push forcibly on all the surfaces. As our piston is the only thing that can move, the high pressure in the cylinder pushes the piston back down the bore until it reaches BDC and can't be pushed any further. This is the end of the ignition/power stoke.

All that is required now is to empty the burnt gas from the cylinder. At this point, the exhaust valve opens and the high-pressure gas starts to make its way past the exhaust valve and into the exhaust pipe. This is helped by the piston, which is coming up the bore towards TDC, driving the gas out of the cylinder.

Once it reaches TDC, the exhaust valve closes and the inlet valve opens ready to start the next combustion cycle. In all the piston has moved in the bore four times and the crankshaft has rotated twice.

That's the simplified view of the four-stroke, although in fact the valves are timed so that the exhaust stays open briefly as the inlet opens to admit the fresh charge, the waste gases helping to draw in the next fresh mixture charge.

Two-strokes

A two-stroke goes through the same combustion cycle as a four-stroke, but in half the time. A two-stroke doesn't have valves in the top of the combustion chamber. Instead, it has holes (ports) in the cylinder wall, which are covered and uncovered by the piston as it rises and falls. By setting the ports at different levels, it's possible to cover and uncover them at the correct times in the induction and ignition cycles.

It's also important to know that two-strokes carry their lubrication in the air/fuel mixture, either pumped in from a separate tank to the crankcases to mix with the fuel or pre-mixed in the fuel tank. This mixture is held in the crankcase, underneath the piston before it enters the cylinder. The oil content in the mixture lubricates the crankshaft and con-rod bearings, and the rise and fall of the piston is used to pump the air/fuel mixture into the cylinder.

With the piston at BDC both the inlet and exhaust ports are uncovered, and fresh mixture is displaced into the cylinder through the inlet port. As the piston rises it first covers the inlet port, stopping any more mixture entering the cylinder and completing induction. As the piston rises further it also covers the exhaust port to seal the cylinder, and compression starts to take place.

The mixture is fully compressed when the piston reaches TDC, and in one movement the two-stroke has completed both induction and compression. The four-stroke's piston has to move twice to do this.

The spark plug now ignites the mixture to give us the power stroke. The piston is then forced back down the bore by the expanding gas until it uncovers the exhaust port. At this point the pressure of the burnt gas starts to escape into the exhaust pipe, completing both ignition/power and exhaust in one more stroke.

In all, the piston has gone up and down the bore once, but has completed all four parts of the combustion process. The crankshaft has gone round only once too. Rather than leave our piston waiting, we should explain that as it travels a little further down it uncovers the inlet port again, allowing fresh mixture to enter the cylinder.

At this point, exhaust gas will still be flowing out through the exhaust port while fresh mixture enters the cylinder via a process called scavenging. The big advantages of a two-stroke are that you get a power stroke for every crank revolution and there are fewer moving parts, which makes the engine cheaper and easier to build. The drawback is they aren't as efficient or economical as four-strokes.

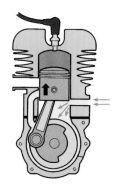

Induction of fresh mixture into crankcase and *compression* of existing mixture in combustion chamber.

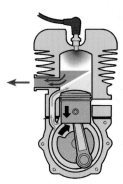

Ignition and exhaust of existing mixture in combustion chamber, and transfer of fresh mixture to combustion chamber.

Engine **layout**

As well as being two- or four-stroke, engines vary in their layout. The simplest is a single-cylinder engine, commonly found in anything from small commuter bikes to thumping supermotos. Normally the cylinder points straight up and sits on top of the crankcases and gearbox. You'll also find singles with their cylinder pointing forwards or at an angle (inclined). But singles are just the start of what's possible

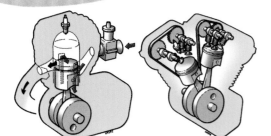

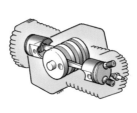

Two-stroke single   *Four-stroke V-twin*   *Four-stroke opposed twin*   *Two-stroke V-twin*   *Four-stroke in-line triple*

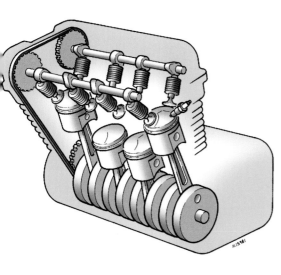

Four-stroke in-line four Honda CBR900RR is one of the finest examples of this layout.

The next stage up from a single is to put two cylinders next to each other and make a parallel twin. This has several advantages because now there are two of everything. Two cylinders mean there is twice as much room to burn fuel, and gives the potential to have twice as many power strokes per crank revolution. But because we need only one crank and one gearbox, the engine doesn't have to be twice the physical size, which is an important factor as far as bikes are concerned.

As well as parallel twins, you'll also see 45°, 60° 70° and 90° V-twins, or opposed twins (BMW Boxers, for example) where the cylinders point in opposite directions. Each has slight advantages and disadvantages over the other but, in general, the most common twins at the moment are V-twins, made popular by Ducati and Harley Davidson.

The engine layout you're most likely to see these days is the in-line four, which is essentially two parallel twins side by side, albeit with a co-joined crank. In-line fours can be found in capacities from 250cc to 1400cc and are widely used since they balance compactness with the ability to make large amounts of power. They also run smoothly because of their configuration and can rev higher, which makes them easy to tune and good for everyday riding. Vibration is quite a big concern on singles and parallel twins. This problem is normally reduced with balancer shafts, although with the right engine layout these are almost unnecessary.

Finally there are a collection of other configurations such as V4s, used by Honda in its VFR sports-tourer range and race bikes, V6s, opposed fours, triples and even in-line sixes, although you won't see many of those around. We're likely to see a host of new configurations in the future as technology developed in GP racing makes its way into road bikes. These could include V5s (Honda's 2002 four-stroke GP bike) and V3s, which are being raced or developed at the moment.

Racing has always improved the breed, and soon we'll be taking our pleasure on a new class of thoroughbred.

Four-stroke V4 is a Honda favourite, this is a VFR800F.

Four-stroke single easiest and cheapest four-stroke to manufacture for reliable performance.

Four-stroke parallel twin backbone of the old British bike industry, finds favour in OHC form today.

Transmission

All the power being generated by your engine has to find its way to the back wheel as efficiently as possible. And that's the job of the transmission or drive train. There are four main elements here – primary drive, clutch, gearbox and final drive.

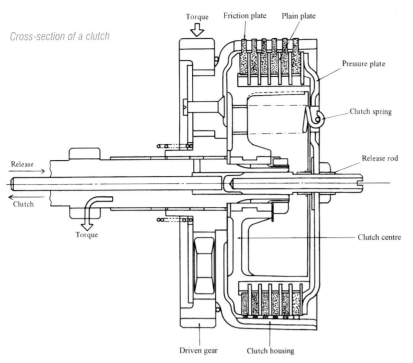

Cross-section of a clutch

Labels on diagram: Torque, Friction plate, Plain plate, Pressure plate, Clutch spring, Release rod, Release, Clutch, Torque, Clutch centre, Driven gear, Clutch housing

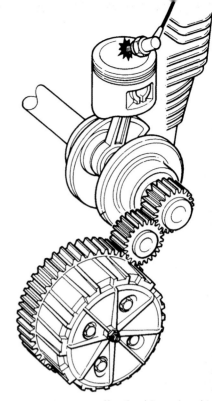

Every powered two-wheeler needs the four main transmission elements to move forward, although these vary in type and detail from bike to bike. There's a further main sub-division of transmission types – manual and automatic. Manual transmission is the most common system for motorcycles, although some bike manufacturers, most notably Guzzi and Honda, have played around with automatic transmission in the past. Automatic transmission is the preserve of mopeds and scooters, although some of these sport manual systems.

Primary drive

This is the link between the crankshaft – spinning merrily round propelled by the con-rods and pistons – and the clutch. The connection is usually achieved either by chain or belt, or more commonly these days, gear. To propel machine and rider forward, especially from standstill and at low engine speeds, we need plenty of torque – the twisting force that ultimately manifests itself at the back wheel.

The primary drive is the first stage in generating sufficient torque to get the bike moving. A typical arrangement is a smaller gear (the input or drive gear) on the end of the crank driving (by gear, chain or belt) a larger gear (the driven or output gear), around the clutch housing. The ratios of these gears dictate by how much the torque at the crank is multiplied. If the input gear has half the number of teeth of the output gear, the output gear turns at half the speed and doubles the torque of the input gear. If the output has three times the teeth, it turns at a third of the speed of the input and produces three times the torque, and so on.

The process of torque multiplication and reduction continues throughout the drive train to deliver the optimum amount of torque for what the rider wants the bike to do.

Clutch

The clutch's job is to disconnect the running engine from the gearbox and final drive. If it wasn't there, the engine would have to be stopped every time the bike pulled up. It also allows drive to be disengaged so you can change gear without crashing through the gearbox and stressing the components. In order to do this smoothly, it has to work progressively via the rider's input to the handlebar lever.

There are different types of clutch around, but they all have one thing in common – they work through friction.

Most manual clutches found on bikes these days consist of a drum or outer driven by the primary, as described above, mounted on the gearbox's input shaft. This is free to turn independently of the input shaft when the clutch is disengaged. The clutch centre is splined to the input shaft. When it turns, the gearbox turns. The drum and the centre are linked by a number of plates, plain steel and friction, which again are steel, but also have inserts of friction material.

The friction plates have teeth on their outer diameter which locate in the drum, and the plain ones have teeth that locate with the clutch centre. The clutch pressure plate pulls the lot together using the clutch springs, and the friction between the sets of plates lets the engine drive the gearbox. When the clutch lever is pulled in, the pressure plate is moved slightly away from the plates, which means there is insufficient friction for the engine to drive the gearbox.

Wet multi-plate clutches are the most common set-up. 'Wet' means the plates run in oil to keep them cool and 'multi-plate' means there is more than one set of plates. The use of numerous plates allows the diameter of the clutch to be kept small, but there is still a sufficient area of friction material to handle the torque generated without clutch slip.

BMW's F650 shows the crank, primary drive, gearbox interface, although the belt final drive is unusual.

Clutch drum driven by primary gears.

Clutch centre connects to gearbox.

Clutch plates alternating plain and friction plates. Friction plates spin with the engine, so when pressed against plain plates, spin the gearbox.

Pressure plate applies and releases pressure on friction plates.

Some designs use single or double-plate clutches – for example, BMW Boxers and Guzzis where the crankshaft is in line with the frame, the clutch mounted on the end of the crank and running at engine speed. These plates are larger in diameter and have to run dry to deal with the torque. As they run at engine speed, torque multiplication takes place elsewhere in the drive train.

Smaller bikes, such as mopeds and scooters, that have automatic transmission run a different type of clutch. Some are governed by centrifugal force, where as the revs rise, shoes like those in a brake drum are thrust into contact with a clutch outer, taking up drive. The other type is called ball and ramp, where as engine speed rises and the clutch outer rotates faster, ball bearings acting on angled ramps against the pressure plate rise on the ramps to engage drive. This type of clutch is very similar to the wet multi-plate units found on bigger bikes.

Manual clutch operation can be by cable or hydraulic. Hydraulic systems are usually found only on high-end sports machines. They provide a lighter action than cable, for the same reasons that hydraulic brakes have more feel and force than cable systems.

Gearbox

The gearbox's job is as simple as its parts look complex. It's there to make the engine turn at a reasonable speed whatever the desired road speed. A side-effect of this is that it dictates the number of powerstrokes needed during each revolution of the rear wheel, as dictated by the need to accelerate machine and rider from rest or low speed.

As internal combustion engines make usable power in only very narrow power bands, gearboxes containing the correct ratios are required to make the most of what is there and keep the powerband as wide as possible. Let's say you're on a sportsbike, accelerating hard in second towards 10,000rpm. Clearly you wouldn't want the rear wheel spinning at the same rate as the engine – you'd almost be clear for take-off. Instead, you want the right amount of torque, as set by the manufacturer getting its torque multiplication sums right, to provide linear acceleration until it's time for the next gearshift. If the ratios are right (and they should be if the manufacturer has been attentive), the rev counter drops to the bottom of the power band when you change gear. Then it rises again as you open the throttle, until you run out of gears, power and, ultimately, road.

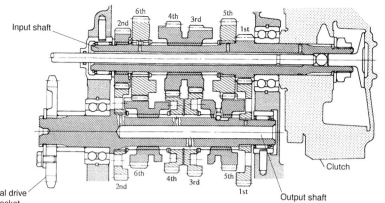

Here's how it all hangs together in a typical constant mesh, six-speed motorcycle gearbox.

Input shaft

6th
2nd
4th
3rd
5th
1st

Clutch

Final drive sprocket

6th
2nd
4th
3rd
5th
1st

Output shaft

Ratios on road bikes are chosen for flexibility rather than outright performance. By contrast, race bike ratios are chosen to work in extremely narrow power bands at the top of the rev range. Hence, first gear on a race bike makes it hard to pull away from the lights without slipping the clutch – but then race bikes only have to pull away from standstill once per outing, where a road bike has to do it many times. That's why it's equipped with higher ratios (lower gears) at the bottom of the 'box.

Gearboxes contain a number of gear pairs, usually between four and six. The principles of torque multiplication apply here too, first gear being a small cog on the input shaft driving a much larger one on the output shaft. At the other end of the scale, top gear consists of a gear on the input shaft that is the same size or sometimes larger than the one on the output. This ensures that there's plenty of thrust in the lower gears for acceleration, yet comfortable cruising in the higher ones with, power permitting, enough oomph for overtaking and so on. Usually gears are in constant mesh, whether they are driving or being driven or not, and slide and engage on their respective shafts as they're selected by the gear shift, which moves the relevant pair of gears together on the shafts.

Final drive

The most common final drive system in current use is chain and sprockets, a small front and larger rear linked by a roller chain. There's also the less common belt type, as found on Harley-Davidsons, for example. As the section on chain care explains, the conventional chain and sprocket arrangement is very susceptible to road dirt and the elements, so regular maintenance is essential to slow the rate of the inevitible wear of both chain and sprockets.

Some bikes use shaft-drive systems. These are relatively low-maintenance and have better longevity than chains and sprockets, but are heavy, adding to unsprung weight, and don't transfer power as efficiently as chains. It's also much harder to change final drive ratios, should you wish to. What's more, there's the problem of torque reaction on a trailing throttle or under hard acceleration as the system struggles to deal with its own backlash between the gear teeth or the sudden take-up of drive. And as chains and sprockets are cheaper to manufacture than shafts, it's likely that manufacturers will stick with those for the foreseeable future.

A BMW F650's final belt drive. Is this the way forward, or have rumours of the chain's demise been greatly exaggerated?

650 cs

Tuning four-strokes

Tuning engines can mean many different things. In some ways, a service is a form of tuning because you adjust components to their optimum settings and replace parts as required. You're effectively tuning the engine to behave as it did when it was new. To most people, though, tuning is about more performance. They want their bike to go faster, and for that the engine needs to make more power and torque.

Engines basically convert the chemical energy in petrol into usable power and torque. So it makes sense that the more petrol an engine can burn, the more power and torque you can get out of it. This is true to a point, but you can't just shove in more fuel, because there won't be enough air to burn it properly unless that side of the induction process is addressed. And even if there is sufficient air, the engine may not make more power if it burns inefficiently, or loses the extra power through friction.

An inlet tract and valve. This is where it all begins, and things have to be right here for your engine to make optimum power.

So tuning can almost be summed up as burning more fuel, extracting energy more completely and losing less of whatever the motor produces. First, look at what's stopping the engine getting that air and fuel in, and make them more efficient. For getting air/fuel into and out of the engine, this means looking at the airbox and filters, carbs or throttle bodies, inlet and exhaust tracts in the cylinder head, valves, camshafts and exhaust system.

Don't charge straight in and cut bits out of the cylinder head hoping to improve flow. Modern computer-designed cylinder heads are exceedingly good already, and it's easier to make them worse rather than better. Most people start by replacing the standard air filter since these are generally quite restrictive. By fitting a filter that can flow air more easily, you've already reduced one of the restrictions – and you've done it without great expense. You also risk making the mixture dangerously lean unless the issue of fuel supply is also addressed.

As the cylinder head is one of the biggest factors controlling how well an engine can breathe, it makes sense to tune it. But this should really be left to professionals, who have the experience to know what works and why. Most amateurs will dive in, make all the ports larger and change the shape to something they think looks nice. But when they run the engine it makes less power. Bigger isn't always best, and once you've ground metal out it's hard to put it back in again.

Perhaps one of the most effective forms of tuning for road bikes is blueprinting. The motivation of blueprinting an engine isn't just to get more performance, although that is invariably a by-product of it. Blueprinting is, as the name suggests, modifying an engine until it is exactly as the original designer's blueprint intended, before the accountants and processes that rule mass-production took over.

Although mass-production means we get our bikes cheaper, it also means there are power-sapping production tolerances to be met. The first bike off the production line might be spot-on, but 500 bikes later the bits in the milling machines will be worn. Of course they're replaced as required but manufacturers still build to tolerances, which means you might get one bike exactly right but another where those key machine tools were at the limit.

We see the results of this most often on the dyno. It's possible to test two bikes of the same age, make and model but see different results (as much as 15–20 per cent) and most of this is down to production tolerances.

When an engine is blueprinted it's stripped down to the individual components and each is measured and weighed to make sure it matches the others. Pistons, for example, will be machined so they all weigh the same, eliminating strain on the crank and con-rods, reducing vibration and giving smoother power delivery. They will also be machined to give the same amount of valve-to-piston clearance in all the cylinders.

This principle is applied throughout the engine until you end up with a perfect engine. It generally makes more power because the tolerances are correct, should be more reliable because it's only tuned to its design spec and is certainly nicer to use.

The next step usually involves component lightening, polishing and other practices of the tuner's esoteric art.

A two-stroke may have fewer moving parts, in that there are no valves and camshafts to worry about, but blueprinting works here too. The main concern is still how the mixture gets in and out of the engine, and how quickly.

Tuning can become extreme, however. And the more power you have, the harder – and more expensive – it becomes to get even more. There will also come a point when your engine becomes so focused it's not very practical or pleasant to ride on the road. It might only make useable power at the top of the rev range and that's no good for road riding. A broad spread through the rev range is best for roadsters. For this reason, it's important to know what you want to achieve through tuning, and why, before you start.

Carburettors

Petrol ignites and burns easily, but getting it to do this inside an engine isn't as simple as it first seems. For complete and efficient combustion, air and fuel need to be mixed in the right proportions. This is usually 12:1–13:1, which means 12–13 pounds of air for each pound of petrol.

The fuel-to-air ratio can change dramatically depending on what an engine is being asked to do. For instance, starting a cold engine might require a mixture as rich as 4–5:1.

That sounds incredibly rich, but bear in mind that this isn't the ratio achieved in the cylinder. Because the engine is starting, the fuel isn't atomised as well as it might be and the low air speed struggles to carry the fuel efficiently. So even before it reaches the cylinder, some of the fuel has dropped out of suspension – effectively making the mixture leaner.

The idea is to end up with a richer than normal mix in the cylinder because a rich mixture is easier to ignite – and that makes starting easier. In contrast, a cruising ratio might be as lean as 18:1.

So much for mixture proportions, but how does a carburettor actually work? Carbs work because they have something called a venturi. This is essentially a restriction where the passage through the carburettor narrows, then opens up again. As air passes through the venturi it drops in pressure, and it is this differential which can be utilised.

Fuel from your tank flows into the carbs and is held in the float-bowl, where it waits until something causes it to do otherwise. In this case, the otherwise is low pressure in the venturi, which is connected to the float-bowl by a passage. Although it's only at atmospheric pressure, the air in the float-bowl is relatively high compared to the venturi. This drives fuel up the passage, through the main jet into an emulsion tube and finally into the air stream, where it is broken down into tiny droplets that are carried into the combustion chamber by the air.

The most common type of carburettor fitted to bikes is the CV (constant velocity) carb. This is a clever device that controls the flow of air through the venturi to help deliver the correct amount of fuel, regardless of how open or shut the throttle plate is, by maintaining the correct pressure in the venturi.

In effect, the rider doesn't directly control the slide in the carb. Instead, the carb monitors the vacuum in the inlet tract, which is controlled by the rider using the throttle plate, and uses this to operate a vacuum slide. The greater the vacuum the more the slide lifts. It sounds complicated but isn't really. It's just a system to help stop the engine bogging-down.

A slide, or flat-slide, carb works in the same way, but the throttle directly opens and closes the slide in the venturi. In effect you control the velocity of air, and therefore fuel.

It's possible to get more power using a flat-slide carb because there is less clutter in the inlet tract when the throttle is wide open. But the drawback is that the rider must have a good understanding of what the engine requires and the necessary skill to operate the throttle accordingly.

You can't just open the throttle with a flat-slide carb to accelerate – especially from low to mid-revs. Because the engine isn't revving very fast, the velocity of air through the carb is relatively slow. Suddenly opening the slide effectively increases the diameter of the venturi, reducing its effectiveness, and also lowers the vacuum in the inlet tract.

This means there isn't enough pressure differential to move enough fuel through the carb and not enough velocity to carry it efficiently to the cylinder. The engine will become starved of fuel and bog. In some cases the engine will recover, but if the revs continue to drop and the throttle remains wide open, the revs fall and the problem gets worse.

CV carbs let the engine run far more smoothly than slide carbs because they avoid this. And they also allow you to ride the bike without worrying about the throttle and fuelling demands of the engine.

A typical bank of CV carbs from an in-line four.

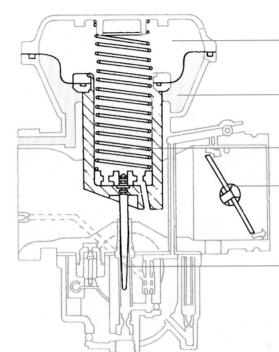

Constant velocity (CV) carburettor

Air is routed up into the vacuum chamber via a hole in the base of the piston.

Air at atmospheric pressure fills the area below the diaphragm.

Return spring helps to stabilise the piston.

Throttle as the throttle is opened, low pressure is created in the vacuum chamber and the piston begins to rise.

Needle the piston has a tapered needle attached which blocks the fuel flow. As it is lifted, petrol is drawn up by the low pressure.

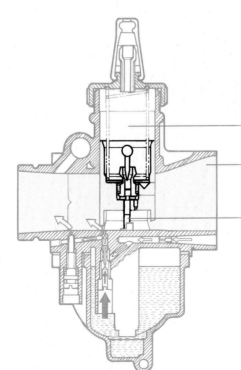

Slide Carburettor

Piston is directly controlled by the twist grip.

Air pressure drops as the piston is lifted and more air flows.

Needle the piston has a tapered needle attached which blocks the fuel flow. As it is lifted petrol is drawn up by the low pressure.

Carburettor **tuning**

Tuning carburettors and actually improving their performance is a true black art, especially as they have been around for so long and most things have been tried already. So the first thing to consider is what exactly you are trying to do.

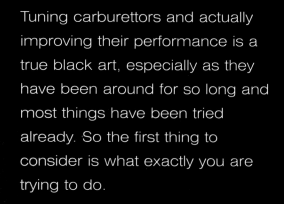

There are many reasons to fiddle with a carburettor. It might be to get rid of that annoying flat-spot at 5000rpm or to make the engine run smoother. Or you may have fitted a new exhaust with different flow characteristics. Whatever it is, chances are it'll be more complicated than you think.

However, there are a few things you can do. The most common alteration to carbs is to balance or synchronise them, assuming there is more than one carb, that is. Balancing the carbs ensures they are all drawing the same amount of air and fuel – so you get the same performance and response from each cylinder. Once adjusted correctly, the power delivery will definitely feel smoother. Unbalanced carbs can even lead to a degree of vibration that feels like serious engine problems.

Balancing is done by connecting vacuum gauges to the inlet tracts and adjusting the synchronisation screws on the carbs. This a very fine way of adjusting the throttle plate so the vacuum in the inlet tracts are the same. Ideally, the vacuum levels of the carbs will match, although sometimes carbs are balanced as pairs, with the inner and outer pairs on a four-cylinder machine running differently. Check your manual if unsure.

It's also important to keep carbs clean – both internally and externally. Dirt tends to accumulate on carbs because of the residue that invariably forms on them. In time, this greasy paste can cause problems and certainly doesn't make it easy to work on or even check the condition of carbs. Careful use of a degreaser is normally enough to keep them clean.

Cleaning carbs internally needs to be done rarely, but if a bike has been stored with fuel in the carbs, it can evaporate from the system and leave a gummy residue, which blocks jets. In this case, the carb should be stripped and cleaned or at least have some aerosol carb cleaner run through it.

It's not so common now, but people used to scrap their existing carbs in favour of ones with bigger throats. The logic is that if more mixture can get into the engine, it'll make more power. While there is a hint of truth about this, it isn't that simple.

As we mentioned previously, carbs mix fuel relative to the vacuum in their venturi. As you get a lower pressure with a smaller venturi, so the reverse is true. Although you increase the flow potential of the engine by fitting bigger carbs, what you normally get is awful fuelling because they're unable thoroughly to mix the correct amount of fuel.

In some ways, a smaller bore carburettor is better for road use because it will improve the mid-range response of the engine. Manufacturers often use this trick when they make less extreme versions of their bikes. Yamaha did this when it fitted the R1 engine into the Fazer 1000.

To set a carb up properly, it's wise to measure the air/fuel ratio in the exhaust. Most dyno houses have this equipment and can run the bike to check that the mixture isn't too rich or lean. To affect the overall ratio of the bike it's necessary to change the main jet. The bigger the hole in it, the greater the flow of fuel and so the richer the mixture becomes.

There are other adjustments too. In most cases, it's possible to 'lift the needle'. This simply means adjusting the height of the needle relative to the slide. Most adjustable needles have three or four grooves at the top, and by moving a clip to different grooves you can raise or lower the needle. This has the effect of allowing more or less fuel to flow through the needle jet for a given throttle opening.

Adjustable needle
The locating circlip can be raised or lowered on the needle to provide fine tuning.

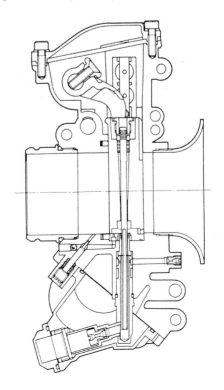

Flat-Slide Carburettor
Mikuni TDMR40, supplied with the Suzuki GSX-R750W race kit. Note angled float bowl and offset main jet, designed to keep the carburettor compact and let it operate at a steep downdraught angle. (Suzuki)

Fuel **injection**

Despite carburettors being refined over many years to a point where they're taken for granted, the world moves on – and in the direction of fuel injection. Fuel injection is not a new technology. In fact, it's been around in cars for so long even the most basic models have it. In bikes, it isn't so common yet and usually only the premier bikes in each class are injected. But having said that, it's come and gone on bikes for the past couple of decades. Until recently, the most common excuse from the manufacturers has been that bikes rev across too broad a range to make efficient fuel injection systems. However, all of that is changing fast.

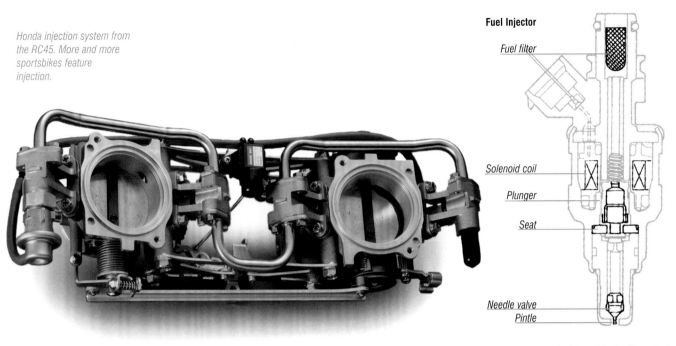

Honda injection system from the RC45. More and more sportsbikes feature injection.

Fuel Injector

Fuel filter

Solenoid coil

Plunger

Seat

Needle valve
Pintle

Inside an injector. The actual engineering looks simple, but injection requires complex electronics to control it effectively.

A fuel injection system is essentially made up of one or more injectors, a number of sensors and a control unit. Unlike carburettors, which are governed by the laws of physics and therefore know what to do intrinsically, a fuel injection system has to be told. For this reason, a fuel-injected bike is covered in sensors.

You might think a cylinder with a displacement of 250cc will suck in a quarter of a litre of air with each induction stroke, but this is not quite the case. Even with the throttle wide open, most engines only fill their cylinders between 80 and 95 per cent of their maximum capacity because there's so little time to do it and so many restrictions. The point at which an engine most effectively fills its cylinders will be when peak torque occurs.

Because the engine doesn't always draw in the same amount of air, the most important thing the ECU (electronic control unit) needs to know is how fast the engine is revving and how far open the throttle is. Using this information, and knowing roughly how well the engine will fill its cylinder under those conditions, it sets off to a library stored in its memory to find out how much fuel to inject.

Unfortunately, that is not enough. If the engine is being started from cold, it needs a rich mixture, so engine temperature needs checking. The system also needs to know the air pressure – higher pressure means denser air, and that requires more fuel to get the correct ratio. Remember, the ratio is by weight, not volume.

As if working out the correct amount of fuel to inject wasn't hard enough, the ECU also has to deliver precisely that amount – and this can be a job in itself. When you turn the key on an injected bike, you'll hear a fuel pump whirr into life. This pumps fuel into a rail connected to the injectors, effectively making them little taps. When an injector opens, fuel flows from the rail into the engine.

The amount of fuel flowing depends on three things: the flow rate of the injector; the amount of time it's open; and the flow rate from the pump. The injector's rating remains the same but the open time and pressure both vary, and these need to be taken into account too.

The list of information required by the ECU goes on, and the more there is, the better the end result will be. Armed with all the information, the ECU determines how long it needs to open each injector to deliver the required fuel. It then sends a timed signal to the injector, which opens and closes a small nozzle in its end. The opening time is a matter of milliseconds.

This is where injectors better carbs, though. By forcing fuel through a nozzle under pressure, the fuel is equally atomised in all conditions. And the smaller the fuel droplets are, the better they can mix with the air. End result: more efficiency and power.

For maximum performance, some bikes have more than one injector per cylinder. The extra injector is normally fitted at the mouth of the inlet tract and only kicks in at high revs. One advantage of this system is that the injected fuel is more evenly spread through the inlet charge, which gives a better burn and more performance.

A single injector, capable of supplying enough fuel at high revs, would only have to open very briefly at lower revs, concentrating the fuel in a portion of the intake air. An injector with a smaller capacity would have to stay open longer to deliver the same amount of fuel, and in that time more air would pass by it.

Electronics also bring a greater degree of control. Most bikes reference different fuel maps depending on what gear they're in. Fuel injection allows manufacturers to control things down to the very last detail, and that means bikes can respond better, whatever our needs.

Exhaust systems

Exhaust systems aren't just there to keep the noise down. In fact, the only reason engines have silencers fitted at all is because legislation says they must – being quiet doesn't improve performance... But even without this legislation, bikes would still have exhaust pipes of some sort because they are just as responsible for engine performance as any other part.

Yamaha exhaust system features that company's famous EXUP valve which helps optimise power delivery.

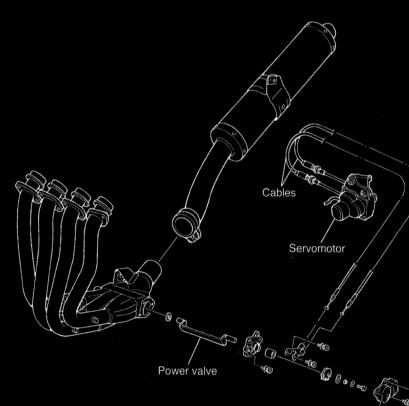

Cables

Servomotor

Power valve

Modern exhaust systems are built from a number of materials. Low-performance or economy bikes still tend towards steel exhaust systems because they're cheap and functional. High-performance bikes use more exotic lightweight materials, such as titanium, and carbon fibre. This has little to no effect on engine power but a large impact on your wallet. They're actually more about saving weight than anything else.

The design of modern sportbike exhausts has come a long way since the late 1990s, and a lot of work goes into them. For starters, they have to be the right bore. In many ways, you'd think a bigger bore pipe would be best because it can flow more gas, but this isn't always the case.

A big-bore pipe helps an engine make good top-end power because it can flow large amounts of gas quickly. However, a smaller bore pipe can give a useful boost to low- and mid-range power by keeping the gas velocity up, which helps it to pull burnt gas from the cylinder.

As well as gas flow, pressure waves can be used in exhaust systems, and are absolutely crucial in two-strokes. These pulses are caused by the flow of gas and by the valves opening and closing. When the exhaust valve closes, it sends a high-pressure wave down the exhaust pipe and part of the energy in the wave will be reflected as a negative wave back down the pipe when it reaches the end. Timed correctly, this negative wave will arrive just as the valve opens and encourage the gas in the cylinder to start moving. This effect only works at certain points in the rev range.

The formation of the pipes has an effect on power too. Some four-cylinder bikes have a 4-2-1, where the four header pipes converge into two pairs, before converging again into a single pipe. Others have a 4-1. There are advantages to each. A 4-2-1 system promotes mid-range power but isn't as efficient at high revs. The 4-1 system is the opposite, boosting top end but sacrificing some mid-range.

Power valves are also fairly common. They can be found in the ports of two-stroke motors and in the exhausts of four-strokes. In each case, they fool the engine into thinking that it has the best of both worlds. They do this by altering the exhaust port timing, the tuned length of the exhaust pipe or the configuration. Either way, the idea is to use the exhaust gas to help get more gas out of the cylinder and so more fresh mixture in.

Two-strokes are perhaps more responsive to the effects of exhaust pipes. You only have to look at their swoopy shapes and bulges to see that a lot of thought goes into them. In general, they aim to return a low-pressure wave at the exhaust port as it opens and a high-pressure wave just before it shuts. This makes a big difference to the scavenging ability of the engine, and can enhance and move the powerband.

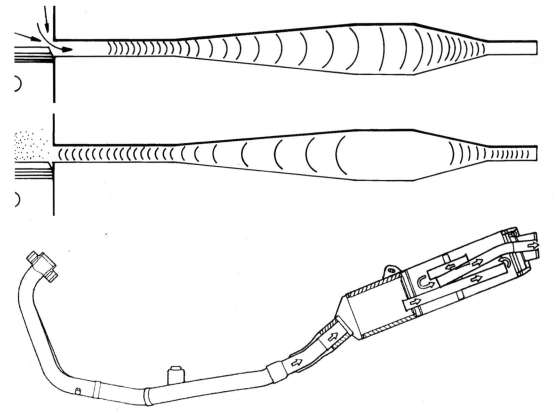

Two-stroke expansion chamber exhaust system
Spent gases rush out as a high-pressure wave, gradually expanding and losing velocity until reaching the reversed cone. Gases are compressed by the reverse cone and a proportion returns as a reverse pulse. This creates high pressure at the exhaust port, stopping fresh mixture escaping down the exhaust.

Four-stroke exhaust
System of internal baffles keeps noise down, hopefully not sacrificing too much power.

Race &
performance exhausts

We've already looked at standard exhaust systems and seen that reducing noise isn't really what they are there for. So when tuning bikes, it makes sense to get rid of the noise restrictions, as these normally work by forcing the exhaust gas back and forth through a series of noise deadening chambers – and that's quite restrictive.

Yoshimura race can
There are dozens of can manufacturers, Yoshimura is one of the longest established.

Harris carbon can
Carbon fibre is a popular material for exhaust cans. And extremely fashionable too.

Yoshimura Tri-oval
Another offering from the celebrated tuning firm. Slimline form gives plenty of ground clearance.

Bike exhaust systems are not made in one piece, which allows just the silencer to be replaced without touching the rest of the system. This is a quick and simple modification, and it's quite cheap too. The standard silencers are normally replaced with slip-on race cans. The slip-on refers to their ease of fitment and the race bit simply means they're not road legal.

In almost all cases, the exhaust gas is free to travel straight through the centre of the can because it does away with the sound chambers. The can is lined with a perforated tube and sound deadening material, though, so it does cut down noise a little bit. Over time, its ability to do this will reduce and eventually it'll need repacking.

By increasing the ability of gas to flow through the exhaust system, it can move faster and in larger amounts. As far as the engine is concerned, this means it can rev more easily because it does not have to push gas through the exhaust system. But there are other implications.

With less pressure in the exhaust, it's easier for burnt gases in the combustion chamber to get out. And the faster that happens, the quicker fresh mixture can be drawn in to replace it. The result is more power, although it's wise to check the bike's fuelling on a rolling road, because fitting an end-can might cause the engine to run lean.

One trade-off might be a slight loss of mid-range power. As new mixture is drawn into the combustion chamber, it can get sucked straight out of the exhaust port.

Race cans flow more gas, so the fuel system must also supply more fuel to keep the correct mixture. This is only a serious problem if the mixture becomes dangerously lean and happens to do so in the type of conditions in which you often ride – say, 7000rpm with part-throttle. Having the bike set-up on a dyno will reveal any potential

problems and also allow the fuelling to be optimised.

As well as replacing the end-can, people often replace the rest of the exhaust system. In the past, they did this because standard systems were built to a price and to give good results over a broad rev-range. By fitting after-market systems, people could pay for performance boosting features that increased engine performance in one area – usually top-end power for racing.

Now, though, many standard high-performance systems already come with features such as tapered header and crossover pipes. Both these features are designed to make best use of pressure waves and pulses travelling backwards and forwards through the exhaust. As with two-stroke exhausts, they're timed to reflect low-pressure waves on to the back of the exhaust valves just before they open, encouraging flow. A well-designed full-system can increase power by 3–10bhp.

Although it's always nice to increase the performance of your bike, there can be drawbacks. Some systems and even end-cans mean you have to remove a centre stand. If this is something you use all the time, it's worth searching around to find a system that lets you retain this.

It is also worth remembering that most race cans and full-systems aren't road legal. So as well as being louder and drawing more attention to yourself, you might end up in trouble with the law.

It should be possible to fit a full system and end-can yourself with only a few tools. Generally, the system will fix to the exhaust ports with two Allen bolts per cylinder, have a couple of brackets under the engine and finally be supported by a bracket or clamp on the end-can. It's important to get a good seal on any joints since gas leaks will reduce performance slightly, but more annoyingly, cause the bike to back fire on a shut throttle. Use an exhaust joint sealer and check for leaks once fitted.

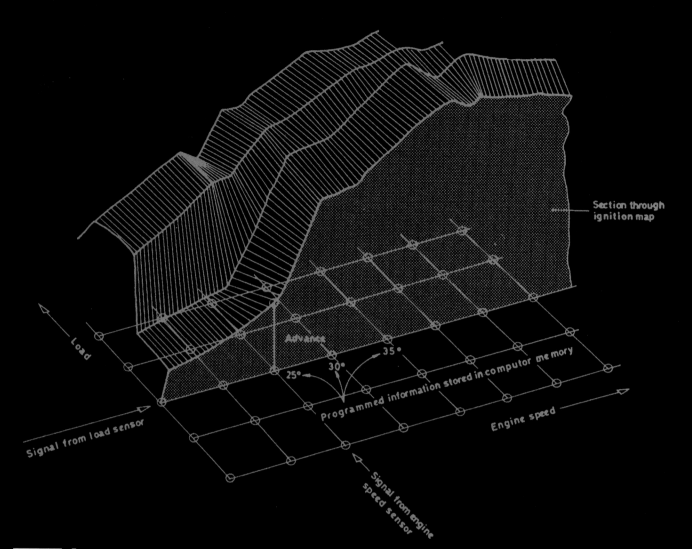

Section through ignition map

Load

Advance

35°

30°

25°

Programmed information stored in computer memory

Signal from load sensor

Signal from engine speed sensor

Engine speed

Electronic **C**ontrol **U**nits & **ignition**

The majority of bikes now have a small black box tucked away somewhere under the plastics – it's the ECU (electronic control unit). These seemingly impregnable boxes control most of the things going on in the engine. But that may not be as much as you think. At most, an ECU governs the fuel injection, ignition timing and sometimes a power valve or two.

Dynojet Power Commander

This clever device allows the info going to and from the ECU to be manipulated to optimise fuelling and/or ignition.

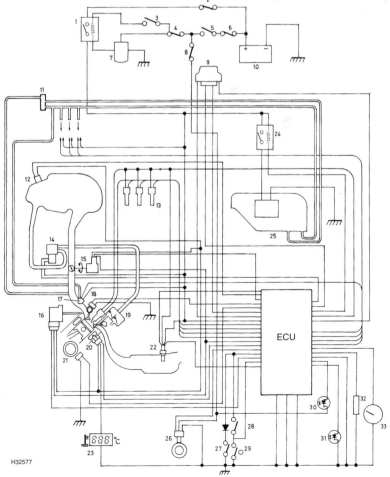

Schematic of a typical modern motorcycle system. At its heart lies the electronic control unit which collects information from sensors all over the bike then tells the key components what to do.

So why have them? Because they're more versatile and accurate than mechanical systems, that's why. They're also smaller, lighter and cheaper to produce.

Fuel injection is perhaps the biggest user of black boxes. We've already touched on carburettors and what a good job they do, despite the many conditions they have to work under. Fuel injection, on the other hand, is essentially dumb and has to be told what to do under each condition it might encounter. For this reason, it needs good, up-to-date information before it makes any decision.

The black box collects information from a number of sensors on the bike. These include throttle position, engine revs, crankshaft position, water temperature, air temperature and air pressure. Generally, more sensors mean the ECU can make a more accurate decision on how much fuel to inject. It then sends a signal to open and close the injector long enough to deliver that pre-cise amount of fuel.

ECUs also control ignition timing. Again, to make the best decision possible, they need information. So at any time, the ECU will know what position the crankshaft is in and what demands are being made of the engine. It then references that information against a table stored in its memory and advances or retards the ignition as required.

In many ways, it's easier to tune bikes using the ECU than it is to do the same job manually. There are several devices available, such as Dynojet's Power Commander and Yoshimura's EMS, which plug into the bike's ECU and alter the signals. Doing this allows

**Four-stroke,
four-valve cylinder**

*A dramatic representation of
what happens inside a
four-stroke bike's cylinders.*

you to manipulate the information being sent to, or
from, the ECU. So you can control the fuelling and
ignition at almost any point in the rev range without
affecting anything else – something that's difficult to
do with carbs or mechanical ignitions. To set it up,
you just need someone with a dyno, load cell and
the necessary software and experience.

The potential to exploit black-box technology is
very exciting. Already we've seen how Suzuki used
it to good effect with its dual throttle-valve injector
bodies. The result is a virtual CV carb with injectors.

In the past, fuel-injected bikes suffered in similar
ways to flat-slide carbs (although to a lesser degree
because of the injectors), because the rider had
direct control over the throttle plate. With its GSX-R
series, Suzuki has incorporated a second throttle
valve controlled by the black box to maintain the
optimum intake velocity – a helping hand on the
throttle, if you like.

In theory, the same unit could also control
variable length inlet tracts to boost mid-range and
top-end power. Honda has already fitted traction
control to some of its bikes, but there's no reason
why this couldn't be extended to sporty models

too. And, with the correct sensors, you could even
end up with a bike that knows when it's raining and
switches to a softer fuel injection map for more
controllable delivery as well as turning on the
traction control system.

Ignition

The ignition is the system responsible for igniting
the air/fuel mixture in the combustion chamber. This
is more difficult than it first sounds, though. For
starters, the mixture has to be ignited at just the
right time to give maximum power, and in engines
this is measured in degrees of crank rotation before
or after the piston is at top dead centre (TDC), or
highest point.

It surprises many people to know that, in many
cases, the air/fuel mixture is actually lit *before* the
piston reaches the top of its stroke. They know that
when the mixture burns it expands and pushes
down on the piston, but what they forget is that the
mixture burns – it doesn't explode.

For this reason, the inertia of the crank is
enough for it to keep turning, despite the burn
starting while it is coming up the bore. The idea

behind starting the burn early is simple. It takes time for the mixture to burn and increase the cylinder pressure.

Sadly, time is something the engine doesn't have (at high revs there are only a few hundredths of a second for the mixture to burn), so by starting the burn early, the burn is more developed as the piston starts on its down-stroke, which is where we want maximum pressure.

It's also worth bearing in mind that as the piston travels down the bore, it increases the volume of the cylinder and reduces the pressure, weakening the effect of combustion. In fact, most of the useful work done by the burnt gas happens in the early stages of the stroke. Ignition is timed to give maximum efficiency on the power stroke.

The burn is started by the spark plug. By jumping a high voltage across a gap, a spark is produced. This excites the molecules adjacent to the spark sufficiently to start the combustion process. From there, the flame spreads out through the mixture, in much the same way as a ripple on a pond, until all the mixture is burnt or something causes it to stop.

There are several things capable of stopping the burn. Over the past few pages, we've mentioned the importance of a good even mixture several times. If the mixture is uneven, this can stop the burn. Think of it like a forest fire.

In ideal conditions, the fire will spread from tree to tree and burn the whole forest. But if the trees are too spread out (that is, they're too lean) the fire won't be able to jump the gap and there will be areas of unburnt trees. This is what happens if there are excessively lean areas in the mixture. There are also small areas around the cylinder walls that don't burn properly because the heat energy for exciting the molecules is absorbed by the metal.

Compression ratios play a role too, and you'll normally find they are increased when an engine is tuned. By compressing the mixture, you're cramming the air and fuel molecules closer together, which makes it easy for each molecule to ignite the next. It's the same as our forest trees when they're planted very close together.

So the conditions have to be right for the mixture to burn. But if the ignition system doesn't deliver enough voltage, or there's a bad connection, the spark may not be strong enough to ignite the mixture properly or even jump the gap at all. If that happens, there will be only a partial burn or possibly no burn at all – a misfire. For this reason, it's important to keep the ignition system in good order.

It's also harder for the ignition to light a lean mixture or one under high compression. In both cases, a stronger spark is required, something that old ignitions sometimes struggled to supply. This is why there used to be lots of aftermarket ignitions for sale. It's not so much of a problem now, because bikes that need it have high-energy ignitions capable of igniting the mixture under normal conditions, and even after the engine has been tuned. They also reduce the frequency of partial burns or misfires.

Ignition reduced to its basics

At the pickup the crank tells the CDI (a basic ECU) where it's at in its stroke. Knowing this, the CDI tells which coil to fire and when. Each pair of coils on a four-cylinder fires both its two plugs simultaneously – the so-called wasted spark, where one plug has no fresh mixture to ignite. The advantage of the system in this case is that only two coils are needed for a four-cylinder bike.

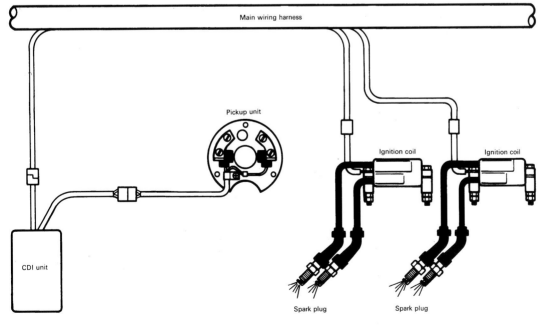

Main wiring harness

Pickup unit

Ignition coil

Ignition coil

CDI unit

Spark plug

Spark plug

Frames

So what does your frame do? At its most basic, it keeps your backside off the floor, your wheels apart from each other, and provides a place for your engine to live. But there is much more to a frame than that.

Looking beyond the fundamentals, it holds the swingarm and forks at the right heights, angles and distances to optimise handling. It must also be rigid enough to keep the wheels in line under the considerable forces of braking, acceleration and cornering. Sufficient rigidity is needed to maintain the steering head's vertical relationship to the machine and swingarm pivot's horizontal relationship regardless of the forces of turning, stopping and accelerating. The design and construction of the frame also has a role to play in insulating the rest of the machine and the rider from damaging and irritating engine vibrations.

A machine's centre of gravity is critical to how it behaves under acceleration, braking and cornering, so the frame is designed with this in mind. As you accelerate, maximum traction through the back tyre is desirable. When you brake, you want traction to be optimised at the front. When cornering, it's best if both tyres grip by the same amount and the bike turns in easily. Generally, these are all improved if the centre of gravity is high, but too high and there can be too much weight transfer, meaning wheelies and stoppies everywhere. If the centre of gravity is lower, the bike will be easier to steer, although more lean is required to make a given turn and there's less traction than with a high centre of gravity.

To provide the best of all worlds, some compromise is required in how the bike's key components are positioned.

When is an **engine** a **frame?**

Some bikes barely have a frame at all, using the engine as a so-called 'stressed member' from which the front and rear ends are hung. In these cases, the engine is effectively the frame. One of the simplest examples to illustrate the concept is the Honda 'semi-pivotless' system (as on the Blade), where the swingarm pivots round a mount at the back of the gearbox casting. Obviously that bike has a frame, as we understand them conventionally, for the front end and engine, so let's take another example of a 'proper' stressed member design. BMW's recent Boxers have the front as well as the rear suspension attached to the engine, with subframes carrying the rest of the bike's components.

Cradle frames

These are a very conventional design and have been around for years. The engine is bolted in a 'cradle' formed by the bottom tubes, and the head is bolted to the top rail or rails. For greater rigidity, there may be a pair of downtubes too, and larger more powerful cradle-framed bikes tend to adopt this design. The most popular material for cradle frames is steel tubing, although box-section steel is sometimes used.

Beam frames

The twin-spar, 'perimeter' or beam frame is very widely used, especially on sportsbikes. Typically two large beams join the headstock to the swingarm pivot although, as mentioned before, some bikes' swingarms pivot off the back of the gearbox. Extruded or box-section aluminium are the most common materials used in these designs, with ally castings for the swingarm pivot, although some still use steel for the whole construction. The frame wraps round the top sides of the engine to make the motor a partially stressed member, its casings being beefed up to improve load-bearing. Some beam frames also feature lower steel rails, which form an additional cradle for the engine.

Spine frames

These are popular on scooters and mopeds and are often made of pressed steel. Honda's Hornet is an example of a larger bike that uses the concept. The Hornet has a box section spine from which the engine hangs, while ally castings provide the swingarm pivot points. Spine frames are well suited to automated mass-production techniques, which explains their appeal to manufacturers of budget machines.

Trellis frames

These usually use the engine as a stressed member. Straight pieces of round or square section material, usually steel, are welded together to form lightweight but very rigid frames. The most celebrated modern example of the trellis is from Ducati. Light, minimalist, but just enough to do the job. Looks gorgeous too.

Other frame stuff

Back in the 1970s and '80s, when engine performance was rapidly eclipsing that of the chassis, a huge frame aftermarket grew up. These days, most standard frames are more than adequate. But if you fancy or require the ultra-trick, there are still plenty of companies out there that will build a bespoke frame. If you're unlucky enough to suffer a spank-up, most frames – apart from the terminally twisted – can be fixed. To check for proper true, the chassis will have to be jigged by a specialist, which means a fairly extensive stripdown. One easier way to check for damage is to look at wheel alignment (see your manual). Sometimes the damage can be seen in obvious folds and buckles in the frame. And if you're a wheelie monster, ham-fisted put-downs might lead to oval bearing housings at the headstock. Steady now.

Front suspension

The front forks are one of the busiest components on any bike. They have to optimise the tyre's contact with the road, both in a straight line and while cornering. They must smooth the ride over uneven surfaces and minimise dive under braking. Then they also need to give the rider adequate feedback about what the front end's doing in any circumstance. Quite a lot to be going on with.

As far as the basic anatomy of motorcycle forks goes, stanchions (also known as sliders) travel up and down the fork leg. There are two basic types in common use these days – right way up (RWU), stanchion above leg and upside down (USD), stanchion below leg. There are other systems, but telescopic forks are by far the most common.

Rebound damping *While the springs will bounce back merrily on their own, the rebound damping uses oil/or sometimes gas forced through valves to slow the process.*

Preload *adjuster takes up sag in the front springs. Doesn't make the spring 'harder', although it can feel that way.*

Compression damping *as with the rebound, uses oil and sometimes gas to slow the bike's progress down the fork's travel.*

Springs

Internal springs take care of the basic rates of dive and rebound. At their cheapest and most basic, springs have equally wound coils, which compress evenly. Because this simple type doesn't become stiffer as it compresses, there's a risk of the forks bottoming out when severe bumps are encountered at speed. Better than these are multi-rate springs, which can be two springs of different strengths, or single springs wound to different rates at either end. The softer spring takes care of smaller bumps and shocks, and as it compresses completely, the second stronger spring or section of spring takes effect.

Best of all are 'progressive' springs, where the distance between the spring's coils gets progressively less along the length of the spring. Progressive springs become stiffer as they compress and less stiff as they lengthen, the rate of which is optimised to account for the weight of the bike and that of a typical rider. The progressive nature of the springs means that small bumps are easily absorbed, and sudden larger bumps can be dealt with without the forks bottoming out.

Damping

When you hit a bump, the fork springs compress. The next thing they want to do is to extend, pushing the bike up – the energy they've just absorbed has to go somewhere. A series of bumps has the potential to tie suspension in knots, the bike bumping and jarring over the irregular surface.

Damping is the method of governing the rate at which the forks dive (compress) and spring back (rebound). Some mopeds, scooters and lightweights get by with no damping at all or rely on friction.

Oil damping is used on other machines. Valves control the rate at which the oil passes on compression and rebound. Gas and air have also been used to assist the damping.

Front suspension adjustment

Budget and smaller capacity bikes often have non-adjustable suspension, and for most riders of these machines, the absence of adjusters will go unnoticed. On larger bikes, particularly sportsbikes and tourers, there are usually four main adjustable factors – preload, height of forks in the yokes, rebound damping and compression damping.

Preload adjustment is found at the top of the forks and alters the effective length of the springs. It doesn't make the suspension softer or harder, but varies the ride height and the amount the bike 'sags' on its suspension. Rebound adjusters are usually concentric with and internal to the preload adjusters and dictate the rate the forks extend after compression. At the bottom of the forks are the compression adjusters, which can be tweaked to control the rate of dive.

When your bike left the dealership when it was new, the suspension should have been set to the base setting suggested by the manufacturer in the owner's manual. These are invariably a best average, for average road conditions, riding style and rider weight. But no road or rider conforms to an average, so feel free to fiddle with the adjusters. Just remember to do it gradually.

And unless you've bought the latest homologation race replica sportsbike, your bike's suspension has been built down to a price. That's not to say it won't meet your needs – and lots of standard forks are excellent – but if you're a trackday demon or an ace on the roads, you might want something with more adjustment. Look at revalving the standard kit or replacing the springs. Or if you want to go all the way, buy some trick aftermarket forks.

Rear
suspension

Like the front forks, the rear shock (or shocks on a twin-shock bike) has plenty to do to. It has to optimise tyre contact with the road in a straight line and in corners; smooth the ride over uneven surfaces; and give the rider feedback about what the tyre's up to. Yet the rear suspension also has an important role in ensuring as much power as possible is delivered to the road without wheelspin or excessive compression and extension. If your bike had no rear suspension and any appreciable power, the back wheel would spend as much time off the road as it would in contact with it.

What's in a shock?

An external spring takes care of the basic rates of dive and rebound and, like the springs in the front forks, it is often 'progressive' or 'multi-rate', so it becomes stiffer as it compresses. As with the front suspension, progressive springs provide a more effective solution than multi-rate springs, which are just two springs of different rates.

On many monoshock bikes, a rising-rate linkage, connecting the shock to the swingarm and frame, means a cheaper-to-manufacture constant-rate spring can be used. All these methods prevent the travel being used up too quickly by severe bumps while making the spring compliant enough to deal with more moderate bumps.

That spring lives outside a damper unit, which is typically oil-filled to control the rates of shock compression and rebound. The oil passes through shim stacks (a bit like washers), which restrict the rate it can pass at.

Shock adjustment

Cheap shocks, as found on budget bikes and many smaller machines, tend to rely on stiff springs and basic damping. More sophisticated shocks combine better multi-rate springs with adjustable damping for improved performance. Many use compressed gas to keep the oil under pressure, which prevents bubbles forming in it and damping being lost when the shock is working hard and fast. Apart from compression and rebound adjusters, some high-end shocks have additional high-speed damping adjusters to give the rear additional help when particularly violent bumps are encountered. Some have ride height adjusters

too to raise the back of the bike and quicken steering.

Rear shock preload adjustment is usually by stepped collar or threaded rings on the shock body. Increasing it reduces sag and the bike sits a little higher. Remote preload adjusters are fitted to some shocks for ease of adjustment. Rebound adjustment is generally found at the bottom of the shock and compression at the top, sometimes on a remote adjuster.

Some shocks are non-adjustable, but it is often possible to fit springs of different rates and have the shock revalved or filled with a different grade of oil to change the way the unit behaves. There are plenty of specialists offering these services.

Most shocks on mass-produced bikes are built down to a budget, but as with front forks, many are excellent and more than adequate for all but racers and trackday nuts. Revalving and springs of different rates are the cheapest ways to tailor the standard equipment to your needs. There's a huge aftermarket out there for riders who simply want replacements and those that want extra performance, providing shocks that are often better and cheaper than original equipment.

The location of monoshocks in particular on a bike means they can get covered in road dirt and water flung off the back wheel. Fitting a hugger will protect the shock from the worst of this. They can run very hot as well because, apart from heat generated in the unit through its operation, it's also sited close to the engine and is away from the flow of cooling air. For that reason, damping systems have become progressively better over the years, especially in high-end shocks. Some keep the damping medium in a separate reservoir sited either remotely or on the back of the shock.

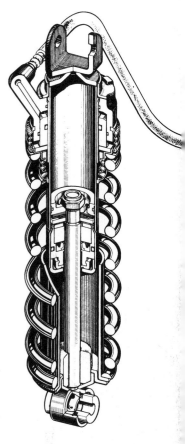

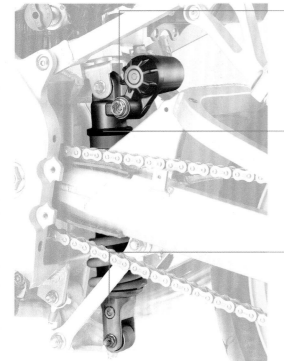

Compression damping Like on the front end oil damping slows the rate of dive. Gas is almost always involved on bigger bikes to help the oil hydraulics out.

Preload This particular shock lacks a remote preload adjuster, making C-spanner induced skinned knuckles a near certainty.

Rebound damping This shock has a screw adjuster for rebound damping which slows the rate the shock extends at. Some others use knurled knobs.

Swingarms

Most swingarms supplied as standard on modern bikes are up to the job they're designed to do. Fundamentally they carry the back wheel, pivot off the back of the frame or engine, and are prevented from slamming the tyre into the underside of the seat by the shocks or monoshock and its linkage.

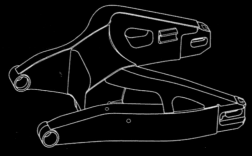

Huge as they are, these ally swingarms provide several times the rigidity of steel for proportionately less weight and allow plenty of bracing to be used for little mass trade-off.

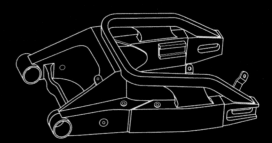

There's a lot more going on beyond the basic functions of a swingarm. As with frames, rigidity is an issue. In the old days, tubular swingarms on puny mounts allowed the wheel to flex sideways, which upset handling, but at that time the power of the bikes and their tyres were such that there weren't too many demands on the (just about) adequate chassis of the era. Gusseting between the two forks of the swingarm and the pivot tube helped prevent flex. The usual material was tubular steel, but as power outputs rose and bikes got better, manufacturers started to use box section designs. The only problem was that the weight penalty started to increase as the section of these swingarms got bigger in line with further power hikes. Bracing got bigger and heavier too.

Modern swing

Today, things are different. Many bikes still use steel swingarms, but tubular ones are usually found only on twin-shock lightweights. Steel box section swingarms are still quite common too, particularly on middleweight budget roadsters.

Aluminium is the thing these days, particularly on high-performance bikes. Obviously it's lighter than steel but not as strong, although an alloy swingarm that's as strong and heavy as a steel arm is stiffer. So it's possible to build alloy swingarms that are just as stiff as steel but lighter. Ally items are often internally and externally braced for more strength. This means the walls of the swingarm can be thinner and hence lighter.

Taking sides

Single-sided swingarms are a race-bred option designed for easy wheel changes in endurance competition. Hyper-rigid, but there's a weight penalty. Ducati top-end sportsbikes have them (although the race bikes use magnesium or carbon while the less exotic street machines use alloy), but the Triumph 955i has gone back to a more

conventional system. Until recently Ducatis used a single-sider pivoting on the crankcase rather than the back of the gearbox or frame, as would be usual practice, because of their long V-twin engines, which had to be mounted far back in the frame because of the cylinder sticking out the front. The Duke's wheelbase would have been too great for quick steering if it used a conventionally mounted swingarm that was long enough to accommodate wheel and shock.

Weight watchers

Swingarms play a big part in the knotty problem of unsprung weight – that's to say, those components which live below your bike's suspension, such as wheels, brakes and swingarms. An amount of the suspension system's weight adds to the unsprung load too. Basically, the lower the proportion of unsprung weight to the sprung mass of the bike (the rest of it), the better the handling. The main reason for this is because unsprung mass gathers momentum on the move, upsetting the suspension. Therefore, a heavy bike on lighter running gear tends to be more composed than a pared-down sportster on the same chassis.

Swing out

So swingarms are a compromise between rigidity and weight. Many aftermarket options offer extra rigidity but not much of a weight advantage. A full works racing swingarm made from something exotic like magnesium or carbon fibre would offer the best of all worlds, but unless you're a full works rider, you probably won't feel any advantage.

There is a healthy swingarm aftermarket too, which first emerged in the old days of flexi-frames and swingarms. Often beautifully engineered with trick bracing, they can also offer the option of adjusting the wheelbase and revised shock linkages. Even these days, the bike manufacturers don't always get it exactly right, so there will always be

Basic tubular steel swingarm, for a twin-shock (left) and alloy single-sider for a monoshock Ducati show both ends of the swingarm pendulum swing. Ducati have now made their race engines short enough to revert to a more conventional and lighter double-sider.

Wheels

Wheels take quite a pounding from the forces of acceleration, braking, the weight of the motorcycle, and irregular road surfaces and potholes. Wheels fall into two main categories – wire-spoked and cast.

Wire wheels

Wire-spoked wheels are less common these days but still find a place on some lightweight road bikes, customs, retros and off-road machines. This last type of bike uses them because of their light weight and ability to take the punishment handed out by off-road riding, thanks in part to their inherent flexibility. BMW's GS series is one exception to the general road bike rule, although it must be said that the GS claims some off-road capability too. The BMW has spoked wheels cleverly laced to allow the use of tubeless tyres – the spokes sit outboard of the tyre bead. Moto Guzzi has adopted a similar system. Tubeless tyres cannot be used on conventional spoked wheels because the air would leak out of the spoke holes.

Cast wheels

Cast wheels have become the norm for most bikes because they're light enough, strong and easy to mass-produce. It wouldn't take long for a modern high-powered superbike to break all the spokes in a wire wheel. In any case, modern radial tyre designs are tubeless, so cast wheels are the obvious choice for most applications. Cast wheels are usually made from a one-piece casting incorporating hub, rim and spokes, unlike the three separate elements of a wire-spoked wheel.

Like so many refinements on modern bikes, cast wheels came from the racing scene, where they were originally made from exotic alloys to cut down on weight. Another advantage was that the hubs could be made narrower than on spoked wheels, allowing more room for the fitment of disc brakes.

The cast wheels on mass-produced road-going machines are made of ordinary aluminium alloys, which are just as stiff but more robust and cheaper (if heavier) than magnesium. However, some top-end production sportsbikes are now being graced with mag wheels and they are available as an aftermarket option.

The wheel deal

The most important thing for a wheel is that it's round. That's not being flippant. If a wheel runs out of true, perhaps because it's been damaged, handling can be upset, tyres wear unevenly and tubeless tyres can deflate. Some run-out is permissible, but if in doubt, have it checked out. Wire-spoked wheels can be trued up if the run-out isn't too bad, and it is possible to have cast wheels repaired, provided the structural integrity of the wheel isn't compromised. But any chunks out of the rim, cracked cast spokes or folds in the rim mean it must be replaced. Also, cast wheels can suffer fractures invisible to the naked eye in an impact, so if you have any doubts, have the wheels checked out by an engineering specialist.

It's important that you have the right tyres on your wheels, that they are correctly aligned and that the bearings are good. See the 'Tyres' and 'Looking after your bike' sections for more information on these areas.

Lighten up

There's a big aftermarket wheel industry, ranging from builders of spoked wheels to companies making competition wheels out of exotic materials such as carbon fibre and magnesium and other light alloys. Apart from looking seriously trick, some of the latter can offer significant savings in unsprung weight. For a basic explanation of this, see the previous pages on swingarms. Another advantage is that light front wheels can help steering because there's less gyroscopic effect to overcome. To understand gyroscopic effect, next time you've got a wheel out of a pushbike, hold the axle and get a friend to set it spinning. Now move your hands up and down and side to side. You'll feel some strong forces at play. But as with most things in biking, there's a compromise. Heavier wheels help with straight-line stability, which is why Honda specifies a heavy tyre for the Gold Wing.

Brakes

Unless you happen to be a speedway rider, you'll appreciate the importance of decent brakes. Apart from a few lightweights, scooters, retros and customs, it tends to be disc brakes all round these days – and even many of the bikes that feature drums on the back opt for discs up front.

Drum brakes

We'll keep it brief on the less common drum brakes. These work by forcing friction-material-lined shoes into contact with the steel or iron-lined inside of the drum by way of a cable or rod-operated cam or cams. Return springs pull the shoes clear of the drum when the brake levers are released.

They do their job adequately on low-powered, light bikes – provided the drum is true, the steel liner is not too worn, the shoes have got enough material on them and the cable's in good nick.

Drum brakes are less efficient at dispersing heat than disc systems. Before the widespread use of disc set-ups, huge drums were used on race bikes and larger road bikes. Under hard use, these brakes would start to 'fade' as the heat built up and braking efficiency was lost.

Drum brakes Simple in operation, but not up to the power, speed and low maintenance requirements of most of today's bikes and riders.

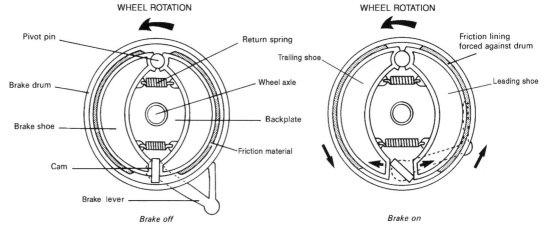

WHEEL ROTATION — Pivot pin — Return spring — Brake drum — Trailing shoe — Brake shoe — Wheel axle — Cam — Backplate — Brake lever — Friction material — **Brake off**

WHEEL ROTATION — Friction lining forced against drum — Leading shoe — **Brake on**

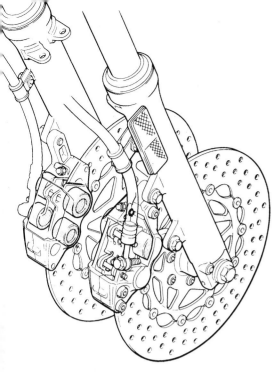

Disc brakes

Disc brakes are far more efficient than drums. We have the aviation industry to thank for disc brakes, but it took a few decades for them to evolve into the hyper-powerful systems used on bikes today.

Pistons operated hydraulically in the calipers from the front or rear master cylinders act on the steel backs of the friction pads, which squeeze the disc.

It's important that the calipers are designed to be rigid. If they were able to flex as the brakes were applied, their efficiency would diminish.

The most basic caliper has a single piston pushing one pad and slides to pull the other (fixed) pad against the disc. An opposed piston caliper has a pair or pairs of pistons pushing the pads. Multi-piston calipers are common on the front of bikes. Four piston (also more commonly known as four-pot) calipers are widely used. Kawasaki, for example, fits Tokico six-pots to some of its sports-bikes. Certain aftermarket calipers have more still. But it's not just down to the number of pistons. Their area and their relationship (ratio) with the master cylinder at the lever is important too; likewise the area of the pads. The piston at the master cylinder has a small area, where the area of the piston(s) in the caliper is large. This gives rise to something called the 'hydraulic multiplier effect', which means that relatively little force at the lever results in far greater forces at the caliper. Different-sized pistons are being used in certain individual calipers now-adays to provide more progressive braking. When you stop applying the brakes, the disc 'pushes' the pad away slightly and a rubber seal between the caliper and piston, shaped to twist a little as the piston moves out, pulls it back in again.

Multi-pot calipers allow longer, narrower pads to be used, meaning the area of the disc they operate on can be narrower and therefore lighter, reducing unsprung weight and gyroscopic forces (see 'Swingarms' and 'Wheels' for explanations of these).

Discs and pads

Discs are usually steel or iron. There's a limit to how narrow and thin they can be, because they have to be strong and there's a lot of heat to dissipate. On many modern designs, the disc can 'float' slightly on its carrier to optimise pad contact and allow a little room for heat expansion, preventing warpage.

Pad friction material is most commonly sintered metal these days because it works well in the wet – something early disc systems tended not to do. Different compounds are available for different applications. Hard brakers and trackday riders will have different requirements from touring riders, for example.

High-end race bikes feature carbon brakes (pads and discs), but the amount of heat that has to be in them to make them work means that they're no good for road bikes.

Likewise, full-on race compound pads might not work as well for standard brake set-ups on the road as they do on the track, although there are many aftermarket pads that offer performance superior to standard kit for everyday use.

Other braking points

Some bikes feature linked braking systems, where application of either the front or rear brake will lead to complete or partial application of the other brake. This is not to every rider's tastes, many preferring individual control of the brakes, although the manufacturers do design these systems for balanced braking.

Other machines feature anti-lock braking systems, usually available as an optional extra, which allow riders to brake as hard as they like without skidding.

The efficiency of your disc brakes relies on correct maintenance of the brake system and periodic changes of the correct type of brake fluid. See your manual or the 'Looking after your bike' section of this book for more details.

Disc brakes Schematic of typical production system on left. Note small diameter yet high bulk of discs. PFM aftermarket system on right has skinny braking area of greater diameter, allowing light but long calipers making for high swept area yet low unsprung weight.

Chassis accessories

There are aftermarket options for every chassis part we've discussed in this chapter, but there are other useful items you might want to consider too.

Grab rails Many bikes, especially sportsbikes, are less than generous in pillion provision. There are aftermarket grab rails to give a passenger something to grab hold of if they don't want to get too intimate with the rider in the absence of standard-fit grab rails.

Huggers Most monoshock bikes have very little protection from road dirt and the elements for the rear shock and its linkages. A hugger mounted to the swingarm will reduce the amount of water and muck being thrown at the shock, swingarm and back of the engine. Most replace the standard chainguard too. There's no problem of fit with better ones, but make sure cheaper items offer enough clearance for the tyre and chain. An undertray for the rear seat unit makes that area easy to clean and keeps crud out.

Rearsets Hard road riders and trackday fanatics might find that standard footpegs don't offer enough ground clearance. Aftermarket rearsets mount the pegs and controls higher and further back to help with this. Many have a huge range of adjustment for peg position to let riders set them for maximum comfort.

Crash bungs Motorcycle bodywork and cycle parts are expensive, so it's worth considering a set of crash bungs just in case the worst happens. Don't go for the cheap minimalist ones that will quickly disappear at the first hint of impact. Buy the type that bolt properly through frame and engine mount. This might mean some drilling of the fairing lowers, but it's worth it if they do their job and prevent your fairing and frame being written off.

Clip-ons If you've gone for racy rearsets, you might find that the handlebars are now in the wrong place. Aftermarket clip-ons usually offer more adjustment than the standard bars fitted to your bike and there's often a weight benefit. Going the other way, riders who find the riding position of their bike too extreme might like to consider bar risers. Remember that cables and hoses might now be too long or too short. Check that everything can still operate freely.

Screens For bikes without screens, there are plenty of bolt-on options to offer a little weather protection. If you have a faired bike and find the standard screen inadequate, there are higher and double-bubble alternatives. But be aware that sometimes all these do is move the windblast to an equally uncomfortable part of your anatomy.

Steering dampers These hydraulic units are designed to prevent tank-slappers (where the bars wobble uncontrollably from side to side) and improve stability. Usually adjustable for damping, they connect between the frame and the forks. The chassis geometry of most modern bikes makes them sufficiently stable most of the time. But some bikes with more radical geometry for quick steering, particularly sportsbikes, can suffer from shakes and wobbles when pushed hard. A decent damper reduces the problem. Some high-end sportsbikes have them as standard, but there's a ready aftermarket supply for bikes that don't, or as improvements over the original equipment.

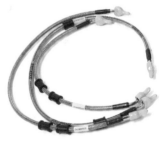

Braided brake hoses These are now fitted as standard on some bikes, but if not they make a huge difference in feel to disc brake set-ups, being less prone to expansion than conventional pipes. Stainless and Kevlar are popular materials for the braided outers of the hoses. The banjos that join the hose to the caliper are available in plated or stainless steel and alloy, but alloy should really only be used on race bikes since road salt can cause dangerous corrosion.

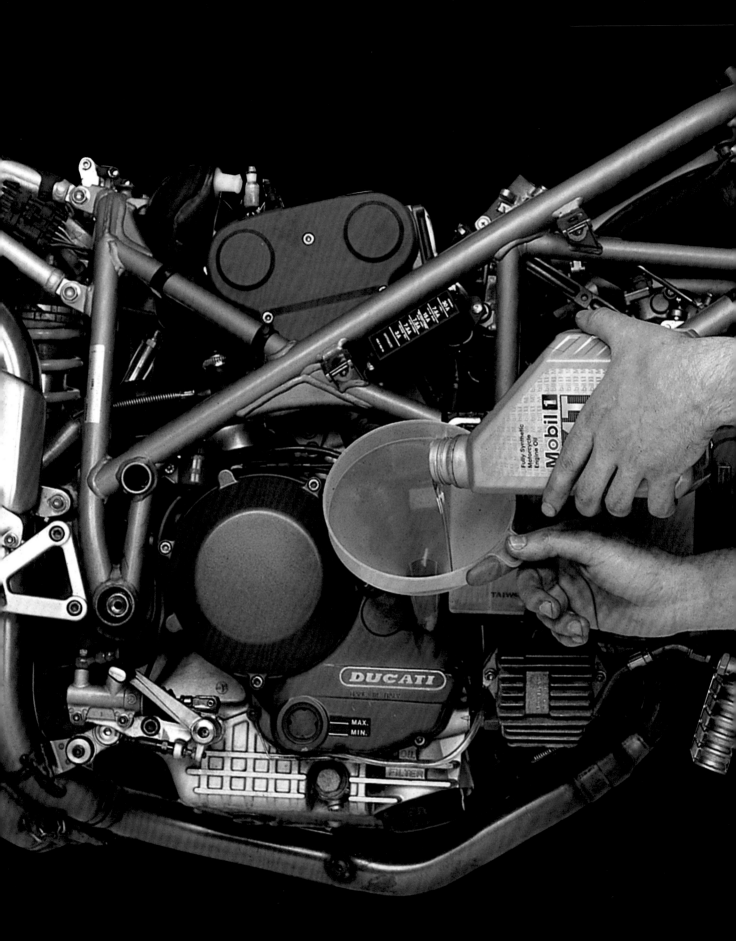

4

Looking after your motorcycle

Tools &
maintenance

Maintenance is vitally important. Just a few simple checks – even a quick glance before you ride – often makes the difference between catching a problem early, and expensive repairs later. It can even help to prevent an accident.

On any vehicle, things wear out, break and come loose. After all, it's simply a collection of parts asked to do fairly extreme things. Just think about the forces acting on a bike and you can imagine how important it is to check that spindles are tight and there's oil in the engine. Of course, you're not going to prevent all failures with maintenance. The idea is simply to prevent the obvious ones so you can spend more time enjoying riding your bike and less time getting it fixed at the dealer.

A comprehensive list of daily and weekly checks can be found in the user's manual, but if you

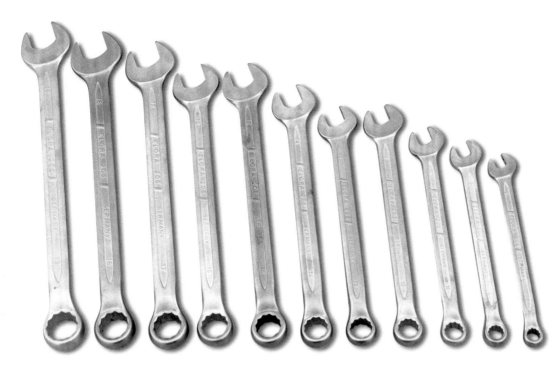

pressures, oil levels and cable adjustments. You should know whether most of these things need adjusting as you ride.

Also, before you ride, just glance at the nuts and bolts you can see. Are any sticking out, indicating they're loose? It does happen, even on brand new machines. If the engine takes longer and longer to start each time you ride, it's a sign that something is beginning to fail, even if it's just the battery. But catching it early means you won't be left stranded. So even with a little mechanical knowledge, you can save yourself money and have peace of mind that certain jobs have been done.

You'll find explanations and suggestions of what to check in the next few sections. By breaking the bike down into sections, looking after it seems less daunting. And as you become more familiar with working on bikes, you should be able to tackle more complicated jobs with ease. The first things you'll need are tools and it's worth making sure you have the right ones.

Tools are an essential part of looking after your bike. Good quality tools of the correct type will enable you to deal with jobs properly. You don't need roll-cabs and chests reaching to the shed roof, but a few quality essentials will go a long way.

Spanners

First and foremost are spanners. A set ranging from 7 to 19mm is good enough to tackle the majority of the fasteners on most modern bikes, although you may want to get two 10, 12 and 13mm spanners since they're popular sizes and sometimes it takes two to undo a component. Owners of some older British and American classics will need the appropriate imperial sizes for their machine. Buy combination spanners – they have an open end and a ring end. There are numerous jaw and ring designs and the more expensive spanners drive on the flats of the fasteners rather than the corners. But don't worry too much about this: quality and comfort are the priorities. Buy the best you can afford, and if you find over time that the most commonly used spanners in the set are wearing badly, replace these with higher quality items. Car boot sales are a great source of second-hand tools for people on a budget, and your money might be better spent there rather than on cheap and nasty new stuff. A couple of small adjustable spanners are a worthy addition to your toolkit, but they're not as good as non-adjustable types because they are often more prone to slipping on fasteners, rounding them off.

This ring spanner drives on the flats of nut and bolt heads, reducing the risk of rounding off through better contact with the component.

This spanner offers more angles of attack, but drives on the corners, giving nuts and bolts a harder time.

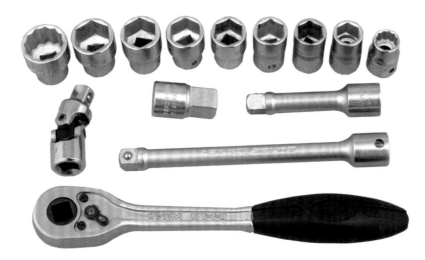

Socket sets

A socket set is vital. As with spanners, cheap stuff is a no-no, so the set you got free with a tenner's worth of petrol will not do the job. Quality is inferior and they're usually useless sizes anyway.

For bike work, $1/4$, $3/8$ and $1/2$ in are the most popular drive sizes, with sockets ranging from 6mm to 24mm in the best sets. Owners of old classics will again require imperial sets. Most sockets have a 12-point design, allowing the socket to fit in more positions and grip bolt heads and nuts snugly, avoiding rounding. However, a six-point design is better in some ways since it's more tolerant of fasteners that have already been slightly rounded. Once you've removed any such fasteners, it's a good idea to replace them with new ones – you might not be so lucky in removing them next time.

Allen, Torx and spline bits are available to fit socket drives, as well as oil filter spinners. Torx and spline-headed bolts are also used occasionally, and you'll need the appropriate sockets.

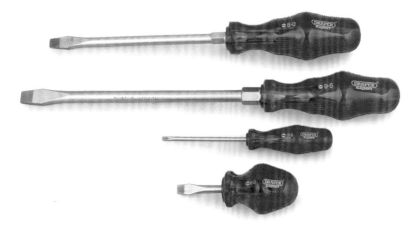

Screwdrivers

It's worth buying good quality screwdrivers as the heads of screws are normally the first casualties of home servicing. Buy screwdrivers with good tips and comfortable handles. A selection of Phillips and flat-bladed screwdrivers is enough for most jobs. Be sure to use the screwdriver that has the best fit to the screw slots you're attacking. If you intend to strip engines, an impact driver that can take sockets as well as screwdriver bits is handy.

Allen keys

Most modern bikes use Allen bolts to hold various things together, so a good set of keys is essential. Better than the classic key shape, consider getting a set of T-bars and some socket-Allen keys. You can use the socket keys to loosen tight bolts and the T-bars to remove them quickly. The most common sizes are 4–8mm, although try to go a little either side of this. Torx and spline keys will be required for some other fasteners.

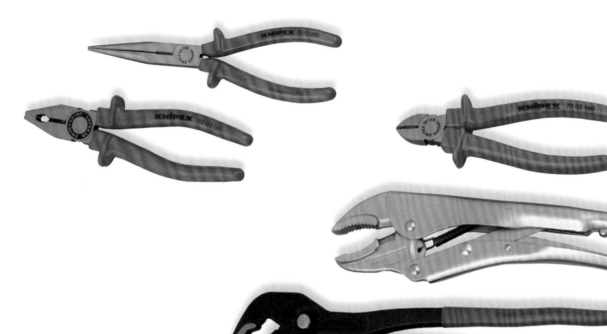

Pliers

As well as a standard set of pliers, long-handled snipe-nose pliers are extremely useful for working on bikes. They allow you to reach deep into the bike through limited gaps. A set of vice-grip pliers will also make life easier.

Torque wrenches

For reassembly, a torque wrench is essential to ensure fasteners are tightened to the correct figures as given in your workshop manual. This will avoid snapped fasteners, stripped threads and distorted casings, or worse. There are two types: the beam type, which uses a pointer on a calibrated scale to show the applied torque; and the pre-set type, where the torque is set with an adjuster and the tool 'gives' or clicks when the fastener is at the proper tightness. You'll need a torque wrench suited towards bike work (the majority of settings needed for bikes are lower than for cars). A tool with a range of 7–100Nm should suffice.

Tool care

Look after your tools and they'll give you years of service. A squirt of WD40 and a wipe with a rag after use is wise. Store them in a decent toolbox, kept in a dry place. If you try to apply some logic to which tool goes where in the box, you'll also save yourself hours of frustration hunting for the right tool.

Cleaning

Cleaning bikes is important. Apart from keeping your bike looking tidy and new for longer, which increases the amount of money you'll get when you resell it, this is a good way of spotting problems before they become too major.

A range of specialist bike-cleaning potions and implements. Beats a sponge and a bucket full of warm water and washing-up liquid. Although that's better than nothing.

When race bikes are cleaned, the mechanics aren't just trying to keep the sponsors happy. As they clean the wheels, they'll be looking for cracks or dents. It's the same with the frame and other parts. Cleaning is the best way of spotting problems before they get serious.

The first thing to do is get rid of the thicker gunge, which, at the rear, normally comes in the form of old chain lube. Some paraffin or other degreaser on a rag will cut through this, and it must be rinsed away afterwards. Avoid using petrol as a degreaser. Apart from being highly flammable, you don't want to get it on your skin. It can also attack some plastic and rubber parts on bikes. Applying degreaser by rag reduces the chances of it getting where it shouldn't, such as in the wheel bearings.

Fresh brake dust can normally be wiped off wheels easily. But old dust, and dust on the calipers, normally needs agitating, which is best done with a short-bristled paint brush or old toothbrush. You can also get special brake dust removing sprays, which are pretty good. Some specialist wheel cleaning fluids are slightly corrosive. Make sure you don't spray or brush any on to unlaquered aluminium. Remember to clean dust from inside the caliper too, and use only brake cleaner or fresh brake fluid. Other solvents might attack the hydraulic seals.

The rest of the bike can be washed normally with water and detergent (dedicated detergent is better than washing-up liquid) then polished. There's a bewildering array of specialised cleaning products on the market. But for general cleaning, you can do all these jobs with one product. Domestic general polishes like Mr Sheen are often ideal. They remove chain lube, dried-on flies, brake dust and clean and polish at the same time – so you only have to do the job once. For dried-on flies and chain lube, spray it on liberally and leave for a minute or two. But try not to do it in conditions where the spray will dry. And remember to use a clean rag on your screen and paintwork. Whole screens have needed replacing because the rag used on them was the same one that cleaned a gritty area of bodywork.

If you're serious about cleaning, or your bike gets particularly filthy, you might want to invest in a jet washer. But don't be too vigourous around wheel, head, swingarm and shock bearings and linkages, since the grease can be forced out, which accelerates wear. The same goes for the chain, so be sure to lubricate it after jet washing.

With your bike cleaned, application of a good polish will bring out the shine, and silicon types claim to provide longer resistance to dirt build-up. Don't go too mad too often with paint-restoring polishes as these are usually mildly abrasive and you might wind up going through the paint. Use specialist polishes on bare aluminium and chrome, a favourite pastime of retro, cruiser and classic enthusiasts.

Chain care

Chains do a lot of work in harsh conditions, so periodic maintenance is essential. Ideally, chains should be inspected every 600 miles. Even a quick once-over and some lube is better than nothing and will increase chain life considerably. The three important chain care jobs are cleaning, adjustment and lubrication.

It's important to keep chains clean because grit and other dirt sticks to the lube and acts as a grinding paste, speeding up the wear process. Clean the chain with something like paraffin to cut through built up lube and then give it a good rinse. Don't leave the paraffin on the chain for ages, though.

Once clean, let the chain dry. If you spray on lube when it's still wet, you'll be trapping in moisture. It's important to know what type of chain you have fitted. Most bikes have O-ring chains, with rubber rings holding lubricant inside the rollers. These should be lubricated with O-ring chain lube. In this case, the lube will protect the outside of the chain and keep the O-rings supple and the grease inside the chain, rather than lubricating the pins.

No matter what type of chain, lube is best applied after a ride, when the chain is warm. This allows better penetration of the lube. When lubing chains,

direct it so it hits in between the plates on both sides of the chain. Also, if you apply it to the lower run of the chain, centrifugal force will take care of lubing the outside. After a few minutes, wipe away any excess – it'll only fling off and make more mess elsewhere.

Automatic oilers are worth a mention because they save time and effort once fitted and extend chain life considerably. They also increase the time required between chain adjustments.

When adjusting chains, it's not only chain tension that's important. Wheel alignment is as crucial and should be checked carefully. Nearly all chain adjusters have some form of indicator, but if you have the time, it's worth double-checking wheel alignment using straight edges or a length of string because some adjusters can be out.

Checking chain tension and wear

To find out the correct tension and permissible chain stretch, check your manual.

With your bike upright (but not with someone sitting on it) and in neutral, push the bottom chain run down and measure the slack midway between the two sprockets. Rotate the rear wheel slightly and check again. Do this at several points along the chain because they wear unevenly, which leads to tight spots. Adjust for the correct tension at the tightest point on the chain.

If your chain is at, or close to, the end of its adjustment, it's worn out. This is best checked with the chain off the bike but can be done while it is still fitted. To do this, remove the chainguard and, with the chain taut, measure a number of links along the top run. Then see how the measurements compare to the spec in your manual. Rotate the rear wheel

and measure various sections of the chain in this way. Any kinking, frozen links or missing O-rings mean that it's time for a new chain.

Check front and rear sprockets for signs of wear too. If either sprocket has teeth that appear bent or 'hooked', do not be tempted to reverse the sprocket – this could lead to sudden failure because the teeth could break off. If either chain or sprockets are worn, replace as a set since one worn item will hasten the wear of the others.

Adjustment

Assuming that the chain and sprockets are still good, they can be adjusted. With the tightest point of the chain at the centre of the bottom run and the bike supported upright (again without someone sitting on it, so either prop the bike securely or have someone hold it from the front), first slacken the wheel spindle. Now loosen the locknuts for the sliding adjusters' screws and turn them equally until the chain is at the correct tension as specified in your manual. Check the wheel alignment marks are in the same place on each side, and that everything is butting up as it should. If not, push the wheel forward or pull it back until they are. Check alignment marks and chain tension again. Once satisfied with everything, tighten the spindle to the correct torque setting in your manual and tighten the locknuts. Make a final check of the chain tension before riding.

Things are slightly different on bikes with eccentric adjusters and single-sided swingarms, but correct chain tension is equally important. Refer to your manual for detailed advice on adjustment.

Remember that if a chain is too tight, it can cause havoc with gearboxes and bearings.

Direct chain lube so it gets between the plates on both sides of the chain. It's best to direct the spray at the lower run while the chain's warm, i.e. after a ride.

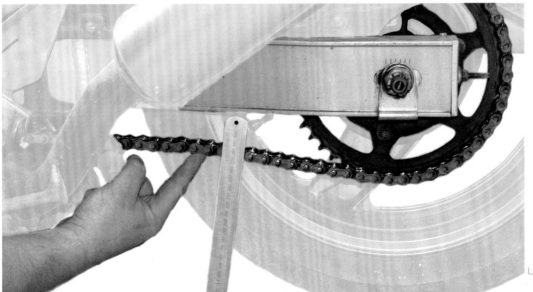

Look for the tightest point on the chain, then adjust as per the measurements in your manual. Some do it by feel. If in doubt use a ruler as shown here.

Brakes

The most important thing about any machine is its capacity to stop. That's why it's vital to keep brakes in good condition, so it stops when you ask it to. All bikes, no matter what their intended use, will use disc or drum brake systems or a combination of both.

Master cylinder reservoir
Check fluid level often, and if it decreases quickly check for leaks in the system. Murky fluid is contaminated and the system should be bled to replace it.

Brake hoses
Most bikes have lines with rubber-type outers that allow expansion over time leading to spongy brakes. Braided hoses are better.

Brake discs
Must be outside minimum thickness. They must also be unwarped or the brakes will judder.

Calipers
Tend to attract road dirt impeding efficiency. Keep 'em clean with regular applications of brake cleaner. Check often for pad wear.

Inspection

The most important thing to check on disc or drum brake systems is the amount of friction material left on the pads or shoes (drum brakes have shoes, discs have pads). The material wears every time the brakes are applied and often wears faster than you might think.

You can check pads simply by looking through the caliper because many pads have wear indicators visible without the need to remove the calipers, but on multi-disc systems bear in mind that pads don't wear evenly. Check all the pads and never allow them to wear so far that the backing plate damages the discs. Drum brakes are harder to inspect and can sometimes require wheel removal, although most drums have wear indicators, which make life easier.

Replacing disc brake pads

Replacing brake pads means removing the calipers and pushing the pistons back with a piece of wood to accommodate the new pads. But before you do this, be sure to clean the pistons as best you can. If you simply push them back, dirt and brake dust can be forced back into the caliper, which can stop the pistons withdrawing properly when you let go of the lever. A squirt of brake cleaner and a wipe is normally adequate.

But be aware that the fluid level can rise as the pistons go back and some may have to be siphoned off. Be careful not to get fluid on paintwork or plastics – it can attack them in seconds.

If necessary, add more brake fluid of the correct type as you pump the calipers up after refitting. Do not allow air to enter the system by letting the fluid level get too low, and make sure you have pumped the brake lever to put the pads back in contact with the disc before riding.

Other brake maintenance

Apart from the pads wearing, there is little else that requires attention. Hydraulic disc systems are self-adjusting, and the only thing to watch is the fluid level in the reservoir. The fluid should be renewed as per the service intervals suggested in your manual.

As the pads wear, more fluid will be taken into the system to take up the slack. If the level drops below the minimum, there is again a chance air will be drawn into the system, which reduces its effectiveness dramatically, making the controls feel spongy. Take a regular look at fluid level indicators on the master cylinders and never let the level drop below the minimum mark. If air does enter the system, the brakes will have to be bled properly.

As drum brake shoes wear, slack in the cables and brake rods will have to be taken up. Check the bike's manual for details of your system. Cables must be in good condition and must be kept correctly adjusted and lubricated.

Disc and drum surfaces need checking too. Discs should be inspected for cracks, as should drums. Discs and drums should also be measured for wear and distortion, and replaced if necessary. The minimum thicknesses are normally stamped on the parts, and can also be found in your manual.

On disc brake systems, the brake fluid, hydraulic seals and hoses degrade over time and must be renewed in accordance with your bike's service schedule. Inspect hoses and unions regularly for signs of leaks and corrosion at the banjos. Brake fluid is hygroscopic and absorbs moisture from the atmosphere over time, impairing braking efficiency and giving a spongy feel at the lever or pedal. So don't neglect replacing it with the correct fluid at the specified intervals, and certainly no more than every couple of years, regardless of mileage. Always use new fluid from a sealed container.

Do not work on a bike's braking system unless you're confident you know what you're doing. Your Haynes manual shows you the correct procedures; for safety's sake follow them to the letter.

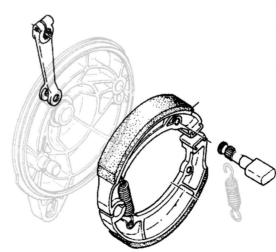

Basic disc caliper (left) and even more basic drum. Don't worry about what type of brakes your bike has too much, they're usually adequate. Pay more attention to maintenance.

Cables

Cables fulfil plenty of useful functions. Apart from where they've been superseded by hydraulic (disc brakes and some clutches) and electrical systems (some speedos, rev counters, chokes and even throttles), cables operate a variety of components just as they have since the dawn of motorcycling.

Simple as cables are, they do require some care and attention for optimum performance. The most common killer is chaffing, where the cable flexes with the steering and wears through the outer casing. Once this happens, corrosion is likely to creep in.

Check for chaffing by inspecting the cables for flat spots. You should be able to see potential problems by turning the steering lock to lock and watching the cables. Cables sometimes fray and snap next to the nipple at the cable end. This is caused by the nipple not being able to rotate in the lever or throttle grip. Before replacing the cable, clean the hole in the lever/grip and smear the nipple with grease.

Routing

When routing cables, the straighter they are the better. Tight bends will make the cable harder to operate, increase the wear rate internally and possibly cause the cable to stick. Bad routing can also cause a cable to operate when flexed. Before replacing a cable, make a note of how the original was routed. Inadvertent operation through bad routing is particularly a problem on the throttle and brakes. If you do fit new throttle cables, always move the bars from lock to lock with the engine running to make sure the throttle doesn't operate. We say throttle 'cables' because almost all modern bikes have one cable to open the fuel supply (accelerator), complemented by one to close it (decelerator).

Cables should also be routed away from components that build up significant amounts of heat, such as exhaust pipes, or outers will melt and internal lubrication will be lost.

Free play on this R1's accelerator and decelerator cables is measured at the throttle itself. Too much or too little, and the cables will have to be adjusted.

Adjustments are made here by pulling the cable outer from the adjuster body. Adjuster and locknut can be seen clearly.

Here are the coarse adjusters at the carburettor end. When fitting cables it's best to take all the adjustment out of the fine adjusters and set the cables up using these coarse adjusters. Then as the cables stretch, the fine adjusters can be used to take up the slack.

Adjustment

Cables must be correctly adjusted for proper operation of controls. There must be adequate free play between the inner and outer so that controls aren't inadvertently operated when the bars are turned or the suspension extends and compresses. For correct cable adjustment, refer to your manual. Most are adjusted by simple barrel and locknut arrangements. In the case of cable clutches and front brakes, it is done by knurled wheel adjusters at the lever end for fine adjustment (as the cable stretches slightly in use), and other adjusters at the gearbox or brake end for coarser adjustment. Some throttle cables have fine adjusters near the twistgrip and coarser ones at the carb/throttle body end too.

Lubrication

As cables get older they get harder to use. This can be caused by fraying of the internal wire, or by dirt build up in the cable. If a cable is frayed, then it should be replaced immediately. If it is simply dirty, then lubricating the cable might displace some of the dirt and also make it easier to use.

It is possible to lubricate cables by creating a reservoir at one end and letting gravity draw lubricant through the cable. A quicker method is to use force. For less than £10, you can buy an adaptor that seals itself around one end of a cable. You then connect an aerosol lubricant (not chain lube) and squirt. The pressure expels dirt and ensures the cable is fully lubricated.

An alternative method is to use a pressure lubricator that is filled with light oil and operated by hand to force the oil through the cable. If an inner cable has a nylon liner, don't use oil to lubricate it. Oil can make the liner swell, and cause the cable to seize. Use a silicone spray instead.

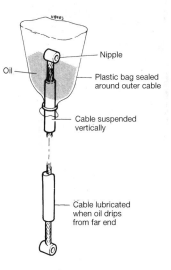

Home-brewed cable lubricator (above). Pressure lubricator (far left) makes the job quick and easy, as does aerosol adaptor (left).

Without oil, engines will do considerable harm to themselves and won't run for long. Oil prevents damage by separating surfaces with a thin film, allowing parts to move past each other with minimal wear or friction.

Oil and filter change

Changing oil is easier on a warm engine because the oil is thinner. Remove the filler first to let the old lube flow more freely.

When removing the oil drain-plug, watch out for the initial gush of hot oil – and for other hot components, such as exhaust pipes. Make sure the drain tray you have under the sump is large enough to hold the used lube.

When fitting a filter, smear a small amount of clean oil evenly around the rubber seal and make sure no dirt has dropped on to the sealing face.

Fill the engine to the correct level with the bike upright – you'll get a false reading if the bike's on its side stand. It's important to use the right grade of engine oil, as specified by the manufacturer, so check your manual.

To top up the engine oil, wipe the oil level inspection window, located on the right-hand side of the engine, so that it is clean. With the motorcycle vertical, the oil level should lie between the maximum and minimum levels on the window. If the level is below the minimum line, remove the filler cap from the top of the clutch cover. Top the engine up with the recommended grade and type of oil, to bring the level up to the maximum level on the window. Re-install the filler cap.

A large part of oil's role is a clean-up job in the motor. Over a period of time, an engine's oil will become contaminated with by-products of the combustion process, including unburnt fuel, moisture from condensation and even coolant from the water jacket. All of this degrades its performance. These problems are on top of the degradation of the lubricant as it performs its basic job of cooling and lubing. Shearing forces break up the oil's molecular structure as it works hard to prevent the engine's key components from grinding themselves to bits, which is exactly what bits of metal flinging themselves at each other several thousands times a minute would inevitably do.

Making the change

Changing a bike's oil involves replacing the oil and filter. It's a good idea to replace them together, or at least fit a new filter every other oil change. Clogged filters can do as much damage as no oil, since they impede correct flow of lubricant, and fitting new filters without changing old oil won't improve the lube's performance.

Most bikes over 125cc have filters. Locations vary but are usually low down on the front or side of the engine for external filters, and underneath for internal ones. Nearly all external filters screw on. There are a number of strap and socket-drive tools available to remove them, and although it works, stabbing them with a screwdriver is best avoided – as anyone who's had an eyeful of hot oil can testify. Replace filters with genuine bike manufacturer parts, or parts of the correct specification.

When disposing of used oil, it's your moral – and

indeed legal – duty to dispose of it correctly. The drain by the back door won't do. Transfer the contents of the oil drain can into the tin your new oil came in, and then take it to the local authority dump, where they'll know what to do with it.

Most modern sump drain-plugs have a magnetic end to catch small pieces of swarf generated by internal engine friction. These plugs should be wiped clean before refitting. It's also advisable to replace the sealing washer with a new one. These are often copper, or another soft metal such as aluminium, and sometimes they have a rubber insert. It's easy to be tempted to turn the washer upside down, assuming it will do the same job as a new one. But this ruse rarely works more than once, and what might start as a messy trickle can quickly turn into a messy and dangerous deluge if the sump plug decides to let go.

When first starting the bike after an oil refill, don't over rev it. It takes a while to fill the filter and build pressure in the system. Until then, you're relying on the oil film on components keeping the key parts safe, so give them an easy time. If the oil pressure warning light doesn't go out after a few seconds, stop the engine immediately. The problem might be down to a multitude of reasons after an engine rebuild. But after a refill, it's more likely to be because of adding too little oil or a major leak from filter or drain-plug – you did remember to refit them, didn't you? We only ask because it's all too easy to forget – and then fail to notice the spreading puddle of fresh lube on the garage floor before realising there is a problem. So never conduct maintenance in a rush. Let the bike idle for a few minutes, before rechecking the oil level.

Oil drain cans/trays sold in car accessory shops are large enough to hold the contents of any bike sump.

Socket wrench driven tool for easy removal of external spin-on oil filters.

Cooling systems

Engines are not very efficient. Most of the energy released during combustion is transferred into heat and escapes into the engine or down the exhaust pipe. All the heat building up in the engine has to go somewhere, or the bike will overheat and the engine will be damaged. That's where cooling comes in.

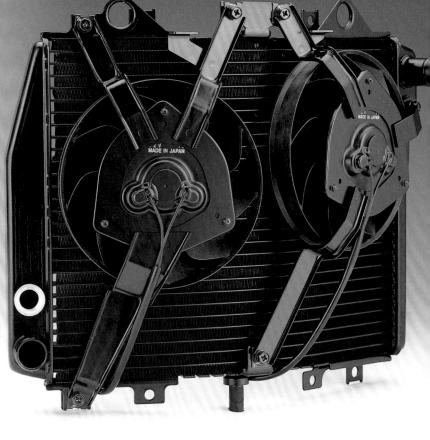

Engines are either air-cooled or liquid-cooled. Liquid-cooling is the most popular choice these days, but is also more complicated. Air-cooled engines are very straightforward. The flow of air over the engine, as the bike moves along, takes the heat with it. Barrels and heads have deep horizontal fins to help with heat dissipation. Problems only arise in very hot climates or if the machine is static or moving slowly for long periods. Some air-cooled bikes have oil-coolers, which look like radiators, to help the lubricant play a more efficient role in taking heat away from the engine. The old Suzuki GSX engines, as still used in the Bandit, are a good example of this. Suzuki describes them as air/oil-cooled.

In a liquid-cooled engine, coolant is pumped through a network of drillings in the motor's castings. Heat transfers to the coolant which then passes through a radiator where it is cooled. If for any reason the coolant doesn't flow, the engine will overheat.

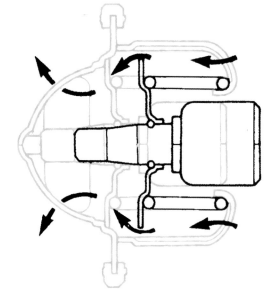

The thermostat lets the engine get up to temperature before opening to allow the coolant to flow to the radiator.

Thermostats

A thermostat in the system gauges when the coolant is up to operating temperature and then allows it to flow to the radiator and the rest of the system. If it wasn't there, the bike would take a long time to warm up. If it fails to open, the engine will overheat. If you suspect the thermostat is faulty, it must be checked. If it is open at room temperature, then it has failed and must be replaced. To test that it opens, heat it in a pan of water and, using a thermometer, check the temperature at which it opens and compare the figure with the spec in your manual. Also check the amount it stays open after being heated at 90ºC for a few minutes and, again, compare this figure with the specifications in your manual.

Temperature sensors

These are mounted in the engine block or cylinder head and are electrical devices whose resistance falls as coolant temperature rises. One brings the electric fan or fans behind the radiator into operation, while another is connected to the temperature gauge on your instrument cluster. On some models, one sensor combines these two operations.

If the fan stays on all the time, doesn't come on at all or cuts in at the wrong temperature, suspect the fan sensor (having first checked the fuse, if the fan doesn't operate at all). Likewise, if the temperature gauge doesn't work or gives clearly inappropriate readings, suspect the sensor.

Both of these sensors can be tested, but the procedure is more complex than for thermostats. See your manual.

Coolant

The most common problem with liquid-cooled engines is lack of coolant. Check the coolant is between the high and low levels on the expansion tank. Don't overfill the system because it has to vent as the liquid expands. Be sure to top up with the correct coolant for your bike.

Leaks reduce a system's effectiveness because coolant can escape and the system doesn't pressurise, reducing the coolant's boiling point. Check hoses and joints for leakage and inspect the radiator too. Sometimes leaks occur internally in the engine for various reasons and these are more serious. Coolant in the oil, which leads to a deposit that looks like mayonnaise, or oil in the coolant is a sign of this.

If the radiator fins have become clogged externally with road dirt or the odd unfortunate pigeon, air can't pass through it and the engine will run hot. Clean it using water from a hose in the opposite direction to which air flows, or, with care, a compressed air line.

Cooling systems are sometimes blocked by corrosion carried into the radiator. Although you can use water (distilled is far better than tap) in cooling systems, it's far better to use dedicated coolant or anti-freeze of the correct type for your bike as both have corrosion inhibitors. Anti-freeze also protects the system during cold weather. Plain water or coolant without anti-freeze can turn into ice, which may lead to cracks in the system. When topping up a system filled with anti-freeze, don't use just water on its own as this will dilute the anti-freeze, lessening its efficiency. For maximum protection, coolant should be replaced every two years, although some systems are sealed for life.

Draining and refilling the cooling system

This is normally done in two stages and must always be done with the engine cold. Remove the pressure cap on the radiator to help the system drain. This must never be removed with the engine hot since scalding coolant and steam may escape and cause injury. When you're sure the engine is cool, remove the cap carefully and slowly with a rag over it. Remember that cooling systems are pressurised and there may still be enough pressure to spit coolant out at you.

Disconnect the hose from the neck of the radiator and use it to empty the expansion tank into a container sufficiently large to hold all the coolant in your bike's system. If any old coolant remains in the expansion tank, remove the tank and tip the fluid out. Next, loosen and remove the lowest coolant hose you can see on the engine. This should drain the radiator and engine. Often there are other drain plugs on the cylinder block and water pump cover. Remove these as well to allow any remaining coolant to escape.

Old coolant must be disposed of carefully, so check with your local authority to find out the location of the nearest dump who can deal with it. Never leave it lying around. It's highly toxic so keep it away from children and animals. Wipe up any spills. Anti-freeze is inflammable as well.

Refill the system, being careful to check for air by squeezing rubber hoses and possibly bleeding the pump if required. Check your manual for the complete procedure for your bike. Remember to fill the expansion tank to the correct level too.

The reservoir is usually mounted on the right-hand end of the radiator. Check that the coolant level is between the 'FULL' and 'LOW' level lines marked on the reservoir.

If the coolant level is low, remove any bodywork obstructing the filler cap. Remove the cap and top up the coolant with the recommended coolant mixture. Fit the cap securely. Then re-install any bodywork.

Bearings

Compared to the engine, a bike's chassis is relatively free of bearings. But chassis bearings require more care than any in the engine, which have a ready supply of warm lubricant to look after them. There are four sets of chassis bearings to check – wheel, swingarm, rear suspension linkages and bushes, and headstock.

The wheel and headstock bearings are perhaps the most important. They're certainly the ones most capable of adversely affecting the handling characteristics. However, checking them is a fairly simple task, especially with a friend helping.

Wheel bearings

To check the front wheel bearings, you need to establish if there is any sideplay. The wheel should be free to spin forwards and backwards. To check bearings, set the steering in the straight ahead position. If you don't have a front paddock stand, ask a friend to lean the bike on its side stand until the front is off the ground. Things are even easier if your bike is equipped with a centre stand – have your helper lean on the back of the bike.

Grab the wheel from one side and try pulling the top towards you while pushing the bottom end away. Any clicking or clunking is likely to be in the bearings, and the wheel should be removed to replace them. The procedure is the same for the rear wheel, and again it's easier if the wheel is off the ground by means of a paddock stand, centre stand (where fitted), or your ever-helpful mate pulling the bike over on its sidestand.

Wheel bearings are usually the ball type, with one pressed into each side of the hub. Chain-drive bikes often have a third bearing in the cush/sprocket carrier assembly of the rear wheel. It's a similar deal with shaft-drive bikes, which often have an additional bearing or bearings in the bevel mechanism for the shaft drive. See your manual for bearing replacement procedure.

Swingarm bearings
As with most bearings, the swingarm's bearings or bushes are easiest checked with the help of a friend.

Wheel Bearings
Side-to-side wheel play or roughness when the wheel is rotated means the bearings are shot.

Swingarm & rear suspension bearings

On bikes with greasing points for these bearings, their life can be considerably lengthened by lubricating as per the maintenance schedule in your manual.

Checking the swingarm pivot bearings is a similar procedure to wheel bearings, but you won't be able to check them on a paddock stand because you need to try to move the swingarm from side-to-side. Use the mate and side stand trick. If the bearings feel suspect, you can carry out the same test with the suspension disconnected from the swingarm. To do this, though, the bike will have to be on a centre stand or stand under the engine or suspended from a beam in the workshop. It's much easier to feel swingarm pivot bearing play this way.

Swingarm bearings will either be bushes or needle, taper or ball roller type. Sometimes there's a combination of types. Refer to your manual for details on replacement.

The suspension linkage on monoshock bikes carries bushes or needle roller or ball bearings. To check for play in these, the rear wheel has to be off the floor with no weight on the swingarm. Grab the top of the rear wheel and pull it upwards. There should be no clunk or free play. Again, refer to your manual for details on replacement.

Steering bearings

Headstock, or steering, bearings need to be checked in two ways. With no weight on the front wheel (time to call on that mate again), move the bars left to right. On models fitted with a steering damper, make sure the damper is backed off to the position of least resistance. Steering action should be smooth and light. Any notchiness or tight spots are signs of bearing damage, and they should be replaced.

Because of the hammering these bearings get, they often work loose. Still with no weight on the front, get someone to push and pull quite hard on the bottom of the fork legs. While they do this, check for small movement by placing your fingers between the back of the top yoke and front of the tank. If you feel movement, the bearings are loose and need adjusting, the procedure for which will be in your manual.

Steering bearings benefit from regular regreasing and being correctly adjusted. The main types these days are taper roller and caged ball, although a few, mainly smaller, bikes still use uncaged balls. These are a laugh-a-minute to fit, since the grease you've used to hold them in the bottom race, while you get the bottom yoke back in, fails to do so, and the tiny balls drop on to the workshop floor.

Bearing markings reveal the bearing type. It can be a lot cheaper to buy from a specialist bearing shop.

Rear suspension bearings and bushes These must be checked with the wheel off the ground and no weight on the swingarm.

Steering head bearings These need to be checked for side-to-side and front-to-back movement. Good handling relies on chassis bearings being in good condition and properly lubed and adjusted.

Electrical

Electrical systems are the most common cause of problems on bikes, so it pays to keep on top of them. Modern bike electrics are becoming increasingly complex but also increasingly robust, making the bikes we ride more reliable at the same time. Just a little bit of care will keep them that way.

Battery
Doesn't last forever, but keep topped-up, with de-ionised water, between the lines so the plates in each cell are covered in non-sealed types. Watch out for build up of clag at the bottom of cells.

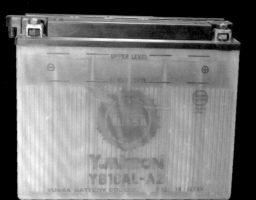

Battery

The obvious place to start is the battery. Unless you've got a modern sealed battery, you need to check it's filled to within the correct levels as indicated on the casing. If low, top it up with a little de-ionised water, but be careful not to get any acidic fluid from the battery on you or your clothes (or the bike). A battery that needs to be topped up too regularly indicates problems with the charging system. Refer to your manual for checks.

It is also well worth ensuring that the battery terminals are tight. These can work loose and cause problems that are hard to trace. A splodge of petroleum jelly or battery grease prevents corrosion forming on the terminals and ensures a good connection.

Typically, a conventional lead acid battery will last for up to three years, provided it is properly maintained and kept charged up when the bike isn't in regular use.

Connectors

Satisfied that the battery is in good condition, it's worth checking the push-fit connectors that link the various electrical components. You'll find these all over most bikes, and if moisture gets in, it can cause failures. Split the connections and spray a little contact cleaner on the pins. Be careful not to spray bodywork or other plastic or painted components since they may be attacked by the contact cleaner.

Smearing a little bit of silicon grease or a squirt of WD40 on the connector body will make them easier to split next time.

Bulbs

Check that your lights work. That might sound simple but it's amazing how easy it is to forget this. It makes good sense before every ride to check head and tail lights, indicators and to apply both brakes to check the brake light and its switches are working – and there are probably some meticulous souls that do. At the other end of the spectrum, there are riders who need to be told their rear light has failed and only notice headlight problems when they can't see in the dark. But it pays to be less slack than this because there is a major safety issue here.

Some bikes seem to get through rear bulbs at an alarming rate. This is often caused by vibration, so make sure the light unit is fitted correctly.

If you notice the direction indicator idiot light on the dash flashing quicker than usual, it's normally a sign one or more of the indicator bulbs have failed.

When performing your routine checks of lights and indicators, give the horn a quick blast to make sure that's working too.

Fuses

The first thing to suspect when an electrical component stops working is its fuse. Bike fuse boxes are usually located in easily accessible places – under the seat, side panel or inboard of the fairing.

There's usually a helpful key on a printed label in the lid of the fuse box to tell you which does what, and sometimes there's a couple of spares too. Some smaller machines just have a single fuse for all the systems, usually found near the battery.

A blown fuse often indicates a short circuit or a faulty electrical component, but sometimes they just blow for no reason, especially on bikes that vibrate a lot. If you replace a fuse and it blows again, the fault requires further investigation. Time to get the manual out. Some bikes use a resettable circuit breaker in place of the main fuse.

Switches

Handlebar switches are probably the most exposed electrical components – particularly on unfaired bikes. It is a good idea, once a year, to remove the switches, scrape away the corrosion, chase out the spiders, and apply a light smear of petroleum jelly to the switch components – metal and plastic.

Connectors
A little bit of preventative maintenance will ensure they keep the electricity flowing to where it needs to go.

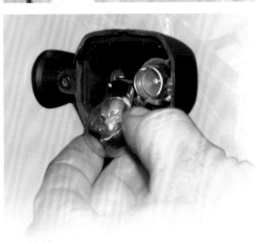

Bulbs do blow now and again, but usually through old age and sometimes vibration. If they persistently fail, there's a problem.

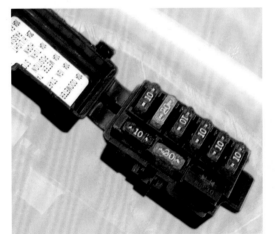

Fuses protect key components from electrical overload damage. Sometimes they just fail. Immediate failure on replacement shows there's a more serious fault.

Blown

Un-blown

A couple more tips

If you use a pressure washer to clean your bike, be careful not to blast electrical connectors or components. Although most systems are designed to be watertight, the force from a pressure washer may be too much.

Side stand kill-switches often get covered in chain lube from the front sprocket. Because they have the ability to kill the ignition system, keep them clean. Don't use solvent cleaners; simply wipe them with a rag and check that they operate freely and smoothly.

MoTs

An MoT certificate is simply a bit of paper stating that a particular bike was in roadworthy condition at the time it was inspected. It's also a legal requirement – every bike over three years old used on the road in the UK has to have one. You can't buy a tax disc without it and your insurance may be invalidated if you have an accident while your bike has no MoT. Here are the areas the MoT inspector will be looking at. You'll save a lot of time and hassle if you look at them yourself before going to the test centre.

Brakes

- Each wheel will be raised off the ground, the brakes operated then released and the wheel spun to check for binding.
- Brake discs will be checked for cracks and to ensure they're securely mounted.
- Pad material will be checked visually on disc systems to ensure the pads aren't on their wear limit.
- Drum brakes will be checked for correct operation of the lever and that the angle between operating cable or rod and the lever on the brake drum isn't too large with the brake applied.
- Brake hoses and their unions will be looked at for bulging in flexible pipes, and signs of corrosion and hydraulic fluid leakage elsewhere.
- Rear brake torque arms will be checked for security and that fasteners are held on by locknuts or split pins.
- ABS-equipped bikes have a self-check warning light in the instrument cluster, and the tester will check that this is working.
- The tester will check braking efficiency, but this is nothing to worry about if you're satisfied your brakes are properly maintained.

Steering

- The front wheel will be raised off the ground and the bars turned from lock to lock to check bars and switches don't foul the tank or trap the rider's thumbs. Busted lockstops and poorly fitted non-standard bars can cause problems here.
- At the same time, the tester will be looking for free steering movement without drag or notchiness caused by incorrectly routed cables or worn or badly adjusted head bearings.
- The tester will look for play in the head bearings by pulling on the bottom of the fork legs.
- Handlebars and controls must be securely mounted, as must the grips.

Wheels and tyres

▸ Cast wheels must be free from cracks. Spoked wheels must have a full complement of spokes, free from corrosion, unbent and correctly tensioned.

▸ Rims must be uncreased and true. Wheels will be raised from the ground and spun to check for truth of tyres and rims, and also to make sure they don't foul mudguards, huggers or suspension components.

▸ Wheel bearings will be checked for excessive wear. See the pages in this chapter on bearings for advice on how to check these.

▸ Tyres will be checked for adequate tread and sidewall, and tread condition. See the section on tyres for more information on this.

▸ Tyres will also be checked to ensure they are of the correct type and match each other front and rear. Tyres must be suitable for road use. Anything marked otherwise will fail the MoT, so hand-cut slicks are out. Direction arrows on the tyres will be checked too.

▸ Security of wheel spindles is another item on the tester's agenda. Where they were fitted as standard, self-locking or castellated nuts with split or R-clips must still be present.

▸ Wheel alignment will also be checked. You can do this yourself by referring to this chapter's section on chains.

Final drive

▸ Chains and belts must be in good condition and at the correct tension. The rear wheel sprocket must be securely mounted on the hub. The overall condition of the sprocket will be checked too.

▸ On shafties, the bevel unit will be checked for leaks that could lead to oil getting on to the rear tyre.

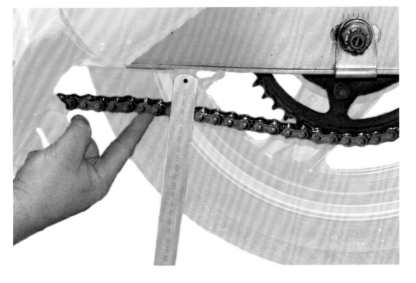

General checks

▶ Remember, the MoT tester isn't looking to catch you out. He's simply checking that your bike is roadworthy and therefore safe. So apart from the items detailed above, check that body panels, seat, mudguard fairings and major fasteners are secure.

▶ All footrests and controls must be securely mounted. Excessive corrosion on the frame or load-bearing components will result in a fail, so check these areas too.

▶ Finally, make sure your bike is presentable. If you wheel it through the door with parts wired on and broken bits dragging on the floor, it's likely you'll be asked to wheel it straight out again. The better the general condition of the bike, the better your chances of an MoT pass.

Exhaust

▶ It must be securely mounted and not fouling rear suspension components.

▶ The bike will be started and the throttle operated to ensure there are no holes or leaks in the entire system, including the collector box, where applicable.

▶ The tester will look for either an original fitment end-can, or the BSAU 193 stamp on the silencer. Bikes made before 1 January 1985 are exempt from this requirement. Anything marked 'race use only' or 'not for road use' will be failed. Overall loudness of questionable cans and systems generally is at the tester's discretion.

Rear suspension

▶ The inspector will have an assistant hold the front of the bike while he or she bounces the rear with the bike off its stand. The inspector is looking for adequate damping in the rear shock(s) while checking nothing is being fouled.

▶ The inspector will look at the shock(s) to check the damper rod(s) aren't corroding and the damping oil isn't leaking.

▶ The swingarm's pivot bearings will be checked, with the rear wheel raised off the ground, by pulling it from side-to-side. At the same time, the rear wheel will be pulled up by its highest point to check for wear in the suspension linkages.

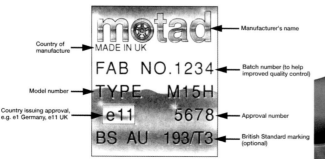

Country of manufacture — MADE IN UK
motad — Manufacturer's name
FAB NO.1234 — Batch number (to help improved quality control)
Model number — TYPE M15H
Country issuing approval, e.g. e1 Germany, e11 UK — e11 5678 — Approval number
BS AU 193/T3 — British Standard marking (optional)

Lights, indicators, horn and reflector

▶ Headlight and tail light must both operate with the switch in high and low beam positions.

▶ With the switch in the parking light position, the front and tail lights must light up.

▶ Indicators must flash at the proper speed and the idiot lights and switch must work properly. If your bike has a hazard warning system, all four indicators must flash when it's operated.

▶ The brake light must come on when each brake is operated. Bikes after 1 April 1986 must have a brake light switch for both front and rear brakes.

▶ The horn must have a continuous tone and sufficient volume.

▶ The headlight beam must be at the right height. The MoT station has equipment to check this. If you think yours is out, check it as per the diagram on this page. Draw a horizontal line on the garage wall at the same height as the centre of your headlight and position the bike as per the distance and angle shown in the diagram. Draw a vertical mark in line with the centreline of the bike. Now take the bike off its stand and sit on it. When the headlight is dipped, the beam on the wall should fall below the horizontal and to the left of the vertical lines.

Front suspension

▶ With the bike off the stand, the tester will sit on it, hold the front brake on and pump the forks up and down to check they don't bind and there's adequate damping.

▶ Fork seals and the stanchion area next to them will be checked, the former for leaks and the latter for pitting or corrosion.

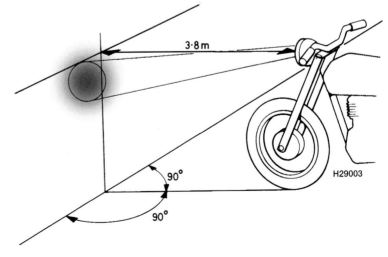

Storage

Unless you're commuting to and from work on your bike, it will probably spend a few months of the year in storage. But storing a bike isn't just a case of putting it in the shed and forgetting about it – not if you want it to be in a decent state when summer returns.

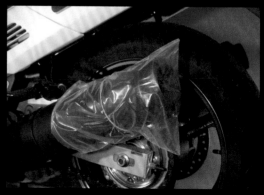

Motorcycles are highly susceptible to corrosion caused by road salt, because their parts are so exposed. Corrosion can start in a matter of days, and is hard to halt. So give the bike a good wash before you put it away, and make sure it's completely dry before it's consigned to the shed.

If the bike is faired, remove the fairing to reach the awkward places underneath. A firm-bristled bottle brush makes life easier and saves your knuckles, although using a pressure washer is perhaps the most convenient and effective method. Just remember not to be too vigorous around steering, suspension and wheel bearings, and electrical components. Lube the chain afterwards too.

Coat the piston bores and rings with oil by removing the spark plugs and squirting around a teaspoon of oil down each spark plug hole. Put the plugs back in and crank the engine over with the kickstart (where fitted), or on the electric start with the kill-switch off. Some bikes only allow the engine to turn with the kill-switch on so the plugs will have to be earthed against the cylinder head – far enough away from the spark plug holes to avoid igniting any fuel vapour in the bores.

Consider draining the petrol or, at the very least, turn the fuel tap off and run the bike until it stops. This prevents petrol residue building up in the carbs and blocking small orifices. Otherwise, turn off the fuel tap and drain the carbs by way of the drain screws at the bottom of the float bowls. If your bike is going to be off the road for a long time, you might want to add fuel stabiliser to the petrol. Otherwise, petrol can go off in storage and you'll need to replace it come springtime. Remember to dispose of old fuel properly.

Completely drained tanks can corrode internally if left for a long time. Remove the tank, pour half a litre of engine oil into it and agitate the tank to coat the inside with oil. Remember to clean the oil out before refilling the tank with petrol. Alternatively, spray the inside of the tank with WD40 or similar.

Air intakes and silencer orifices can be plugged or covered in polythene to prevent build up of condensation. Run the bike until it's hot, allow to cool, then cover.

Most batteries, even new ones, will discharge if the bike is unused over the winter. The problem is worse if the bike is alarmed, no matter how small the drain. A trickle charger helps keep batteries topped up, without damaging them. It's best to remove the battery from the bike and keep it in a place where there's no danger of it freezing.

If it's an unsealed type, ensure there's enough electrolyte in it.

If the bike is liquid-cooled, check it has anti-freeze in. It takes only one freezing night to do expensive damage. Corrosion inhibitors in the anti-freeze will help prevent internal damage to the cooling system. And if the bike is chain driven, make sure it's lubed – a rusty chain wears faster. While lubing, you might consider a light coat of WD40 or

similar on the wheel rims if they're chrome, and on fork sliders and other exposed metal parts. Remember not to spray the brake discs however.

Finally, check tyre pressures. A bike stood for several months on flat tyres is likely to deform them so badly that they lose their shape, or even worse, develop splits. Deflate by no more than 5–10psi. If your bike has a centre stand, put it on that with blocks of wood under each wheel to save them from damp. If possible, store the bike on paddock stands so that the wheels are off the ground. If you haven't got any such stands, rotate the wheels periodically so they're not standing on the same section of tyre.

Tempting as it is to start the engine every so often, try not to unless you intend to let it get up to operating temperature. If the engine isn't thoroughly warm, condensation is likely to form in the engine and contaminate the oil, possibly causing internal corrosion.

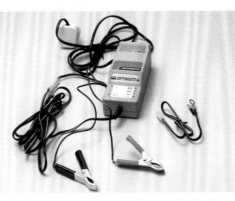

Trickle chargers keep batteries in optimum condition.

Disconnect the battery while your bike's in storage.

If a cable-operated clutch sticks in storage, tie the lever back to see if it frees.

Is your bike **legal?**

Numberplate

It was popular over the past few years, for aesthetic reasons, to replace the standard numberplate on sportsbikes with a smaller one. However, the law is specific about numberplates and requires them to be a certain size, with letters of a certain size and spacing. Anything else is illegal, and will probably get you stopped.

Exhaust pipe

Aftermarket exhaust cans are the most popular thing people fit, either because they want the extra noise and performance, or simply because after a crash it's a cheaper alternative to buying a replacement stock silencer. However, unless the exhaust meets Government noise requirements and is marked to say so, it is illegal for road use. Most race cans have a 'not for road use' marking and removing this doesn't make it legal.

Headlight cover

The law says forward-facing lights should be white and rear-facing lights should be red. Any departure from this is illegal. Headlight covers are often fitted to colour match with the bodywork. These are illegal. Clear covers are useful because they prevent costly stone damage to the headlight.

Bigger tyres

Although not illegal, fitting larger or smaller tyres than those recommended by the manufacturer is inadvisable. More than anything, it will affect the bike's handling, and there's a chance your insurance company could use it as an excuse not to pay out in an accident.

Paintwork

There is no law against what colour your bike can be, although you couldn't get away with having it painted like a police bike. It's generally frowned upon to have race-like numbers on it.

Pillions

So long as the bike was designed to take pillions, and so long as the person riding pillion can sit with their feet on the pegs, it's okay for them to ride pillion. The only real legal requirements are that they wear a helmet and that you're licensed to carry them. Some insurance policies exclude cover for pillions, so it's worth checking your own policy.

Trouble shooting

When things go wrong, as they sometimes do, don't panic. A motorcycle is a mechanical entity and as such is governed by rules of basic engineering and mechanics. By applying a little logic it's reasonably easy to drill down to the root of a problem, and even if your own mechanical skills or workshop resources don't stretch to it, you'll be able to point the guys in the shop in the right direction.

To help you see the trees from the forest, there follows some basic fault-finding material which will at least guide you in the right direction. Two-stroke riders can ignore any references to valves and camshafts, of course, but the rest of the material pretty much applies regardless of engine type. Remember this is a general guide, so for specific treatment of problems refer to the Haynes manual for your bike.

Engine doesn't start or is difficult to start

Starter motor doesn't rotate

Engine kill switch OFF.
Fuse blown. Check main fuse and starter circuit fuse. See your Haynes manual.

Battery voltage low.
Check and recharge battery.

Starter motor defective.
Make sure the wiring to the starter is secure. Make sure the starter relay clicks when the start button is pushed. If the relay clicks, then the fault is in the wiring or motor.

Starter relay faulty.
See your Haynes manual.

Starter switch not contacting.
The contacts could be wet, corroded or dirty. Disassemble and clean the switch. See your Haynes manual.

Wiring open or shorted.
Check all wiring connections and harnesses to make sure that they are dry, tight and not corroded. Also check for broken or frayed wires that can cause a short to ground (earth). Refer to the wiring diagram in your Haynes manual.

Ignition (main) switch defective.
Check the switch according to the procedure in your Haynes manual. Replace the switch with a new one if it is defective.

Engine kill switch defective.
Check for wet, dirty or corroded contacts. Clean or replace the switch as necessary.

Faulty neutral, side stand or clutch switch.
Check the wiring to each switch and the switch itself according to the procedures in your Haynes manual.

Starter motor rotates but engine does not turn over

Starter clutch defective.
Inspect and repair or replace. See your Haynes manual.

Damaged idle/reduction or starter gears.
Inspect and replace the damaged parts. See your Haynes manual.

Starter works but engine won't turn over (seized).
Seized engine caused by one or more internally damaged components. Failure due to wear, abuse or lack of lubrication. Damage can include seized valves, followers, camshafts, pistons, crankshaft, connecting rod bearings, or transmission gears or bearings. See your Haynes manual for engine disassembly.

No fuel flow

No fuel in tank.

Fuel tank breather hose obstructed.

Fuel tap filter or in-line filter (carburettor models) or fuel pump assembly filter (fuel injection models) clogged.
Remove the tap or pump and clean or renew the filter. See your Haynes manual.

Fuel line clogged.
Pull the fuel line loose and carefully blow it through.

Float needle valve clogged (carburettor models).
For all of the valves to be clogged, either a very bad batch of fuel with an unusual additive has been used, or some other foreign material has entered the tank. Many times after a machine has been stored for many months without running, the fuel turns to a varnish-like liquid and forms deposits on the inlet needle valves and jets. The carburettors should be removed and overhauled if draining the float chambers doesn't solve the problem.

Fuel pump or relay (fuel injection models) faulty.
Check the fuel pump and relay. See your Haynes manual.

Engine flooded (carburettor models).
Float height too high. Check as described in your Haynes manual.

Float needle valve worn or stuck open.
Dirt, rust or other debris can cause the valve to seat improperly, causing excess fuel to be admitted to the float chamber. In this case, the float chamber should be cleaned and the needle valve and seat inspected. If the needle and seat are worn, then the leaking will persist and the parts should be replaced.

Starting technique incorrect.
Under normal circumstances (i.e. if all the carburettor functions are sound) the machine should start with little or no throttle. When the engine is cold, the choke should be operated and the engine started without opening the throttle. When the engine is at operating temperature, only a very slight amount of throttle should be necessary. If the engine is flooded, turn the fuel tap OFF (where fitted) and hold the throttle open while cranking the engine. This will allow additional air to reach the cylinders. Remember to turn the fuel tap back ON after the engine starts.

Engine flooded (fuel injection models).
Faulty pressure regulator – if it is stuck closed there could be excessive pressure in the fuel rail. Check as described in your Haynes manual.

Injector(s) stuck open, allowing a constant flow of fuel into the engine.
Check as described in your Haynes manual.

Starting technique incorrect.
See advice as for carburated bikes. But remember some fuel injected bikes have no choke lever and most have no manually-operated fuel tap.

No spark or weak spark

Ignition switch OFF.

Engine kill switch turned to the OFF position.

Battery voltage low.
Check and recharge the battery as necessary. See your Haynes manual.

Spark plugs dirty, defective or worn out.
Locate reason for fouled plugs using spark plug condition chart and follow the plug maintenance procedures. See your Haynes manual.

Spark plug caps faulty.
Check condition. Replace if cracks or deterioration are evident. See your Haynes manual.

Spark plug caps not making good contact.
Make sure that the plug caps fit snugly over the plug ends.

Ignition control unit (carburettor models) or ECM (fuel injection models) defective.
Check the unit, referring to your Haynes manual for details.

Pulse generator defective.
Check the unit, referring to your Haynes manual for details.

Ignition coils defective.
Check the coils, referring to your Haynes manual.

Ignition or kill switch shorted.
Usually caused by water, corrosion, damage or excessive wear. The switches can be disassembled and cleaned with electrical contact cleaner. If cleaning does not help, replace the switches referring to your Haynes manual.

Wiring shorted or broken between:
a) Ignition (main) switch and engine kill switch (or blown fuse)
b) Ignition control unit or ECM and engine kill switch
c) Ignition control unit or ECM and ignition coils
d) Ignition coils and spark plugs
e) Ignition control unit or ECM and pulse generator.

Make sure that all wiring connections are clean, dry and tight.
Look for chafed and broken wires.

Compression low

Spark plugs loose.
Remove the plugs and inspect their threads. Reinstall and tighten to the specified torque. See your Haynes manual.

Cylinder heads not sufficiently tightened down.
See your Haynes manual. If a cylinder head is suspected of being loose, then there's a chance that the gasket or head is damaged if the problem has persisted for any length of time.

Incorrect valve clearance.
Check and adjust the valve clearances as per your manual.

Cylinder and/or piston worn.
Excessive wear will cause compression pressure to leak past the rings. This is usually accompanied by worn rings as well. A top-end overhaul will be required.

Piston rings worn, weak, broken, or sticking.
Broken or sticking piston rings usually indicate a lubrication or carburation problem that causes excess carbon deposits or seizures to form on the pistons and rings. Top-end overhaul will again be necessary.

Piston ring-to-groove clearance excessive.
This is caused by excessive wear of the piston ring lands. Piston and ring replacement will be called for.

Cylinder head gasket damaged.
If a head is allowed to become loose, or if excessive carbon build-up on the piston crown and combustion chamber causes extremely high compression, the head gasket may leak. Retorquing the head is not always sufficient to restore the seal, so gasket replacement is needed too.

Cylinder head warped.
This is caused by overheating or improperly tightened head bolts. Machine shop resurfacing or head replacement and a new gasket will be needed.

Valve spring broken or weak.
Caused by component failure or wear; the springs must be replaced.

Valve not seating properly.
This is caused by a bent valve (from over-revving or improper valve adjustment), burned valve or seat (improper carburation) or an accumulation of carbon deposits on the seat (from carburation or lubrication problems). The valves must be cleaned and/or replaced and the seats serviced if possible or replaced by an engineering shop.

Stalls after starting

Improper choke action (carburettor models).
See your Haynes manual.

Ignition malfunction.
See your Haynes manual.

Carburettor or fuel injection system malfunction.
See your Haynes manual.

Fuel contaminated.
The fuel can be contaminated with either dirt or water, or can change chemically if the machine is allowed to sit for several months or more. Drain the tank and float chambers. Also check that fuel can flow freely.

Intake air leak.
Check for loose carburettor or throttle body-to-intake manifold connections, loose or missing vacuum gauge adapter screws or hoses, or loose carburettor tops.

Engine idle speed incorrect.
Turn idle adjusting screw until the engine idles at the specified rpm in your manual. On fuel injection models, check other components as specified in your Haynes manual.

Rough idle

Ignition malfunction.
See your Haynes manual.

Idle speed incorrect.
See your Haynes manual.

Carburettors or throttle bodies not synchronised.
Adjust with vacuum gauge or manometer set as described in your Haynes manual.

Carburettor or throttle body or fuel injection system malfunction.
See your Haynes manual.

Fuel contaminated.
The fuel can be contaminated with either dirt or water, or can change chemically if the machine is allowed to sit for several months or more. Drain the tank and float chambers as per your manual.

Intake air leak.
Check for loose carburettor or throttle body-to-intake manifold connections, loose or missing vacuum gauge adaptor screws or hoses, or loose carburettor tops.

Air filter clogged.
Clean or replace the air filter element.

Poor running at low speeds

Spark weak

Battery voltage low.
Check and recharge battery.

Spark plugs fouled, defective or worn out.

Spark plug cap defective.
See your Haynes manual.

Spark plug caps not making contact.

Incorrect spark plugs.
Wrong type, heat range or cap configuration. Check and install correct plugs.

Ignition control unit (carburettor models) or ECM (fuel injection models) defective.
Check as per instructions in your manual.

Pulse generator defective.

Ignition coils defective.

Fuel/air mixture incorrect Carburettor mods

Pilot screws out of adjustment.
See your Haynes manual.

Pilot jet or air passage clogged.
Remove and overhaul the carburettors. See your Haynes manual.

Air bleed holes clogged.
Remove carburettor and blow out all passages. See your Haynes manual.

Fuel level too high or too low.
Check the float height as detailed in your manual.

Carburettor intake manifolds loose.
Check for cracks, breaks, tears or loose clamps. Replace rubber intake manifold joints if split or perished.

Fuel/air mixture incorrect Fuel injection models

Fuel injection system malfunction.
See your Haynes manual.

Fuel injector clogged.
See your Haynes manual.

Fuel pump or pressure regulator faulty.

Throttle body intake manifolds loose.
Check for cracks, breaks, tears or loose clamps. Replace rubber intake manifold joints if split or perished.

Fuel/air mixture incorrect All models

Air filter clogged, poorly sealed or missing.

Air filter housing poorly sealed.
Look for cracks, holes or loose clamps and replace or repair defective parts.

Fuel tank breather hose obstructed.

Compression low

Spark plugs loose.
Remove the plugs and inspect their threads. Reinstall and tighten to the specified torque in your manual.

Cylinder heads not sufficiently tightened down.
If a cylinder head is suspected of being loose, then there's a chance that the gasket and head are damaged if the problem has persisted for any length of time. The head bolts should be tightened to the proper torque in the correct sequence described in your manual.

Incorrect valve clearance.
This means that the valve is not closing completely and compression pressure is leaking past the valve. Check and adjust the valve clearances.

Cylinder and/or piston worn.
Excessive wear will cause compression pressure to leak past the rings. This is usually accompanied by worn rings as well. A top end overhaul is necessary.

Piston rings worn, weak, broken, or sticking.
Broken or sticking piston rings usually indicate a lubrication or carburation problem that causes excess carbon deposits or seizures to form on the pistons and rings. Top-end overhaul is necessary.

Piston ring-to-groove clearance excessive.
This is caused by excessive wear of the piston ring lands. Piston and probably ring replacement is necessary.

Cylinder head gasket damaged.
If a head is allowed to become loose, or if excessive carbon build-up on the piston crown and combustion chamber causes extremely high compression, the head gasket may leak. Retorquing the head is not always sufficient to restore the seal, so gasket replacement is necessary.

Cylinder head warped.
This is caused by overheating or improperly tightened head bolts. Machine shop resurfacing or head replacement is necessary.

Valve spring broken or weak.
Caused by component failure or wear; the springs must be replaced.

Valve not seating properly.
This is caused by a bent valve (from over-revving or improper valve adjustment), burned valve or seat (improper carburation) or an accumulation of carbon deposits on the seat (from carburation, lubrication problems). The valves must be cleaned and/or replaced and the seats recut or replaced if possible.

Poor acceleration

Carburettors or throttle bodies leaking or dirty.
Overhaul them.

Fuel injection system malfunction.
Faulty fuel pump, or pressure regulator (fuel injection models).

Timing not advancing.
The pulse generator or the ignition control unit or ECM may be defective. If so, they must be replaced with new ones, as they can't be repaired.

Carburettors or throttle bodies not synchronised.
Adjust them with a vacuum gauge set or manometer.

Engine oil viscosity too high.
Using a heavier oil than that recommended can damage the oil pump or lubrication system and cause drag on the engine.

Brakes dragging.
Usually caused by debris which has entered the brake piston seals, or from a warped disc or bent wheel spindle. Repair and replace as necessary.

Poor running or no power at high speed

Firing incorrect

Air filter restricted.
Clean or replace filter.

Spark plugs fouled, defective or worn out.

Spark plug caps defective.

Spark plug caps not in good contact.

Incorrect spark plugs.
Wrong type, heat range or cap configuration. Check and install correct plugs listed in your manual.

Ignition control unit or ECM defective.

Ignition coils defective.

Fuel/air mixture incorrect Carburettor models

Main jet clogged.
Dirt, water or other contaminants can clog the main jets. Clean the fuel tap filter, the in-line filter, the float chamber area, and the jets and carburettor orifices.

Main jet wrong size.
The standard jetting is for sea level atmospheric pressure and oxygen content.

Throttle shaft-to-carb body clearance excessive.
Check manual for inspection and renewal.

Air bleed holes clogged.
Remove carburettor and blow out all passages.

Fuel level too high or too low.
Check the float height.

Carburettor intake manifolds loose.
Check for cracks, breaks, tears or loose clamps. Replace rubber intake manifold joints if split or perished.

Fuel pump, where fitted, faulty.

Fuel/air mixture incorrect Fuel injection models

Fuel injection system malfunction.

Fuel injector clogged.

Fuel pump or pressure regulator faulty.

Throttle body intake manifolds loose.
Check for cracks, breaks, tears or loose clamps. Replace rubber intake manifold joints if split or perished.

Fuel/air mixture incorrect All models

Air filter clogged, poorly sealed or missing.

Air filter housing poorly sealed.
Look for cracks, holes or loose clamps and replace or repair defective parts.

Fuel tank breather hose obstructed.

Compression low

Spark plugs loose.
Remove the plugs and inspect their threads. Reinstall and tighten to the specified torque.

Cylinder heads not sufficiently tightened down.
If a cylinder head is suspected of being loose, then there's a chance that the gasket and head are damaged if the problem has persisted for any length of time. The head bolts should be tightened to the proper torque in the correct sequence.

Incorrect valve clearance.
This means that the valve is not closing completely and compression pressure is leaking past the valve. Check and adjust the valve clearances.

Cylinder and/or piston worn.
Excessive wear will cause compression pressure to leak past the rings. This is usually accompanied by worn rings. A top-end overhaul is necessary.

Piston rings worn, weak, broken, or sticking.
Broken or sticking piston rings usually indicate a lubrication or carburation problem that causes excess carbon deposits or seizures to form on the pistons and rings. Top-end overhaul is necessary.

Piston ring-to-groove clearance excessive.
This is caused by excessive wear of the piston ring lands. Piston and probably ring replacement is necessary.

Cylinder head gasket damaged.
If a head is allowed to become loose, or if excessive carbon build-up on the piston crown and combustion chamber causes extremely high compression, the head gasket may leak. Retorquing the head is not always sufficient to restore the seal, so gasket replacement is necessary.

Cylinder head warped.
This is caused by overheating or improperly tightened head bolts. Machine shop resurfacing or head replacement is necessary.

Valve spring broken or weak.
Caused by component failure or wear; the springs must be replaced.

Valve not seating properly.
This is caused by a bent valve (from over-revving or improper valve adjustment), burned valve or seat (improper carburation) or an accumulation of carbon deposits on the seat (from carburation or lubrication problems). The valves must be cleaned and/or replaced and the seats serviced or replaced if possible.

Knocking or pinking

Carbon build-up in combustion chamber.
Use of a fuel additive that will dissolve the adhesive bonding the carbon particles to the crown and chamber is the easiest way to remove the build-up. Otherwise, the cylinder heads will have to be removed and decarbonised. Rare with modern fuels.

Incorrect or poor quality fuel.
Old or improper grades of fuel can cause detonation. This causes the piston to rattle, thus the knocking or pinging sound. Drain old fuel and always use the recommended fuel grade.

Spark plug heat range incorrect.
Uncontrolled detonation indicates the plug heat range is too hot. The plug in effect becomes a glow plug, raising cylinder temperatures. Install the proper heat range plug.

Improper air/fuel mixture.
This will cause the cylinders to run hot, which leads to detonation. Clogged jets or an air leak can cause this imbalance.

Miscellaneous causes

Throttle valve doesn't open fully.
Adjust the throttle grip freeplay.

Clutch slipping.
May be caused by loose or worn clutch components. Refer to your manual for clutch overhaul procedures.

Timing not advancing
Faulty ignition control unit or ECM.

Engine oil viscosity too high.
Using a heavier oil than recommended can damage the oil pump or lubrication system and cause drag on the engine.

Brakes dragging.
Usually caused by debris which has entered the brake piston seals, or from a warped disc or bent axle. Repair and replace as necessary.

Overheating

Engine overheats

Coolant level low.
Check and add coolant.

Leak in cooling system.
Check cooling system hoses and radiator for leaks and other damage. Repair or replace parts as necessary.

Thermostat sticking open or closed.
Check and replace.

Faulty radiator cap.
Remove the cap and have it pressure tested.

Coolant passages clogged.
Have the entire system drained and flushed, then refill with fresh coolant.

Water pump defective.
Remove the pump and check the components.

Clogged radiator fins.
Clean them by blowing compressed air through the fins in the reverse direction of airflow.

Cooling fan or fan switch fault.

Firing incorrect

Spark plugs fouled, defective or worn out.

Incorrect spark plugs.

Ignition control unit or ECM defective.

Pulse generator faulty.

Faulty ignition coils.

Fuel/air mixture incorrect
Carburettor models

Main jet clogged.
Dirt, water or other contaminants can clog the main jets. Clean the fuel tap filter, the in-line filter, the float chamber area, and the jets and carburettor orifices.

Main jet wrong size.
The standard jetting is for sea level atmospheric pressure and oxygen content.

Throttle shaft-to-carburettor body clearance excessive.

Air bleed holes clogged.
Remove carburettor and blow out all passages.

Fuel level too high or too low.
Check the float height.

Carburettor intake manifolds loose.

Check for cracks, breaks, tears or loose clamps. Replace rubber intake manifold joints if split or perished.

Fuel pump faulty.

Fuel/air mixture incorrect
Fuel injection models

Fuel injection system malfunction.

Fuel injector clogged.

Fuel pump or pressure regulator faulty.

Throttle body intake manifolds loose.
Check for cracks, breaks, tears or loose clamps. Replace rubber intake manifold joints if split or perished.

Fuel/air mixture incorrect
All models

Air filter clogged, poorly sealed or missing.

Air filter housing poorly sealed.
Look for cracks, holes or loose clamps and replace or repair defective parts.

Fuel tank breather hose obstructed.

Compression too high

Carbon build-up in combustion chamber.
Use of a fuel additive that will dissolve the adhesive bonding the carbon particles to the piston crown and chamber is the easiest way to remove the build-up. Otherwise, the cylinder heads will have to be removed and decarbonised.

Improperly machined head surface or installation of incorrect gasket during engine assembly.

Engine load excessive

Clutch slipping.
Can be caused by damaged, loose or worn clutch components. Refer to your manual for overhaul procedures.

Engine oil level too high.
The addition of too much oil will cause pressurisation of the crankcase and inefficient engine operation. Check specifications and drain to proper level.

Engine oil viscosity too high.
Using a heavier oil than recommended can damage the oil pump or lubrication system as well as cause drag on the engine.

Brakes dragging.
Usually caused by debris which has entered the brake piston seals, or from a warped disc or bent axle. Repair and replace as necessary.

Lubrication inadequate

Engine oil level too low.
Friction caused by intermittent lack of lubrication or from oil that is overworked can cause overheating. The oil provides a definite cooling function in the engine. Check the oil level.

Poor quality engine oil or incorrect viscosity or type.
Oil is rated not only according to viscosity but also according to type. Some oils are not rated high enough for use in this engine. Check the specifications section in your manual and change to the correct oil.

Miscellaneous causes

Modification to exhaust system.
Most aftermarket exhaust systems cause the engine to run leaner, which makes them run hotter. When installing an accessory exhaust system, always rejet the carburettors or tweak the fuel injection by means of an aftermarket black box. Invest in some dyno time to get the set-up right.

Clutch problems

Clutch slipping

Clutch cable incorrectly adjusted.
Check and adjust.

Friction plates worn or warped.
Overhaul the clutch assembly.

Plain plates warped.

Clutch springs broken or weak.
Old or heat-damaged (from slipping clutch) springs should be replaced with new ones.

Clutch release mechanism defective.
Replace any defective parts.

Clutch centre or housing unevenly worn.
This causes improper engagement of the plates. Replace the damaged or worn parts.

Clutch not disengaging completely

Clutch cable incorrectly adjusted.
Check and adjust.

Clutch plates warped or damaged.
This will cause clutch drag, which in turn will cause the machine to creep. Overhaul the clutch assembly.

Clutch spring tension uneven.
Usually caused by a sagged or broken spring. Check and replace the springs as a set.

Engine oil deteriorated.
Old, thin, worn out oil will not provide proper lubrication for the plates, causing the clutch to drag. Replace the oil and filter.

Engine oil viscosity too high.
Using a heavier oil than recommended can cause the plates to stick together, putting a drag on the engine. Change to the correct weight oil.

Clutch release mechanism defective.

Loose clutch centre nut.
Causes housing and centre misalignment putting a drag on the engine. Engagement adjustment continually varies. Overhaul the clutch assembly.

Gear changing problems

Doesn't go into gear or lever doesn't return.

Clutch not disengaging.
See above.

Selector fork(s) bent or seized.
Often caused by dropping the machine or from lack of lubrication. Overhaul the transmission.

Gear(s) stuck on shaft.
Most often caused by a lack of lubrication or excessive wear in transmission bearings and bushings. Overhaul the transmission.

Selector drum binding.
Caused by lubrication failure or excessive wear. Replace the drum and bearings.

Gearchange lever return spring weak or broken.

Gearchange lever broken.
Splines stripped out of lever or shaft, caused by allowing the lever to get loose or from dropping the machine. Replace necessary parts.

Gearchange mechanism broken or worn.

Jumps out of gear

Selector fork(s) worn.
Overhaul the transmission.

Gear groove(s) worn.
Overhaul the transmission.

Gear dogs or dog slots worn or damaged.
The gears should be inspected and replaced. No attempt should be made to service worn parts.

Abnormal engine noise

Knocking or pinking

Carbon build-up in combustion chamber.
Use of a fuel additive that will dissolve the adhesive bonding the carbon particles to the piston crown and chamber is the easiest way to remove the build-up. Otherwise, the cylinder head will have to be removed and decarbonised. Rare with modern fuels.

Incorrect or poor quality fuel.
Old or improper fuel can cause detonation. This causes the pistons to rattle, thus the knocking or pinging sound. Drain the old fuel and always use the recommended grade.

Spark plug heat range incorrect.
Uncontrolled detonation indicates that the plug heat range is too hot. The plug in effect becomes a glow plug, raising cylinder temperatures. Install the proper heat range plug.

Improper fuel/air mixture.
This will cause the cylinders to run hot and lead to detonation. Clogged jets or an air leak can cause this imbalance.

Piston slap or rattling

Cylinder-to-piston clearance excessive.
Caused by improper assembly. Inspect and overhaul top-end parts.

Connecting rod bent.
Caused by over-revving, trying to start a badly flooded engine or from ingesting a foreign object into the combustion chamber. Replace the damaged parts.

Piston pin or piston pin bore worn or seized from wear or lack of lubrication.
Replace damaged parts.

Piston ring(s) worn, broken or sticking.
Overhaul the top-end.

Piston seizure damage.
Usually from lack of lubrication or overheating. Replace the pistons and have the cylinders rebored as necessary.

Connecting rod upper or lower end clearance excessive.
Caused by excessive wear or lack of lubrication. Replace worn parts.

Valve noise

Incorrect valve clearances.
Adjust the clearances.

Valve spring broken or weak.
Check and replace weak valve springs.

Camshaft or cylinder head worn or damaged.
Lack of lubrication at high rpm is usually the cause of damage. Insufficient oil or failure to change the oil at the recommended intervals are the chief causes.

Other noise

Cylinder head gasket leaking.

Exhaust pipe leaking at cylinder head connection.
Caused by improper fit of pipe(s) or loose exhaust flange. All exhaust fasteners should be tightened evenly and carefully. Failure to do this will lead to a leak.

Crankshaft runout excessive.
Caused by a bent crankshaft (from over-revving) or damage from an upper cylinder component failure. Can also be attributed to dropping the machine on either of the crankshaft ends.

Engine mounting bolts loose.
Tighten all engine mount bolts.

Crankshaft bearings worn.

Camshaft drive assembly defective.

Abnormal clutch noise

Clutch outer drum/friction plate clearance excessive.

Loose or damaged clutch pressure plate and/or bolts.

Transmission noise

Bearings worn.
Also includes the possibility that the shafts are worn. Overhaul the transmission.

Gears worn or chipped.

Metal chips jammed in gear teeth.
Probably pieces from a broken clutch, gear or shift mechanism that were picked up by the gears. This will cause early bearing failure.

Engine oil level too low.
Causes a howl from transmission. Also affects engine power and clutch operation.

Final drive noise

Chain not adjusted properly.

Front or rear sprocket loose.
Tighten fasteners.

Sprockets worn.
Renew sprockets.

Rear sprocket warped.
Renew sprockets.

Rubber dampers in rear wheel hub worn.
Check and renew.

Abnormal frame and suspension noise. Front end noise

Low fluid level or improper viscosity oil in forks.
This can sound like spurting and is usually accompanied by irregular fork action.

Spring weak or broken.
Makes a clicking or scraping sound. Fork oil, when drained, will have a lot of metal particles in it.

Steering head bearings loose or damaged.
Clicks when braking. Check and adjust or replace as necessary.

Fork yokes loose.
Make sure all clamp pinch bolts are tightened to the specified torque.

Fork tube bent.
Good possibility if machine has been dropped. Replace tube with a new one.

Front axle bolt or axle clamp bolts loose.
Tighten them to the specified torque.

Loose or worn wheel bearings.
Check and replace as needed.

Shock absorber noise

Fluid level incorrect.
Indicates a leak caused by defective seal. Shock will be covered with oil. Replace shock or seek advice on repair.

Defective shock absorber with internal damage.
This is in the body of the shock and can't be remedied. The shock must be replaced with a new one.

Bent or damaged shock body.
Replace the shock with a new one.

Loose or worn suspension linkage or swingarm components.
Check and replace as necessary.

Brake noise

Squeal caused by pad shim not installed or positioned correctly (where fitted).

Squeal caused by dust on brake pads.
Usually found in combination with glazed pads. Clean using brake cleaning solvent.

Contamination of brake pads.
Oil, brake fluid or dirt causing brake to chatter or squeal. Clean or replace pads.

Pads glazed. Caused by excessive heat from prolonged use or from contamination.
Do not use sandpaper, emery cloth, carborundum cloth or any other abrasive to roughen the pad surfaces as abrasives will stay in the pad material and damage the disc. A very fine flat file can be used, but pad replacement is suggested as a cure.

Disc warped.
Can cause a chattering, clicking or intermittent squeal. Usually accompanied by a pulsating lever and uneven braking. Replace the disc.

Loose or worn wheel bearings.
Check and replace as required.

Oil pressure indicator light comes on

Engine lubrication system

Engine oil pump defective, blocked oil strainer gauze or failed relief valve.
Carry out oil pressure check as per manual.

Engine oil level low.
Inspect for leak or other problem causing low oil level and add recommended oil.

Engine oil viscosity too low.
Very old, thin oil or an improper weight of oil used in the engine. Change to correct oil.

Camshaft or journals worn.
Excessive wear causing drop in oil pressure. Replace cam and/or cylinder head. Abnormal wear could be caused by oil starvation at high rpm from low oil level or improper weight or type of oil.

Crankshaft and/or bearings worn.
Same problems as above. Check and replace crankshaft and/or bearings.

Electrical system

Oil pressure switch defective.
Check the switch according to the procedure in your manual. Replace it if it is defective.

Oil pressure indicator light circuit defective.
Check for pinched, shorted, disconnected or damaged wiring.

Excessive exhaust smoke

White smoke

Piston oil ring worn.
The ring may be broken or damaged, causing oil from the crankcase to be pulled past the piston into the combustion chamber. Replace the rings with new ones.

Cylinders worn, cracked, or scored.
Caused by overheating or oil starvation. The cylinders will have to be rebored and new pistons installed.

Valve oil seal damaged or worn.
Replace oil seals with new ones.

Valve guide worn.
Perform, or have performed, a complete valve job.

Engine oil level too high, which causes the oil to be forced past the rings.
Drain oil to the proper level.

Head gasket broken between oil return and cylinder.
Causes oil to be pulled into the combustion chamber. Replace the head gasket and check the head for warpage.

Abnormal crankcase pressurisation, which forces oil past the rings.
Clogged breather is usually the cause.

Black smoke
Carburettor models

Main jet too large or loose.
Compare the jet size to the Specifications in your manual.

Choke cable or linkage shaft stuck, causing fuel to be pulled through choke circuit.

Fuel level too high.
Check and adjust the float height(s) as necessary.

Float needle valve held off needle seat.
Clean the float chambers and fuel line and replace the needles and seats if necessary.

Black smoke
Fuel injection models

Fuel injection system malfunction.

Black smoke
All models

Air filter clogged.

Brown smoke
Carburettor models

Main jet too small or clogged.
Lean condition caused by wrong size main jet or by a restricted orifice. Clean float chambers and jets and compare jet size to Specifications in your manual.

Fuel flow insufficient.
Float needle valve stuck closed due to chemical reaction with old fuel. Float height incorrect. Restricted fuel line. Clean line and float chamber and adjust floats if necessary.

Carburettor intake manifold clamps loose.

Faulty fuel pump.

Brown smoke
Fuel injection models

Fuel injection system malfunction.

Faulty fuel pump or pressure regulator.

Brown smoke
All models

Air filter poorly sealed or not installed.

Poor handling or stability

Handlebar hard to turn

Steering head bearing adjuster nut too tight.
Check adjustment as described in your manual.

Bearings damaged.
Roughness can be felt as the bars are turned from side-to-side. Replace bearings and races.

Races dented or worn.
Denting results from wear in only one position (e.g. straight ahead), from a collision or hitting a pothole or from dropping the machine. Replace races and bearings. Steering stem lubrication inadequate. Causes are grease getting hard from age or being washed out by high pressure car washes. Disassemble steering head and repack and/or replace bearings.

Steering stem bent.
Caused by a collision, hitting a pothole or by dropping the machine. Replace damaged part. Don't try to straighten the steering stem.

Front tyre air pressure too low.

Handlebar shakes or vibrates excessively

Tyres worn, out of balance or at incorrect pressures.

Swingarm bearings worn.
Replace worn bearings.

Wheel rim(s) warped or damaged.
Inspect wheels for runout.

Wheel bearings worn.
Worn front or rear wheel bearings can cause poor tracking. Worn front bearings will cause wobble.

Handlebar clamp bolts loose.

Fork yoke bolts loose.
Tighten them to the specified torque in your manual.

Engine mounting bolts loose.
Will cause excessive vibration with increased engine rpm.

Handlebar pulls to one side

Frame bent.
Definitely suspect this if the machine has been dropped. May or may not be accompanied by cracking near the bend. Replace the frame if it can't be safely straightened.

Wheels out of alignment.
Caused by improper location of spindle spacers or from bent steering stem or frame.

Swingarm bent or twisted.
Caused by age (metal fatigue) or impact damage. Replace the arm.

Steering stem bent.
Caused by impact damage or by dropping the motorcycle. Replace the steering stem.

Fork tube bent.
Disassemble the forks and replace the damaged parts.

Fork oil level uneven.
Check and add or drain as necessary.

Poor shock absorbing qualities

Too hard:
a) Fork oil level excessive.
b) Fork oil viscosity too high. Use a lighter oil (see the Specifications in your manual).
c) Fork tube bent. Causes a harsh, sticking feeling.
d) Shock shaft or body bent or damaged.
e) Fork internal damage.
f) Shock internal damage.
g) Tyre pressure too high.
h) Suspension adjusters incorrectly set

Too soft:
a) Fork or shock oil insufficient and/or leaking.
b) Fork oil level too low.
c) Fork oil viscosity too light.
d) Fork springs weak or broken.
e) Shock internal damage or leakage.
f) Suspension adjusters incorrectly set

Braking problems

Brakes are spongy, or lack power

Air in brake line.
Caused by inattention to master cylinder fluid level or by leakage. Locate problem and bleed brakes. Cable problem on drum brakes.

Pad or disc (or drum/shoes) worn.

Brake fluid leak.

Contaminated pads/shoes.
Caused by contamination with oil, grease, brake fluid, etc. Clean or replace. Clean disc/drum thoroughly with brake cleaner.

Brake fluid deteriorated.
Fluid is old or contaminated. Drain system, replenish with new fluid and bleed the system.

Master cylinder internal parts worn or damaged causing fluid to bypass.

Master cylinder bore scratched by foreign material or broken spring.
Repair or replace master cylinder.

Disc warped/drum out of true.
Replace disc/drum.

Brake lever or pedal pulsates

Disc warped/drum out of true.
Replace/skim.

Spindle bent.
Replace spindle.

Brake caliper bolts loose.

Brake caliper sliders damaged or sticking (rear caliper), causing caliper to bind.
Lubricate the sliders or replace them if they are corroded or bent.

Wheel warped or otherwise damaged.

Wheel bearings damaged or worn.

Brakes drag

Master cylinder piston seized.
Caused by wear or damage to piston or cylinder bore. Incorrect cable/rod/shoe adjustment on drum systems.

Lever sticky or stuck.
Check pivot and lubricate.

Brake caliper binds on bracket (rear caliper).
Caused by inadequate lubrication or damage to caliper sliders.

Brake caliper piston seized in bore.
Caused by wear or ingestion of dirt past deteriorated seal.

Brake pad/shoe damaged.
Pad/shoe material separated from backing plate. Usually caused by faulty manufacturing process or from contact with chemicals. Replace.

Pads/shoes improperly installed.

Electrical problems

Battery dead or weak

Battery faulty.
Caused by sulphated plates which are shorted through sedimentation. Also, broken battery terminal making only occasional contact.

Battery cables making poor contact.

Load excessive.
Caused by addition of high wattage lights or other electrical accessories.

Ignition (main) switch defective.
Switch either grounds (earths) internally or fails to shut off system. Replace the switch.

Regulator/rectifier defective.

Alternator stator coil open or shorted.

Wiring faulty.
Wiring grounded (earthed) or connections loose in ignition, charging or lighting circuits.

Battery overcharged

Regulator/rectifier defective.
Overcharging is noticed when battery gets excessively warm.

Battery defective.
Replace battery with a new one.

Battery amperage too low, wrong type or size.
Install manufacturer's specified amp-hour battery to handle charging load.

Glossary

A

Accelerator pump A carburettor device for temporarily increasing the amount of fuel.

Air filter Either a paper, fabric, felt, foam or gauze element through which the engine draws its air.

Air/fuel ratio Proportions in which air and fuel are mixed to form a combustible gas.

Alternator A generator of alternating current (a.c.) electricity.

ABS (Anti-lock braking system) A system that prevents the wheels locking up under braking.

Ampere-hour (Ah) Measure of battery capacity.

Antifreeze A substance (usually ethylene glycol) mixed with water, and added to the cooling system, to prevent freezing of the coolant in winter.

Anti-dive System attached to the fork lower leg (slider) to prevent fork dive when braking hard.

Aspect ratio With a tyre, the ratio of the section's depth to its width.

ATF Automatic Transmission Fluid. Often used in front forks.

Axle A shaft on which a wheel revolves. Also known as a spindle.

B

Backlash The amount of movement between meshed components. Usually applies to gear teeth.

Ball bearing A bearing consisting of a hardened inner and outer race with hardened steel balls between the two races.

BDC Bottom Dead Centre – denotes that the piston is at the lowest point of its stroke in the cylinder.

Bearings Used between two working surfaces to prevent wear of the components and a build-up of heat.

Belt drive Drive by a belt. Typical applications are for drive to the camshafts and transmission, and sometimes to the rear wheel.

Bevel gear Gear with slanted teeth, a pair of such gears turning the drive through ninety degrees.

BHP Brake horsepower.

Bias-belted tyre Similar construction to radial tyre, but with outer belt running at an angle to the wheel rim.

Big-end The larger end of a connecting rod and the one mounted on the crankpin.

Bleeding The process of removing air from an hydraulic system.

Bore Diameter of a cylinder.

Bore:stroke ratio The ratio of cylinder diameter to stroke. When these are equal the engine is said to be square.

Bottom Dead Centre (BDC) Lowest point of piston's stroke in the cylinder.

Bottom-end An engine's crankcase components and all components contained there-in.

BTDC Before Top Dead Centre in terms of piston position. Ignition timing is often expressed in terms of degrees or millimetres BTDC.

Bush A cylindrical metal and/or rubber component used between two moving parts.

C

Caliper In an hydraulic brake system, the component spanning the disc and housing the pistons and brake pads.

Cam chain The chain which takes drive from the crankshaft to the camshaft(s).

Cam follower A component in contact with the camshaft lobes, transmitting motion to the valve gear.

Camshaft A rotary shaft for the operation of valve gear in poppet valve engines.

Carburettor Mixes variable volumes of air and fuel in the correct ratio.

Catalytic converter A device in the exhaust system of some machines which converts certain pollutants in the exhaust gases into less harmful substances.

Centrifugal To be thrown outwards. An outward force on an object moving around a point.

Charging system Description of the components which charge the battery.

Clutch A device for engaging or disengaging the engine from the driving wheel.

Coil spring A spiral of elastic steel.

Compression Squeezing smaller, particularly a fresh charge of mixture in the cylinder by the rising piston.

Compression damping Controls the speed the suspension compresses when hitting a bump.

Compression ratio The extent to which the contents of the cylinder are compressed by the rising piston.

Concentric Tending to a common centre.

Connecting-rod The rod connecting the piston to the crankshaft via the big and small ends.

Constant rate A spring is this when each equal increment in load produces an equal change in length. (Contrast with multi-rate and progressive rate.)

Crankcase The chamber which carries the crankshaft.

Crankshaft A forged component, using the principle of the eccentric (crank) for converting the reciprocating piston engine's linear power pulse into rotary motion.

Cross-ply tyre Form of tyre construction in which the wraps of fabric in the tyre carcass are laid over each other diagonally instead of radially (see radial ply).

Cush drive A shock-absorbing component in a transmission system.

Cylinder head Component closing the blind end of the cylinder. Houses the valve gear on a four-stroke engine.

D

Damper A device for controlling and perhaps eliminating unwanted movement in suspension systems.

Detonation Explosion of the mixture in the combustion chamber, instead of controlled burning. May cause a tinkling noise, known as pinking, under an open throttle.

Diaphragm The rubber membrane in a master cylinder or carburettor which seals the upper chamber.

Disc brake A brake design incorporating a rotating disc onto which the brake pads are squeezed.

Displacement The amount of volume displaced by the piston of an engine on rising from its lowest position to its highest.

Dog A projection from a moving part, mating with another dog or a slot. Used in gearboxes to connect two pinions on a shaft.

Double-overhead camshaft (DOHC) An engine that uses two overhead camshafts, one for the intake valves and one for the exhaust valves.

Downdraught Downward inclination of the induction tract, usually the carburettor too.

Dry sump Four-stroke lubrication system in which the oil is carried in a separate oil tank and not in the sump.

Duplex Two. A duplex frame has two front down tubes. A duplex chain has two rows of rollers (a simple chain has one).

E

Earth Usually the negative terminal of a battery, or part of the earth return.

Earth return The path of an electrical circuit that returns to the battery, utilising the motorcycle's frame.

ECU (Electronic Control Unit) A computer which controls (for instance) an ignition system, or an anti-lock braking system.

EMS (Engine Management System) A computer controlled system which manages the fuel injection and the ignition systems.

Expansion chamber Section of two-stroke engine exhaust system so designed to improve engine efficiency and boost power.

F

Final drive Description of the drive from the transmission to the rear wheel. Usually by chain or shaft, but sometimes by belt.

Firing order The order in which the engine cylinders fire, or deliver their power strokes, beginning with the number one cylinder.

Flat twin (or four/six) An engine with horizontal adjacent or opposed cylinders, thereby having a flat configuration.

Float A buoyant object. Used in a carburettor to open and close the fuel inlet valve to maintain a constant fuel level.

Float chamber A carburettor component used to stabilise the fuel level in the carb.

Float level The height at which the float is positioned in the float chamber, so determining the fuel level.

Flywheel A rotating mass of considerable weight and radius, used to smooth out power impulses at the crank.

Four-stroke An operating cycle for an internal combustion engine in which combustion takes place on every other ascent of the piston. See also Two-stroke.

Freeplay The amount of travel before any action takes place, for example, the distance the rear brake pedal moves before the rear brake is actuated.

Friction The resistance between two bodies moving in contact with each other and relatively to each other.

Front fork Telescopic tubes incorporating springs and dampers used to provide a suspension system for the front of a motorcycle.

Fuel injection The fuel/air mixture is metered electronically and directed into the engine intake ports (indirect injection) or into the cylinders (direct injection). Sensors supply information on engine speed and conditions.

Fuel/air mixture The charge of fuel and air going into the engine.

Fuel level The level of fuel in a float chamber. Can be altered by changing the float level.

Fulcrum The point about which a leverage system pivots.

Fuse An electrical device which protects a circuit against accidental overload.

G

Gasket Any thin, soft material – usually cork, cardboard, asbestos or soft metal – installed between two metal surfaces to ensure a good seal.

Gear A component, often circular, with projections for the positive transmission of movement to a companion gear which may, or may not be, of the same shape and size.

Gearbox An assembly containing the transmission components used in varying the ratio of the gearing.

Gear ratio The ratio of turning speeds of any pair of gears or sprockets, derived from their number of teeth.

Gudgeon pin The pin, usually made of hardened steel, linking the piston to the small end of the connecting rod.

H

Helical gears Gear teeth are slightly curved and produce less noise than straight-cut gears. Often used for primary drives.

HT High Tension Description of the electrical circuit from the secondary winding of the ignition coil to the spark plug.

HT lead A heavily insulated wire carrying the high tension current from the coil to the spark plug.

Horizontally-opposed A type of engine in which the cylinders are opposite to each other with the crankshaft in between.

Hub The centre part of a wheel.

Hydraulic A liquid-filled system used to transmit pressure from one component to another. Common uses on motorcycles are brake and clutch actuating mechanisms.

Hygroscopic Water absorbing. In motorcycle applications, braking efficiency will be reduced if DOT 3 or 4 hydraulic fluid absorbs water from the air – care must be taken to keep new brake fluid in tightly sealed containers.

Hypoid oil An extreme-pressure oil formulated to stand up to severe and unique conditions in hypoid transmission gears.

I

lbf ft Pounds-force feet. An imperial unit of torque. Sometimes written as ft-lbs.

Ignition advance Means of increasing the timing of the spark at higher engine speeds. Done by mechanical means on early engines or electronically by the ignition control unit on later engines.

Ignition timing The moment at which the spark plug fires, expressed in the number of crankshaft degrees before the piston reaches the top of its stroke, or in the number of millimetres before the piston reaches the top of its stroke.

Injector Equipment for squirting a fluid. Used for both fuel and oil.

Inverted forks (upside down forks) The sliders or lower legs are held in the yokes and the fork tubes or stanchions are connected to the wheel axle (spindle). Less unsprung weight and stiffer construction than conventional forks.

J

Jet A hole through which air, fuel or oil passes, the size of the jet determining the quantity.

Joule The unit of electrical energy.

K

Kickstart A crank, operated by foot, for starting an engine.

Knock Similar to detonation, with same end results, but only the end gases in the far reaches of the combustion chamber ignite. The knocking sound, also known as pinking, occurs when the central and outer flame fronts meet.

L

Lambda (λ) sensor A sensor fitted in the exhaust system to measure the exhaust gas oxygen content (excess air factor).

Land The raised portion between two grooves (e.g. between the ring grooves in a piston).

Layshaft In a 'direct top gearbox' a gearbox shaft parallel to the mainshaft and carrying the laygears with which the mainshaft gears mesh to achieve ratio change.

Leading link A form of front suspension using a pivoting link – approximately horizontal – with the axle in front of the pivot.

LT Low Tension Description of the electrical circuit from the power supply to the primary winding of the ignition coil.

Lubricant A substance, usually an oil, interposed between rubbing surfaces to decrease friction.

M

Main bearing The principal bearing(s) on which a component is carried but usually reserved exclusively for the crankshaft.

Mainshaft A principal shaft, as in an engine or a gearbox.

Master cylinder The operator end of an hydraulic control system.

Monoshock A single suspension unit linking the swingarm or suspension linkage to the frame.

Multigrade oil Having a wide viscosity range (e.g. 10W40). The viscosity ranges from SAE10 when cold to SAE40 when hot.

Multi-rate A spring which changes length unequally for equal increments of load. (Contrast with constant rate and progressive rate.)

N

Needle roller bearing A bearing made up of many small diameter rollers of hardened steel, usually kept separated by a cage. Often used where lubrication is poor.

Negative earth Using the negative or minus pole of the battery as the earth.

Nm Newton metres used to measure torque.

O

Odometer A mileage recorder.

Oil injection A system of two-stroke engine lubrication where oil is pump-fed to the engine in accordance with throttle position.

Oil pump A mechanically-driven device for distributing oil around a four-stroke engine or pumping oil into a two-stroke engine.

Overhead valve (OHV) A four-stroke engine with the valves in the cylinder head and operated by pushrods.

Overhead cam (OHC) As above but with the camshaft contained in the cylinder head and operated by chain, gear or belt from the crankshaft.

P

Pinking The noise arising from Detonation and Knock.

Pitch The nominal distance between two specified points such as gear teeth, spring coils or chain rollers.

Plug cap A cover over the top of a spark plug that transmits the HT voltage from the coil and lead to the plug.

Plug lead A heavily insulated wire carrying the high tension current from the coil to the spark plug.

Port Strictly, a hole or opening but also used to described the transfer ports in a two-stroke engine.

Power band The band of rpm in which the engine produces really useful power.

Pre-ignition Auto-ignition taking place before the desired moment and happening, not by sparking, but by incandescence.

Pre-load (suspension) The amount a spring is compressed when in the unloaded state. Pre-load can be adjusted by gas, spacer or mechanical adjuster. Determines ride height.

Premix The method of engine lubrication on older two-stroke engines. Engine oil is mixed with the petrol in the fuel tank in a specific ratio.

Primary gears The pair of gears connecting the crankshaft to the clutch in a unit construction engine.

Progressive rate A spring that progressively deflects less for equal increments in load (see Constant rate and Multi-rate).

Pushrod A stout rod used to transmit a push as in clutch or overhead-valve operation.

R

Radial ply tyre Form of tyre construction in which the wraps of fabric in the tyre carcass are laid over each other radially, and not diagonally.

Radiator Device for losing heat.

Rake The angle of the steering axis from the vertical.

Rebore Removing the worn surface of a cylinder to create a new working surface.

Rebound damping A means of controlling the oscillation of a suspension unit spring after it has been compressed.

Rectifier Electrical device passing current in one direction only (and thus a wave), used to convert alternating current into direct current.

Reed valves A valve functioning like a reed, with pressure causing the 'flap' to open or close.

Regulator Device for maintaining the charging voltage from the generator or alternator within a specified range.

Relay An electrical device used to switch heavy current on and off using a low current auxiliary circuit. Relays are used to switch heavy currents such as for the starter motor.

Rim The edge, margin or periphery. In the case of a wheel, the part that carries the tyre.

Rising rate Condition set up using a three-way linkage between the swingarm and the shock absorber to give progressive suspension action.

Roller bearing One containing rollers as the support medium, and not balls.

rpm Revolutions per minute.

S

Seizure The binding together of two moving parts through pressure, temperature or lack of lubrication, and often all three.

Shaft drive A method of transmitting drive from the transmission to the rear wheel.

Shock absorber A device for ironing out the effects of riding over bumps in the road to give a smooth ride.

Single-overhead camshaft (SOHC) An engine that uses one overhead camshaft to operate both intake valves and exhaust valves via rockers.

Small-end The smaller end on a connecting rod to which the piston is attached.

Spark plug Device for arcing an electric current, as a spark, between two electrodes inserted in the combustion space.

Spindle The fixed rod about which an article turns or perhaps swings in an arc.

Sprocket Toothed wheel used in chain drive.

Stanchion In a telescopic front fork, that tubular part attached to the fork yokes and on or in which travels the moving slider.

Steering head The part of the frame which houses the steering stem.

Stroke The distance between the highest and lowest points of the piston's travel.

Sub-frame The rear part of a motorcycle frame which carries the seat, rear lighting and electrical components.

Sump Chamber on the bottom of a four-stroke engine that contains the oil.

Swingarm Supports the rear wheel and rear suspension.

T

Taper rollerbearing A hardened steel roller, being tapered instead of cylindrical.

Tachometer Rev-counter.

Thermostat Controls the flow of engine coolant into the radiator.

Timing The opening and closing points of valves and the moment of ignition in the engine cycle.

Top Dead Centre (TDC) Highest point of a piston's stroke.

Top-end A description of an engine's cylinder block, head and valve gear components.

Torque A twisting force about a shaft, measured in Nm, kgf m or lbf ft.

Trail The distance between the point where a vertical line through the wheel axle touches the ground, and the point where a line through the steering axis touches the ground.

Twistgrip Rotary throttle control on the right handlebar, operated by twisting.

Two-stroke An operating cycle for an internal combustion engine in which combustion takes place on every ascent of the piston. The four events (induction, compression, ignition, exhaust) in the engine cycle are thus completed in two strokes (one up, one down) of the piston. See also Four-stroke.

U

Unsprung weight Anything not supported by the bike's suspension (i.e. the wheel, tyres, brakes, final drive and bottom (moving) part of the suspension).

Upside down forks (inverted forks) In contrast to conventional forks, these have the inner tube at the bottom, connected to the wheel axle, and acting as the slider, moving in the outer tube.

V

Valve A device through which the flow of liquid, gas or vacuum may be stopped, started or regulated by a movable part that opens, shuts or partially obstructs one or more ports or passageways. The intake and exhaust valves in the cylinder head are of the poppet type.

Valve seat That part of the cylinder head against which the valve face seats and seals.

V-engine A motor with its cylinders arranged in V formation.

W

Watercooling Engine cooling system which uses a recirculating liquid coolant which passes through channels in the engine castings and externally through a radiator.

Water pump A mechanically-driven device for moving coolant around the engine.

Wet sump Conventional four-stroke engine lubrication system in which the oil is carried in a pan (sump) on the bottom of the crankcase.

Wheelbase The distance, between the axles of the front and rear wheels.

Y

Yokes Connect the steering stem to the front forks.

Index

Photos:
Tom Critchell,
John Noble,
Phillip Tooth,
Aprilia, BMW, CCM,
Ducati, Harley-Davidson,
Honda, Hyperbolt, Italjet,
Kawasaki, KTM, Suzuki,
Triumph, Yamaha

**Author
Acknowledgements:**
Bob Gray
the late John Robinson,
Louise McIntyre,
Simon Larkin,
Luke Brackenbury,
Tom Critchell (again)

Written by
Alan Seeley
Design
Simon Larkin
Technical editor
Martynn Randall
Editor
Peter McSean
Project Manager
Louise McIntyre

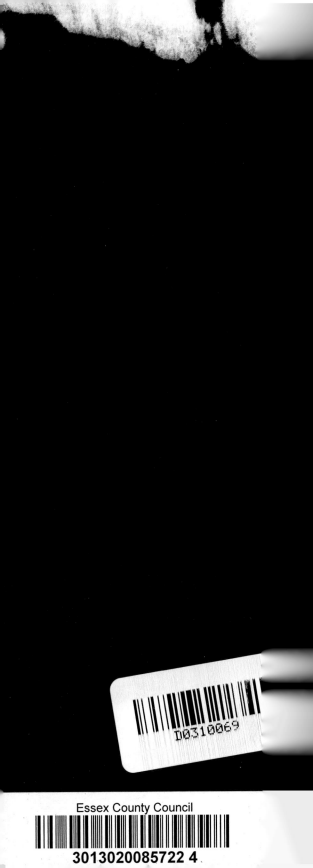

The Man Who
Sold The World

David Bowie and the 1970s

The Man Who
Sold The World

DAVID BOWIE AND THE 1970s

PETER DOGGETT

THE BODLEY HEAD
LONDON

Published by The Bodley Head 2011

2 4 6 8 10 9 7 5 3 1

Copyright © Peter Doggett 2011

Peter Doggett has asserted his right under the Copyright, Designs
and Patents Act 1988 to be identified as the author of this work

First published in Great Britain in 2011 by
The Bodley Head
Random House, 20 Vauxhall Bridge Road,
London SW1V 2SA

www.bodleyhead.co.uk
www.vintage-books.co.uk

Addresses for companies within The Random House Group Limited can be found at:
www.randomhouse.co.uk/offices.htm

The Random House Group Limited Reg. No. 954009

A CIP catalogue record for this book
is available from the British Library

ISBN 9781847921444 (HBK)
ISBN 9781847921451 (TPB)

The Random House Group Limited supports The Forest Stewardship Council (FSC®), the
leading international forest certification organisation. Our books carrying the FSC label are
printed on FSC® certified paper. FSC is the only forest certification scheme endorsed by
the leading environmental organisations, including Greenpeace. Our paper procurement
policy can be found at www.randomhouse.co.uk/environment

Typeset by Palimpsest Book Production Limited,
Falkirk, Stirlingshire
Printed and bound in Great Britain by
Clays Ltd, St Ives PLC

Contents

Introduction

People look to me to see what the spirit of the 70s is, at least, 50%
of them do – critics I don't understand. They get too intellectual.
   David Bowie, 1973

I

Historians often prefer to ignore the rigid structure of the calendar
and define their own decades. These can be 'short' or 'long', lasting
six years or sixteen: for example, the 'short' sixties might be bracketed
by the impact of Beatlemania in 1963 and the Manson murders in
1969; their 'long' equivalent could stretch from Harold Macmillan's
'never had it so good' speech in 1957 to America's withdrawal from
Vietnam in 1973. What unifies these artificial eras is a sense of identity
that marks them out from what came before and after.

Perhaps anticipating that the seventies might be less susceptible
to easy categorisation than its over-mythologised predecessor, David
Bowie effectively imposed his own 'long' margins on the decade. At
the start of 1969, he wrote 'Space Oddity' [1], a song that punctured the
global admiration for the Apollo mission to the Moon. His hero, Major
Tom, was not making a giant leap for mankind, but sitting in the alienated exile of a lunar capsule, unwilling to come back to Earth. In 1980,
Bowie returned to the scenario of that song in 'Ashes To Ashes' [184],
to discover that his reluctant hero was still adrift from humanity, as if
the previous eleven years had changed nothing. 'Space Oddity' turned

David Bowie into an uneasy pop star; 'Ashes To Ashes' marked the end of his long decade of stardom, during which he had tested the culture, and his own personality, to the limits of their fragile endurance.

Like the Beatles in the decade before him, Bowie was popular culture's most reliable guide to the fever of the seventies. The Beatles' lives and music had reflected a series of shifts and surges in the mood of their generation, through youthful exuberance, satirical mischievousness, spiritual and chemical exploration, political and cultural dissent, and finally depression and fragmentation. The decade of David Bowie was altogether more challenging to track. It was not fired by idealism or optimism, but by dread and misgiving. Perhaps because the sixties had felt like an era of progress, the seventies was a time of stasis, of dead ends and power failures, of reckless hedonism and sharp reprisals. The words that haunted the culture were 'decline', 'depression', 'despair': the energy of society was running out, literally (as environmentalists proclaimed the imminent exhaustion of fossil fuel supplies) and metaphorically. By the decade's end, cultural commentators were already defining the era in strictly negative terms: the chief characteristic of the seventies was that it was not what the prime movers of the sixties had hoped it would be.

This was not, at first sight, the stuff of pop stardom. The Beatles would have struggled to capture the hearts of their generation had they preached a message of conflict and decay, rather than idealism and love. What enabled David Bowie to reflect the fear and chaos of the new decade was precisely the fact that he had been so out of tune with the sixties. He was one of the first pop commentators to complain that the optimism that enraptured the youth of the West in the mid-sixties was hollow and illusory. His negativity seemed anachronistic; but it merely anticipated the realisation that Western society could not fuel and satisfy the optimism of sixties youth culture. 'Space Oddity' aside, his work of 1969/70 failed to reach the millions who heard the Rolling Stones' *Let It Bleed* or John Lennon's *Plastic Ono Band*, two albums that also tore away the pretensions of the recent past. But even those records paled alongside the nihilistic determinism of Bowie's first two albums in his new guise as cultural prophet and doom-monger.

Bowie might have maintained a fashionable gloom for the next decade, and turned his sourness into a calling. Instead, he embarked on a far more risky and ambitious course. Unable to secure a mass audience for his explorations of a society in the process of fragmentation, he decided to create an imaginary hero who could entrance and then educate the pop audience – and play the leading role himself. Since the start of his professional career as an entertainer in 1964, he had used his brief experience as a visualiser in an advertising agency to rebrand himself in a dozen different disguises. Now he would concentrate on a single product, and establish a brand so powerful that it would be impossible to ignore. The creation of Ziggy Stardust in 1972 amounted to a conceptual art statement: rather than pursuing fame, as he had in the past, Bowie would act as if he were already famous beyond dispute, and present himself to the masses as an exotic creature from another planet. Ziggy would live outside the norms of earthly society: he would be male and female, gay and straight, human and alien, an eternal outsider who could act as a beacon for anyone who felt ostracised from the world around them. Aimed at a generation of adolescents emerging into an unsettling and fearful world, his hero could not help but become a superstar. Whereupon Bowie removed him from circulation, destroying the illusion that had made him famous.

What happened next was what made Bowie not just a canny manipulator of pop tastes, but a significant and enduring figure in twentieth-century popular culture. He channelled the momentum of Ziggy Stardust's twelve months of fame into a series of artistic and psychological experiments that tugged at the margins of popular entertainment, and at the cohesion of his own psyche. Between 1974 and 1980, Bowie effectively withdrew from the world around him and created his own microculture – a bewildering landscape in which nothing was fixed and everything familiar was certain to change shape before the observer's eyes.

Bowie's methods were simple, and devastating: he placed himself into alien environments and cultures (New York, Los Angeles, Berlin; R&B music, experimental rock, ambient soundscapes), turned them to his own devices, and then systematically demolished what he had just created. In each situation, he pushed himself, and his surroundings, to their limits, to see whether they would crack or bend. Then he moved on, relentlessly and compulsively, to the next incarnation. Ultimately, he succeeded in shedding all the skins and disguises he had worn since 1964, and all of the cultural debris, to arrive in 1980 enervated, disgusted, exhausted, free. Then he, like Ziggy Stardust, disappeared.

What linked the sounds of the seventies, Bowie once said, was irony; and there was irony aplenty when he chose to reappear in 1983 – not as a restless investigator of fresh cultures and techniques, but as nothing more disruptive than the professional entertainer who had been hiding beneath his skins from the beginning. The irony was that his audience was so desperate to believe he was still the David Bowie of 1972, 1976 or 1980 that they ignored his artistic inertia and greeted him as a conquering hero – Bowie therefore becoming exactly the mainstream success that he had parodied in the seventies. Only in the nineties did his work rekindle the spirit of more interesting times; by then, the world at large was interested in him as a figure of nostalgia, not a creative artist. But that is another story.

II

Fragmentation was central to Bowie's seventies. He pursued it in artistic terms by applying cut-up techniques to his language, subverting musical expectations, employing noise as a way of augmenting and substituting for melody, using a familiar formula and distorting it into an alarming new shape. He applied the same tools to his identities and images, assembling each different persona from the remnants of the past. Even Ziggy Stardust, the guise in which Bowie left his most enduring mark on the decade, was assembled like a collage from a bewildering variety of sources, despite his appearance of having stepped fully formed from a passing flying saucer. Elements of Ziggy came from pop: from Judy Garland, the Rolling Stones, the Velvet Underground, the Stooges, the Beatles, Elvis Presley, Little Richard. Strands of pop art were also visible in his disguise, from Richard Hamilton's assimilation of science fact and science fiction to Andy Warhol's obsession with surface and the borrowed sheen of stardom. Through Ziggy, Bowie was also able to access themes that preoccupied the wider culture: the ominous hum of apocalypse, the fear of decay, the compulsive attraction of power and leadership, the search for renewed belief in a time of disillusion. Ziggy represented the 'over-man' that

Bowie had discovered in the writings of Nietzsche; the Führer who had commanded magnetic attention in Germany; the pop icons who had peopled Bowie's own dreams; the struggle of Western civilisation to adjust to a world order that had slipped beyond its control.

Yet fragmentation wasn't just an artistic technique for Bowie; it became the only way in which he could transcend his own psychological heritage. He was born into a family web of mental instability, frustrated ambition and emotional repression. In his teens, he had become aware that authentic emotional responses could not always be controlled; that self-expression could carry someone beyond the acceptable borders of sanity. He had always imagined that success would offer him stability, that he could only become himself in the eyes of an audience; and to achieve that aim, he was prepared to unmake and remake his identity as often and as radically as he needed to. This fluid sense of the self was what enabled him to explore such varied terrain, as an artist and a human being. The pioneering psychologist William James once recounted his own unmaking of identity: 'It consisted in a gradual but swiftly progressive obliteration of space, time, sensation and the multitudinous factors of experience which seem to qualify what we are pleased to call our Self.' He described this process as 'mysticism'; and in his exploration of Buddhist meditation in the late sixties, Bowie would have arrived at a similar sense of what psychologists call 'undifferentiation'. As the seventies progressed, he explored a variety of ways of achieving this state. The most commonplace, for a rock star of his era, was through drugs, which inflated his ego, fuelled his restless creativity, and threw his senses into disarray. From his complex family background came the tantalising, terrifying notion that madness – psychosis, schizophrenia – might be a means of establishing his identity, and destroying it in the same moment. He spent a decade trying to avoid what his grandmother called the family curse, and then several more years creating his own form of psychosis with cocaine and amphetamines.

In place of Buddhist meditation, he became obsessed in the seventies with the exploration of the occult: the search for hidden powers and meanings, the attempt to reach beyond the conscious into a realm of unimaginable riches and danger. And it was that quest for something beyond that also inspired his artistic experiments, encouraging him to reach through or around familiar techniques to access material and methods that would help him to overcome the limitations and repressions of the everyday world around him. He would use erratic combinations of all four methods of escape – hallucination, meditation, madness, innovation – throughout the decade, taking fearful risks with his health and sanity, sabotaging key personal relationships, and creating a body of work that surpassed anything in rock for its eclecticism and sense of daring.

III

'This is a mad planet,' Bowie said in 1971. 'It's doomed to madness.' Or, as novelist William S. Burroughs had written four years earlier: 'abandon all nations, the planet drifts to random insect doom'.

Since the late sixties, the notion that mankind was facing apocalyptic disaster had begun to infect every vein of Western society. Cultural critic Susan Sontag noted that the awareness of fear created its own reality: 'Collective nightmares cannot be banished by demonstrating that they are, intellectually and morally, fallacious.' The global bestseller of the early 1970s was Hal Lindsay's recklessly naïve *The Late Great Planet Earth*, which twisted the Christian scriptures to suggest that apocalypse would soon emerge from the Middle East. Lindsay's book was no more rational than thousands of similar explorations of religious paranoia that had been published down the centuries, but it had found its perfect moment. Its alarmist arguments resonated through the popular press, and prepared the ground for the ultra-conservative brand of evangelical Christianity that would help to propel Ronald Reagan into the White House a decade later.

If Hal Lindsay's dread was superstitious, it chimed with the sobering warnings of the scientists who predicted environmental disaster for mankind. The debate had been simmering since the early 1960s, erupting into mainstream culture in the form of tabloid headlines or science fiction dystopias. The threats were so immense – a new ice age, global warming, mass starvation, the exhaustion of water, food or fuel – that it was easier to ignore them than tackle them. They merged seamlessly into the recurrent fear of global annihilation via nuclear warfare, meeting on the equally uncertain ground of nuclear power. As if to signal that the new decade would force these environmental monsters into our everyday lives, the BBC launched a television series in February 1970 called *Doomwatch*, about a governmental department whose brief was nothing less than the preservation of mankind against overwhelming natural (and extraterrestrial) threats. Hollywood extended the theme with the disaster movies that captured the popular imagination for much of the decade.

In the teeth of *Jaws* and *The Towering Inferno*, there was something intolerably mundane about financial catastrophe, and the pervasive sense of decline that afflicted the West (and particularly Britain) through the early seventies. Successive leaders had been preaching economic doom since the mid-sixties, to the point where the pronouncement in late 1973 that Britain was facing its gravest economic crisis since the end of the Second World War sounded almost comfortingly familiar. Industrial unrest triggered strike action amongst key workers, and periodically during the decade the UK population was returned to the age of candlelight, as regular power cuts restricted television broadcasts, closed cinemas, darkened neon advertising displays, cancelled sporting fixtures, and of course deprived homes and offices of light, warmth and electricity. These episodes occupied no more than a few weeks of the decade, but they left such a mark that they remain the dominant folk memory of the 1970s.

The optimism associated with scientific progress, which flowered briefly as man landed on the Moon and Concorde broke the sound barrier, was soon replaced by a debilitating sense of dread; science seemed as likely to spark the end of civilisation as it did to solve mankind's problems and fulfil its desires. Even computers, the wondrous creation of post-war technology, threatened to become the instruments of repression rather than liberation. It was no accident that in 1970 David Bowie wrote a song entitled 'Saviour Machine' [24], around a scenario in which an all-powerful computer becomes so bored with eliminating mankind's needs that it begins to invent fresh crises to keep itself interested.

If computerisation, with its taint of depersonalisation and callous, robotic indifference,* threatened society as a whole, then the growth

---

* Which was exactly the quality that the German rock band Kraftwerk exploited during the seventies, exerting a huge influence over Bowie's work in the second half of the decade.

of urban terrorism across the West brought the shudder of imminent extinction into daily life. Television news bulletins showed planes being hijacked, politicians kidnapped and murdered, shops and hotels exploding without warning; the implicit message was that nobody was safe, and any stranger could be the agent of sudden death or maiming. Car bombs, the murder of athletes at the Olympic Games, random shootings, picket-line confrontations, the unstoppable force of flood or famine: these dissociated threats were woven into the psychological landscape of the age, preparing civilisation for the savage hand of apocalypse to descend.

In economic terms, none of these threats left a deeper mark on the decade than the Yom Kippur War of 1973, a brief conflict between Israel and its Arab neighbours that pushed the oil-producing nations of the Middle East into imposing a jolting rise in the cost of the oil they supplied to the West. Commentators routinely compared oil-hungry Britain to the Weimar Republic from which Hitler's Nazi party had emerged. 'Declinism was an established British state of mind,' the historian Andy Beckett has written, 'but during the mid-70s it truly began to pervade the national consciousness . . . It darkened the work of artists, novelists, dramatists, film-makers and pop musicians . . . And it shifted in tone: from the anxious to the apocalyptic.' And so it was that in 1975 David Bowie, who had been exiled in the USA for 18 months, began to offer a running commentary on the state of the nation in which he was no longer resident, which could be summar-ised in a sentence: Britain needed a strong leader, and fascism would produce a strong leader. That was the point where the apocalyptic imagery with which he had been toying on his early- to mid-seventies albums collided with the side effects of his 'undifferentiation', with catastrophic (if short-lived) results for his reputation.

The reaction to his quasi-fascist statements (one of the sparks that fired the creation of the Rock Against Racism movement) shocked Bowie into a realisation of how removed he had become from British culture, and from a solid sense of his own position in the world. He no longer masqueraded as a commentator on British affairs; even the election of Conservative politician Margaret Thatcher as the country's first woman prime minister in 1979 was allowed to pass in silence. Instead, he took up residence in Berlin, a city that epitomised the Nazi past with which he had long been fascinated and the experimental music of so-called 'Krautrock'; and also an arena in which political ambiguities were still too close to the surface for him to offer ill-informed generalisations about the state of the world. In Berlin, he would concentrate on personal rehabilitation, and musical transformation – the latter enabling him to escape the accusations of irrelevance that were now being flung at almost all of his contemporaries.

IV

We are passing through terrible times, when everybody wants attention, but nobody quite knows how to command it.
Howard Zinker, *Rolling Stone* magazine, 1971

In March 1974, David Bowie travelled to Paris and then to Cannes, where he boarded the SS *France*. His destination was New York, where he would assemble the pieces for his most lavish stage presentation of the decade: the *Diamond Dogs* tour. He did not realise that, at the age of 27, he had broken his bonds to England, or that he was destined for the two most turbulent years of his life on America's opposing coasts. Nor was it apparent to anyone that this voyage marked a crucial moment in his career as a musician. Until this point, he had used the tools and techniques of mainstream rock and pop to promote themes and obsessions that were radical and dramatic in their impact. Now, in America, Paris and then Berlin, he would leave his mark on the decade in a different way, by inventing styles and hybrids that would inspire generations of young musicians. The David Bowie of the early seventies was a conventional pop star who acted as a social revolutionary. From 1974 until 1980, he was an experimental rock artist who managed to attract a mass audience for some of the most challenging music of his career.

The primary purpose of an entertainer is to find an audience, and retain its attention. During the sixties, Bowie was unashamedly an entertainer, but one who found it impossible to focus on who he was, what he was trying to convey, and who he was attempting to impress. The success of his 'Space Oddity' single in 1969 appeared to have solved all three conundrums; in fact, it merely illustrated the hollowness of the goal that had sustained Bowie for the previous six years.

His 1969 LP *David Bowie* and 1970's *The Man Who Sold The World* were vehicles for self-analysis and bitter reflections on the culture around him. They spoke *for* him, but not *to* anybody – not, at least, until they were rediscovered by the mass audience who were entranced by his later incarnations. *Hunky Dory* in 1971 was a collective of attractively accessible pop songs, through which Bowie tested out his feelings about the nature of stardom and power. *Ziggy Stardust* was his commercial breakthrough in 1972; on that record, the concept was everything, the music firmly lodged in the mainstream. 1973's *Aladdin Sane* allowed Bowie to continue his explorations of fame, within familiar rock formulas. His second album that year, *Pin Ups*, was a fashionable exercise in nostalgia, the comfortable refuge of a society in disarray. Finally, the *Diamond Dogs* album in 1974 brought together all the themes with which he had been toying since 1969, in service of a dark study of cultural disintegration.

Little of the music on those albums was beyond the imagination of Bowie's peers; much of it was overtly indebted to his predecessors, especially the Beatles and the Rolling Stones. What marked Bowie out as a unique talent were the themes of his songs, and the ways in which he sold them (and himself). Nobody had ever manipulated the tools of pop stardom so blatantly, and with such stunning impact. Rather than destroying pop's mystique as well as his own, his Ziggy Stardust charade became the most glittering image of the age. Central to its appeal was the way in which it offered one of the key motifs of the seventies: androgyny. By portraying – and, to every appearance, being – a bisexual rock star for whom camp was an instinctive playground, Bowie broke startling new terrain. As the openly gay eighties star Marc Almond recalled of Bowie's epochal July 1972 appearance on *Top Of The Pops*, 'Next day, all hell broke loose in the playground. Bowie was a queer, and if you like him you must be queer too.' Previous pop stars had been willing to flirt with 'queer' imagery, and then coyly withdraw the offer. What set Bowie apart was his lack of shame; his openness to what he called (in 'Changes', [48]), 'the strange'. He broke down powerful but invisible barriers, and made it impossible for them to be reinstated. After Bowie, ambiguity of gender and sexual preference became a common attribute of a pop star, rather than an unmentionable secret.

The resonance of that manoeuvre would endure for the rest of the decade, particularly in the USA. The year of his arrival, 1974, began with rock culture apparently being threatened with harsh restrictions upon its activities as a result of the oil crisis afflicting the West. Instead, the industry careered into an era of extreme decadence and profligacy. Rock was no longer a badge of the counter-culture; it was a multimillion-dollar branch of the entertainment business. Its economic power was reflected by the lucrative arena tours staged by all major artists (Bowie included); by the plethora of expensively packaged double or even triple albums that were catapulted into the marketplace (Bowie contributing with his *David Live* set); by music's invasion of television, film and the stage; and by the prevalence of cocaine abuse that fuelled the industry's arrogance and self-confidence, sapped its creativity, and reinforced a culture of hubris that would lead inevitably to the invention of punk rock. This rambunctious intruder did not destroy the superstar system or its attendant extravagances: superstars still filled arenas, and issued multiple-album chronicles of their exploits. But punk did provide an iconoclastic style, ethos and brand that would enable a dozen alternative forms of music to emerge and flourish during the eighties and beyond.

Bowie's contribution to this culture of excess, and its antidote, was as ambiguous and bewildering as the music he created during the second half of the seventies. At the same time, he fuelled the savage beast of consumerism, offering peerless rock-disco crossovers that became major US hits; and undermined it, with a succession of albums that demanded their own musical genres. *Young Americans* suggested new ways for rock performers to utilise the sound of black America; *Station To Station* distilled the essence of German rock, the dance floor and occult speculation into a genuinely shocking (and yet commercially viable) new sound; *Low* and *'Heroes'* demonstrated the era's fragmentation of style, society and self; *Lodger* invented the unhappy tradition of rock stars acting as instant authorities on the Third World; and *Scary Monsters* compressed a decade of Bowie identities, and approaches, into a stirring (if often uneasy) blend of rhythm and dissonance that would set the benchmark for the years ahead.

No other pop artist (in any medium) was as restlessly inventive in the seventies as David Bowie; none took as many risks, so obsessively avoided the safety of repetition, or stretched himself and his audience

so far. Little wonder, then, that it would take the following decade
for Bowie, and his contemporaries, to assimilate everything that he
had achieved, and move beyond it.

V

In 1976, cultural commentator Tom Wolfe coined a phrase that would
endure as a capsule summary of the era unfolding around him: 'The
Me Decade'. He described it in terms that seemed particularly pertinent to David Bowie: 'The new alchemical dream is: changing one's
personality – remaking, remodelling, elevating, and polishing one's
very self . . . and observing, studying, and doting on it.' Two years
later, another writer, Christopher Lasch, portrayed what he called *The
Culture of Narcissism*, and especially 'the narcissistic preoccupation with
the self'. It betrayed, he said, 'the anxieties of a culture that believes
it has no meaning'.

The preoccupations of this decade and culture, spiralling out from
their birthplace on the American West Coast, were psychotherapy,
spirituality, personal awareness, human potential – an entire process
of unbecoming one's temporal self in order to become the deeper and
more meaningful self beneath. A 1975 article in the magazine *Harper's*
laid out the consequences of this immersion in individuality: 'Our
therapies become a way of hiding from the world, a way of easing
our troubled conscience . . . What disappears in this view of things
is the ground of community, the felt sense of collective responsibility
for the fate of each separate other . . . The self replaces community,
relation, neighbour, chance or God.'

That 'felt sense' began to die as soon as the participants in the sixties
counter-culture realised that their dream of a transformed society was
too utopian to succeed. They saw the gleam of optimism fade as the
global anti-war movement fragmented into factional infighting; as
the totems of the hippie culture, from revolutionary leaders to rock
stars, opted for lucrative self-mythologising rather than the defiance
of opposition; as the wider consumerist culture enveloped and then
repackaged the symbols of rebellion as (another Tom Wolfe phrase)
radical chic. In place of utopia, it was strangely comfortable to lean
on apocalypse – an eschatological obsession that was fuelled by the

belief that the dominant culture was too corrupt and diseased to survive. But survive it did, reinforced by the generation who had once pledged to destroy it.

So the collective energy of the counter-culture dissipated into spasms of individualism, each convulsion representing a desperate grasp for meaning and purpose. Instead of mass movements, some of the young focused on personal salvation and transformation, which might be religious or political or psychological, and lead them into obscure cults or terrorist cells or psychiatric wards. The underground magazines that had once been filled with political manifestos were now dominated by interpretations of ancient runes and manuscripts, from the Bible to the prophecies of Nostradamus, any of which could be manipulated to prove that humanity was entering its end times. Then the underground papers died, or became the new establishment; just as the rock stars who preached violent revolution in the late sixties turned into the professional nostalgists of the seventies and beyond.

From his secluded standpoint in 1990, David Bowie the ageing rock star attempted to explain how this process had affected him and his peers: 'In the 70s, people [of] my age group were disinclined to be a part of society. It was really hard to convince yourself that you *were* part of society. It's like, "OK, you've broken up the family unit, and you say you're trying to get out of your mind and expand yourself and all that. Fine. So now that you've left us, what are we left with? Cos here we are, without our families, totally out of our heads, and we don't know where on earth we are." That was the feeling of the early 70s – nobody knew where they were.'

Bowie's immediate response to that disabling sense of confusion was to shift ground – invent new identities, constantly alter and update his musical style, discover new ways to access his creativity, keep himself and his observers guessing. 'I change my mind a lot,' he admitted. 'I usually don't agree with what I say very much. I'm an awful liar.' To remain eternally fascinating, he had to change his mind, and his story: from one interview to the next, he would be capable of delivering violently opposed, but devoutly sincere, explanations of himself and his work. He learned how to invite or repel the attentions of the media as the situation required: he would distance himself from the commonplace duties of an entertainer promoting himself and his product, but then treat the lucky few who were allowed access as if they were not only close personal friends, but also uniquely acute observers of his career. 'That's it, exactly!' he would say when a journalist ventured a theory about a song or a change of direction; the interviewer would leave with a glow of triumph, and Bowie would survive with his mystique untouched.

Not just his mystique; but his 'self' – which is what, ultimately, makes David Bowie such a perfect exemplar of Tom Wolfe's 'Me Decade'. It was not that Bowie was preternaturally selfish, or arrogant, or self-obsessed, or closeted, although (like every rock star) he could be all of those things. What gave him his 'Me Decade' was the fact that, in the end, all of his creativity was focused on himself; just as even the most outside-oriented of artists cannot help but reveal themselves in their work. He set himself the task of exploring, quite fearlessly, what it was to exist amidst the turmoil of culture that was stumbling in search of a purpose and direction. By chronicling his own perilous journey through the decade, he encapsulated the spirit of the age, in all its anarchic disarray. His seventies was not the decade of the political historian, charting the progression from Wilson to Thatcher, or Nixon to Reagan; it was the decade of a sensitive man caught in the midst of a psychodrama that became a public spectacle, inspiring music that was as restless and creative as the man himself.

Bowie began his 'long' seventies by trying to sell himself to the public; and ended it by cancelling the sale. He was the man who sold himself to the world; and who sold the world an unrivalled vision of its own dreams, fears and possibilities.

VI

The unashamed model for this book is Ian MacDonald's pioneering study of the Beatles' songs, *Revolution In The Head*. At the time of his death, MacDonald was under commission to write a similar book about Bowie and the seventies. His editor is also mine, and a casual conversation provoked the idea of discovering whether Ian had completed any part of his text before his death. When it became apparent that, sadly, he hadn't, my editor asked if I would be interested in taking on the task myself.

One thing should be clear: this is definitely not an attempt to imagine and recreate the book that Ian MacDonald would have written. Although I remain a great admirer of his work, our views on the Beatles, and doubtless David Bowie, were very different. But I would have loved to have read his take on this subject; I hope that he would have found mine intriguing as well.

Early in this project, I realised that every Bowie fan carries a different version of the artist in his or her heart. His career has been so eclectic and multifaceted that it can support multiple interpretations. This is, unashamedly, mine – the work of someone whose relationship with Bowie's music has undergone almost as many changes over the past forty years as the man himself. During that time, there have certainly been periods (much of the eighties, for example) when I felt that each new, and disappointing, manifestation of Bowie's career ate away at the lustre of what had gone before. Then, as the nineties progressed, it became obvious that he had succeeded in reconnecting with his artistic selves, and compressing them into work that may not have been as radical as the peaks of his seventies catalogue, but still demonstrated a fierce critical intelligence alongside his enduring musical skills.

Writing this book has allowed me the delightful indulgence of being able to study a collection of music that, I sincerely believe, bears comparison with any comparable catalogue within the very broad remit of popular entertainment. I have been thrilled by Bowie's versatility, touched by his emotional commitment; most of all, stunned by the daring with which he approached a genre (rock, in its broadest sense) that was becoming increasingly conformist during the course of the seventies. At a time when pop artists are encouraged to repeat themselves endlessly within crushingly narrow margins, his breadth of vision and sense of adventure remain truly inspiring.

A word, finally, about the structure of this book. After an initial study of how David Jones of Brixton, Bromley and Beckenham became the David Bowie of the 'long' seventies, the book is focused squarely on the songs – numbered [in square brackets] in chronological order of composition, where that is possible to determine. When that information isn't available, as with all of Bowie's albums after 1975, the songs are covered in the order in which they appear on those records. (Songs recorded and written between 1963 and 1968 can be found in the Appendix, numbered [A1] etc.) Interspersed among those song-by-song studies are brief reviews of every commercial project Bowie undertook during this time frame; and short essays on the major themes in his work and times, from the occult to glam rock, fashion to fascism.

Ian MacDonald was a trained musicologist, and *Revolution In The Head* sometimes tested the understanding of anyone who lacked his grounding in musical theory. I have chosen to take more of a layman's path through Bowie's music, assuming only a limited knowledge* of musical terminology, and the ability to grasp how (for example) a change from minor to major chords in a song can alter not only the notes that Bowie sings, but the emotional impact that those notes have on the listener. Musicology aside, I have employed the widest possible parameters for my critiques of each song: examining the words, the music, how they fit together, how they are performed, how they affect the audience, what they represent in Bowie's career, what they tell us about the wider culture, and what influenced him to create them. The result – I hope – is a book that examines David Bowie the artist, rather than the celebrity, and helps to explain the significance of a song catalogue that is as revealing a guide to the seventies as the Beatles' music was for the sixties.

---

* For example: I have used the abbreviations for chords – Am for A minor, etc. – that will be familiar to anyone who has ever strummed a guitar. On occasions, I have also employed the Roman-numeral system of denoting chords within a particular key. I-vi-IV-V, for example, refers to a chord sequence that begins with the tonic or root chord of the key, moves to a minor sixth (minor denoted by being in lower case), then a major fourth and major fifth. In this instance, this sequence denotes a series of chords that will be instantly recognisable to anyone who has ever heard fifties doo-wop music: in the key of C major, it equates to a sequence of C-Am-F-G.)

The Making of
David Bowie: 1947–1968

The past loads us with guilt. Annihilation can at least be
guaranteed to exonerate us, to cancel all those inherited debts.
Peter Conrad, cultural historian

I

David Bowie was born, under another name, in a city still bearing the
visible scars of war. His family was the haphazard creation of desires
indulged years before his birth; it bequeathed to him the psychological
inhibitions and thwarted dreams that had restricted the lives of his
father and mother. He emerged in 1963 in the planet's most vibrant
city, in time to witness – and participate in – a brief flowering of
creativity and freedom, which has passed into our collective myth as
the era of 'Swinging London'.

In all human history, he might have reflected, there was scarcely a
more welcoming time and place to be alive. He was young, attractive,
creative, ambitious, self-confident, charismatic, flexible, impression-
able, warm and – so one mentor after another declared – a star in the
making. He might become a singer, a composer, a poet, a dramatist,
an actor, a mime artiste, an advertising executive, a television personality, a sculptor, a painter, a model, a hero, an idol, or some fabulous
collage of all these possibilities. Yet for most of the 'short' sixties, bar
a fleeting period of public acceptance as the era closed, David Bowie
was awkwardly out of kilter with the times. He was always there,

on the fringes of Soho or Carnaby Street, the King's Road or South Kensington, Mayfair or Piccadilly, familiar but strangely elusive, alive but never quite where he needed to be. He was held back not by any lack of talent – far more ephemeral and less attractive figures achieved far greater success during the 1960s – or determination; but by a void invisible to the naked eye, which nullified every move he made. He did not entirely know who he was, or who he was intended to be. He was a charming vacancy, an elegant decoration on the lapel of a decade overstocked with such fripperies.

No wonder, then, that when the artificial construct of a fresh decade was signalled on the calendar, Bowie was ready to create a persona more appropriate for the new age. He would cast off his past and fashion a renewed, endlessly fluid sense of self out of his own imagination. By becoming something *other*, he would refuse to be enclosed by gender, by race, by style or by reality. He would become a creature in a state of constant metamorphosis, no longer seeking to capture the spirit of the age but inviting the age to follow him. At the height of his fame, he would reassure his audience: 'You're not alone – give me your hands' [61], and then stretch out his own emaciated arms towards them, coyly allowing the tips of his fingers to graze theirs for an instant, before he withdrew, keeping their tantalising dream of contact alive while remaining ultimately aloof and alone.

Yet the David Bowie who formed and inhabited the shell of Ziggy Stardust carried the dubious inheritance of his troubled family in his genes. No matter how convincing his fantasy, and how often he boasted that he no longer related to his past, he was still the son of Haywood Stenton 'John' Jones and Margaret Mary 'Peggy' Burns; the half-brother of Terry, Annette and Myra; the child of Brixton, the schoolboy of Beckenham and Bromley, the cynical advertising trainee of the West End, the frustrated hero of countless adolescent dreams of transcendence and fame. Ziggy Stardust may have sold himself as a man from Mars, but he lived in Beckenham, an unambitious suburb of south London, in close vicinity to the family web that he had spent a decade struggling to escape.

II

The setting was mundane: the future David Bowie was born David Robert Jones, the son of a charity worker and a cinema usherette, in a three-storey terraced house in Brixton, a working-class area of south London that would soon become synonymous with its community of economic migrants from the Caribbean. He entered this world 17 months after the end of the Second World War, on 8 January 1947 – the twelfth birthday, so he would discover many years later, of a child from Tupelo, Mississippi, named Elvis Presley. The Brixton boy later claimed to have been 'absolutely mesmerised' by this coincidence: 'I was probably stupid enough to believe that having the same birthday as [Elvis] actually meant something.'

Like Presley, whose father spent much of his son's childhood in jail, Bowie's family was shaped by scandal. His parents were not married until he was eight months old, because his father was waiting to divorce his first wife. The social taint of illegitimacy marked out the Jones family, as both John Jones and Peggy Burns had already spawned children out of wedlock, amidst the moral confusion of a society at war. The young Bowie quickly became aware that 'belonging' was a complicated issue for his family, in which blood ties could be disowned or forgotten without warning.

John Jones has been described as 'a withdrawn and emotionally stunted young man who found it hard to display his feelings', but this belied his reckless streak of romanticism. On the verge of inheriting a trust fund at 21, he met a young cabaret performer who billed herself as 'the Viennese Nightingale'. Rather disappointingly, her name was Hilda Sullivan, of Irish-Italian descent, but John was ravished by her talent and potential. He offered to marry her, and bankroll her career, a combination that Hilda found difficult to resist. Much of his inheritance was channelled into a touring revue in which she was the star. When this failed, he diverted the remainder of his fortune into a drinking club in London's bohemian district of Fitzrovia, exotically named the Boop-A-Doop. Within a few months, his money was exhausted, the club closed and – so Bowie alleged later – John Jones became an alcoholic down-and-out, before rousing himself as a hospital porter and then, in 1935, joining the Dr Barnardo's children's charity. (This swift turn of events suggests that Jones' alcoholism may well have been overstated by his son.)

Having separated during this period, husband and wife were reunited a few months later – whereupon Jones embarked on an affair that produced a daughter, Annette, in January 1938. Strangely, this mishap seems to have strengthened the ties between John and Hilda, who agreed to raise the child as her own. They were parted again while John was serving with the 8th Army in North Africa, and recognised that their marriage was over, but continued to plan for Annette's future. When he was demobbed, Jones returned to Dr Barnardo's, where he acted as publicity officer, persuading stars of stage and screen to lend their names to the charity's work. One lunchtime in early 1946, he was served at the Ritz Cinema café in Tunbridge Wells by a 31-year-old waitress named Peggy. Within weeks, they were living together; by April, she was pregnant.

For another woman, this might have been an unbearable disgrace, but Peggy Burns had grown used to outraging bourgeois morals. She was one of six children of a First World War veteran with a dubious record of heroism, and a mother who insisted that her bloodline was destined to be cursed by madness. Indeed, three of Peggy's siblings spent time in mental institutions. Her own history was tangled enough: she was reputed to have run with the 'blackshirts' of Oswald Mosley's British Union of Fascists, while simultaneously staging an affair with a Jewish Frenchman. She fell pregnant, and her son Terence – originally given the old family name of Adair, but later known as Terry Burns – was born in November 1937.

During the war, Peggy became involved with a married man, and had a second child, Myra Ann, who was swiftly exiled into adoption. When Peggy met John Jones, each partner must have welcomed the other's tarnished history as a means of exculpating their own. Indeed, John's life had recently become even more confused: he had bought a house with his estranged wife in Brixton, which they rented out with the intention of presenting it to Annette when she came of age. Hilda generously allowed John and Peggy to live there, while a divorce was obtained as speedily as the law would allow – which proved to be some seven months after David Jones was born.

There were now four children, then: David, the symbol of John and Peggy's union, who spent his entire childhood with his parents; an older son who was alternately accepted and rejected for the next decade; one daughter who had been adopted and forgotten; and an older girl who was only sporadically a member of the household. Terry was belatedly welcomed into the Jones home when he was ten and David was a baby. Family witnesses from these years each had their own prejudices and agendas: Bowie's early biographers were told, for example, that John Jones resented Terry's presence under his roof, because the boy resembled his father too closely; and also that Peggy showed little affection towards her elder son, and began to erect an emotional barrier between herself and David once he became a child rather than a baby. She withheld physical affection from her children; John doted on his younger son but frequently scolded his stepson Terry; while the two boys, who shared a room in the Brixton house, established a tight bond.

Like Edward Heath, the British prime minister between 1970 and 1974, Bowie was raised as the favoured younger son: the cherished, blameless scion of family hopes, appearing all the more perfect alongside the flagrant flaws of the elder sibling, and carrying an assurance of entitlement into adulthood. His aunt recalled, however, that although Bowie relished his good fortune, he also felt guilty for prospering so blatantly at his brother's expense. Adolescence being a trial of identity in even the most well-adjusted family, Terry must have experienced extreme alienation from his parents, and from the outside world. His enthusiastic young brother became his ideal protégé, confidant and ward: as Terry's mental health declined over the next decade, so David inherited the cultural script that Terry had imagined for his own life.

Given the tender rapport between the two boys, it seems insufferably cruel that when the Jones family moved from Brixton to a succession of small houses in the borough of Bromley, Terry was not invited to join them. By the time he had begrudgingly been allowed into their home in Plaistow Grove, Beckenham, he was awaiting his compulsory National Service with the Royal Air Force. He was squeezed into the tiny box room alongside David's larger bedroom, and as soon as his call-up papers arrived, John Jones demonstrated his feelings by knocking through the partition wall, creating a more spacious room for David and effectively signalling Terry's banishment from the family.

David was rarely short of companionship after Terry's departure. At least two of the friendships he made in Beckenham have survived to this day, with George Underwood (musical collaborator and designer) and Geoff MacCormack (backing vocalist and companion on Bowie's mid-seventies tours). At home, the family was augmented by the arrival of his slightly older cousin Kristina, whose mother had been consigned to a mental hospital. It was she who introduced the nine-year-old Bowie to the transcendent power of rock 'n' roll, as she jived around the sitting room to Elvis Presley's 'Hound Dog' with an abandon that David found both compelling and slightly disturbing. John Jones' job led him to meet British stars such as Tommy Steele, and he would frequently allow his son to accompany him and spend a few golden moments with these other-worldly icons.

In drab mid-1950s Britain, which was still cowed by the memory of Nazi air raids and food rationing, rock 'n' roll slapped luminous strokes of colour across the monochrome landscape. The Jones household was shadowy, musty, cramped, repressed; the flamboyant gestures of the early rock pioneers pushed back the walls, opening a world of possibility and pleasure that was painfully out of sync with middle-aged reality. A similar explosion of mental and sexual energy was being experienced in homes across the land. For the ten-year-old Bowie, the cannonball propulsion of Little Richard's 'Long Tall Sally' and the Alan Freed Rock and Roll Band's 'Right Now, Right Now' – or the menace of Screaming Jay Hawkins' 'I Put A Spell On You' and Bo Diddley's experiments with African rhythms – seemed as exotic as the science-fiction melodramas he watched on the minuscule screen of the Joneses' black-and-white television.

Bowie's world changed significantly when he was eleven. His cousin Kristina emigrated to America, and vanished from his life for fourteen years. Meanwhile, he moved to Bromley Technical High School – its name a sign that its pupils were expected to learn practical rather than academic skills. Two months later, Terry was demobbed from the air force, and arrived home to discover that his stepfather no longer wanted him in the house. He spent a year lodging in north London, before finding accommodation closer to Beckenham.

Terry now re-entered David's life as an influential force, described in one account as 'a man, handsome and muscular, witty and worldly-wise'. Working in the City, he gravitated towards the clubs, coffee bars and prostitutes of Soho, and on Friday evenings he would regularly escort David around central London's seamy nightlife, pointing out the call girls on corners and in exotically lit doorways, sneaking him into jazz clubs, and buying his younger brother Cokes in bohemian bars. He also began to expand David's mental horizons, introducing him to modern literature and jazz. 'It was Terry who started everything for me,' Bowie recalled. 'Terry was into all the Beat writers, Jack Kerouac, Allen Ginsberg, Gregory Corso, Lawrence Ferlinghetti, William Burroughs and John Clellon Holmes, and he'd come back home to Bromley with the latest paperbacks tucked away in a coat pocket. He was into everything, reading up the early drug writers, Buddhism, poetry, rock and jazz, especially the saxophone players John Coltrane and Eric Dolphy . . . His mind was open to everything . . . He was rebelling in his own way . . .' Bowie might have been talking about his future self. Once more, Terry was shaping his brother's mental terrain, providing the inspiration that had been so poignantly lacking from his own adolescence.

The education Bowie received from his brother was reinforced in 1960 when he was accepted into an experimental school programme masterminded by teacher Owen Frampton (father of future rock star Peter, who was three years Bowie's junior). Bowie would sometimes later pretend that, like many of his fellow British rock stars, he had attended art college, but Frampton's curriculum, based around art, handicrafts and design, occupied an equally pivotal role in his development. Frampton encouraged his naïve interest in Kerouac and Coltrane, and by 1961 Bowie had been introduced to the era's most symbolic literary influences, from Baudelaire to Orwell, Sartre to Colin Wilson. Nothing in his background had prepared him for this expansive artistic landscape.

There were now two contrasting but reconcilable strands to Bowie's life: his fascination with existentialism, beat and the bohemian lifestyle; and his immersion in US youth culture, via movies, rock 'n' roll and jazz. In his early teens, his father gave him an alto saxophone – in white plastic, like that played by free jazz innovator Ornette Coleman. His teacher, Ronnie Ross, encouraged him to listen to Charlie Parker, the bebop pioneer who built dynamic dimensions of sound on the foundation of Broadway standards and familiar blues changes. Parker's conscious steps into atonality were the missing link between the orthodox harmonies of 'trad' jazz and the fearsome sheets of sound unleashed by Terry's jazz hero John Coltrane. Not that Bowie's education ended there: Terry also encouraged him to soak himself in the daredevil rhythms and unfettered melodicism of Eric Dolphy, whose most ambitious album (*Out To Lunch!*) was released just as Bowie abandoned his commitment to jazz in early 1964. 'I tried passionately at that time to believe I liked Eric Dolphy,' Bowie recalled. 'I'd been forcing myself at first to listen to modern jazz, fighting myself to understand what it was I loved about it, but I really didn't know. I couldn't digest it yet.'

Besides the iconoclastic music suggested by his brother and his teacher, Bowie was exposed to more direct showcases for the saxophone. Many of the early rock 'n' roll records, by Little Richard and the Coasters, Lloyd Price and Elvis Presley, featured the 'yakety' staccato sax of King Curtis, or the guttural roar of Boots Randolph. Although the British 'trad jazz' heroes of the age, such as Acker Bilk, Kenny Ball and Chris Barber, often excluded saxophone from their arrangements, there were many showbands on the club circuit who offered a danceable medley of big-band jazz, R&B, rock and pop – Peter Jay and the Jaywalkers, for example, or Sounds Incorporated – and when Bowie saw them in early 1960s package shows at the Odeon cinemas in Lewisham or Streatham, he could imagine himself on stage. 'I spent my days thinking about whether I was gonna be a rock 'n' roll singer or if I was gonna be John Coltrane,' he recounted many years later. Emulating Coltrane required genius and technical prowess that was beyond him at 14; and he wasn't yet confident about his voice. A few weeks after his fifteenth birthday, with a year or more of school ahead of him, he joined a budding local showband, named the Kon-Rads, as saxophonist and occasional vocalist.

The surviving photographs of the group, in their matching blazers with grammar-school piping, identify Bowie as the youngest and, so it seemed, cheekiest member, his hair crafted into an approximation of a quiff, an Artful Dodger smile flickering across his face. 'He was a very charming, pleasant young man, who quickly developed real aspirations of stardom,' remembered the Kon-Rads' drummer, David Hadfield. 'The Kon-Rads gave him the opportunity to help him create a mental picture of his own career. With us, he started to evolve his own ideas of image and theatrics – the first sparks of what he later became. He could see real potential in what we were doing, but he was young and impatient.'

When Bowie joined up, it was still nine months before the Beatles would release their first single; eighteen until the Rolling Stones' debut. For a rock group, the successful template was the Shadows, all guitars and matching dance steps; so Bowie's only apparent route to fame involved seizing the spotlight as a vocalist. By October, when the Beatles' 'Love Me Do' was issued, Bowie was styling himself David Jay (the resemblance to Peter Jay was not coincidental) and singing approximately a quarter of the Kon-Rads' live repertoire: lightweight American pop for the most part, with only Joe Brown's ballad 'A Picture Of You' betraying even a hint of his London origins. This was teen entertainment that wouldn't upset elder members of the family, with none of Coltrane's startling cacophony or Little Richard's audacious swagger. There was applause and even adulation, however, and like any 15-year-old, Bowie relished the sexual attention sparked by his performances.

Bowie's enthusiasm for school soon paled by comparison. He was still reading voraciously, and filling sketchbooks with designs for stage uniforms, but none of that coincided with his school curriculum. Neither was there a clear connection between the controlled exuberance of the Kon-Rads, neatly parcelled into unthreatening three-minute vehicles for teenage romance, and the limitless horizons that tantalised him in the pages of his brother's beat literature, or in the transcendent and frankly unsettling vastness of Coltrane or Dolphy's saxophone solos.

Several events in the summer of 1963 altered Bowie's sense of himself, and his potential future. He left Bromley Technical High School with a single O-level qualification in art – evidence of his failure to engage with academic requirements. In a time of virtually full employment, and a booming economy desperate for teenage fodder, he found it easy (with Frampton's assistance) to secure a job as a trainee commercial artist in a Bond Street advertising agency. If he'd been asked to symbolise the spirit of the age, he could hardly have manufactured a more convincing image: by day, he helped to fashion the dreams of consumerism; by night, he lived out the wildest of those dreams as – within the London borough of Bromley, at least – a pop star.

III

This sunny snapshot of Swinging London was shadowed by an alarming development in his family life. By summer 1963, Terry Burns' behaviour was beginning to worry Bowie, and his parents. His mother Peggy, quite capable of acting erratically herself, recognised the signs of the family curse, the schizophrenia that had afflicted her mother and several of her siblings. When Terry's grasp on reality began to waver, Bowie not only suffered the fear and distress of watching his much-loved brother slowly slip into another, terrifying psychological world, but also began to realise that the Burns heritage of instability could extend to his own generation.

Terry continued to live independently for several more years. But Bowie could no longer rely on his strength and vigour. During an uncharacteristically candid interview with the journalist Timothy White in late 1977, he shone a momentary flashbulb on how he experienced his brother at this time: 'He cried an awful lot at an age when I had been led to believe that it was not a particularly adult thing to do . . . he would seem miserable.' Bowie recalled that in his final months at school, 'I became very withdrawn', and felt that he must have 'repressed a lot of strange things I thought about or saw in my mind'. He believed that his brother, and other relations, had experienced similar visions and fantasies, but been unable to repress them: 'I know insanity happened frequently within my family. A lot of institutions kept cropping up to claim various members, most of it coming out of bad experiences, loneliness, in-built caution with other people . . . I tried to sort it out for myself to prevent it.'

In the same interview, he admitted that 'the first time I felt uncomfortable' was when he was reading *Metamorphosis*, Franz Kafka's tale of psychological and physical transformation, with its suggestion that our shared humanity might be ripped away in a night's sleep, to reveal a bestial creature within. Turning the pages of Kafka, and watching his own brother's transformation, he must have felt like an explorer walking over a fraying rope bridge towards a dense cloud of fog.

By 1970, when Bowie was a pop star and Terry was living in an asylum, there was an organised revolt against the savage division of mankind into 'sane' and 'insane'. Organisations such as People For A New Psychiatry, and the Campaign Against Psychiatric Atrocities

(CAPA), founded by patients and mental health practitioners, offered a new approach to 'madness'. CAPA saw insanity as a convenient way of enforcing political control, and said that the inability to exist within a repressive capitalist society was nothing less than a badge of honour: 'People who break down because they cannot find a way to live sanely in an insane society are shattered forces of change. Kept whole and mended, restored to themselves, they might threaten. So whilst they are broken and defenceless, the lackeys of the power system step in and make new men and women of them . . . new but no longer themselves.' The moral was simple: 'The sane make war, slaughter each other by the million, lock people up for years, for life. The mad take trips, talk strangely, act oddly, but they rarely kill each other and they don't imprison and oppress. So are they really mad? Are the others really sane?'*

Bowie would have seen that manifesto in the pages of a paper he read avidly, the *International Times*, and it helped to shape his 1970 album *The Man Who Sold The World*. In 1963, when there was no underground press in Britain to represent what would soon become known as a counter-culture, and Bowie read nothing more radical than the *Daily Mirror*, the nature of insanity was only being challenged by psychotherapists such as R.D. Laing, whose analysis of the family culture of schizophrenia still casts an intriguing light on the extended Jones household. Laing baulked at the idea of schizophrenia as a disease of the psyche. Behaviour that was categorised as schizophrenic, he argued, was not 'a biochemical, neurophysical, psychological fact'; instead, it was 'a social event', a product of relationships within the family. He insisted that 'each person does not occupy a single definable position in relation to other members of his or her own family . . . People have identities. But they may also change quite remarkably as they become different others-to-others . . . Not only may the one person behave differently in his different alterations, but he may experience himself in different ways.'

Imagine Terry Burns, then, already ostracised from his mother and stepfather; unwelcome in his family home; his room physically obliterated as soon as he joined the air force; being raised amongst

* The same argument had been propounded by surrealists such as the poet Paul Eluard in the 1920s.

a female line of relatives for whom madness was not so much a fear as an expectation; growing to feel, perhaps, that schizophrenia might represent a way of belonging to his family in a profound sense that was otherwise unavailable to him. Yet within that family unit, he has one person, his half-brother David, who accepts him, respects him, trusts him, regards him as a source of knowledge and experience. Using Laing's logic, it is easy to imagine how Terry might submit to the tradition of 'insanity' presented by his mother; while in his relationship with David, the same chaotic emotional responses that his family classed as 'madness' might become a means of exposing his young sibling to the artistic potential of life. The more exuberant Terry would become when talking about literature or music, the more likely it is that David would be enraptured by his example; and, at the same moment, that his mother and stepfather would see not *joie de vivre*, but the unmistakable traits of insanity.

That visceral sense of life was encapsulated for Bowie in a book that Terry gave him, and which he acknowledged as a major influence on his teenage self: Jack Kerouac's *On The Road*. Set in the year of Bowie's birth, 1947, *On The Road* is the exemplar of the beat generation – a manifesto to the wild impulse to go, get gone, change, keep pushing out and on and over the limits, in cars, in the free-form extravagance of bebop jazz, on pills and weed and beer, in lust and in the sheer necessity of moving to keep from standing still. Its ethos is speed – the Benzedrine pills that propel the body through all-night stands, the cars that career across state lines at midnight, the conversation that pulses back and forth across smoke-filled rooms, everything that let its characters realise that 'we were leaving confusion and nonsense behind and performing our one and noble function of the time, move. And we moved!'

Speed and motion governed everything *On The Road*, from sex ('the one and only holy and important thing in life') to writing ('you've got to stick to it with the energy of a benny addict') and bop ('going like mad all over America'). In a key passage, Kerouac proclaims that 'the only people for me are the mad ones, the ones who are mad to live, mad to talk, mad to be saved, desirous of everything at the same time, the ones who never yawn or say a commonplace thing, but burn, burn, burn like fabulous yellow roman candles exploding like spiders across the stars'. Bowie would meet those spiders again later; but in Kerouac's desperate yearning for the extreme he would have recognised his own relentless desire to change and burn, and his brother's wild enthusiasms.

Kerouac, and the savage pile-up of imagery in Allen Ginsberg's epic poem *Howl*; the tortured extremities of William Burroughs' *Naked Lunch*, and the elemental clamour of John Clellon Holmes' *Go*: that perverse and electrifying set of images jangled Bowie's nerves and roused his adrenalin just as Little Richard and John Coltrane had done. Rock 'n' roll and bop – and now beat literature – precluded the need for chemical stimulation, although that merely added to the heightened surge of energy. In 1963, Bowie was a cauldron of excitement, on stage and in his head, while being told that one vital source of that adrenalin, Terry's quicksilver mind, was not to be trusted. Doctors and psychiatrists prescribed drugs for his elder brother, which subdued his brain, and set a distance between the two young men that would rarely be bridged again. Only the imprint of Terry's influence remained, a cocktail of art and experience that amounted to a vision of life's possibilities and perils.

IV

While his head reeled with the restlessness of Kerouac's wanderers and the twitching pulse of rock 'n' roll, there was little room in Bowie's consciousness for the demands of school – or, after July 1963, his new career in advertising. His employment lasted no more than a year, and on the rare occasions when he discussed it in interviews, he tended to dismiss it as either a bore, or else a disappointment. ('It was diabolical. I never realised that to be an artist meant buckling under so much,' he declared in 1971.) Occasionally, seeking to prove a point about the Orwellian nature of modern society, he would hint that he had witnessed advertising as a dark, controlling force, lending another interpretation to 'diabolical'. 'I've been in the media, I used to be a visualiser for an advertising agency,' he said in 1975. 'They are killers, man . . . They're dealing with lives, those ad agencies.'

The TV series *Mad Men* has lent advertising in the early 1960s a lustre that Bowie might not have recognised. There was a clear gap between New York, where young ad men were (in Tom Wolfe's phrase) the 'masters of the universe'; and London, where most agencies were run in a frosty atmosphere closer to a law office than an adventure playground. In his move from technical school to a desk as a trainee commercial artist, though, Bowie represented the changing nature of the industry. As elsewhere in Swinging London, it was becoming possible for a working-class boy to attain a senior position in an agency. What agencies desired from their 'creatives', according to a 1963 survey, was a list of qualities that Bowie exemplified: 'creative imagination, visual awareness, marked powers of analysis and synthesis, judgement, curiosity, clarity of thought and expression, observation, versatility, flexibility and psychological insight'. Almost all of those assets were evident in his later musical career.

Despite Bowie's insistence that his advertising employment was little more than a charade, he demonstrated enough promise during his year in the West End to be promoted from trainee commercial artist to junior visualiser. His first role involved illustrating other people's ideas, and as a trainee he would often have done nothing more creative than draw boxes around illustrations and insert lettering into existing designs. As a junior visualiser, however, he was being inducted into the world of what the American writer Vance Packard called, in a celebrated exposé, *The Hidden Persuaders*. Visualisers were creating the concepts and images that the commercial artists would illustrate; alongside the copywriters, whose territory was strictly words, they would bring alive the products and campaigns of their clients. 'The basic purpose of visualization is to communicate,' noted an advertising handbook of the times. 'Only elements that carry forward the advertising message should be included – all others should be discarded.'

In keeping with Bowie's 'diabolical' verdict, Packard believed that advertising agencies 'see us as bundles of daydreams, misty hidden yearnings, guilt complexes, irrational emotional blockages. We annoy them with our seemingly senseless quirks, but we please them with our growing docility in responding to their manipulation of symbols that stir us to action.' From there, reasoned Packard and (in *Brave New World Revisited*) the novelist Aldous Huxley, both writing in the late 1950s, it was a comfortable step to using the tools of the advertising trade to control a populace in the service of political power, whether that was democratic or (the advertising ethos at its devilish zenith) dictatorial. 'Find some common desire, some wide-spread unconscious fear or anxiety,' Huxley wrote; 'think out some way to relate this wish or fear to the product you have to sell; then build a bridge of verbal and pictorial symbols over which your customer can pass from fact to compensatory dream, and from the dream to the illusion that your product, when purchased, will make the dream come true.' And so the public laps up a new soap powder, a magazine, a pop star or, as Huxley reasoned, a Hitler. Small wonder that one mid-sixties advertising chief on Madison Avenue conceded: 'The techniques of persuasion by which the Russians seek to subvert governments, win the allegiance of new countries, and turn every political situation to their own advantage, are fundamentally the same psychological devices that we apply daily in selling products to consumers, and selling ideas at home.'

Bowie's awareness of the malevolent power of the advertising industry would only crystallise as he experienced its effects at first hand, as a performer rather than a visualiser. More immediately, the agency ethos altered the way in which he viewed himself, and the Kon-Rads. 'His main contribution [to the band] was ideas,' recalled David Hadfield. 'He had thousands of them, a new one every day – that we should change the spelling of our name, or our image, or our clothes, or all the songs in our repertoire. He also came up with lots of black-and-white sketches of potential advertising campaigns for the band. Many of them were great ideas, but it was impossible to put them all into practice.' Hadfield's testimony suggests that much of Bowie's working day was devoted to selling and rebranding the Kon-Rads, rather than the agency's clients. It also confirms how seriously Bowie took the power of the hidden persuaders. For the remainder of the 1960s, he would present himself to the public in a bewildering variety of guises, as if he was still at his desk in Bond Street, presenting potential campaigns to his superiors. His willingness to pursue a dozen contradictory ideas at the same time, effectively damning them all, reflects the fact that he never moved beyond junior roles during his brief advertising career. Only in the 1970s did he realise what his agency bosses could have told him: to sell a product (or a career), it was not helpful to suggest that it was endlessly versatile but with no particular purpose. What he needed was to fix on a single brand, an image that would grab the public's attention and be burned indelibly into their collective memory.

V

In the mid-1960s, Bowie was too blinded by the idea of success to establish a single identity in a long-term campaign. Like Kerouac's 'mad ones', he was 'desirous of everything at the same time', and heedless of the effect that his single-minded pursuit of stardom would have on those around him. In just three years, he would work his way through six bands, repeating an often callous pattern of behaviour. Each time, he would pour energy and enthusiasm into the project, and then abandon his comrades at the first sign of resistance. 'David wasn't really prepared for failure,' reflected David Hadfield. 'He started to push for a break-through, and when it didn't come, he decided to leave.'

Bowie's intuition that the Kon-Rads were not a viable vehicle for his career was entirely correct: their image and their repertoire looked backwards, rather than anticipating the rampant changes ahead. After seeing the Rolling Stones perform on the same bill as Bo Diddley and Little Richard at the Lewisham Odeon in October 1963, he was desperate to perform R&B rather than teen pop. He was several years younger than the Stones and their British blues contempo-raries (though a full sixteen months older than the precocious Stevie Winwood of the Spencer Davis Group, and three years the senior of Little Stevie Wonder). If there was something faintly ridiculous about 20-year-old Mick Jagger wading into the territory of full-grown bluesmen such as Muddy Waters and Howlin' Wolf, then the barely 17-year-old David Jones was an even less convincing messenger from the Deep South. Like thousands of his peers, however, the man who had yet to christen himself David Bowie soaked himself in righteous rhythm and blues, soul and gospel, black by affiliation if unmistakably paleface in appearance.

He began 1964 in a blues duo with his friend George Underwood, the Hooker Brothers, before the two teenagers formed a five-piece R&B band, the King Bees (named after a Slim Harpo tune that was already in the Rolling Stones' repertoire). He knew that the Beatles' success had been masterminded by the manager of a Liverpool music shop, Brian Epstein; and his agency contacts told him that no entrepreneur in London was sharper and more successful* than the Rolls-Colston

---

* Though not for long: his company went into voluntary liquidation in July 1964.

tycoon, John Bloom. So Bowie sold himself as a good investment to Bloom, an approach so cheeky that, rather than discarding the boy's letter, Bloom passed it to show-business manager Leslie Conn. After a year in which the Beatles and their ilk had rewritten the rules of the London music industry, no self-respecting impresario could afford to ignore an aspiring set of moptops. Conn realised the appeal of the singer he described (exaggerating by an inch or two) as 'a handsome six-footer with a warm and engaging personality', and Bowie's persistence was repaid when the King Bees were offered a bottom-level recording contract with the ugly duckling of the Decca Group of Companies, Vocalion Records. Though the group was ostensibly a collective, 'Davie Jones' was picked out for special billing.

Although Conn announced that Davie Jones had 'all it takes to get to the show business heights', the King Bees' single, 'Liza Jane' [A2], was lost amongst more convincing releases. Two months later, Conn introduced Bowie to the more proficient Manish Boys, who initially struggled to secure a record contract. David had been asked to leave his advertising job, having slept at his desk once too often. But his basic knowledge of branding, his father's PR connections, and Conn's unashamed gift for hype delivered a publicity coup. The specifics were Bowie's invention; John Jones then persuaded journalist Leslie Thomas (author of *The Virgin Soldiers*, the movie of which would later feature a momentary appearance from Bowie) to fashion them into a story for the *London Evening News*.

The pitch was simple. Teenager David Jones from Bromley was so tired of being insulted because he wore long hair that he had formed the International League for the Preservation of Animal Filament. (A week later it was the Society for the Prevention of Cruelty to Long-Haired Men.) 'Anyone who has the courage to wear hair down to his shoulders has to go through hell,' announced Jones with the conviction of a man who had recently been assaulted in Maidstone for his effeminate hair. 'Everybody makes jokes about you on a bus, and if you go past navvies digging in the road, it's murder!' The story was picked up by BBC TV's popular magazine show, *Tonight*, and Bowie was duly interviewed alongside fellow members of his society (which was purely an invention).

As a ten-day wonder, the Long-Haired Men crusade satisfied its initial purpose to win Bowie publicity. As an advertising campaign, it lacked a vital ingredient, a physical product to sell: the Manish Boys didn't release a single [A4] for another four months. Yet the hype was instructive: Bowie had learned that by making an outlandish announcement, and risking an image that blurred feminine and masculine, he could command the attention of the media.

The following month, the Manish Boys were included on a brief package tour headlined by the Kinks – whose leader, Ray Davies, belied the jagged aggression of their records with the overt feyness of his demeanour on stage, twisting his wrists coyly and mincing in front of the microphone. It was a studied exercise in camp, the hallmark of which, said cultural commentator Susan Sontag, was 'the spirit of extravagance . . . The androgyne is certainly one of the great images of camp sensibility . . . To camp is a mode of seduction.' Bowie quickly learned to mimic both Davies' arch, self-mocking persona and his idiosyncratic approach to songwriting. His fellow musicians recognised that his personality in front of an audience had altered, without quite understanding how or why.

In April 1965, Bowie auditioned for another R&B-inspired band, the Lower Third; within days of being recruited, he had ousted the existing vocalist and assumed control. The other band members were alarmed to discover, however, that their first record was credited solely to 'Davy Jones'. Next time, they were assured, things would be different. Before then, another spate of rebranding was required. 'Davy Jones' was signed to the Kinks' label, Pye Records, by producer Tony Hatch, who pointed out quite sensibly that there were already two singers of that name in the marketplace: a black American transplanted to Europe, and a Mancunian actor who had starred in *Coronation Street* and enjoyed West End and Broadway success as the Artful Dodger in Lionel Bart's stage musical, *Oliver!*. This was a level of fame beyond anything glimpsed by John Jones' boy, who took the opportunity to offer an alternative trade name, with which he had been toying since the days of the Kon-Rads: David Bowie.*

* The name was inspired by the legendary Wild West character Jim Bowie, creator of the 'Bowie knife'. David would later claim that he had chosen it for its incisive, knife-like qualities, but this was retrospective reasoning; the simple fact was that he had enjoyed Richard Widmark's portrayal of Bowie in the 1960 Western epic, *The Alamo*. In a bid for individuality, he chose to ignore the US pronunciation of the name (*Boo*-ie); he preferred to rhyme the first syllable of his adopted surname with 'mow', and not 'wow', as is commonly assumed.

VI

Every aspect of Bowie's career was now in constant flux. During 1965, he found a new manager – albeit on a low budget – called Ralph Horton. As a favoured son, Bowie knew how to command affection where it was needed, and he began to stay at Horton's home regularly to cement their business relationship. A few months later, Horton told his successor, Kenneth Pitt, that David was 'mixed up', a polite way of suggesting ambiguity in the singer's sexual orientation. By presenting a persona that was at least open to the polymorphous, Bowie was broadening his prospects of acceptance, just as he would with his music.

During 1964 and 1965, Bowie updated his appearance with almost manic regularity. The slicked-back quiff of the Kon-Rads was super-seded in the King Bees by bouffant hair that was an exhibition of the stylist's art – teased, sculpted, blow-dried and waved, and adding several valuable inches to his height. A first hint of the alien was apparent in the early summer of 1964, when alongside the more conventional moptops of his colleagues, Bowie's hair looked as if it had been created by the designers of a 1950s science fiction B-movie, to disguise the unearthly origins of the man with the pointed head. As he prepared to abandon the King Bees for the Manish Boys, his coiffure was reshaped into an exquisite fringe that ran along his eyebrows and down his sculpted cheeks, before falling across his shoulders like a lawn sweeping away from a stately home. For his television defence of the hirsute, his mop was softened and evened to look like a pre-pubescent schoolgirl; but left to grow untroubled by the barber's scissors into the early months of 1965, it arrived at a shaggy rebelliousness that was, probably by design, identical to the image cultivated by the aptly named Pretty Things, the Rolling Stones' primary rivals for media outrage and parental disapproval.

Alongside his new identity as Bowie, he restyled himself in summer 1965 as a mod. His close contemporary and friend Marc Bolan, another client of Leslie Conn who traced an equally erratic course through the 1960s, had identified himself with the self-styled modernist movement since his early teens. The term originally identified a working-class elite of fashion-conscious self-stylists, committed to constant innovation and renewal under the sway of designers from Milan and Paris; by 1965, it had become an attitude and style with a dress code as strict as any

English public school, in which a misplaced jacket button or trouser hem could signal ignominy.

If the Who's Pete Townshend was the unchallenged poet of this exclusive, near-paranoid mentality, Bowie presented himself as its Prince Charming, as if his entire adolescence had been the prelude to the moment when the peacock could unfurl its feathers. He sported dogtooth or tweed, Carnaby Street or King's Road as the month demanded, his jeans or corduroy cut tight to his pipe-like legs.

Bowie's allegiance to the mod community was confirmed by his hair, described quaintly in the *Kentish Times* as a 'long back and sides'. With its pudding-basin fringe and loosely enforced side parting, it looked haphazard at first, as if Peggy Jones had taken a pair of blunt scissors to her wriggling son. But it was simply another badge, an instant symbol of affiliation that placed Bowie squarely into the same camp as London contemporaries such as the Small Faces and the Action.

His stage repertoire with the Lower Third encompassed such unlikely fare as a blues-tinged interpretation of 'Chim-Chim-Cheree', from the children's film *Mary Poppins*; and the 'Mars' theme from Gustav Holst's orchestral suite *The Planets* – which Bowie first heard as the theme to the 1950s TV science fiction series *Quatermass*. Though he was still prepared to offer his mod audience some familiar slices of American soul, much of his act comprised original material. In late 1965, he introduced two songs that, in their autobiographical scope and musical invention, had no obvious precedents in his music: 'The London Boys' [A21], a harrowing slice of Soho life as experienced via teenage naivety, and the gloriously narcissistic 'Can't Help Thinking About Me' [A14]. Within weeks, he was performing with yet another group, the Buzz.

Bowie was a recognisable figure on the London music scene by now, personable, amenable, and unconventionally handsome. He had a handful of supporters in the pop press, who guaranteed him a modicum of regular coverage; he could fill prestigious clubs such as the Marquee, which staged a series of Sunday-afternoon shows under the title *Bowie Showboat*. He was, in mod parlance, a 'face'; but still not yet twenty, he was gaining a reputation as a quality performer who didn't, quite, have star quality. He had recorded for three of Britain's four major record corporations (Philips had yet to bite), without conspicuous success. His songwriting was becoming increasingly inventive, and there were signs that he felt confined by his mod status, as evidenced by his choices of finale for his stage act with the Buzz: either 'You'll Never Walk Alone' or Anthony Newley's 'What Kind Of Fool Am I'. This was decidedly passé material for an avowed modernist. And indeed, by August 1966, he claimed to be composing a stage musical with 'Downtown' composer Tony Hatch, and announced one solid ambition: 'I'd like to get into cabaret, obviously.'

Kenneth Pitt had been introduced to Bowie after one of the *Showboat* performances at the Marquee, and a mutual rapport had been established. Bowie was impressed by Pitt's experience as an agent for stars such as Manfred Mann and Bob Dylan; Pitt was won over by Bowie's idiosyncratic performances and unabashed charm. 'Nobody at that time knew he was gay except for me and Ralph Horton,' Pitt declared later. 'David would have gone to any extreme at that time to avoid it being known.' What's obvious in retrospect was that Bowie was prepared to be whatever anyone who wielded power and influence wanted him to be. When it suited him, any of these identities could be discarded with ease, as a more lucrative prospect entered his horizon. This was the mercurial client whom Pitt agreed to manage in 1966. For the next three and a half years, he would be Bowie's single-minded mentor, introducing the 19-year-old to cultural and social influences that he could never have discovered in Bromley or Beckenham – and reawakening those he had already forgotten.

VII

There must be a hole in a man who gets up on a stage and cries, 'Look at me! Look at me!' I am still a paramount egotist forever watching myself. Why? A kid needs all the attention he can get, all the affection. He works for it. He was born with an engaging little face and nothing more. So he uses his cuteness to get love. The process continues throughout his life, into maturity. He sharpens and hones that ability until it is an art. Acting, when you boil it down, is just a plea for approval, for love.

Anthony Newley, *Daily Express*, 1963

The man with 'a hole' in his personality, the 'paramount egotist', was a star of rare versatility. If Anthony Newley had been American, he would have occupied a place in the Rat Pack pantheon alongside Sammy Davis Jr. The British public, however, tends to distrust performers who exhibit more than one talent; they're seen as pompous, pretentious, arrogant, all adjectives that were thrown at Newley during his lifetime.

Little more than a decade after his death, he is a mostly forgotten figure, often reduced to nothing more than a footnote in the career of a man he never met: David Bowie. This is scant reward for a decade of wild creativity, in which Newley moved like quicksilver from cabaret to film stardom, scored hit records as a teen idol, comedian and crooner, penned two successful musicals, composed some of the most enduring British show tunes of the 1960s, conquered television as an entertainer, comic actor and tragedian, wrote the original theme tune for the James Bond movie *Goldfinger*, starred in *Dr Dolittle*, concocted a best-selling album of political satire with Peter Sellers, married Joan Collins to become part of the nation's highest-profile celebrity couple, and then followed Sinatra to Las Vegas – all this between 1959 and 1969. He invented a new strand of surreal television comedy that paved the way for the Monty Python troupe; mastered song-and-dance and mime; and, in a groundbreaking 1961 drama that mixed comedy with existential protest, tackled a theme that would haunt David Bowie a decade later: the helplessness of the entertainer when faced with the imminent extinction of mankind. He was a true giant of British popular culture, but the solitary mark he has left on the rock generations is that he inspired Bowie to record 'The Laughing Gnome' [A37].

Newley could not muster much enthusiasm for Bowie or his music. 'Never cared for his performances,' he admitted in 1975. 'Sort of unisexless, wouldn't you say?' In later years, Bowie would laugh affectionately when Newley's name was mentioned, like a gangster being reminded of a vintage heist with a tragic flaw. Before 'The Laughing Gnome' re-emerged to embarrass him in 1973, however, he was more prepared to admit to this influence. 'I was Anthony Newley for a year,' he said earlier that year. 'He was once one of the most talented men that England ever produced.' He would consistently ask interviewers if they remembered *The Strange World of Gurney Slade*, a 1959 ATV series that ran to just six half-hour episodes. Its gimmick, startling for the times, was that Newley would find himself stumbling from one inexplicable mishap to the next, while providing all the dialogue as a stream-of-consciousness voiceover – like the bizarre love child of Virginia Woolf and Mr Bean.

Kenneth Pitt remembered the series well, and cemented his bond with Bowie by showing him offcuts from the filming of the 1962 drama *The Small World of Sammy Lee*. Set in a suitably enclosed milieu that barely extended beyond the square mile of Soho, *Sammy Lee* was a virtual one-man showcase for Newley as a strip-club compère with a seamless line in suggestive patter, plenty of self-hatred and a doomed proclivity for owing bookmakers money. Like *Gurney Slade*, it established the distinctive Newley persona: a tragic hero who is incapable of meeting any crisis without a gag. With his deadpan cockney humour and almost annoyingly consistent charm, Newley was the prototype for one of Bowie's standard ways of greeting the media: he would fall naturally into the role of the south London cheeky chappie who insists that you really shouldn't take anything too seriously, darling, otherwise where would we all be?

There were other Newleys who left their mark on Bowie: the exaggerated London barrow-boy vocalist of novelty singles such as 'Strawberry Fair' and 'Pop Goes The Weasel'; the writer of melodramatic, breast-beating West End ballads such as 'Who Can I Turn To?' and 'Once In A Lifetime'; the mime artiste and occasional clown he portrayed in his award-winning musical *Stop The World, I Want To Get Off*; and the star facing humanity's final curtain in the 1961 BBC drama *The Johnny Darling Show*. Most of all, Newley made it possible for David Bowie to embrace his London heritage, in the same way that the Beatles had opened up Liverpool to the world. He was not the only star of the rock 'n' roll era who proudly displayed his roots in the Big Smoke: in fact, there was a brief but proud tradition of entertainers who shifted from rock to show business, including Tommy Steele, Joe Brown and Mike Sarne. What Newley offered, and they didn't, was a sense of a deeper humanity; like Bowie, he inhabited his characters with such precision that it was impossible to distinguish the man from the masks.

Kenneth Pitt's professional involvement with Newley allowed Bowie to reconnect with an artist whose work he had adored when he was 13. Pitt's influence certainly didn't end there: he introduced the young singer to the sumptuous aestheticism of Oscar Wilde and

Aubrey Beardsley; encouraged him to read Christopher Isherwood's stories of life in pre-war Berlin; and invited him to attend West End shows. In Pitt's account, Bowie was constantly altering his image and his obsessions: 'To begin with, he had a scruffy period when he wouldn't change his clothes and my secretary kept telling me how worried she was that he wasn't eating . . . and then we had a Bob Dylan period, when he dressed in black and went all introvert . . . and then he went hippie, like everyone else, wearing beads and bangles . . . and now we were back to Newley, whom he'd been listening to before in 1960 and 1961.'

In London, it was a time of cultural ferment, in which novelty was king. Pitt's expansive knowledge of popular music enabled him to imagine a career for Bowie beyond the apparently ephemeral life-span of a rock singer. In August 1966, so Bowie archivist Kevin Cann discovered, Pitt introduced him to Carl Davis, an American composer and orchestrator who was a decade older than Bowie. Their brief was to compose songs for a short musical film, a task that allowed Bowie to distance himself from the material he was writing. Though he has never discussed his brief collaboration with Davis, it seems to have inspired him to attempt something entirely new: a series of character songs that were deliberately nostalgic (capitalising on the London fad for reviving Edwardian fashion) and theatrical.

This session secured Bowie a rare opportunity to record an album for Decca Records' newly launched vehicle for contemporary pop and easy listening, Deram. It was a sign that his potential extended well beyond the mod audience, for whom singles would have been more appropriate. He would now demonstrate his remarkable ability to separate his life into several discrete parcels, simultaneously inhabiting a variety of contradictory roles. For Deram, he was the miniaturist, creating tiny affectionate portraits of British life, often reaching back into the nation's imagined past. Meanwhile, he and Pitt continued to toy with ambitious plans for cabaret performances and stage musicals. The Buzz had become the latest casualties of his shift in perspective, but rather than gathering a small group of baroque musicians to accompany his latest compositions, he joined forces with an existing London band, the Riot Squad, with whom he began to explore the margins of contemporary rock culture. Having been reminded of Anthony Newley's early-sixties novelty hits, he had also begun to write in a similar vein himself, concocting the notorious 'The Laughing Gnome' [A37] and 'Over The Wall We Go' [A36].

These songs, so Bowie reflected many years later, were 'fumblings about how to bring theatricality to pop music or rock. It stems from the very English thing, the idea of music hall and vaudeville . . . I would probably have gone on to all that, pantomimes, musicals and that sort of thing, if I hadn't been so stubborn and hard-headed about doing something that had to do with art.' At the age of 20, he was prepared to accept success however it came. He clearly sensed that 'art' and 'entertainment' might be mutually contradictory for him, and his magpie enthusiasm for new forms of expression – one minute he claimed to be designing clothes for John Stephen, the next he was planning a film career – ensured that he would rarely concentrate on one method of stimulation for too long. Bowie was learning (and borrowing) from everyone, whether that was Frank Zappa (whose anarchic Mothers Of Invention material he persuaded the Riot Squad to tackle on stage) or Cliff Richard (Britain's most polished pop star, whom Bowie saw in *Cinderella* at the London Palladium). No avenue was closed, no possibility rejected, no style discarded as too crass or embarrassing. Yet there was a wilful streak in this young man that encouraged him to reject Swinging London at the peak of its iconic power; and to subvert opportunities for self-promotion, simply because he could. 'When I wanted David to be extrovert, he wanted to be introvert,' Pitt complained in the mid-seventies. 'When I wanted him to wear beautiful clothes, he wanted to wear dirty clothes. This glamorous creature that comes on with all this make-up was once totally introvert and colourless.'

VIII

The lure of the Swinging Sixties – the myths of Carnaby Street and flower power – both enticed and repelled Bowie. He could recognise the thrill of dressing sharp and loud, of flitting from woman to woman (or man) in search of a momentary thrill, of waving his peacock feathers as a sign that he was alive. Yet like George Harrison of the Beatles, who looked at Carnaby Street and saw only spiritual emptiness, Bowie was racked by the conviction that there must be more.

'As far as I'm concerned the whole idea of Western life – that's the life we live now – is wrong,' he declared in 1966. 'The majority [of people in London] just don't know what life is.'

Before the Beatles inaugurated an era of pop spirituality with their sponsorship of Maharishi Mahesh Yogi, Bowie was staking his allegiance to the mystic East. He was, he proclaimed, a Buddhist who was fascinated by Tibet. 'I'd like to take a holiday and have a look inside the mountains,' the budding cultural tourist said. He also claimed to be fascinated by astrology and reincarnation – anything that would explain and expand his life on the planet. As he admitted, though, 'These are hard convictions to put into songs.' At a formative age, he had read Christmas Humphreys' book *Zen Buddhism*,* a suitably enigmatic account of the spiritual path that vanishes at the moment you begin to glimpse it. Humphreys declared that Zen was 'incommunicable', and then devoted 200 pages to proving himself right, although his failure still offered the stuff of temptation: '[Zen] climbs, with empty hands, from the level of "usual life" to the heights of spiritual awareness. The effort is terrific; the results are commensurate.' For a creative person like Bowie, who was conscious of the fleeting moment of creation and the distraction of goals, Humphreys' conception of Zen must have sounded both familiar and bewitching: 'Zen is not a new thing but a new way of looking at things. It is a new vision with the old eyes.'

The Beatles had the advantage of being able to immerse themselves in the spirit of the East with only self-imposed distractions. Bowie, by contrast, was scratching for a living, searching for acceptance, struggling to remain immune from his past. On 22 February 1967, he accompanied his brother Terry to a concert by the overpoweringly loud rock band Cream. As they walked home afterwards, the increasingly disturbed Terry fell to the ground in terror, convinced that the earth was opening up beneath his feet in flames. The chronology is uncertain, but around this time Bowie's brother had returned to London after several months, expecting to live with his aunt Pat – only to discover that she and her husband had emigrated to Australia without telling him. Scarred by the apparent rejection, he is said to have run away to Chislehurst Caves in Kent (Bowie and the Buzz

---

* Van Morrison would later acknowledge the same influence, in his song 'Cleaning Windows'.

had performed there the previous year), where he was discovered in a state of profound emotional dislocation, and escorted back to the Jones household by the police. Henceforth he would spend his weekends with his mother and stepfather, and then stay in a mental hospital between Monday and Friday.

It's clearly not a coincidence that Bowie now began to spend as much time as he could at Kenneth Pitt's London flat, becoming a full-time resident in June 1967. Terry had once been his family protector and spiritual guide; perhaps it had simply become too uncomfortable for David to witness his brother's disintegration; perhaps the Jones house in Plaistow Grove, Beckenham, was now too cramped for creative endeavour; perhaps Bowie simply needed to be closer to London's media and artistic milieu. Whatever the rationale, the two men's relationship gradually faded away, even if the memory of what Terry had been, and what he had become, continued to shape Bowie's mental landscape for many years to come.

'One puts oneself through such psychological damage in trying to avoid the threat of insanity,' he told the BBC in 1993. 'You start to approach the very thing you're scared of.' To alleviate this pressure, Bowie depended on his creativity: 'I felt that I was the lucky one [in the family] because I was an artist, and it would never happen to me. As long as I could put those psychological excesses into my music and into my work, I could always be throwing it off.' During the remainder of the sixties, and for much of the seventies, he pursued a ferocious working schedule, as if constant exertion – the flood of songs, film treatments, scripts and artworks that he produced, even when he was supposed to be resting between tours – would keep madness at bay. Creative output also blocked another avenue of negativity: 'I was convinced I wasn't worth very much. I had enormous self-image problems, and very low self-esteem, which I hid behind obsessive writing and performing. I was driven to get through life very quickly. I thought I didn't need to exist. I really felt so utterly inadequate. I thought the work was the only thing of value.'

His lack of self-esteem must have been reinforced when *David Bowie* – the album, and its attendant image – was launched, to a minimal response from the public. It had the misfortune of being released on the same day as the Beatles' epochal *Sgt. Pepper* album, but Bowie and Pitt's loyal supporters in the media ensured that it did at least receive a modicum of press coverage. 'David Bowie has no great voice,' one review stated, but 'he can project words with a cheeky "side" that is endearing yet not precocious', while his work was 'full of abstract fascination'. In an apt summary of Bowie's current situation, the journalist suggested that he could 'make quite a noise on the scene if he gets the breaks and the right singles'. Prestigious though his album was, it effectively suffocated his career. Until a month before its release, he was still performing with the Riot Squad, incorporating a psychedelic lights show, surreal sound effects and garish make-up into his act. The *David Bowie* LP bore no relation to this persona, and few of its songs could be performed without orchestral musicians. Bowie and the Riot Squad parted company in May, with the bizarre result that he celebrated the release of his album by not performing a conventional 'pop' gig for the next 14 months. Any momentum created by his years of performances at venues such as the Marquee was lost.

Instead, Pitt encouraged Bowie to look beyond the vicissitudes of the pop charts for more enduring success – a far-sighted view that would reward the singer, if not his new manager. His publisher, David Platz, urged him to pen English lyrics for songs from Israel and France, the most notable of which would provide the biggest hit of Frank Sinatra's career – though not, sadly, utilising Bowie's translation [A50]. He also continued to write deliberately commercial pop songs ('top ten rubbish', he called them, though none came remotely close to achieving that status) in the hope of attracting other artists.

Meanwhile, Bowie won the starring role in a short silent film entitled *The Image*, filmed in September 1967. Written and directed by Michael Armstrong, it was ostensibly a tale of obsession in the vein of Henry James' 'The Story Of A Masterpiece', though it carried a subtext of homosexual self-loathing so obvious that perhaps its creator was blind to its implications. An artist has painted a portrait of a mysterious young man, and then finds the incarnation of his picture at his door. He is so unnerved by this apparition that he kills the youth, only for him to reappear continually in his house. The haunted artist then destroys his painting, and immediately drops dead. Bowie's role required nothing more demanding than a fixed expression and the ability to tumble down a few stairs. But he achieved this with sufficient panache for Armstrong to offer him the lead role in a screenplay based around Offenbach's opera *Orpheus in the Under-world*, which updated the plot by centring it on a pop singer who is torn apart by his fans – an uncanny precursor of the Ziggy Stardust myth five years later.*

'I want to act,' Bowie had announced in 1966. 'I'd like to do character parts. I think it takes a lot to become somebody else.' His subsequent career as an actor, certainly until the early eighties, merely demonstrated the truth of what he was saying, as he found it difficult to escape a sense of self-consciousness that left the audience constantly aware that they were watching David Bowie rather than a fictional character. Yet in his music, he found it natural to 'un-become' himself, or at least offer an array of different aspects to his personality.

IX

Two other routes to that 'un-becoming' were available to him in late 1967. Neither promised financial reward: despite Pitt's moral and monetary support, Bowie was forced to take part-time jobs just weeks after his album was released, as a cleaner and an assistant in a West End photocopy shop.† Hence the attraction of escape, which led him to explore the possibility of becoming a Buddhist monk. He had befriended an American record producer, Tony Visconti, who introduced him to the guru Chimi Youngdong Rimpoche at the Tibet Society in Hampstead. By the end of the year, he and Visconti were at the Samye Ling Tibetan Centre in Scotland. 'I was a terribly earnest Buddhist at the time,' he admitted in 1969. 'I had stayed in their monastery and was going through all their exams, and yet I had this feeling that it wasn't right for me. I suddenly realised how close it all was: another month and my head would have been shaved.'

---

* The British Board of Film Censors effectively sabotaged the project by informing Armstrong that the screenplay's homoerotic ambience made it impossible to film within the existing censorship laws.

† Typically, Bowie was able to create mythology out of this depressing interlude. In 1975, he recalled: 'I used to work for two guys [presumably in the copy shop] who put out a UFO magazine in England. And I made sightings six, seven times a night for about a year, when I was in the observatory. We never used to tell anybody.' A few seconds later, he talked about 'media control . . . It's just so easy to do.' Indeed, he could have lectured on the subject.

He embellished the story for William Burroughs in 1973: 'About two weeks before I was actually going to take those steps, I broke up and went out on the street and got drunk and never looked back.' What had he learned from this episode? 'To try and make each moment of one's life one of the happiest, and if it's not, try to find out why.' It was an admirable philosophy, though not one that he would be able to follow in the years ahead.

'I decided that as I wasn't happy,' he claimed in 1969, 'I would get right away from it all. I vanished completely for a year. No one knew where I was.' He certainly wasn't at the heart of London's youth culture, at the UFO Club or at Middle Earth; neither was he visible in Grosvenor Square, protesting against US involvement in Vietnam, or joining the hippy campaigns against the repressive drug laws, or supporting black power, or lining up in the student revolts, fired into action by the tear gas on the streets of Paris, Berlin or London. At the moment when many of his generation regarded their youthfulness as a revolutionary act, and their political activism as a basic function of being alive, he was absent, apparently uninterested, definitely uninvolved.

So determined was Bowie to remain silent, in fact, that he began to experiment with a medium in which he would not be allowed to use his voice. In July 1967, he was introduced to dancer and mime artiste Lindsay Kemp, who was using Bowie's album as interval music for a London show entitled *Clowns Hour*. Besides his classical training and innate physical skill, Kemp was powered by a fearless drive to confront his audience and destroy their inhibitions – which led to his being branded 'lewd and obscene' and banned from performing in various parts of Europe. While Buddhism offered Bowie freedom from desire and ambition, Kemp was able to dangle the more enticing prospect of liberation from dread and self-restraint. Although other artists, from Mick Jagger to Andy Warhol, may have left a more recognisable mark on Bowie's career, it was Kemp who allowed him to recognise his scattered selves and let them loose upon the world.

'I knew we shared a common joy,' Kemp remembered. 'I said, "We have to be together, we have to have a child between us." It was like Isadora Duncan when she first saw Nijinsky. It wasn't just because I wanted to screw him, although I must say that was at the back of my mind.' 'He lived on his emotions,' Bowie noted, 'he was a wonderful influence. His day-to-day life was the most theatrical thing I had seen, ever. It was everything I thought Bohemia probably was.'

Kemp introduced Bowie to the discipline of mime, its code, its emblematic characters, such as Columbine, Pierrot and Scaramouche. 'Lindsay Kemp was a living Pierrot,' Bowie recalled. 'He lived and talked Pierrot. The stage thing for him was just an extension of himself.' Some of Kemp's literary influences, such as Wilde and Joyce, were familiar to Bowie from Kenneth Pitt's bookshelves; others, notably the French novelist and playwright Jean Genet, were a revelation. Bolstered by fame several years later, Bowie would intervene to settle an artistic quarrel between Kemp and Genet; in 1967, he was simply entranced by Genet's celebration of transgression in his rococo descriptions of thievery, male prostitution and suicidal despair. '[Genet] has come', said critic David Mairowitz in 1966, 'out of his private erotic cave to say "shit" to "our" world' – which was exactly the spirit that Kemp admired, and that Bowie could not help but ingest.

Three months after their first meeting, Bowie joined Kemp and his partner Jack Birkett in *Pierrot in Turquoise* at the Oxford Playhouse. While Kemp and Birkett acted out a scenario of erotic infatuation that was heightened by Kemp's passion for his new recruit, Bowie played the aptly vague role of Cloud, which required him to perform songs from his LP, and flit ethereally across the stage, demonstrating the bare minimum of mime expertise. 'I enabled him to free the angel and demon that he is on the inside,' Kemp reflected many years later. That perhaps explained why Kemp essayed a token slash at his wrists with a knife during a subsequent engagement at an arts centre in Lancashire, taking to the stage that evening bandaged and with bruised ego because he had discovered Bowie in intimate congress with the troupe's costumier, Natasha Korniloff.

Bowie channelled what he had learned from Kemp into a brief but compelling reincarnation as a solo mime artiste at several 1968 rock concerts. He had written a short sketch entitled 'The Mask', in which – symbolically, in the light of his own shifts of identity – a performer becomes so closely attached to a stage disguise that his public can no longer distinguish man from mask. The piece ends with the performer being strangled by the mask, a symbolic fate that haunted Bowie for much of the seventies as his various images threatened to overshadow his own fragile identity. His most ambitious venture into mime also betrayed his interest in Tibetan Buddhism. 'Jetsun and the Eagle' was a twelve-minute performance (a lifetime for a solo mime artiste in front of a rock audience) inspired by the Chinese Communist 'rape' of Tibet, prompting outraged dissent from Marxist traditionalists .in the stalls.

The combination of Buddhist transcendence and Kemp's raw connection with emotion plainly unlocked Bowie's creativity in late 1967 and early 1968. Besides a steady output of songs, many of which remain unheard to this day, he wrote the script for a radio play entitled *The Champion Flower Grower*, which was rejected by the BBC; and also composed the skeleton of a rock opera, *Ernie Johnson* [A51], about a suicide party. Yet this was not the stuff of financial success, a dream that Pitt – and Bowie, when he was in Pitt's presence – continued to pursue. The two men prepared a tentative track listing for a second album, centred once more around character-based vignettes, despite knowing that Decca's enthusiasm for Bowie had dimmed markedly. Meanwhile, the singer maintained at least the veneer of enthusiasm for a significant rebranding of his career, which would involve abandoning all the trappings of rock in favour of a hip, upwardly mobile and effervescently young approach to cabaret.

Would the David Bowie whose mind and body were being schooled by Lindsay Kemp, or the David Bowie who dreamed of suicide parties, really have been content to package himself as Carnaby Street's rival to Andy Williams? The truth is that Bowie was prepared to follow any path that seemed to offer him a destination.

Indeed, rather than offering the public one solid, unmistakable product, the Bowie of 1968 was a veritable supermarket of fleeting passions and wild fancies. Recognising that the most efficient way of capturing this mercurial talent might be to commission a TV special called something like *The Many Faces Of David Bowie*, Kenneth Pitt began to test enthusiasm in the television industry for a showcase that would sell his star-in-the-making. To be comprehensive, such a project would need to offer a dozen different Bowies: the Anthony Newley imitator, the soul/blues mod, the Kinks-inspired commentator on contemporary life, the avant-garde rock experimentalist, the crooner, the Edwardian revivalist, the purveyor of children's and novelty tunes, the composer of boutique pop songs, the mime artiste, the actor, the folk musician and the co-star of a Simon & Garfunkel tribute act.

These final two identities both emerged late in 1968, as Bowie, his girlfriend Hermione Farthingale and guitarist/vocalist Tony Hill (swiftly replaced by John Hutchinson) formed a trio called Turquoise, in honour of Kemp's *Pierrot in Turquoise*. Their original intention was to merge folk in the Peter, Paul and Mary tradition (square, in other words, but with the faint air of hipness) with poetry and mime, in the spirit of counter-culture poetry/music clubs across the country. Within a couple of weeks, Turquoise became Feathers, their repertoire stretching from Bowie originals to songs by the Belgian composer Jacques Brel, the Canadian poet Leonard Cohen and the Byrds.

Feathers survived for less than four months, but events during their brief lifespan established Bowie's direction for the decade ahead. At a September 1968 show at the Roundhouse in London, they were watched by a young American called Mary Angela 'Angie' Barnett, who briefly met Bowie after the performance. Accompanying Barnett was Calvin Mark Lee, shortly to join the staff of Mercury Records, whose enthusiasm for Bowie's music (and appearance) would prove to be crucial for the singer's immediate career.

Meanwhile, Pitt's energetic pursuit of Bowie's TV showcase had ended in failure, so he opted to pursue a lower-budget effort himself. Under the working title of *The David Bowie Show*, it limited Bowie's 'faces' by excluding his more experimental leanings and concentrating on material he had already recorded for Deram. Feathers appeared in several of the brief segments that made up the programme, while Bowie also offered his well-practised mime routine. Pitt encouraged him to compose one additional song in a contemporary vein, perhaps to bolster his client's enthusiasm for this strangely retrospective project. Bowie began to explore a scenario based loosely on America's attempts to land a man on the Moon.

Gradually, Bowie's options were narrowing. Late in the filming, his relationship with Farthingale disintegrated, instantly reducing Feathers to the Simon & Garfunkel-inspired duo of Bowie & Hutchinson. His efforts to secure a major role in the British war comedy *The Virgin Soldiers* had ended in rejection, though the director let him appear on screen for a handful of frames as an anonymous extra. Lindsay Kemp was launching a new mime vehicle solely for himself and his boyfriend,

Jack Birkett. Established stars were showing a marked reluctance to cover Bowie's songs, despite all efforts by his publishers to promote him as the British equivalent of Burt Bacharach. Pitt's cabaret schemes had been sunk by a lack of enthusiasm from entrepreneurs and singer alike. Of the dozen Bowie 'faces' available to Pitt as *The David Bowie Show* was hatched, only the duo with Hutchinson seemed to carry any significant commercial promise. Pitt, however, had reckoned without the power of the song that Bowie had penned specifically for the show: 'Space Oddity' [1].

The Songs of
David Bowie: 1969–1980

[1] SPACE ODDITY (Bowie) [see also 177]

Initially recorded February 1969; *Love You Till Tuesday* film. Demo recorded
March 1969; *David Bowie (Deluxe Edition)* CD. Re-recorded June 1969; single
A-side. Italian vocals overdubbed December 1969; Italian single A-side.

'Imagine the 1990 version of *All Our Yesterdays** with "Space Oddity"
being used in the way they use "Roll Out The Barrel" in documen-
taries about the First World War now,' David Bowie exclaimed on
the eve of mankind's first steps on the Moon. 'What a groove!' He
was being unduly cautious: the BBC first broadcast 'Space Oddity'
during its television coverage of the Moon landing on 20 July 1969. 'I
want it to be the first anthem of the Moon,' Bowie had said, 'play it
as they hoist the flag, and all that.' In the same interview, he offered
a less idealistic view: 'I suppose it's an antidote to space fever, really.'

Thanks in part to the revisionists who insist that the Moon landing
was faked, that 'space fever' has barely survived forty years of damp-
ened expectations, though the event itself retains its iconic significance.
In January 1967, author John Michell (who was convinced that the
Age of Aquarius would be marked by visits from flying saucers) wrote
impatiently: 'Some event is awaited which will inspire us with a new
ideal and open our minds to a further realization of our potential.
What form this event will take is impossible to say, for it will involve
us in experiences and visions for which we lack any precedent and
cannot therefore express in language or even in thought.' So staggering to the mind was the concept that humans could walk on the
surface of a dead planet 250,000 miles away that the successful mission
of Armstrong, Aldrin and Collins in July 1969 was widely greeted as

---

* *All Our Yesterdays* was an ITV series that ran from 1960 to 1973, comprising nostalgic
excerpts of 25-year-old newsreel footage.

our species' single greatest achievement. Yet this was not a bloodless triumph: a few days after Michell had dreamed of the unprecedented, the initial Apollo crew of three had been burned to death inside a space capsule on the launch pad in Florida.

'If we die, we want people to accept it,' said one of those astronauts in 1965. 'We are in a risky business and we hope that if anything happens to us it will not delay the program. The conquest of space is worth the risk of life.' Had he lived, Gus Grissom might have revised his opinion. The ultimate tragedy of the Apollo programme was that space was conquered, but proved to be a cul-de-sac. Despite the initial glory of *Apollo 11*, and the near-disaster of *Apollo 13*, manned trips to the Moon failed to hold the American imagination, or – amidst a global recession – justify the staggering expense. After *Apollo 17* returned safely in December 1972, further missions were cancelled. Physically and psychologically, the programme led nowhere; yet it had achieved its seldom-voiced objective, of demonstrating to the world that Western democracy could outstrip the repressive utopianism of Soviet Russia, which had pledged to beat America to the lunar surface.

Within months of the *Apollo 11* landing, there were reports that American scientists were investigating whether a nuclear bomb could be exploded on the Moon, and the seismic results studied, as a means of determining the planet's make-up. True or not, the story reinforced the mistrust felt by many in the Western counter-culture about this triumph of the capitalist will. Just before *Apollo 11* was launched, underground journalist Alex Gross complained: 'the people running the space programme have jumped into something so big that not even they are able to cope with it psychologically, they haven't a clue what the effects of landing on the Moon will be . . . [They] are in utter and absolute awe before the enormity of space and the challenge it presents to all earthbound preconceptions.' Assigned to cover Apollo for *Life* magazine, American novelist Norman Mailer noted how all metaphysical concerns about the mission were masked in scientific sterility designed to excise emotion from the quest. 'The publicity image of a spaceman at work is of an automaton rather than a human being,' David Bowie said in July 1969. 'My Major Tom is nothing if not a human being.' As such, he was as much an outsider as Bowie had been from the hedonistic optimism of late-sixties pop culture, a distance he had already declared in songs such as 'The London Boys' [A21] and 'Join The Gang' [A27].

'It's only a pop song, after all,' Bowie said dismissively of 'Space Oddity' in November 1969, but it signalled his immunity to 'space fever', and in a wider sense his alienation from the collective fantasy – over- and underground – that mankind was embarked on a voyage towards progress and enlightenment. Greeting the dawn of 1969, the London underground newspaper *IT* had wondered: 'The question for us now is whether we can make as much progress inside our own heads and the heads of our friends to lay the foundations for an intergalactic life more meaningful than our present earthbound condition.' Bowie's answer in 'Space Oddity' (written shortly after that editorial appeared in a paper that he read avidly) was that life on the Moon, or en route to the stars, was just as hollow as it was at home. At the moment when mankind had transcended its 'present earthbound condition', Bowie was already inhabiting the world of the future decade, in which space travel would be a desperately expensive and ultimately anachronistic irrelevance.

The 'Space Oddity' scenario of an astronaut marooned in space was commonplace in science fiction: three of the tales in Ray Bradbury's collection *The Illustrated Man*, already an influence on Bowie's 'Karma Man' [A48], explored variations on this theme. It was cemented in the mind of Bowie's generation by Stanley Kubrick's film, *2001: A Space Odyssey*, the clear source for the song's title.* In *2001*, space voyagers were threatened and betrayed by their ship's computer, 'Hal'. Bowie has always described the film as the primary influence on 'Space Oddity': 'I related to the sense of isolation,' he explained. A less celebrated inspiration may have been a BBC TV drama entitled *Beach Head*, broadcast as the song was being written, which portrayed the unrelenting ennui of a space pilot, thus anticipating the alienation that haunts 'Major Tom'. In either case, the scenario represented a central theme of the existential literature – Camus, Sartre, Genet – that Bowie had devoured in recent years: an individual's alienation from society, and from himself. Like the astronauts on the Moon, Major Tom could look back at Earth and reflect on its perilous, insignificant place in the heavens.

* The American rock band the Byrds pre-empted Kubrick by several months with their own 'Space Odyssey'; they later recorded a tribute to the *Apollo 11* astronauts.

Bowie's alienation from his career, which had apparently stalled in the summer of 1968, had exhausted his previously prolific output of songs. Now facing a TV special for which there was no guaranteed audience, and which was based around material he'd written more than a year earlier, he was encouraged by his manager, Kenneth Pitt, to pen 'a very special piece of material that would dramatically demonstrate David's remarkable inventiveness and would probably be the high spot of the production'. The TV special's director, Malcolm Thomson, claimed that he and his girlfriend Susie Mercer contributed ideas to the song-writing process; likewise Bowie's musical partner John Hutchinson took credit for refining the structure of the song. Meanwhile, Marc Bolan – himself an inveterate magpie – insisted that 'I wrote part of "Space Oddity", and it was me who suggested that he sang the song like the Bee Gees.' '"Space Oddity" was a Bee Gees type song,' Hutchinson agreed. 'David knew it, and he said so at the time.' Though there were vague similarities to the structure of the Bee Gees' first hit, 'New York Mining Disaster 1941', the comparison owed more to the haunting atmosphere of both songs, in which minor chords were left to hover at the end of the opening lines, leaving the listener uncertain where they might touch down.* The 'Space Oddity' chords may have been determined by Hutchinson, as Bowie originally conceived the melody using a Stylophone, a newly marketed electronic keyboard aimed at (affluent) children. Its unmistakable buzz was a striking feature on the final record.

Hutchinson's contribution was apparent from the floating Fmaj7[†] that opened the song, portraying the astronaut adrift in space. He must surely have suggested the almost ethereal sequence of 'ninth' chords that portrayed the spaceman hanging free, setting up the final verse in which the spaceship had taken control of its occupant. This interlude, filled on the record by a Mick Wayne guitar solo that seemed to be testing out the walls of Major Tom's prison, was introduced by a dramatic quartet of 'barre' chords.[‡] They were reminiscent of similar

---

* Compare also the construction of Simon & Garfunkel's 'Save The Life Of My Child' on the *Bookends* album, which Bowie studied closely in 1968.
† This chord recurred on other songs Bowie wrote during their collaboration, then vanished from his repertoire.
‡ The C chord that established the key was played higher up the guitar neck than its companions, despite occupying a lower place on the scale.

motifs used in Jimmy Webb's songwriting during 1967/68, notably on the Fifth Dimension's 'Carpet Man', one of the period's more extravagant pop productions. Throughout, Paul Buckmaster's string arrangement cast an eerie shadow: it evoked the unsettling modernist music written in Vienna in the early years of the century, against the softer and more conventionally melodic 'string' parts contributed by Rick Wakeman's Mellotron.

The lyrical content of the song was a more authentic reflection of its creator, especially when Bowie spotlighted the power of the media and the advertising industry to reach out into space and demand to own a stake in a man who was exiled from the rest of humanity. There was a cheeky reference to another study of aliena-tion, as Bowie borrowed the musical ascent from the Beatles' 'A Day In The Life'. And note also the strange vocabulary of the radio transmissions between Earth and space – Ground Control instead of Mission Control, 'engines on' for 'ignition', and the unmilitary combination of rank (Major) and first name (Tom). But then Bowie never claimed that 'Space Oddity' was anything other than a fiction, in which orthodoxy didn't apply.

Between February 1969, when the song was taped for the *Love You Till Tuesday* film, and June, when the single was recorded, 'Space Oddity' underwent one crucial change. In February, and on the subsequent demo session, it was a duet performance by Bowie and Hutchinson – a dialogue, effectively, with Hutchinson on the ground (supported by Bowie's high unison or harmony) and Bowie in space. Ninety seconds passed before Major Tom answered Ground Control's urgent enquiries, and Bowie's voice was heard in eerie solitude.

A month later, the act known as 'David Bowie + Hutch' made a demo tape of ten songs:* though eight of the ten were written by Bowie, the intention was clearly to market them as a duo, mirroring Simon & Garfunkel in the distinction between songwriter (Bowie/

---

* All Bowie biographers agree that this artefact was taped in the Mercury Records office, and was aimed at the record company's executives. But internal evidence leads me to believe that it was recorded at Bowie's home, for the ears of Bob Harris, the future BBC disc jockey then working for the London listings magazine *Time Out*. Harris had secured prestigious London gigs for Turquoise the previous year, and continued to promote Bowie's cause throughout 1969.

Simon) and arranger (Hutchinson/Garfunkel). Only when financial problems forced Hutchinson to leave London around April 1969 did David Bowie become, once more, a solo act, in time to sign a deal with Philips/Mercury Records in June. There he recorded this remarkably accomplished song in a voice coloured by his respect for the work of John Lennon; and later, under request from the company's Italian office, struggled manfully with the demands of a translation in that language, only discovering after the event that his rewritten words had nothing to do with space (or oddities) at all. Separating those two recording sessions was a long period of frustration, in which 'Space Oddity' was deemed to be too controversial for prime-time radio airplay when flesh-and-blood astronauts were risking their lives; and then, finally, commercial acceptance, the dream that Bowie had been pursuing since 1963. Although America remained immune to the single's charms until 1972, British sales took the record to no. 5 in the national chart. Only then did Bowie discover that success did not guarantee satisfaction or self-esteem.

Sound and Vision #1: *Love You Till Tuesday*

Filmed January/February 1969;
unseen until home-video release, 1984.

The David Bowie on display in his 1969 TV special – titled after a single that had flopped nearly two years earlier – was a chirpy, camp, sometimes sensitive clothes-horse from Carnaby Street who resembled no one on the pop scene more than Peter Noone of Herman's Hermits. He was a passable mime, an unlikely rock 'n' roller (as he proved when mimicking Elvis Presley's pelvis-thrusting as he lip-synced to 'Let Me Sleep Beside You' [A47]) and a rather clumsy actor, trying his best to sell songs he had long since outgrown. So deadening and coy was the overall effect, in fact, that even the debut of 'Space Oddity' [1] must have made little impression on the hapless TV executives who received copies of this low-budget showcase. So it is not at all surprising that, despite issuing excited press releases about the prospect of a screening in Germany, Kenneth Pitt was unable to secure any interest in *Love You Till Tuesday* during 1969. Instead, he retained the reels and the copyright, and the special received a belated premiere on video cassette in 1984, when Bowie's career was altogether more secure.

Above all else, the TV special demonstrated that neither Bowie nor Pitt knew what to do next, or which version of Bowie they were trying to market. The inclusion of several clips featuring the members of Feathers – who broke up as the filming concluded – simply clouded the issue. In retrospect, the collapse of Bowie's relationship with Hermione Farthingale was a pivotal moment in his career. It freed him to work as a duo with John Hutchinson, who helped to widen his musical vocabulary; and it also provided him with a sharp emotional focus, reflected in the songs that poured out of him over the next few weeks. 'With a guitar and memories of Hermione on my back, I thumbed through my mind and got involved with writing,' Bowie told disc jockey John Peel. 'I have walked through no less than fifteen songs in two weeks and some of them were very bad.' Meanwhile, there was one quantifiable benefit from the TV special: without it, he would probably never have written 'Space Oddity' – a song that was perfectly timed to capture the imagination of a record company.

Before then, Bowie the mime artiste was added to the bill of a short tour starring Tyrannosaurus Rex, the cult hippy duo fronted by his friend Marc Bolan. One reviewer noted that Bowie 'was convincing in his act as an old man carried into the world of fantasy by smoking a fragment of "pot", also as a man who eventually becomes famous by donning a mask which eventually sticks to his face'. But mime would never make Bowie famous; the songs that he wrote in the spring of 1969 held more promise.

[2] JANINE (Bowie)

Demo recorded March 1969; unreleased. Re-recorded July 1969; *David Bowie [Space Oddity]* LP.

'Janine', Bowie announced on his 1969 demo tape, 'is named after a girl who I met once and is the girlfriend of a guy called George [Underwood], who does very nice album covers'. Less charitably, he added later: 'It's how I *thought* he should see her.' Yet the character of 'Janine' was virtually absent from the song; the focus was on the narrator, whose deliberately obtuse* use of language helped to isolate him from his lover. Bowie may have been using the disguise of his friend to explore facets of his own psyche that he was unwilling to confront. Certainly, as an artist who set out to blur his own identity (Jones? Bowie? Ziggy Stardust?), it was telling that he chose to investigate that theme so openly: if Janine murdered the narrator, it would be someone else who died, he declared, not him.

This psychological complexity was strangely at odds with the playful exuberance of the music, Bowie and Hutchinson ending the demo with the wordless chorus from the Beatles' 'Hey Jude',† and Bowie drifting into an impression of Elvis Presley on the record. The latter was wonderfully chaotic, like a herd of buffalo careering through the studio, with Mick Wayne's electric guitar cutting across the Dylan-esque acoustic guitar changes that rooted the song,‡ while Bowie plucked haphazardly at an African thumb piano. Almost shouting a high harmony behind his chorus vocal, Bowie stretched himself to an A beyond his normal range.

[3] An Occasional Dream (Bowie)

Demo recorded March 1969; unreleased. Re-recorded July 1969; *David Bowie [Space Oddity]* LP.

Nothing in the 'David Bowie + Hutch' repertoire recalled the music of Simon & Garfunkel more than their demo recording of this melancholy reflection on a love affair, which ended with an arpeggio chord that demanded to lead into Simon's 'The Sound Of Silence'. Hutchinson's blueprint was followed exactly in the studio, suggesting that guitarist

---

* For example, Bowie used 'collocate' instead of 'organise', for no apparent reason except to show off his vocabulary; coincidentally, or not, T.S. Eliot had talked of 'collocation' in the notes to *The Waste Land*. Another obscure reference may have been sparked by the death of the Polish 'outsider' artist Nikifor in October 1968.

† Bowie briefly intended to re-record 'Janine' as a follow-up single to 'Space Oddity' [1], incorporating parts of another Beatles song, 'Love Me Do' – which he later added to 'The Jean Genie' [65] in his 1973 concert repertoire. 'Janine' could certainly have been retooled for the Ziggy era with only a modicum of effort.

‡ The unexpected surge into an E major chord at the start of the verse's second line added a macho defiance to an already abrasive lyric.

Keith Christmas – a singer-songwriter whom Bowie perhaps envisaged as Hutch's successor – had listened attentively to the demo. It was a subtle, flowing arrangement, with unexpected shifts of key and mood, and discreet application of woodwinds, but elegantly constructed (in a way that much of Bowie's earlier material was not) to allow smooth transition between otherwise dissonant elements. Trapped in the circularity of the chorus, the melody soared only when Bowie recalled the fantasy that gave the song its name, and as it escaped its shackles in the final movement, his voice conjured an eerie anticipation of the man who would croon 'Wild Is The Wind' [131].

So personal was the lyrical landscape of the song, with its talk of a 'Swedish room',* that the inspiration can only have been the collapse of Bowie's relationship with Hermione Farthingale in February 1969, recalled with almost manic obsession. He couldn't bear to 'touch your name', he insisted, though by the time his album was completed in September, he was prepared to use it openly in a song title [5].

[4] CONVERSATION PIECE (Bowie)

Demo recorded March 1969; unreleased. Re-recorded August/September 1969; single B-side.

Intended until late in the day for the 1969 *David Bowie* album, 'Conversation Piece'† might have tilted the record too pointedly towards the melancholy folk rock of his post-Hermione self-pity. It had the tightly restrictive melodic range of a French *chanson*, a modulation introduced only to shake off the air of gloom, and an ending that neatly embraced both prevailing keys. Oboe added decoration to what would otherwise have been a maudlin tune, and on the single occasion when the instrument ran off its country-tinged rails into an accidental discord (just after Bowie sang 'so rudely'), it was masked by the subtle use of strings – a combination that led the ear to believe it was hearing a steel guitar.

---

* This cannot help but recall the romantic bathos of the Beatles' 'Norwegian Wood', though Bowie was referring to the dream of Scandinavian bourgeois comfort marketed today by the IKEA chain.
† The title told its own story: this was a conversation piece, or conceptual artwork; and also nothing more than a 'conversation piece', hardly worth anyone's attention, in the same protest-too-much tradition as 'I'm Not Losing Sleep' [A19].

Two years earlier, Bowie had employed his own mask to distance himself from his characters: he was the storyteller, the entertainer, the Actor (as he would bill himself on *Hunky Dory*). Here, as on 'Space Oddity' [1], where Major Tom's alienation became his own, his characters were infested with his emotions. On his 1967 debut album, 'Conversation Piece' might have been called 'College Clive': the heart-rending tale, ladies and gentlemen, of a young man who read so many books that he could no longer connect with the real world. The 1969 incarnation of David Bowie wallowed in his narrator's narcissistic agony, and the realisation that he could no longer 'read' conversation, on the page or in real life. His voice was a warm, husky purr, but the ghost of Hermione lingered over the track like a Gothic mist.

[5] LETTER TO HERMIONE (AKA I'M NOT QUITE) (Bowie)

Demo recorded March 1969; unreleased. Re-recorded August / September 1969; *David Bowie [Space Oddity]* LP.

The lingering resonance of the 12-string acoustic guitar encourages experimentation with chord shapes not found in the instruction books. Hanging open chords that would sound one-dimensional on a 6-string instrument suddenly assume three-dimensional form on a 12-string. Hutchinson and Bowie's investigations of chord variations lacking a root, by simple dint of lifting a finger from the fretboard, created the lush, appealingly unfulfilled landscape of this study in lost love and emotional transference. The latter turned Bowie's unashamed acknowledgement of his deepest passion into an admission – possibly unconscious, though painfully obvious in retrospect – that his pain had warped his sense of reality.

William Burroughs once described the tape recorder as 'an externalised section of the human nervous system', allowing someone to transfer unpleasant memories from the brain on to an external object, where they could be manipulated into a form that was easier to bear. Bowie later told Burroughs that 'I'm not at ease with the word "love" ... I gave too much of my time and energy to another person, and they did the same to me, and we started burning out against each other.' He was referring, of course, to Hermione Farthingale, the subject of this song, whose loss pervaded so much of his work in 1969. More dramatically, and perhaps more truthfully, Bowie once recalled that being in love 'was an awful experience. It rotted me, drained me, and it was a disease.' But that was a retrospective judgement: when he wrote the song he initially titled 'I'm Not Quite' (itself a telling phrase, in isolation), he was still besotted with her memory. Throughout three beautifully sung verses, he wrapped his feelings around his fantasy of Hermione, in the desperate hope that they might become her own emotional skin. After describing the perfection of her life without him, he wondered if she might, just once, have called out his name, 'just by mistake'. As teachers of Latin grammar would understand, there are some verb forms that anticipate the answer 'no'.

Yet it would require a hard heart not to be touched by the open naivety of this performance – a nakedness that Bowie would not repeat until the *Low* album. His voice grew husky and cracked with tears during the second verse, and unlike his laughter-to-order on 'Love You Till Tuesday' [A39], this time it felt unfeigned. Keith Christmas set harmonics ringing on his guitar, sparkling like raindrops on a sunlit lake. And nothing spoke deeper than the scat vocal that began and ended the song, and which – to judge from their acoustic demo – was a Hutchinson innovation, in the style that David Crosby would soon make his own.

Hermione's memory was rarely far from Bowie's mind during the summer of 1969: chronicler Kevin Cann notes that when he attended the Malta Song Festival in July, he wrote new words for a local folk song, which he titled 'No One Someone', and devoted to a girl who 'loved to walk by the neon-lit fountains . . .' Yet by November, he had mustered sufficient self-protection to boast, 'I've never had any traumas with girls.'

[6] LOVER TO THE DAWN (Bowie)

Demo recorded March 1969; unreleased.

This four-minute acoustic demo captured the gestation of one of Bowie's weightiest compositions, 'Cygnet Committee' [8]. It demonstrated the gulf between the melancholy romanticism of his collaborations with John Hutchinson and the harsh eye of his subsequent solo work; and also shed intriguing light on the balance of creative power in the 'Bowie + Hutch' partnership.

As recorded in spring 1969, and presumably intended for their duo album, 'Lover To The Dawn' introduced the opening theme of 'Cygnet Committee', but only as an intricate instrumental guitar passage, and included almost all of the second section, with its singing sparrow. Rather than entering the mythical terrain of 'Cygnet Committee', it moved through a series of sequences that were lopped from the later song – including a blatant imitation of the 'hey, hey, hey' refrain from Paul Simon's 'Mrs Robinson'. The object of their lament was, inevitably, a young woman maligned as 'bitter' and 'crazy' because she no longer wanted to associate with these perfectly nice young men. The Hermione resonance lived on.

Yet this was far from being a vehicle for Bowie's sadness, in the vein of 'Letter To Hermione' [5]. It was Hutchinson who took centre stage here, with Bowie adding a harmony line that pushed his voice to its upper limits. In this form, it was a rather disjointed, derivative and jaundiced pastoral, taking the Beatles' 'Mother Nature's Son' and the entire *oeuvre* of Donovan as its model. Stripped of most of Hutchinson's decorations, it would soon become something altogether more intimidating.

The demo tapes that 'David Bowie + Hutch' recorded in the early weeks of 1969 also included revivals of the blighted 'Ching-A-Ling' [A55] and the more passable 'When I'm Five' [A53]; and two cover versions, Lesley Duncan's* 'Love Song' and 'Life Is A Circus', by the harmony band Djin, both vehicles for duets in the Simon & Garfunkel style.

Bowie's partnership with Hutchinson ended for economic, rather than musical, reasons. For several weeks, Bowie continued to consider himself a member of a duo, and it was definitely in that guise that he submitted a demo tape to Mercury Records' London office, staffed by his friend and, apparently, occasional lover, Calvin Mark Lee. Mercury duly offered him a recording contract, by which time he was a solo artist. Lee was also responsible for another, equally momentous liaison: he reintroduced Bowie to 19-year-old Angie Barnett, who became his

---

* Rumour has it that Lesley Duncan was Bowie's lover in 1968; 'Love Song' was later recorded by another of Duncan's friends, Elton John.

girlfriend. Bowie shamelessly moved her into the house that he was sharing with another sexual partner – with whom he was also engaged in his most committed espousal of the late-sixties counter-culture.

[7] WILD-EYED BOY FROM FREECLOUD (Bowie)

Recorded June 1969; single B-side. Re-recorded August 1969; *David Bowie [Space Oddity]* LP.

The first Arts Lab was founded by Jim Haynes in Drury Lane, London. It was, Haynes declared, 'an "energy centre" where anything can happen depending upon the needs of the people running each individual Lab and the characteristics of the building. A Lab is a non-Institution . . . a Lab's boundaries should be limitless.' The venue hosted art exhibitions by Yoko Ono and John Lennon, among many other happenings, and attracted curious visitors from across London. Among them was David Bowie, who by spring 1969 was living with underground journalist Mary Finnigan in Beckenham. As the Arts Lab ethic spread across the country, they launched a local venture at a pub in Beckenham High Street: a Folk Lab, initially, designed as a fund-raising focus for a wider Arts Lab collective. As a demonstration of Bowie's almost invisible profile as a musician, he and Finnigan listed their home phone number in underground newspaper advertisements for their enterprise.

'The plan is to turn on the adults by spearheading the project at children,' Finnigan announced. 'Initially, we will run Saturday morning poetry, music and mime scenes for children, gradually expanding to include theatre projects for kids.' Bowie, she said, 'is enthusiastic about teaching mime, music and drama to kids'. His affinity with children was apparent from songs such as 'There Is A Happy Land' [A25] and 'When I'm Five' [A53]; his own experience of childhood was more ambiguous. At 22, he admitted that 'I feel almost middle-aged physically. I often regret not leading a more normal teenage life.'

His idealism and regret informed the parable of the 'Wild-Eyed Boy From Freecloud': an innocent boy is threatened with hanging by his fellow citizens, and is rescued by the mountain on which he lives, which destroys the village to save his life. 'Everything the boy says is taken the wrong way,' Bowie explained, 'both by those who fear him and those who love him. I suppose in a way he's rather a prophet-figure.' The song added another dimension: the boy's persecution was sparked by a fear that his madness might be contagious. Allowed to speak, though, he uttered nothing more insane than a cry of universal humanity: the hippie equivalent of Ziggy Stardust's 'you're not alone' [61]. Twenty years later, Bowie reflected: 'I always felt I was on the edge of events, the fringe of things, and left out. A lot of my characters in those early years seem to revolve around that one feeling.'

'Wild-Eyed Boy From Freecloud' was a courageous attempt to deal with this isolation on an almost operatic scale. Trapped in his prison, the boy was represented by the endless circularity of a D chord with a descending root, from which there was no escape; even a key shift led inexorably back down the scale to captivity. As the scene cut to the mountain, announced with a strident C major chord, the ground began to slide, and after a series of unexpected key changes, Bowie proclaimed the boy's apparent freedom with a defiant declaration of identity. Then the action began to race, with a flurry of abrupt tonic/ subdominant and tonic/relative-minor chord changes – before, inexorably, the initial theme returned, to signal that hope had died. The melody kept close to the action, the boy's plaintive cry reaching to Bowie's familiar high G, and then being knocked back to earth.

In its initial reading, the song was played out starkly against acoustic guitar and an almost aggressive, chopping cello played by Paul Buckmaster. When re-recorded for the *David Bowie* LP, it was left to gasp beneath an epic arrangement ('I heard a Wagnerian orchestra in my head,' admitted producer Tony Visconti), tonally rich and extravagant to the point that it sapped the drama from the story. This time, Bowie's voice cracked emotionally on the final line, but it was a gesture too far, the wave of an actor's hand.

The sparse original arrangement was issued as the B-side to 'Space Oddity' [1] on 11 July 1969. 'Never have I been so flipped out about a single,' enthused one of Mercury Records' US executives. But he warned: 'I've been quite concerned about the record's ending. I've been worried that some programmers might not play it, what with the space shot and all.' In America, the single's negative slant on the space mission smothered its commercial prospects; in Britain it took seven weeks to make the Top 50 sales chart. By then, Bowie's enthusiasm for his success had been jolted by the unexpected death of his father on 5 August. 'David's career would have turned out differently had his father lived,' Kenneth Pitt reflected later. '[John Jones] would have continued to be the moderating influence David needed.'

[8] CYGNET COMMITTEE (Bowie)

Recorded August / September 1969; *David Bowie [Space Oddity]* LP.

Written almost simultaneously, 'Cygnet Committee' and 'Memory Of A Free Festival' [9] documented the extremes of Bowie's reaction to the hippy movement, and his Arts Lab experiment as a microcosm of that ideal. 'Here we are in Beckenham,' he said as 'Space Oddity' [1] was released, 'with a group of people creating their own momentum without the slightest concern for attitudes, tradition or pre-ordained moralities. It's alive, healthy and new, and it matters to me more than anything else.' In September, as 'Space Oddity' finally charted, three months after it was released, he was still suffused with optimism: 'I run an Arts Lab which is my chief occupation. I think it's the best in the country. There isn't one pseud involved. All the people are real – like labourers or bank clerks.' Yet by the end of the month he had completed this long, near-hysterical account of betrayal, disillusion, greed and defiant individualism, which concluded one side of his album, while his radiant-eyed account of the Arts Lab festival closed the other.

By November, he was declaring that the hippy movement was dead,* its followers 'materialistic and selfish'. 'These people,' he said dismissively, 'they're so apathetic, so lethargic. The laziest people I've met in my life.' Hippies were no more motivated than anyone else: everyone was 'crying out for a leader'. Like Bob Dylan, who was fighting off all attempts to co-opt him as the figurehead of a counter-cultural revolution, Bowie wanted nothing more than to be allowed to live. That single word, screeched over and over like a victim's final cry for help, provided the climax to a song that cast off the comfortable slogans of the counter-culture, the catchphrases of the Beatles or the

---

* He wasn't alone in this complaint: Kevin Ayers' 'Song For Insane Times' pursued a similar theme.

MC5 that were bandied around the underground press as gestures of solidarity. A year later, in a song Bowie much admired ('God'), John Lennon compressed the death of idealism into a single phrase: 'The dream is over.' Bowie, still grieving for Hermione and his recently deceased father, struggling to adjust to the commercial recognition that had been his sole aim since 1963, needed more than nine minutes to spit out the emotional debris.* In interviews before his father's death, Bowie talked warmly of what 'we' could achieve with the Arts Lab. After his bereavement, he was a defiantly singular 'I'.

His vehicle, ironically, was a remnant of the dream, as – following a brief prelude, which sounded as if the musicians were uncurling themselves after long hibernation – 'Cygnet Committee' was constructed around the delicate skeleton of 'Lover To The Dawn' [6]. Its first two sections were retained intact, with another paean to Hermione fleshing out the previously instrumental opening. Once more, Bowie was 'The Thinker',† but now he eschewed romance in favour of a bitter excoriation of all those who had drained his energy, sapped his will, even exhausted his money: the price of his fame. From a defiant movement through the key of F, a rhythm guitar stabbing the third beat of every bar, he gave way to self-pity, unloading himself across the familiar I-vi-IV-V chord progression (in C) that underpinned a thousand maudlin fifties teen ballads. And then the dance began again, with Hermione recollected as a touchstone of truth, before the betrayed Thinker was replaced by the voice of the crowd, ungrateful and unworthy, revealing their subterfuge like pantomime villains. Bowie's language grew even more bombastic, passion replacing poetry, adding up to total condemnation of the values of the counter-culture. One by one, the hollow slogans of the failed revolution were tossed aside, Bowie ranting like a Hitlerian Dalek, the band chaotic in their excitement, an electronically treated harpsichord swaying from side to side across the stereo spectrum.

Finally, Bowie escaped the tight four-chord restraints of the song

---

* Speaking in America more than a year later, Bowie claimed: 'I basically wanted [the song] to be a cry of "fuck humanity"', before adding with more than a degree of creative imagination, 'it's a dialogue between a left-wing capitalist and a real revolutionary'.

† And 'older': he held the first syllable, his voice cavernous with echo, with a keening croon that would reappear at the climax of 'Wild Is The Wind' [131].

with a desperate cry for freedom: 'Live!' He had finally shed his illusions: having dominated his songwriting for months, Hermione vanished from his landscape. Even before he had become a star, Bowie had glimpsed the cannibalistic relationship between leader and followers, idol and fans, guru and disciples. Yet he was still drawn towards pursuing fame, influence, the trappings of a god – a tension that would haunt the decade ahead.

[9] MEMORY OF A FREE FESTIVAL (Bowie)

Recorded September 1969; *David Bowie [Space Oddity]* LP. Re-recorded March/April 1970; single A/B-sides.

Five days after his father's funeral, when he was 'in a completely catatonic state', Bowie performed at the Growth Summer Festival and Free Concert in Beckenham. It was the epitome of counter-cultural eclecticism: besides an array of folk and rock musicians, the event offered 'a barbecue, exotic tea stall, poster & original artwork stall, Transmutation paper & magazine shop, candy floss, street theatre, puppet theatre, jewellery & ceramics stall, clothes shop, fuzz-nut shy, assault course, Tibetan shop, Culpepper herb and food stall, etc.'. The Beckenham Arts Lab collective (alias Growth) had expanded in four months from a sparsely attended folk club in the back room of a pub to a celebration of summer optimism filling a local park.

Growth organiser Mary Finnigan recalled that Bowie was 'vile' that day, castigating his fellow activists as 'mercenary pigs' because they had allowed the stalls to raise money for their activities – which was the avowed aim of the festival. 'He hated us for it,' she said, 'and I hated him.'

Yet within three weeks, Bowie had written and recorded 'Memory Of A Free Festival', the anthemic climax to his second album. 'We go out on an air of optimism, which I believe in,' he explained. 'I wrote this after the Beckenham Festival, when I was very happy.' What he created was a fantasy, a melding of other people's experiences of Beckenham with news reports of the Woodstock gathering in upstate New York that same weekend, filtered through a science-fiction sensibility that passed control of earthly happiness from the hippies to visitors from the stars. It climaxed in a simple chant, inspired by the elongated ending of the Beatles' 'Hey Jude' the previous year, which celebrated the arrival of the Sun Machine, inaugurating a party that would no doubt stretch out into the galaxies.*

Amidst the celebration, however, Bowie acknowledged that this was all fiction – one with which he was prepared to play along, but a simulacrum of reality nonetheless. Then he immersed himself in the innocence of fantasy, amongst Venusians, Peter (Pan?), and the rest, with people passing bliss among the crowds, and Bowie himself fixed on the overpowering Buddhist enlightenment of Satori. As a growing chorus joined his anthem to the Sun Machine, he let the myth run free, his own memory of a particular free festival fading into the 'summer's end' of 1960s idealism.

This required a giant leap of faith, so it was apt that the music began with what sounded like an uncertain church organ.† To hint that we were in a dream world, the organ (and Bowie's voice) drifted very slowly back and forth between the stereo speakers. At the height of the fairy tale, with tall Venusians mingling in the crowd, Bowie soared like a choirboy to a top A. Then there was a flurry of sound, an unthreatening counterpart to the anarchic cacophony of the Beatles' 'Revolution 9', before a fuzz bass stabilised the tempo, and Bowie announced the joyous coming of the sun.

In the mythology of the 1960s, Woodstock was followed by the shambolic Altamont festival in December 1969; the Moon landing of July led to the near-disaster of *Apollo 13* in April 1970; and, after Bowie was pulled on to the pop circuit to promote 'Space Oddity', the Beckenham Arts Lab folded back into a folk club, and then vanished, as did the national movement inspired by Drury Lane. When 'The Prettiest Star' [13] failed to extend his career as a pop star, his record company suggested that he should re-record 'Free Festival' as a single for the very different summer of 1970.

It was a significant moment in Bowie's career: his first recording session with guitarist Mick Ronson, his creative foil for the next three

---

* Compare the 'Cygnet Committee' [8] nightmare of a 'love machine' on 'desolation rows'.

† It was a Rosedale chord organ, played by Bowie; he could press buttons to trigger wheezing chords, though he was restricted to a choice of twelve, the major and minor chords of A, B♭, C, D, F and G, which – apart from a solitary Em – determined the structure of the song.

years. With the song now split across both sides of a single, Ronson dominated the finale, his Eric Clapton-inspired tone subordinating the chorus choir. Earlier, he had taken his turn as each instrument slowly entered the scene, and an instrumental flourish (a signal of allegiance to progressive rock, not pop) marked the end of each verse. But the most significant change came from Bowie himself: the vulnerable idealist of 1969 was now a recognisable prototype for Ziggy Stardust at his most swaggering, drifting into a phrase or two in mock-cockney as a proud badge of identity, rather than a throwback to the music hall as in 1967. Ironically, while the song was now tighter and more focused than before, it appeared at a time when rock festivals were torn between chaos and commercialism, and bliss was no longer being passed among the crowd.

[10] GOD KNOWS I'M GOOD (Bowie)

Recorded September 1969; *David Bowie [Space Oddity]* LP.

The final two songs recorded for Bowie's second album offered variants on the African rhythm brought to rock 'n' roll by Bo Diddley, and employed most famously on the Rolling Stones' 'Not Fade Away' and George Michael's 'Faith'. Bowie transported it to acoustic 12-string guitar for this trivial extrapolation of a 1969 tabloid story about a shoplifter. Rhythm aside, his obvious influence was Bob Dylan, Bowie throwing around flamboyant metaphors (the 'spitting', 'shrieking' cash machine) and emphasising apparently random syllables in what he clearly believed to be an imitation of the master. Only in the chorus (echoed for dramatic effect) did he step outside his familiar folk guitar changes in A minor, landing on an E major at the end of each line to accentuate the moral crisis at hand.

[11] UNWASHED AND SOMEWHAT SLIGHTLY DAZED (Bowie) (inc. [11A] Don't Sit Down)

Recorded September 1969; *David Bowie [Space Oddity]* LP.

'Unwashed' was ostensibly the most conventional rock recording on Bowie's second album, the electric blues workout of its second half almost erasing what had gone before. Within a few days, however, Bowie was capable of revealing two ambiguous 'explanations' for the song: that it was 'about a boy whose girlfriend thinks he is socially inferior' (a theme that first surfaced on 'I'm Not Losing Sleep' [A19] in 1966), and then that it 'describes how I felt in the weeks after my father died'. What was most shocking wasn't the comic-book violence of its imagery – the rotting flesh and rats of a heavy-metal nightmare – but the swiftness of the transition from the 'pretty girl' who glimpsed Bowie from her window, to the revenge exacted on her accursed father.*

Like several songs of this period (notably 'Cygnet Committee' [8]), 'Unwashed' sounded as if it had been assembled piecemeal, wandering through a succession of major chords in a desperate attempt to find a home. It eventually settled on C, and a slowed-down, souped-up reproduction of the Rolling Stones' 'Not Fade Away', escaping the formula only for two Dylan-inspired[†] runs from G and then F back to the key chord at the climax of the chorus. After Bowie had exhausted his self-disgust and his social inferiority complex, the band took control, their leader contributing a single scared-sheep bleat in imitation of his friend Marc Bolan, before the brass and Benny Marshall's blues-wailing harp brought the track home.

Original pressings of the album, and the most recent CD reissue, separated this track from 'Letter To Hermione' [5] with a 40-second audio-verité extract from a jam session around the 'Unwashed' chords. Pointless and disruptive, it barely deserved the honour of its own title: 'Don't Sit Down'. The album is stronger without it.

---

* The music reflected the abrupt transition, veering from the soft, hanging and heavily echoed 12-string chords of the opening bars, accompanied only by the tap of a cymbal and an electric guitar heavy in reverb, to the rough-edged knife of a rock band.
† The Dylan references didn't end there: the title was only an adverb short of sounding like a refugee from *Blonde On Blonde*; while the track was performed with the same chaotic daring, all missed changes and dropouts, as the most anarchic moments of *Highway 61 Revisited*. Some other moments to treasure: the voice steering left for the first verse, right for the second, and eventually finding the middle of the road; Bowie's American pronunciation of 'tomatoes'; and the way he defused the incendiary (for 1969) word 'phallus', by pronouncing it 'fey-less'.

David Bowie LP (alias *Space Oddity*)

Recorded June–September 1969;
released November 1969 (UK), January 1970 (US).

Like Zager & Evans' 'In The Year 2525', a transatlantic hit single in late summer 1969, 'Space Oddity' [1] was such an obvious novelty for the pop audience – indelibly linked to the Apollo missions – that it sapped rather than reinforced Bowie's prestige as a performer. Fans at his live performances reacted ecstatically to the song, then ignored everything else he offered them. A similar fate awaited *David Bowie*, his second album release of that title – replacing the 1967 model with the same lack of regret that Ford might have applied to the launch of a new Escort. Only when it was reissued in 1972, with a *Ziggy Stardust*-era cover portrait, was the record renamed *Space Oddity*.

If the original intention was to stress that Bowie could not be defined by one song alone, it was a disaster in marketing terms. Like its Deram predecessor, the 1969 *David Bowie* offered no more clue to its contents than a striking colour photograph of its creator – his Dylan (circa 1966) perm merging into an op-art array of blue circles taken from the *Planetary Folklore* portfolio by the Hungarian artist Victor Vasarely. The artist was seeking to create a sense of movement: superimposed with Bowie's staring face, his painting lost its purpose. So did the Beckenham Arts Lab: as Bowie complained in 1971, 'We found that the mass percentage of the people that came just came to be entertained. The participation element was gone.' With his idealism punctured, he viewed his success purely in financial terms. 'The money I'm making now will make a nice nest egg,' he explained, 'and if the bubble bursts, I'll be able to live quite comfortably for a couple of years on the proceeds.' Would success, however short-lived, go to his head? 'I can take it all in my stride. I'm not a particularly excitable person.'

Elsewhere, he revealed that 'I never plan ahead, and I'm very fickle. I'm always changing my mind about things.' He presented a different persona in every situation: meeting an interviewer whose interests went beyond pop, he would talk knowledgeably about authors such as André Gide, Oscar Wilde and Dylan Thomas. Confronted by skinheads after a poorly received solo performance, he promised to act as their spokesman in the underground newspaper *International Times*. The paper's in-house 'skin' duly announced the launch of a regular column: 'He's a good

bloke, and on our side, in spite of his long hair, and he should have a
lot of interesting things to say.' But none of Bowie's thoughts on the
skinhead lifestyle ever appeared in print. Meanwhile, he was toying with
the idea of assembling a rock band, having borrowed the services of
Junior's Eyes for his late 1969 tour commitments; while at the same
time giving serious consideration to starring in a stage adaptation of a
novel by Sir Walter Scott at the Harrogate Theatre. This was still the
butterfly Bowie of 1967, uncertain how to meet the new decade, and
unable to fix on a saleable brand that could quell his growing feelings
of restlessness and inertia.

[12] LONDON BYE TA-TA (see also [A52] & [14]) (Bowie)

Recorded January 1970; *David Bowie [Space Oddity] (Deluxe Edition)* CD.

The success of 'Space Oddity' [1] demanded a follow-up, and though
Bowie had toyed with a ditty entitled 'Hole In The Ground'* before
Christmas, that wasn't it. Neither, it transpired, was this remake of
an unreleased song from 1968, despite press reports that it had been
scheduled as his next single, and several broadcast performances
by Bowie. It might have been a more productive choice than 'The
Prettiest Star' [13], thanks to an arrangement that featured spiky
electric guitar, a three-woman vocal chorus in the gospel-flavoured
style that was fast becoming de rigueur on the London rock scene,
and a boogie riff that looked ahead to 'Suffragette City' [59] two
years hence.

[13] THE PRETTIEST STAR (Bowie) (see also [71])

Recorded January 1970; single A-side.

Bowie promised an ecstatic climb to the summit in the final verse
of this spring 1970 single, and if – as is commonly supposed – it was
inspired by Angie Barnett, the woman who became his wife two weeks

* This throwaway song was gifted to Bowie's friend George Underwood, but did
nothing to revive a recording career that had extended to one 1965 single under the
pseudonym 'Calvin James'.

after it was released, then it was uncannily prophetic (professionally, if not personally). The song garnered a huge audience when it was revived on *Aladdin Sane*, but this blueprint is rumoured to have sold no more than 1,000 copies. 'I think a lot of people were expecting another "Space Oddity",' Bowie mused as it became clear the single would not be a hit.

The flaw was not Bowie's delightful melody, tripping around the key of F like a party of revellers from *The Great Gatsby*; or the words, sufficiently romantic to make any recipient swell with pride; or indeed the intimate, breathy vocal, with Bowie purring like Eartha Kitt draping herself across a chaise longue. What damned the single commercially was, in retrospect, its main attraction for collectors of rock trivia: the only memorable musical collaboration between two sixties mods who had spent the decade vainly chasing a vision of stardom, Bowie and Marc Bolan. Tony Visconti produced them both, and engineered this uneasy alliance, in which Bolan extemporised a solo around the verse melody. (Typically, Bolan later claimed that he also 'wrote the middle bit' of the song.) The problem was not the notes, but the ambience, which left Bolan's guitar as the sonic focus of the track, with an edginess that grated against the voice and rhythm section. The lethargic nature of the latter didn't help, either. Only Bowie's personal stake in the song could have persuaded him that this was his best shot at radio airplay.

Two weeks after the release of 'The Prettiest Star', Bowie and Angie became husband and wife. 'She's an American citizen, and if I hadn't married her, she'd have had to leave the country,' Bowie explained a few months later. 'But for that, I don't think we'd have got married at all.' The couple embarked on what both agreed should be an 'open marriage' – a fashionable concept of the times, and also the title of a best-selling 1972 study of 'free love' by the anthropologists Nena and George O'Neill. By 1977, Nena O'Neill had written a retraction, entitled *The Marriage Premise*, having discovered that few of her original interview subjects had succeeded in keeping their open marriages intact. Neither would David and Angie Bowie.

In a coincidence that symbolised the directionless nature of his career, 'The Prettiest Star' was released on the same day as *The World Of David Bowie*, a budget-priced (less than £1) album of his Deram recordings. Bowie was allowed to select and sequence the tracks, retaining most of his 1967 *David Bowie* LP but substituting three songs that the record company had chosen not to release: 'Let Me Sleep Beside You' [A47], 'Karma Man' [A48] and 'In The Heat Of The Morning' [A49]. Although the album's appearance did provide a degree of publicity, it also suggested that he was already a man of the past, his 'World' circumscribed by music he had recorded several years earlier.

[14] THREEPENNY PIERROT (Bowie)

[15] THE MIRROR (AKA HARLEQUIN) (Bowie)

[16] COLUMBINE (Bowie)

Recorded January / February 1970; Scottish TV.

Finding himself in Scotland at the same time as Lindsay Kemp, Bowie agreed to participate in a Scottish TV production of *Pierrot In Turquoise*, which he had last performed in March 1968. Of the three musical pieces fashioned for the show, 'Threepenny Pierrot' was a simple keyboard reworking of 'London Bye Ta Ta' [A52 & 12] sung at breakneck speed with lyrics inspired by the *commedia dell'arte* archetype. 'Columbine' (Harlequin's perennial love interest) and 'The Mirror' were brief new compositions, adhering to theatrical need and to the folk ambience of his early 1969 songs, though there was a stridency to the delivery of 'The Mirror' that betrayed a new self-confidence waiting to be captured on record. Once again, though, this was a gesture to the past rather than the future.

[17] AMSTERDAM (Brel; trans. Shuman)

Recorded February 1970; BBC Radio. Re-recorded summer 1971; single B-side.

In the music of Jacques Brel, which he discovered second-hand, Bowie found the same relish for the sweat, semen and soul of everyday life, in all its passion and mundanity, that he had admired in the pages of Jean Genet. There was none of Genet's extravagant campness in Brel; instead, the Belgian master of the declamatory *chanson* delivered bulletins of blood-soaked humanity straight from an open vein. Despair and mortality were his battlefield, and nowhere was his scalpel wielded with more zeal than in his lurid evocation of the port of Amsterdam.

Brel's tumultuous rendition (recorded live in 1964) accentuated his melody's similarity to the traditional 'Greensleeves', rising to an ecstatic climax that roused his audience to uproar. Tortured pop star Scott Walker felt Brel as a kindred spirit, and he interpreted 'Amsterdam' in 1967 in a hushed croon, disguising the potentially offensive word 'pisses'* and avowing that the whores had 'promised their love', not 'given their bodies'. The translation[†] he was bowdler-ising was by lyricist Mort Shuman, who belied his past as a hit song-writer for Elvis Presley with his libretto for the musical *Jacques Brel Is Alive And Well And Living In Paris*. Bowie saw a London performance of the show in July 1968, and almost immediately began to perform 'Amsterdam' himself.

Unable to master the emotional terrain of the song in a February 1970 BBC performance, he was equal to its demands by 1971. Returning to the BBC that year, he phrased every line like an actor utterly confident of his lines, switching his mood stylishly between lines. His studio rendition, not released until 1973, was more strident, a showcase for his vocal range rather than for his interpretative talents. He continued to tease out the full range of Brel's implications, on this song and 'My Death' [64], until the end of the Ziggy era.

[18] THE WIDTH OF A CIRCLE (Bowie)

Recorded February 1970; BBC Radio. Re-recorded April/May 1970; *The Man Who Sold The World* LP.

'I don't want to be one of those singers whose career depends on hit singles, and they are virtually dead for six months of the year,'

---

* American singer John Denver recorded the song in 1970: he doesn't piss but 'spits'.
† Walker claimed that he originally learned the songs from Brel's original record-ings, as translated for him by a German girlfriend, a claim that led him into dispute with Shuman.

Bowie remarked in November 1969. He had glimpsed the success that had been his goal since he joined the Kon-Rads, and found it deeply troubling. The failure of 'The Prettiest Star' [13] demonstrated that, far from establishing him as an artist of integrity, the sales of 'Space Oddity' [1] had actually narrowed his commercial brand: in the eyes of the public, he was simply the man who sold the space song. 'I throw myself on the mercy of an audience,' he said, 'and I really need them to respond to me. If they don't, I'm lost.' In the same interview, he noted wistfully that 'it's a bit early in life for all my ideas to have dried up, isn't it?' – an effective admission that he felt creatively bankrupt.

At heart, he still believed that his primary purpose was to please a mass audience: 'I'm determined to be an entertainer; clubs, cabaret, concerts, the lot.' He had little sympathy with the rock underground: 'It seems to me that they have expanded their own personal little scenes to a certain extent, and then they stop, content to play to the converted. For some reason, even the words "entertainer" and "cabaret" make them shudder.' In a musical world no longer attempting to span a widening chasm of taste, between pop and rock, commercial and underground, mass and elite, he was aligning himself firmly with the majority.

'What the underground has got to remember is they're still a minority, and they're not representative of the youth,' John Lennon noted at the start of 1970. 'And that's what we've got to realise, that we haven't got youth sewn up, by any means. We haven't even converted our own contemporaries, we're not even communicating fully with *them*.' Bowie concurred: 'It's not that they *want* to communicate, particularly. A lot of them haven't anything at all *to* communicate. I want my songs to be known, otherwise I wouldn't go on writing, because I don't write for myself.'

'The Prettiest Star' aside, however, Bowie wrote nothing between September 1969 and April 1970 that made the slightest concessions towards an audience. 'All my songs are very personal,' he admitted in March, 'and I combine this with an exaggeration so the meaning is clearly brought home to the listener.' This exaggeration was certainly evident in the new material he performed for BBC Radio in February and March, but the intended audience appeared to be Bowie himself, seeking to divine his lack of connection with the world.

In an attempt to bridge that gap, he formed a band who were known, variously, as Harry the Butcher, David Bowie's Imagination and, ultimately, the Hype. Alongside his established friend/bassist/producer Tony Visconti, he recruited two former members of a Hull-based R&B band called the Rats: drummer John Cambridge and guitarist Mick Ronson. In Ronson, Bowie had happened upon someone who was not only a guitar virtuoso, with an utterly distinctive tone, but also a classically trained musician capable of concocting orchestral arrangements. Ronson and Cambridge were invited to join David and Angie at their gothic Beckenham residence, known as Haddon Hall. They discovered that their hosts were not only keen buyers of art deco and art nouveau – in keeping with the contemporary revival of both styles – but also avid collectors of sexual conquests, often from the gay club on Kensington High Street known as the Sombrero (or 'the Chinese takeaway', to many of its denizens).

Within a fortnight, Bowie and the Hype were appearing at the Roundhouse, a counter-culture bastion in north London, dressed as cartoon superheroes. 'I was in silver lamé and blue silver cloak and silvered hair and blue hair and the whole thing, glitter everywhere,' Bowie recalled sheepishly. 'We died a death. [But] I knew what it was I wanted to do, and I knew it was what people would want eventually.' It was, in hindsight, a nativity scene for glam rock – designed not by Bowie, but by his wife and Tony Visconti's girlfriend Liz. He had yet to fashion appropriate music for this exaggerated image, however. His Roundhouse set included not only 'The Width Of A Circle' and 'The Prettiest Star' [13], but also a cover version of Van Morrison's 'Cyprus Avenue' from the *Astral Weeks* album – unlikely fare for a glam-rock pioneer.

The same confusion clouded Bowie's future plans. He originally intended his next album to be half acoustic, half electric, and 'The Width Of A Circle' was one of only three songs he presented at the sessions for *The Man Who Sold The World* that were written for acoustic guitar. It was premiered as his first performance with Mick Ronson at a BBC concert in February 1970. This rendition opened with Bowie establishing the key via an E/E7 variation on acoustic guitar, followed by a simple Ronson riff running down the scale of A but ending short of the root, which emerged as the first of just two verses began. Then the focus was on Ronson's skills as an improviser, on both electric and acoustic instruments. A month later, at another BBC appearance, the song had grown a Hendrix-inspired feedback introduction, reminiscent of 'Purple Haze'; a wordless vocal motif, echoing Ronson's riff, first in unison, then in wildly erratic harmony, finally as a group chorale; and a three-chord-trick instrumental passage that set up the last return to the Valkyrie vocal chorus.

'We had been playing [it] live,' bassist Tony Visconti claimed in his memoir, 'but we felt like it needed another section . . . after one take we broke into a spontaneous boogie riff. Afterwards, we listened to a playback of the boogie jam for a laugh, and we decided to make this a permanent part of the song. We put the track "to bed" with the promise that David would come up with lyrics and melody at a later date.' As the second BBC recording proved, half of the 'boogie jam' was already present in skeletal form before they reached the studio; what Ronson and Visconti added, in their role as musical directors, was a structure that provided a dramatic pause at the end of every four repetitions, breaking the jam into verse form.

Establishing a pattern that would hold for most of the tracks recorded for *The Man Who Sold The World*, Bowie then had to create a song to fit the musical structure. What emerged was a disturbing fable that mixed violent homoeroticism with an occult sense of the uneasy balance between god and demon.

'A lot of my compositions are very much fantasy tales,' Bowie conceded in March 1970, and the original two-verse skeleton of 'The Width Of A Circle' fitted this description. In a whimsical manner reminiscent of *Alice's Adventures in Wonderland*, his narrator met his alter ego in the form of a monster, engaging in a circular dialogue as unenlightening as Mr Jones' efforts in Bob Dylan's 'Ballad Of A Thin Man'. As augmented three months later, though, the tale took a turn into darkest night, as the narrator 'smashed my soul', flirted with fleshly pleasures, and met a God who carried him into the depths of hell. But this was no ordinary inferno: its language was intensely physical, mingling fear with ecstatic lust amidst imagery that suggested a shocking, eviscerating, thrilling baptism into anal intercourse. Through it all, the Bowie character repeated greedily, 'Do it again', while a Greek chorus warned, 'Turn around, go back.' There was nothing camp here, nothing suggestive: this was a dangerous sexual encounter, painted in lurid, compelling detail. Or was it? Though the erotic intensity was unmistakable, it is just as easy, in retrospect, to read this tale as Bowie's attempt to rationalise his new business relationship with the enticing but intimidating Tony Defries; or as a graphic account of spiritual crisis; or as low comedy. 'I very much doubt whether anyone could decipher that song correctly on my level,' Bowie admitted in 1971. His own explanation didn't help: 'I went to the depths of myself in that. I tried to analogise the period of my life from when I left school to that time . . . just for my own benefit, not really for any listener's benefit.' Forty years on, the circle remains unbroken.

During the pause between recording the accompaniment and the vocal of 'The Width Of A Circle', Bowie had – almost accidentally – engineered a coup in his management set-up. Kenneth Pitt was ousted, after four years of loyal devotion, and replaced by two show-business lawyers, Laurence Myers and Tony Defries. Myers ran Gem Productions from an office in Regent Street, and initially both Defries and Bowie were Gem employees. Soon Defries assumed control of the singer's affairs, ultimately buying out Myers' stake in Bowie and forming his own organisation: the modestly titled MainMan. Defries, so Pitt said acidly, 'is a man with legal knowledge who set up a business wherein they had a product to market called David Bowie'. Myers was more generous in his appraisal of his one-time partner: '[Defries] absolutely *believed* that David was, and would be, the greatest star in the world, and he acted accordingly.'

[19] THE SUPERMEN (Bowie)

Recorded April/May 1970; *The Man Who Sold The World* LP. Re-recorded November 1971; *Glastonbury Fayre* LP.

Now that Bowie had shed his allegiance to the underground, having appeared at the Beckenham Arts Lab for the last time on 5 March 1970, his mind was focused entirely on esoteric interests. For the next year, he would view the world from a perspective that was obsessed with mythology, the limits of human power, and the mysteries of the occult. Like 'The Width Of A Circle' [18], 'The Supermen' betrayed his recent speculations. Though Friedrich Nietzsche's *Übermensch* was the initial spark for this song, it occupied an entirely different meta-phorical realm: a science-fiction re-enactment of the trials of the Greek pantheon of gods, or the deities of H.P. Lovecraft's Cthilhu mythos. Their curse was immortality – punishment, perhaps, for their perfec-tion. Yet 'The Supermen' was less a narrative than a series of ghastly images, its words chosen for their assonance and rhyme, for effect rather than meaning.

John Cambridge later attributed his axing from Bowie's group to difficulties with this track, and his drumming on its initial airing, a BBC Radio One session in March 1970, was anything but propul-sive. To deepen the wound, his replacement Woody Woodmansey opened the studio recording by skipping expertly around his kit. A rowdy monkish chorus announced the portentous two-semitone rise at the heart of the song, while Ronson's guitar churned as if it were stirring cement. Bowie's voice entered like a south London devil, twisting his vowels into mutations of cockney dialect, his phrasing clipped and triumphant. For the chorus, his voice was doubled, one fiend in each speaker; by the second verse, it had become an inhuman rant, made all the more ominous by the relentless cohesion of the band. This was a new persona for popular music: eerie, compel-ling, utterly contemporary, and as far removed from the Bowie of 'Space Oddity' [1] (let alone 'Love You Till Tuesday' [A39]) as it was possible to imagine.

To heighten the sense that an old order was being expelled, the track crushed a path from the opening F and G major chords to the climactic C of the chorus with scant regard for the niceties of key signatures, while Ronson's extended guitar solo was enacted over mock-orchestral barrages of chords in pairs with the same reck-less abandon for convention. 'We came up with outrageous sonic landscapes,' Tony Visconti told Bowie biographer David Buckley, 'which was kind of prescient for the sound that Queen eventually came up with.' Only the dying fade of Bowie's voice at the end of each chorus, plummeting nearly an octave into the depths, hinted that even the gods might be stricken by human emotions.

The song was re-recorded with the Spiders From Mars, with an acoustic opening verse, the following year, and included on the album that commemorated the first Glastonbury festival. Bowie had origin-ally agreed to give the festival organisers, Revelation Enterprises, a song from his performance there in June 1971, but then decided that it might muddy the Ziggy Stardust brand. 'It's a shame,' said Barry Everitt, who assembled the album. 'He didn't like [his live tape], because it was very simply, beautiful and gentle. It was David on his own, David the man, not Ziggy.' Revelation announced solemnly: 'The tape will remain in our vaults until the revolution.' Its current whereabouts – like those of the counter-cultural revolution – are unknown.

The Lure of the Occult

A sense of the occult – the hidden, the esoteric, the satanic, the alien, the mythological, the divine – pervaded Bowie's songwriting in 1970 and 1971, from the graphic imagery of 'Width Of A Circle' [18] to the parade of possibilities that was 'Quicksand' [50]. In seeking out information and answers about the unknown, Bowie was reflecting a wider obsession in the culture around him. It was a multifaceted quest, which ranged from a cultish interest in witchcraft or devil-worship to a profound exploration of the limits of human consciousness. Running through it all was the conviction – already a manifesto amongst the youthful counter-culture – that conventional explanations of the world, and mankind's place within it, were ineffective and partial.

This dissatisfaction was displayed in a bewildering variety of ways and arenas. The late sixties saw a dramatic rise of interest in witchcraft, not least because relaxed censorship laws allowed the distribution of sensational films that claimed to reflect the witch trials and inquisitions of earlier centuries but were actually a smokescreen for nudity and sexual violence. The endlessly popular 'satanic' novels of Dennis Wheatley found a fresh audience amongst teenagers eager to be scared and titillated. The Rolling Stones toyed with demonic imagery in their songs and stage performances, and were briefly taken seriously as representatives of the devil, until the weakness in their facade was exposed by the tragic fiasco of the Altamont festival in December 1969.

It became deeply fashionable to be fascinated by Aleister Crowley, the so-called 'Beast' of British occultism: Crowley's long-suppressed manuscripts were published, and rock stars competed to drop his name. In 1967, the year in which his face appeared on the cover of the Beatles' Sgt. Pepper album, he became something of a posthumous icon amongst the British underground, as familiar a hero as Timothy Leary or Allen Ginsberg. Crowley was joined in the occult pantheon by the veterans of long-defunct organisations like the Hermetic Order of the Golden Dawn (from which he had been expelled in 1898). Names such as Madame Blavatsky, Annie Besant, Gurdjieff and Rasputin were revered for their teachings, and even more for the exaggerated tales surrounding them.

There was a more peaceful strain of mystical exploration, stretching from Big Sur's Esalen community in California to Glastonbury Tor, which would later be gathered together under the rather baggy heading of 'New Age'. There were best-selling books about the lost continent of Atlantis, about alien visits from far-flung stars, about the myths of King Arthur, and the prevalent belief in flying saucers (alien abduction would only become an obsession later in the decade). People pursued ley lines, rubbed crystals, revived long-dead pagan rituals, and prayed to gods once feared and revered by their distant ancestors. In London, there was sufficient interest in this multifarious field to inspire the opening of a shop devoted to the esoteric, Dark They Were & Golden Eyed.

As Bowie recorded The Man Who Sold The World, a weekly magazine entitled Man, Myth & Magic was achieving enormous sales (not least because of its regular pictures of naked witches). Tabloid newspapers also discovered that being able to uncover witches' covens and blood-drinking cults in rural English beauty spots was a guarantee of increased circulation; once again, the promise of nudity and orgies was a heady attraction. Alex Sanders and his wife Maxine Morris became notorious as the monarchs of British witchcraft; Sanders even issued a record of his incantations (which was swiftly withdrawn from sale). Rock bands such as Black Sabbath and Black Widow traded on their supposed involvement with spells and demons.

In California, meanwhile, notoriety on the Crowley scale attended the Church of Satan, founded in 1966 by the self-styled 'Black Pope', Anton LaVey. He declared the time of the church's inauguration to be Year One, Anno Satanas, and flaunted the names of celebrities who had previously expressed even the mildest interest in his activities, notably film stars Marilyn Monroe and Jayne Mansfield (both of whom had soon met untimely ends), and song-and-dance-man Sammy Davis Jr. In 1969 LaVey published The Satanic Bible, which was a veritable instruction book for a lascivious lifestyle. 'Instead of commanding our members to repress their natural urges,' he explained, 'we teach that they should follow them. This includes physical lusts, the desire for revenge, the drive for material possessions.' A rock star's bible would surely have carried a very similar set of commandments.

All this was sensationalism, and was exploited as such. But besides these lurid attractions, David Bowie became engrossed in a more positive area of exploration, as exemplified by Colin Wilson's panoramic study of *The Occult*, published in 1971. It's difficult to imagine that Bowie did not read this book, as it explored all of his interests in the field over the next few years, from the *I Ching* to the Kabbalah, Crowley to Rasputin, alien visitations to reincarnation. Through it all, Wilson propounded a simple message, which was effectively reproduced (in negative form) in the chorus to Bowie's 'Quicksand' [50]: human beings must escape the habit of allowing self-imposed restrictions to limit their awareness of the world beyond everyday consciousness. Exactly that quest would intrigue Bowie throughout the next decade, to be achieved by any means necessary.

[20] AFTER ALL (Bowie)

Recorded April/May 1970; *The Man Who Sold The World* LP.

The only song on *The Man Who Sold The World* that suggested it might have been fashioned for Bowie's original concept of a half-acoustic album was 'After All', a companion piece to 'All The Madmen' [23] insofar as it explored the nature of innocence beyond the corrupting claims of adulthood. Its protagonists were children; its ostensible moral, almost banal in its simplicity, was that children represented the pure spirit of mankind, and adults were merely children in aged skin. Those poetic champions of childhood, the Williams Wordsworth and Blake, would have approved: Wordsworth's tale of the 'strange adventures' of 'The Idiot Boy' made explicit the links between the equally innocent pleasures of childhood and insanity. But as the song unfolded, the child narrator mouthed more unsettling concepts from the realms of Zen Buddhism and the satanist dilettante Aleister Crowley.

Crowley's gargantuan *Confessions* had recently been published in full, laying bare his belief that humanity should be divided between a Nietzschean elite of supermen and 'a caste of "men of earth", sons of soil, sturdy, sensual, stubborn and stupid, unemasculated by ethical and intellectual education' to act as their slaves. 'After All' recast that differentiation in terms of innocence and experience, leaving the listener to wonder whether the innocents might actually be more corrupt, and more threatening, than their age-tarnished counterparts. Like the chant that ended 'All The Madmen', the refrain here was a Dada-esque tag for a children's skipping game, albeit one enacted in slow tempo. Delivered by a crowd (growing menacingly in size) of vari-speed 'children', it gradually became eerie with repetition, as if it had tapped into the dark side of the collective unconscious.

Bowie added to the mystery with a vocal so gentle that one almost needed to apply a mirror to see if he were still alive. There was a constant sense of ebb and flow in the music, as the descending cycle of Em/Em7/A/Am* chords that fuelled the verse was replaced by the gradual rise up the scale into the chorus, echoed by a delicious falling away as an A minor guitar chord was augmented by a finger running slowly down the final frets of the first string. It was an intrusion when three sudden notes from Visconti's bass signalled a modulation into an instrumental revisiting of the verse by synthesiser ('a passion of mine at the time', he admitted) and pipe organ, a section that sounded as if it had been pasted into Bowie's sonic picture as an afterthought. 'After All' was more rewarding under a delicate touch, such as the Stylophone creeping into the chorus, and the Woodmansey cymbal taps answered each time by a tom-tom salute.

[21] RUNNING GUN BLUES (Bowie)

Recorded April/May 1970; *The Man Who Sold The World* LP.

'The seventies are exploding,' announced the Weatherman collective of young American revolutionary activists in January 1970. 'Armed violence is in the air . . . In Seattle, two kids are stopped on the street for a hippie check, attack the pig, rip off his piece, and blow

---

* This represented a minor variation on the D/D7/G/Gm pattern that opened 'Lover To The Dawn' [6], which was itself a transposition of the E/E7/A/Am of the Beatles' 'Dear Prudence', released about a month before Bowie wrote that song.

his head off. It's happening.' They believed that peaceful defiance of the American state had failed: only the gun and the bomb could topple the war machine. Weatherman's anger was heightened by the belief that American soldiers were committing genocide in the name of freedom: in November 1969, the public had belatedly learned of the killing in March 1968 of several hundred Vietnamese civilians by a company of US infantrymen, in the so-called My Lai massacre.

The protagonist of 'Running Gun Blues' seemed to have stepped straight from that nightmare, driven to kill 'the gooks' with no more compunction than the cast of a zombie movie. Bowie approached him with the same playful amusement he gave the characters on his 1967 album, his gruesome relish in the opening verse a masterful piece of emotional dissociation. An eerie whine from a Moog synthesiser suggested that we had tripped into a twilight zone where murder was a game without consequences. Then a crunching electric guitar entered the scene, representing the corporate military might behind this maverick barbarian. This was the natural territory of the Who, and the resemblance was heightened by the extended drum fills and by Bowie's melismatic swagger, which it was easy to imagine Roger Daltrey's voice reproducing. The track became an exercise in hard-rock dynamics, highlighting the fearsome power of this short-lived band.

[22] SHE SHOOK ME COLD (Bowie)

Recorded April/May 1970; *The Man Who Sold The World* LP.

'Mick Ronson, Woody Woodmansey and I were working out most of the arrangements [for *The Man Who Sold The World*] by ourselves in David's absence,' producer Tony Visconti told Bowie biographer David Buckley. In a less guarded moment, he would insist that 'The songs were written by all four of us. We'd jam in a basement, and Bowie would just say whether he liked them or not.' Several years after he parted company from Bowie, Ronson was asked whether he felt that he and Visconti had effectively composed the music for the album. He started to agree, and then told the interviewer that he would rather not talk about it.

What's beyond dispute is that many of the songs on *The Man Who Sold The World* were recorded in two stages, often several weeks apart. The band (sometimes with Bowie contributing guitar, sometimes not) would record an instrumental track, which might or might not be based upon an original Bowie idea. Then, at the last possible moment, he would reluctantly uncurl himself from the sofa on which he was lounging with his wife, and dash off a set of lyrics. In this haphazard way, his initial batch of completed compositions – three or four at most – was extended to fill an entire 40-minute album, on which he received the sole composing credit for every track. 'The only thing that I didn't think was quite as gentlemanly as it could have been was that he never shared publishing then,' Angie Bowie reflected many years later. 'In terms of kudos and feeling that one is valued, it would have been nice for Mick Ronson to have had publishing credits on some of the songs that he contributed a great deal to.'

Aural evidence alone suggests that, on this song at least, Ronson's contribution extended beyond augmenting Bowie's ideas. The lumbering guitar melody that dominated 'She Shook Me Cold' was instantly reminiscent of one of Ronson's musical heroes, Jeff Beck – emulating the style of his 1968 album *Beck-Ola*. Perhaps it was coincidental that Bowie's lyric was based around a title ('You Shook Me') from Beck's previous album, *Truth*. The working title for this entertaining medley of hard-rock clichés ('Suck') captured its primitive sexuality, which was the theme Bowie expanded for his vampiric lyrics. He assembled them from fragments of imagination and memory, borrowing 'Love In Vain' from Robert Johnson via the Rolling Stones, a violent sexual image from a song he'd later revive on *Pin Ups* [84], and 'Golden Hair' from the title of a recently released piece by one of his own heroes, Syd Barrett. 'I see it now as a summary of England,' he declared in a particularly obfuscatory 1971 interview.

[23] ALL THE MADMEN (Bowie)

Recorded April/May 1970; *The Man Who Sold The World* LP.

'"All The Madmen" was written for my brother and it's about my brother,' Bowie revealed in 1971. 'He's the man inside, and he doesn't want to leave. He's perfectly happy there . . . and he's always very happy to see us, but he never has anything to say.'

During 1969, Bowie's half-brother Terry Burns was living in the Cane Hill asylum in south London. Like most of Britain's mental hospitals, it was a vast Victorian institution, whose inhabitants underwent a strict regime of care that involved heavy doses of sedative drugs, electro-shock therapy and, in some cases, a haphazard method of excising parts of the brain known as lobotomy. Many patients quickly slipped into a culture of dependence that did nothing to aid their return to the outside world: the suppressed emotions and physical torpor induced by their diet of chemicals left them unable to respond to, or with, any state of reality. Others were pacified into a state where they could be released to their families. A more progressive regime was slowly introduced into British asylums during the seventies.

In the spring of 1970, as the sessions for *The Man Who Sold The World* began, Terry arrived at the bohemian enclave that was Bowie's portion of Haddon Hall – shared with his new wife, Angie, his producer Tony Visconti, and assorted musicians, roadies and associates. It was a volatile environment for rehabilitation, and despite David's attempts to provide his brother with security, Terry soon had to return to Cane Hill.

'Our alienation goes to the roots,' wrote radical psychiatrist R.D. Laing in the late sixties. 'We are bemused and crazed creatures, strangers to our true selves, to one another, and to the spiritual and material world – mad, even, from an ideal standpoint we can glimpse but not adopt.' He was describing the world beyond the asylum, where 'we who are still half alive' were condemned to 'reflect the decay around and within us'. This was the landscape of 'All The Madmen', the song Bowie composed soon after Terry's departure, in which he channelled his brother's alienation from the 'real' world in a remarkable display of empathy.

Most commentators have assumed that Bowie was writing from his own perspective, watching his 'friends' picked off by madness. He often employed different narrative voices within the same song, but on this occasion his role was clear: he had thought himself inside his brother's head, and captured the insecurity of a man who can endure the prison in which he lives, but cannot face the 'sadmen' of civilisation. What was genuinely chilling was the gradual realisation that the narrator had the choice of whether or not to pass as 'sane' in the eyes of those on the 'far side of town'. He presented himself quite deliberately as 'mad', twisting a familiar pop phrase* to offer behaviour that was guaranteed to be considered 'insane'. The song ended with a comfortingly meaningless chant, part Dada, part children's rhyme, that became an anthem for those inside the asylum. But the price to be paid for that comfort was, by the standards of those outside, quite terrible: lobotomy, EST, Librium, loss of libido.

The music expressed the value of that bargain. As the chorus proclaimed the narrator's sense of belonging with the insane, it surged into a defiant A major chord, finally escaping the narrow straitjacket (between Dm and G) that had confined the opening verses. The guitar solo maintained that theme of playful liberation, as if announcing a courtly dance. Instead, Bowie employed an unexpected jump-cut: a disarming glimpse of madness seen from outside, as four speaking voices competed for attention. Two of them were recognisably Bowie, and unmistakably 'simple', in the parlance of the times, offering eloquent nonsense; a third reinforced them in the stuffy tones of a BBC announcer. The sense of disconnection was profound; only a small child,[†] a gentler incarnation of a vari-speed gnome, could relate to this unreality. 'He followed me home, Mummy,' the child's voice explained. 'Can I keep him?' It was every parent's nightmare; every sane man's stereotype of the threat posed by those who were different from you and me.

The other side of madness was what endured, however, as a Moog synthesiser traced gambolling violin melodies, and the final chorus – a surreal cousin to the coda of 'Memory Of A Free Festival' [9] – revealed its roundelay in B minor.[‡] It was a stunning conclusion to a masterpiece, all the more impressive for having been constructed around a rhythm track that had impatiently been awaiting its burden for several weeks.

* The first line of the Beatles' 'You've Got To Hide Your Love Away', in fact.
† The child/madman nexus of innocence was explored further in 'After All' [20].
‡ The chord quartet achieved the illusion of constantly rising, like the Penrose Stairs in Escher's *Ascending and Descending*.

[24] SAVIOUR MACHINE (Bowie)

Recorded April/May 1970; *The Man Who Sold The World* LP.

Stripped of its vocal – in the shape, therefore, which it assumed until Visconti chivvied Bowie into composing a song – 'Saviour Machine' would have been a highlight of *The Man Who Sold The World* purely as an instrumental. It faded in as if we were eavesdropping on some secret collaboration between Cream and Carlos Santana, matching the British blues band's sturdy dynamics with the Latin-rock guitarist's joyous fluidity, while the spirit of Jimi Hendrix guided Ronson's solo. The album's very own saviour machine, a Moog synthesiser, ran lightning-quick string arpeggios that would have boggled Vivaldi's imagination, before reincarnating itself as a trumpet. And then it all faded into the distance: you could imagine that in some other dimension, the band kept playing, for the delight of any planet that strayed momentarily across their path.

It was a testament to Bowie's skill, then, that under duress he was able to concoct a composition that did not betray the intensity of the track. Like the well-intentioned but ultimately destructive Mountain of 'Wild-Eyed Boy From Freecloud' [7], the computer created by President Joe (shades of Major Tom) is damned by its own omnipotence. A world without evil and want is too dull for the Saviour Machine, which hates the species that gave it life, and urges them to destroy it before it allows its boredom to wipe them out first. Bowie's vocals reinforced the irony: metallic and machine-like as the human narrator, crooning like a martyr to give the computer voice.

[25] BLACK COUNTRY ROCK (Bowie)

Recorded April/May 1970; *The Man Who Sold The World* LP.

The creation of this track spotlighted the haphazard nature of Bowie's creativity during these sessions. He arrived at the studio with a fragment of a melody, a repeated phrase that ended with a swift rise and fall. Then he guided Visconti and Ronson as they fleshed out his theme into a song structure. Reckoning that it sounded like the Birmingham band the Move, he spontaneously named the wordless backing track 'Black Country Rock' in their honour. Only in the final days of the album sessions did he arrive with a skeletal set of lyrics that – bar another fleeting reference to madness and its unique perspective – were merely functional.

His approach to the vocals epitomised his casual attitude to the song. For the verse, he imitated the way in which Ray Davies satirised the aristocracy on songs such as 'Dedicated Follower Of Fashion', before switching his attention to an old friend. 'David spontaneously did a [Marc] Bolan vocal impression because he ran out of lyrics,' Tony Visconti recalled. 'He did it as a joke, but we all thought it was cool, so it stayed.'

That 'tribute' aside, the track was memorable for the musicality that the band introduced, notably the distressingly brief circular guitar lick that acted as a prelude, the expanding density of the central guitar riff (first doubled, then trebled, and finally harmonised as well) and the machine-gun stutter of Woodmansey's drum fills.

[26] THE MAN WHO SOLD THE WORLD (Bowie)

Recorded April/May 1970; *The Man Who Sold The World* LP.

There were precursors: a Robert Heinlein science-fiction tale from 1949 entitled 'The Man Who Sold The Moon'; a 1954 DC comic, 'The Man Who Sold The Earth'; a 1968 Brazilian political satire that flitted across the arthouse movie circuit, *The Man Who Bought The World*. None of them has an apparent thematic link to one of Bowie's most enigmatic songs, written and vocalised over an existing backing track while the clock counted down for completion of the album to which it lent its name. Its lyrics have proved to be infuriatingly evocative, begging but defying interpretation. Bowie himself has contributed nothing more helpful to our understanding than a teasing suggestion that the song was a sequel to 'Space Oddity' [1], an explanation designed to distract rather than enlighten (as the song said, 'Who knows? Not me'). Looking back on this period from the vantage point of 1990, however, Bowie reflected that 'I felt very ephemeral. I didn't feel substantial. I didn't feel a particular sense of self. It seemed that I had to extract pieces from around me, and put them onto myself to create a person. I was having a real problem. I felt invisible.'

'The Man Who Sold The World' was essentially an unconscious

reflection of a piece of self-knowledge that was beyond Bowie's reach in 1970. At the time, there was probably no conscious design in a set of words that suggested more than they defined. Any concrete meaning had to be imposed to the listener's satisfaction. For example: it would be possible to read the song as an acknowledgement of the mysterious connection between David Bowie (who isn't there, because he doesn't actually exist) and David Jones (who does exist, but is effectively dead to the world). Which is the man who sold* (himself to) the world? Maybe they both are. Or neither of them. Like the question of who killed President Kennedy, or what happened to the crew of the *Mary Celeste*, the mystery is more satisfying than any solution.

But not as satisfying as the track, a compact, elegantly assembled piece that featured none of the metallic theatrics found elsewhere on the album. It was hypnotic from the start, when Ronson's guitar nagged repeatedly at the same riff while Bowie's acoustic shifted ground beneath it. The chord structure was equally treacherous, repeatedly augmenting its key of F with an A major chord borrowed from the relative minor scale of Dm. Every musician played his part: Visconti's bass ran scales under the chorus, and a melody elsewhere; Woodmansey left ecstatic drum rolls deep in the mix, and Latin-flavoured percussion trembling on the surface; Ronson conjured a momentary howl of feedback to announce the chorus. But it was the human voice that conveyed the true strangeness of the song, heavily phased during the verse (and briefly doubled, which came as some surprise, as Bowie slyly admitted), compressed (and again double-tracked) for the chorus, and then bursting into a haunting chorale in the final refrains, more rushing to join the crowd with each repetition, filling out the spectrum from bass to alto – facets every one of the single, tangled identity that was the song's enigmatic subject.

---

* In the same year, novelist J.G. Ballard noted that, 'The exterior landscapes of the 70s are almost entirely fictional ones created by advertising . . . We move through a landscape composed of fictions.' In that context, it would be simple for someone to be there, and not there at all.

The Man Who Sold The World LP

Recorded April/May 1970;
released January 1971 (US), April 1971 (UK).

Disconnections made up the shattered framework for this record, almost every facet of which was fragmented and ambiguous. 'It was meant to be our *Sgt. Pepper*,' claimed producer Tony Visconti, who in the same interview noted: 'David didn't really care too much about this album.' His verdict was based on the memory of countless recording sessions at which the artist was, at best, a fleeting presence. 'David was so frustrating to work with at the time of this album,' Visconti concluded. 'I couldn't handle his poor attitude and complete disregard for his music.' Producer and musicians were left to assemble many of the tracks around the hint of a Bowie melody, or a muttered suggestion of a mood. Then, with the studio budget about to run dry, Bowie forced himself to compose the songs that would fill the backing tracks. This modus operandi proved to be unusually effective, and *The Man Who Sold The World* introduced many of the themes and obsessions that would fill his work for the decade ahead: madness, alienation, violence, confusion of identity, power, darkness, sexual possession.

After the rush to complete the record, there was an infuriating delay. 'It's been a waste of a year,' Bowie reflected when the album finally appeared in 1971. Business disputes were to blame: his new manager, Tony Defries, was anxious to prove himself as a major force in Bowie's career, and also to test the strength of the deal that his client had signed with Mercury Records. Critical opinion was almost entirely positive: Bowie's long-time supporter, the journalist Penny Valentine, proclaimed that 'There can't be another writer/performer around today who is even halfway near doing what Bowie has achieved', and added that Bowie displayed 'all the melodramatic power of Dylan crossed with the Demon King'. 'His unhappy relationship with the world is traced to his inability to perceive it sanely,' wrote Bowie's most perceptive American critic, John Mendelsohn, emphasising that – unconsciously, at least – the singer empathised with the theorists of the radical psychology movement.

In Britain, a record that was filled with propulsive hard rock was issued in a cover that, as Bowie noted slightly tongue-in-cheek later, 'was a parody of Gabriel Rossetti. Slightly askew, obviously.' He was clad in 'a man's dress' designed by Michael Fish,* recumbent on a chaise longue like Mrs William Morris in one of the Pre-Raphaelite artist Rossetti's many sketches of women draped decoratively across furniture (and 'slightly askew' because Bowie was, despite his attire, a man). The personality of the record and that of its cover were utterly at odds – as were the mock-Rossetti design and the Mike Weller cartoon that filled the US album cover, showing a rifleman in a Stetson (modelled on a photograph of John Wayne) against the backdrop of the asylum in which Bowie's brother Terry was a resident. That picture, even after being vandalised by Mercury Records' US office, did at least chime with the prevailing theme of madness: the 'man's dress' heralded an entirely different mindset, anticipating the androgynous look that would soon become one of the decade's prevailing images. For the moment, it simply confused those who might have been attracted by the music.

The Man Who Sold The World only charted after it was reissued in 1972, in the wake of *Ziggy Stardust* and with a more obvious cover design. Back in 1970, the album's completion marked the end of Bowie's brief liaison with the Hype. Mick Ronson and Woody Woodmansey returned to Hull, and Tony Visconti opted to work with the altogether more active Marc Bolan instead. So it was that between 1 August 1970 and 20 June 1971, David Bowie made no public appearances – his second such 'retirement' in just three years. It was an unusual way of pursuing stardom.

[27] TIRED OF MY LIFE (Bowie)

Recorded *c*. September 1970; unreleased.

Bowie's description of his mental state in 1970 was suggestive of a man battling clinical depression: 'I used to have periods, weeks on end, when I just couldn't cope anymore. I'd slump into myself – I felt so depressed, and I really felt so aimless and this torrential feeling of "What's it all for, anyway?"' While there were personal reasons for his despair – the hollowness of fame, the Arts Lab debacle, his brother's illness – he was also reflecting the ennui and disillusionment that were haunting youth culture.

---

* The owner and designer of the Mr Fish store in London also created man's dresses for Mick Jagger.

John Lennon reflected at the start of the year that 'a lot of people are in what they term as the Post-Drug Depression period, where there's no hope and they're all hooked on various whatevers'. The hard-rock music that was becoming the lingua franca of young teen-agers – epitomised by Black Sabbath, Led Zeppelin, Uriah Heep, Deep Purple – was loud, relentless, crushing, and best experienced with a dose of a 'downer' like Mandrax. Among those who wanted a more lyrical connection with their music, the two most prominent performers of 1970 were James Taylor, a melancholy folk songwriter with a heroin addiction, and Neil Young, whose voice was almost a parody of extreme dejection, a lonesome, wasted whine that masked his wit and poetic insight.

Bowie credited Neil Young as an influence on several occasions during this period, and 'Tired Of My Life' – a gorgeously maudlin acoustic lament, supported by countless vocal harmony parts in the style of Young's musical playmates, Crosby, Stills & Nash – clearly bore his mark. It combined the melodic flavour of 'Don't Let It Bring You Down' with the vocal blend of 'Tell Me Why', both featured on Young's September 1970* album, *After The Goldrush*. Had Bowie retained the services of John Hutchinson in 1969, and never met Mick Ronson, this is the music that he might have been selling to the world. Instead, he filed this song away, but never forgot it: an entire melodic section, and two full lines of lyrics, were revived for 'It's No Game' [180/181] in 1980.

[28] HOLY HOLY (Bowie)

Recorded November 1970; single A-side. Re-recorded November 1971; single B-side.

Billed as 'the first haunted song' by its plucky PR team, 'Holy Holy' might have been better described as 'cursed'. Issued as a single, it was intended to be the focus of a six-week marketing campaign, involving copious press adverts and themed carrier bags. Instead it limped into

---

* Kevin Cann's admirable Bowie chronology suggests this song dated from the May sessions for *The Man Who Sold The World*. If so, it displayed Bowie's uncanny ability to predict the future.

the shops quietly in January 1971, and promptly disappeared – forever, as (almost alone in Bowie's catalogue) it has never been reissued.* It was Bowie's solitary collaboration with the instrumentalists behind the Blue Mink group of session musicians (contemporary hitmakers in their own right with 'Melting Pot' and 'Good Morning Freedom'), but its blatant musical prototype was Marc Bolan's T. Rex. Bowie's single was recorded as Bolan's 'Ride A White Swan' climbed the charts, and from the distinctive warble in his voice to the 'lie-lie-lie' chorus at the end, 'Holy Holy' sounded like a conscious attempt to mimic (or parody) the vehicle for Bolan's success.

It's been claimed that the song reflected Bowie's interest in the occult, but a more convincing explanation is that, like 'The Prettiest Star' [13], it was a private message to his wife, signalling devotion within the acceptance of an open marriage. It was more of an exercise in assonance than communication, however, from the first line to the final chorus. It opened with menacing E-F footsteps, which chased the melody through the opening line, and only allowed the song to root itself in the chorus. A repeated flamenco rhythm from Alan Parker's electric guitar introduced a mock-operatic feel, which had also been present in some of the arrangements on *The Man Who Sold The World*. But the overall effect was of a basket of ideas that had been thrown together haphazardly without a clear design.

Bowie returned to the song during the *Ziggy Stardust* sessions a year later, electrifying the clockwork mechanism of the original recording. Under Mick Ronson's guidance, this rendition was faster, punchier and more powerful, with Bowie's voice echoed and compressed like one of Dr Who's deadliest enemies.

[29] HOW LUCKY YOU ARE (AKA MISS PECULIAR) (Bowie)

Recorded November 1970; unreleased.

If 'Holy Holy' [28] retained some of the hard-rock dynamics of *The Man Who Sold The World*, 'How Lucky You Are' represented a clear step into a new – and mightily productive – arena for Bowie. Until

* The 1990 CD of *The Man Who Sold The World* claimed to include this track, but contained the 1971 re-recording instead.

now, his songs had been composed on acoustic guitar, or simply as melodies, translated into musical form by his accompanists. Now, for the first time, he was writing on piano, an instrument that would transform his style over the next year. If his playing was still rudimentary – triads in the right hand, a single left-hand finger for the bass note – it allowed him to explore harmonic movements that were less obvious on guitar, experimenting with what happened if he retained the basic shape of a chord but simply moved one finger up or down the keyboard. The piano didn't immediately cure his perennial problem with constructing a song: the middle section of 'How Lucky You Are' was as chaotic as anything on his 1965 demo tapes. But the speed at which his confidence at the keyboard progressed was a sign that it enabled him to approach his creativity with a clear mind, unhindered by the risk of tumbling into his own clichés.

That said, 'How Lucky You Are' was a strange place to begin, its waltz tempo first resembling a Eurovision Song Contest entry and then a lost song from *The Threepenny Opera*. Like 'Holy Holy', it ended with a wordless vocal chorus, building a bridge between Kurt Weill and Paul Simon's 'The Boxer'. Its lyrics were its most puzzling feature, however, their incoherence demonstrating the extent of the erotic fixation and concomitant self-disgust that were apparently their spark. They must have sounded uncommonly strange to the ears of Tom Jones, to whom this song was sent as a possible single by Bowie's publisher.

Besides his demo, Bowie also supervised a second version of 'How Lucky You Are', sung by his friend Micky King (see [36]).

Bowie and the Homo Superior

Bowie was 23 years old when he wrote 'The Supermen' [19], which, he explained the following year, 'was about the *homo superior* race'. The phrase has been traced back to *Odd John*, a 1935 novel by science-fiction author Olaf Stapledon, in which *Homo sapiens* does not make way for *Homo superior*, but attacks him. It was subsequently used by many other SF authors, though Bowie himself was responsible for widening its circulation. In 'The Supermen', however, he was using *Homo superior* as a translation of one of the most misunderstood concepts in the history of philosophy: the *Übermensch* described by Friedrich Nietzsche.

Academics are still debating the implications and meaning of Nietzsche's noun, often translated into English as 'superman' or, more literally, 'over-man'. Bowie subsequently admitted that he had skimmed Nietzsche's work at the start of the seventies, and pretended to understand it – intrigued, it seems, by the influence that Nietzsche had on the philosophy of the Nazi Party. In that 1971 interview, he made the connection explicit, before burbling unintelligibly about Hitler* and 'the Magic Wine', and the risk that modern man might 'have given birth to *homo superior* prematurely'.

So it's not surprising that Bowie's grasp of the *Übermensch* was partial and confused: that he missed Nietzsche's contrast between two avenues that mankind could follow now that God was dead – the *letzte Mensch*, or 'last man', a mediocrity brought to a state of apathy and exhaustion by the mirage of democratic equality; and *Übermensch*, a flash of lightning strong enough to exist beyond the comforting illusion of equality and ethics, who will illuminate the truth for those bold enough to follow him. Nietzsche animated this choice in *Also Sprach Zarathustra*,† in which the prophet's warnings are ignored by weak humans who prefer the 'last man' to the 'over-man'. It was much easier for Bowie to gloss over the philosophical debate, and hold firm to the attraction of the *Übermensch* – or, in SF terms, the *Homo superior* – as a superior species with powers excelling our own. Hence the link with the Nazi Party, and its dream of Aryan stormtroopers and maidens, who could populate an ideal Reich that would last a thousand years. By toying with Nietzsche's terminology, Bowie was indirectly reflecting a surge of interest in the philosopher that pervaded the work of French theorists in the decade ahead. There were new editions of Nietzsche's works; a collection of his letters; a sense that, 25 years after the end of the Second World War, the core of Nietzsche could be retrieved from the Nazis' deliberate perversion of his writings.

This enthusiasm somewhat incongruously tumbled into the field of rock music, where it became a commonplace for artists and critics with a smattering of education to talk knowledgeably about the gulf between Dionysian and Apollonian qualities, again using terms employed by Nietzsche. Foremost among these philosophical pretenders was Jim Morrison of the

* Bowie admitted to being 'overwhelmed' by the Nazis' methods, which he described as 'diabolical' – the same adjective he applied to the advertising industry.
† Nietzsche's book inspired Richard Strauss to compose the music that became the theme to the film *2001: A Space Odyssey* – a connection that may also have brought the philosopher to Bowie's attention.

Doors, who quite deliberately fashioned his public persona as an embodiment of Dionysian frenzy and spontaneity. The same tag was soon applied to Bowie's future friend, Iggy Pop of the Stooges.

Imagine, then, the confusion in Bowie's head at the end of the sixties, with a dangerous smattering of Nietzschean knowledge colliding with a (perennially) fashionable obsession with Hitler and the Nazis, a sense of disillusionment about the hippy movement, and a feeling of drift in his own life. Beyond his personal experience, the daily newspapers reported on Britain's economic and political lethargy, alongside summaries of the rabble-rousing speeches given by maverick Tory MP Enoch Powell. This was a time when, as historian Andy Beckett has indicated, 'a certain feverishness seized some of those involved in British right-wing politics . . . [with] the belief that British decline had worsened into national crisis; the need for a strong, quite possibly authoritarian right-wing government to stop the slide'.

So it was that Bowie, attempting to condense these vague ideas into a philosophy, could utter these comments in a December 1969 interview aimed at a teenage pop audience: 'This country is crying out for a leader. God knows what it is looking for, but if it's not careful it's going to end up with a Hitler. This place is so ready to be picked up by anybody who has a strong enough personality to lead. The only person who is coming through with any strength is Enoch Powell. He is the only one with a following.'

Bowie didn't imagine that Enoch Powell was the *Homo superior*; nor Hitler, for that matter. But like his infatuation with the occult, his flirtation with Nietzsche and the Nazis tapped into his nagging belief that there was more to life (and his life) than the daily obsessions of the media and the herd; that there was an additional dimension beyond the everyday; that the people needed to be led by a 'superman', whatever that might entail. Later in the decade, these elements would combine with extreme cocaine paranoia to send Bowie's political thinking into a state of crisis. Before then, they would congeal in his mind, and help to create the conditions whereby he would seek to portray that 'superman' – not as a political dictator, but as a rock star.

[30] OH! YOU PRETTY THINGS (Bowie)

> Demo recorded January 1971; unreleased. Re-recorded June/July 1971;
> *Hunky Dory* LP.

Bowie had spent years attempting to craft hit singles for other performers, his failure a cause of much frustration for his loyal publishers. As part of Tony Defries' 'new broom' approach to his client's career, Bowie signed a five-year publishing deal with Chrysalis Music in October 1970, thereby removing his new songs from David Platz's Essex Music and assigning them to a newly formed Chrysalis affiliate, Titanic Music. Under the contract, he was given a £5,000 advance (20 per cent of which went straight to his managers), a very substantial sum for the time. He was now freed from the necessity to scrape a living on the road, and was able to concentrate on his songwriting.

'All of a sudden, all these great songs started appearing,' recalled Chrysalis executive Bob Grace. 'We used to do all his demos at the Radio Luxembourg studios in London, which was cheap, and that suited us, because David was writing so much stuff.' 'Oh! You Pretty Things' was one of the first songs Bowie completed under the new deal, and Grace took the demo tape to the Midem music business gathering, where he gave it to producer Mickie Most. Within a matter of weeks, Bowie had finally achieved his aim of writing a hit for another artist, with a song that was a vividly personal reflection of his own psychological landscape. The recipient of this attractive but lyrically unwieldy gift was Peter Noone, whose boy-next-door looks and voice had brought him fame in the 1960s as the lead singer of Herman's Hermits.* His approach to the song involved a total lack of engagement with its darker, occult-inspired themes, altering the word 'bitch' to 'beast' and, more significantly perhaps, beginning his record with the chorus.

For it was the descending diatonic major progression of the chorus (repeated by Bowie in 'Changes' [48] and 'All The Young Dudes' [62], and a familiar motif in the work of Paul McCartney) that undoubtedly

---

* Though they came from Manchester, the Hermits had enjoyed huge success in the USA with revivals of cockney music-hall novelties, which may have encouraged Bowie to explore similar themes during his Deram years.

sold this song, and has ensured its enduring popularity among those who have never grappled with its philosophical conceits, and probably assumed that Noone and Bowie were singing 'gotta make way for the wholly superior'. Only the lyric sheet revealed that Bowie's fixation was actually the *Homo superior*, his conception of Nietzsche's *Übermensch*. Others have noted his references to *The Coming Race* (a prophetic nineteenth-century novel by Bulwer-Lytton), and the Golden Ones (probably inspired by the 1890s occult obsessives of the Temple of the Golden Dawn), while there was an H.G. Wells resonance to his concern about 'the world to come'.

There was no doubting the extent of Bowie's interest in the occult, or his preoccupation with the fate of *Homo sapiens*. Yet, as journalist Michael Watts noted perceptively in 1972, 'His other great inspiration is mythology . . . he has crafted a myth of the future.' It was derivative, and peopled with other people's characters, but its fatalism was entirely Bowie's own. So was the domestic scenario of the opening verse, in which Bowie either inherited or revisited a vision of the Earth cracking open that had been experienced by his brother Terry. In a 1976 BBC Radio interview, Bowie all but admitted that the vision had been his own: 'According to Jung, to see cracks in the sky is not really quite on . . . I thought I'd write my problems out.' But then Bowie has often been, by accident or quite consciously, his own least reliable chronicler.

Nor was he an infallible pianist, though the experiments he'd begun on 'How Lucky You Are' [29] came to fruition on 'Oh! You Pretty Things'. Having played piano on Noone's record (albeit proving unable to perform the song in its entirety without running aground), he had become sufficiently proficient by summer 1971 to prefix his own recording with a 2/4 introduction in F, feeling his way through some appropriate chord changes,* via a brief stop at 3/4 time, towards the final destination of Gb in a 4/4 tempo. The results were charmingly naïve, if occasionally faltering, and quite free of the flourishes that a more accomplished musician might have provided. As if in keeping, Bowie's vocal was also quite unadorned, presented so starkly, in fact, that it was almost unsettling. He accentuated the evil word 'bitch' as

---

* He emerged with a set of chords that were perfectly feasible for a piano player, but fiendishly difficult to transpose to guitar.

if to revenge himself for Peter Noone's timidity, and stretched himself to new levels by hitting a high B at the top of the chorus. That had unexpected consequences when he was unable to rise to the challenge at a BBC concert in June 1971, his voice cracking apart in an eerie replica of the ground in the opening verse. For subsequent performances – at a BBC TV studio in January 1972, for example – he would carefully avoid taking a similar risk, and aim low rather than high.

[31] HANG ONTO YOURSELF (Bowie)

Demo recorded January 1971; unreleased. Re-recorded February 1971; Arnold Corns single. Re-recorded November 1971; *Ziggy Stardust* LP.

'I didn't believe it till I came here, got off the plane,' Bowie commented on his first trip to the USA, in January 1971. 'From England, America merely symbolizes something, it doesn't actually exist. And when you get off the plane and find that there actually is a country called America, it becomes very important then.' Like every British child of the rock 'n' roll era in the years before cheap transatlantic flights, Bowie could barely imagine reaching the soil from which Little Richard, Elvis Presley and Chuck Berry had grown. America's streets were filled with pop poetry, its cities as resonant as the birthplace of any religion.

After a year of ennui bordering on depression at home, this semi-mythical landscape replenished Bowie's energy. 'I think I've been in prison for the last 24 years,' he commented incredulously. 'I think coming to America has opened one door.' Over the next few months, he would write as many songs as he had in the previous three years. 'I got very sharp and very quick,' he explained in summer 1971. 'Somehow or other I became very prolific. I wanted to write things that were more *immediate*.'

This surge of creativity was stimulated by the music he heard during his trip, especially the garage rock of the Stooges and the Velvet Underground. Before Bowie's dextrous rewriting transformed it into a key piece of *Ziggy Stardust* mythology, 'Hang Onto Yourself' was born as an instant response to hearing the Velvets' final album with Lou Reed, *Loaded*. Extracting the spirit of Reed's 'Rock And Roll', Bowie combined it with a lyrical steal from the same album's 'Sweet Jane' (although his narrator was on a radio show, not in a rock 'n'

roll band like Reed's protagonist) and some classic rock 'n' roll reference points. The three-chord guitar opening was pure Eddie Cochran,
while the insistent 'come on' in the chorus brought back memories
of Cochran's 'C'mon Everybody', Chuck Berry's 'Come On' and the
chorus of the Beatles' 'Please Please Me'.* With its attractively familiar
chord changes and instantly accessible structure, 'Hang Onto Yourself'
fulfilled Bowie's desire of creating something 'more immediate' than
the songs he'd written in recent years.

Having taped a multi-instrumental demo in America, Bowie recorded
the song with a band a week after his return, alongside 'Moonage
Daydream' [32]. His double-tracked vocal was an even clearer acknowledgement of his debt to Reed, but the performance lacked the velocity
or punch to sell the song's undoubted commerciality.

Nine months later, it was a very different song that found its way into
the repertoire of the Spiders From Mars. (This is a useful point at which
to recall Jack Kerouac's 'spiders across the stars' in the most memorable
passage of *On The Road*.) Bowie had raised the melody by two semitones,
and written two entirely new verses, excising the borrowed mythology
and creating a legend of his own. There was a groupie and the object
of her adoration, the Spiders themselves, who could move like 'tigers
on Vaseline' – conjuring the vision of magnificent cats sliding out of
control on a newly varnished floor. The propulsive thrust of the band
would be reproduced endlessly later in the decade as the prototypical
British punk sound, but there was a swagger and arrogance to Bowie's
performance (the chuckle as he announced his tiger simile, for example)
that few in any genre could muster.

[32] MOONAGE DAYDREAM (Bowie)

> Demo recorded January 1971; unreleased. Re-recorded February 1971; Arnold
> Corns single. Re-recorded November 1971; *Ziggy Stardust* LP.

Like 'Hang Onto Yourself' [31], 'Moonage Daydream' would long
since have been forgotten had it survived only in the version Bowie
recorded in the Radio Luxembourg studio in February 1971. At this

---

* It has been alleged that 'Please Please Me' was actually a song about mutual
masturbation, which lends a new frisson to the title of 'Hang Onto Yourself'.

point, it consisted of a playful science-fiction-inspired chorus, two nondescript verses with a single memorable line, and an arrangement that not only racked his voice like a martyr under the Inquisition, but virtually defined the word 'shambolic'. (That it was still released as a single by the pseudonymous Arnold Corns in May says much about the depth of Bowie's commitment to this strange side-project, more of which later.)

Chorus and key line – that gloriously emblematic phrase about the holiness of 'the church of man-love', which must have delighted Bowie's mother – were retained for the Spiders From Mars in November. By then, Bowie had wallowed in another bout of self-mythology, declaring himself an alligator (strong and remorseless), a mama/papa (and thereby fashionably gender non-specific), a space invader (alien and phallic), and even a pink monkey-bird, gay slang for a recipient of anal sex. His carefree imagery heightened the erotic fantasy of the chorus, a wet dream that was 'moonage' for the era of the Apollo missions – and also, perhaps, for the tradition of what Robert Graves called 'muse poetry', linked to ancient cults that worshipped the Moon, accessing the imagination without involving the intellect. As occult historian Colin Wilson noted in 1971, 'The moon goddess was the goddess of magic, of the subconscious, of poetic inspiration.' Hence a 'Moonage Daydream' might represent an ecstatic, instinctive path to creativity – or, more banally, nothing more substantial than a homage to Marc Bolan's brand of lyrical imagery. His last single under the name Tyrannosaurus Rex in 1970 had, after all, been called 'By The Light Of A Magical Moon'.

Learning from the vocal agonies of the initial recording, the Spiders tackled the song three semitones lower than before. After Ronson's declaration of intent with a piledriver D chord, there was a moment's pause for the shock to resound, before Bowie launched into his vocal, his rounded tone far removed from the metallic rasp of his 1970 recordings. The electric thrust of the opening bars was deceptive, as the first voice was powered by Bowie's acoustic, and Ronson only reappeared late in the chorus. Saxophone and penny-whistle* danced a prim duet

---

* This element of 'Moonage Daydream' was adapted from the introduction to the Hollywood Argyles' 'Sho' Know A Lot About Love', the flipside of 'Alley Oop', from which Bowie quoted in 'Life On Mars?' [52].

over a sliding major-chord progression for the solo, echoed by electric guitar, before Ronson introduced a lush, hopeful string arrangement for the return of the chorus, climaxing in a steep pizzicato descent. Only in the final moments did Ronson's guitar provide the climactic release that the daydream demanded, continually returning to the same motifs as if in ecstatic spasm.

[33] LADY STARDUST (Bowie)

Demo recorded March 1971; unreleased. Re-recorded November 1971; *Ziggy Stardust* LP.

As America had been robbed of the opportunity to gaze upon Bowie in his 'man's dress' on the cover of *The Man Who Sold The World*, the singer brought that vision of loveliness to life when he first visited the country. The Bowie whom John Mendelsohn of *Rolling Stone* magazine met in California during January 1971 was 'ravishing, almost disconcertingly reminiscent of Lauren Bacall, although he would prefer to be regarded as the latter-day Garbo'. He was wearing 'a floral-patterned velvet mini-gown . . . fine chest-length blond hair and mod nutty engineer's cap that he bought in the ladies' hat section of the City of Paris department store in San Francisco'. This exotic creature was both male and female, straight and gay, and even the land that had spawned a male hard-rock band called Alice Cooper was taken by surprise.

On his return from the States, Bowie began to erase gender distinctions in his songs. 'Lady Stardust' moved painlessly back and forth from 'he' to 'she' like the hero(ine) of Virginia Woolf's novel *Orlando*.* 'She' has long been identified with the late Marc Bolan, who shortly before his death claimed that he and Bowie had enjoyed a gay flirtation, though stopping short of penetration. Bowie critic Nicholas Pegg astutely remarked on the similarity between Lord Alfred Douglas' famous admission, 'I am the love that does not speak its name', and Bowie's 'love I could not obey'. In his piano demo, Bowie opened another can of allusions, to Peter forsaking Jesus in the garden of

---

* 'Freud maintained that individuals alternate between male and female personae', noted cultural historian Peter Conrad.

Gethsemane, though this had been removed later in the year. (As 'sighed' replaced 'lied', Bowie pushed his ever-expanding vocal range to a falsetto C#.)

Whether or not Bolan was the intended subject of the song (and the references to his hair and animal grace certainly fitted), the finished record sounded like a pastiche of a mutual acquaintance, and another pop star who was familiar with sexual confusion: Elton John. Bowie could hardly have concocted a more exact imitation of Elton's mannered tone, the way he held his notes, and the echoed combination of tambourine and snare that were hallmarks of albums such as *Elton John* and *Tumbleweed Connection*. Only the slow descent over major chords in the chorus established Bowie's ownership of the song.

[34] RIGHT ON MOTHER (Bowie)

Demo recorded March 1971; unreleased.

'Right On Mother' was presented to Peter Noone at the same time as 'Oh! You Pretty Things' [30], and was indeed taped as the singer's next single, though without repeating its predecessor's success. Beneath its kitchen-sink drama scenario of a young man daring to live with his girlfriend before marriage, it had a personal edge for Bowie, suggesting that his mother had suffered some difficulty in accepting his increasingly camp persona of recent months. As he declared proudly 'I'm a man', his voice soared defiantly to a high C, as a demonstration of how he had liberated himself in recent months. His piano accompaniment, similar to that on his earlier gift to Noone, carried this song deep into the territory of Paul McCartney's 'Martha My Dear' and 'Honey Pie'.

[35] ZIGGY STARDUST (Bowie)

Demo recorded March 1971; unreleased. Re-recorded November 1971;
Ziggy Stardust LP.

Written within days of each other, 'Lady Stardust' [33] and 'Ziggy Stardust' were always intended as partners. They offered starkly different portraits of the same protagonist: while 'Lady Stardust' left the tale unfinished, with no hint at a denouement beyond a vague air of melancholy, 'Ziggy Stardust' was a birth-to-death chronology, from his shocking, Hendrix-like arrival to the moment when 'the kids' killed 'the man'. It was the equivalent of finding a complete gospel amongst the Dead Sea Scrolls, giving context to everything around it on the *Ziggy* album. If Bowie was, as he later claimed, thinking from the start about fashioning a theatrical rock opera, then this song could have acted as its overture – or, if he preferred to keep the ending a surprise, it could have reappeared throughout the musical as a running commentary on its star.

As early as his spring 1971 demo, Bowie recognised that a song this pivotal required a fanfare: a simple but stunningly effective combination of tonic and dominant chords (the latter with a hammered 4th), followed by the familiar (for guitarists) shifting-bass run from C to Am, and assuredly back to the root. Bowie's acoustic 12-string survived on to the record, beneath Ronson's electric fuzz guitar and, almost unnoticeable unless you knew it was there, a 'jingle-jangle', Byrds-inspired riff from a second electric. Then Bowie's voice arrived, like a meteor from a distant galaxy, with the phrase that defined his hero: 'Ziggy played guitar'. Whether his inspiration was Hendrix or Bolan mattered less than his checklist of rock-star characteristics: the drugs, the enormous cock, the too-wasted-to-leave-the-room pallor. The climax was inevitable, as it has been played out countless times before and after Ziggy: ego, alienation (who would want to get close to a leper Messiah?), disintegration. Ziggy was, after all, the Nazz, a name that neatly referenced early bands led by contemporary rock stars Todd Rundgren and Alice Cooper (who also fronted his own set of Spiders in 1965), but ultimately led back to the hip raconteur Lord Buckley, and his tales of Jesus of 'Naz'. That story also resulted in death, followed by a mysterious afterlife, acolytes, sceptics, and all the other paraphernalia associated with the premature demise of modern-day icons, from Monroe and Dean to Hendrix, Presley, Lennon and Cobain. If the biblical gospels were an attempt to prejudice the verdict of history, then 'Ziggy Stardust' had the same clinical effect upon Bowie's creation, who has passed into legend as the ultimate rock superstar.

Even within the song, however, a multiplicity of voices offered their testimony – heavily echoed in the first and last* verses, intimate and close in the second, then doubled in the chorus like a zealot shouting in each ear. That chorus was already eerie, creeping down to the oscillation between E and F chords that found a happier home here than on 'Holy Holy' [28], and also rekindled memories of the Who's 'Boris The Spider' scurrying across the floor. The final masterstroke, the one major addition to the song after Bowie's original demo, was the reprise of the announcement that 'Ziggy played guitar'. Bowie held the note defiantly, his voice finally sliding away, and prompting Ronson's guitar to offer the same tribute. Then, after one of the most perfectly judged pauses ever captured on vinyl, there was 'Suffragette City' [59] – a last-minute addition to the mythology.

[36] RUPERT THE RILEY (Bowie)

Recorded by Micky King's All Stars, April 1971; unreleased.

The mock-Californian vocal harmonies and lovingly recorded car engine on this playful tribute to Bowie's vintage motor suggested that during his first trip to California in January he had bought a recent Beach Boys' single, the B-side of which ('Susie Cincinnati') was an affectionate celebration of a taxi driver that opened in remarkably similar style.† Like all good car songs, it carried some sexual innuendo, but its intention was merely to amuse. Bowie hoped that it might spawn a musical career for his friend Micky 'Sparky' King, a rent boy whom he and his wife had met at the gay mecca of the Sombrero Club in Kensington. ('I would try and get anyone who would open their mouths to do my songs,' Bowie recalled in 1998.) In the event, the track wasn't released, but it lingered in Bowie's memory: its 'beep-beep' chorus (borrowed from the Beatles' 'Drive My Car') not only reappeared in 'Fashion' [185], but was probably the melodic ancestor of the 'transition/transmission' refrain in 'TVC15' [129].

---

* And double-tracked here too, leading to the strange effect of two voices both declaring that 'I' had to break up the band.
† So did several older Beach Boys tracks, though, from '409' onwards.

[37] LIGHTNING FRIGHTENING (AKA THE MAN) (Bowie)

Demo recorded April 1971; *The Man Who Sold The World* extended CD.

Given unwarranted prominence in Bowie's catalogue by its inclusion on the 1990 CD of *The Man Who Sold The World*, this simple three-chord jam session, with minimal lyrics, was notable only for its antecedents: Marc Bolan's equally simplistic compositions for T. Rex (though he rarely committed anything this laboured to tape), and more specifically, 'Dirty Dirty' from the debut album by Neil Young's backing band, Crazy Horse. The CD on which this appeared credited it as a collaboration with Tim Renwick, Tony Visconti and John Cambridge, suggesting a pre-spring 1970 date; Bowie archivist Kevin Cann opts for April 1971, and claims that its actual title is 'The Man'. Imported copies of the *Crazy Horse* LP would have reached British stores by that date, supporting Cann's theory.

The Making of a Star #1: Arnold Corns

'Lady Stardust', 'Ziggy Stardust', and soon 'Star' [38]: the recurrent symbolism in David Bowie's songwriting during the early months of 1971 was not a coincidence. Since the beginning of his career, he had been putting into practice the rudimentary theories of advertising and marketing that he had learned as a teenager at his Bond Street agency. He knew how to present and sell an image, how to win publicity, how to rebrand his product – himself – if the public didn't like it. He had also experienced, in the wake of 'Space Oddity' [1], the discomfort of achieving success on other people's terms.

   He was now, effectively, a performer without an audience. He had no regular band, a recording contract with a label who had been unable to sell his two previous albums and an image that had won him more notoriety than respect. But he had, at last, conceived the ultimate product, a brand that he could sell to the world with utter sincerity and conviction: the perfect rock 'n' roll star. He would be male and female, king and queen, alien and human, transcendental and sublime; he would inspire his audience and belong to them, ultimately *be* them, become the incarnation of their dreams, lusts and fears.

   His star would be, in the jargon of the advertising industry, a 'trade character', a brand so powerful that it would demolish everything in its path. And it would arrive fully grown, already invested with the glory that lesser mortals – such as David Bowie – could spend precious years trying in vain to achieve. Bowie would be creating not just a star, but a guaranteed route to stardom.

He was not yet ready to assume this role himself, however. His manager, Tony Defries, was telling him to wait for a more lucrative recording contract to be signed. And there was also a hint of reticence, of insecurity, in Bowie's actions: a feeling that, after his hollow success with 'Space Oddity', he lacked the confidence or the will to put himself forward as the focus of all this desire and expectation.

Meanwhile, he was writing and recording demos of songs that his publisher, Bob Grace, rated as a commercial proposition. Grace was eager to reap some financial reward for his investment in Bowie's potential: with Peter Noone's cover of 'Oh! You Pretty Things' [30] not yet in the charts, Grace and Bowie decided to lease two of the demos to the small B&C Records label. They could not be issued under Bowie's name, as he was still under contract to Mercury. So necessity and fantasy were combined: Bowie's initial demos of 'Moonage Daydream' [32] and 'Hang Onto Yourself' [31] would become the vehicle for an entirely imaginary star. He would be able to test out the potency of his dream, without risking his own reputation.

His sacrificial lamb was a 19-year-old designer called Freddie Burretti, whom Bowie had met at the Sombrero. He was known professionally as Fred of the East End, and once Bowie began to wear his designs, he was able to open a boutique entitled Play It Cool & Play It Loud. That was exactly the spirit Bowie wanted for his imaginary star. There was one problem: Burretti couldn't sing. And one solution: he wouldn't need to. Years before Milli Vanilli scandalised the American rock industry by using two male models to 'front' music that they hadn't made, David Bowie was attempting to play exactly the same trick on the pop audience.

First the two men appeared together on the cover of the 'sex education' magazine, *Curious*, while Freddie also posed with a snake wrapped around his waist. (Bowie was soon claiming that Burretti had come up with the idea before Alice Cooper.) Bowie touted his protégé around the London pop papers, announcing that Freddie was actually Rudi Valentino, the leader of a band called Arnold Corns. 'I believe that Rudi will be the first male to appear on the cover of *Vogue* magazine,' he boasted. 'I believe that the Rolling Stones are finished, and that Arnold Corns will be the next Stones . . . [Rudi] will be the next Mick Jagger.' Burretti wasn't quite so confident: 'Really I'm just a dress designer,' he said apologetically.

Despite Bowie's assurances that his prototype of 'Moonage Daydream' was 'unique, there's certainly nothing to compare with it', the first Arnold Corns single was a flop. The experiment was extended to two further songs [43/44], one of which Burretti was allowed to sing (though his voice was carefully buried in the mix). But B&C didn't release another Arnold Corns single until after Bowie himself had become a star, and because Bowie officially didn't perform on the records, his management was unable to exert any control over the process of marketing and sales. Neither Bowie nor Tony Defries would make that mistake again.

[38] STAR (Bowie)

> Demo recorded May 1971; unreleased. Re-recorded November 1971;
> *Ziggy Stardust* LP.

'I believe in fantasy and star images,' Bowie said in 1971. 'I am very aware of these kinds of people and feel they are very important figures in our society. People like to focus on somebody who they might consider not quite the same as them. Whether it's true or not is immaterial.' So it's surprising that he made strident attempts to dispose of 'Star' to other artists, giving a copy of his May 1971 demo to at least two other bands. Maybe he was wary of capitalising himself on the rock 'n' roll star mythology; maybe he distrusted the song's blatant commerciality. In either case, he heavily rewrote the lyric (as he had 'Hang Onto Yourself' [31]) for *Ziggy Stardust* as a young man's fantasy, almost erotic in its narcissism, in which reality (joining the British Army in Belfast, trying to change the world) paled alongside the 'wild mutation' of rock stardom. The final lines revealed the scenario: the narrator was lulling himself to sleep by dreaming of fame, as the 15-year-old Bowie might have done when he first joined the Kon-Rads. 'Watch me now,' he muttered, echoing the proud boast from the Contours' early sixties dance-floor anthem 'Do You Love Me'.

There were other ghosts afoot during the recording, with the exaggerated backing vocals mimicking a dozen Beatles songs, from 'Baby

It's You' via 'Girl' to 'Sexy Sadie' and 'Happiness Is A Warm Gun' – Bowie claimed it was 'Lovely Rita', though that's less easy to hear. Like John Lennon, Bowie must have relished the affectionate doo-wop throwback of Frank Zappa's album *Ruben & The Jets*. There was also a hint of the Who's 'Pinball Wizard' (another sales pitch for a superstar) in the triple contact of Mick Ronson's plectrum as he hit the power chords beneath the frantic, stumbling* introduction. The song was elegantly constructed, too, with verse and chorus nearly replicating each other (separated by a three-beat pause when four was what the ear expected), a guitar interruption offering a series of abrupt tonic-dominant shifts, and a coda that took an unexpectedly flattened route home from C to the key chord of G as if to signal the transition from daydream to the oblivion of sleep.

[39] KOOKS (Bowie)

Recorded June 1971; BBC Radio. Re-recorded July 1971; *Hunky Dory* LP.

As Bowie was launching his initial experiment in creating a rock star, he decided that he was ready to resume his own career as a public figure. He had been using a shifting group of session musicians and acquaintances (some of whom were ostensibly members of Arnold Corns) for his recording work this year, but now he was keen to recruit a full-time band. His initial impulse was to reform the Hype, but as he was estranged from his previous bassist, Tony Visconti (who was still masterminding Marc Bolan's star-making machinery), he required a replacement. Mick Ronson and Woody Woodmansey returned to Haddon Hall from Hull with the perfect candidate: another local musician, Trevor Bolder. And so, though he didn't yet realise it, Ziggy Stardust had acquired his Spiders From Mars. The ensemble debuted at a haphazard but joyful performance for BBC Radio, at which Bowie allowed several of his friends – George Underwood and Geoff MacCormack from Bromley, Dana Gillespie from his Marquee days, and Mark Carr-Pritchard from the Arnold Corns sessions – to share his spotlight.

* The stuttering effect was achieved by piano and bass playing quavers in 4/4 time, and Woody Woodmansey mimicking the distinctive drum motif from Jimi Hendrix's 'I Don't Live Today'. Once Ronson was added to the mix, the impression of manic impatience was unmistakable.

Their performances included covers of Chuck Berry's 'Almost Grown' and Ron Davies' 'It Ain't Easy' [41], while George Underwood sang Bowie's 'Song For Bob Dylan' [40] and Dana Gillespie made his 'Andy Warhol' [47] her own. But Bowie also introduced some more personal material.

An unfinished song about an unconventional family Bowie had met in Chiswick – musically inspired by Neil Young's equally fragmentary 'Till The Morning Comes' – swam into sharp focus once his son Zowie was born in May 1971. Four days later, he performed the song on BBC Radio, and its inclusion on *Hunky Dory* ensured its enduring appeal amongst those who were less entranced by his explorations of politics, psychology and occult elsewhere on the album. The instrumental hook was that guitarist's favourite, the movement between D major and D sustained 4th, with a subtle switch to D7 for the second line. The rest appeared seamless, with the C-Am drift of the chorus giving way to a more definite set of major chords for the verse. Some flamboyant, rollicking piano heightened the vaudeville* feel of the latter portion of the song, while bassist Trevor Bolder contributed a simple reprise of the melody on trumpet.

Any minor complication was reserved for the lyrics, with their repeated question – '*will* you stay' – allowing the subject an element of free will that the more obvious alternative ('*won't* you stay . . .') would have denied. The 'story' also suggested an element of fantasy that didn't, perhaps, bode well for the child's welfare. Bowie's bohemian rhapsody included another disavowal of his school days, in the vein of 'Can't Help Thinking About Me' [A14].

[40] SONG FOR BOB DYLAN (Bowie)

Recorded June/August 1971; *Hunky Dory* LP.

'Dylan belongs in a very personal way to everyone who digs his music,' a British underground newspaper declared in 1970. 'He existed in our heads, we absorbed him and his music wholesale.' So deep was this identification that those who aligned themselves with the

---

* There were hints in 'Kooks' that Bowie might have been familiar with Kevin Ayers' earlier exploration of similar musical territory, 'The Clarietta Rag'.

counter-culture needed to believe that Bob Dylan shared their values and ideals. When the singer-songwriter refused to lead the protests against the Vietnam War, or comment on the repression in Nixon's America, there was a very real sense of outrage amongst his peers and fans. Dylan preferred to tease his followers with his indifference to their cause: 'How do you know I'm not, as you say, *for* the war?' he said in a 1968 interview. Country Joe & the Fish issued a song in 1970 entitled 'Hey Bobby', complaining, 'Where you been? We missed you out on the streets.' By the end of the year, self-styled 'Dylanologist' A.J. Weberman had founded the Dylan Liberation Front in New York, whose manifesto was simple: 'Free Bob Dylan From Himself'. John Lennon was among those who proudly wore the Liberation Front badge.

Bowie's decision to add his name to those placing responsibility for social change on Dylan's shoulders was intriguing, to say the least, especially given that he was also beginning to explore the demands of stardom in his songs. One wonders whether he connected the fate of 'Ziggy Stardust' [35], killed by his fans, with the pressure that was being exerted upon Dylan.* His excuse was that the song was written to reflect the views of his friend George Underwood, who duly performed it during Bowie's June 1971 BBC concert in an attractively Dylanesque voice. By 1976, however, Bowie had concocted a faintly ridiculous rationale: 'It laid out what I wanted to do in rock. It was at that period that I said, "OK, if you don't want to do it, I will." I saw the leadership void.' However much sense this made to him retrospectively, there was nothing in the song to support this explanation.

Not that the song was fully coherent, in any case. The simple finger-pointing of the verses (constructed around chord changes familiar from Dylan's work) and the final lines of the chorus were separated by a shift of perspective that gave the song its working title ('Here She Comes'), and muddied its narrative. Who was the person who could tear everything to pieces with his cat claws? This was purely personal iconography, which read like a lost fragment from 'Queen Bitch' [45], especially as its original title recalled a song by Lou Reed, the ostensible inspiration for the latter composition.

* Later that year, Dylan responded by recording a protest single, 'George Jackson', only for his Liberation Front to complain that he was being insincere.

More intriguing was Bowie's decision to address Dylan by his real name of Robert Zimmerman, just as John Lennon had done on 'God' a few months earlier. By distinguishing 'artifice' from 'reality', he was begging a comparison with his own multiple identities of David Jones, David Bowie and, very soon, Ziggy Stardust.

[41] IT AIN'T EASY (Davies)

Recorded July 1971; *Hunky Dory* LP.

American singer-songwriter Ron Davies introduced this song on his eponymous 1970 album as a slice of Louisiana folk-blues. The US band Three Dog Night, who had a penchant for translating rock iconography into Top 40 pop, softened the song's rural edges. But it took David Bowie's band of friends and neighbours, at his 3 June 1971 BBC concert, to bring out the gospel-soul potential of the chorus, with Dana Gillespie's powerful voice evoking comparisons to Bonnie Bramlett's adventures with the Delaney & Bonnie big band. This was mainstream early seventies Americana, a sound that was re-created on British records by Joe Cocker, Eric Clapton and Elton John, making it all the more strange that Bowie chose to revisit the song in the studio – considering it first for *Hunky Dory*, and then imposing it on *Ziggy Stardust*, when it had no sonic or thematic links with either. Though Gillespie's wailing voice ensured that the chorus, at least, was respectable, Bowie doomed his performance by assuming a strangulated vocal tone that was, presumably, meant to sound both Southern and intense, without achieving either aim. As this performance proved, he was never less convincing than when trying to be the kind of transatlantic rock star that he was usually content to parody.

[42] BOMBERS (Bowie)

Demo recorded *c.* June 1971; unreleased. Re-recorded July 1971; *Hunky Dory* extended CD.

'Kind of a skit on Neil Young' was how Bowie described this song in early 1972, more than six months after he had first taped a solo demo and performed it for BBC Radio. Aside from a couple of lyrical references* that might be coincidental, however, the comparison did little to elucidate a strangely theatrical song about aerial warfare, as if the London music hall of the 1930s had decided to tackle the conflict in Vietnam. Bowie's voice was gleeful, sardonic, clipped, exaggeratedly mock-English – a whole spectrum of hyperbolic mannerisms, in fact, as one might expect from a mime artiste suddenly allowed to speak after a lifetime of silence. As Bowie admitted, it was positively 'queer', and decidedly camp, placing 'Bombers' into the same satirical territory as the 1969 film *Oh! What A Lovely War*. Camp, too, was the final, vaudeville verse, in which Bowie soared to a falsetto C reminiscent of one of his musical heroes of the time, Tiny Tim. The air of mockery was reinforced by the musical subversion of modulating suddenly into a flat key at apparently random moments of the melody – as in the rise to the chorus, where a predictable set of chord changes, C-Dm-Em-F, slipped back into an unexpected E♭ before achieving the obvious safety of the final G chord.

[43] LOOKING FOR A FRIEND (Bowie/Carr-Pritchard)

Recorded June 1971; BBC Radio & Arnold Corns single. Re-recorded November 1971; unreleased.

Whether performed with Mark Carr-Pritchard at the BBC, attempted in the studio as an Arnold Corns single, or briefly considered for *Ziggy Stardust*, 'Looking For A Friend' was doomed to sound like a reject from the Rolling Stones' *Sticky Fingers* album – Mick Ronson heightening that impression with some Mick Taylor-inspired lead lines on the radio performance. After a nod to Bob Dylan's 'The Times They Are A-Changin'', the lyric swiftly degenerated into a coy, camp collection of clichés, which Bowie didn't even attempt, as he had with earlier Arnold Corns songs [31/32], to revamp for his own purposes.

---

* The old man could have come from the first line of Young's 'Don't Let It Bring You Down', also an apparent influence on 'Tired Of My Life' [82]; while 'Right Between The Eyes' was the title of a recently released song by Young's CSNY bandmate, Graham Nash, though it was also where Captain Marvel zapped the tiger on the Beatles' 'Bungalow Bill'.

[44] **MAN IN THE MIDDLE** (Carr-Pritchard, possibly with Bowie)

Recorded June 1971; Arnold Corns single.

The last of the four Arnold Corns recordings relegated Bowie to the role of supporting player, while the song's chief composer, Mark Carr-Pritchard, offered a gloriously detached lead vocal. The lyrics might easily have been a portrait of Bowie in his 'I'm gay' persona.

[45] **QUEEN BITCH** (Bowie)

Recorded July 1971; *Hunky Dory* LP

'It's time to be proud of making it with other guys, time to get out of the guilt-ridden ghettos of the gay world,' wrote underground journalist Jim Anderson in 1970. He continued: 'So long dinge queens, toe queens, leather queens, size queens, cottage queens, hair fairies, fag hags and chubby chasers. There's no need any longer to shriek or camp about like hysterical birds of prey, no need for that bitchy defiance. You can relax. The world in the 70s will be one vast erogenous zone with that most natural and persistent of sexual variations, homosexuality, an integral and vital part of the kaleidoscopic world of human sexuality.'

For those flirting with the naughtiness of the 'guilt-ridden ghettos', however, the old stereotypes were too attractive to abandon. Hence 'Queen Bitch', a cornucopia of camp terminology, overtly pitched as a tribute to Lou Reed and the Velvet Underground, the only rock artists at ease in this louche milieu.* So the song has been widely assumed to be directed at Reed himself, even though in 1971 there was no sign of his mincing in satin and tat, as Bowie claimed.

I'd like to propose a different reading, and suggest that in 'Queen Bitch' – and perhaps the chorus to 'Song For Bob Dylan' [40] as well – Bowie was acting as a 'queen bitch' himself and revenging himself on an old friend. When the song was written, Marc Bolan had escaped his own ghetto as a hippy pixie poet and become the most successful

---

* Besides the reference to the 'V.U.' on the back cover of *Hunky Dory*, 'Queen Bitch' utilised a variation on the central riff of Reed's 'Sweet Jane'. Bowie also referred to Sister Flo, an obvious reference to the Velvets' 'Sister Ray'.

British pop star since the Beatles. Music journalist Penny Valentine, a long-time promoter of Bowie's cause, would soon note that Bolan occupied 'an amazing position unequalled by anyone else in contemporary music. [He represents] the new Presley image, surrounded by the same fanatical devotion that James Dean once reaped.' That quote was printed a few days before *Hunky Dory* was released and widely ignored by the public.

Having known, and competed against, Bolan since 1964/65, Bowie was understandably jealous when his rival achieved such startling success. 'We were all green with envy,' he recalled many years later. 'It was terrible: we fell out for about six months. And he got all sniffy about us who were still down in the basement.' The fact that Bolan's hits were being produced by Bowie's estranged friend Tony Visconti can't have eased his pain. So it's not far-fetched to imagine that Bowie might retaliate in song. As Bowie mistrusted his rival's sincerity, he could easily have imagined that Bolan could slash him with his claws while masquerading as a friend, as the chorus to 'Song For Bob Dylan' suggested; likewise, Bolan could have been the painted lady whom Dylan could destroy with a return to his mid-sixties acerbity. Extend the fancy, and look at 'Queen Bitch' in that light: the track opened with a Bolan-esque piece of scat, used a Bolan-esque turn of phrase to describe a hat, and concluded jealously that he could do better than that – as he had proved on the (British) cover of *The Man Who Sold The World*. Add in some malicious gossip from the London clubs, and a sense of bitterness that it could have been him . . .

Far-fetched or otherwise, this theory doesn't account for the superbly simple production of the finished record, trebling the basic riff with two electric guitars and one acoustic, that blend being an intrinsic part of Bowie's sound in 1971/72. (Note how Bowie chuckled as he sang 'false claims', followed instantly by the guitar in the left-hand channel fumbling its chords.) Like a method actor, he tossed in perfect, apparently off-the-cuff interjections between lines, the epitome of the streetwise rock star, and typical of this remarkable pastiche of rock sponaneity.

[46] FILL YOUR HEART (Rose)

Recorded July 1971; *Hunky Dory* LP.

American singer-songwriter Biff Rose is fated, at best, to pass into the history of popular music as a footnote to Bowie's *Hunky Dory* album, most listeners being unaware that Bowie was not himself the composer of 'Fill Your Heart'. Though Bowie first heard the song on the debut album by the freakishly falsettoed novelty act Tiny Tim, he was led to obtain a copy of Rose's own LP, *The Thorn In Mrs Rose's Side*. There he found a jaunty tea-party arrangement of Rose's mock-hip tale of living like a freak, 'Buzz The Fuzz', which he reproduced – copying all of the mannerisms and asides – during several live and radio performances during 1970/71.

He adopted an equally faithful attitude when covering 'Fill Your Heart', his arrangement of which was practically identical to Biff Rose's, except that where the American glided and swung, Bowie bounced from side to side like a marionette. Bowie and Ronson did at least have the grace to credit Rose's original arranger, Arthur G. Wright, on the sleeve of *Hunky Dory*.

Andy Warhol: Pop to *Pork* and Back Again

Like David Bowie, Andy Warhol had started out in advertising – the difference being that whereas Bowie merely soaked up half-understood ideas from his agency life, Warhol mastered his trade, and turned it into a philosophy of art. Warhol's trademark was the inauthentic: the flowing signature that appeared beneath his ad-agency drawings in the fifties bore his name, but had actually been drawn by his mother. He shamelessly employed assistants to create 'his' art; the Warhol-branded feature films were directed by Paul Morrissey. Though he was a genuinely accomplished artist with a pencil or brush, Warhol chose to manipulate other people's images rather than create his own. He was hailed as the progenitor of pop art, a genre he neither conceived nor introduced to the American public. His achievement was to take a movement that had been propounded as an intellectual critique of prevailing trends in art, and turn it into a frothy, cynical and clever piece of media manipulation.

Like Bowie in the decade ahead, Warhol had invented a persona with which to fool and manipulate the public – only his character bore his own name, not that of a fictional spaceman. The public Warhol barely spoke or moved, preferring to let the denizens of his Factory studio make the noise. His ethos was that nothing meant more than it seemed to mean: 'If you want to know all about Andy Warhol,' he insisted, 'just look at the surface of my paintings and films and me, and there I am. There's nothing behind it.' Just as Christopher Isherwood (in the story sequence *Goodbye to Berlin*) had likened his gaze to that of a camera, Warhol offered himself as the ultimate voyeur, collecting experiences and people without ever apparently interacting with them. Bowie borrowed Warhol's rhetoric just after he had portrayed the artist in song [47]: 'I'm just picking up on what other people say . . . I'm not thinking for myself anymore . . . I'd rather retain the position of being a Photostat machine with an image.' Or, in Lou Reed's take on the Warhol stance, embodied in a Velvet Underground song: 'I'll Be Your Mirror'.

Bowie could never have maintained this facade of indifference for more than a few weeks: he was too enthusiastic a participant in the decadent adventure of life. But his choice of Warhol as artistic mentor in 1971 reflected the American's pervasive influence on British culture. Prints of Warhol's movies were seized from London cinema clubs by police on the grounds that they might be obscene (when they were merely dull). The Rolling Stones' 1971 album *Sticky Fingers* bore a Warhol cover design. There was a sizeable retrospective of his art at the Tate Gallery in February and March 1971, when a documentary about his work was banned from British TV. No wonder that, in seeking out modern icons to portray in song, Bowie should alight on the flat surface of Warhol's bloodless image.

That May, a play named *Pork* opened in New York's East Village. Written and directed by Anthony Ingrassia, it was billed as a Warhol production, having been based, Ingrassia explained, on a 29-act Warhol script that would have taken 200 hours to perform. Like Warhol's 'novel' *A*, his script was merely a transcript of conversations and phone calls made at the Factory, recorded by Brigid Polk (hence the play's title). The Factory regulars were portrayed onstage by struggling actors from the fringes of the Warhol milieu, with Tony Zanetta – soon to become the US president of Tony Defries' MainMan organisation – playing 'B Marlowe', an artist who was wheeled around the stage on an office chair, taking Polaroids of the debauchery unfolding around him.

This deliberately outrageous production (promising 'explicit sexual content and "offensive" language') transferred to the London Roundhouse in July

1971. The cast of *Pork* visited a Bowie concert; he repaid the compliment, and took them to his risqué nightspot of choice, the Sombrero. *Pork* star Wayne County complained later: 'All the while he was studying our make-up for his own future use. His whole look came from us.' County was nursing a grudge against MainMan for not making him a star. But Bowie undoubtedly learned about New York's peculiar brand of decadence from the *Pork* ensemble, many of whom would subsequently join his manager's staff. He was already acting out another Warhol obsession, by gathering a collection of friends and admirers around him and branding them as 'superstars' – a scheme that resulted in attempts to launch two mates from school, a former girlfriend and a Sombrero rascal as recording artistes, albeit with minimal success. Within weeks, Bowie was in New York himself, meeting Warhol (who thoroughly disapproved of his tribute in song) and the artist's former protégé, Lou Reed. By then, the London boy was beginning to feel like an insider rather than a voyeur, assuming a thick coating of self-confidence that would fuel him through the years ahead.

[47] ANDY WARHOL (Bowie)

Recorded June/July 1971; *Hunky Dory* LP.

Within a few weeks* of Warhol's retrospective exhibition at the Tate, Bowie penned this ambiguous tribute to the man he would describe later in 1971 as 'one of the leaders' of 'the media of the streets, street messages'. He offered it immediately to his long-time friend Dana Gillespie, the current partner of his manager, Tony Defries. She performed it in the strident style of Curved Air vocalist Sonja Kristina at a BBC performance in June. Her studio rendition, produced by Bowie, appeared on an acetate LP that Defries utilised to promote both Gillespie and Bowie in America, but Bowie instantly undercut its value by recording it himself for *Hunky Dory* as a late substitution for the crass 'Bombers' [42].

Like Warhol's art, the song hinged around the act of repetition, and the haphazard consequences of reproducing an original concept. All commercial songwriting depended, to some extent, on repeating

---

* The song was carbon-dated perfectly; Britain's currency was decimalised, and 'new pence' substituted for old, on 15 February 1971.

a phrase, or a motif, or a melody; the purpose of a chorus was to focus the audience's attention on something familiar. 'Andy Warhol' employed those inevitable tricks, then reinforced them with a calculatedly repetitive melody, a playful spoken-word introduction that dissolved Warhol's very name into a collision of random syllables, and a coda of endless open-tuned chords, as similar and different as Warhol's subtly varying screen-prints. Meanwhile, the lyrics emphasised Warhol's blurring of life and art.

The deceptively simple structure of the song also erased boundaries, as a 6-string acoustic ran repeatedly (of course) up the scale of Em, while its 12-string counterpart pushed the verse and chorus, in flamenco style, towards A major (in an E Dorian mode). The coda was a delicious medley of handclaps, guitar harmonics and chords reminiscent of Led Zeppelin's acoustic material (notably 'Friends') on their recently released third album. A more famous example of pop art (in both senses of the term) bracketed the song, with the introductory laughter and closing applause recalling the sound effects on the Beatles' *Sgt. Pepper* album.

[48] CHANGES (Bowie)

Recorded *c*. June/July 1971; unreleased demo, and *Hunky Dory* LP.

Changes: emotional, psychological, existential, changes in style and sound, but undeniably, and primarily, physical. This was a song, after all, built around minute shifts of the fingers on the keyboard, a process of experimentation by a man whose technical inadequacies as a pianist liberated him to face the strange* if he found it and embrace the obvious just as readily. As he revealed onstage a few months later, he didn't know the chord changes on guitar. He didn't know them on piano either, but he followed his fingers as they crept slowly up and down the keyboard, augmenting familiar shapes, or simply reproducing them a step or two along the ivories. As its title suggested, 'Changes' was constantly changing, sometimes in the left hand (where he followed the diatonic major descent of 'Oh! You Pretty Things' [30] in the chorus, all the way through the bass scale

---

* I can't be the only person who bought the album without a lyric sheet, and assumed for years that Bowie was singing 'Turn and face the strain' in the chorus.

from C down to D), and almost always in the right. It was as if the piano accompaniment was scared to rest in one place for more than a couple of beats, in case it would be hemmed in or halted. By restlessly moving, it kept its options open and its spirit alive. Perhaps there was a deliberate irony, though, involved in composing a song called 'Changes' in which the opening chords were repeated – in reverse – over the final bars, so that after several minutes of constant mutation, the pianist's hands began exactly where they had started, tracing the symmetrical shape of a C major 7th chord, with four fingers equally spaced along the keys.

Changes as a statement of purpose: it was the first song on *Hunky Dory*, the first his audience had heard of him since *The Man Who Sold The World*, and where was the doom-racked rocker and his metallic power trio? Neither was this a throwback to the atmospherics of 'Space Oddity' [1], or the unwieldy prophecies of the *David Bowie [Space Oddity]* album. This was pure, unashamedly melodic, gleefully commercial, gorgeously mellifluous pop. It could have been called anything – imagine he sings 'ch-ch-ch-chases' instead – and it would still have been a musical metamorphosis of Kafkaesque proportions.

Changes as a manifesto: this was the retrospective interpretation, after a decade of innovation, in which *Young Americans* could not have been predicted from *Diamond Dogs*, or *Station To Station* from *Young Americans*, or *Low* from *Station To Station*. Bowie was the so-called chameleon of pop, and look! He'd already predicted the future back in 1971. But he could just as easily have been looking back from that vantage point at his equally bewildering reincarnations since the Kon-Rads, the stuttering sense of identity that had allowed him to be mime artiste *and* blues-wailing rocker, prophet of doom *and* cheeky clown. And think for a second of the self-confidence required to launch yourself at the world with a manifesto of change, when you have no idea whether anybody will even notice your existence.

Changes as a faith in fate and chance: Bowie was intrigued by the lessons of the *I Ching*, the Chinese Book of Changes, founded on the polarisation of yin and yang, positive and negative, good and evil, action and stasis and, as Colin Wilson noted in 1971, 'the creative drive of the conscious mind and the receptive quality of the subconscious'. When these two forces were separated from their yin/yang relationship, Wilson insisted that the result was 'a condition of vital stagnation' – life enmired in quicksand, no less. Yet this polarisation could take place against the constant flowing of the river of impermanence: as Christmas Humphreys wrote, 'Life is flow, and Zen is the flow of it.' Humphreys again: 'Satori [already referenced by Bowie in his 'Free Festival' song [9]] is the world of perpetual now and here and this, of absolute, unimpeded flow.' And in this flow of perpetual nowness, change was not a choice but a fact of life, however the *I Ching* fell.

Changes as self-healing: you could take the first verse of the song as the heart of a musical drama, in which we've already witnessed our hero in hot pursuit of himself, with a cast of oddballs at his heels, unable to realise until the closing number that the only way he can locate his real identity is to stop for a second, and just be himself, and realise that – look, the typist at the next desk, she's actually the girl of his dreams. That's 'Changes' as the story of Billy Liar in Keith Waterhouse's novel of the same name (and Waterhouse was one of Bowie's favourite authors in the 1960s). Or you could read 'Changes' as pure Bowie autobiography (except that experience tells us there is never anything 'pure' about Bowie's accounting of himself). It was all there: the dead-end streets of Bromley, Beckenham, Soho and Kensington; the success of 'Space Oddity', which proved to be 'not so sweet'; the withering awareness of himself as a faker (or, as he credited himself on the sleeve of *Hunky Dory*, 'the actor'). And it was all out of his control: he knew that time would change him, but he couldn't trace time. His life was impermanent, but every reincarnation would leave him unchanged. It was the curse of eternal life, played out at the speed of light – or life, as Bowie would suggest in a title on *Low* [188].

Changes as rock criticism: the stammering voice of the Who's 'My Generation' was the obvious reference point, as Pete Townshend's mod narrator wanted to 'die before I get old'. In the final chorus of 'Changes', Bowie warned Townshend and his fellow rock 'n' rollers that ageing was the fate that awaited them all (Townshend and Daltrey are in their sixties as I write, still performing 'My Generation' for money). Rock, he complained around the time he wrote the song, 'has become the new extension of factory work'. Bowie had stepped off the production line; he could look forward to a life of 'strange fascination' (at least until 1980).

Changes as immortality: not just the satisfaction of summarising your life at the age of 24, past and future, without narrowing down any of your options; but also of knowing that you have created a perfect pop record, with an unforgettable chorus, and enough sonic scenery to ensure that it would never stale through repetition. His ramshackle piano demo, taped in the Radio Luxembourg studio, demonstrated the strength of what he'd written; though he stumbled over the piano chords, his multi-dubbed harmonies and vulnerable handclap percussion would have sold the song to any Peter Noone who'd been lucky enough to wander within earshot.

But the record was something else entirely, a masterpiece of production (credit Ken Scott, whose first record in that role this was) from Rick Wakeman's flowing piano to Bowie's beautifully poised alto sax solo over the final descending chords. The saxophones were there at the start, in fact, alto and tenor side by side in the lead-up to the first verse; so too were the strings, the sole accompaniment for the piano during that verse. Bowie's voice was the purest instrument on display, however. It entered warm but hushed, almost impossibly intimate through headphones, then soared as Bowie 'turned' (and it was impossible not to see him on a West End stage, throwing his arms wide to the audience). Every syllable was perfectly clear, the hallmark of a trained actor. Then, the chorus: and suddenly a rush of voices from either side, not the accent-less English we'd heard so far, but the unmistakable sound of London, as many as five different Bowies combining to give him, and us, the command to face the strange. We know now that the strange was only just beginning.

[49] EIGHT LINE POEM (Bowie)

Recorded June/July 1971; *Hunky Dory* LP.

Designed to sound like a continuation of 'Oh! You Pretty Things' [30], 'Eight Line Poem' was, at least, eight lines long. (The change in piano tone proved that the two were recorded separately.) Was it a poem? Well, there was a metaphor linking the cactus and the prairie; an internal rhyme ('tactful cactus'); and a striking image in the last line. None of it opened *out*, however; it was a lock with only one key.

So 'Eight Line Poem' was more intriguing as a performance: sparse and sometimes uncertain piano, wobbling across the speakers like a sine wave, country-tinged guitar, and a vocalist who crammed five different personae into those eight lines. Two highlights: the Hank

Williams-inspired yodel of the cacti; and the way that his 'collision' fell almost an octave, echoed as if it was plummeting down a mineshaft. The inspiration? Haiku; the imagist poets; or perhaps Bowie had been playing Neil Young's 'Birds' idly to himself, and allowed himself to dream – but not to rethink what he had written.

[50] QUICKSAND (Bowie)

Recorded July 1971; demo & *Hunky Dory* LP.

> The only thing that emerges with any certainty from the study of spiritualism and occultism is that our normal, sane, balanced standpoint is built upon quicksand, since it is based upon a commonsense view of human consciousness that does not correspond to the facts.
>
> Colin Wilson, *The Occult*, 1971

How could Bowie complain that he had lost his creative power on a song (and an album) that demonstrated precisely the opposite? Because 'Quicksand' – like 'Sound And Vision' [136] five years later – was written *about* a lack of inspiration, as a means of *accessing* the inspiration that he had been searching for. Like 'Oh! You Pretty Things' [30] and 'Changes' [48], it chronicled his confused but dogged attempts to explore the limits (if they existed) of human potential. Through the index of possibilities that the song (re)presented, Bowie held fast to one core belief. Conscious, intellectual thought would not allow him to penetrate beyond the realm of everyday existence, into whatever lay beyond: spontaneous creativity, self-awareness, spiritual discovery or transcendence. Thought, as Colin Wilson suggested, was a form of quicksand, that allowed consciousness – with all its traps of self-doubt and self-deception – to keep the unconscious beyond reach. So 'Quicksand' was a song to himself, and his unconscious (what the poets of old would have called his muse): a plea to be shown the way, or ways, of reaching through, or beyond, or above – whatever metaphor worked for Bowie to be able to touch a realm that his conscious mind told him was an illusion. The very existence of this song (and its neighbours on *Hunky Dory*) demonstrated how profoundly his plea was answered.

It was surely not a coincidence that 'Quicksand' was written in

America, of which Bowie said in 1971 that it had 'opened one door', and a crucial one at that. Like his readings in the occult, which had preoccupied him for the previous year or more, America offered alternate views of his future; took him out of his everyday environment, and the thinking associated with it; and freed him to experience life in a more direct and fulfilling way. Everyone is familiar with the feeling of liberation that can come on holiday, when you decide to quit your job, leave your partner, or simply stop worrying about the mundane pressures of life at home. Except: when you get home, it takes only a few minutes for the old routine to regain control, and all of that transcendence is lost. Bowie's breakthrough – his escape from the quicksand – was that he was able to use his first visits to America as a means of avoiding those traps. Hence 'Changes': Bowie had discovered how to access his unconscious and bring its treasures to the surface.

Yet, as the small print of 'Quicksand' revealed, this was not a painless or reliable process. 'Sometimes I don't feel as if I'm a person at all,' he let slip in a 1972 interview. 'I'm just a collection of other people's ideas.' And here they were, a bewildering collection of voices, each threatening to impose thought on to the unconscious. Many of them were tantalising, because they seemed to be seeking the same thing as Bowie: that explained the appeal of the occult teachings of the Order of the Golden Dawn, or the man who effectively destroyed that organisation, Aleister Crowley. No wonder Bowie declared that he was torn between light and dark – white and black magic, trusting in human potential or seeking the help of Satan. From Nietzsche he had already felt the lure of being human, with potential of becoming a 'superman'; he had been raised in a culture soaked in the 'bullshit faith' of Christianity. Most of all, he had been attracted for many years by the promise of transcendence offered by Zen Buddhism,* the philosophy of which was neatly summarised in the chorus. Now even Buddhism might be suspect in Bowie's search for enlightenment – a quest for the total goal that, as he admitted elsewhere in the song, terrified him at the same time that he realised its inevitability.

This was a song that begged for academic annotation, to discuss whether, for example, Churchill's lies were those alleged in a notorious

---

* Bowie's 'Bardo' wasn't a French actress but the situation of the human soul between death and rebirth in Tibetan Buddhism.

late-sixties play about the death of the Polish wartime leader Sikorski; or whether he was considering intimacy with a snake because he had recently attended a late-night screening of the classic film noir, *Kiss Of The Viper Woman*. But in the context of this song, all that is quicksand: conscious, distracting thought; a neurotic need for explanation and consistency. The music offered another choice: between the tight and tense melodic framework of the verses, almost Dylanesque in their construction, with a questioning rise at the end of several lines; and the choruses, which were all ebb and flow, effortlessly sweeping to a high B♭ with an ease that suggested Bowie had already discovered one way of transcending the everyday.

On his original acoustic demo (included on the extended CD of *Hunky Dory*), Bowie set the song higher than on the finished record, with the result that he sounded like a child bewildered by ideas beyond his grasp. The ragged edge to his voice also conveyed the immediacy of the song's drama: he did not yet know whether he could escape the quicksand. All of that uncertainty had vanished when the song was recorded professionally – the irony being that it was the careful nature of the arrangement, the product of conscious thought rather than unconscious instinct, that conveyed the power of Bowie's message. The opening gambit of acoustic guitar and shimmering vibes gave way to an epic canopy of sound, with massed guitars (and multiple Bowies, in the chorus) decorated by a lavish string score, Rick Wakeman's flamboyant piano, and a succession of urgent drum fills from Woody Woodmansey. Yet the genius of Ken Scott's production was that the overwhelming impression left by 'Quicksand' was of a solitary man looking for a solution, the almost decadent arrangement merely reinforcing the existential drama of Bowie's song.

[51] THE BEWLAY BROTHERS (Bowie)

Recorded July 1971; *Hunky Dory* LP.

Bowie told producer Ken Scott that the final track on *Hunky Dory* was deliberately meaningless,* designed to bamboozle American rock

---

* John Lennon had played the same trick on the Beatles' 'I Am The Walrus' and 'Glass Onion', both of which, coincidentally, were engineered by Scott.

critics with its obscure imagery. The artist was merely covering his tracks. 'I like "The Bewlay Brothers" so much, only because it's so personal,' Bowie conceded in 1972. 'I'm sure it doesn't mean a thing to anybody else, and I'm sorry if I inflicted myself upon people with that track.' He subsequently told his cousin that it was actually a portrait of his relationship with his brother, Terry, and confirmed this interpretation during a 1977 radio interview. Certainly the song retained great significance for him, as he used its name for his music publishing company, founded in 1976. But the title was only obliquely personal: Bewlay's was a chain of London tobacconists (something Bowie signalled at the start of the track by striking a match and lighting up).

Even though none of his potential audience would have been able to pierce the skin of his secret, Bowie made sure that he kept any identifying details under heavy wraps. Only an occasional reference to madness and mental dislocation suggested the subject of his song. This dense, deliberately obtuse lyric was as much about the play of language and the joy of its sound as it was about two human beings. The first line insisted that it was all mythology – or, like Herman Melville's epic novel, 'a whale of a lie'. It would be possible to deconstruct every line in search of meaning: was the reference to a dress harking back to the cover of The Man Who Sold The World? Were the Moonboys a teenage gang in Beckenham? But the song didn't respond on those lines.

You could learn more from the cramped melody of the verses, and their suburban claustrophobia, and the way that the chorus burst into open space when 'we were gone' – liberated, or unrestrained by the bounds of sanity, perhaps. The initial intimacy of the vocal, matter-of-fact like a well-worn story, gave way to the double- or triple-tracked voice of the chorus, attacked by the sweeping gulls of Mick Ronson's interjections of backwards guitar. From the second verse, the singer was accompanied by a spoken voice, as if his personality was shearing apart. A sense of urgency took hold, which grew until the strange relief of the coda. Then a mock-cockney music-hall ditty (compare Cream's 'Mother's Lament', and remember Terry Burns' breakdown after a Cream concert) mutated into a congress of hobgoblins, as the vari-speed voices of 1967 returned with evil intent: the stuff of nightmares, conjuring up the eerie mental landscape of the man who had once shaped Bowie's world.

[52] LIFE ON MARS? (Bowie)

Recorded August 1971; *Hunky Dory* LP.

Having lost the race to the Moon, the Soviet Union redirected their space scientists into another battle with the USA: the first landing of a probe on Mars. Two Russian craft were launched on 19 and 28 May 1971, with the admirably simple names of *Mars 2* and *Mars 3*; on 30 May America retaliated with *Mariner 9*, which trumped its rivals by arriving in Martian orbit first. Even though an earlier mission, *Mariner 4*, had debunked the notion that there were canals on Mars, and therefore some form of recognisable life form, this flurry of interplanetary activity was enough to spark headlines around the world, asking the age-old question: is there life on Mars?

David Bowie had already decided to claim Ziggy Stardust's backing band as Martian invaders: the Red Planet had fascinated him since he was a child, when he had heard Holst's *The Planets* suite, and he had later devoured science fiction about Mars, such as Ray Bradbury's *The Martian Chronicles* (published in Britain as *The Silver Locusts*). But 'Life On Mars?' had no connection with our planetary neighbour, beyond a title that was simply a reference to a media frenzy, of the same brand that could envelop a film star and a fan in a symbiosis of desire.

Ironically, the song developed out of a side effect of that relationship. Bowie had watched enviously as Frank Sinatra, whose movie persona he admired, had achieved the biggest success of his recording career with 'My Way'. Like Bowie's own 'Even A Fool Learns To Love' [A50], it was an English adaptation of Claude Francois' 'Comme d'Habitude' – the publisher of which had opted for Paul Anka's interpretation rather than Bowie's own. It was impossible to fault that decision on artistic grounds, but the perceived slight still rankled with Bowie, who determined to exact his revenge by reusing elements of the song to his own purposes. Hence the coy dedication on the back cover of *Hunky Dory*: 'Inspired by Frankie'. Carefully avoiding copyright infringement, he borrowed the chord sequence from the opening lines of 'My Way' and reproduced it as the opening to 'Life On Mars?' – but with a different rhythm and melody line.

Like 'Changes' [48], 'Life On Mars?' evolved on the piano, with a single-finger bass line descending in the stately fashion that was something of a *Hunky Dory* trademark. Once it was transferred from the fumbling hands of Bowie to the classically trained Rick Wakeman, the accompaniment assumed flamboyant proportions. It was an epic journey from the single piano note that opened the song to the climax of Mick Ronson's gargantuan orchestral arrangement. Besides his own guitar fanfares (and a solo apparently inspired by George Harrison's 'Something'; producer Ken Scott recalled that Ronson nailed it in a single take), Ronson's score featured grim-reaper cellos, echoing the bass in the chorus, and a tumultuous finale involving a full string section making eight descents in just two bars, each beginning a note above where its predecessor had ended, till it gained the force of a river torrent. After the cellos made one last climb up the scale, *2001*-style timpani sounded a funereal farewell. But Wakeman's piano refused to die with the rest, and tinkled on until, deep in the mix, a phone began to ring and a voice could be heard saying, 'I think that's the one.'

Bowie's vocal – also a first take, according to Scott – was equal to the majesty of the arrangement, as he hit a high B♭ at the end of the chorus, and held it for three whole bars. The passion of that climax contrasted with the acerbic, almost nasal tone of the verses, Bowie's sardonic voice rising to exasperation as he lamented the predictability of Hollywood. (I prefer to think that it's not a coincidence that while Bowie was lambasting Hollywood, he revised a line from the Hollywood Argyles, whose 1960 hit 'Alley-Oop' ended with a very similar reference to a caveman.) America's movie capital was the key motif of the song, a manufacturer of dreams and stars that have become stale with repetition. The girl in the first verse – a refugee from 'The London Boys' [A21], perhaps – can no longer believe in the fantasies she is being fed.

As Bowie widened his sights, so more icons crumpled beneath his gaze: Mickey Mouse, Lennon (up for sale, like any other pop star, regardless of his political ideals), all the heroes of those hordes of what Leona Helmsley would call 'the little people'. And where did that leave Bowie, pouring out his heart one more time for people he despised, over a chord sequence that everyone had heard ten times or more? The clash of cynical despair and passionate commitment was almost shocking – not least for what it revealed about how Bowie saw his own role as a star in the making, at the end of this remarkable performance of a deeply unsettling song.

Hunky Dory LP

Arguably the most commercial album David Bowie ever released, *Hunky Dory* was a statement about stardom, and the creation of fame, by a man who was not yet a star. In retrospect, when so many of its songs have become pop standards – 'Life On Mars?' [52], 'Changes' [48], 'Oh! You Pretty Things' [30] among them – it seems remarkable that *Hunky Dory* didn't establish Bowie as the most credible successor to the Beatles that the new decade had yet produced. Instead, it passed almost unnoticed, its profile erased rather than boosted by Bowie's decision to proclaim 'I'm gay' a few weeks after it was released.

There have been rumours since that either Bowie, or Tony Defries, or both of them, chose not to promote *Hunky Dory* in anything like an orthodox fashion, because they were holding back for the launch of *Ziggy Stardust* just seven months later. 'It was an interim project to get me through the recording contract,' Bowie explained later, 'which meant that I had to have an album out.' If *Hunky Dory*'s quality had won out, and the album had been a significant success, then the *Ziggy* experiment might have been abandoned: the impact of *Ziggy* was all the more intense because it was unexpected.

If that album represented a concept being brought to life, then its predecessor was an attempt to explore what stardom, and notoriety, might represent. 'Song For Bob Dylan' [40] and 'Andy Warhol' [47] examined two of the era's dominant figures in pop art (in the widest sense); 'Life On Mars?' asked whether, ultimately, everyone was for sale; 'Changes' found Bowie testing out his own willingness to adapt or compromise to achieve success.

The album cover was both ironic and iconic in its use of star imagery: Bowie arrived at the photo session clutching a volume of Marlene Dietrich portraits, and singled out the image that he wanted Brian Ward to replicate. This was stardom of the old school (a theme he would revisit on *Young Americans*), and the result was a photograph every bit as ambiguous about its gender as 'Lady Stardust' [33]. Indeed, Bowie's new record company, RCA,* had to be persuaded to accept the design, because they feared that the W.H. Smith chain would refuse to display such a confusing image of a man.

The London underground newspaper *International Times* astutely noted that *Hunky Dory* 'has very little to do with David Bowie the poet, something to do with David Bowie the performer, lots to do with David Bowie the artiste, and most of all with David Bowie the public relations expert. He's caught up in a lot of games, so he plays them properly.' And the games were only just beginning. Alongside the strength of his songs, Bowie was teaching his audience that all stardom is an illusion, everything authentic is a fake. It was time for Ziggy Stardust to ram the lesson home.

* The RCA deal had been secured by Tony Defries in September 1971, after he had agreed to buy Bowie out of his Mercury contract, and hence secure the future rights to his 1969 *David Bowie* LP and *The Man Who Sold The World*.

[53] ROUND AND ROUND (Berry)

Recorded November 1971; single B-side.

When the Rolling Stones covered Chuck Berry's 'Around And Around' (the B-side of his 1958 'Johnny B. Goode' single) in 1964, they were acknowledging one of their heroes, in the studio where the original recording had been made. By 1971, when Bowie and the Spiders revived the song for *Ziggy Stardust*, they had shortened the title and quickened the pace, in the same way that Elvis Presley was speeding through his fifties hits in Las Vegas, in a vain effort to make them seem as exciting as they had once been. Throughout the seventies, it was almost obligatory for rock bands of every ilk to offer their audiences an encore of fifties rock 'n' roll classics: it was, they assumed, the shared heritage of their audience. Some artists made a living from pretending that the fifties had never ended (Sha Na Na, the Wild Angels); others, such as the Flamin' Groovies (particular favourites of Bowie's at this point), channelled the spirit of Berry, Jerry Lee Lewis and Little Richard into their contemporary music, as if the sixties had never happened. Or as Marc Bolan explained in 1971: 'What I've been trying to do is recapture the feeling, the energy, behind old rock music without actually doing it the same technically.'

Bowie's performance of 'Round And Round' seemed to have been conceived in a similar spirit. Had it been included on *Ziggy*, as he originally intended (and as the title track, no less), it would have punctured any fantasy that the Spiders were exotic rock stars from another planet. They'd have been exposed, instead, as leaden-footed and crass, fronted by a man who had learned little about how to generate rock 'n' roll excitement since 'Liza Jane' [A2] in 1964. Mick Ronson's instantly recognisable guitar sound – the tonal product of a wah-wah pedal, a Marshall amp and a 1968 Les Paul – was perfect for Bowie's material, but overdramatic for a 12-bar rock 'n' roll tune. The Spiders' 'Round And Round' worked only if the previous inter-pretations could be wiped from history.

Berry's song wasn't the only borrowed tune to feature in the Spiders' stage shows, though it was their solitary homage to the fifties. Bowie preferred to revisit more recent memories, which is why he treated Cream's 'I Feel Free' to a turbulent makeover, Ronson regularly indul-ging in a lengthy guitar solo while Bowie changed costumes backstage. Lou Reed's 'Waiting For The Man' [A44] and 'White Light/White Heat' were also in Ziggy's repertoire: 'white light makes me sound like Lou Reed', Bowie sang hopefully but not entirely accurately. His occasional version of the Beatles' 'This Boy', a B-side from 1963, was interesting to imagine but not to hear. More intriguing, in retrospect, was the medley of two contemporary James Brown cuts that Bowie concocted in 1972, combining 'You Gotta Have A Job' with 'Hot Pants'. This was unusual territory for a rock band: although mod acts such as the Who had tackled some of Brown's early R&B hits, no British performers had dared to attempt the propulsive funk that was his current bag. Bowie's audience must have been baffled as he strutted the stage like the R&B legend he'd dreamed of becoming in 1965, manfully squeaking his soprano sax in imitation of Brown's side-kick, Jimmy Parker. All would become clearer in 1974, despite Bowie's promise two years earlier that 'I'm never going to try and play black music because I'm white. Singularly white!'

Glad to Be Gay

In 1971, Bowie visited America in a man's dress and told the *Daily Mirror*, 'My sexual life is normal.' In 1972, he told *Melody Maker*'s Michael Watts, 'I'm gay, and I always have been, even when I was David Jones.' Watts astutely noted Bowie's 'sly jollity' during that January interview: the campness of someone who presented himself as 'a swishy queen, a gorgeously effeminate boy', and displayed gay magazines prominently on his coffee table when journalists were due. Sexual preferences aside, this was a carefully chosen pose, for all Bowie's subsequent claim that 'It wasn't a premeditated thing.' It certainly worried his mother, who asked him, 'What's happening, David? Are you changing your sex?' 'Don't believe a word of it, Mum,' Bowie assured her.

The music business had a glorious tradition of gay managers, lyricists and, no doubt, performers; but no celebrity had chosen to 'out' himself as flamboyantly as Bowie, others preferring to let their audiences assume (the painter David Hockney, with his delicious canvases of young male swimmers) or vehemently deny the slightest vile implication (Liberace). Homosexuality had been legal for consenting adults in England and Wales for less than four years, and in America gay liberation was the last and slowest of the sixties counter-culture movements to be accepted by the so-called New Left.* The British censors had baulked at the publication of Jean Genet's novels, while Hubert Selby's *Last Exit to Brooklyn* in 1966† aroused outrage not merely for its savage rape scene, but for the impunity with which its author described his male characters as 'she'.

Bowie's openness to the idea of bisexuality was presumably what had encouraged Kenneth Pitt to arrange his client an interview with the newly launched magazine *Jeremy* (promising 'out of this world gay fashion, humour and fiction') in 1969. But Bowie was not yet ready to launch a crusade. It was more than two years later – after the formation of the Gay Liberation Front, from which he made sure to distance himself; after the editor of another gay magazine, *Spartacus*, was arrested for sending indecent literature through the post; after the release of films centring around bisexual relationships, such as Pasolini's *Teorema* and Schles-

---

* The gay seventies was effectively delineated by the Stonewall riots in Greenwich Village in June 1969 – the same week that Judy Garland died in London – and the murder of Harvey Milk in November 1978.
† A ban on sales of the book in Britain was overturned on appeal in 1968.

inger's *Sunday Bloody Sunday* (for which Pitt had secured Bowie an audition) – that he was finally prepared to admit to his diversity of sexual choices, and more importantly use bisexuality as a fashionable PR tool. Pitt was given no credit; this was a Bowie/Defries production. Within a few months, Bowie was placing his arm casually around Mick Ronson's shoulders on *Top Of The Pops*; and miming fellatio to Ronson's guitar on stage, producing an image that was immediately milked by Defries' organisation for its full shock value.

In 1969, Bowie would have been breaking genuinely new – and potentially threatening – ground. By 1972, the US garage rock band Alice Cooper were already ensconced as rock's cartoon transvestites, with Alice himself noting, 'Everyone is part man and part woman, and the people who are threatened by us haven't dealt with their own sexuality. People are really surprised when they meet us and find out that we're all straight.' He would soon be reinforcing that point by boasting about the 14–16-year-old girls who dominated their audience: 'We get so much action from them, it's untrue.' If gay stars were still shocking, seventies society chose not to be concerned about rock's infatuation with what was lasciviously known as 'jailbait'. Yet Bowie's 'I'm gay' statement won him more publicity than his recent *Hunky Dory* album, preparing a reputation that would serve him well when he donned the disguise – the week after that interview appeared – of the gender-ambiguous, alien-origin Ziggy Stardust. If Ziggy was a cartoon like Alice, at least he existed in three dimensions.

Together, these two reprobates certainly left their mark. One American rock writer noted that 1972 had become 'the year of the transvestite'. Bowie's buddy Mick Ronson was persuaded to board the wagon: 'I'm gay,' he explained helpfully, 'inasmuch as I wear girls' shoes and have bangles on my wrist. I get offers, too – but I don't accept them.' Established British star Cliff Richard, for whom the very existence of sexuality seemed troubling, was certainly shocked: 'Bowie is physically a man no matter what he does, and I think it must be pretty confusing for his audiences. I mean, it doesn't help young people when they see him like that.' It took Lou Reed – the man who would pose with a boyfriend named Rachel on an album cover, and then deny every imaginable rumour about himself a decade later – to separate artifice from action: 'Just because you're gay doesn't mean you have to camp around in make-up. You just can't fake being gay. If they claim they're gay, they're going to have to make love in a gay style, and most of these people aren't capable of making that commitment. And that line – "everybody's bisexual" – that's a very popular thing to say right now. I think it's meaningless.'

Bowie continued to milk the image of bisexuality throughout Ziggy's lifetime, aided by a growing entourage replete with gays, transvestites and every variant between. In later years, he was altogether more ambiguous on the subject. For example, in 1976 he was able to tell one interviewer, 'It's true, I am a bisexual,' adding that he adored Japanese boys in their late teens; while telling another, 'Positively not. That was just a lie . . . They gave me that image . . . I never adopted that stance. It was given [to] me.' He completed his denials by pretending in the latter interview that he had never heard of Lou Reed until he was compared to him in 1971 (see [A42]).

A more sensible Bowie came clean to Paul Du Noyer in 2002: 'I found I was able to get a lot of tension off my shoulders by almost "outing" myself in the press in that way . . . I wasn't going to get people crawling out the woodwork saying, "I'll tell you something about David Bowie that you don't know." It perfectly mirrored my lifestyle at the time. There was nothing that I wasn't willing to try.' That was the spirit of Ziggy, recalled in a more accepting age by a man who no longer needed to care about his image. In any case, hyped or otherwise, his pronouncement in January 1972 genuinely cheered those who knew precisely which way they were leaning. As Boy George recalled in his autobiography, 'Even if Bowie's claim that he was bisexual was a fashionable hoax, he marginalized himself for a sizeable chunk of his career. He took a risk that nobody else dared and in the process changed many lives.' Tom Robinson, whose 'Glad To Be Gay' in 1977 became the uncompromising anthem that Bowie was unwilling to provide, noted: 'When Bowie came up with *Hunky Dory*, I knew what he was talking about, and it affected my life in an enormous way. Had that message been stronger, and not broadcast on the radio, I'd never have heard it.' Bowie's hype became a generation's lifeline.

[54] VELVET GOLDMINE (Bowie)

Recorded November 1971; single B-side.

'Probably the lyrics are a little too provocative,' Bowie warned in 1972 about this teen sex fantasy oozing with references to oral sex. Though he sold himself as a King Volcano, by the second verse he was already exhausted. Like 'Sweet Head' [55], 'Velvet Goldmine' was recorded for *Ziggy Stardust*, but sensibly exiled: even after John Lennon had posed naked on an album cover,* the pop world was not ready for a star who suggested bathing his lover's face in semen.

The song was a tribute to the creative possibilities aroused by the Velvet Underground, rather than a pastiche of their sound(s); music-ally, it owed more to a fusion of Gene Vincent's fifties rock 'n' roll and the electric thrust of Marc Bolan. It burst into action without even a minimal fanfare, as if the narrator was ready to explode, the combined electric/acoustic guitar assault grinding back and forth relentlessly across the tonic-subdominant chord change. But the guitars disap-peared in the chorus, an altogether more sinister exercise in minor chords – more apt for the Berlin cabaret than New York's Lower East Side. By the close, it sounded like a parade of Nazi troops humming their way to the front line (compare 'Ching-A-Ling' [A55]), accompa-nied by operatic guffaws – a heady cocktail for Ziggy's admirers to swallow.

[55] SWEET HEAD (Bowie)

Recorded November 1971; *Ziggy Stardust* extended CD.

The effect of introducing 'Sweet Head' and 'Velvet Goldmine' [54] to the sketchy scenario of *Ziggy Stardust* would have been profound. Was Ziggy, one wonders, specifically designed to be the first outwardly gay rock 'n' roll star?[†] He would certainly have been the first to sing about 'spics' and 'blacks', language that located the opening verse in the heart of the borderline racist, white supremacist Teddy boy culture that was the British guardroom of rock 'n' roll in the mid-fifties.

That language littered the opening chapters of Nik Cohn's novel, *I Am Still The Greatest Says Johnny Angelo*, and 'Sweet Head' suggested that regardless of the sexual inclinations of 'Brother Ziggy', he and

---

* Lennon's offending photo – it prompted a police investigation – was on his *Two Virgins* collaboration with Yoko Ono. More than 30 years after 'Velvet Goldmine', the proudly 'out' Rufus Wainwright talked of being 'baptised by cum' in 'Gay Messiah', and people were still shocked.

[†] That role may originally have been intended for Freddie Burretti, the effectively non-singing frontman of Arnold Corns.

Johnny Angelo were very much cut from the same egomaniacal cloth. (Note the way in which Bowie issued instructions to whichever groupie, of whatever gender, happened to be servicing his mighty organ.) That made them blood brothers to the genuine fifties rockers, men like Jerry Lee Lewis, who could easily have sung, like Bowie, about their desire for the young* and the loud. For the first and, arguably, only time in his career, Bowie set out to re-create the sound of the fifties, as filtered through the young American sensibility of bands such as the Flamin' Groovies and the MC5. His vocal was stuffed with bravado, fleet-footed, sneeringly confident, rolling his 'rrrs' and turning 'wall' into a feline howl.

After a power-chord introduction (A major to A6), Bowie built the bulk of 'Sweet Head' around the simple E-A progression that was, insisted his friend Lou Reed, the heart of rock 'n' roll. Only the middle section dipped briefly into the vulnerability of a minor chord, before reverting to the swagger of the majors. Bowie delivered the most convincing rock vocal of his entire career, only to sideline this stunning performance in favour of more subtle, and cerebral, material.

Several other songs were apparently recorded by the Spiders during this period, but permanently shelved, including 'The Black Hole Kids', 'It's Gonna Rain Again' and 'Only One Paper Left'.

[56] FIVE YEARS (Bowie)

Recorded November 1971; *Ziggy Stardust* LP.

Bob Dylan once claimed† that he wrote 'A Hard Rain's A-Gonna Fall' in response to the Cuban missile crisis, filling each line with the ingredients for an entire song because he was afraid the world would

---

* Lewis sabotaged his career in 1958 by bringing his 13-year-old wife on a British tour. Maybe he had just arrived too soon: by 1972, the British underground press was openly carrying adverts for child pornography, with one 'naturist photographer' in Northampton offering 'deprived town kids' the chance of 'free weekend holidays' in a 'well-known naturist club' if they would model for him in the nude. Magazines legally available by postal subscription in the early seventies included *Kidds* and *Boys International*.

† As Dylan historian Clinton Heylin subsequently revealed, the song was actually composed before the Cuban stand-off: Dylan was as keen a mythologist of his own life as Bowie.

end before he could finish them all. 'Five Years', the first act of *Ziggy Stardust*, was Bowie's equivalent: snapshots of the end times, which were survived only – like cockroaches after a nuclear holocaust – by the ominous drumbeats that had introduced the song. His jump-cuts through urban decay moved from a market square that might be in England to a fantasy America of symbols and stereotypes – the Cadillac, the 'black', the 'queer', and a girl carelessly fixated on her milkshake, mocked by Bowie in a sarcastic recitative. His narrator watched dispassionately at first, before his humanity took hold, and he was seized by the urgency of imminent apocalypse. But crisis seemed surreal, and once again Bowie identified himself as an actor. (In an amusing echo of a *Monty Python* catchphrase, he also complained that his brain hurt.)

Bowie's vocal was certainly delivered with an actor's certainty. As he moved almost imperceptibly from calm to hysteria, his voice nearly shredded under the strain, culminating in a primal scream reminiscent of John Lennon's anguish on his 1970 song, 'Mother'. That was not a coincidence: 'Five Years', which used the I-vi-IV-V structure of a thousand doo-wop songs, was set to a stark, minimal piano accompaniment in the 'Mother' style, gradually becoming more ornate until it sounded like another song from the same Lennon album, 'God'. But whereas Lennon stripped down his accompaniment to a basic trio, Bowie's song added an autoharp to emphasise key chords, and then acoustic guitar and strings for the second verse. By the finale, the orchestral players were fighting for air against amplified guitar static, scraping despairingly at their own instruments while the last of the human race screamed around them.

There were just five years* left, Bowie insisted till the last, but the apocalypse was unfolding right now, regardless of what he had promised. Had he telescoped time, replaying his warning to prove that he had been right? Or was he demonstrating the powerlessness of the prophet? That ambiguity reverberated through the album that followed, undermining trust in soothsayers, heroes and even starmen from beyond our world.

---

* One possible source for this line was a television drama in the BBC's *Doomwatch* series, broadcast around the time he wrote the song: as one of the characters proclaimed, its theme was 'We've got twenty years!' before mankind was destroyed.

[57] SOUL LOVE (Bowie)

Recorded November 1971; *Ziggy Stardust* LP.

'Soul Love' followed 'Five Years' [56] on *Ziggy*, and mimicked its portentous drum rhythm (and the priest amongst its cast of characters). After the panoramic vision of the apocalypse, it apparently offered a more optimistic landscape, with bongos and acoustic guitar signalling mellow fruitfulness. Then Bowie's voice appeared: dull, jaded, depressed, sapped of vitality, as if he'd stumbled briefly into a warning of *Low* spirits five years ahead.

The word 'soul' rarely entered Bowie's vocabulary ('Lady Grinning Soul' [74] being another rare exception): his occult studies had taught him that the soul was vulnerable to unwelcome claimants, while he may have mistrusted the facile boast of soulfulness that had become a rock cliché. There was little in 'Soul Love' to inspire braggadocio: this was a song of stifled creativity and cynicism. Its brief libretto destroyed all illusions – religion, politics, romance, idealism – while retaining the outer vestiges of a musical form that was usually devoted to the banalities of teenage infatuation, the three-minute pop song.

This appeared a tame example of the genre, its melody rising in wary steps over conventional chord changes. But two minor excursions in the chorus told a darker story. As Bowie subverted the romantic theme in the chorus, he introduced an E major chord ('sweeping') in place of the expected minor, to strengthen the image of love's carelessness. Then he used a vulnerable E♭ to interrupt the G major theme, highlighting the weakness of 'all I have', and the hollow nature of fantasy.

Even on this (apparently) slightest of Ziggy songs, the attention to musical detail was stunning. Mick Ronson added sparkles of guitar harmonics to the verse, and Bowie's saxophone kept relaxed company. Meanwhile, the backing voices wailed like harpies, as if fifties doo-wop had become the devil's music. Bowie's lead vocal, defeated at first, bit back with the spirit of Ziggy himself in the chorus, before dropping apparently random cockney vowel sounds in the final verse, to add a cynical veneer to an already enervated vision of humanity and its follies. On this album, it seemed, no love could stand unchallenged.

[58] SHADOW MAN (Bowie)

Recorded November 1971; unreleased.

The similarity of 'Shadow Man' to the sound of the Rolling Stones in 1971 – all elongated Southern (US) vowels and swaggering power chords – suggests that, like 'Looking For A Friend' [43], the song was intended for a band who would be Bowie-but-not-Bowie: not the Spiders From Mars in this instance, but Arnold Corns. The melody was clearly constructed around the framework of the chords, and the contrivance involved was perhaps too obvious: the song seemed to lead towards a dramatic chorus that wasn't there. Bowie revisited the song early in the twenty-first century as a power ballad, perhaps indulging the entertainer he might have become if his 1968 cabaret act had ever reached the stage.

The Making of a Star #2: The Birth of Ziggy Stardust

Nobody believed that Arnold Corns were the new Rolling Stones, or that Rudi Valentino could topple Mick Jagger. (Their music wasn't even momentarily convincing.) Bowie realised that sooner than anyone, and began to sketch out a more ambitious vision of stardom, and how it might be manufactured.

That was a pejorative concept in 1971, and for many years afterwards; late sixties rock was, by definition, authentic, the anti-pop, anti-hype, anti-commercial refuge for those fans who wanted their music to have a meaning as well as a backbeat. The true badge of authenticity was a connection – real or feigned, it didn't matter – with rock's roots in working-class American styles such as blues, soul and country. Emotional openness was de rigueur; a link to the soil a distinct advantage (which is why it became a cliché, in the wake of the Band's *Music From Big Pink* album, for British musicians to 'get their heads together in the country'). The most authentic performers of all, such as Bob Dylan and the Band, were steeped in American folk traditions, grew ragged beards, abandoned the city, and spoke for a community that believed that it had escaped the vacuity of consumerism – despite the fact that its messages from the country arrived in shrink-wrap with a sales sticker on the front. Only much later would it become apparent to many observers that the most authentic personae of the era were also the most elaborately constructed. As Bowie reflected three decades later, 'Realism, honesty and all these things that came out of the late 60s had got really boring to many jaded people going into the early 70s.'

As early as 1971, he was speaking for the jaded minority: 'I think [rock] should be tarted up, made into a prostitute, a parody of itself.' Nothing could be more self-parodic than for him to live out John Lennon's sarcastic line from his 1970 single, 'Instant Karma!', daring his listeners to imagine themselves as superstars. Lennon wasn't the only person confronting the emptiness of stardom: it was implicit in Delaney Bramlett's tawdry tale of a 'Groupie' (smoothed for commercial acceptance by the Carpenters into 'Superstar'); in the Kinks' cynical *Lola Vs. Powerman & The Moneygoround*, with its tales of music-business chicanery and media manipulation; and even in the musical *Jesus Christ Superstar*, which repositioned the gospel story in the world of first-century AD public relations.

'I really wanted to write musicals more than anything else,' Bowie claimed in 2002. 'Some kind of new approach to the rock musical, that was at the back of my mind. The initial framework in '71, when I first started thinking about Ziggy, was as a musical-theatrical piece. [But] I couldn't afford to sit around for six months and write up a proper stage piece. I was too impatient.'

The textbook for doomed rock 'n' roll romanticism was *I Am Still The Greatest Says Johnny Angelo*, a novel published in 1970* by the young journalist and rock historian Nik Cohn. The author based his hero's stage performances on the mid-sixties pop icon P.J. Proby, but in his closeted stardom, Johnny Angelo is also Elvis Presley, the Bob Dylan of 1966, Howard Hughes, and every other idol isolated from reality, and his audience, by fame. Johnny lives by Tarot readings and omens, surrounded by a lickspittle entourage, and respects only 'violence and glamour and speed, splendour and vulgarity, gesture and combustion'. More pertinently to Ziggy, and Bowie, 'he was all things at once, masculine and feminine and neuter, active and passive, animal and vegetable, and he was satanic, messianic, kitsch and camp, and psychotic, and martyred, and just plain dirty'. Eventually he becomes locked into a bored ritual of stardom: 'I mean

---

* The book originally appeared as a hardback in 1967, when Cohn was 21; and was then rewritten, with scarcely a sentence remaining intact, for the 1970 paperback edition. The original text, reissued by Savoy Books during the eighties, is almost fascist in its attitude to violence and glamour; the revised version is more subtle, and more convincing.

to make an ending, a final explosion and, when it's done, I shall cease.' Johnny stages a confrontation with the law, and his story ends in an orgy of murder and bullets.

Out of Johnny Angelo's staged martyrdom; Marc Bolan's transformation from hippy to teen idol; Erich von Daniken's claim (in his book *Chariot of the Gods*) that the planet had been visited, and civilisation set in motion, by extraterrestrials; the deaths of performers such as Brian Jones, Jimi Hendrix and Janis Joplin; his own experience of fame with 'Space Oddity' [1], and of hero-worshipping Little Richard and Elvis: out of all these images and more,* Bowie began to assemble an imaginary star whom he could impersonate and ride to his own stardom. Later, he would adopt a fashionable cynicism towards his creation: 'Most people still want their idols and gods to be shallow, like cheap toys. Why do you think teenagers are the way they are? They run around like ants, chewing gum and fixing onto a certain style of dressing for a day; that's as deep as they wish to go. It's no surprise that Ziggy was a huge success.' But by early 1972, when he chanced upon the signifiers of Ziggy's identity – the cropped red hair, the jumpsuit, the glitter and panache – he was operating with one eye on his career, the other trained affectionately on Ziggy's disciples, who deserved a star worthy of their devotion.†

Ziggy's hair was chopped, coloured and allowed to stick up perkily on top of his head in January 1972. For a TV appearance, he donned a codpiece, a bomber jacket and trousers rolled up to reveal red and black plastic platform boots. At the end of that month, Bowie's manufactured idol – dressed in a jumpsuit made from what he later called 'a quite lovely piece of faux-deco material' – made his debut on the tiny stage of the Toby Jug public house in Tolworth for an audience who, if they were expecting anyone, might have assumed that they would see the David Bowie of *Hunky Dory* or even 'Space Oddity', not a space oddity of an entirely different complexion. The artiste had no doubt what would happen next: 'I'm going to be huge,' he promised a few days earlier, 'and it's quite frightening in a way, because I know that when I reach my peak and it's time for me to be brought down, it will be with a bump.'

---

* He would more recently credit the American rocker Vince Taylor and the madcap Legendary Stardust Cowboy as Ziggy's prime inspirations, preferring to name the obscure rather than the obvious.

† By early 1972, many rock critics were echoing this review of a T. Rex concert in *International Times*: '[Bolan] had a potential riot force under his control and could have used it to direct them into something worthwhile – made them THINK. But he's into self-adoration.'

[59] SUFFRAGETTE CITY (Bowie)

Recorded February 1972; *Ziggy Stardust* LP.

The only popular song to incorporate 'suffragette' into its title before *Ziggy Stardust* was 'Sister Suffragette' from the musical *Mary Poppins*, and that arguably had more to do with women's liberation than Bowie's 'Suffragette City', despite the claims that he subsequently made on the latter's behalf. His offering was nothing more, or less, than a collage of his rock 'n' roll influences: a sexually charged catchphrase borrowed from Charles Mingus via the Small Faces,* some 'White Light/White Heat' vocal interplay and sonic thrust from the Velvet Underground, a little *Clockwork Orange* imagery ('droogies'), a line from John Lennon's 'I Found Out', some Bolan boogie, some Flamin' Groovies speed, some Jerry Lee Lewis swagger, and a dose of hard-rock theatrics to wrap it up. Bowie heightened the feeling of playful pastiche by switching vocal personae every few words, sometimes mock-threatening, sometimes sarcastic, sometimes merely alive with the joy of fronting an electric band.

Not that the band was that simple: there was an almost inaudible acoustic guitar, as usual, supporting Ronson's hyper-powered electric, while what registered as a saxophone was actually created using an ARP synthesiser. Bowie dreamed up that synth riff, producer Ken Scott found an appropriate sound on the Trident Studios ARP, and Ronson pushed the keys. The backing vocals skipped from left-hand speaker (first verse) to right (second), to add another layer of contrivance. There was even a trick in the (entirely major-chord) fabric of the song. While many classic rock songs, such as the Rolling Stones' 'Brown Sugar' and the Kinks' 'All Day And All Of The Night', were raised on a three-chord structure spaced two and three semitones apart (e.g. E-G-A, or A-G-C), Bowie used tighter two-semitone gaps (F-G-A), leaving the ear

---

* 'Wham Bam Thank You Ma'am' appeared on the jazz bassist's 1961 album, *Oh Yeah*; and it was also the title of a Small Faces rocker in 1967. The Small Faces were an underrecognised influence on this era of Bowie's career, from Steve Marriott's cockney delivery of 'Lazy Sunday' and 'Rene' to their regular combination of rich acoustic and raunchy electric guitars, as heard throughout *Ziggy Stardust*. Paul Trynka's excellent 2011 Bowie biography suggested that the group had briefly considered including him in their ranks in 1965. Meanwhile, Bowie told a TV audience in 1999 that he and Marriott had thought about forming an R&B partnership called 'David & Goliath'. Pardon my scepticism about both stories.

to expect a softer A minor as the root of the song, only for a decisive A major chord to appear in its stead. This simplest of manoeuvres, performed quite unconsciously, gave 'Suffragette City' its unrelenting power, causing every deviation from the basic riff to sound transitory and quickening the desire for the root chord to return. And it did, over and over, until the band veered out of the chorus into a teasingly held E major chord, begging for a resolution back to A. 'Wham bam thank you ma'am,' Bowie cried gleefully after a fake ending, before the band went round again, and this time delivered the relief of a last climax, as Bowie shrieked: 'Suffragette!' To every man his own fantasy . . .

[60] **STARMAN** (Bowie)

Recorded February 1972; *Ziggy Stardust* LP.

If Bowie was indeed 'the actor', as he claimed on *Hunky Dory*, then this was his finest performance. It was also a triumph of the techniques he had learned in advertising, from the casual (but carefully anticipated) way in which he draped his arm around Mick Ronson's shoulders on *Top Of The Pops*, through the juxtaposition of old and new Bowie voices in the double-tracked chorus, to his assumption of superstar status on the back of what was, after all, only a no. 10 success in Britain (and a no. 65 damp squib in America, where it was killed by Elton John's 'Rocket Man', itself little more than an imitation of 'Space Oddity' [1]). Even before *Ziggy Stardust* was released, 'Starman'* was a blatant exploitation of an album, and an image, to which it was largely peripheral. Ultimately, it was simply – like 'Space Oddity' before it – a space-age novelty hit, and the fact that Bowie dropped it from his live set as early as he could hinted that it was too calculated a move even for this evangelist of self-recreation.

But 'Starman' was something else: a superbly constructed pop record. Bowie made no attempt to hide the fact that the octave jump in the chorus ('Star-*man*') mirrored the rise in Judy Garland's 'Over The Rainbow' ('some-*where*'); he even combined the two melodies in

---

* The word may have been lodged in Bowie's memory since his teens, when he first came across the Robert Heinlein science-fiction novel *Starman Jones*. As with Philip K. Dick's *The World Jones Made*, how could the young David Jones, already a SF aficionado, resist books that included his name in their title?

a showcase London performance. But whereas the Garland song used its cathartic rise to introduce a refrain that was emotionally, and melodically, expansive, the leap in Bowie's song was followed by a more uncertain melody, reflecting his character's innate lack of confidence. All around the starman, however, his presence evoked anticipation (the link between the verse and the chorus was the guitar figure from the Supremes' 'You Keep Me Hanging On') and then joyous relief, when he commanded the children to boogie, and Mick Ronson's guitar led the Spiders in a relaxed swagger through territory that Marc Bolan (the prince of 'cosmic jive') would have recognised as his home turf. Which begs the question: was 'Starman', like 'Lady Stardust' [33], another song written with Bolan in mind? If so, it was a tribute that worked as a palace coup. The wordless chorus that brought 'Starman' to its fade was interpreted by Bolan as a steal from his 1971 hit 'Hot Love'.

The tentative opening chords – the subdominant chord followed by the major 7th of the root – were played out on a 12-string acoustic that was echoed across the stereo channels, and answered by the occasional strum of a 6-string, until the starman and the verse arrived, and the guitar was crammed back into a single speaker. Ronson only introduced his electric guitar for the heavily phased 'radio signal' from space, and to prove that we really hadn't strayed very far from Kansas after all, a warmly romantic string arrangement carried us through the chorus. Only when the band obeyed the instruction to boogie, perfectly mimicking the T. Rex style, did a rock sensibility briefly assume the spotlight. If the starman was going to blow our minds, it would be as a pop idol, not a rock 'n' roller.

[61] Rock 'n' Roll Suicide

Recorded February 1972; *Ziggy Stardust* LP.

Like 'Starman' [60], which was designed as a hit single, 'Rock 'n' Roll Suicide' was meticulously contrived* to perform a specific role in Bowie's

---

* One wonders whether Bowie watched a BBC TV film called *Herostratus*, screened in 1967 and again in 1970: its hero wishes to commit suicide in public, and hires an advertising agency to promote the event. It's such an archetypal Bowie theme that it would be disconcerting to learn that he didn't see it. In the interests of historical accuracy, one should also note that Lou Reed claimed that Bowie had written this song 'for' him – though whether that meant 'about him' or 'for him to sing' isn't clear.

career. Placed at the end of *Ziggy Stardust* (and at the end of Ziggy's final performance in 1973), it appeared to let the curtain fall on a theatrical narrative. The equation was implicit: Ziggy had allowed himself to be killed by his fans, so he was a suicide* in all but deed. But Bowie was cleverer than that. Whoever was performing this song, whether it was the creation of David Jones or David Bowie, was addressing his audience – and every alienated individual in that audience – rather than himself. They were the victims; he reassured them 'you're not alone', begged them to stretch out their hands, let them just touch the end of his fingertips, and then abandoned them in a state of hysteria.

That proclamation of union between artist and audience was never enacted with such passion as in the life of Judy Garland. Diagnosed as bipolar, indeed containing multiple personalities, she played out an incurably dramatic ritual of courtship with her fans. Her moment of 'suicide' came with her final season at the London Palladium, in January 1969, where she tested the patience of her admirers beyond sufferance by arriving on stage (if at all) hours late, to the point that they pelted her with breadsticks. She died in June 1969 of barbiturate poisoning, having virtually ceased to eat several months earlier. Elton John connected the dots from Garland to Bowie: 'I'll always remember going out for dinner with him and Angie when he was Ziggy Stardust. It was a fabulous dinner, and over dinner he admitted to me that he always wanted to be Judy Garland, and that's the God's honest truth.'

Garland's tortuous example aside, the cry of 'you're not alone' in 'Rock 'n' Roll Suicide' was borrowed from Mort Shuman's translation of the Jacques Brel song 'Jef'. Brel's solace for loneliness was sex; Bowie's was a show of awareness that his fans were suffering all the anguish of adolescence. Instead of sending them each a copy of 'Can't Help Thinking About Me' [A14], to show that he'd been there too, he acted the kindly uncle, or big brother perhaps, who understood their agonising lack of self-confidence.

As he rose to the challenge of matching their hysteria, his voice changed from the urgent intimacy of the opening lines, through the metallic screech he'd used on his 1970 album, into a throat-scarring

---

* Bowie admitted in March 1972, just after he'd written this song: 'I get worried about dying . . . Last month, it was being killed on stage. Not here [in Britain] so much. In America. I know that one day a big artist is going to get killed on stage, and I know that we're going to go very big. And I keep thinking – it's bound to be me.'

roar, way beyond his vocal range. A song that had begun with an
unadorned acoustic guitar was now a tumultuous wash of sound, with
strings and brass trying to contain the frenzy, until Ronson's guitar
seized the moment of release, and caringly guided the track down
to a calming D♭ chord. It was echoed an octave lower by the string
quartet – the final sound to be heard on this quintessential rock album.

As early as the second line of the song, Bowie substituted a major
chord where the key strictly required a minor, as a warning of imminent
danger. When the cigarette* reached the mouth, the E major introduced
a haunting moment of doubt, quickly defused by the more predictable
changes that made up the verse. By the end of the third verse, when
things were so confused that an American car ('Chev brakes') was
joined by a British utility vehicle ('the milk float'), the prevailing key
was starting to crack under the strain, and the song veered into G♭ for
6 bars, and finally into D♭ for 12 bars of desperate reassurance. In the
final two bars, the arrangement incorporated all three of the song's key
chords, in the order in which they had originally appeared – as elegant
a landing from a space fantasy as it would be possible to conceive.

The Making of a Star #3: *The Rise And Fall Of Ziggy Stardust And The Spiders From Mars* LP

On 15 July 1972, David Bowie and his band performed at Friars, a club
held inside the assembly hall in the Buckinghamshire town of Aylesbury,
for the third time in less than a year. On his previous visits, he had been
an amiable, approachable figure, happy to chat to audience members
after the show as a friend rather than an icon. Now he was accompanied
by a coachload of journalists flown in by MainMan from America; flanked by
security guards; preceded on to the stage by strobe lights and Walter Carlos'
theme from the movie *Clockwork Orange*; and then kept safely apart from

* Bowie credited Baudelaire as the source for the 'time takes a cigarette' line, though
this was definitely not the case. Bowie encyclopedist Nicholas Pegg, with his typically
rigorous research, identified a similarity with a verse by the Spanish poet Manuel
Machado, which begins '*La vida es un cigarillo . . .*', or 'Life is a cigarette . . .' There
is only one problem: as far as I know, Bowie could not read Spanish in 1972, and I
have been unable to locate a prior English translation of the poem, which is entitled
'"Tonas" y Lavinias'. So the final piece of this mystery remains.

the same fans whom he'd greeted warmly a few months earlier. They wrote distressed letters to the pop press: what has happened to David Bowie?

It was not Bowie who appeared at Friars that night, however, but Ziggy Stardust: the conceptual art project who had become a rock 'n' roll star. 'I'm continually aware that I'm an actor portraying stories,' Bowie admitted the following day, 'and that's the way I wish to take my performance.' Ziggy was the guise he had chosen to adopt, 'for a couple of months'. In an unguarded moment, he could confess that impersonating Ziggy had imposed a bizarre sense of dissociation from his 'real' self: 'It's a continual fantasy . . . I'm very rarely David Jones any more. I think I've forgotten who David Jones is.'

Seven weeks earlier, when *The Rise And Fall Of Ziggy Stardust And The Spiders From Mars* LP was released, David Jones/Bowie was not a star – not in the way that Marc Bolan was, or Alice Cooper. MainMan hyped the record as if he had already achieved that status, boasting that his previous album, *Hunky Dory*, was 'now high in the US charts' – which was true, as long as you regarded a placing of no. 185 as 'high'. Bowie and his management had effectively decided to let *Hunky Dory* succeed or fail by itself, and to focus their energy on the *Ziggy* concept. But six weeks after its release, the 'Starman' single, which was intended to stir up anticipation for the album, had still not charted. The success of *Ziggy*, and with it Bowie's entire credibility as a pop performer, was in the balance.

The initial response to the album was lukewarm. Nick Kent in *Oz* magazine complained that Bowie was attempting to 'hype himself as something he isn't'. The rock paper *Sounds* noted that the record 'could have been the work of a competent plagiarist . . . a lot of it sounds as if he didn't work on the ideas as much as he could have done'. This was the verdict of reviewers who had raved over the dense, philosophical songs on Bowie's earlier albums, and could not relate to the apparently simplistic rock mythology of *Ziggy Stardust*. By contrast, Michael Watts of *Melody Maker* – to whom Bowie had made his 'I'm gay' boast earlier in the year – immediately understood the singer's intentions: the album, he wrote, 'suggests the ascent and decline of a big rock figure, but leaves the listener to fill in his own details, and in the process he's also referring obliquely to his own role as a rock star and sending it up'.

The challenge for journalists who believed passionately in the authenticity of their idols was to accept that distance, irony and fiction could be acceptable methods of confronting the star-making machinery of rock. They had baulked at CBS Records' publicity campaign for 'The Rock Revolutionaries', in which a multinational media corporation attempted to use the symbolism of 'revolution' – the radical touchstone of the age for Western youth – as a means of selling plastic product. Now Bowie was expecting them to deal with an artist who was quite blatantly using rock iconography to sell himself, and the illusion of stardom, as commodities. ('I'm very much a conglomerate figure,' he admitted in 1972. 'It's a visual exercise in being a parasite.' He could not be accused of covering his tracks.)

Only in retrospect* would the audaciousness of Bowie's manoeuvres be appreciated and understood. In June 1972, several emblematic TV appearances (notably on *Top Of The Pops*) combined with the undeniable commercial appeal of 'Starman' [60] to create exactly the degree of stardom for Ziggy Stardust that Bowie had envisaged. The audience for these records had not graduated through the dense lyrical explorations of Bowie's beliefs and fantasies that made up the *David Bowie* (1969 edition), *The Man Who Sold The World* and *Hunky Dory* LPs. If they knew Bowie at all, it was as the avowed bisexual who had written 'Oh! You Pretty Things' [30]. Analysis of the shifting viewpoints and incomplete narrative of the *Ziggy Stardust* album could come later. Before then, the British pop audience – and especially those among them who were confused about their own identities, sexual or otherwise – welcomed the arrival of a home-grown performer as daring and provocative as Alice Cooper, as tuneful as the Beatles, and more mysterious than Marc Bolan could ever hope to be.

By the time of his Rainbow concerts in August, where he presented a theatrical concept featuring a mime troupe (the Astronettes) led by his one-time mentor, Lindsay Kemp, Bowie was stardom personified, his concept brought to ecstatic, multicoloured life. But the intensity of his personification was already beginning to show. When he arrived in America the following month, he told *Newsweek* magazine that 'I'm not what I'm supposed to be. What are people buying? I adopted Ziggy onstage, and now I feel more and more like this monster and less and less like David Bowie.' His star had become a straitjacket, one that he would struggle to slough off for the next year and beyond.

---

* By the rock press, at least. Theatrical reviewers were altogether more perceptive, and less surprised. The magazine *Plays & Players* compared Bowie's performance at the Rainbow Theatre in London to that of Joel Grey, the arch, camp master of ceremonies in the film *Cabaret*, and concluded that 'the entire evening seemed like a tribute to Judy [Garland]'. Bowie must have been delighted.

[62] ALL THE YOUNG DUDES (Bowie)

> Recorded by Mott the Hoople, May 1972. Recorded by Bowie, December 1972; *RarestOneBowie* CD.

A derivation, first of all: in classic Hollywood Westerns, 'dudes' had blown in from the city, and didn't fit. Folk/blues pioneer Lead Belly sang about 'The 25-Cent Dude' in the 1940s. The Hollywood Argyles, the studio collective who recorded the much-loved (by Bowie) 'Alley-Oop', had a 1965 single entitled 'Long Hair, Unsquare Dude Called Jack', though it's unlikely that Bowie would ever have heard it. More likely he found his dudes in African-American (and lesbian) slang, where a 'dude' was simply a man. After Bowie gave this song to Mott the Hoople, 'dudes' entered the rock vocabulary as a synonym for 'the kids', though it was so linked to the seventies that it has only been used ironically since then. And even in 1972, the 'boogaloo' was a dance craze that was strictly passé. If the boogaloo dudes did indeed carry the news, they may have been reading yesterday's papers, to quote another band.

Though Bowie wrote the song, and co-produced it (and its subsequent album) with Mick Ronson, it was Mott the Hoople who *owned* it. They invented two of the record's chief attractions: the opening guitar motif by Mick Ralphs, and the quite terrifying valedictory monologue from Ian Hunter. Bowie never came close to matching it, either when he laid down a guide vocal in 1972, re-cut the song insipidly during the *Aladdin Sane* sessions in 1973 (though it was left unreleased), or included it on *David Live* in 1974. The last of those three efforts was the most beguiling, as Bowie held back the tempo and returned the song to Mott's key (D), though that (and certain chemical strains on his voice) left him unable to hit, or ultimately even attempt, any of the high notes.

But he did write the song, which was greeted as the teen anthem of the era (alongside Alice Cooper's 'School's Out') and, ironically, outsold his own 'Starman' in Britain and America. It was a melodic return to the territory of *Hunky Dory*, with its diatonic major descent, and the slow glide of his left hand down the bass keys of his piano.* Verse and chorus followed essentially the same path, though the verse offered a variation that used an unscheduled E major chord in the

---

* Bach's 'Air on the G String', as heard for many years on the television advertisements for Hamlet cigars, was the obvious comparison.

same way as 'Rock 'n' Roll Suicide' [61] (announcing the delinquent), and the chorus detoured from C into B♭ for two bars, requiring an interlude of three chords in 3/4 time to regain the predominant key. If the music revisited the familiar moves of 'Changes' [48] and 'Oh! You Pretty Things' [30], the lyrics updated the lives that Bowie had chronicled in 'The London Boys' [A21]. Life was over at twenty-five, he had one of his characters suggest, having just celebrated his own twenty-fifth birthday. The song doubled as an incisive piece of rock criticism: it was an elder brother, not a dude, who was still fixated on the Beatles and the Stones. A new generation required new idols, and Bowie was prepared to provide them.

Glam, Glitter and Fag Rock

One of the great strengths of the early 70s was its sense of irony . . . There was a very strong sense of humour that ran through the early British bands: myself, Roxy Music, Marc . . . Whatever came out of early 70s music that had any longevity to it generally had a sense of humour underlying it.

David Bowie, 1991

In Britain, it was glitter rock; in America, fag rock or drag rock. 'I don't know anything about fag rock at all,' Bowie insisted in September 1972. 'I think glam rock is a lovely way to categorise me, and it's even nicer to be one of the leaders of it.' Given his unwillingness to fit into anyone else's straitjackets, his polite acquiescence to this US interviewer was presumably an early example of that sense of irony he boasted about twenty years later.

Three months earlier, *Sounds* journalist Steve Peacock had been able to survey what he dubbed 'glitterbiz' without mentioning Bowie's name. Then 'Starman' became a hit single, and the perceived pioneers of 'glitter rock', Alice Cooper and Marc Bolan, had a serious rival. But not that serious: looking back almost forty years later, what is most striking about Bowie's career-establishing appearance on *Top Of The Pops* in July 1972 is not the casual way in which he drapes his arm around Mick Ronson's shoulder as they lean in together for the chorus of 'Starman', but the beaming smile that rarely leaves Bowie's lips. It's the hallmark of confidence, no doubt, and the knowledge that he is about to stun British reserve out of its lethargy.

But it's also the brand of a man who is not taking any of this remotely seriously: who knows, in fact, that there are few things more ridiculous than posing as a red-haired spaceman on prime-time BBC television, apart from the fact that it is about to make him irreversibly famous.

In the brief period between the coining of 'glam rock' and Bowie's realising that it was important not to be typecast, he claimed that he had actually invented the genre by posing in a dress on the cover of *The Man Who Sold The World*. That was a blatant attempt to steal the limelight from his rival Marc Bolan, who had sprinkled his face with glitter before his own *Top Of The Pops* debut with T. Rex a few weeks before Bowie's album was released. He would have had more credibility had he staked his 'glam' reputation on his February 1970 appearance at the Roundhouse, where he had masqueraded as a glittery 'Rainbowman'. That aside, he knew that it was Bolan who had introduced British teenagers to the possibilities of gentle reinvention with a packet of glitter; and Alice Cooper who had taken on the responsibility, like Mick Jagger a decade earlier, of outraging parents and press with his shocking antics on stage.

Steve Peacock's account of the visual hedonism in British pop circa June 1972 concluded: 'If you look at what's happened in ten years, we'll see that it's the music that's lasted, and the glittering gimmicks have come and gone.' That was both true, and wildly mistaken. So potent was the appeal of glam, with its triumphantly banal anthems, outrageous sense of camp, and deliberately amateurish presentation, that after the initial enthusiasm had ebbed away, to be followed by a suitably embarrassed pause from all involved, it was reborn as the definitive sound of the seventies. Even today, the caricatured sexuality* of Gary Glitter and the flagrant bandwagon-jumping of Sweet offer instantaneous memories of the era of power cuts and strikes, all the more potent for the fact that neither act (then) demanded to be taken at all seriously.

Anyone who watched *Top Of The Pops* could reproduce Bolan's glitter or Sweet's mock-Cherokee make-up after a visit to Woolworth's.

---

* That sexuality was to be seen in a different light many years later, after Glitter's imprisonment on charges of possessing child pornography. As one of his former press agents told me on the day Glitter was arrested, 'We always knew Gary liked young girls, but we didn't realise how young.' For me, the power of glam's ironic sex appeal was proven in the late seventies, when I worked in an office alongside a teenage girl who appeared to be entirely sane, apart from her claim – entirely a fantasy, I'm sure – that she was living with the almost forgotten glam-rock star Alvin Stardust. As Bowie realised much earlier, stardom exists as long as an artist's fans believe he is a star.

(Bowie once described the Ziggy Stardust look as being 'Nijinsky meets Woolworth's', as effective a summary of glam's clumsy genius as any.) Glam's essence was entertainment, and that was both its appeal and, for many of its protagonists, its curse. By June 1973, Marc Bolan was declaring: 'I don't want to go on the road now for fear of being involved in the dying embers of glam rock. I don't feel involved in it, even if I started it. It's not my department any more, and personally I find it very embarrassing.' But he was too closely tied in to the glam aesthetic to be accepted outside it, and he died without registering another Top 10 single or album. Around the same time, Bowie expressed his concern that 'The Jean Genie' [65] had (on some charts) reached no. 1, in case it meant that he had become a pop star, rather than an enigmatic icon. But the pretensions he carried – and the sense of mystery that was his trademark – ensured that he was never in danger of becoming trapped by a single image, as Bolan was. He alone was able to complain that he actually wasn't very interested in rock, while maintaining all the trappings of a rock superstar.

Bowie's skill was being able to live out the dictum of rock critic Simon Frith: 'Rock is entertainment that suggests – by its energy, self-consciousness, cultural references – something more.' He achieved this almost instinctively, whereas Roxy Music, his most cogent rivals as intelligent seventies pop stars, deliberately used their art-school background as a resource. They were a conscious evocation of classic pop-art principles, deftly using the clichés of fifties and sixties rock to satirise pop's superficiality, while employing irony and camp as a way of distancing themselves from the purely ephemeral pap around them. Roxy's frontman, Bryan Ferry, was Bowie's only serious rival as the self-constructed symbol of seventies pop art, though it was his short-term colleague Brian Eno who proved to be more influential on the decades to come (and on Bowie himself).

Although Bowie gave every sign of wishing that he could have enjoyed Ferry's past – with its apparently seamless journey from miner's son to art-school aesthete – he had stumbled upon a less certain but more enduring way of translating constant artistic innovation into a credible career. It would be his destiny to extend the genre of glam rock, and then transcend it, while his peers struggled to escape its curse.

[63] JOHN I'M ONLY DANCING (Bowie) (see also [117])

Recorded June 1972 and January 1973; both single A-side.

The setting: the Sombrero Club in London's Kensington Church Street. The clientele: all of the city's hippest queens and most available boys. The visitors: David and Angie Bowie, plus whichever of their straight friends they could tease into accompanying them. The scenario: boy arrives with boy, but dares to dance with another he/ she. Cue the chorus . . . and remember that Bowie claimed in 1972, 'I don't know anything about fag-rock at all.'

Some antecedents: the opening riff used the most familiar chord change in rock 'n' roll, but at a speed that harked back to the version of 'Pontiac Blues' R&B veteran Sonny Boy Williamson recorded with the Yardbirds in 1963. Mick Ronson's stuttering final G chord stemmed from a later Yardbirds incarnation, responsible for the 1966 single 'Shapes Of Things'. Bowie's 'oh lawdy' interjection, meanwhile, pre-dated the British blues boom by conjuring up visions of Al Jolson in blackface, waving his jazz hands at the camera as the talkies began.

Having slowed his output since the torrent of 1971, Bowie could write nothing except hit singles. That such an uncompromisingly gay song should reach the UK charts (and receive BBC airplay) testified to its naked panache, from the explosive drumbeats across the opening riff to the guitar noise echoing eerily between the speakers at the climax. Bowie's voice was harsh and brittle, but still soared to a crazily high falsetto D as he expressed his needs. Rarely were the Spiders' rhythm section of Trevor Bolder and Woody Woodmansey so central to the impact of a Bowie recording, with Bolder's bass walking up and down the E minor scale during the first half of the chorus, before dealing out notes an octave apart with consummate ease. Besides the resonant acoustic guitar, Ronson laid down a grumbling electric figure beneath the verse, as if trying to emulate a saxophone, before adding a police siren wail to the chorus. The collective effect was propulsive and hypnotic; but still Bowie wasn't satisfied.

The Spiders duly returned to the song during the *Aladdin Sane* sessions, and without any fanfare their second attempt was substituted for the first, though by then sales of the single had dried up. The retread was faster, more unhinged and added a saxophone to replace Ronson's imitation; but it sacrificed two of the most thrilling aspects of the original, the percussive arrival and the marching bass. In one respect, though, it was arguably more satisfying: if the guitar crescendo of the first recording hinted at orgasm, the second took it all the way.

Transformer: Bowie and Lou Reed

Four years after being introduced to the music of Lou Reed and the Velvet Underground by Kenneth Pitt [A42/A44], David Bowie was elated to witness a performance by the band during his first visit to America in January 1971. He went backstage to congratulate Reed, and was embarrassed to discover that the man he was calling 'Lou' was actually Doug Yule, who had assumed leadership of the Velvets after Reed's departure a few months earlier. When he returned to the States in September, Bowie endured an uncomfortable meeting with Reed's one-time 'producer', Andy Warhol, before finally connecting with the composer of the Velvets' most enduring material at Max's Kansas City that evening.

The pair struck up a slightly awkward friendship, blighted by Reed's fragile emotional state and legendarily spiky personality. They met again when Reed travelled to London to record his first solo record, a self-parodic, self-titled disappointment. Reed proclaimed that Bowie was 'the only interesting person around. Rock 'n' roll has been tedious, except for what David has been doing.' Bowie responded by offering to produce an album for Reed. 'The people I was around at the time thought Bowie would be the perfect producer for me to make a record that would sell,' Reed said cynically a decade later. First, Bowie set out to introduce the American to his own burgeoning audience, and Reed made his British concert debut as a guest at Bowie's acclaimed* performance at London's Royal Festival Hall on 8 July 1972. Tony Defries made strident attempts to shepherd Reed into his MainMan empire: 'He was always running around telling people he was my manager, which he wasn't, although he tried,' Reed complained. In tribute to Bowie's influence, Reed even sported glitter and eyeshadow for his early UK gigs, before reverting to the leather-clad image that he found more comfortable. During a brief pause in Bowie's schedule, he and Ronson acted as co-producers (with the trusted Ken

* 'A Star Is Born!' exclaimed the *Melody Maker* headline, in another of Bowie's increasingly frequent comparisons to Judy Garland; *Record Mirror* announced that Bowie 'will soon become the greatest entertainer Britain has ever known'.

Scott in the supporting role of engineer) for the best-selling album of Reed's entire career: *Transformer*.

Although it was Bowie's involvement that sold the project, Ronson was the principal creative force on the record, as an arranger and multi-instrumentalist. Bowie's chief role was to keep his troubled artist awake and interested, while encouraging Reed to exploit some of the more outré themes that he had introduced with the Velvet Underground – erotic obsession, transvestism, drugs, bisexuality. 'There's a lot of sexual ambiguity in the album,' Reed conceded, 'and two outright gay songs.' He and Bowie duetted on the deliciously camp trifle of 'New York Telephone Conversation', while Reed also explored the full perversity of the Warhol milieu – most famously on 'Walk On The Wild Side', a triumph of Ronson's arranging skills and Herbie Flowers' bass-playing, and arguably the most explicit song ever given airplay by naïve British radio producers. The album also provided another showcase for Bowie and Ronson's increasingly inventive use of backing vocals, which had begun to assume a Beatlesque variety and confidence.

Within months of the album's completion, Reed's trust in Bowie's motives had begun to evaporate. 'I don't know what he was up to,' he complained of his fan-turned-producer, 'I honestly don't know.' But he was presumably assuaged by the belated success of 'Walk On The Wild Side' and the sales of *Transformer*, which lived up its title by turning a cult artist into a mainstream rock star, for the next decade and beyond. In that context, it hardly mattered that, as one long-time admirer noted, *Transformer* was merely 'a collection of songs witty, songs trivial, songs dull, songs gay, songs sad, none of them really much cop'. (One of those songs, 'Wagon Wheel', is now often claimed to have been a Bowie composition, despite being credited to Reed. But that seems unlikely, given that Reed recorded an acoustic demo of the song several months before he began working with Bowie.) If that judgement was harsh, it also reflected the extent to which Reed had allowed his own personality to become subsumed into Bowie's. He did not respond to Bowie's invitation to produce his next record, the magnificent *Berlin*, a song cycle fuelled by paranoia and pain, which left its mark on Bowie's *Diamond Dogs*. The two briefly considered another joint venture in 1979, until their discussions ended in a fist-fight. Only in the nineties would both men's egos have subsided to the point that they could collaborate without fear of being scarred by the comparison.

[64] **MY DEATH** (Brel; trans. Shuman)

Performed live 1972/73; *RarestOneBowie* CD.

The second of Bowie's homages to Jacques Brel – after 'Amsterdam' [17] – was mediated through the dual prisms of Scott Walker, who recorded 'My Death' on his 1967 debut solo album, and lyricist Mort Shuman, whose English translation was included in the theatrical show *Jacques Brel is Alive and Well and Living in Paris*, and was made available to Walker several months before the show premiered off Broadway. Both Walker and Elly Stone, who sang Shuman's adaptation on stage, assumed that mortality demanded a portentous delivery, and Bowie followed suit when the song* joined his live repertoire in 1972. It allowed him to experiment with the mannered crooning that he would later adopt on the *Station To Station* album, while thematically it reinforced the imminent conclusion of his adventures with Ziggy Stardust. 'I can't think of a time that I didn't think about death,' he admitted in 1997. Sadly, Bowie seemed not to have heard Brel's uproarious original recording from 1960, which treated death with cavalier contempt, marching in military fashion over its pretensions to importance.

[65] **THE JEAN GENIE** (Bowie)

Recorded October 1972; single A-side and *Aladdin Sane* LP.

'In England, David Bowie may become – may already be – a real star, but in the American context he looks more like an aesthete using stardom as a metaphor . . . I felt unsatisfied; more than that, I felt just the slightest bit conned. Something was being promised that wasn't being delivered.' That was the verdict of American critic Ellen Willis on Bowie's third US appearance, at New York's Carnegie Hall on 28 September 1972. 'I had flu that night,' Bowie said a decade later. 'I'll never forget that.'

Bowie had arrived amidst a publicity campaign worthy of Hollywood's most brazen myth-makers. At a time when other British acts (notably Marc Bolan's T. Rex) were struggling to establish themselves

---

* His arrangement used the same chord sequence as the opening section of 'After All' [20].

in the USA, MainMan booked their artist into major arenas and halls on the back of two singles ('Changes' [48] and 'Starman' [60]) that had failed to climb higher than the low 60s on the Hot 100 chart. It was effectively the Ziggy Stardust coup played out on an international stage: an imaginary star demanding instant reverence and respect.

Even with a roving spotlight lighting up the sky outside, and an audience including Andy Warhol and his Factory entourage, plus celebrities such as Tony Perkins, Alan Bates and Lee Radziwill, more than 500 of the 2,800 tickets for the Carnegie Hall show could not be sold, and had to be given away (with MainMan's approval) to ensure a full house. Elsewhere, in Cleveland, Memphis and Detroit, MainMan's strategy worked. But across the South and the Midwest, the tour was a disaster. Only 500 seats were sold for the 5,700-capacity Kiel Auditorium in St Louis; and just 250 for a show in Kansas City, during which Bowie got drunk and fell off the stage. Other concerts were cancelled to avoid a similar fate. Most embarrassing was Bowie's visit to San Francisco, for two nights at the Winterland Arena. Unfortunately for him, the Cockettes – an ultra-camp cabaret troupe, starring future film star Divine alongside Goldie Glitters and Paula Pucker – were staging a new revue that weekend at the Palace Theater. Much of his potential audience chose to sample the delights of their nude ballet and risqué song-and-dance routines, rather than his somewhat tamer form of flamboyance.

The US tour took an enormous mental toll on Bowie: each successive week saw him ingesting more cocaine and less food. Yet there were compensations: he recruited a key musical collaborator, jazz pianist Mike Garson; was introduced to the New York Dolls; and struck up a lasting friendship with Iggy Pop, who invited him to mix the amateurishly recorded tapes for the third Stooges album, *Raw Power*.

Meanwhile, Bowie channelled his bus-window impressions of America into the songs that would fill his next album. A simple process of addition produced one of his most enduring singles: he took the guitar riff* from the Yardbirds' arrangement of Muddy Waters' 'I'm A Man'; combined it with the climactic build on a repeated chord that

---

* Bowie's memory of this riff may have been jogged when it was revived as the central motif of 'Keep That Fire Burning', on a 1971 album by Tucker Zimmerman, who not only performed alongside Bowie at the Beckenham Arts Lab but was also a friend of Tony Visconti. Zimmerman was not, however, Bob Dylan's cousin, which was how he had been billed in Beckenham.

the Yardbirds used on another R&B standard, 'Smokestack Lightning'; created an imaginary character out of his observations of Iggy Pop; and found a title by playing with the name of Lindsay Kemp's literary hero, Jean Genet. He honed his ideas at the RCA Studios in Nashville, and 'The Jean Genie' was recorded in New York a few days later. It was rush-released in Britain, coinciding with another RCA release, 'Blockbuster' by the Sweet, that was built around the same Muddy Waters riff (and in the same key). To Bowie's chagrin, 'Blockbuster' narrowly outsold 'The Jean Genie'; the British rock press loyally assumed that Sweet had 'copied' Bowie, but neither act had heard the other's record in advance.

The 'classic' roots of Bowie's record – its slightly wheezy blues harp, and snake-rattle percussion – ensured its longevity: if 'Starman' was the sound of 1972, 'The Jean Genie' might have been recorded in 1966, or indeed 2006. Its lyrics created instant rock 'n' roll mythology, touching on fashion, drugs and rampant sexuality, with a nod to the Max's Kansas City scene in New York, where everyone had been familiar with the powder known as Snow White. His vocal had a playfulness that undercut the menace of the band, which was deliberate; his rhythm guitar occasionally missed its entrance into the chorus, which was not. But 'The Jean Genie' was never intended to be about antiseptic perfection: its selling point was exuberance, not exactitude.

[66] WATCH THAT MAN (Bowie)

Recorded January 1973; *Aladdin Sane* LP.

In September 1972, David Bowie witnessed two consecutive shows in the Oscar Wilde Room of Max's Kansas City by the New York Dolls, whose transparent assemblage of classic rock images proved more enduring than the brittle collision of influences that comprised their music. Though their commercial impact was negligible (neither of their albums reached the US Top 100 chart), they represented America's most committed response to the British glam-rock movement – not least because they owed their fashion sense to the same west London stores and stalls that were frequented by Bowie and Bolan. The Dolls' guitarist, Johnny Thunders, also pre-empted the early punk bands by sporting a swastika armband for confrontational effect.

In New York, the band attracted the attention of homosexuals, transvestites and those few members of the Warhol entourage who didn't fit comfortably into either category. So it was inevitable that Bowie would seek them out. 'He's a collector,' said his producer Ken Scott, 'of anything and everything, experiences, influences, the lot.' Bowie was reported to have told the Dolls at their first encounter that they had 'the energy of six English bands'. It was that spirit that he attempted to capture on 'Watch That Man', a decadent collage of impressions from Max's (notably his meetings with Wayne County and Cyrinda Foxe), the Sombrero in Kensington, and the pages of Evelyn Waugh's *Vile Bodies* (whose characters would not yet have become bored with the jazz standard 'The Tiger Rag', which became little more than a cliché after Benny Goodman's hit version in 1936). As for the focal point of the action, he was a chancer, a hipster, a voyeur, and a star;* the verses were his, but the perspective (and the key) changed for the chorus, where he was now the one being watched.

Maybe the basis of life as a chancer (and a star) was taking inspiration wherever it could be found. The structure of the chorus – punch the first syllable, then pause for effect – was reminiscent of a track Bowie had recently produced for Mott the Hoople, 'Momma's Little Jewel'. The vocal blend – lead buried deep in the mix, female backing almost more prominent – was identical to the sound of the Rolling Stones' newly released *Exile On Main Street* album. The rest was pure hard-rock theatricality, from the viscous layers of guitar to the boogie-woogie lines of the bass, and the guttural grunt of Bowie's saxophone holding up the bottom end.

[67] PANIC IN DETROIT (Bowie)

Recorded January 1973; *Aladdin Sane* LP.

Politics as passion or politics as posture: that choice shaped rock's involvement with radical activism during the late sixties and early seventies. In the motor city of Detroit, blues fan, beat poet and

---

* There was a playful allusion to the line from John Lennon's 'I Found Out' – 'a throwback from someone's LP', as Bowie put it – about being harassed on the phone, previously referenced on 'Suffragette City' [59].

perpetual dissident John Sinclair responded to the defiance of the Black Panther Party in Oakland, California, by forming the White Panther Party, whose manifesto demanded 'rock 'n' roll, dope and fucking in the streets!'. Police brutality in the city provoked extensive riots amongst the African-American community in 1967, and Sinclair aligned his Panthers with those seeking to banish racism from the streets and end the war in Vietnam. In 1969, he was jailed for possession of a small amount of marijuana; a prolonged protest campaign, climaxed by a concert featuring John Lennon, brought about his release. Meanwhile, the rock band that Sinclair had managed, the MC5, carried the Panthers' manifesto into thousands of homes via their debut album, *Kick Out The Jams*.

Some of that history was available to Bowie as a gentle reader of the music press; the rest he learned from Iggy Pop when the pair met again in Detroit in October 1972. Not an instinctively political being, Bowie chose to satirise* the cult of John Sinclair, by comparing him to rebel martyr Che Guevara, who even by 1972 was being admired more for his rock 'n' roll image (a mustachioed Jim Morrison) than for his example as a guerrilla fighter. The subsequent 'panic' told us more about the narrator's sense of irrelevance than about any political realities.

That provided a thematic link with Bob Dylan's 'All Along The Watchtower', which used a similar† three-chord riff to underpin its apocalypse. Like 'The Jean Genie' [65], and indeed Iggy & the Stooges' '1969', Bowie's recording harked back to the swampy R&B records that came out of Chicago in the fifties, all maracas and tom-toms, creating a tension that pulsed and grew until a single cymbal crash signalled the way out of the chorus/chaos. The entire track seemed on the verge of that electronic sound distortion known as phasing, which finally won sway in the instrumental break, mimicking the 'train' drums of Jimi Hendrix's 'Gypsy Eyes'. All the sense of disturbance that Bowie's lyrics couldn't satisfy was provided by the turbulence of the final moments, as Ronson's guitar filled the right-hand speaker with wave after wave of dive-bombing sirens, and female voices wailed demonically.

---

* Bowie's narrator merely wants the autograph of the man who has inspired him to destroy a slot machine: not exactly the overthrow of the military-industrial complex. And why else would Bowie tell us about the rebel's diesel van if not for comic effect?
† Dylan played Am-G-F; Bowie used Bm-G-A.

All this was in keeping with what one journalist at the time, paraphrasing Bowie's explanation, called 'a vague feeling of impending catastrophe', a conviction that 'the Americans he had met were poised unknowingly on the lip of a cataclysm that would rock the world'. Partly that reflected the milieux in which he had chosen to mix; partly it represented a transference of his own unease on to a nation that was politically and economically troubled, but lacked the cripplingly defeatist mentality that afflicted Bowie's homeland during this era.

[68] DRIVE-IN SATURDAY (Bowie)

Recorded January 1973; *Aladdin Sane* LP.

Before the movie *American Graffiti* legitimised fifties teenage life as a subject for nostalgia* rather than ridicule, the drive-in was a peculiarly American phenomenon, as alien to Europe as the science-fiction landscape of Bowie's song. The song's location was the future, when sixties icons such as Mick Jagger and Twiggy (the Wonder Kid) were as archetypal as anything conceived by Jung, and – as in the 1967 movie *Barbarella* – lust was a thing of the past, only accessible from ancient videotapes. It's one of the ironies of 'Drive-In Saturday' that technology that sounded so advanced in 1973 is now laughably passé. But then Bowie was a much better alarmist than he was a futurologist. A few months before he wrote the song, he warned British pop fans that they needed to 'face up to a future which is going to be controlled by the Pill, and by sperm banks . . . Man and woman will change . . . I want to be very optimistic. But I have a hard time being optimistic about the future.' He conjured up his anachronistic desire by placing it in a mythical version of the 1950s, the tapes providing a 'crash course' for the ravers of the future, even though 'ravers' was decidedly sixties slang. Along the way, he tipped his hat to the T. Rex hit 'Get It On' and to the New York Dolls' drummer Sylvain Sylvain, whilst preparing his public for the intended launch, the following year, of a group called the Astronettes.

The fifties landscape also permeated the music, from the arpeggio

---

* This theme was mined for comic effect in the TV series *Happy Days*, and the movie *Grease* – itself based on a musical play that hit Broadway in summer 1972.

plucking of the opening E chord to the re-creation of the era's vocal group sound – lush but not quite perfect,* as you'd expect from denizens of the future. Like a Saturday-morning movie serial, the song depended on maintaining anticipation: the opening V chord established a tension that was immediately resolved at the start of the verse, which itself ended in a cliff-hanging B7 chord, preparing the way for the small leap up (and down, from the key of A into G) of the chorus. There were other signals of the era, from the Duane Eddy-style lead guitar to the Phil Spector-inspired percussion. Bowie originally requested Spector's services as producer for *Aladdin Sane*, but failed to make contact with him. The dense, luxurious sound of the chorus hinted at the effect that he had hoped Spector's presence might bring. Within a few months, this epic re-creation of a lost era would itself become a cliché, in the skilled hands of Roy Wood's Wizzard ('Angel Fingers' and 'See My Baby Jive' being prime examples).

[69] TIME (Bowie)

Recorded January 1973; *Aladdin Sane* LP.

Melodic and structural similarities between the chorus of this song and 'Oh! You Pretty Things' [30] weren't an accident, as both were composed during Bowie's piano experimentation of 1971. Indeed, a prototype of 'Time', titled 'We Should Be On By Now', was given to his friend George Underwood that summer, complete with its playful, clock-watching lift from Chuck Berry's fifties rock classic, 'Reelin' & Rockin''.[†]

Extended and rewritten as 'Time', the song not only shifted its chronological focus from the fifties to the thirties, via the ambience of Mike Garson's Berlin-cabaret-club piano, but also renewed one of the most unsettling concepts of the twentieth century: relativity. As cultural historian Peter Conrad noted, before 1900, 'Time flowed always at the same reliable speed: space, by contrast, was immov-

* Vocal group hits of the fifties were invariably built around the I-vi-IV-V chord sequence; the verses of 'Drive-In Saturday' utilised I-vi-iii-V instead.
† Similarly, Marc Bolan had concluded the 1971 T. Rex hit 'Get It On' with a line from another vintage Berry composition, 'Little Queenie'.

able. Then, in the twentieth century, the universe suddenly ceased to obey these laws. Time adopted variable, unsynchronised tempi, and space too became mobile.' In Bowie's fevered imagination, as in the temporal realm of modernism, time could shift and bend like a note on his blues harmonica: yesterday's apocalypse might be previewed today. To add to his perturbation, he had recently become obsessed with the culture of a country he had yet to visit, Japan, where verb formations took no account of time existing in the past or the future: everything was in the present tense; everything was happening simul-taneously. Time, then, could be both Life and Death; and, in its latter form, it claimed Bowie's friends, such as Billy Dolls.*

'Time' opened to the distant sound of Garson's piano, offering vaudeville clichés with a distinctly European flavour. Bowie's voice entered with a lingering echo delay, as if to demonstrate time in action. Once the initial verse was over, we were returned to familiar territory, another diatonic descent in the tradition of the 'Changes' [48] chorus, with backing vocals marking out the root of each chord. But the decadent romanticism of the song abruptly gave way to horror: Bowie could only voice that with a scream, answered a few bars later by slowly declining howls from Mick Ronson's guitar. The eeriest moment of the song, however, came when yet another of his wordless choruses – remember 'Ching-A-Ling' [A55] and 'Velvet Goldmine' [54] – turned into a cacophonous march, with massed Bowies accompanied by saxophone and flute. It was like a scene from Christopher Isherwood's evocations of 1930s Berlin, which – in another reversal of time – had recently been revived in the movie *Cabaret.*

[70] ALADDIN SANE (1913–1938–197?) (Bowie)

Recorded January 1973; *Aladdin Sane* LP.

While 'Time' [69] could have been subtitled '1973–1933', the title track of *Aladdin Sane* was both more and less specific. Bowie's inspiration was

---

* Alias Billy Murcia, original drummer of the New York Dolls, who died – ostensibly of a drug overdose although no drugs were found in his body – in November 1972, little more than six weeks after Bowie had partied with him in Manhattan.

Evelyn Waugh's 1930* novel *Vile Bodies*: 'The book dealt with London in the period just before a massive, imaginary war,' he explained. 'People were frivolous, decadent and silly. Somehow it seemed to me that they were like people today.' The closest that Waugh came to anointing a hero in his novel was with Adam Symes, who tells his lover: 'Nina, do you ever feel that things simply can't go on much longer?' While the characters frolic in cavalier ignorance, war is declared during a Christmas Eve carol service, and Symes finds himself 'on a splintered tree stump in the biggest battlefield in the history of the world . . . The scene all round him was one of unrelieved desolation.' It was a fine epigraph for a pop album at the height of the supposedly hedonistic genre of glam rock.

The feeling of two worlds moving at different speeds – glamour and apocalypse, frivolity and war – was emphasised by the way the song was constructed. The verse repeated a virtually identical theme over and over, while the accompaniment constantly shifted its ground, using chords that only a pianist could have conceived. Then, by instinct rather than musical training, Bowie added to the sense of dislocation by launching his chorus melody on a high A (against a movement from G to F major chords), and then continuing to build his theme out of notes that didn't appear in the chords beneath them.

Though the song was unmistakably Bowie's creation, its landscape belonged to jazz keyboardist Mike Garson. His flamboyant glissandi in the verse, the ultimate signs of romanticism, heightened the feeling of decadence – while his extended solo, a phenomenal improvisation around the simplest of changes, stabbed at the keys with reckless flamboyance, apparently unhinged but thrillingly controlled. There were other magisterial but more subtle touches throughout: the eighth-note caresses of the cymbal with a brush over the opening chords, the cameo appearances by a twisting acoustic guitar, the single delayed saxophone note repeated after Garson's showcase, the voice vanishing into echo on the final call of 'sane'. And one touch of amused guilt: Bowie briefly offered a line or two from the Drifters' 'On Broadway' to acknowledge the similarity between the roots, if not the ambience,

---

* 'I just work out probabilities,' Bowie explained as he was finishing the album, 'pick incidents that happen in the 30s and 40s and push them through to the 80s and see what conclusions could come from what happened then.'

of the two songs. Finally, there was a slow decaying of sounds, some tonal, some merely an interruption, a long-held bass note from the piano, one last defiant flourish – and then silence.

Fashion: Turn to the Left

Stanley Kubrick's film of Anthony Burgess' novel *A Clockwork Orange* was premiered in January 1972, the same month in which David Bowie ventured into the outside world under the guise of Ziggy Stardust. The choreographed violence of Malcolm McDowell (as 'Alex') and his fellow 'droogs' would, Burgess predicted, encourage imitations: 'After seeing *A Clockwork Orange*, a lot of boys will take up rape and pillage and even murder,' he declared. 'Therefore all art should be banned.' He was being both ironic and searingly truthful, and Kubrick would soon take him at his word, preventing the film from being screened in Britain until after his death.

Such was the ease with which irony and outrage merged in the early seventies that David Bowie, who loved Burgess' book and saw an early screening of the film, was able to translate the uniform in which the droogs dispensed their rape and murder into a distinctive brand for a pop group. 'I got most of the look for Ziggy from that,' he recounted in 1993. 'I liked the malicious, malevolent, vicious quality of those guys.' But he insisted that he had stripped the violence from their image, while being able to retain 'that terrorist, we're-ready-for-action, kind of thing'. The film toyed with a series of troubling equations: art as voyeurism, voyeurism as violence, violence as Nietzschean ecstasy. Burgess insisted that he had looked back for inspiration, rather than forward: *A Clockwork Orange* was a report on the world of the fifties and early sixties, not a forecast of a dystopian future. In Bowie's hands, however, everything became futuristic, and everything ironic.

The missing, essential ingredient in that equation was 'style', a quality that had obsessed Bowie since his earliest adventures in Soho with his brother Terry at the dawn of the sixties. A decade later, he both reflected and invented the styles of the age, drawing on not only futurism and violence, but also several other vital facets of the seventies: androgyny, individuality, eclecticism. In fashion as in history, this was a decade that was defiantly not its predecessor, but which could not escape being influenced by the recent past. Hence Bowie's importance as a catalyst, for the way in which he compressed symbols from the fifties and sixties – from SF movie costumes to the stage garb of the classic rock 'n' rollers – into a series of images that always appeared to be pointing the way ahead. Throughout the sixties, you could understand exactly where youth culture had arrived by looking at Bowie's hair and clothes. In the seventies, people studied Bowie to find out the ways in which they would soon be selling themselves to the outside world.

Cultural commentator Peter York wrote that Bowie's distinctive contribution to style in the seventies was that he introduced 'the idea of conscious stylisation – oneself as a Work of Art – to a wider audience than ever before'. To an extent, 'oneself as a Work of Art' was also a definition of the mod subculture of the sixties. What Bowie added was an understanding that 'oneself' need not stop at surface appearance, but could become a conceptual art project encompassing every facet of existence.

His influence on appearance was immense, however, provoking thousands of so-called 'Bowie kids' to mimic him. (They needed to look sharp in every sense of the phrase, however, to avoid seeming tragically anachronistic. Woe betide the fan who arrived for a Bowie concert in 1976 wearing Ziggy make-up, only to discover that the once-alien rock star was now masquerading as the star of a Leni Riefenstahl documentary.) The cropped hair sported by Bowie and his wife Angie was similar to the feather cuts of female suedeheads at the start of the seventies, but it was Ziggy who made it into a mainstream badge of pride. But whereas Bowie commissioned what he called his 'cosmic Clockwork Orange jumpsuits' from Freddie Burretti and his 'impossibly silly "bunny" costume' (cut unflatteringly short: a hot pants jumpsuit) from Japan's hottest designer, his fans had to concoct his image out of home-styled hair and accessories from Woolworth's.

Bowie himself was both a peacock and a magpie, borrowing looks and styles wherever he could find them. Two years before he visited Japan for the first time, he (like many others) was enraptured by the designs of a designer named Kansai Yamamoto,* who staged his first London show in 1971. Bowie credited him as the source for Ziggy's dyed hair: 'He had just unleashed all the Kabuki- and Noh-inspired clothes on London, and one of his models had the Kabuki lion's mane on her head, this bright red thing.' Yamamoto subsequently created many extravagant costumes for

---

* Other Japanese designers of the time also left their mark, notably Kenzo Takada and Issey Miyake.

Ziggy's final months in the spotlight. 'He has an unusual face,' he said of Bowie, adding: 'He's neither man nor woman.'

If Yamamoto was the first designer to adopt Bowie as a deliciously angular model, the singer continued to prowl the most fashionable stores in London and New York for inspiration. They in turn created their fantasies out of nostalgia. Vintage clothing stores – The Last Picture Frock, Nostalgia, Paradise Garage – were (comparatively) cheap, ecologically efficient at a time of industrial disputes and material shortages, and conveyed glamour borrowed* from bygone ages. This applied especially to the thirties chic that passed rapidly from artists such as Lindsay Kemp (with his ostrich feather fans) into the mainstream, growing more popular as the West drifted further into recession – as if the only way of coping with a return to the economic emergencies of the pre-Second World War era was to reinvent its style as well. By mid-decade, people were reading Stella Margetson's *The Long Party*, a study of 'high society in the 20s and 30s', watching Robert Redford glide effortlessly through the depression-free gardens of *The Great Gatsby* and, perhaps, reaching for the sleeves of either *Pin Ups* (with its back cover portrait of Bowie in a Tommy Roberts suit, like a twenties Chicago gangster) or *Young Americans* (with classic-era Hollywood cover portrait). Many of the symbols of mid-seventies fashion – platform shoes, flyaway lapels, high-waisted flares – originated in the thirties, though few of those who adopted them in 1973 wanted to hear that their grandparents might have worn the same styles.

It was Tommy Roberts who, in 1970, opened Mr Freedom on London's Kensington Church Street. Like Bowie, the store offered a choice of identities to borrow or reconfigure, from the art deco of the thirties through fifties rock 'n' roll to sixties pop. As *Vogue* magazine declared, 'there are no rules in the fashion game now. You're playing it and you make up the game as you go.' Marc Bolan could have acquired an entire wardrobe at Mr Freedom, his skeletal figure acting as the perfect show pony for its hip-hugging reflective trousers and tight-cut jackets. Among the store's designers was the delightfully named Pamla Motown, whose cropped red hair and androgynous face marked her out as a hybrid clone of Bowie and his wife. A minute's walk from Mr Freedom was the Biba store on Kensington High Street, which brought the revivals of deco, nouveau and the belle époque within reach of the girl on the street.

---

* At its most extreme, this trend could encourage the singer-songwriter Gilbert O'Sullivan to brand himself as a deprived working-class kid, in ragged pullover and schoolboy shorts.

Biba also attracted the attention of the tiny urban guerrilla cell known as the Angry Brigade, who exploded a bomb inside the store on May Day 1971. In the terrorist fashion of the times, they issued a communiqué to explain their assault on the cult of selling: 'Life is so boring there is nothing to do except spend all our wages on the latest skirt or shirt. Brothers and Sisters, what are your real desires? The only thing you can do with modern slave-houses – called boutiques – IS WRECK THEM. You can't reform profit capitalism and inhumanity. Just kick it until it breaks.'

Theirs was a lone voice. Novelist J.G. Ballard might have noted cynically that 'The next religion might come from the world of fashion rather than from any conventional one', but even those who advocated the overturning of conventional morals and the hollowness of social thinking were far from immune to the pull of fashion. And so it was that Malcolm McLaren, a fellow traveller of the iconoclastic situationist movement, found himself in 1972, running a vintage clothes shop on the premises that had previously held the iconic sixties boutique Hung On You, and then two of the stellar influences on the new decade, Mr Freedom and Paradise Garden. McLaren leased the building at 430 King's Road in Chelsea for the remainder of the decade, and the changing names of his business told their own story: from Let It Rock to Too Fast To Live, Too Young To Die; then Sex; and finally Seditionaries, by which time McLaren was notorious as the manager of a rock band who compressed the world-weary contempt of the Angry Brigade into a single message: 'Anarchy In The UK'. Anthony Burgess must have nodded sagely in recognition.

[71] THE PRETTIEST STAR (see also [13]) (Bowie)

Recorded January 1973; *Aladdin Sane* LP.

Amidst the rock 'n' roll swagger and almost sickly decadence of *Aladdin Sane*, the revival of Bowie's little-known 1970 single 'The Prettiest Star' seemed anachronistic – neither contemporary nor apocalyptic enough to fit the album's themes. It certainly received a more sympathetic arrangement than before, being taken at an altogether faster pace. Mick Ronson replicated Marc Bolan's original guitar solo, but this time it sat within the track, rather than outside it. While doo-wop vocals and country-tinged piano lent the song a late-fifties feel, the middle section featured a quartet of male voices that conjured up the world of Edward VII, as if the entire performance were an exercise in demonstrating the supple nature of time.

Bowie's own status as 'the prettiest star' in the glam-rock field – or at least Marc Bolan's closest rival – was evidenced by the amount of memorabilia that was now on the market to tempt his fans. Besides the usual posters (more often than not carrying photographs from the 'Space Oddity' [1] era, as his management – in an early example of multimedia control – controlled the image rights on Ziggy Stardust portraits), it was also possible to buy Bowie pillowcases, alongside those featuring Bolan, Donny Osmond and David Cassidy.

[72] LET'S SPEND THE NIGHT TOGETHER (Jagger/Richards)

Recorded January 1973; *Aladdin Sane* LP.

Variously described by critics down the years as camp, bisexual or gay, this riotous assault on a Rolling Stones single from 1967 was more accurately a celebration of Bowie's utter dominance over the world around him. Other covers of classic rock tunes during the Ziggy era (from 'This Boy' to 'I Feel Free') were conventional or ill-conceived; but 'Let's Spend The Night Together' jettisoned the tight control of the Stones original and thereby set the entire tradition of sixties rock aflame.

The Spiders set out their manifesto from the start: a crushing guitar chord, savage smears of synthesised* noise, and Mike Garson's fearless romp through all the major chords from D to F♯, casting key signatures to the winds. Thereafter they settled for inflamed Chuck Berry riffs, while Bowie sang as if he were setting fire to every line. In the most daring, ridiculous moment, he broke the song down into a fifties-styled monologue, a pastiche of Paul Anka's mock-sincerity on 'Diana', perhaps. 'Let's make love,' he purred, and was answered by two orgasmic spurts of Ronson's guitar, the briefest and most brutal

---

* 'The idea was to fuck the sound up, give it some, "whoa, what's that?",' Bowie recalled in 1991. 'That was the first time I used synthesisers, the wobbly noise on the break.' He was forgetting that Visconti, Scott and Ronson had already played synthesisers on his earlier records.

of couplings. Spend the night? On this evidence, Bowie could hardly bear to spend two minutes with his battered victim.*

[73] CRACKED ACTOR (Bowie)

Recorded January 1973; *Aladdin Sane* LP.

Crack the image; smack the face; inject the smack; suck up the fantasy; suck up the phallus. Three layers of prostitution collided on Hollywood's Sunset Strip in this song: offering money for sex; sex for drugs; worship for fame. 'They were mostly older producer types, quite strange looking, quite charming, but thoroughly unreal,' Bowie recalled of the Strip's clients. The 50-year-old star (insert your own choice of name) of 'Cracked Actor' was 'stiff on his legend': erect, famous, over the hill, effectively dead. He despised the whore, 'a porcupine' of dope tracks, and the whore despised him. It was just another sales transaction in the city of dreams. The rhythm guitar cranked mechanically up and down its succession of barre chords with a whore's indifference, while Ronson wavered between grunts of feedback and howls of equally contrived ecstasy. This was standard early-seventies hard-rock raunch, with a jaded air of glam, enlivened by a suitably flashy vocal, with Bowie building himself up to a climax that was stolen by Ronson's insistent guitar solo.

It was probably not a coincidence that the age differential between whore and trick in this song exactly mirrored the gap between Marlon Brando and Maria Schneider in the cinematic tale of erotic obsession, *Last Tango In Paris*, which was premiered in New York during Bowie's autumn 1972 US tour. The film provoked shocked headlines around the world for its graphic sexual context, although only the woman was seen in a state of full-frontal nudity – because, claimed director Bernardo Bertolucci, he identified himself completely with Brando's character, and could not bear to expose 'himself' on screen. Bowie himself would not be so reticent before the decade was out.

---

* Small wonder, then, that Keith Richards took great delight in erasing Bowie's handclapped contribution to the basic track of the Rolling Stones' 1974 single, 'It's Only Rock & Roll', and replacing it with his own.

[74] LADY GRINNING SOUL (Bowie)

Recorded January 1973; *Aladdin Sane* LP.

Legend has it that 'Lady Grinning Soul' was an ecstatic love song to the soul singer Claudia Lennear, best known as the supposed inspiration for the Rolling Stones' 'Brown Sugar', and perennial back-up to white rock stars who required some authentic African-American passion in their work. The pair certainly met towards the end of his late 1972 US tour, and the song was written and recorded immediately after his return. But despite the regularity with which she has been named as the subject of both songs, a reliable source for this attribution is difficult to find.

Whoever she was, no muse could have wished for a more vivid or affecting portrait, especially from a man who, during that same tour, described himself as 'a very cold person . . . a bit of an iceman'. After the octave jump of the first two syllables, Bowie delivered much of the song beyond the high G that he used to regard as the top of his range, as if to demonstrate his vulnerability and commitment, his voice aching with loss and desire. His musicians were equally sensitive to the moment, Mike Garson wrapping Bowie's delicious melody in a wrap of semi-classical, ultra-romantic flourishes; Trevor Bolder offering some equally sensitive bass accompaniment; Mick Ronson summing up the moment with a flamenco-inspired solo as beautiful as Bowie's obsession. They were drifting across a gossamer-light song, its verse a succession of tentative, tender steps up the scale; the chorus floating back and forth between B♭ and B natural, melancholy and joy, memory and anticipation, with the equally uncertain closing movement (G♯m-G-G♯m) suggesting that he already knew that their love affair was over.

Aladdin Sane LP

The figure on the album cover that was trumpeted on its launch as the most expensive design of all time was the archetype of artificiality – glittered, painted, dyed, decorated with a lightning flash, its flesh marble-cold and deformed with a silver teardrop, sculpted, epicene, emaciated, haughty, vulnerable and ultimately alien. 'David Bowie Aladdin Sane', read the lettering, as if the two personae were interchangeable (and as if Bowie might indeed be a lad insane). Which is exactly what Bowie's fans assumed, and hoped: that here was another character as striking and persuasive as Ziggy Stardust, ready to lead them on a second adventure into the outer limits of sexuality and identity.

Initially, Bowie was at pains to play down these expectations. 'I don't think Aladdin is as clearly cut and defined a character as Ziggy was,' he insisted. 'Aladdin is pretty ephemeral.' The album, he explained, was 'my interpretation of what America means to me. It's like a summation of my first American tour.' But so relentless was the demand for Aladdin Sane to exist inside Bowie's skeleton that the singer eventually gave in, and began to talk about the character as if he were more than simply a set of photographs, a pose and a song. For example: 'Aladdin Sane was a schizophrenic. That's why there were so many costume changes, because he had so many personalities.' Among them, presumably, was Ziggy Stardust – or vice versa – because there was no break in Bowie's schedule, or change of presentation, to differentiate the star of one album from the icon of the next. Fans chose not to ponder the philosophical dilemma – was Ziggy performing as Aladdin Sane, or was Aladdin playing Ziggy's songs? – and simply wallowed in the decadence of it all.

Neither at the time was there any exploration of the lightning bolt across Aladdin's visage – mirroring the flash that was to be found on the flag of the Hitler Youth, was doubled to produce the insignia of Heinrich Himmler's SS cadre, and was also a Tarot symbol for the card known as the Tower, denoting the need to reconstruct oneself. The bolt had been seen on a gown designed by Kansai Yamamoto for Bowie to wear on stage, though photographer Brian Duffy recalled that Bowie's inspiration was actually a similar symbol used by Elvis Presley – and Bowie himself, fleshing out his portrait of the imaginary Mr Sane, contended that 'I thought [Aladdin]* would probably be cracked by lightning.'

Ultimately, Bowie's original explanation – that here was a slightly deranged report on the American scene, from the distorted vision of

---

* Aladdin was an intriguing choice of name, in any case: a pantomime favourite – indeed, portrayed on stage by Cliff Richard, no less – he was first encountered in *The Arabian Nights*, as a poverty-stricken young man who had been given a magic ring with which he could achieve his heart's desires. All comparisons with the life of a rock star from a working-class family in south London were, of course, coincidental.

a rock star – was quite accurate. There was no narrative or theme to *Aladdin Sane*, beyond the sense that civilisation could not continue as it was without toppling into apocalypse: a clear case of personal crisis infecting the world beyond. As such, it was arguably a more 'real' album than *Ziggy Stardust*; and, also arguably, a more rewarding one at this distance, its Stones-inspired, vivid production enduring better than the somewhat flat sonic canvas of *Ziggy*. But *Ziggy* had an impact beyond the duration of its songs; *Aladdin Sane* was its songs, its sleeve, and nothing more. It did not solve the problem of where Bowie might take his Ziggy character, or abandon him: it simply compounded the pressure, and his fame.

[75] ZION (AKA ALADDIN VEIN AKA TRAGIC MOMENTS) (Bowie)

Recorded *c.* July 1973; unreleased.

'Zion' was allegedly recorded for *Aladdin Sane*; meanwhile, Bowie declared that *Tragic Moments* was a work-in-progress during the *Pin Ups* sessions later in the year, intended as 'a musical in one act . . . probably running straight through both sides'. He then played journalist Martin Hayman a long instrumental, 'a highly arranged, subtly shifting piece of music with just a touch of vaudeville'. That description fits the piece of music circulated amongst fans under the title of 'Zion': it opened with the piano motif that would later grace the 'Sweet Thing' medley [100] on *Diamond Dogs*, moved through a weighty Ronson guitar riff reminiscent of the Who's 'I Can See For Miles', and then into a wordless Bowie melody that sounded like a close cousin of the Beatles' 'I'll Follow The Sun' – and still on, via a jazzy descent into a piano section that could have featured on *Hunky Dory*, and finally back through the first two movements, to close with a typical Mike Garson flourish. It could almost be the overture for a rock opera; or a skeleton for the 1984 musical; or an attempt to marry half a dozen different themes and moods into a coherent whole, which Bowie chose to abandon.

The Unmaking of a Star #1: Rock 'n' Roll Suicide

As a piece of theatre, it could hardly have been bettered. David Bowie's performance at the Hammersmith Odeon in London on 3 July 1973 had reached its final encore. Before his by now traditional rendition of the elegiac 'Rock 'n' Roll Suicide' [61], he stunned his audience – and at least two members of his band – by announcing that 'this is the last show we'll ever do'. Cue screams and cries from his audience; startled glances from his rhythm section, who would never work together with Bowie again; banner headlines in the pop press; and knowing nods from those who had anticipated just such an outcome all along.* Bowie could not be accused of having hidden his intentions. The previous winter, he had signalled his discontent with the pressure of enacting Ziggy Stardust, night after night across Britain, North America and Japan: 'I feel as though I'm on a tightrope more and more, a kind of precipice.' By January 1973, he was telling a British pop magazine that 'I'm not too sure when I'll be appearing on stage in this country again . . . I may be concentrating on films in the future.' Within his organisation, Mick Ronson recalled: 'David's retirement was first talked about a few months before, at the start of the British tour. It was never a definite thing, but everything seemed to lead up to that Hammersmith show like it was the last time.' The concert was recorded and filmed by a documentary crew, for an album tentatively titled Bowie-ing Out.

There were countless reasons for Bowie to step off the treadmill. He was completing a two-month tour of British cinemas, theatres and civic halls: 61 shows in 53 days, crossing the country's notoriously inadequate road system for a diet of anonymous hotel rooms, scrambled meals and relentlessly enthusiastic fans. After a brief pause, he was booked to endure an even more enervating schedule in America. 'There was a time when what I was doing didn't seem to resemble anything anybody else was doing,' he recalled in 2000, describing his personality as 'out of sync, not in touch'. Cocaine was now his main nutrient, with all its attendant fears and excesses: 'You start on this trail of psychological destruction, and you become what's called a drug casualty at the end of it all.'

* Compare the retirement speech given by Ray Davies of the Kinks less than two weeks later, at the end of their performance at the White City festival. In severe mental distress, the Kinks' leader announced that this would be his final gig, but his words were masked by applause and extraneous noise over the PA system. Davies had taken an overdose of pills before he went on stage, but survived, and was back on the road within two months.

Bowie was exhausted beyond simple repair; he was bored with the repetition, of the constant ringing in his ears, the feelings of staleness and circularity. He did not want to be Ziggy Stardust, or perhaps even David Bowie, though he did not know what would remain if he gave up both of these assumed identities. There was also the problem of his band: not just that he wanted a new sound behind him, but the embarrassing fact that two members (Bolder and Woodmansey) had discovered that another member (Garson) was earning enormously more per show than they were, and so they wanted a raise that their manager, Tony Defries, would not grant them.

Defries had another excellent reason for encouraging Bowie to stop. The proposed US tour was being promised as the most elaborate piece of staging in rock history: the stage would be covered in a large plastic bubble, surrounded by a skin beneath which gases of various colours would be pumped during the performance, to alter Bowie's hue and maybe even, as far as the audience were concerned, his size. It sounded an incredible idea; and incredible it was, as there was no money in the MainMan budget to cover the expense, while RCA Records – who had cleverly been landed with the fees for the loss-making 1972 US tour – were not about to be fooled again. Bowie's US tour receipts could not possibly match the hype that surrounded him, so the planned itinerary would have been financially disastrous for MainMan; whereas operating on a restricted budget and smaller scale would have destroyed Defries' reputation for grand gestures and *coups de théâtre*.

So the American tour could not happen, although Defries dared not let his client find out why, for fear of losing face where it mattered most. Meanwhile, Bowie prevaricated, which is one reason why his band weren't told in advance. As Mick Ronson admitted, 'In the end it was almost a last-minute decision.' If Bowie's bodyguard, Stuey George, was to be believed, it wasn't even the singer's choice: 'His manager decided just before he went on. He didn't react instantly; he didn't think about it until he'd done half the show . . . He said, "What am I going to do?", and his manager said, "Don't you worry, leave it all to me. I'll tell you what we are going to do after."' So, according to this account by someone who was at Bowie's side for almost every moment he was off-stage, Bowie swallowed hard and did as he was told. Then – the eternal mythologist – he phoned the pop press the next day and explained that he had elected to quit because he wanted to concentrate on working in films (notably a screenplay based on Robert Heinlein's SF novel, *Stranger in a Strange Land*) and 'various activities that have very little to do with rock and pop'. MainMan added that Bowie would now be 'writing the script' for his future: not just the Actor, then, as he'd been credited in the small print on *Hunky Dory*, but the Author as well. Soon he was rationalising his retirement as a conceptual climax to a conceptual experiment in inventing and achieving rock stardom. 'The star was created,' he said, as if he were talking about a robot he'd invented; 'he worked; and that's all I wanted him to do. Anything he did now would just be repetition.'

The tedium of life on the road aside, Bowie – acting as and on behalf of Ziggy Stardust – was being more astute than perhaps he realised. By 1973, most of his peers and elders in the business of rock 'n' roll were already leaving their peak of innovation and creativity behind, and embarking on the long (and, as it proved, highly lucrative) process of reproducing and feigning their youthful passion for audiences who pretended that the excitement was still real. 'Will this be the last time?', the media asked at the start of each Rolling Stones tour, before realising that in the hands of the Stones, the Who and countless others, rock would pass almost without notice from an embodiment of youthful rebellion into a highly rewarding pension plan.

Bowie could foresee the cynicism ahead, and several weeks before he retired Ziggy Stardust from the stage, he decided to come clean. 'Maybe I'm not into rock 'n' roll,' he confessed to the *New Musical Express*. 'Maybe I just use rock 'n' roll. This is what I do. I'm not into rock 'n' roll at all . . . it's just an artist's materials.' But his words didn't make sense from a rock star, to an audience for whom rock was a shared language, their way of comprehending the world around them. So nobody, perhaps even Bowie, understood them. It was like Hamlet, at the denouement of his tragedy, holding his script up to the audience and declaring that it was all a facade. Better to do what Bowie did: announce his retirement, and then immediately throw himself into a frenzy of activity and creativity that convinced his public his retirement was simply a career move.

One thing was certain: David Bowie would no longer be Ziggy Stardust (or, for that matter, Aladdin Sane). There would be no more Spiders From Mars. So Bowie had to face an uncertain future without the props that had served him so well. He had created a rock star, and destroyed him. The challenge was to invent a second act for what had been intended as a one-act drama.

[76] ROSALYN (Duncan/Farley)

Recorded July 1973; *Pin Ups* LP.

Bowie's first step after his apparent retirement was to travel to Paris with all but one of the Spiders (Aynsley Dunbar replacing Woody Woodmansey), and record an album of songs from the heritage of British rock, 1964–7. The sessions lasted for just three weeks, during which time he also began to sketch out plans for an elaborate piece of rock theatre; and produced a single for another veteran from the mid-sixties, Lulu.

Other motives aside, *Pin Ups* allowed Bowie to repay some overdue debts. His first single with the King Bees in 1964 [A2] had been an obvious attempt to emulate the Pretty Things' own debut, 'Rosalyn', a riot of teenage lust and excess energy. Their hallmark was the slurred, snarling voice of Phil May, compared to whom Mick Jagger sounded like an elocution coach. By 1973, Bowie had realised that he couldn't match May for incoherent aggression, so he substituted adolescent contempt instead, otherwise mirroring the original arrangement with skill but little passion.

[77] HERE COMES THE NIGHT (Berns)

Recorded July 1973; *Pin Ups* LP.

In tackling this 1965 single by Them, Bowie was competing with one of Britain's great vocal stylists, Van Morrison. Writer/producer Bert Berns had compelled Morrison to record the song, and a hint of his disdain could be heard in his rasping approach to the chorus. Elsewhere, he managed a reasonable facsimile of the uptown soul sound of Ben E. King, best known for 'Stand By Me' and 'Spanish Harlem'. Bowie's attempt to channel King, via Morrison, resulted in a sly croon, reminiscent of his mid-sixties imitations of American R&B, while Aynsley Dunbar's drums reduced the playful skip of the original to a plod. The rather awkward, almost squawking saxophone solo was presumably the work of Bowie himself, rather than session professional Ken Fordham, who played elsewhere on this album.

[78] I WISH YOU WOULD (Arnold)

> Recorded July 1973; *Pin Ups* LP.

One of just two songs on *Pin Ups* not to be offered in the same key as the original models, 'I Wish You Would' was also the album's first major piece of reinvention. Bowie's arrangement hinted that he had begun to soak up the mechanical, European (and defiantly non-American) rhythms of Kraftwerk. Mick Ronson's contribution was to transfer 'I Wish You Would' from the repertoire of the 1964 line-up of the Yardbirds (with blues purist Eric Clapton on guitar), into the pop-art-oriented Yardbirds sound of 1966/67, when (Ronson's hero) Jeff Beck and then Jimmy Page were at the helm. One of Page's trademarks was playing his guitar with a violin bow; Ronson and Bowie enlisted an electric violin player (from the French band Zoo) to similar effect. His spectacular inventiveness, culminating in a menacing rumble of feedback that suggested a distant explosion, provoked Bowie into an impressive imitation of Page's colleague in Led Zeppelin, Robert Plant. On every level – from classic rock cover to conceptual art project – this was a stunning success.

[79] SEE EMILY PLAY (Barrett)

> Recorded July 1973; *Pin Ups* LP.

If 'I Wish You Would' marked one chronological extreme of the *Pin Ups* repertoire (the Yardbirds were performing Billy Boy Arnold's American R&B tune by the end of 1963), 'See Emily Play' represented the other. Pink Floyd's second single, originally issued in June 1967, was the only song tackled by Bowie that came from the era of full-blown psychedelia. Written by Syd Barrett, an influence on Bowie's song-writing in the late sixties and early seventies, Pink Floyd's record was a breathtaking mixture of electronic experimentation and commercial pop.

Realising that it would be pointless to imitate their pioneering exploits in sound, Bowie chose to lean on his strengths: the hard-rock theatrics of Mick Ronson's guitar, his own insight into the psychology of alienation, and his willingness to use vivid colours in his arrangements. Pink Floyd's trippy playfulness was forgotten;

instead, Bowie introduced the eerie vari-speed vocal ensemble he'd used on 'After All' [20] and 'The Bewlay Brothers' [51], as if he was signalling that there was an inevitable path from the lysergic adventures of the so-called 'flower-power' era to mental disintegration. Mike Garson's typically free-spirited keyboard solo revived memories of his work on 'Aladdin Sane' [70], while alluding to Wagner's 'Also Sprach Zarathustra' theme.* Ronson's string arrangement widened the cultural horizons still further, as it moved seamlessly back in time from the twelve-tone experiments of the early twentieth century to close with a melody borrowed from a Beethoven symphony.

[80] EVERYTHING'S ALRIGHT (Crouch/Konrad/Stavely/ James/Karlson)

Recorded July 1973; *Pin Ups* LP.

Few records issued during the British beat boom of 1963/64 came close to matching the naïve excitement of the debut single by the Mojos, who were briefly one of the rawest of the era's Liverpudlian bands. Everything thrilling about their performance – Stu James' rasping vocal, the untutored energy of the band, the sense that nobody quite knew what was going to happen next – was lost in Bowie's arrangement, which sounded like a parody of rock 'n' roll from a West End show. His track had no centre, least of all his own vocal performance, which slipped from shoddy Elvis impression to mock-R&B without any apparent purpose. The final insult was the Beatles pastiche (from the climax of 'She Loves You') of cooing vocals and major 6th chord: it was impossible not to imagine the entire band going down on their knees and posing for the camera with their 'jazz hands' held high.

---

* This music now held several layers of resonance: besides its use in the soundtrack to *2001*, and its links via Wagner to Nietzsche and Hitler, it had also been borrowed by Elvis Presley to signify his imminent arrival on stage – neatly linking several areas of Bowie's obsessive interest.

[81] **I Can't Explain** (Townshend)

> Recorded July 1973; *Pin Ups* LP.

The Who's first single under that name, 'I Can't Explain' was a compact portrait of mod incoherence, sweetened just enough by producer Shel Talmy to pass as an acceptable 1965 pop hit. Bowie trimmed the signature guitar riff from four chords to three, lowered the key from E to C, cut the tempo, and emerged with a track that approximated the feeling of swimming underwater. Strangely, this rethinking worked, from the crunch of guitar, cymbal and steam-whistle sax that opened the song, through Bowie's intensely arch vocal interpretation, set to a robotic dance rhythm. Mick Ronson reproduced the famous guitar solo from Johnny Kidd & the Pirates' 1960 hit 'Shakin' All Over' to add to the joyous sense of confusion.

Bowie chronicler Kevin Cann suggests that an earlier version of this song was recorded during Ziggy Stardust's brief infatuation with covering rock standards in 1972 (see [53]). The Spiders certainly performed the song in concert a full year before the *Pin Ups* sessions.

[82] **Friday On My Mind** (Vanda / Young)

> Recorded July 1973; *Pin Ups* LP.

As an exhibition of the dynamics of pop music, the Easybeats' 1966 single 'Friday On My Mind' was virtually unbeatable. It captured perfectly the essence of the divide between the working week and the weekend, the tight, almost neurotic tension of the verses exploding into the release (and relief) of the chorus. Bowie's reinterpretation completely ignored that dichotomy, acting instead as a demonstration tape of the Many Voices of David Jones – every one of them a pastiche, from Peter Sellers to Elvis Presley. He also introduced a layer of background vocals that robbed the song of its anxiety (and at one point reached an unfeasibly high E, the summit of his vocal exploits during the seventies).

[83] SORROW (Feldman/Goldstein/Gottehrer)

Recorded July 1973; *Pin Ups* LP.

The one performance on *Pin Ups* that suggested a real emotional commitment to the song, rather than distant nostalgia for the memory of a record, was Bowie's revival of 'Sorrow' – originally cut by the US garage band the McCoys, smoothed out for British consumption by the Merseys in 1966, and recalled affectionately by George Harrison during the fade-out of the Beatles' 'It's All Too Much' the following year. If the cumulative effect of *Pin Ups* was to remind Bowie of the bands he'd wanted to lead in the mid-sixties, 'Sorrow' seemed to evoke an entirely different career path, in which he might have abandoned rock entirely to become an elegant interpreter of pop's many facets – a cross between P.J. Proby and Scott Walker, perhaps.

There was a very real sense of melancholy to his vocal, with none of his customary theatricality, yet at the same time an amused playfulness, as if sorrow was all he had long since grown to expect. The arrangement was rich, with tenor sax to the fore, baritone honking underneath, strings that shimmered to eerie effect, an elegiac piano coda, and an entire verse on which Bowie was supported by urgent backing vocals, representing his last vain opportunity to break free.

[84] DON'T BRING ME DOWN (Dee)

Recorded July 1973; *Pin Ups* LP.

The successor to 'Rosalyn' [76] in the Pretty Things' 1964 release schedule, 'Don't Bring Me Down' represented British sixties pop at its most carnal. When Phil May snarled that he had laid the heroine on the ground, any crime seemed possible. Bowie had already discovered he couldn't out-growl May, so once more he subjected the song to parody, crooning away all the lustful aggression of the original. Mick Ronson's guitar offered some compensation, though any impact of his solo was lost amidst the cluttered mix. Even when Bowie tried to sound like a confused adolescent, he emerged gauche, not wired. May had sung with a mixture of anger and amazement; Bowie seemed supremely self-satisfied, ridding this erotic encounter of all its apocalyptic edge.

[85] SHAPES OF THINGS (Samwell-Smith/McCarty/Relf)

Recorded July 1973; *Pin Ups* LP.

Mick Ronson had emulated Jeff Beck's vicious, stuttering finale to the Yardbirds' 1966 'freakbeat' single on 'John I'm Only Dancing' [63]. Faced with the song itself, he dragged out the repeated growl of guitar to the point of self-parody (and then repeated the trick on 'Anyway Anyhow Anywhere' [86]). The Yardbirds' guitarists always stole attention from the band's rather anonymous singer, Keith Relf, but Bowie avoided that fate with a deliberately mannered lead vocal (note the bizarre vowel sounds of 'shapes' and 'lonely'), heavily phased voices in the chorus, some cacophonous antics from saxophone and bass, and a string section that continually tried to pull the track into a different key. The core of the Yardbirds' record was Beck's solo, played with a violin bow over howls of feedback. Ronson probably realised that he couldn't surpass it, so he settled for a showcase of two harmonised guitar lines, supporting rather than overshadowing Bowie's starring role.

[86] ANYWAY ANYHOW ANYWHERE (Townshend/Daltrey)

Recorded July 1973; *Pin Ups* LP.

Nothing on *Pin Ups* came closer to replicating the sound of the original record than Bowie's rendition of the Who's second single from 1965. The blueprint was all about tension and release, with Nicky Hopkins' piano valiantly attempting to stabilise the track while Keith Moon's drums rumbled and Pete Townshend unleashed a masterfully controlled blast of dynamic aggression, shaping his guitar feedback into an expression of teenage frustration.

Bowie was 26, not 19, so he had to manufacture the adolescent fury of his voice. Aynsley Dunbar valiantly emulated Moon's chaotic frenzy behind the drum kit, deliberately echoing the percussive crescendos that had powered the Who's 1966 single 'Happy Jack', while his cymbal crashes were carefully phased. Ronson added some flickers and snorts of guitar feedback to the mix, while Bowie topped them both with a final screech of falsetto.

[87] WHERE HAVE ALL THE GOOD TIMES GONE (Davies)

Recorded July 1973; *Pin Ups* LP.

Ray Davies of the Kinks was already lamenting the end of an era in 1965, when most of his contemporaries believed that it was only just beginning. Like Davies, Bowie was a defiant non-believer in the manifesto of sixties optimism, so the Kinks' ramshackle exercise in disgust and ennui was the perfect choice to bring down the curtain on an album, and an era. Bowie certainly achieved the required degree of disinterest in his vocal, only marshalling a more metallic sound (reminiscent of his own 1970 recordings) in the chorus. Around him, the band tried to imitate the Kinks without capturing their essence, though Mike Garson's vaudeville piano did at least hint at Davies' love of the London music hall.

Sixties Nostalgia and Myth: *Pin Ups* LP

Pin Ups was an exercise in pop art: a reproduction and interpretation of work by other artists, intended for a mass audience. The British pioneer and theorist of pop, Richard Hamilton, had re-created Marcel Duchamp's 'The Bride Stripped Bare By Her Bachelors'; Andy Warhol used newspaper photographs and consumer graphics as the canvases for his art. 'I don't know whether I want to be a commercial artist again,' Bowie had pondered during the sessions for an album that epitomised the brand.

The singer became a brand himself – a pop-art pop artist, indeed – with the release of *Pin Ups*: for the next two years he would no longer be 'David Bowie' but merely 'Bowie'; paving the way, perhaps, for future incarnations as Pedigree Bowie, New Improved Bowie and of course Original Bowie.

This album of defiantly unoriginal material was also a sure way of not giving any new Bowie songs to his music publishers, both of whom were in dispute (with each other and with MainMan as Bowie's representatives) during the period that the album was recorded. And this may ultimately have been the primary reason for the project – a way of continuing Bowie's career beyond the retirement of Ziggy Stardust, without having to reveal a fresh direction or surrender any valuable copyrights.

Yet the primary impact of *Pin Ups* was as a fashionable utilisation of nostalgia, which was already – alongside the craze for androgyny – emerging as one of the dominant themes of the early seventies. ('It sometimes looked as if the originality of 70s designers lay in their flair for deciding what period style to use next,' journalist Norman Shrapnel reflected in 1980.) In pop rather than pop-art terms, Bowie's album was a cheeky way of copying and overshadowing *These Foolish Things*, an album of rock and pre-rock standards by Roxy Music singer Bryan Ferry, which had been much longer in the making than *Pin Ups*. The two albums ultimately emerged on the same day, Bowie gaining more sales, Ferry better reviews. Yet while Ferry ranged across the decades in search of suitably arch material, Bowie chose to concentrate on his own past: not his adolescence, as John Lennon was then attempting with Phil Spector on the album belatedly released in 1975 as *Rock & Roll*, but the years in which he had battled in vain to establish himself alongside the likes of the Who and the Kinks. It seemed as if everyone in British pop was remembering the fifties and early sixties, from Elton John's 'Crocodile Rock' to 10cc's 'Donna' and Wizzard's 'Ball Park Incident', taking a self-conscious look back at an era they had originally experienced without a hint of irony. Bowie, by contrast, was tackling a more immediate version of the past, as if to prove that he could have been a contender after all.

Once he had re-imagined the mid-sixties, Bowie's passion for nostalgia knew no bounds. His next target was his own recent past. First he used pop star Lulu to reinvent 'The Man Who Sold The World' and 'Watch That Man'. '[Bowie's] in show business, and knows where it's at,' declared Lulu, who had bonded with Bowie in a hotel bar over their shared passion for Anthony Newley's show tunes. And then he reincarnated Ziggy Stardust for American eyes only, for a TV project known as *The 1980 Floor Show*. It allowed him to reprise the highlights of *Pin Ups* and two of his earlier hits, preview his scheme for a musical based around a George Orwell novel, and revisit one of the more enduring singles of the sixties, Sonny & Cher's 'I Got You Babe', in the erratic company of one of that decade's most emblematic figures, Marianne Faithfull. One minute Ziggy was a prophet of the new; the next, he was selling the past to an audience desperate to believe that it could return again: tomorrow's nostalgia today.

[88] GROWIN' UP (Springsteen)

Recorded July 1973; *Pin Ups* extended CD.

The commercial impact of *Greetings From Asbury Park NJ*, the debut album by the American singer-songwriter Bruce Springsteen, was minimal in 1973. Its influence on David Bowie was brief, but intense. Springsteen represented a fabulous collage of classic American symbols: Chuck Berry's command of teenage iconography; James Dean's almost delinquent sullenness; Bob Dylan's lyrical extravagance; the ephemeral glory of pop, mixed with the gutsy authenticity of soul. Rock critics initially greeted him as 'the new Bob Dylan', and within a year journalist Jon Landau could proclaim, 'I have seen Rock 'n' Roll Future, and its name is Bruce Springsteen' (Landau was rewarded with a multi-decade career as Springsteen's producer-turned-manager, as if to spite every journalist who had ever crafted a cruel review). Bowie bought into the hype early, but unlike the press, he was not impressed by Springsteen's manic live shows, which belonged to a very different theatrical tradition from his own.

In the aftermath of his celebration of British pop on *Pin Ups*, Bowie began to assemble material for an American equivalent, including the Velvet Underground's 'White Light/White Heat' (the exhilarating backing track for which was bequeathed to Mick Ronson) and the Beach Boys' 'God Only Knows'. Both of those songs were acknowledged as classics; by approaching Springsteen's catalogue, Bowie would be conferring some sort of princely tribute on a performer who was two years younger than himself. On the evidence of his cover of 'Growin' Up', and his subsequent rendition of 'It's Hard To Be A Saint In The City' [122], an entire album of *Bowie Sings Springsteen* might have been a worthier project than *Pin Ups*.

Guitarist Ronnie Wood augmented Ronson for this session, treating Springsteen's song with a disregard for the niceties of rhythm that was well suited to his own band, the Faces, but less appropriate here. That problem faded in the heat of Bowie's vocal performance: taking the song in a higher key than Springsteen, he pushed himself to his physical limit, rasping into falsetto and leaving a raw throatiness in his wake. This imperfection was strangely affecting, betraying his absolute engagement with the song. These early forays into the highest reaches of his vocal range proved to be a rehearsal for his later experiments with soul music.

By the end of 1973, Springsteen's launch would appear understated alongside the publicity campaign focused on another new American singer-songwriter: Jobriath. Billed as 'The First Gay Rock Star', he was flamboyantly hyped by his manager, Jerry Brandt, as 'a composer, arranger, singer, dancer, painter, mime artist, ballerina, woman, man' who would soon be 'the biggest artist in the world'. When Brandt was asked about his client's similarity to Bowie, he dismissed the comparison contemptuously: 'David Bowie has taken his best shot. He's tacky and he can't pirouette and he can't move and he's rigid and he's scared to death . . . It's just like the difference between a Model A Ford and a Lamborghini.'

Billboards on Sunset Strip and promises of a live show that would be extravagant beyond Bowie's imagination failed to translate into a career strategy, especially when Jobriath's concert debut proved to be spectacularly short on pizzazz. By early 1975, Jobriath – like Ziggy Stardust – had announced his retirement, the only difference being that Ziggy had become a star, while Jobriath was a laughing stock. Little attention was paid to the perfectly respectable blend of Bowie, Stones and cabaret influences that comprised his two albums, and Jobriath died from AIDS in 1983 without any public recognition. The utter failure of Brandt's PR strategy emphasised the skill of Tony Defries' handling of David Bowie; and also the subtle difference between launching a 'Gay Rock Star' and a rock star who said 'I'm gay' with a smile on his face and a twinkle in his eye.

[89] MUSIC IS LETHAL (Battisti; trans. Bowie)

Written for Mick Ronson.

The end of Ziggy Stardust, and the consequent demise of the Spiders From Mars, need not have signalled the end of Bowie's working relationship with Mick Ronson. That was a matter of choice, from a man who, less than two years later, would tell an interviewer: 'I honestly can't remember Mick that well these days. He's just like any other band member that I had.' During the final Ziggy tour, he had already begun to downplay Ronson's contribution, preferring to regard him as someone who could translate Bowie's creative impulses rather than, as most objective observers remember him, an artistic contributor in his own right.

The two men had very different temperaments: in an otherwise warm tribute after Ronson's death in 1993, Bowie said that his one-time musical collaborator lacked ambition, and would have been content to sound like Jeff Beck or Free's Paul Kossoff. 'I just gave up trying to get him to come out and see other bands or listen to interesting musics,' Bowie recalled. 'You'd mention anything new, and his pet phrase was, "Don't need to".' But it's hard not to conclude that ego – Bowie's need to be seen as master of his own destiny – played an equally large part in the severing of their partnership.

As recompense for his loyalty, Bowie and Tony Defries agreed to support Ronson's launch as a solo artist, and the MainMan hype machine was set in motion on the guitarist's behalf. To publicise his first solo album, *Slaughter On Tenth Avenue* (named after a movie theme that Bowie had suggested he should record), the Rainbow Theatre in London was booked for a prestigious debut performance. It proved to be little more than a disaster, not just because Ronson was never a strong vocalist in isolation, but because he presented himself like someone who didn't believe he deserved to be in the spotlight. Bowie went backstage during the intermission to offer encouragement, and briefly considered joining Ronson on stage, before realising that this would only highlight the gulf in charisma between the two artists. Neither man could have been delighted that the only song in Ronson's repertoire that roused the crowd was Bowie's 'Moonage Daydream', as if fans had half-closed their eyes and imagined that Ziggy himself were there.

Ronson's solo career ran aground after two albums – the second more cohesive than its predecessor, though it lacked the attraction of any material from Bowie (bar the abandoned backing track for 'White Light/White Heat' from the *Pin Ups* sessions). By contrast, Bowie had a hand in three songs on Ronson's debut – among them this rather embarrassing adaptation of an intimate ballad by the Italian singer Lucio Battisti. He certainly seemed to have learned little about the art of translation since his ill-fated attempt to secure the English-language rights to Claude François' 'Comme D'Habitude' in 1968 [A50]. The song required an intensely personal lyric, open to the dramatic potential of tiny incidents within a relationship; Bowie delivered an almost hysterical parody of Jacques Brel's most lubricious work, cramming in words as if he were being paid by the syllable.

[90] HEY MA HEY PA (Ronson/Bowie)

Written for Mick Ronson.

Working around a framework erected by Mick Ronson was hardly a new experience for Bowie: unlike the songs for *The Man Who Sold The World*, this melody was supplied by Ronson, reducing Bowie's role to lyricist. Both men's recent influences were on brazen display. While Ronson's music betrayed his enthusiasm for Todd Rundgren's dazzling exhibition of pop and electronics on *A Wizard A True Star* ('Zen Archer' was the closest equivalent here), Bowie continued to pay homage to the streetwise sensibility of Bruce Springsteen – albeit via parody. His tale of J.J. Dean and Pigsty Paul was a blend of comic-book Western and a schoolboy's version of a James Dean scenario.

[91] GROWING UP AND I'M FINE (Bowie)

Written for Mick Ronson.

It was surely no coincidence that having recorded Springsteen's 'Growin' Up' [88], Bowie borrowed that title for another gift to Mick Ronson. Stylistically, though, it was a throwback to the days of *Hunky Dory*, diatonic descent in the chorus and all. If that automatically sparked thoughts of the Beatles, the resemblance was reinforced by the melodic similarity between the finale to the chorus and Paul McCartney's 'Mother Nature's Son'; while Mike Garson's piano introduction had the same quality of music-in-motion as George Harrison's circular guitar opening to 'I Want To Tell You'.

The lyrics might have been written by the narrator of 'Can't Help Thinking About Me' [A14] to explain why he was abandoning his teenage friends in favour of a woman. Like the most existential of mods, he mapped out his previous life in epic terms. Then love intervened, bringing with it a strident middle section that seemed to have stepped from the score of *West Side Story* – itself an influence on Bruce Springsteen, completing this circle of adolescent melodrama.

[92] I AM DIVINE (Bowie)

Recorded by the Astronettes, November 1973.

In November 1973, Bowie interrupted the sessions for his next album to pursue a musical fusion that his own previous work had barely dared to touch. He revived the name of the Astronettes – used for his backing vocalists at the Rainbow in 1972, and mentioned as an aside in 'Drive-In Saturday' – for a loose vocal group based around his school friend Geoff MacCormack and his intimate companion Ava Cherry. With session singer Jason Guest, they formed a black/white, male/female combination that allowed Bowie to explore what he could achieve with contemporary forms of soul music, without the pressing necessity to be making a conceptual statement at the same time.

His manager Tony Defries retained the rights to an entire album's worth of Astronettes tapes when the pair separated in 1975, though they weren't released until 1994. The song selection betrayed several of Bowie's private obsessions: Frank Zappa, Roy Harper, standard songs, even the Beach Boys' 'God Only Knows' (cut at these sessions in an arrangement he clearly copied for his 1984 album *Tonight*). As a commercial (rather than archival) release, the album subsequently titled (by Defries) *People From Bad Homes* would have damaged Bowie's reputation if it had appeared at the time – which is presumably why he chose to leave it unfinished.

Of the four songs that Bowie contributed to the project, 'I Am Divine' gave the most accurate indication of what would happen when he visited Philadelphia the following year for the *Young Americans* sessions. Indeed, it would have been a worthy contender for that album, its rhythmic breakdowns and disco-funk arrangement providing a thrilling vehicle for the glorious voice of Geoff MacCormack. The combination of R&B trademarks – gospel voices, wah-wah guitar – with the daredevil piano of Mike Garson was positively inspired, Garson's ability to send out jazz feelers across the standard funk changes making one wish that he had survived in Bowie's band long enough to participate in *Young Americans*. Besides the ecstatic rush of the music, the track had its biographical intrigue: its portrait of a megalomaniac contained a sly reference to someone who considered himself the 'MainMan' – which was exactly how Tony Defries used to sign his seventies correspondence.

[93] I AM A LASER (Bowie)

Recorded by the Astronettes, November 1973.

Of interest solely because Bowie returned to the song briefly in 1974 [111], and then rewrote it as 'Scream Like A Baby' [187] in 1980, 'I Am A Laser' was a ghastly exercise in theatrical soul that contained some of the most embarrassing lyric-writing of his entire career – patronising, clichéd, ultimately laughable. In other circumstances, a couplet about the excitement of a 'golden shower' might have been amusing; given to Ava Cherry as a statement of power and pride, it was nothing less than insulting.

[94] PEOPLE FROM BAD HOMES (Bowie)

Recorded by the Astronettes, November 1973.

Bowie's mid-sixties songwriting demos [A8–A13] illustrated that writing to a pop formula did not come naturally. 'I Am A Laser' [93] and 'People From Bad Homes' confirmed that he found it no easier to come to terms with the demands of R&B. No reputable music publisher would have offered him a contract on the basis of those two songs – though the latter was marginally more effective, thanks to its vague similarity to the Drifters' 'On Broadway' (as quoted in the play-out of 'Aladdin Sane' [70]) and the brief spasm of excitement spurred by the opening to the chorus. As yet, Bowie had no reliable guide for constructing a soul melody, or indeed an appropriate lyric: 'People From Bad Homes' had a tune that seemed to be running a bar or two behind the band, and a social-comment lyric that was little more than inane. It left at least a subliminal mark on its creator, however, as the title reappeared in the lyrics to the altogether more successful 'Fashion' [185] in 1980.

[95] **THINGS TO DO** (Bowie)

> Recorded by the Astronettes, November 1973.

After two songs that displayed little flair for melody or structure, 'Things To Do' did at least provide the Astronettes with an adventurous backing track – the only indication in Bowie's song catalogue of his passion in 1973 for the Latin music he'd heard in New York's clubs. Musically, this was strongly inspired by the Cuban standard 'Oye Como Va', recorded by Santana on their *Abraxas* album in 1970. Its basic chord sequence (Cm-E♭-Fm) and bubbling percussion were pure Latino; but Bowie had yet to learn that on a track dominated by congas, the drummer did not need to match their frenetic pace, and 'Things To Do' sometimes suggested that the Muppets puppet Animal had entered the studio. The Astronettes grasped the special harmonic blend of the Latin sound, but were hampered by a melody that merely filled the track, rather than enhancing it.

[96] **1984/DODO** (Bowie)

> Recorded *c.* September 1973; *Sound + Vision* CD set.

[97] **DODO (AKA YOU DIDN'T HEAR IT FROM ME)** (Bowie)

> Recorded September 1973; *Diamond Dogs* extended CD.

[98] **1984** (Bowie)

> Recorded October 1973–February 1974; *Diamond Dogs* LP.

'I'm an awful pessimist,' David Bowie conceded in 1973. 'That's one of the things against me. I'm pessimistic about new things, new projects, new ideas, as far as society's concerned.' He was not alone. In America, the Watergate scandal was undermining the public's faith in the nation's most trusted institutions. Across the West, a new era of austerity loomed, as the Yom Kippur war sparked an energy crisis that soon led to what the British Chancellor of the Exchequer,

Anthony Barber, described as the nation's 'gravest economic crisis' since the Second World War.

It was a season for visions of apocalypse and repression, which for Bowie reinforced the impact of a train journey across the Russian continent in April and May. The grim bureaucracy and acute poverty of the fabled Communist paradise stoked his prevailing sense of panic and claustrophobia in the run-up to his final tour as Ziggy Stardust. Back in London, he told his wife, 'After what I've seen of this world, I've never been so damned scared in my life.' So intense was his feeling of dread that he vehemently resisted the notion of compressing his experiences into an album. 'If I ever wrote about it, it would be my last album ever,' he said. 'I don't think I'd be around after recording it.'

It was hardly a coincidence that instead he chose to map out a rock musical around George Orwell's fictional re-creation of a Stalinesque society, *Nineteen Eighty-Four*. Other musicians had flirted with Orwell's theme, notably the rock band Spirit, whose '1984' single was banned by many US radio stations in 1969 for its political content; and jazz drummer Hugh Hopper, who issued an instrumental album entitled *1984* in 1973. But Bowie's fantasies, as ever, were fashioned on an epic scale: a Broadway revue with a huge cast, and perhaps a television film to document it for posterity. Instead of resting after completing *Pin Ups*, he threw himself into a week-long frenzy of writing, and emerged with a skeleton script and several songs that would propel the action forward.

There was a certain irony in Bowie's attempting to translate the devious operations of Orwell's (or more accurately Big Brother's) Ministry of Truth into song. Minitrue's constant rewriting of history was no more audacious than Bowie's ability to fashion a fresh version of his own past whenever he was confronted with a microphone. But his sincerity was transparent: nothing he had conceived since the original blueprint of the Ziggy Stardust project had exerted such a hold over his imagination. So his sense of disappointment – almost betrayal – when the proposed musical had to be abandoned was crushing.

The problem was simple, and intractable: 'Mrs Orwell refused to let us have the rights, point blank. For a person who married a socialist with communist leanings, she was the biggest upper-class snob I've ever met in my life. "Good heavens, put it to *music*?" It really was like that.' Not that Bowie was given singular treatment:

so protective was Sonia Orwell of her late husband's legacy, and so appalled had she been by a 1955 film adapation, that she had turned down everyone who approached her wishing to translate *Nineteen Eighty-Four* into another medium. As her biographer noted, 'Rejected applicants inevitably found her approach tiresome and high-handed.' Bowie was left to mould his Orwell-inspired rock musical into something equally apocalyptic, but sufficiently removed from the original to keep Sonia's lawyers at bay.

Without access to Bowie's notebooks from the period, it's impossible to determine how thoroughly he had sketched out the scenario for *Nineteen Eighty-Four*. Several songs – 'We Are The Dead' [102] and 'Big Brother' [103] amongst them – explored themes or phrases that can be traced back to Orwell's novel. Others, composed during his experimentation with lyrical cut-ups, were sufficiently vague to fit into almost any category, and could perhaps have been revised to make them more specific. Some ('Rebel Rebel' [101] is the most notable example) were difficult to imagine inside even the loosest *Nineteen Eighty-Four* frame. It was also not clear whether Bowie was intending for the narrative to be carried forward entirely in song; or whether he would create dialogue to link the musical segments.

The medley of '1984' and 'Dodo' – his first studio work on *Nineteen Eighty-Four*, and his last with both producer Ken Scott and the remnants of the Spiders – provided a clue as to how the album might have been constructed, if not the stage musical it was meant to accompany. With its cinematic scoring and constant iteration of the title, '1984' would have provided a striking theme for the project, even if its links with Orwell's book were more suggestive than representational. 'Dodo', meanwhile, was a tightly assembled series of snapshots and incidents that could be located (with some musical licence) in the novel. It is possible to imagine an entire album in a similar vein: a collage of emblematic fragments linked by repeated themes, spotlighting selected crisis points and characters from Orwell's imagination, carefully scored to ensure continuity of tone as much as storyline. But it would have required a degree of concentration and focus that was perhaps beyond the mercurial Bowie at this stage of his career.

'1984' and 'Dodo' were clearly intended from the outset to stand as one discrete piece of music: they were previewed in that form during Bowie's last television appearance with the Spiders From Mars, in

October 1973. Issued as a single, it might have altered the public perception of Bowie, and certainly banished all memories of *Ziggy Stardust*. It would have revealed him as the first major rock act to incorporate the stylistic innovations of a generation of US soul performers who had been invited to score so-called 'blaxploitation' movies in the early seventies. Instead, it languished in Bowie's archives until it was exhumed for the retrospective *Sound + Vision* project in 1989.

With its chattering wah-wah guitar deep in the mix, and its dramatic, percussive blend of bass and piano, the '1984' theme was instantly reminiscent of Isaac Hayes' 'Theme From *Shaft*'. The use of strings evoked another 'blaxploitation' soundtrack, Curtis Mayfield's *Superfly*. But there was much more to the arrangement than pastiche: the repeated use of a cavernous bass-drum beat that was detuned as an eerie commentary on the landscape; the four-note piano motif that underpinned the verses; the almost visual impact of the strings, from the cellos introducing the middle section to the spectacular swirl and fall of the violins that ended it; and the way in which the vocal chorus filled out the sound palette, from baritone to soprano, building on the root of the first verse, and then a harmonic third in the second.

Drums and piano (the latter offering a variation on the opening to Strauss' 'Also Sprach Zarathustra') signalled the switch to the much sparser soundscape of 'Dodo'. The song focused initially on Orwell's doomed lovers, Winston and Julia, before switching to Winston's neighbour, the hapless Mr Parsons (who is betrayed by his own child in the novel), and then to the world that those children would inherit. Cellos and electric piano dominated the arrangement, while Mick Ronson laid a surf-guitar motif under the chorus in a surreal juxtaposition of moods. Then the '1984' theme returned, its rhythmic string score acknowledging the pioneering work of Philadelphia soul producers Kenny Gamble and Leon Huff.

Once the *Nineteen Eighty-Four* musical was abandoned, 'Dodo' was isolated as a possible duet vehicle for Bowie and Lulu. That might explain Bowie's casual vocal on the surviving mix of the separated song, pitched two semitones above the original recording (presumably for Lulu's benefit, although Bowie was not there to hear the results. 'No Bowie?' Lulu said when she arrived at Olympic Studios, before adding her voice like a true professional). There was no such prevarication about '1984', which was stripped of its 'Dodo' elements and retooled for the *Diamond Dogs* album, at a harsher tempo and with the *Shaft*-inspired wah-wah guitar of Alan Parker at the front of the mix. The full dramatic potential of the piece was laid bare here, from the tinkling siren (played on electric piano) that introduced and closed the track to the eight-to-the-bar cymbal rim-shots that sizzled beneath the keynote riff. Once again, Bowie found room amidst the drama for subtle, sometimes almost puzzling sonic touches – the harpsichord that was audible during the verses, the Byrds-inspired electric guitar beneath the middle section, and the electric piano decorations in the final verse that operated in a different key to the rest of the track, perhaps meant to symbolise Winston Smith's separation from Big Brother's society. The only weakness of the track was the rather redundant third verse, added when the two halves of the medley were separated. One mystery remained: was Bowie warning of the 'savage jaw' of 1984 – Big Brother's harsh words, perhaps, plus the image of a rabid, slobbering hound – or the 'savage lure', which enabled Big Brother to retain power? The naked ear suggested the former; the printed sheet music insisted the latter.

[99] (ALTERNATIVE) CANDIDATE (Bowie)

Recorded January 1974; *Diamond Dogs* extended CD.

The deluxe *Diamond Dogs* reissue of 2004 unveiled this 'Alternative' version of a song that was subsequently incorporated into a medley with 'Sweet Thing' [100]. It was described as 'a demo for proposed 1984 musical', although its thematic link with that project was difficult to determine. Some courageous fans have provided elaborate and highly creative 'interpretations' of the lyrics, linking them with the *Nineteen Eighty-Four* narrative.* But there was little internal evidence to support such a theory, beyond a mysterious sense of dissatisfaction, as felt by Orwell's Winston Smith (and characters in thousands of other novels). More persuasive was the idea that this was one of Bowie's first experiments with the cut-up technique, to fill out a track for which he had a title but no song. Everything operated just outside the realm of logic, though

---

* The teenagewildlife.com forum hosted one such discussion.

Bowie's self-description as the 'Fuhrerling' was not only alarming and prophetic, but also pre-dated Nick Lowe and Elvis Costello's 'little Hitlers' by half a decade. The very title of 'Candidate' was emblematic at a time when the Watergate scandal was beginning to bite, however, and Richard Nixon's defiant words ('I am not a crook') were slowly being stripped of their sincerity.

Only the first two lines of this composition reappeared in the later incarnation of the song, set to a different melody. No musical element of the 'Alternative Candidate' track survived the transition, in fact: while the released 'Candidate' revolved around a single three-chord sequence, the 'Alternative' comprised several different sections welded together. But there was musical promise: not in the very lackadaisical melody, but in the syncopation of the drums and piano in the introduction, and the way in which the strings oozed eerily beneath an aggressive wah-wah guitar line. Note also the second use of the 'detuned' drum sound first heard on '1984/Dodo' [96].

The Art of Fragmentation

The primary source for Bowie's lyrics during the *Diamond Dogs* sessions was a collection of notebooks, in which he had written hundreds of phrases and lines. Flashes of inspiration were recorded there, alongside images borrowed from books, TV advertisements, even the labels stuck on the Olympic Studios mixing consoles. He had already discovered the value of introducing chance into his creative process; but on this album, and again in 1977 on much of *'Heroes'*, he elected to rely explicitly upon an accidental collision of images rather than orthodox narrative techniques. He was encouraged in this direction by his November 1973 meeting with the author William S. Burroughs (motto: 'mix your own linguistic virus'), an encounter engineered by the editors of *Rolling Stone* magazine. To prepare for the interview, Bowie immersed himself in Burroughs' novel *Nova Express*, the third of his books (after *The Soft Machine* and *The Ticket That Exploded*) to depend on the cut-up technique pioneered by his friend Brion Gysin. Gysin in turn acknowledged the influence of Dada and surrealist writers such as Tristan Tzara, who had assembled poetry by cutting random words out of newspapers. 'Cut up everything in sight,' Gysin once wrote. 'Make your whole life a poem.'

The 'poem' of Burroughs' *Nova Express* was obscure to anyone who wasn't under chemical influence or acutely alert to the sound, rather than the meaning, of words. Bowie qualified on both counts, describing the cut-up technique as 'a very western Tarot' and using it as a substitute for the random significance of the *I-Ching*. 'My thought forms are already fragmented, to say the least,' he admitted in 1975. 'I've had to do cut-ups on my writing for some time, so that I might be able to put it all back into some coherent form again. My actual writing doesn't make a tremendous amount of sense.' Faced with a society that he imagined was deconstructing itself, and a personality that was in danger of fragmenting, he found a rationale in cut-up that eluded him elsewhere.

He was hardly the first musician to utilise similar techniques: Stravinsky had compressed fragments of folk tunes into *The Rite of Spring*; Pierre Boulez pioneered the operation of chance as a compositional method in the fifties; the Beatles* chopped up tapes of fairground organs and threw them to the ground during the recording of *Sgt. Pepper*. Steve Reich's pioneering minimalist piece, 'It's Gonna Rain', evolved when two recordings of the same speech pattern accidentally ran out of phase with each other. Brian Eno would later incorporate elements of chance into his fundamental theories of composition: hence the working title of the third album he made with Bowie, *Planned Accidents*. Bowie met Brion Gysin in 1976, and for the next decade Gysin pursued the dream of persuading him to star in his screenplay of Burroughs' most famous novel, *Naked Lunch*. Meanwhile, Bowie would return to cut-up – this time facilitated by a computer program – in the mid-nineties, as a way of triggering a creative leap of faith during the assembly of the *1.Outside* project.

Back in 1973/74, however, when he allowed cut-up to shape the 'Sweet Thing' medley [100] and the title track of *Diamond Dogs* [107], the technique he'd borrowed from Gysin and Burroughs performed a different set of functions. It enabled him to convey a sense of apocalyptic decay, one of the themes that followed him from *Nineteen Eighty-Four* into *Diamond Dogs*. More pertinently, perhaps, it was a way of distancing himself from his work – or, to be more accurate, shifting the location of his involvement. On the cut-up songs, there was no personal disclosure or commitment in

---

* One of the hazards of chance was demonstrated when they reassembled the pieces of tape, and discovered that the result sounded too similar to the original recording. So their cut-up had to be manipulated quite deliberately to replicate the effect they had hoped to create by accident.

the lyrics; but on 'Sweet Thing', in particular, Bowie invested almost frightening levels of passion in his performance, which spoke more eloquently
than his words. Only when he adopted the musical language of American
soul later in 1974 did he find a way of combining words and music as a
means of emotional expression.

[100] SWEET THING/CANDIDATE/SWEET THING (Bowie)

Recorded January/February 1974; *Diamond Dogs* LP.

Nothing on *Diamond Dogs* illustrated the album's creative enigma
– emotional commitment, lyrical dissociation – as vividly as this
extended* exercise in romantic image-mongering. All attempts to
translate this musical extravaganza into a narrative form, whether
inspired by *Nineteen Eighty-Four* or *Diamond Dogs*, were doomed to
failure: there was no sweet thing, no candidate, no characters at all.

Yet the song contained several of Bowie's most enduring images:
photographs (taken with instinctive perception by Robert Doisneau,
perhaps) so emblematic that it is difficult to believe one hadn't
witnessed them being played out. There was the couple caught in a
doorway; or, later, the same pair glimpsed as they threw themselves
into a river, hand in hand. There was Bowie himself, crooning in a
voice drenched in despair; or conjuring up 'papier mâché' icons of
semi-mythical figures such as Charles Manson or Muhammad Ali. And
finally, one stunning piece of self-revelation (or was it prophecy?), as
Bowie asked himself about life in the 'snowstorm' of cocaine, at a time
when rock 'n' roll life was in total, unquestioning thrall to tooting and
snorting the septum-rotting, brain-shrinking powder.†

That ultimate self-condemnation aside, what mattered in this song

---

* It was listed as three separate pieces on the album cover, but finally recognised as
a single entity when Bowie assembled the *iSelect* compilation in 2008.
† Bowie's original lyric sheet indicated that this was a late addition to the song.
Indeed, he continued to alter the words until recording was completed. The first
two lines of 'Candidate', which set up the song title, weren't included in the lyric
sheet he took into the studio, which contained references to the French Revolution
that – aside from a line about 'les Tricoteuses', the women who knitted as heads
rolled – were excised from the final performance.

was sound and the visions it implied, not the literal meaning of the words. Bowie was effectively painting with the colours of music – the tonal scope of his own crooning voice, the comfortable growl of a baritone saxophone, the crisp richness of an acoustic guitar, the gamut of sounds that could be created by his Moog synthesiser, and above all the rococo flourishes of Mike Garson's keyboards. You could replace Bowie's English words with any other language, and lose none of the effect; even the voice was merely a constituent part of the canvas, no more or less important than any other.

The fundamental structure of this epic was simple enough: 'Sweet Thing' was based around a conversation between variations of C and D major chords, occasionally rising to E minor at moments of emotional stress. Its chorus introduced the sequence (Dm-Am-G) that also ran throughout 'Candidate'. And when 'Sweet Thing' returned, so did its familiar chords. Connecting these elements were interludes that explored more foreign territory, switching their key signature at will, but inevitably reverting to the original root. In the end, the most jarring of these interruptions veered into quasi-mechanical noise (worth comparing with the conclusion of Eno's 'Dead Finks Don't Talk', taped a few months earlier), with a slippery bass-line that prepared the ears for the simple chord change at the heart of the next track, 'Rebel Rebel'.

That was merely the landscape for the drama, however, which began with what sounded like a homage to the famous crescendo from the Beatles' 'A Day In The Life' (a song that Bowie would later reference on 'Young Americans' [113]). Slowly the colours emerged: sustained and phased guitar, synthetic (Mellotron) woodwind, Bowie's almost conversational croon. After the pinched yet desperate vocal harmonies of the chorus, the scene expanded to rival any of Phil Spector's 'Wall of Sound' extravaganzas, filling out the sonic and emotional palettes from a Japanese koto to a rainbow of saxophones. And so it continued: a perfectly restrained but emotive guitar solo, the marching drums that introduced the 'candidate' motif, a growling fuzz bass guitar, eventually every instrument in the studio hammering the beat as Bowie's multi-dubbed vocals neared a hysterical climax. And there was still the reprise of 'Sweet Thing' ahead, with electronic strings rising tentatively and falling quickly away as Bowie considered the snowstorm, Garson's piano reeling off epic flourishes, and the final climb to a vocal pitch that even Bowie could not have believed he could reach, a high D that dragged saxophones and keyboards in its wake – until the almost banal rock cacophony of the transition stripped away the humanity and left nothing of the romance but the squeal and grind of machinery.

[101] REBEL REBEL (Bowie)

Recorded January 1974; UK single A-side. Overdubbed/remixed April 1974; US single A-side.

Within the context of *Diamond Dogs*, 'Rebel Rebel' acted as the musical continuation of the 'Sweet Thing/Candidate/Sweet Thing' [100] medley: it began with the chord change (D to E) that had been prefigured by the bass guitar slide underpinning the medley's final chaotic moments. In isolation, it was a magnificent pastiche of the Rolling Stones' sound, with the same timeless quality as 'The Jean Genie' [65]. But whereas 'The Jean Genie' was as tight as an overwound alarm clock, 'Rebel Rebel' had a swaggering insouciance, reinforced by the deliberate indifference of Bowie's vocal. Its axis was a simple guitar riff around D, E and A chords, concocted by Bowie and then augmented by session musician Alan Parker, who added the downwards trail at the end of each line. (The melody of the verse followed Bowie's guitar line, not Parker's.)

Bowie had begun to socialise with the Rolling Stones in 1973: Mick Jagger had attended Ziggy's farewell party, like the king acknowledging and recognising a distant claimant for his crown. The intention behind 'Rebel Rebel' was to outdo the tired self-parody of the Stones' most recent album, *Goats Head Soup*, and Bowie duly emerged with a stronger and more enduring* single than Jagger's next offering, 'It's Only Rock & Roll'. Its wordless vocal riff repeated and therefore satirised the hook of the band's recent US single, 'Doo Doo Doo Doo (Heartbreaker)'. Meanwhile, the key line of the lyric, about

---

* In Britain, at least, Bowie also outsold the Stones. Journalist Roy Carr saw 'Rebel Rebel' as 'a premeditated rewrite' of the Stones' 'Satisfaction', and noted: 'Seemingly, the only explanation for such a "lift" is Bowie didn't want to risk covering a Stones hit for *Pin Ups*.'

the ambiguity of sexual identity, harked back to the insults that the Stones' appearance had provoked back in 1964.*

The track was certainly worthy of inclusion on any of the recent Rolling Stones albums, its raw-edged guitar being introduced against a click track, and then the visceral punch of bass and drums, while acoustic guitar and piano languished deep in the mix. 'Rebel Rebel' was pure attitude from start to finish: the essence of adolescent defiance, guaranteed to bring out the teenager in all who heard it.

Bowie wasn't satisfied with creating a perennial dance-floor anthem. For US consumption, he treated the track to a Latin dub mix, issued as a summer 1974 single, two decades or more ahead of its time. He effectively buried the signature rock riff of the original beneath phasing, sine-waves of percussion, acoustic guitar and an otherworldly bank of backing vocals, each line preceded by a rush of backwards echo, as if time were being sucked into a vacuum.

[102] WE ARE THE DEAD (Bowie)

Recorded February 1974; *Diamond Dogs* LP.

Winston and Julia embark on their forbidden romance in Orwell's novel in the knowledge that 'what was now happening could not last long. There were times when the fact of impending death seemed as palpable as the bed they lay on.' In their final moments before discovery, Winston considers the closed lives of those who exist in the world of Big Brother with the hope of freedom for their distant descendants. '"We are the dead", he said.' And with that pronouncement, their illusion of freedom is ended.

Like Winston and Julia, Bowie's 'We Are The Dead' was constantly pulled between two spheres of existence. Its verses fleshed out the stunted humanity of Winston's life, from his first encounter with Julia to his vain hope of marking their union with a child. Its chorus, an

---

* Bowie had, of course, exploited exactly that controversy with his 'long hair' media hype that winter. To add to the saga, Wayne County – briefly a client of MainMan at this point of his/her career – later claimed that Bowie had based his song on elements of a demo tape that he had recently sent to Tony Defries. One of County's songs, 'Queenage Baby', questioned whether the protagonist was a boy or a girl, a dilemma that could just as easily have been applied to County him/herself.

amalgam of accident and intention from Bowie's experiments with cut-ups, evoked menace and confusion in equal proportion, while beneath the relentless decline of the chords,* a chorus of soulless voices crooned that they were the new boys, the dogs, the dead.

The treatment of Bowie's voice brilliantly reinforced his lyrical intentions. It entered with a slap across the electric piano introduction, and was then heavily echoed throughout the verse, almost half a beat behind, to emphasise Winston's tentative belief in Julia. The chorus, however, was an ocean of emotional commitment, bringing all of Winston's anguish to the surface – and, with the references to bankers and the bankrupt, resonating beyond the Oceania of 1974 into the second decade of the twenty-first century.

[103] BIG BROTHER (Bowie)

Recorded February 1974; *Diamond Dogs* LP.

'Big Brother is watching you' was the warning – or perhaps promise – that restrained the characters in Orwell's novel. Big Brother may not have existed; it was enough that his subjects believed that he did. Orwell portrayed his image as a grim bureaucrat, 'black-haired, black-moustachio'd, full of power and mysterious calm'. Bowie's narrator – perhaps one of the subjects of Oceania deranged by the enforced hysteria of the 'Two Minutes Hate' (see [104]) – envisaged him as the Apollo of Greek mythology, the exemplar of beauty and light. Like Orwell's 'little sandy-haired woman', who cries out 'My Saviour!' when she sees Big Brother's picture, the chorus echoed a passionate cry for belonging from an artist who was a natural outsider. Only with a reference to chemical excess that sounded like an uncanny prediction of Bowie's immediate future was there any personal resonance. The fact that its unembellished voices and acoustic guitars sounded like an addendum to 'The Bewlay Brothers' [51] merely added to the surreal sense that this fragment belonged elsewhere.

---

* The very structure of the song exemplified the split in perspective: the chorus ran grimly down the scale of D♭ major – a chord that never appeared in the song – from Cm to F, before walking up a different scale – C major – back to the original Cm. Meanwhile, the backing chorus started its fall on F, against the C minor chord; and finished at C, against the F chord, as if all polarities had been reversed.

That diversion aside, 'Big Brother' was as expansive as its subject's powers, opening with a vocal chorus produced by a machine, alongside a Mellotron trumpet motif* – an immediate sign that humanity was in the shadows. Bowie compensated with a soaring vocal, doubled by a voice an octave higher that might have been on the edge of insanity – or simply trying to connect with its emotions within the restraints of Big Brother's society.

[104] CHANT OF THE EVER-CIRCLING SKELETAL FAMILY (Bowie)

Recorded February 1974; *Diamond Dogs* LP.

From the cry for 'Big Brother' [103], Bowie's electronic soundscape led inevitably into the ritualistic 'chant of humanity' – his equivalent to the 'Two Minute Hate' in Orwell's novel, in which the citizens of Oceania were required to vent their anger and contempt for Big Brother's enemies. As the final track on *Diamond Dogs*, it was an uncompromisingly bleak portrait of mankind.

Orwell's Hate began with 'a hideous, grinding screech, as of some monstrous machine without oil', and climaxed in 'a deep, slow, rhythmical chant . . . a heavy, murmurous sound, somehow curiously savage'. Bowie's musical equivalent was pitched somewhere between a robotic, futuristic dance track, and an inhuman assault on the senses. Every iota of sound was under stress – reversed, synthesised, phased into a distortion of reality. Eventually the recognisable instruments (electric guitar, bass, Latin percussion) were suppressed beneath a reverberating rhythmic effect that was sound itself, the aural equivalent of a barrage of strobe lightning. To reinforce the banality and repetition of this mindless convulsion, Bowie added the most skeletal and meaningless dance lyrics, before the cacophony focused into the brutal metallic rasp of mutated syllables – 'bro' and 'riot' merged into an aural weapon.

That almost indecipherable sound was then repeated *al fin* in an eerie homage to the pioneering minimalist music of the American composer Steve Reich a decade earlier. Reich's 'It's Gonna Rain' used tape loops and time delays to create a pulsing hammer of noise from

---

* Despite what some critics have written, this was not a quote from Miles Davis' *Sketches Of Spain* album.

the voice of a Pentecostal preacher. Kevin Ayers, whose musical path often crossed with that of Bowie in the early seventies, had already exploited Reich's example on 'When Your Parents Go To Sleep' a few months earlier, but Bowie extended the technique to confrontational ends.

[105] ROCK 'N' ROLL WITH ME (Bowie / MacCormack)

Recorded February 1974; *Diamond Dogs* LP.

Only one song on *Diamond Dogs* could reliably be located as a contender for the lost *Ziggy Stardust* stage musical. Its subject was the ambiguous liaison between star and audience: the pull between the ecstatic lure of the stage, and the pressurised capsule of fame. Bowie triumphantly located a door marked 'OUT', as if voicing Ziggy's intention to escape the spotlight. The gloriously commercial chorus,* which would have guaranteed substantial success had this song been issued as a single, signalled Bowie's (and Ziggy's) awareness of the gulf between the image and reality of fame. Later in 1974, Bowie summarised the song's message to his Messiah-hungry audience: '*You're* doing it to *me*, stop it!'

The prevailing mood was anything but exuberant. Though the refrain begged for a stadium of flag-waving fans, Bowie's voice was fired with desperation to be released, while the back-up singers sounded distinctly resigned to their fate. Even Bowie's baritone sax seemed to be acting as a depressive, while the gospel-flavoured piano emphasised that there was at least one soul at stake. Relief came only in the smallest of signs: the gorgeous texture of the acoustic guitar, for example, filling in the pauses between lines with delicious passing chords.

The credited co-writer, Geoff MacCormack, told David Buckley that his contribution to the song was minimal: 'I started fiddling around with a chord sequence [on piano] . . . David said, "Hang on a minute, play that again!" So it was very much accidental . . . I wouldn't have dreamed of sitting down and saying, "Oh, let's write a song together."'

---

* The repeated journey from C major to F and back to C offered only a slight variation on the structure of Bob Dylan's 'Girl From The North Country', incidentally.

[106] FUTURE LEGEND (Bowie; inc. 'Bewitched' by Rodgers/Hart)

Recorded February 1974; *Diamond Dogs* LP.

Alongside his cover of John Lennon's 'Across The Universe' [168], this brief prelude to the *Diamond Dogs* album ranked as Bowie's greatest creative misstep of the decade. The transitory allure of its mutant iconography and sub-William Burroughs imagery quickly palled, becoming more laughable with every passing year. Equally silly was the climactic 'genocide' line, which was presumably meant to match the impact of the Rolling Stones' self-congratulatory introduction to their *Get Yer Ya Ya's Out* live album.

Beyond the zombie chic and (Burroughs') *Wild Boys* derivatives, however, 'Future Legend' did offer some signposts, forwards and back. Its surreal collage owed something to Frank Zappa's 'Help I'm A Rock', a Bowie favourite of 1966. Even more distant was the Rodgers & Hart tune 'Bewitched',* one of three guitar themes running simultaneously beneath his monologue. The title of 'Future Legend' was suggestive in itself: the apocalypse was no longer 'Five Years' [56] ahead, as on *Ziggy Stardust*, but any day now. (Looking forward to his reincarnation as a soul singer, Bowie briefly imitated the melody of the hit song of that name from 1962.) Most significantly in the context of what was to come, the sonic landscape of this track was severely distorted – a clamour of phasing, echo, synthesised sound, vari-speed vocals and feedback, all contributing to a canvas that was rotting from within.

[107] DIAMOND DOGS (Bowie)

Recorded February 1974; *Diamond Dogs* LP.

The song existed before Guy Peellaert's cover artwork for the album, begging the question: who or what are the diamond dogs? They could be the canine equivalents of Burroughs' *Wild Boys*; or, as one rock journalist of the era suggested, a reinvention of the loyal beast from Harlan Ellison's apocalyptic science-fiction tale, 'A Boy And His Dog'.

---

* 'Bewitched' was the epitome of a hit song: no fewer than nine different versions reached the US chart in 1950, five of them appearing in the Top 10. Bowie would most likely have heard the song from Frank Sinatra, in the 1957 movie of Rodgers & Hart's stage musical *Pal Joey*.

Historians of science might remember Isaac Newton's dog Diamond, which unfortunately destroyed manuscripts detailing twenty years of his master's research. Those of a more metaphorical bent might recall that dogs are man's best friends, and diamonds are a girl's best friends: at least according to cliché and popular song.

Then again, who is Halloween Jack, aside from a character who lives atop a mansion that bears the name (reversed) of a major US bank, Chase Manhattan? Many Bowie aficionados credit Jack as a Bowie 'identity', following Ziggy and Aladdin, but there was little hint in this song that he occupied more than a cameo role. Could he have any ties to Robert Neville, hero of the 1971 movie *The Omega Man*, a futuristic man/dog/apocalypse film that was set in March 1975 – 'any day now', indeed, in 1974? Or, as elsewhere on the *Diamond Dogs* album, was Bowie merely using cut-up chance and a little sleight of hand to create an appropriately fantastic but vague vision of what Alvin Toffler's 1970 best-seller called *Future Shock*? The lyrics were certainly full of allusions, notably referencing Tod Browning's controversial* 1932 movie *Freaks*, which had been a cult item in London's cinema clubs since finally being passed fit for public exhibition in 1963. But why Tarzan? And why mutate Donovan's 'Season Of The Witch' into a bitch? Literal translation of the song did not bring you any closer to its heart, and Bowie's after-the-fact explanations were no more convincing than the spontaneous *Ziggy Stardust* myth that he related to William S. Burroughs during their meeting in late 1973.

For a real sense of civilisation collapsing, the music was a more reliable guide. It began in applause, cheekily stolen from the Faces' recently completed *Overture And Beginners* live album, beneath which the scratchiest of rhythm guitars (one loud and confident, the other soft and erratic) embarked on a precarious series of slides between major chords. Eventually the track fell cacophonously into the key of A, over a drum pattern last heard on a late-fifties Bo Diddley record. While Bowie happily spewed out his lyrical disconnections, he was

---

* Adults suffering from ill-health were advised not to attend screenings when the film originally opened in America. Bowie relished the explorations of similar territory in the uncompromising photography of Diane Arbus, who committed suicide in 1971, apparently unable to bear the gulf between her vision of humanity and that shared by the masses. A major retrospective of her work opened in New York the following year.

accompanied by wildly distorted* backing vocals. That dislocation paled alongside what happened next: 'Will they come?' the strange voices asked, and in reply the drums began to play *between* the beats of the bar, as if time had come off its hinges. The track kept building from there: layer upon layer of keyboards, guitars, saxophones, dog imitations, *noise*, none of it centred around anything. So primal was its interpretation of rock 'n' roll that it was easy to make comparisons – to the Velvet Underground's 'Waiting For The Man' [A44], perhaps, or a loose rendition of the Rolling Stones' 'Brown Sugar'; or, given that Bowie seems to have studied the work of Kevin Ayers with some care, the opening of 'Stop This Train' from Ayers' *Joy Of A Toy* album in 1969. Ultimately, though, 'Diamond Dogs' created its own universe: ramshackle, amateurish, weirdly compelling, as jarring in its way as punk would become two years later.

Diamond Dogs LP

When *Diamond Dogs* was complete, MainMan promised that the record 'conceptualises the vision of a future world with images of urban decadence and collapse'. That sounded like an all-purpose description, which might just as well have been applied to the *Nineteen Eighty-Four* project.* In fact, what was striking about *Diamond Dogs* was how consistently it avoided direct political and social relevance: the individual images that Bowie had assembled carried less cultural significance than their fragmentary state. So this was neither a soundtrack for a lost musical (although that didn't prevent Bowie from dreaming), or a work of social analysis, but an attempt by the artist to explore the impact that those themes had exerted on his psyche. *Diamond Dogs* also explored some of the fixations of the pop-art school of the fifties – the nexus between science fiction, catastrophe and consumerism, for example – but within an entirely personal landscape.

* Indeed, Bowie originally intended to make the connection quite obvious, by titling this record *We Are The Dead*, after both a song [102] and a memorable line of dialogue from Orwell's book. He was persuaded that this might antagonise Sonia Orwell's lawyers into claiming that he was trying to pass off his record as an interpretation of her husband's novel.

---

* Tony Visconti, who helped Bowie complete the album, explained that Bowie's voice had been mutated by a primitive electronic sampler known as a 'Keypex': 'we used the Keypex to key the vocal to a 20-cycle-per-second oscillator tone, which created a quavering effect'.

That dream of Bowie's, the notion (shared by Pete Townshend of the Who and Ray Davies of the Kinks) that an album needed stage or screen to assume its full three-dimensional power, led him to boast almost immediately that there would soon be a *Diamond Dogs* musical or movie. To facilitate the latter idea, he constructed a miniature landscape and models of his intended characters in his New York hotel room, and then filmed them, all the time narrating the key elements of his screenplay. 'I wanted to make a film of *Diamond Dogs* so passionately,' he revealed in 1980, when he was still hoping to issue his trailer as a video-cassette. 'I had the whole roller-skating thing in there. We had no more cars, because of the fuel crisis . . . Also, I had groups of these cyborg people wandering around looking so punky.' But the narrative needed to fuel a movie was more difficult to grasp.

With three decades' hindsight, Bowie dismissed *Diamond Dogs* as 'my usual basket of apocalyptic visions, isolation, being terribly miserable'. Participants in the 1974 sessions at Olympic Studios, where Bowie shared his time with Brian Eno, who was mixing *Here Come The Warm Jets* down the corridor, remember an altogether more positive artist – energised, restlessly creative, bouncing back and forth between his white Perspex guitar, his Mellotron and his synthesiser. *Rolling Stone* magazine may have complained that the finished record was 'simplistic and murky . . . muddy and tuneless', but that was the way Bowie wanted it. To that extent, *Diamond Dogs* anticipated the sonic audacity of *Low* and *'Heroes'*, at the same time as it capsized the vessel of classic rock.

None of this was apparent at the time, and – in Britain, at least – the album was widely regarded as a severe disappointment, ameliorated only by the rowdy genius of the 'Rebel Rebel' [101] single. There was much talk, too, about Guy Peellaert's cover design, on which Bowie metamorphosed into a mutant canine, just as the inner gatefold of *Aladdin Sane* had seen his body morph into a creature without sexual organs. Peellaert, however, had painted the Bowie dog with a penis and balls, which had to be airbrushed into decency before the record was released. Censored or otherwise, the *Diamond Dogs* sleeve marked the end of a year of semi-affectionate sparring with Mick Jagger, who had made the mistake of boasting to Bowie that the next Rolling Stones album would feature a Peellaert design. 'Mick was silly,' Bowie conceded. 'I mean, he should never have shown me anything new.' And with a swagger in his step, he set off for America, his three-year experiment with the rock template fashioned by the Stones and the Beatles at an end.

[108] CAN YOU HEAR ME (Bowie)

Recorded August, November/December 1974; *Young Americans* LP.

Bowie's journey from rock to soul began with this sensuous and elegant ballad, written to prove his conviction that his friend Lulu was 'a real soul singer'. In April 1974, he boarded the SS *France* for New York, to begin preparations for an extravagant American tour. When he checked into the Sherry-Netherland Hotel, Lulu was already in residence, and the following day he produced her still unreleased version of the song, commissioning a string arrangement from Mick Ronson (their last musical collaboration of the decade). 'Lulu's got this terrific voice,' he said excitedly after the session, 'and it's been misdirected all these years. People laugh now, but they won't in two years' time, you see!' The session, which also allowed him to revamp 'Rebel Rebel' [101] for its US single release, marked his first encounter with guitarist Carlos Alomar, who would soon join his band, and remain a vital collaborator for the rest of the decade.

'Can You Hear Me' re-emerged during Bowie's Philadelphia sessions in August, its intense 'take it in right' vocal interplay inspiring the creation of another song [119]. Ostensibly a romantic ballad, for someone whom Bowie refused to name, it also awoke some internalised demons. As on 'It's Gonna Be Me' [116], he expressed his boredom with the parade of sexual partners available on tour. More urgently, the song's title expressed a more existential fear: could his perception of reality be trusted? Did he really exist at all? 'I set out on a very successful crusade to re-establish my own identity,' he said later of this period. 'I stripped myself down, and took myself down, and took myself apart, layer by layer. I used to sit in bed and pick on one thing a week that I either didn't like or couldn't understand. And during the course of the week, I'd try to kill it off.' All of which may explain the apparent – with Bowie, reality and artifice were always difficult to separate – emotional openness of his performance.

Like 'It's Gonna Be Me', 'Can You Hear Me' captured the mood of Southern rather than Philly soul, as if it had been cut during Elvis Presley's 1969 sessions at American Studios in Memphis. Indeed, Bowie had envisaged producing an entire album for Lulu in exactly that location. The signifiers of 'Southern' identity were the gospel-tinged piano, the tight and terse guitar figures, and the sense of space in the arrangement. Where Philadelphia reasserted itself was in the strings (added by Tony Visconti in London, ironically enough) and in the intimacy of the relationship between Bowie and his background singers, especially during the play-out, as the band vamped modestly over a C major chord. His lead vocal, slightly compressed and rigidly controlled in the opening verse, slowly began to betray the depth of his commitment, the edges almost cracking with emotion as he stretched out all the possible implications of the gorgeous melody.

The Heart of Plastic Soul

'White rock has lost its contact with the dance by straying too far from black beginnings; black music is struggling to define its own integrity in the throes of new developments in the popular idiom comparable to the be-bop pioneers' impact on 40s jazz. Whatever next? I suggest black 'n' white music.' That was *NME* rock critic Ian MacDonald in 1975. For another voice, try Ron Ross from the US magazine *Circus*: 'Any artist who will mean as much to as many in the 70s as the Beatles did in the 60s is going to have to involve black listeners in the same way Stevie Wonder or Jimi Hendrix involved whites.'

For the generation of white musicians who emerged in the mid-sixties, particularly in Britain, black American music represented a touchstone of authenticity – a jewel that they could reproduce in paste, but never hope to match. As American producer Tony Visconti noted in 1974, 'Every British musician has a hidden desire to be black. They all talk about "funky rhythm sections", and their idols are all black blues guitarists.' Talking of Bowie, he added: 'He's been working on putting together an R&B sound for years.' Like the Beatles, the Rolling Stones, the Who, and many more besides, Bowie had set out in 1964 with the intention of sounding as if he had been born in Harlem, rather than pre-immigration Brixton. A decade later, he boasted: 'It's only now that I've got the necessary confidence to sing like that. That's the kind of music I've always wanted to sing.'

Not that one could have deduced that from the music that he – or, for that matter, the Beatles, the Stones or the Who – had recorded between

1967 and 1970. All of those acts felt as if they had progressed beyond the need to imitate their black American idols. They were under more direct influences: psychedelic drugs, literature, radical politics, street protests, the decline of a traditional national identity. None of them lost their passion for R&B or soul, but they now inhabited what felt like a more complex universe, which the simple verities of the blues were inadequate to reflect.

Instead, American soul music came to meet them: alongside the rise of black nationalism and black power, the Black Liberation Army and the Black Panthers, performers such as Curtis Mayfield, James Brown, Marvin Gaye and Sly Stone began to sketch vivid portraits of a black nation in revolt, under threat and forced to confront the starkest economic realities of the age. Only when the black liberation movement was destroyed by covert government interference (the Nixon administration's infamous COINTELPRO initiative), the ghettos of America's cities were flooded with cheap heroin and cocaine, and the revolution of 1970 was repackaged as 'blaxploitation' chic in movies such as *Shaft* and *Superfly*, did the culture of US soul slide back into escapism and hedonism, the righteous blast of funk giving way to the dance-floor metronome of disco.

That's a very simplistic overview, of course, which glosses over complex social transformations and political initiatives, and underplays the richness of America's black music during the early to mid-seventies. It was the latter that attracted David Bowie when he moved to New York in 1974. He hung out at the Pierre Hotel, ordering steaks that he never ate and $100 bottles of vintage champagne, before heading uptown to the Apollo and downtown to Max's Kansas City – sampling the best of the era's sweet soul in Harlem, and an altogether more chaotic brew in the East Village. He wasn't alone in his obsessions: Mick Jagger, John Lennon and Elton John were all about to welcome contemporary black American influences back into their music, to disguise the hollowness of their closeted rock culture. But Bowie, ever the stylist at heart, was entranced as much by dance moves and fashions as by music. He fell for the clichéd swagger of what Tom Wolfe, in an essay entitled 'Funky Chic', called 'the Pimpmobile Pyramid-Heel Platform Soul Prince Albert Coat Got-to-get-over look of [New Haven's] Dixwell Avenue', in which 'all of them, every ace, every dude, [were] out there just getting over in the baddest possible way, come to play and dressed to slay'. As Bowie recalled nearly thirty years later, 'it was an attempt to turn the visual around as well as the music' – an escape route from his image as a space invader, his obsessions with political apocalypse, his hard-rock clichés, his emotional repression; a reconnection with the body that he was already subjecting to torture by starvation and drug addiction; an expression of (there was no other word for it) soul.

In the remainder of 1974, therefore, he channelled his soul obsessions into one tour that was meant to promote *Diamond Dogs*, and one that clearly wasn't; and into a series of recording sessions whereby the strategies of contemporary black music enabled him to explore psychological terrain left untouched by his rock stardom.

[109] KNOCK ON WOOD (Floyd/Cropper)

[110] HERE TODAY AND GONE TOMORROW (Bonner/Harris/Jones/ Middlebrooks/Robinson/Satchell/Webster)

Performed live 1974; *David Live* LP [109] and extended CD [110].

Bowie promised 'some silly ones' during the July 1974 *Diamond Dogs* concerts taped for *David Live*, no doubt leading some in the audience to expect a live debut of 'The Laughing Gnome'. Instead, he worked his way gently towards a contemporary soul sound via two vintage offerings. In 'Knock On Wood' he was tackling a song so well-known that it was virtually a cliché, having entered the repertoire of every British R&B band in the late sixties. While Eddie Floyd's 1966 original was tightly controlled, relying on its brass section to help it swing, Bowie increased the tempo and let Earl Slick's guitar dominate the arrangement, with an inevitable reduction in subtlety.

Few, if any, of Bowie's following in 1974 would have been familiar with 'Here Today And Gone Tomorrow', a 1968 single by the Ohio Players. Even in 1968 it must have sounded like a throwback, to the era when Smokey Robinson was crafting a succession of hits for the Temptations. Aside from lowering the key, Bowie did little to amend the Ohio Players' arrangement, delivering a faithful but ultimately pointless reproduction of the original.

The Unmaking of a Star #2: *David Live* LP

The mid-seventies was the last era of rock history in which concert tours by major artists were not routinely documented for posterity. David Bowie undertook two lengthy excursions across the United States and Canada in 1974: the first, designed to promote *Diamond Dogs*, was recorded for the album *David Live*, but only a few fragments of concert footage have survived; the second, for which he abandoned the scenery and iconography of *Diamond Dogs* and set out to prove himself a soul singer, was glimpsed briefly in the 1975 BBC TV documentary *Cracked Actor*, but otherwise exists only in memory and on illicit tapes made by audience members. For fans in Britain, famine replaced glut: after two years of frantic touring activity, Bowie was not seen on stage for almost three years.

David Live was roundly criticised on its release in October 1974: one of Bowie's staunchest supporters, journalist Charles Shaar Murray, wrote: 'He seems to be kicking and screaming in a vain attempt to break out of the boundaries imposed on him by the songs, as if he needs them to say more than they are capable of saying; as if they had lost so much of their original meaning to him that he must infuse the lyrics with a desperate theatricality simply in order to convince himself that the songs have not yet become totally impotent.' The staging of the tour was certainly theatrical. Bowie had become obsessed with German expressionist cinema of the silent age, and the treacherous, angled surfaces of the most enduring example of the genre, *The Cabinet of Dr Caligari*, were a major influence on the *Diamond Dogs* scenery. Everything in *Caligari* was off-balance, as befitted a film about madness and the uncertainty of identity – themes that were close to Bowie's heart. For the *Diamond Dogs* tour he combined the tilting floors of *Caligari* with the inhuman cityscape of Fritz Lang's film *Metropolis*, which he had seen for the first time in January 1974.

Lang had arrived in New York a few months before he began shooting *Metropolis* in 1926. He saw the city as 'the crossroads of multiple and confused human forces', though implicit in his film was the belief that love could overcome the confusion and break through the overpowering modernity of a technocratic society. In Bowie's hands, this theme became more vague: instead of Metropolis, his designers built Hunger City, with skyscrapers that seemed to be decaying before the audience's eyes. Yet the singer, his band (positioned modestly stage right, as if observing proceedings) and his two 'dogs' (singing dancers) never fully interacted with this vision. Songs were staged in a series of tableaux: Bowie was carried over the audience on a boom, mimed a boxing bout, or ran with a street gang, but never captured the focused intensity of the silent movies that ran through his imagination.

Critics lamented his vocal inadequacies (as *David Live* proved, his off-stage habits had cut away at his range) and the band's lack of engagement with the music. Meanwhile, the gadgets didn't always work, the venues didn't sell out (especially in the South, in cities such as Nashville, Tampa, Charlotte and Greensboro, where the arena was only 20 per cent full), and the running costs were enormous. Even the taping of *David Live* during a six-show run at the Tower Theater in Philadelphia was problematic: the band mutinied over a pay dispute before they went on stage; and the intended producer, Tony Visconti, only arrived after the shows.

When the first tour ended in New York, a chance discussion with a MainMan employee forced Bowie to face an uncomfortable truth: he had misunderstood the entire nature of his business relationship with Tony Defries. What he had signed and what he had chosen to believe were diametrically opposed. He had imagined that he must be the co-owner of MainMan alongside Defries; instead, he was merely one of the company's employees, albeit the single most profitable individual on the staff. Bowie felt betrayed, and his personal relationship with Defries effectively ended at that point. His first decision in his new state of awareness – like Adam and Eve after they'd tasted the apple – was to cover himself up, to lessen his liabilities: specifically, he ordered that the next leg of the tour, due to open in September on the West Coast, should proceed without the ruinously expensive scenery and special effects.

He also revamped his live band, replacing several experienced musicians with young black hopefuls from New York. Shepherded by Mike Garson, and led vocally by the then-unknown Luther Vandross, they were allowed to open the subsequent shows, to the disgust of many fans who had come to see Ziggy Stardust, not an unknown band of R&B singers. Although much of the material and arrangements remained intact (including Bowie's reduced range), publicity centred around the handful of new songs that Bowie had added to the repertoire, all of which revealed a strong soul influence. Reviewers were virtually unanimous: as a soul man, Bowie was 'a non-singer of the Lou Reed school', 'lightweight', 'hoarse', 'undistinguished', 'raw, uneven and generally strained'.

It was now impossible to describe Bowie without mentioning his emaciated appearance, his skull clearly visible beneath his skin, like one of Egon Schiele's distorted portraits of sickness. Associates had been worrying about his attitude to food since the late sixties, when Ken Pitt's secretary complained that he never seemed to eat. His bodyguard during the Ziggy tours, Stuey George, talked as if he were a wilful, self-destructive child: 'You'd give him something to eat and he'd say he'd have it in a minute, so that in the end you would have to take the work off him. Many times he would go for days without eating, then he couldn't get any food down. We had to fix Complan [a nutritional food supplement] and make him eat.' By 1974, he would taste a little milk or cheese in the early hours, but otherwise ingest nothing but alcohol. Observers guessed that he weighed no more than seven stone. Journalists noted that he was 'almost ravaged, beyond belief'.

He was also trapped in a routine of epic drug use. It was, said guitarist Earl Slick, 'self-destruct time'. That was a more accurate summary than Slick perhaps realised. On 23 October 1974, Bowie returned to his hotel after a gig in Chicago to watch an *In Concert* TV special based on the final Ziggy show the previous year. He could hardly have been taken by surprise to see the broadcast: he had remixed the tapes of the performance a few days earlier, for this exact purpose. But as he saw himself at the height of his powers just fifteen months earlier, in a state of benign innocence about his financial situation, something inside of him cracked. 'I nearly threw myself out of the window,' he revealed later, claiming that Defries had never told him about the film. 'I saw everything for the first time. And I nearly threw myself out. I was trying, but they stopped me. I just couldn't take it.' A week later, as if nothing had happened, he was back on stage in New York. 'I saw everything for the first time': where he had been, what he had become, what he had believed, how he had been manipulated, what lay ahead. It was too much reality to bear.

During his run at the city's famous Radio City Music Hall, he filmed an appearance on Dick Cavett's TV chat show, sniffing uncontrollably, tapping a cane on the floor incessantly as he spoke, singing with passion but little voice, and resembling a famine victim. A few weeks later, he was spotted in a New York club with Bob Dylan, 'moving very strangely, looking very thin, and also a bit crazed'. It was this man who recorded one of the most directly emotional albums of his career; and then resolved to overturn the business relationship that had guided him to fame and all its attendant curses.

[111] I Am A Laser (Bowie)

[112] Shilling The Rubes (Bowie)

Recorded August 1974; unreleased.

A spontaneous decision led David Bowie to Sigma Sound in Philadel-phia, the base for Gamble & Huff's sweet-soul empire. He booked the studio for two weeks, naïvely assuming that he would be working with the musicians he had heard on hits by the O'Jays, Harold Melvin & the Blue Notes and the Three Degrees. But they were engaged elsewhere, so it was a mixture of New York players and local singers who accompanied him as he attempted to confect his own facsimile of the Philly soul sound. Beyond that, his agenda was vague. This was not a project built around a concept, unless you included one possibility that flitted across his mind: the enticing but commercially perilous idea of chronicling his feelings about his career, and more specifically his declining relationship with the MainMan, Tony Defries.

Hence 'Shilling The Rubes', street slang for a form of exploitation that was second nature to any huckster or (as Bowie knew from experience) salesman. Rumour had long suggested this as a possible song title from these sessions, though with no evidence to support it until 2009, when a private vendor on eBay briefly posted samples of these two songs (plus working versions of 'After Today' [114] and 'Young Americans' [113]) to prove that he did indeed possess original tapes from the Sigma Sound project. And there, at last, was 'Shilling The Rubes' (take 1), a slow, dramatic variation on the James Brown ballad tradition ('It's A Man's Man's Man's World' being the closest equivalent). Only a minute of the song circulated before the tapes were withdrawn: enough merely to show that Bowie intended to pin a businessman to the wall with bitter humour.

A slightly longer extract of 'I Am A Laser' (marked simply 'Lazer' on the tape box) also surfaced, with an entirely different feel to the Astronettes' version [93], and totally rewritten verses – one of which began by referring to the rumoured working title for the album, *The Gouster* (a youth fashion of the fifties and sixties that could best be defined by borrowing a song title from New York Dolls vocalist David Johansen: 'Funky But Chic').

[113] YOUNG AMERICANS (Bowie)

Recorded August & November 1974; *Young Americans* LP.

Note the title: it never appeared in this song, where everyone – he, she, I – wanted 'the young American'. So did every advertising executive in the nation, every politician, every pop star. As a temporary immigrant, albeit one who was being advised not to return home for tax reasons, and who would never be resident in Britain again, David Bowie knew the pull of the mythical young American only too well, as it had dragged him from south London, via the media of movies, rock 'n' roll and beat literature, to New York, California and now Philadelphia, in his quest to become what he had worshipped since he was a child. On one level, then, 'Young Americans' was the portrait of a fantasy: the global dream of how it would feel to have life laid out before you in the land of plenty.

Yet there was more to this myth than simple obeisance to the Yankee dollar, and all it could buy. In the summer of 1974, with Watergate on the news, unemployment lines around the block, the economy on the edge, being young and American was a less certain fate than the myth allowed. The dream might already be over; childhood affluence and teenage promise snuffed out in a moment of economic decline, where the young Americans might have to 'die for the fifty more' years. After the opening verse of the song, with its moment of sexual passion so transcendent that she doesn't even care if he takes her behind the fridge,* it's only a moment before they're married, and he's the breadwinner on his knees in despair, not lust. Even the Barbie Doll on the poster (movies, records, advertising, it didn't matter) had suffered a broken heart as the myth disintegrated. Yet the power of fantasy, of the ad man's game and stardom's sheen, was so overwhelming that it could replenish itself even at times of national dread, to the point where young Americans had already forgotten their vanquished president (who'd resigned days earlier, prompting his successor to promise,

---

* Or maybe the bridge, which is what one printed lyric sheet suggested; Bowie definitely sang 'fridge' every night on stage, though. Contemporary reviewers were equally baffled by whether 'your mamma' was suffering from 'cramps' or 'crabs', one ungracious British pop paper even suggesting that the latter must be a reference to Bowie's wife.

optimistically: 'our long national nightmare is over') – and maybe couldn't even remember yesterday.

There was another layer to American mythology that Bowie only began to explore after he'd questioned the nation's collective memory (and, incidentally, changed the song's key). He was working in a studio run by black entrepreneurs, with mostly black musicians, on music that was inspired by the sound of black America. As a kid, that had been the most seductive part of the myth, before he knew what it meant to be black in this land. Now, after the official end of segregation and the supposed death of discrimination, what was black America, the youngest America of them all? Was it the high, quasi-feminine falsetto voice of a sweet soul band? Or the pimp and hustler stereotypes that peopled the so-called 'blaxploitation' movies? What did it mean to process your hair, or shape it into an Afro, using Afro-Sheen? What was the black identity in America, when the black nation was crippled by fantasy just like the white, and divided between the ghetto and the self-improving middle class? Where did that leave soul music? And, as Bowie sang with a mighty octave-and-a-half leap, was there nothing that could make him 'break down and cry'?

That was merely the last of a series of questions posed by the would-be young American who had grown up surrounded by myths, and no longer knew which to believe or follow. By the end, he was barely coherent, flashing out images and fragments of sentences that didn't run together, as a cacophony of American voices and myths filled his mind. All of this was in the song – material for sociological disserta-tions and psychological reports, a dazzling series of snapshots of real America and mythical America and Bowie's place in the country and the myth. And none of it seemed to be thought, merely felt, as if it had emerged in automatic writing, and he had found the courage to let it stand as a genuine, unfeigned response to the mystery of what America represented in 1974.

Bowie could hardly have offered more commitment to the song, vocally or lyrically, if he'd been speaking in tongues: the change of key midway not only refocused the lyrical theme, it also pushed his voice to its limit. Yet for a song of such intensity, the musical framework was refreshingly loose, following a simple I-ii-IV-V chord sequence through the verse and chorus. The band reached out for attention at the start – one of those percussive intros that were ubiquitous in 1974's soul music, followed by a run down the keyboard – and then lay back, with plenty of space in the arrangement, and only David Sanborn's word-in-your-ear saxophone coming close to rivalling Bowie's insistence. As they would throughout the Philadelphia sessions, the backing of Luther Vandross, Ava Cherry and Robin Clark filled out the vocal spectrum around and against Bowie's lead, never becoming caught up in his hysteria. Musically simple, lyrically fragmented, emotionally inspired, 'Young Americans' presented a Bowie who had never been heard on record before, catching almost everyone who had followed him by surprise.

[114] AFTER TODAY (Bowie)

Recorded August 1974; *Sound + Vision* CD.

Throughout the sixties, Bowie rarely dared to attempt singing anything above a high G. Yet the chorus of this song barely ventured below that point, provoking one of his most enthusiastic, if erratic, attempts at a falsetto vocal. Like the Bee Gees, whose 'Jive Talking' would soon feature even more extreme displays of the art, Bowie was clearly enraptured by the tradition (particularly in Philadelphia) of sweet-soul groups with a soaring male lead. While they tended to concentrate on ballads, Bowie let rip on this frenetic disco-funk tune, rather generic in nature, but none the less energised for that. Its working lyrics carried a vague message of encouragement to a friend or lover, but would surely have been replaced if 'After Today' had become a serious contender for his next album. Throughout, David Sanborn's saxophone mimicked the physical strain of Bowie's voice with playful accuracy.

[115] WHO CAN I BE NOW? (Bowie)

Recorded August & November 1974; *Young Americans* extended CD.

It was a title that seemed to summarise Bowie's strange journey. There was a real contempt in his voice as he recalled the drudgery of adopting a new disguise, as if all the allure of 'Changes' had been stripped away, to reveal the puppet-master going through the motions.

The boundary lines between spiritual desolation and romantic despair were blurred throughout this exercise in gospel-soul, which was naggingly reminiscent of John Lennon's 1973 song, 'Out Of The Blue'. The two compositions shared a circularity of structure, and a familiar melodic descent that was most obvious in the bass-line. But where Lennon sought solace in love, Bowie's narrator was concerned with a more profound dilemma about the purpose of existence itself. 'Who Can I Be Now?' exhibited many of the trademarks of the Philadelphia sessions: gospel-tinged piano, saxophone as an expression of pain, call-and-response vocal interplay. But despite Bowie's full-blooded performance, it was perhaps a shade too mechanical (note the additional half-bar needed to travel from verse to chorus) to stand up to the scrutiny of a place on the *Young Americans* album.

[116] IT'S GONNA BE ME (Bowie)

> Recorded August, November & December 1974; *Young Americans* extended CD.

One of the most remarkable performances of Bowie's career, 'It's Gonna Be Me' was a consummate display of his vocal artistry, a naked revelation of the man behind the art, and a dexterous piece of character acting – begging the question of who exactly was holding this thinnest of masks. It staked his claim to be ranked as a soul singer alongside the likes of Aretha Franklin and Dusty Springfield, over a perilously bare gospel-soul track that apparently left him nowhere to hide. And it raised the tantalising question of whether he could (or indeed should) have taken a train to Tennessee with this song, 'Who Can I Be Now?' [115] and 'Can You Hear Me' [108] in his sack, and begged a Southern producer like Chips Moman or Dan Penn to help him record a *Bowie In Memphis* album, the way that countless others before him had done (Dusty Springfield, Elvis Presley, Cher and Lulu amongst them).

Not that Moman or Penn could have improved on this Tony Visconti production,* which reinforced the Bible-fearing starkness of piano, bass and drums, and let the human voice carry the emotional burden – either Bowie's alone, racked with guilt and self-doubt, or

---

* Visconti preferred the arrangement with overdubbed strings, heard on the most recent reissue of *Young Americans*, to the unadorned mix included on the 1991 CD.

supported by the tonal richness of the background vocals through the chorus. At its confessional peak, there was just singer and piano, which held back as if to give Bowie room to feel. There was nothing modernist about this arrangement, nothing of the 1970s; this was how the gospel of truth had been presented for decades in the churches of the South, and that tradition lent Bowie's crisis an eerie sense of a soul at stake. He responded with a voice that signified reality, rather than artifice: 'pure' soul, not the crooning, whispering persona who inhabited the other ballads from these sessions.

But this was simply a performance. Like 'Can You Hear Me', 'It's Gonna Be Me' was ostensibly the confession of a casual seducer, who had suddenly awoken to the audacity of his crimes, glimpsed his own hollowness, and realised that he had let slip the possibility of authentic love. His victim had been robbed of her virginity, her purity, her holiness; qualities that his false display was bound to destroy. He was pleading for a second chance, to be born again in a world of understanding and compassion. He traced out the scenario – he'd run to her door, she'd dissolve tearfully into his arms, and then what? She'd forgive him? He'd apologise? No, he'd be strong, time and again. In the end, it was all about the man, and when the key changed in the final bars of the song, the penitent was once again the smooth seducer, awaiting another victim in another city. Was the penitent Bowie? Only if, in the purity of his soul, he talked like Frank Sinatra in a saloon bar, calling 'Hit me, Jack' to the band. But the artifice was full of artistry.

[117] JOHN, I'M ONLY DANCING (AGAIN) (Bowie)

Recorded August & November 1974; single A-side.

Critics and fans alike were alarmed by the radical reinvention of several of Bowie's most distinctive songs during his 1974 US tours. These qualms would have multiplied exponentially had he remained faithful to his original decision to include this lengthy mutation of his 1972 hit single [63] on the album he was recording in Philadelphia. Perhaps feeling that he had never quite reached the core* of

---

* His second recording of the song had been intended for the *Aladdin Sane* album, but was omitted at the last minute.

the song – which had, moreover, yet to be released in the USA at this point – he stripped it bare of everything but the essentials of the chorus, and remodelled it as a lengthy genre exercise in disco. If the original arrangement was pure London, the product of nights at the Sombrero Club, then 'Again' owed its life to his hedonistic nights in venues like the drag-queen capital of the East Village, Club 82 (or the Anvil, or Club 220) – the long, ecstatic play-out matching the stimulant-fuelled excesses of the midnight hours. The reference in the revised lyrics to 'Charlie' suggested at least one illicit source of inspiration. There was no hint as yet of Bowie's later proclamation that the 'endless numb beat' of disco was 'really dangerous'; for the moment, he preferred the interpretation that disco broke down social barriers between black and white, male and female, gay and straight. As one historian noted, 'It obviously threatened suburban white boys who found it too feminine, too gay, too black', although 'the black musical establishment hated disco just as fervently as the white rock-and-rollers did . . . they dismissed it as bleached and blue-eyed funk'. By the late seventies, when Bowie had lost his enthusiasm for the genre, performers black and white alike were being forced to assimilate disco into their natural style, from the host of soul performers who sacrificed their individuality in favour of generic dance-floor fodder to the cash-in manoeuvres of the Beach Boys ('Here Comes The Night') and Paul McCartney ('Goodnight Tonight').

Instead of the original two-chord guitar shuffle, the 1974 arrangement began with a defiantly machine-made vamp up and down the scale, vocoder, electronic keyboards and synthesisers combining to abstract effect. Then humans intervened, with bass and drums thudding eight-to-the-bar to introduce the frantic funk rhythm of the verse, with its parade of seventh chords, chattering guitar motifs, and syncopated breakdown as a finale. Bowie's pleasure at being able to toss off lyrics based on nursery rhymes, innuendo and improvisation was plain to hear. He reduced the Watergate crisis haunting the American nation to a banal remark, alluded to a line from the standard song 'Ain't She Sweet', and even sneaked in a reference to the Velvet Underground's 'White Light/White Heat'. The chorus pitched one of Bowie's more elegant vocal personae against crooning background voices (one of them his own), using more ethereal variations of the original chord phrasings. In its unexpurgated version, however, the song was dwarfed by the dual-phase play-out, the first dominated by almost hysterical interplay between Bowie and his singers, the second devoted to equally madcap instrumental revels. The results still sounded sufficiently strange, and *au courant*, to produce a hit single five years later.

[118] SOMEBODY UP THERE LIKES ME (Bowie)

Recorded August & November 1974; *Young Americans* LP.

> Really, I'm a one-track person. What I've said for years under various guises is, 'Watch out, the West is going to have a Hitler!' I've said it in a thousand different ways. That song is yet another way.
>   David Bowie, August 1974

Aldous Huxley was the first commentator to recognise the similarities between the techniques used by the advertising industry, and the way in which Adolf Hitler was 'sold' to the German public in the thirties. His account of Hitler's emotional manipulation of his audiences read like an account of a performance by a teenage pop idol: 'Strong emotion (as every actor and dramatist knows) is in the highest degree contagious. Infected by the malignant frenzy of the orator, the audience would groan and sob and scream in an orgy of uninhibited passion. And these orgies were so enjoyable that most of those who had experienced them eagerly came back for more.' The next step was to 'brand' Hitler as an ad agency would brand cigarettes: 'Hitler induced the German masses to buy themselves a Fuhrer, an insane philosophy, and the Second World War,' Huxley concluded. The historian of fascist iconography, Steven Heller, has taken the comparison further: 'It could be argued that this self-proclaimed artist [Hitler was an aspiring painter] conceived his horrific plans as a massive socio-political *Gesamtkunstwerk* (total work of art) built on the notions of racial purification, nationalist regeneration, and world domination. These were integrated in an overall graphic scheme . . . [which] ultimately became a textbook example – indeed, a perverse paradigm – of corporate branding.'

Bowie recognised the insidious attraction of the Nazi brand, allowing it to influence his iconography (the 'SS' lightning flash across his face on the cover of *Aladdin Sane*) and staging (the stark spotlighting of the stage on his 1976 world tour). He also knew the potency of his own branding as a star: what else was Ziggy Stardust but a demonstration of that effect? 'Somebody Up There Likes Me' (its title purloined from a 1956 Paul Newman movie about boxing champ Rocky Graziano) explored his confusing relationships with advertising, stardom and power. It built upon the melodic framework, though with a revised chord structure, of 'I Am Divine' [92] – a song that, like his more recent 'Shilling The Rubes' [112], seemed to have a specific predator in mind. Now Bowie was casting his net into an ocean of sharks, himself included.

At times, he sounded like a jaundiced political commentator of the old school, complaining that in the TV age, appearance counted more than substance. The obvious target was 'Tricky Dicky' Nixon, who had just resigned from the US presidency because of his involvement in the Watergate scandal, and the frequent target of the question: 'Would you buy a used car from this man?' Yet Bowie's attack on Nixon seemed tame alongside more pointed barbs from singers such as Stevie Wonder (whose attack on the former president, 'You Haven't Done Nothin'', charted the week that Bowie's sessions began). What gave Bowie's lyric its bite was his willingness to extend his cynicism beyond the political arena and into his own backyard, where a star such as Valentino – or David Bowie – had the power to sell his audience anything under the innocent guise of his own stardom, and where the star's relationship with his manager might resemble that between Faust and Mephistopheles.

By accident or design, the instrumental accompaniment for this exploration of cunning and deceit was coloured by the facsimile of an orchestral string section, as conjured up on a synthesiser. Over this lush background, David Sanborn's defiantly harsh saxophone sounded a wake-up call. Bowie, meanwhile, phrased with the confidence of a born charmer, or a natural salesman, eventually adopting an array of different vocal personae like a one-man Sly & The Family Stone, a different mood for every moment and every pair of ears. Seduction had rarely seemed so attractive, or so menacing.

[119] RIGHT (Bowie)

Recorded August & November 1974; *Young Americans* LP.

This song was titled 'Right' (rather than, for example, 'Never No Turning Back', the most constant refrain) more, one imagines, to continue Bowie's vague theme of using a single evocative word* to define his R&B pieces – though it begged confusion with the 'take it in right' chorus of 'Can You Hear Me' [108]. Nothing he'd written to date had been draped around such a skeletal frame: a slight movement between Fmaj7 and E major for the choruses, after which band and vocalists alike vamped at length over that solitary E chord.

Those choruses were, effectively, self-help mantras, the second of which had the distinctly personal context of assuaging Bowie's fear of flying. They could also be interpreted more widely, as commentary on a relationship – which was then acted out in vivid colours by the extended interplay between lead and background vocalists, Bowie shifting like a well-oiled actor from pleading to insisting to shrieking for control. As the BBC documentary *Cracked Actor* revealed, this apparently spontaneous call-and-response routine between Bowie and his backing vocalists was meticulously planned.

[120] WIN (Bowie)

Recorded November/December 1974; *Young Americans* LP.

Much of this song seemed to exist in that slightly delirious space between drunkenness and morning, where tones matter more than words, and nothing you say would make much sense in the piercing light of day. Nothing was quite in focus: instruments shimmered and echoed, David Sanborn's saxophone flittered up the scale and out of earshot, Bowie's voice swayed between a whisper and a sultry croon, then gradually slipped into desperation as the sexy woman who'd lit his fire refused to believe his reassurances. Whereas 'Right' [119] had set up a dialogue between lead and backing vocalists, in 'Win' the

* He was perhaps following the lead of the Ohio Players, originators of 'Here Today And Gone Tomorrow' [110], whose hits included 'Pain', 'Pleasure' and, perhaps inevitably, 'Ecstasy'.

chorale was there simply to support Bowie's point of view: I must be right, he seemed to be saying, all these other people think so too. Totalitarianism assumes many forms.

Rarely was it enacted in such intimate terms, however. Bowie softened his chords throughout the verses by adding a major 6th, creating the sense of unfinished business – and making the climactic shift to an E major chord seem all the more conclusive. Amidst the delicate emotional drama of the song, it was easy to miss some of the more subtle elements of the arrangement, such as the cello section introduced portentously, and the Beatlesque (from the *Abbey Road* era, to be exact) guitar chords unwinding beneath the chorus.

[121] FASCINATION (Vandross/Bowie)

Recorded November/December 1974; *Young Americans* LP.

During Bowie's late 1974 US tour, 23-year-old background vocalist Luther Vandross was allowed to open the show with his self-penned paean to the power of soul, 'Funky Music (Is A Part Of Me)'.* Bowie begged to be allowed to tinker with the lyric for his own purposes, presumably feeling that he needed to prove his funkiness rather than boast about it. 'Funky Music' duly became 'Fascination', with the barest of chorus rewrites, and verses that were revamped only where strictly necessary. The Vandross arrangement was also retained almost unchanged, as an utterly contemporary slice of funk, over which Bowie exhibited his range of vocal personae – from breathy confidant to sly lothario. By mid-point, he had become so dazzled by his own dexterity that he felt the need to ensure he was still feeling something. 'I like fascination', he sang, 'still – tick!', checking the box marked 'soul'.

Where Vandross was celebrating his cultural heritage, Bowie was playing an altogether more cunning game. Out of his mouth, 'Fascination' was a celebration of male lust and power. But two other connotations of the title, both of which he had recently encountered, may have influenced his choice of noun. In the book *Occult Reich*, which he had given to several friends, he had read that 'Fascination' had

---

* He recorded it in 1976 as leader of the vocal group Luther, scoring a minor hit on the US soul charts.

once been an alternative name for hypnotism, originally regarded as 'one of the occult arts . . . a spell cast by wizards'. In *City Of Night*, John Rechy's ground-breaking novel about homosexual relationships, however, 'F*A*S*C*I*N*A*T*I*O*N' shone from the front of a gay nightclub, enticing every he/she in the vicinity to fall under its spell.

[122] IT'S HARD TO BE A SAINT IN THE CITY (Springsteen)

Recorded November 1974 & September–November 1975;
Sound + Vision CD.

The second of Bowie's Bruce Springsteen covers was billed as an out-take from the *Station To Station* sessions when it was released belatedly in 1989. But he certainly attempted this song in Philadelphia during November 1974, on a night when Springsteen visited him in the studio; and many fans believed that they recognised a Tony Visconti string arrangement in the mix, alongside an Earl Slick guitar track presumably overdubbed in 1975. Yet the song wasn't one of those for which Visconti supervised orchestral accompaniment in December. The clinching argument seemed to be the unmistakable presence of Mike Garson's keyboards over the closing bars, suggesting that at least part of this track did pre-date the creation of *Station To Station*.

The finished piece emphasised the stark difference in approach between the two sets of sessions: other artists could have picked up a year-old track and continued happily in the same vein, but Bowie brought a markedly different sonic agenda to each project in the seventies. If the 1974 track had been intended as a faithful tribute to Springsteen's urban romanticism, then the addition of Slick's bombastic guitar and cacophonous drums undermined the pretensions of glamour, as if Travis Bickle from Martin Scorsese's movie *Taxi Driver* had wandered on to the set of *West Side Story*. Bowie, meanwhile, drew on a wide palette of vocal identities, imitating Springsteen at one moment, squeezing his throat into an agonising falsetto the next. The result hinted that his enthusiasm for the naïve imagery of Springsteen's work might have waned after spending more than 18 months in America.

[123] FOOT STOMPING/SHIMMY LIKE KATE (Collins/Rand; Smith/Goldsmith)

Recorded for NBC TV, November 1974; *RarestOneBowie* CD.

This medley of early sixties R&B hits would have been forgotten had Bowie not performed it during his rather alarming appearance on the NBC TV staple, *The Dick Cavett Show*, and guitarist Carlos Alomar then twisted the riff at the heart of the arrangement into the skeleton of 'Fame' [125].

'Foot Stomping' was written and recorded in 1961 by the Flares, a Los Angeles-based vocal group who had earlier scored memorable hits as the Jacks ('Why Don't You Write Me') and the Cadets ('Stranded In The Jungle'). 'Shimmy Like Kate' was a 1960 adaptation – by the Olympics, of 'Western Movies' fame – of a New Orleans jazz tune known as 'I Wish I Could Shimmy Like My Sister Kate'. The Olympics' producers took the writing credit on their single; jazzman Armand Piron originally copyrighted the tune, to the disgust of other Crescent City players who had known it for decades.

Bowie's medley found him rasping as he had with the King Bees a decade earlier, though now it was 'exhaustion' rather than inexperience to blame. On the same show, he delivered equally ragged but compelling renditions of 'Young Americans' [113] (having perfected the Elvis moves he'd been parodying in his *Love You Till Tuesday* film in 1969) and '1984' [98].

[124] ACROSS THE UNIVERSE (Lennon/McCartney)

Recorded January 1975; *Young Americans* LP.

While producer Tony Visconti was in London, supervising string overdubs and the final mixing sessions in the belief that the *Young Americans* album was complete, Bowie covertly arranged a collaboration with John Lennon in January 1975. Perhaps believing that the Beatle would only attend if he had a personal stake in the session, Bowie announced that he wished to record 'Across The Universe', a song that had caused Lennon immense difficulty in the late 1960s before being remixed by producer Phil Spector for the Beatles' *Let It Be* LP.

At a period of creative inertia, Lennon had toyed with a simple chorus around the Indian spiritual phrase, *'jai guru dev'*. Later, as he seethed silently in bed after an argument with his wife Cynthia, he began to channel his frustration into a song that celebrated the poetic muse, and the triumph of the unconscious over intellectual intention. He combined this with the Indian chorus, added a refrain to the effect (rather inaccurate, as it transpired) that nothing in his life was about to change, and emerged with a song that he proposed as a potential Beatles single. Instead, he struggled to bring his creation to life, remaining dissatisfied with the two strikingly different mixes of the song issued by the group.

Lennon can hardly have been more encouraged by Bowie's deliberately bombastic interpretation, which seemed to have been inspired by *Pussy Cats*, the gloriously ramshackle album that Lennon had recently produced for Harry Nilsson. In particular, he channelled Nilsson's ragged version of 'Many Rivers To Cross', itself intended as a tribute to Lennon's own vocal sound. Bowie double-tracked his voice for much of the song, as Lennon always did, and by the climax he was roaring in an uncanny imitation of his collaborator's more throat-searing moments. Earlier, his voice had sounded so mannered that he might have been parodying Bryan Ferry. Either way, it was a bizarre way of impressing Lennon, especially as he chose to ignore the *'jai guru dev'* refrain that was at the heart of the song. But the ex-Beatle generously heard him out, adding some distinctive guitar touches to the spaces where his spiritual mantra had once been.

A veteran of his own managerial disputes with former financial guardian Allen Klein, Lennon was able to advise Bowie during the disintegration of his relationship with Tony Defries. He subsequently wrote a song about Bowie. Its identity was never confirmed, but 'She's A Friend Of Dorothy's', an unissued Lennon composition from circa 1976/77, was an intriguing portrait of a multi-personalitied denizen of Manhattan and Hollywood high-life, with a penchant for bisexuality. 'I never really knew what he was,' Lennon recalled affectionately in 1980, 'and meeting him doesn't give you much more of a clue, because you don't know which one you're talking to.'

[125] FAME (Bowie / Alomar / Lennon)

Recorded January 1975; *Young Americans* LP.

> I wouldn't inflict fame on my worst enemy.
>   David Bowie, 2002

For all his attempts to master the sweet sound of Philadelphia soul, it was a track recorded almost by happenstance in New York that finally carried Bowie's music on to R&B radio stations, and also produced his first major US hit single.* The track emerged during a jam session at which John Lennon was present, and to which the ex-Beatle made the briefest of lyrical contributions, which was enough to win him a co-writing credit. Mick Ronson must have wondered at the injustice of life.

Numerous explanations have been offered for the creation of this track, both from participants and supposed bystanders, and they are so contradictory as to be (collectively) worthless. It is possible, of course, that while John Lennon believed they were reworking 'some Stevie Wonder middle eight', and the co-composer, Carlos Alomar, felt they were revisiting his arrangement of the R&B oldie 'Footstompin', Bowie had a Machiavellian plan to create a magnificent hybrid of rock and funk. Or, more likely, a bunch of seasoned musicians in a professional studio fell into a riff (more accurately, an interlocking collection of riffs) and hardened it until it felt tight enough to crack. They emerged with something that was right in the pocket of black American music at the beginning of 1975: a cousin of Kool & the Gang's 'Hollywood Swinging' (check the rapidly stroked rhythm guitar against Alomar's), James Brown's 'The Payback',† or the recent no. 1 hit, 'Do It (Til You're Satisfied)' by the B.T. Express. Other potential sources of inspiration included the Rascals' 1972 single 'Jungle Walk', the Average White Band's 'Pick Up The Pieces', and a highly uncharacteristic funk track,

---

* 'Fame' topped the *Billboard* Hot 100 for two weeks in late 1975. In Britain, however, where Bowie hadn't performed live for two years, it barely scraped into the Top 20, continuing a run of underwhelming sales that stretched back to 'Diamond Dogs' [107] and was only ended by a reissue of the six-year-old 'Space Oddity' [1].

† Brown brazenly used the 'Fame' backing track, or at least a close facsimile of it, as the basis of his 1975 single, 'Hot'. Bowie was prepared to sue him for plagiarism, but didn't bother when Brown's single proved to be a comparative commercial failure.

'Brighter Day', by Bowie's Beckenham friend Keith Christmas, issued shortly before 'Fame' was recorded.

So complex was the relationship between the motifs offered by the electric piano, the guitar, the bass and the drums that one could waste pages of prose or musical transcription describing how they work. But what made them function was accident and instinct, not planning – which is why it didn't matter when the drummer turned the beat around, and encouraged the bassist to mess with an entirely different pattern for a few bars; or when the acoustic guitar dropped in and out of the track at apparently random intervals. Even the vocal interjections weren't consistent. But one of them, at some point during the session, hit upon the word 'fame'.

To Bowie in January 1975, 'fame' meant not only his own stardom, and the impending lawsuits sparked by the sudden ending of his relationship with manager Tony Defries; it also meant *Fame*, a painfully expensive musical theatre project masterminded by Defries, using money from MainMan, the company built around Bowie's fame. The show was an examination of another icon, Marilyn Monroe, and it closed after exactly one night on Broadway (having already flopped off-Broadway). For MainMan, this failure was near-ruinous; for Bowie's faith in his manager, it was traumatic. Every time in 'Fame' that Bowie snapped back with a cynical retort about its pitfalls, he had his manager and his manager's epic folly in mind: 'bully for you, chilly for me', as the most often quoted line had it.

In overall effect, 'Fame' resembled Sly Stone's 1970 masterpiece 'Thank You Falettinme Be Mice Elf Again', another combination of danceable funk skeleton and viciously pointed lyrics. Like Sly's Family Stone, Bowie's record employed an array of vocal sounds – all his own, bar the occasional piped voice of Lennon. Most striking of all was the electronically mutated 'fame' that ran down three octaves, from Yoko Ono soprano to Johnny Cash basso profundo. Fame, it seemed to suggest, was an all-enveloping, artificial construction, in which it was impossible to locate the authentic human being. Which is why Bowie must have relished the idea of achieving his pinnacle of fame with a record designed to expose the emptiness at its heart. As he said of stardom in a contemporary interview, 'There's no gratification in it.'

By the time 'Fame' was recorded, Bowie had already broken off relations with Tony Defries. Legal correspondence between MainMan and

Bowie's chosen representative, Michael Lippman, took on an almost metaphysical tone, with Defries' office announcing that they were suspending 'the running of time' and Lippman telling Defries that he was 'hereby terminated effective forthwith'. While papers and writs went back and forth, Bowie was hiding out in a cheap apartment in New York, where (according to his girlfriend of the time, Ava Cherry) he claimed that he was being haunted by 'psychic vampires'. She, in turn, described him as appearing 'very upset and emotional and hysterical'. He automatically soothed himself with work, supposedly painting 200 pictures and penning three film scripts in less than two months.

It soon became apparent that, regardless of what he believed and how he felt, Bowie was legally signed to MainMan's management, and Defries had kept carefully to the terms of their original contract. His only means of escape was to make a settlement, which effectively entailed doing what Defries wanted. Bowie cried when he read the final agreement, but signed it anyway. It entitled MainMan to joint ownership with Bowie of all his work to date, allowing either party to exploit them as long as the proceeds were shared. In addition, MainMan would receive 16 per cent of Bowie's gross income from records issued and songs written between the signing of the settlement and the end of September 1982, and 5 per cent of his receipts from live appearances. The company would be entitled to those percentages in perpetuity, beyond Bowie's death.*

So Bowie moved ahead without the manager who, he was forced to concede in later years, had contributed enormously to the impact of his work on a public which had shown a strong resistance to his activities ('Space Oddity' excepted) before Defries' reign began. He considered himself scarred by the experience, but free. Every time over the next five years that he wrote a song, or made a record, however, he knew that one sixth of what he had created was owned by a man and a company he had grown to despise. It was a dilemma that was bound to spark conflict in his heart: could he still be inspired when he knew that Defries was a beneficiary of his inspiration, or would the knowledge sour every song he composed?

---

* This arrangement remained in place until the mid-nineties, when Bowie made a one-off payment to release himself from any financial obligations to Defries and MainMan.

Young Americans LP

The cover of *Young Americans* – an airbrushed studio portrait that belonged in a thirties film annual – was as deceptive about the record's contents as the photograph of Bowie in his man's dress on the sleeve of *The Man Who Sold The World*. No wonder that critics assumed the entire exercise was a pose, an attitude that Bowie appeared to validate when he described the album in 1976 as 'the definitive plastic soul record . . . the squashed remains of ethnic music as it survives in the age of Muzak rock, written and sung by a white limey'.

A year earlier, he had been more protective, claiming that *Young Americans* was the first of his records since *Hunky Dory* four years earlier that he actually enjoyed. 'Basically, I haven't liked a lot of music I've been doing the past few years,' he said. 'I forgot that I'm not a musician, and never have been. I've always wanted to be a film director, so unconsciously the two mediums got amalgamated. I was trying to put cinematic concepts into an audio staging. It doesn't work.'* Indeed, he almost callously dismissed the run of albums from *Aladdin Sane* to *David Live*: 'It wasn't a matter of liking them, it was, "Did they work or not?" Yes, they worked. They kept the trip going. Now, I'm all through with rock 'n' roll.'

That might have been more apparent had Bowie elected to release his original track selection for the album, which was then known as *Fascination*. It would have included his disco remake of 'John I'm Only Dancing (Again)' [117], alongside two epic soul ballads, 'It's Gonna Be Me' [116] and 'Who Can I Be Now?' [115]. By removing those songs in favour of his collaborations with John Lennon, Bowie not only gained a valuable publicity angle, but also distanced himself from the emotional extremities of those ballads, emerging with a record in which self-disclosure was masked by the stir caused by his daredevil mutation into a Philadelphia soul man.

* Almost inevitably, he soon changed tack, suggesting that he had written a *Young Americans* screenplay, about a non-American astronaut signed up for the US space programme. Bizarrely, he claimed that the movie would be set in 1952, five years before the launch of the first space rocket. Needless to say, nothing more was ever heard of the project.

Sound and Vision #2: *The Man Who Fell To Earth*

Bowie's manager between 1970 and 1975, Tony Defries, has commonly been portrayed in a negative light by biographers. Yet he had a keen awareness of his client's potential, and how to exploit it. 'I think he's very much a 70s artist,' Defries commented in 1972. 'Bowie, to me, is going to be the major artist of the 70s. In 1975, he will be at his peak in music. What he does after that is going to depend on what his talents are in other fields. I want to see him in film.'

Aside from Bowie's endless ideas for movie versions of his albums, the most coherent plan for a film project during the early seventies was an adaptation of Robert Heinlein's science-fiction epic, *Stranger In A Strange Land*. Bowie would, of course, have played the messianic leading role. When that project foundered (if indeed it was ever more than a Defries negotiating lever), Bowie was open to further suggestions. In 1974, he met film director Nicholas Roeg, creator of three of the most compelling films of recent years: *Performance*, *Walkabout* and *Don't Look Now*. Roeg offered Bowie the leading role in a script that had originally been intended for TV, then as a pilot for a TV series, and as a feature film only when Roeg's prestigious services were secured. The screenplay was an adaptation of *The Man Who Fell To Earth*, a 1963 novel* by Walter Tevis, which treated a science-fiction plot to the conventions and manners of literary fiction. Tevis' alien hero, Thomas Jerome Newton, travels to Earth in search of the water that can keep his own planet alive. He is defeated not just by the bureaucracy and suspicion of the Earth's people, but by his own Hamlet-like reticence and sense of futility. This was SF as existentialism, with a main character who is six foot six tall but otherwise strangely familiar: 'His frame was impossibly slight, his features delicate . . . He weighed very little, about ninety pounds.' Newton cannot comprehend the melodic complexity of classical music, but relishes the simpler tonalities of the blues. Near the end of the novel, he records an album (condensed on to a small steel ball, in an eerie precognition of the digital age) called 'poems from outer space, by "the visitor"'. This allowed the

---

* The novel was republished in a slightly amended form after the release of the film. The time frame was shifted from 1972–6 to 1985–90; the 'LP albums' became, in a mistaken glimpse into the future, 'quadrophonic albums'; a record company lost its tag as 'merchants of the really far out'; and Tevis inserted a single ironic reference to the Watergate scandal. Unlike most film novelisations, however, no attempt was made to iron out the discrepancies between the novel and the screenplay, or to add any descriptions of Bowie or the other actors.

film's designers to mock up a more conventional sleeve for an imaginary 'Bowie' LP entitled *The Visitor*.

Roeg certainly knew what he'd found in Bowie, whom he described as a 'very strange and different kind of human being. He's a great charmer, also very cold. What is attractive about him is he has no sentiment at all.' The combination of charm and *froideur* was perfect for the role. 'It required non-acting,' Bowie said of the film later, 'because the character of Newton that I played is a very cold, unexpressive person.' Bowie and/or Newton exemplified what the radical psychiatrist R.D. Laing described as the 'unembodied' self, 'always at one remove' from the outside world. That was a stance that Bowie found it hard to escape once the filming was completed.

The release of the film was shrouded in corporate intrigue: changes in distribution, enforced cuts, the employment of a psychiatrist by the film company to explain to them exactly what was happening on screen. Eventually 22 minutes were cut from the US print, to remove the most graphic sexual sequences (including a shot of Bowie's penis) and impose an orthodox narrative technique on a film that quite deliberately concentrated on episodes in Newton's earthly progress, rather than a seamless transition of plot in keeping with Hollywood tradition.

Bowie had undertaken the project on the understanding – never solidified in his contract – that he would be providing the soundtrack for the film. There were reports that he would concoct a title song, alongside other new compositions, while the film would also include 'Space Oddity' and Elton John's 'Rocket Man'. In fact, he laboured with Paul Buckmaster on a set of mostly instrumental recordings, only one of which [198] was ever released. When he discovered that he was only being asked to submit music for approval, he threw a tantrum and refused. Instead, Roeg employed the equally mercurial John Phillips, the drug-obsessed former leader of the Mamas & the Papas. In an oblique pun, the closing credits were accompanied by Artie Shaw's recording of the standard tune 'Stardust': the sole concession in the film to Bowie's 'real' identity. Freed from the responsibility for the soundtrack, Bowie was free to concentrate on his next album, whilst exploring the farthest limits of his own 'unembodied' psyche.

The Unmaking of a Star #3: Cocaine and the Kabbalah

> I just wish Dave would get himself sorted fucking out. He's totally
> confused, that lad . . . I just wish he could be in this room, right
> now, sat here, so I could kick some sense into him.
>   Mick Ronson, 1975

Cocaine was the fuel of the music industry in the seventies. Audiences
were still more likely to have smoked dope, or swallowed the 'downers'
known as Mandrax in Britain and Quaaludes in the USA. Rock stars in
search of a cure for the burdening necessity of sleep could rely on the
artificial energy of amphetamines (with the attendant risk of psychosis).
Where casual sex and the dance floor collided, there was likely to be
amyl nitrate or, in America, PCP (alias angel dust). But the drug that kept
rock 'n' roll buzzing, sealing deals, deadening sensibilities and providing a
false sense of bravado and creative achievement, was cocaine. Bowie's
arrival in America in 1974 coincided neatly with the rapid growth of the
cocaine-producing industry in Colombia, which within two years had
corrupted that nation's political structure to such an extent that the
most notorious traffickers (such as Pablo Escobar Gaviria) were effectively beyond prosecution. Like heroin at the start of the decade, cocaine
flooded into America, despite the efforts of federal law-enforcement
agencies to stem the tide.

Bowie was, and has been, more candid about his drug use during this
period than most of his contemporaries, and various associates have fleshed
out the picture. 'I've had short flirtations with smack and things,' he told
Cameron Crowe in 1975, 'but it was only for the mystery and the enigma. I
like fast drugs. I hate anything that slows me down.' So open was his drug
use that the normally bland British pop newspaper *Record Mirror* felt safe
in 1975 to describe Bowie as 'old vacuum-cleaner nose'. His girlfriend in
1974/75, Ava Cherry, recounted that 'David has an extreme personality, so
his capacity [for cocaine] was much greater than anyone else's.' 'I'd found
a soulmate in this drug,' Bowie told Paul Du Noyer in 2002. 'Well, speed
[amphetamines] as well, actually. The combination.' The drugs scarred his
personal relationships, twisted his view of himself and the world, and sometimes delayed recording sessions, as Bowie waited for his dealer to arrive.
As live tapes from 1974 demonstrated, they also had a profound effect on

his vocal range. Yet the effect on his creativity was minimal: cocaine took its toll on his internal logic, not his abilities to make music.

'Give cocaine to a man already wise,' wrote occultist Aleister Crowley in 1917, '[and] if he be really master of himself, it will do him no harm. Alas! the power of the drug diminishes with fearful pace. The doses wax; the pleasures wane. Side-issues, invisible at first, arise; they are like devils with flaming pitchforks in their hands.' Bowie's 'side-issues' were rooted in his unsteady sense of identity; he talked later of being haunted by his various characters, who were threatening him with psychological oblivion. When he described the Thin White Duke of 'Station To Station', he was effectively condemning himself: 'A very Aryan, fascist-type; a would-be romantic with absolutely no emotion at all but who spouted a lot of neo-romance.' Michael Lippman, Bowie's manager during 1975, said his client 'can be very charming and friendly, and at the same time he can be very cold and self-centred'. Bowie, he added, wanted to rule the world.

It was not entirely helpful that a man who was bordering on cocaine psychosis should choose to immerse himself in the occult enquiries that had exerted a more intellectual fascination over him five years earlier. The sense that his soul was at stake was exacerbated by the company he kept in New York at the start of 1975: Led Zeppelin guitarist Jimmy Page, a fellow Crowley aficionado; and occult film-maker Kenneth Anger. In March that year, he moved to Los Angeles, where he was reported to be drawing pentagrams on the wall, experimenting with the pack of Tarot cards that Crowley had created, chanting spells, making hexes, and testing and investigating the powers of the devil against those of the Jewish mystical system, the Kabbalah. He managed to survive the filming of *The Man Who Fell To Earth* by assuming the emotionally removed traits of his character in the movie. But back in California, as he tried to assemble a soundtrack for the film and also create the *Station To Station* album, he slipped back into a state of extreme instability. Michael Lippman remembered 'dramatically erratic behaviour' on Bowie's part. 'Everywhere I looked,' the singer explained to Angus MacKinnon in 1980, 'demons of the future [were] on the battlegrounds of one's emotional plane.'

That was the emotional landscape against which he wrote the songs on *Station To Station*: in retrospect, it is surprising that the results were not more extreme. By the time the album was completed, Bowie was suffering severe, sometimes nearly continuous hallucinations, which ensured (perhaps fortunately) that his memories of this period remain sketchy. The impact on those around him was more immediate; when the singer left the Lippmans' residence at the end of December (and quickly launched a lawsuit against his recent protector), his traumatised manager could only express relief, coupled with fear at what might happen next. Bowie attributed his survival to an unnamed friend, who 'pulled me off the settee one day, stood me in front of the mirror and said, "I'm walking out of your life because you're not worth the effort"'. This jolted Bowie enough to propel him through a major tour, still flirting with the worst of his curses, before he chose quite deliberately to crash-land in Berlin, and offload all his burdens, nightmare by painful nightmare.

[126] STATION TO STATION (Bowie)

Recorded September–November 1975; *Station To Station* LP.

Much of *The Man Who Fell To Earth* was filmed in Albuquerque – the so-called 'Duke city'. And it was there that David Bowie, who was unmistakably thin, and white, began to write a book of short stories entitled *The Return of the Thin White Duke*. It was, he explained, 'partly autobiographical, mostly fiction, with a deal of magic in it'. Simultaneously, he was telling journalist Cameron Crowe: 'I've decided to write my autobiography as a way of life. It may be a series of books.' Or, as printed in *Rolling Stone* magazine at the time, it might be the briefest and most compressed of autobiographical fragments, which suggested he would have struggled to extend the entire narrative of his life beyond a thousand words.

Instead the Thin White Duke returned in this song, which it would be easy to assume must therefore have been autobiographical. But Bowie's landscape was more oblique than that: not least because, in the tradition of 'The Bewlay Brothers' [51], this was a song with lyrics that suggested more than they revealed, as if they had been written in a strictly personal code – an occult language, then, in every sense of the adjective.

Even if Bowie saw himself as the Thin White Duke, another duke was at the heart of the action: Prospero, the rightful Duke of Milan, exiled on an island in Shakespeare's *The Tempest*. It is Prospero whom

Bowie misquotes in the song, Shakespeare's original line being: 'We are such stuff as dreams are made on.' (The same speech refers, as does Bowie, to 'thin air'.) Prospero, like Bowie's Duke, is a master of magic, who can command the elements while 'lost in my [magic] circle'. And he can also cast a spell – throwing darts,* perhaps – over lovers' eyes, as he does with his daughter Miranda and her paramour, Ferdinand, during the course of the play.

Shakespeare, however, was only one source for a song rich in borrowed imagery. This ranged from the vaguely ridiculous (compare Bowie's drinking stanza to the chorus from *The Student Prince* made famous by Mario Lanza) to the deliberately hidden (or occult). Only the keenest of occult scholars would have recognised *White Stains* as the title of a slim volume of verse by Aleister Crowley (Bowie may have owned a copy as early as 1969, as there were apparent allusions to Crowley's poem 'Contra Conjugium TTB' in 'Cygnet Committee' [8]). Likewise, few amongst Bowie's audience in 1976 would have been familiar with the Jewish mystical system of the Kabbalah, with its septhiroth (or stations, if you like) separating Kether (the realm of spiritual transcendence; the Crown of Creation, as the rock band Jefferson Airplane put it) from Malkuth (the conduit for divine revelation to reach the physical world). 'All the references within the piece are to do with the Kabbalah,' Bowie claimed in 1997, not entirely accurately. Then there was the strange reference to the European canon (or, at a stretch, 'cannon'), which was a pretentious way of summarising Bowie's interest in Brechtian theatre and Kraftwerk; and the final choruses of the song, which (canon aside) seemed to offer an account of all-powerful love (nature unknown).

With that, the lyrics came full circle, from the Duke's command over lovers to the lovers' loss of control over themselves. In a song this esoteric, it may or may not be significant that Aleister Crowley's pack of Tarot cards represented Art and Lovers as complementary icons; that a dart, or arrow, was a symbol of direction revealing the dynamic of the True Will; that the Kabbalistic Tree of Life referred to a 'heavenly bow and arrow' . . . almost every line could be glossed

* There is a long tradition of darts, or arrows, being used as a weapon in combat between deities, or between God and the devil: see, for example, St Paul's Epistle to the Ephesians (6:16), in which he offers 'the shield of faith' to 'quench all the fiery darts of the wicked one'.

and interpreted, without coming any closer to Bowie's intentions.

Take a step back, and consider the basic themes: magic, and the arts of legendary magicians, fictional and otherwise; the Kabbalah's mystical account of progress from Kether to Malkuth; love; cocaine. Just as 'Quicksand' [50] offered a catalogue* of avenues open to the inquisitive imagination of David Bowie circa 1971, so 'Station To Station' presented a more confused (because Bowie was more confused) medley of the themes that were haunting his nightmares in the final weeks of 1975. Yet he could surely not have expected his fans to deduce more from the lyrics than that he had invented a new character, called the Thin White Duke, who took cocaine.

What rescued 'Station To Station' from utter obscurity and his audience from alienation was the music. The song comprised a complex arrangement of fragments in the vein of a progressive rock suite (imagine something by early-seventies Genesis or mid-seventies Jethro Tull), connected by the sonic impact of Bowie's remarkable 1975/76 band, and the mannered flexibility of his voice. Like the howls of wind that opened Van Der Graaf Generator's 'Darkness (11/11)' a few years earlier, the eerie train effects that signalled the beginning of the *Station To Station* album were both symbolic and visceral. The train (created by guitar with flangers/phaser and delay effects) ran from right to left across the stereo divide before disappearing into a tunnel with a howl of feedback. Gradually the band awoke: percussion knocking, a keyboard stabbing repeated chords in and out of key, bass, drums, a second keyboard, and finally a gargantuan atonal guitar riff (played by Bowie and Earl Slick with syncopated accents across three bars in 4/4 and one in 2/4). This train was no express, bound for glory; its lumbering progress suggested a force too evil to stop.

More than three minutes after the album began, Bowie finally made his entrance alongside the Duke, still unwilling to settle comfortably into a recognisable key signature. The uneasy relationship between the two identities was mirrored by the way in which their voices were sometimes in orthodox harmony, sometimes in unison, sometimes

---

* The missing link between these two songs, in thematic terms, was provided by an artist in whose work Bowie had immersed himself around 1974: Peter Hammill. '(In The) Black Room' from his 1973 album *Chameleon In The Shadow Of The Night* was preoccupied with various adventures of the spirit, from the Tarot and religious belief to psychedelic drugs.

(as when surveying the trail from Kether to Malkuth) a whole octave apart. Bowie announced his arrival in double-voice, one echoed and tired, the other almost hysterical, as if under attack from the wicked one's fiery darts.

A thud of drums signalled a change, of tempo, key (now strictly orthodox) and intentions: Bowie had entered the landscape of mountains and sunbirds, prodded by a burbling electric guitar. After three lines (accompanying the drinking episode) built around the slowest of turnarounds (like a train that had reached the end of its journey), there was finally the joyous relief of cocaine, and love. Here was Bowie's first nod of recognition to the so-called 'motorik' sound of Krautrock, as the ominous Wagnerian strains of the early segments of the song were succeeded by the propulsive dance rhythms of the finale. Only a churl would have worried that the theme of this cathartic moment was that it was too late – suggesting that the spiritual journey might not lead to salvation.

[127] GOLDEN YEARS (Bowie)

Recorded September–November 1975; single & *Station To Station* LP.

In isolation, this was Bowie's most perfect exhibition of disco music as an art form – a tightly controlled, intensely hypnotic weave of electronic certainty and human vulnerability. At its heart was a simple two-chord* (F♯E) groove reminiscent, in very different circumstances, of 'Aladdin Sane' [70]. In keeping with the restlessness of the lyric, however, the song was actually set in the key of B major, never actually arriving at its root chord – although one of the two guitar riffs that shaped the groove was solidly based there. The magical ingredients were percussive: the rattling of sticks against the hi-hat cymbal from the start, the startling clack of woodblocks, the sudden drum fills. Bowie straddled all these elements with consummate ease, channelling the spirit of Elvis Presley (to whom he sent a tape of the song) in the verses, then touching a haughtier, more strident tone in the chorus.

---

* Carlos Alomar created a three-chord riff out of those two majors in the left-hand channel, voicing his F♯ with a barre C chord on the 6th fret before moving to the more predictable barre E chord on the 2nd.

Seductive and knowing, he sounded like the most arrogant and yet attentive of lovers, promising a full millennium of fidelity. But in the wake of the occult excursion of 'Station To Station' [126], 'Golden Years' began to display another face. 'Invoke often', wrote Aleister Crowley of the holy names, and in his belief system, the 'higher self' was represented by the Holy Guardian Angel. Sure enough, it was an 'Angel' that Bowie invoked throughout the song, each time cloaking the word in an otherworldly echo. In this light, the most innocent of lines began to assume menacing proportions: the thousand years sounded Hitlerian; the instruction to his love to rise suggested that he / she was actually dead. No wonder that the supposedly pure message of love carried a darker (literally) subtext: 'run for the shadows', Bowie insisted repeatedly, as if only in darkness could he feel truly safe.

[128] WORD ON A WING (Bowie)

Recorded September–November 1975; *Station To Station* LP.

Context was all in the first half of *Station To Station*: after two flir-tations with darkness, Bowie seemed to utter a plaintive cry to the Christian God, and to Jesus, the 'sweet name' of his childhood prayers, for salvation. Three years later, Bob Dylan's apparent 'conversion' to evangelical Christianity sparked unease and contempt from many of his followers. Bowie's equally stark avowal of faith – in equally dire personal circumstances – caused barely a whisper.

In part that was because few of Bowie's fans looked to him for spiritual guidance, although he had been far more consistently vocal about matters metaphysical (and socio-political, for that matter) than Dylan. Only when he knelt to the ground during the Freddie Mercury tribute concert in 1992 to recite the Lord's Prayer before a packed Wembley Stadium, and a global television audience, did his religious conduct arouse any comment. There was also a profound distinction of tone: where Dylan hectored his audience, and the wider society beyond, Bowie offered an intimate relationship with the divine spirit, part confession, part conversation, part plea for help.

Typically, he was ambiguous about his motives. He claimed in a 1976 interview that he had written the song 'when I felt very much at peace with the world. I had established my own environment with

my own people for the first time . . . What better way can a man give
thanks for achieving something that he had dreamed of achieving,
than doing it with a hymn?' Four years later, his explanation was very
different: 'There were days of such psychological terror when making
[*The Man Who Fell To Earth*] . . . It was the first time I'd really thought
seriously about Christ and God in any depth, and "Word On A Wing"
was a protection. It came as a complete revolt against elements that
I found in the film.'

'Word On A Wing' was cleverly placed on the (vinyl) album,
opposite the similarly titled 'Wild Is The Wind' [131] – a stark contrast
between romantic love and religious devotion, each delivered with
unshakeable conviction. Both conveyed loss of control, to the extremes
of passion and despair; but both were the product of consummate
professionalism. Arguably Bowie has never sounded more desolate on
record than when he almost cried the words 'Oh Lord', late in this
song, twisting the first syllable in pain, holding tight to the second
in hope. But his absolutely precise phrasing proved how carefully
he'd planned the moment: this was an accounting of the soul, not a
spontaneous outburst from its depths. That attention to detail was
evident throughout his performance, in the way that his voice was
mixed right in the listener's ear, without a trace of echo or artifice,
in the opening verse; then echoed as if from the heart of a church as
he serenaded the sweet angel of salvation; and finally left harsh and
strident as he offered his prayer. To reinforce the appropriate mood,
there was the synthesised sound of a church organ – and then, as the
track died away, the electronic 'voice' of an 'Ave Maria', the symbol
of the Catholic mass.

For once, Bowie's lyrics disavowed his natural inclination for metamorphosis. Like 'Station To Station' [126] and 'TVC15' [129], however,
'Word On A Wing' was awash with changes – of tone, of production,
of musical structure. It repeated the trick of 'Golden Years' by opening
with the dominant chord of the key of B major (on synthesiser),
though this time he swiftly resolved matters in a hesitant piano motif.
Thereafter he utilised as wide a palette of instrumental textures as of
vocal settings, with the tension of a howling guitar buried deep in the
mix like a hidden emotion, while vibes and acoustic guitar signalled
humanity. What remained in the mind, though, was the prayer –
and the taint of the grand illusion which, like the class interests that

united warring nations in Jean Renoir's thirties film of the same title, threatened to be more enduring than any hope of salvation.

The religious yearning of 'Word On A Wing' was embodied in a gold cross that Bowie was given by his then manager Michael Lippman during the *Station To Station* sessions. 'He also asked to have a mezuzah up in his room,' Lippman recalled, referring to the scriptural parchment that orthodox Jews often wear around their neck, or fix to a doorpost, 'because of his revival and belief in religion, and because he felt that it would create more security for himself.' Bowie admitted in 1977 that 'I'd been pretty godless for a few years. [My faith] became part of a new positive frame of mine that I have about trying to re-establish my own identity for myself – for my own sanity . . . It's part of coming down from the high mountain of fabrication.'

Bowie was hardly alone amongst his generation in searching for a credible sense of self amidst the consolations of religion. The seventies was an era of spiritual hope and also self-deception, in which those who had lost faith in the political and social certainties of the sixties reached out for the comfort of a more arcane belief system. Besides the tiny Church of Satan in California, former hippies were attracted by ISKCON, the International Society for Krishna Consciousness, financially supported by ex-Beatle George Harrison but thrown into confusion in 1977 by the death of its leader, Swami Prabhupada. Harrison's seventies songs were rich in Krishna terminology, alongside concepts he had learned from another former guru, Maharishi Mahesh Yogi. Maharishi's brand of transcendental meditation famously won over the Beatles and the Beach Boys in 1967; within five years, he had launched a Meditation University in Iowa, and formulated a World Plan to carry his philosophy around the world.

Equally ambitious was the Reverend Sun Myung Moon, who formed the Unification Church (colloquially known as the Moonies) in 1954, and who brought it to America in 1972, from where he sent missionaries around the world. So too did the young Guru Maharaj Gi, who declared his leadership of the Divine Light Mission at the age of eight, after his father's death. He staged a heavily hyped spiritual gathering in the enormous Houston Astrodome in 1973, before scandal eroded his church's reputation.

While attendance at traditional Anglican services dipped, more contemporary Christian sects began to flourish during the seventies, promoting the so-called 'Jesus revolution'. Among them were the Jesus Movement, the Jesus Army and, more controversially, the Children of God. This last group adopted as many identities as Bowie across the decade, among them Teens for Christ, Revolutionaries for Jesus and the Jesus Children (referenced in a Stevie Wonder song). Wonder wasn't the only musician intrigued by their message: Fleetwood Mac guitarist Jeremy Spencer abandoned his career to follow the sect in 1971. For a year or two the Children of God infiltrated the last bastions of the counter-culture with their orange Jesus stickers and Jesus comics. Then their avowedly celibate leader was found to have taken a second wife, and also sampled the delights of other members' spouses. By 1978, he was encouraging young women known as God's Whores to practise Flirty Fishing, using their charms to entice gullible young men to join the cause. More conventionally minded members of the Children of God had already broken away to form the less scandalous Family of Love.

While Jehovah's Witnesses vainly awaited the end of the world, apparently scheduled for 1975, other groupings watched for flying saucers to arrive and carry the faithful few to heaven on another planet. The Scientologists followed an equally mysterious doctrine, written by science-fiction novelist L. Ron Hubbard, whose first novel (*Slan*) assumed the imminent arrival of his own brand of *Homo superior*, 'a new race of supermen' who represented 'the next evolutionary step'. Bowie might have recognised the pervasive influence of Friedrich Nietzsche. Of all the religions and cults active in the seventies, however, none might have amused or appalled Bowie more than the Church of All Worlds. It based its philosophy on another SF novel: Robert Heinlein's *Stranger in a Strange Land*, a film adaptation of which Bowie was rumoured to be considering in 1973. What Bowie called 'the high mountain of fabrication' stood tall and proud throughout this decade.

[129] **TVC15** (Bowie)

Recorded September–November 1975; *Station To Station* LP.

Few (vinyl) sides in Bowie's catalogue could rival the wilful eclecticism of the second half of *Station To Station*. It was as if he had thrown the entire post-war history of popular music into a bag, and juxta-posed elements at random – the aural equivalent of the Burroughs/Gysin cut-up technique, perhaps. 'TVC15' exemplified that method in miniature, deploying a distinct sound picture for each section of the song. What opened like a New Orleans piano 12-bar blues from the early fifties (a blend between Huey Smith's 'Rockin' Pneumonia' and Professor Longhair's 'Hey Now Baby', seasoned with the Climax Blues Band's recently released 'Loosen Up') was soon deluged with two layers of echoed guitar, a synthesised siren, and a saxophone burping as if it wanted to become a tuba. Amidst that joyous collision of sound, Bowie* reeled off a nonsense tale of a carnivorous television – *Attack Of The Killer TV* if it had been a 1953 B-movie, perhaps. The idea was a joke, of course, but it chimed with the counter-culture's distrust of the media, and consumer culture: the situation lamented by the philosopher Herbert Marcuse in *One Dimensional Man*, whereby 'people [only] recognise themselves in their commodities; they find their soul in their automobile, hi-fi set, split-level home, kitchen equipment'.

While the New Orleans piano provided continuity, the song mutated into a two-word interlude ('transition/transmission') that hinted at significance but was simply an evocative use of wordplay. And then there was a deliciously playful chorus, in the tradition of the Beach Boys' *Smile* project, augmented with handclaps, guitars pretending that they were cellos, and a saxophone in a world of its own, while more and more Bowies were added to the mix. By the end, all these elements seemed to be locked into a pattern, as if machines had taken over a discotheque.

[130] STAY (Bowie)

Recorded September–November 1975; *Station To Station* LP.

This was a song about misunderstanding and indecision, clouded by chemical influence. 'That was recorded very much in our cocaine frenzy,' Carlos Alomar told Bowie biographer David Buckley. Yet it

---

* His unadorned vocal, briefly harmonised at the end of each verse, was later joined by a humming chorale, and an occasional interjection of what sounded like 'chew', but was more likely 'Jim', in honour of Jim Osterberg – Iggy Pop – who had provided him with the song's scenario.

was performed with utter conviction, and a staggering command of dynamics. There was effortless self-confidence in the way that Earl Slick's four-bar guitar riff was able to pause twice for two whole beats, to let the echo resound across the speakers. Gradually the other instruments entered: the thud of kick drum and bass guitar; synth strings and percussion; another howling guitar from Slick, answered by more gentle motifs from Carlos Alomar – each provoking a subtle rearrangement of the rhythm, until the band had settled into a jerky, almost mechanical, ritual of funk. (The slow build-up of sound harked back to cinematic soul epics such as the Temptations' 'Papa Was A Rolling Stone' and Isaac Hayes' 'Theme From *Shaft*' three years earlier.) Slick carried the uniform shape of a 9th chord up and down the fretboard for the verse, before dropping out and letting Dennis Davis' drums shoot adrenalin into Bowie's ennui. After drifting through the verses in double-tracked unison, his voice broke into two parts for the chorus, restrained in the lower register, almost histrionic an octave higher. And then the band was set free, with layers of guitars piled up beneath Slick's solo, each offering a subtly different variant on the main theme.

[131] WILD IS THE WIND (Tiomkin/Washington)

Recorded September–November 1975; *Station To Station* LP.

Such was the power of Bowie's international following by 1976 that he was able to indulge himself with material that would have crippled his career a decade earlier. Certainly his audience would have been unlikely to remember this theme song from a 1957 movie melodrama, sung by Johnny Mathis* with schmaltzy reverence. Unlike Bowie, they might also have been unfamiliar with Nina Simone's reinvention of the song as an eerily placid investigation of romantic hypnosis. It appeared on her 1959 LP *At Town Hall*; then again (in a more extended live rendition from 1964) as the title track of a 1966 album. It was the latter that Bowie adopted as his template, rendering a precise imitation of many of Simone's mannerisms and choices of phrasing, before

---

* The *Miami Herald* review of a Bowie concert in November 1972 noted that his voice 'has an original timbre, so far as rock is concerned, though it derives from the Beatles and possibly Johnny Mathis'.

allowing himself off the emotional leash, and up to an ecstatic high B in the finale.

Without stretching his persona in the slightest, it was easy for Bowie to prey on the more ethereal elements of Simone's performance, and extend them into a gothic display of quite deliberate affectation. His voice progressed from almost total detachment through an extravagant display of quivering vibrato to the verge of hysterical despair, all without losing control for a second. At the end of an album in which sonic distortion was the norm, there was something unsettling about an arrangement built around gentle strokes from Carlos Alomar's electric guitar, with only the occasional knocking of woodblocks to disturb the mood. When drummer Dennis Davis finally provided emotional release with a four-bar gallop around his kit, topped with an orgiastic cymbal crash, the intrusion was almost shocking.

Station To Station LP

'I really, honestly and truly, don't know how much longer my albums will sell,' Bowie admitted a few weeks after signing his severance agreement with Tony Defries. 'I think they're going to get more diversified, more extreme and radical right along with my writing. And I really don't give a shit.' It would have been understandable if Bowie had reacted to the demands of his settlement by vowing not to record until it expired in 1982; or perhaps set himself to create the most uncommercial material imaginable, to ensure that Defries would effectively be earning 16 per cent of nothing from his work. Instead, he was able to make music that was totally uncompromising, utterly unlike anything he had recorded to date, and yet unexpectedly commercial. Indeed, *Station To Station* charted higher (no. 3) on the US album charts than any of his previous work: in those terms, at least, it remains the most successful album of his career in North America.

In subsequent decades, Bowie would declare himself unable to recall the creation of the album: 'I have serious problems about that year or two. I can't remember how I felt.' His memory of the subsequent tour survived until 1980, at least, when he declared: 'I was out of my mind totally, completely crazed.' It was, he summarised in 1997, 'a miserable time to live through', promoting an album that he now heard 'as a piece of work by an entirely different person'. Yet as the record appeared, he visualised it in similar terms to those he'd applied to *Young Americans* a year earlier: '*Station To Station* is probably the first album where I've got down to what I really think.' In which case, his mind was a mess of spiritual contradictions, defiant bombast, and unashamed romanticism.

The other participants in the creative process remembered *Station To Station* in terms that were almost symbolic of the seventies Bowie: he arrived with melodic fragments and vague concepts instead of finished songs, then constantly changed what he had recorded, rewriting lyrics even when tracks were supposedly complete. Yet unlike albums such as *Lodger* and *Scary Monsters*, where the fragmentary nature of the compositions was allowed to stand, he succeeded on this record in unifying and focusing his vision for each song, just as he had (in a very different milieu) on *Hunky Dory* and *Ziggy Stardust*.

As evidence that, no matter how scattered his brain cells by emotional dislocation and chemical imbalance, he could still persuade them to work at some level of co-ordination, his 1976 world tour translated that focus into performances of almost mesmeric intensity. He claimed that he was only performing for the money: 'This time I'm going to make some. I think I deserve it, don't you?' But there was clearly a more personal agenda in play, or else he would not have challenged his audience so directly. Beyond his diehard fans, he was now filling large arenas – the venues he'd left half-empty in 1972 and 1974 – in the expectation of an evening of hedonistic rock/disco music in the vein of his most recent hits, 'Fame' [125] and 'Golden Years' [127]. Instead, as he had done with the sound collage that preceded the *Diamond Dogs* concerts in 1974, Bowie consciously challenged the audience's desires. First, they had to listen to an extensive portion of Kraftwerk's catalogue before the show began – not with a radio anthem but with a screening of Dali and Buñuel's 1929 surrealist masterpiece *Un Chien Andalou*. Notoriously, the film includes a scene in which an eyeball is cut open with a razor; it was greeted in some American venues with laughter, and in others by outrage so vocal that, on at least one occasion, Bowie had to abandon the screening and hastily take to the stage. Bowie's experimentation didn't end with the visual non sequiturs and unsettling imagery of the surrealists; his performance was staged under extreme white lighting* in honour of the way in which Bertolt Brecht's plays were presented by the Staatstheater in Berlin during the late

---

* There was another potential source for Bowie's fascination with white light: Alice Bailey's book, *A Treatise on White Magic*, which suggested White Light (her capitals) as a source of transcendence and healing.

twenties. Surrealism on film; expressionist lighting: Bowie explained that 'I'm trying to get over the idea of the European movement' (or canon). Or, as he reflected in 1989, there were 'a bunch of lights, but we didn't do anything. I walked about rather haughtily.' He sang and spoke haughtily, as well, with consequences that would soon become apparent.

Fascism: Turn to the Right

In October 1973, at the height of the glam-rock boom, the ITV network broadcast a documentary entitled *The Messengers*. It was advertised as follows: 'Two superstars of their time. Marc Bolan, idol of today's youth, and Adolf Hitler, hero of a revitalised nation a generation ago. Two people, totally different but both subject to mass adulation.' If Bowie watched the programme – and how could he have resisted the coupling of a rival with the century's most notorious dictator? – one hopes that he would have found the comparison crass, or amusing, or ridiculous. Or is it possible that it planted a seed that would only sprout two years later?

By the summer of 1975, Bowie was in America, wrestling with demons literal and metaphorical, and conjuring with the perilous juxtaposition of mind-altering drugs and occult experimentation. He was reading avidly about magic and religion, while dipping into a travelling library of volumes about the Third Reich. He was fascinated by the way in which the Nazis had transformed an ancient religious symbol, the swastika, into something that the world would remember as a badge of evil; and by their quest* for the Holy Grail of Arthurian legend. To assuage his various obsessions, he bought multiple copies of *Occult Reich*, a thin and mildly sensationalist account of the Hitler regime's dabbling with mythology and the super-natural, which he handed out to friends and strangers. The book offered a panorama of rumour and suggestion, each brief chapter providing enticing details of such themes as Hitler's ability to predict the future; the power of hypnosis, otherwise known as 'fascination' [121]; Kirlian photography and 'bio-plasmic energy' (a Bowie passion; he was given a Kirlian camera by a US academic); the origins of the Nazi salute in the nineteenth-century

---

* A quest which, it transpires, was the invention of seventies writers: although SS leader Heinrich Himmler did encourage the Ahnenerbe group to investigate the prehistoric origins of the Aryan race, this did not entail a search for a secret/symbol that might bring the Nazis supernatural power, despite what Indiana Jones might believe.

rituals of the Hermetic Order of the Golden Dawn; Hitler's insistence on working by night and sleeping by day (with which Bowie could have empathised); numerology (a subject of enduring interest to Bowie at this point); the links between Tibetan Buddhism and the Nazis; and Hitler's observations on the Nietzschean concept of the 'superman'. This was, in other words, an anthology of speculation about subjects in which Bowie had a peculiar interest, almost as if it had been designed with his fevered imagination in mind.

In addition, Bowie was attempting to win any one of a number of film roles that all, coincidentally, required him to play a Nazi; and speaking all too freely to journalists while under the influence of an exotic blend of chemicals. Not having set foot in Britain for more than a year, he had decided he was an expert about the country's political, social and economic ills – which were sufficiently alarming to have inspired a number of covert right-wing groups to plan a coup against a government that they believed (quite erroneously) was laden down with Communist sympathisers. These small organisations included GB75, led by Colonel David Stirling; Civic Assistance, headed by General Sir Walter Walker; and the less militaristic National Association for Freedom. In vastly different ways, they sought to impose repressive control on a nation that, they complained, was heading for ruin. Britain's 'official' fascist political parties had been undermined for years by internal feuding and incompetent organisation. But the apparent backing for their cause from senior military officers encouraged the National Front to regroup, and gain at least 10 per cent of the vote in many areas during the 1976 local elections.

This was the arena in which Bowie chose to plant his own rather bedraggled flag, based on a cocktail of ill-digested reading and cocaine. He uttered similar phrases in several interviews during late 1975 and early 1976: 'I could have been Hitler in England . . . England's in such a sorry state . . . You've got to have an extreme right front come up and sweep everything off its feet and tidy everything up . . . I believe very strongly in fascism . . . Adolf Hitler was one of the first rock stars.' It did not help that he had set out on his 1976 world tour with a visual identity – sculpted cheeks, dyed hair swept back across his head, stern black costume – that encapsulated Hitler's vision of the perfect Aryan icon. Nor that he was rumoured to have been photographed outside Hitler's bunker in Berlin, giving a Nazi salute. Nor that when he returned to Britain on 2 May 1976, he stood up in the back of a limousine and was caught by a photographer apparently giving his followers that same salute. This he denied most vehemently, and quite justly: the picture was a split-second image of an arm in motion, not raised to greet the Nazi hordes. Fans responded in kind at the Wembley Arena shows that followed, as if Bowie really were the dictator he had fantasised about in his interviews.

After Eric Clapton stood on stage in Birmingham a few weeks later and delivered what was widely interpreted as a racist rant (for which he apologised in mealy-mouthed fashion), and a riot broke out at the Notting Hill Carnival between black partygoers and white police, a group of activists formed an ad hoc organisation called Rock Against Racism. Its first newsletter included a potent photographic montage, in the tradition of Heartfield and Grosz's satirical ridiculing of the Nazi leaders. Lined up as if they were sharing a stage were the unmistakable figures of Adolf Hitler, maverick Tory politician and racial controversialist Enoch Powell – and David Bowie. Soon the Musicians' Union was debating Bowie's 'fascist' remarks, and threatening to sanction or ban any members who uttered similar comments in the future. Meanwhile, the leaders of the National Front welcomed him as a convert to their cause, a theme they were still pursuing well into the eighties. Bowie later claimed that he had deliberately fashioned his 1976 'identity', the Thin White Duke, as a fascist: 'the best way to fight an evil force is to caricature it'. Even more ludicrously, he tried to argue that his naïve intervention in British politics 'did some good because, for the first time, it brought to the fore that the National Front are a fascist party. Until then the National Front were nice and polite.' At least he dismissed fascism as 'an idiot's dream', though without acknowledging the true identity of the idiot in question.

[132] SISTER MIDNIGHT (Bowie/Alomar/Pop)

Performed live 1976; unreleased by Bowie.

Like 'Golden Years' [127], 'Sister Midnight' – in all its incarnations – was built around a two-semitone slide: up and down for the introduction, down and back up for the verse. It emerged as the lead track of Iggy Pop's *The Idiot*, and then in disguise as the framework for 'Red Money' [173] on *Lodger*. But first it was prepared for, and occasionally performed during, Bowie's *Station To Station* tour in 1976. In rehearsal, it was arguably his purest engagement with funk, slapped through its repeated chord change by a fretless electric bass. Bowie treated it as a vocal gallery, showing off his clipped voice, his falsetto, his croon, even a quasi-sexual series of groans. The identity of 'Sister Midnight' was irrelevant: she was merely a cipher, who could send him soaring to the Moon or falling to Earth (like the spaceman he had recently played on celluloid) without either journey seeming to register on his emotions.

By the time it reached the stage, something of the track's simplicity had been lost, and 'Sister Midnight' quickly vanished from Bowie's repertoire. It took a new set of lyrics, and a less cluttered attitude, both supplied by Iggy Pop, for the song to regain its relentless momentum.

The Actor and the Idiot: Bowie and Iggy

Iggy Pop and Lou Reed were the two touchstones of Bowie's rock sensibility in the early seventies. If Reed represented the Warhol milieu, New York cool and lyrical precision, Pop was raw Detroit muscle, Dionysus to Reed's Apollo: untutored, stumbling, an accidental genius, an idiot savant.

Most of the shambling qualities that Bowie admired in his theoretical Iggy Pop were the product of drugs. During Bowie's 1972 US tour, another Iggy was sometimes visible: smart, articulate, even erudite. But his unpredictability made it impossible for the two men to maintain a relationship longer than Bowie required to mix Iggy's third album with the Stooges, *Raw Power*. Bowie's manager, Tony Defries, added the Stooges to his roster in 1972, but cancelled their weekly retainer when it became obvious that it was supplying stimulants, not provisions.

Just over two years later, Iggy was in a Los Angeles mental hospital, and Bowie visited him bearing the gift of cocaine. Within a few weeks, they were sharing a recording studio, and Bowie had penned a screenplay in which Pop could star. Then their sessions collapsed, and Bowie lamented: 'He'll never make it to the recording studios in time. Iggy's doomed.'

Their paths inevitably crossed during Bowie's 1976 US tour, at which point Pop became a solid member of his entourage. They journeyed together to Russia, and were photographed in Moscow's Red Square. When Bowie had fulfilled his European tour dates, the pair settled at the Chateau d'Herouville near Paris with the rhythm section from his live band.

There they recorded the backing tracks for around ten songs, before adding Iggy's vocals in Munich – and then mixing the results in Berlin, where Bowie and Pop rented an apartment. Bowie had entered the studio hoping that they might emerge with a single of 'Sister Midnight' [132]; instead, they completed an album, *The Idiot*, which Pop described as 'a cross between James Brown and Kraftwerk'.

Iggy's album propelled Bowie into the sessions for *Low* – an enervating project that would have required any other performer to rest after its completion. Instead, Bowie agreed to accompany Pop on brief tours of Britain and America, as his virtually anonymous keyboardist, resisting all demands from the audience to perform his own material.* He even broke a self-imposed five-year ban on flying to visit America with the band – perhaps because, as he admitted later, their collective drug intake was 'unbelievable'. In one of the more surreal moments of either man's career, they appeared as guests on *Dinah!*, an afternoon chat show hosted by forties big-band singer Dinah Shore. Their union survived long enough to record a second album in Berlin, *Lust For Life*, during the making of which Bowie banished Pop from the studio because of his excessive (even by the standards of the time) cocaine abuse.

What did Bowie gain from this collaboration, besides the garage-punk prestige of working with the ramshackle prince of the genre? He was undoubtedly able to sustain the creative freedom he enjoyed at the Iggy Pop sessions when he almost immediately began work on his own, more focused projects, *Low* and *'Heroes'*. In retrospect, it is a shame that the pair did not manage a third collaboration† before the *Lodger* sessions. More importantly, their partnership did not rob Bowie of words (which were, after all, in short supply on the *Low* album). His contribution to both Iggy records was purely musical: that is, he would participate in the haphazard studio creation of riffs and chord changes, and perhaps suggest a tune, before letting Pop pen the lyrics. His role was similar to that of Mick Ronson during the creation of *The Man Who Sold The World*: which is why the songs from *The Idiot* and *Lust For Life* have not been examined individually in this book.

---

* Several songs from this tour were included on the subsequent live album *TV Eye*, which – like Bowie's *Stage* – was motivated by the need to fulfil a recording contract.
† Instead, Bowie made a fleeting visit to the recording of Pop's 1979 album *Soldier*, encouraging him to concoct a libellous account of adventures in high society. Iggy subsequently rewrote the lyrics under the no doubt ironic title of 'Play It Safe'.

The reception of both records was coloured by reviewers' attitudes towards Iggy Pop. Those who wanted their Iggy to be incoherent and self-destructive (as on the Stooges' live album, *Metallic KO*) accused Bowie of taming their hero. Others assumed that this limp-wristed glam-rocker was merely stealing some of Pop's punk-rock credibility. Then there were those who took Pop's reputation at face value and heard, on *The Idiot*, music that Nick Kent* described as 'totally riveted and fettered to a thoroughly unhealthy aroma of evil and twilight zone zombie-time release'. *The Idiot* was certainly riveting: it moved at a majestically slow pace, like some vast overladen pantechnicon that was uncomfortable taking corners (probably because Bowie insisted on choosing rehearsals rather than final takes, and often the band would not have changed chord or tempo at the same time). With one exception, it was built around the simplest of chord structures, often underpinned (or sometimes undermined) by a simultaneous collection of riffs, each musician contributing his own. Some songs matched the Kraftwerk/James Brown hybrid that Iggy promised; whereas 'Baby' and 'China Girl' hinged around a more orthodox verse/chorus structure. The exception mentioned above was 'Tiny Girls', introduced by a 'cool' jazz-style saxophone melody from Bowie, which elegantly shifted key on three occasions, before a more orthodox (for this album) form of minimalism resumed control. Repetitive and haphazard, *The Idiot* represented the music that might have been made by a garage rock 'n' roll band in 1962 if their nutrition had been restricted to downers and beer.

By contrast, *Lust For Life* (the title, borrowed from a novel and movie about Vincent Van Gogh, said it all) was cleaner, more propulsive, and altogether more definite: polished masters instead of rehearsals, in other words. These were songs, not spontaneous collisions of ideas, though still often rooted in late-fifties and early-sixties rock 'n' roll. *The Idiot* would never have produced an anthem if Bowie hadn't revisited 'China Girl', in an altogether lighter frame of mind, six years later; *Lust For Life* was full of them, from the glorious title track and the emblematic 'Some Weird Sin' to the hypnotic riff behind 'The Passenger' (one of two songs for which Bowie didn't receive a composing credit). Any extreme moments here

* Kent's recent memoir, *Apathy For The Devil*, suggests that he was describing his own late seventies life as much as *The Idiot*. In a 1976 interview, he recalled meeting Bowie three years earlier: 'He was getting into his King of Decadence trip and I didn't like it . . . I got a bad feeling from him – he had this Nazi aura, very unfeeling and very unhuman.' He went on to accuse Bowie of being 'a real plagiarist . . . a very over-rated figure'.

came from Pop's lyrics, and were delivered with a wry grin (see the cover for confirmation: no expressionist angst here). There were none of the ambiguous chord changes heard on the previous record's 'Nightclubbing' or 'Funtime', where each band member sounded as if he had his own vision of where the song should go next, and was stubbornly sticking to it.

Iggy later explained that Bowie had concocted several of the *Lust For Life* songs by copying the basic structures of rock standards, but there were almost too many candidates to make a definite identification of the original sources. Two albums, then, from two distinct personalities; two methods for Bowie to access his own creativity without spilling any seed.

[133] SPEED OF LIFE (Bowie)

Recorded September 1976; *Low* LP.

The sessions for *Low* were undertaken against a background of extreme turbulence in David Bowie's personal life. 'He was, in my opinion, unquestionably at his lowest ebb,' recalled his one-time manager, Michael Lippman. 'He was emotionally distraught.' Bowie's distress had been triggered by a series of meetings designed to produce a compromise solution to his business difficulties with Lippman – during which he was reported to have accused everyone around him of only being interested in his money.

In theory, Bowie and his family were now resident in a Swiss villa on the shore of Lake Geneva, chosen by his wife Angie. But instead Bowie had opted to remain in Paris and Berlin with Iggy Pop (not least because he had become temporarily infatuated with a Berlin cabaret owner, a transsexual named Romy Haag). When Angie arrived to remonstrate with him, he told her he wanted a divorce – though only after discussions so heated that Bowie collapsed with chest pains, and was taken to hospital with suspected heart disease. Angie subsequently told journalists that he was merely suffering from stress and depression.

Meanwhile, Bowie had invited Brian Eno and Tony Visconti to collaborate with him: Visconti as a trusted friend, Eno because Bowie admired his ambient *Discreet Music* album, and the minimalist rock experimentation of his *Another Green World* LP. Together they assembled the album that began with that (previously) most unimaginable of artefacts: a David Bowie instrumental. Its title was close to his heart. 'People simply can't cope with the rate of change in this world,' he noted in 1977. 'It's all far too fast. Since the industrial revolution there's been this upward spiral with people desperately trying to hang on, and now everybody's started to fall off. And it'll get worse. There's not really a cause for hope.' 'David works very fast,' said Brian Eno in 1976 of their collaboration on *Low*. 'He's very impulsive, and he works like crazy for about two hours or sometimes three-quarters of an hour – and then he takes the rest of the day off. And in that time, he does an incredible amount, very well, very quickly and faultlessly. Whereas what I do is to – quite slowly – build things up over a period . . . Very slow.'

Bowie and Eno elected to work with Tony Visconti on *Low* after the American producer rang Bowie and boasted that he had a gadget that 'fucks with the fabric of time'. 'I heard that it could change the pitch of a sound without changing the speed,' Visconti explained to Bowie biographer David Buckley. 'My brain nearly exploded when I found what I could do with drums. By lowering the pitch of a live drum, then feeding it back, I got a sort of infinite dropping of pitch, ever renewing itself.'

So the speed of life on *Low* was fast, the way that Bowie loved to work but feared to live; and slow, like Eno's painstaking tapestries of sound; and not to be trusted, because their music 'fucks with the fabric of time'. And time, as Albert Einstein could have told them, was infinitely flexible, transforming everything it touched as certainly as Tony Visconti's Eventide Harmonizer. In the four traumatic years since *Aladdin Sane*, when 'Time' [69] had been a glamorous, nearly unimaginable concept, Bowie had witnessed its cruelty and trickery at first hand – the way it extended pain into an eternity and compressed happiness into the twitching of an eye. On a record that boldly chose to confront Bowie's own experience of eternity, and compress the images of himself that he shared with the outside world, it made perfect sense for the opening instrumental to credit the 'Speed Of Life', a subject too profound for words.

Hence this remarkable track, which began with a fuzzy keyboard searching for direction, before being kicked into order by the most aggressive snare drum sound yet captured on recording tape. 'Speed

Of Life' rekindled the glorious tradition of rock 'n' roll instrumentals from the late fifties, augmented to reflect the pace of technological invention over the previous twenty years. Beneath the sonic playfulness of treated drums, mutated guitar and keyboards that mimicked prehistoric birds, the primary riff could have been performed by a fifties horn section with answering handclaps. Not so its companion, set to a more unsettling semitone fall (D♭-C), through which a rhythm guitar chattered like a telegraph machine – itself one more victim of the relentless speed of life.

[134] BREAKING GLASS (Bowie/Davis/Murray)

Recorded September–November 1976; *Low* LP.

After years of attempting to translate music into theatrical or cinematic extravaganzas, Bowie had finally recorded an album that begged to be represented on film. The movie of *Low* would have required a simple but chilling technique: episodic scenes of psychological disintegration, viewed just out of focus, each one fading swiftly to a black screen. For 'Breaking Glass', a single close-up on the hero's face would have sufficed, documenting the disconnection between emotion and appearance.

In just six masterful lines, and less than two minutes of music, Bowie had succeeded in capturing a state of total dislocation between two people – or, to be more accurate, between one person and his perception of the world. It didn't matter whether, as many commentators have suggested,* the 'awful' design that the narrator drew on the carpet was, or was not, the 'Tree of Life' from Kether to Malkuth (see [126]). No sooner did he command his companion to avert his/ her eyes from his 'awful' drawing than he barked, 'See!' Such was the fracture between his conduct and his self-awareness that when he declared that he would never touch his companion again, the only sensible response would be: 'Thank God.'

Bowie's vocal was virtually robotic; certainly stripped of humanity,

---

* These suggestions depended upon the belief that the 'Tree of Life', and the Kabbalah beyond it, were intrinsically 'awful', because of their occult connotations, and moreover that Bowie agreed with this verdict. Case not proven on either count, I believe.

even when double-tracked in the chorus: two madmen were no more comforting than one. The soundscape was uncertain: cymbals and drums crashed in reverse, appearing from their own echoes. Both of his commands – listen, see – were followed by bursts of electronic sound between the speakers, obeying some logic that was entirely his own. This was desolation in miniature: fade quickly to black.

[135] WHAT IN THE WORLD (Bowie)

Recorded September–November 1976; *Low* LP.

In a sequence of songs that owned up to depression and alienation, 'What In The World' was the exception. Not that those conditions weren't present; but Bowie's narrator deflected them on to a girl who was entombed in her room. 'What In The World' treated her like a foreign object, before Bowie decided that, despite it all, he was still prepared to allow himself to sample her love. (The repetitions of 'for your love' by Bowie and his guest vocalist, Iggy Pop, were a homage to the Yardbirds' 1965 single of that name.) So this wasn't a song about a depressed girl, after all; the star of the show was a man who could only view her through the prism of his own lust. Bowie could not be accused of tumbling into romantic clichés.

The song's emotional dislocation was matched by the mechanical nature of Bowie's lead vocal, which by the second verse could barely muster the energy to change notes. That sense of imprisonment – in the room, in the ego – recurred in the structure of the song, with its repeated chord changes between major chords two semi-tones apart (F-E♭; later D-C). Only during the brief seconds when Bowie was admitting to some emotional involvement was there any respite, as a descending bass-line offered a hint of some traditional pop romanticism, only to be shut down immediately. Nor did the musical accompaniment lighten the gloom: everything was as synthetic and pre-programmed as Bowie's responses, from the treated drums at the start (supported by what sounded bizarrely like an electronic wobble-board) to the staccato attack of the guitar solo.

[136] Sound And Vision (Bowie)

Recorded September–November 1976; *Low* LP.

Some statistics, first of all: 'Sound And Vision' ran for 183 seconds.* No human voices were heard for 46 seconds, when the backing singers crooned a two-note descent; no hook for 74 seconds, until Mary Hopkin (then married to producer Visconti) provided a deceptively playful word-less chorus. Not until 88 seconds had passed did David Bowie's voice appear, posing a question with which his admirers could surely identify.

Like 'Quicksand' [50], 'Sound And Vision' was Bowie's admission that his creative inspiration had disappeared: cunningly, he used a confession of artistic bankruptcy to spark his muse back to life. Hence the tension that haunted the first side of *Low*: Bowie no longer knew whether he could function as the artist he had once been. 'Sound And Vision' didn't promise that he could reconnect with the outside world (it was telling that he chose not to promote this record in any way), but it did at least reconnect him with himself; and as such it was arguably one of the most important songs he had ever written.

It was also a consummate pop record, as tightly produced as any disco classic of the era: indeed, it might well have registered with the public just as strongly as an instrumental, with Hopkin's vocal as the focus. Its glassy sheen was constructed from metallic elements – the sizzle of a cymbal on the third beat of each bar, guitar reverb on the first beat, a mock-reggae rhythm in the right channel, the defining guitar riff in the left, and then the whiniest of electronic strings, running down the key of G. Bowie's lead vocal was lugubrious and almost apologetic; his harmonies ludicrously affected, suggesting he didn't believe in his renaissance. And at the end, the track faded quickly away, as if trying to erase its own existence.

[137] Always Crashing In The Same Car (Bowie)

Recorded September–November 1976; *Low* LP.

Bowie explained this song with a charming anecdote about the time when he had chased a drug dealer around the car park of a Hollywood

* Tony Visconti revealed in his autobiography that the track had originally featured several other verses, which were edited out during the mixing process.

hotel, recklessly sideswiping anything within automobile range. His ability to deliver flagrant inaccuracies within the utterly unreliable context of a promotional interview, and with a poker face, has been a hallmark of his entire career.

Regardless of its truth, his tale was irrelevant in the context of *Low*. Driving was central to the mystique of American rock 'n' roll: brand names and car chases littered the writing of Chuck Berry and Bruce Springsteen. In US popular culture, the automobile signalled freedom, movement, direction, identity, individuality in the instant of signing up for a collective fantasy. In the seventies novels of the British writer J.G. Ballard, driving was hazardous, directionless, maniacal, suicidal, murderous. 'I think the twentieth century reaches its purest expression on the highway,' he wrote in a 1971 essay. 'Here we see all too clearly the speed and violence of our age, its strange love affair with the machine and, conceivably, with its own death and destruction.' His 1973 fiction *Crash* eroticised the phenomenon of the automobile accident, equating the puncturing of the flesh by twisted steel with the bodily invasion of sexual intercourse. The narrator grows 'to accept the perverse eroticism of the car-crash, as painful as the drawing of an exposed organ through the aperture of a surgical wound'. Reviewers were less accepting: the *New York Times* declared *Crash* to be 'hands down, the most repulsive book I've yet to come across . . . Believe me, no one needs this sort of protracted and gratuitous anguish.'

Man and machine had become indissoluble; just as in the sonic landscape of *Low*, technology had enabled the synthesis of computer and creator. In a Ballardian universe, the car was a vehicle for the human in the same way that the body was a vehicle for the soul or mind. This was the ultimate driving metaphor; life on the road, not as a touring musician but as a passenger of the human condition. You could get a paint job, but it was still the same car.

Bowie's lead vocal on this track – placid, isolated, cocooned in echo, reduced to little more than a whisper – accentuated the sense of remorseless circularity. When he briefly broke out for a repeated cry of 'yeah', he sounded hollow, not liberated; it was like a cynical pastiche of the Beatles' life-affirming chorus from 'She Loves You' an aeon before. Behind Bowie, keyboards and guitars mapped out the same featureless landscape – repetition, an unbroken drone – in a world of distortion: a suitably inhuman and unreal setting for a drama in which identity had been sacrificed.

[138] BE MY WIFE (Bowie)

Recorded September–November 1976; *Low* LP.

David and Angela Bowie were still married, if effectively estranged, when Bowie wrote this apparently straightforward song. But it was not intended for a specific target: 'It could've been anybody,' he admitted. Just as his car was a symbol for his life, so a wife was the totem of what his life was missing: a symbol of belonging, of (in every sense of the word) engagement, the opportunity for empathy, a public gesture of normality. So this was not a marriage proposal but a confession of living outside and beyond, of restless movement and an empty heart. It was not a conventional declaration of romance: 'share my life' was not an enticing suggestion. As Bowie said later, 'It was genuinely anguished, I think.' His qualification was an attempt to soften the blow for himself.

Who was delivering this message? A Londoner, audible as such for the first time since he had left Britain in 1974; someone who didn't reveal his emotions lightly; who preferred the clipped irony of the Englishman abroad. On *Young Americans*, two years earlier, Bowie might have opened his heart like a soul singer; here he preferred to adopt a low profile. So the listener had to search out his intentions in the music – in the predictable Am/G/F chord structure of the opening line, which was then subverted by being left hanging on the G chord next time around; in the wry smile of a vaudeville-style piano, masking the clown's tears; in the suppressed emotion of the strident piano chords that completed each line; and in the animal howl of the guitar solo.

[139] A NEW CAREER IN A NEW TOWN (Bowie)

Recorded September 1976; *Low* LP.

Bowie identified 'A New Career In A New Town' as the 'most narrative' piece on *Low* – a judgement that was either playful or devious, as the track was purely instrumental. If there was a sense of movement and progression beyond the title, then it was in the juxtaposition of 'old' and 'new' Bowie styles: the collision between the synthesised percussion,* ambient drone and sonic manipulation of the opening section, and the more traditionally rhythmic blend of rock and funk that provided the main theme. The latter hinged around the classic 'doo-wop' chord sequence (I-vi-IV-V), utilising a repetitive keyboard motif against a blues harmonica that was strangely reminiscent of the 1970 UK novelty hit 'Grooving With Mr Bloe'.

The Art of Minimalism

The division of *Low* into 'experimental rock' and 'ambient' sides mirrored two of the major influences on this era of Bowie's career: minimalist music and the German tradition dubbed (by British journalists) 'Krautrock'. Each of them offered a conscious shift of perspective away from the dominant cultures of the age. The minimalists represented a return to simplicity and melody after decades in which classical music had been dominated by the modal compositions of the modernists. Rather than returning to the orthodoxies of previous centuries, however, they preferred to use repetition to capture the spirit of the age, and subtle variations on that repetition to express individuality. The two premier figures in this field were Steve Reich and Philip Glass (whom Bowie and Brian Eno saw in 1970 performing 'Music With Changing Parts' at the Royal College of Art in London). Reich's work favoured the intervention of juxtaposition and chance, as part of what he called 'music as a gradual process'; Glass preferred to introduce deliberate variation into an area of repetition. Each composer had his 'school' of admirers and copyists.

'Krautrock', meanwhile, was a defiantly German answer to the Anglo-American dominance of the global rock industry, arriving at both repetition and atonality as an electronic means of extending musical boundaries while imposing tight restraints on artificial notions of novelty. The racism implicit

---

* The initial syn-drums mirrored those on Kraftwerk's *Radio-Activity* album, paced between the title track and 'Geiger Counter'. Ralph Hutter described his band's rhythm as 'this metallic, metronomic beat', adding proudly: 'We play automatic music.'

in the 'Krautrock' name was exposed when one surveyed the remarkable range of music that it pigeonholed: everything from the ethereal, almost ambient textures of Tangerine Dream's synthesised compositions to the confrontational rock and sound experiments of Faust. Can were perhaps closest to their American psychedelic contemporaries; Kraftwerk relied on almost robotic formality; and NEU! divided their three albums between raucous rock assaults and deceptively simple synthesiser pieces.

Both schools were reflecting techniques and theories that were current in the contemporary visual arts, from the repeated motifs of the op-art painters to the self-imposed asceticism of those European artists who set themselves the task of endlessly reproducing the same canvas (among them Daniel Buren, Olivier Mosset and Niele Toroni).

If Bowie's conduit to the minimalists was Brian Eno, he had discovered the 'Krautrock' tradition first-hand. The link between the two schools was electronic, and more specifically synthetic: the Moog synthesiser and its cousins introduced new textures, encouraged the mechanisation of music-making, and proudly displayed their 'non-human' tones. There was no more a definitive 'Krautrock' sound than there was a single technique of minimalism, but both of them marked a step away from the traditions in which Bowie and his peers had been raised. The German bands deliber-ately refused to use the clichés of British and American rock, especially its roots in the blues; the minimalists, equally consciously, rejected the harsh dissonance of the post-Schoenberg schools.

In Brian Eno, Bowie found a partner who was comfortable with both innovations: sonically and theoretically daring, not least in his willingness to allow quiet, almost inaudible sounds into a (music) world dominated by noise. (He defined minimalism as 'a drift away from narrative and towards landscape'.) Eno contributed another vital ingredient, in the form of his *Oblique Strategies* cards. Their instructions, like the verbal art concepts of the Fluxus group in the sixties, encouraged participants to jettison their instinctive responses to the problems of creativity. The cards in Eno's pack were as potent and jolting as anything in Aleister Crowley's Tarot: they might, for example, encourage an artist to 'Abandon normal instruments' (see [171]), 'Give way to your worst impulses', 'Make a sudden, destruc-tive unpredictable action' or, indeed, 'Just carry on'.

Over the course of three albums made with varying degrees of collabor-ation, Bowie and Eno exploited many of these suggestions, and ignored as many more. The cards provided a playful theoretical backdrop to a series of projects that extended both men's musical vocabularies, but depended (as *Lodger* proved) on Bowie being willing to risk more than his colleague. Or perhaps it wasn't a risk at all: Bowie had no wish to continue the career he had been pursuing, and *Low* was an abrupt and challenging way of disrupting it. For those who had taken little notice of the computerised rhythms of Kraftwerk, the apparently seamless patterns of Philip Glass and Steve Reich, the sparse landscape of NEU! and the deconstructive impulses of Faust, *Low* sounded completely revolutionary. Even for those who knew its antecedents, the album (and its successor) wrenched both its creators and its listeners out of their comfortable familiarity.

[140] WARSZAWA (Bowie / Eno)

Recorded September 1976; *Low* LP.

'Music carries its own message,' Bowie told Angus MacKinnon in 1980. 'Lyrics are not needed because music does have an implicit message of its own; it makes its case very pointedly. If that were not the case, then classical music would not have succeeded to the extent that it did in implying and carrying some definite point of view, some attitude which presumably can't be expressed with words.'

As on 'Subterraneans' [143], Bowie employed the human voice on 'Warszawa' to sing words that had no meaning in any language, but were chosen for their phonetic sound. So his voice became another instrument, alongside the treated piano, bass drone, and synthesised orchestra (strings, church organ, woodwinds); and like them, it was translated through technology, as Tony Visconti recalled: 'To make him sound like a boy I slowed the tape down about three semitones and he sang his part slowly.'

The title of 'Warszawa' was intended to supply the meaning that the words did not express: Bowie explained that it reflected the sadness of the Polish peasants he had glimpsed during a train journey from Berlin to Moscow. Yet the framework of the piece had been prepared by Eno while Bowie was enduring business meetings in Paris. Perhaps that was why, of all the instrumentals Bowie and Eno created for *Low* and '*Heroes*', 'Warszawa' sounded the most carefully scored, with no hint of randomness or accident.

The piece opened tentatively, as if searching for safe ground, with an ambiguous A minor chord, a rising motif resolving in A major that was reminiscent of the famous opening to Strauss' 'Also Sprach Zarathustra', and a second climb to a repeated C major chord, which suggested that it might determine the key signature for the entire piece. Instead, a hauntingly simple melody rose above an F♯ chord, was briefly echoed, and then answered by a second line that ended in mid-air on F, begging for completion. Again the ground shifted: another melody vied for supremacy, but was finally set aside as Eno elegantly steered the piece from F♯ into E, at which point Bowie's monkish vocal chorale chanted lines that sometimes sounded traditionally Western, and at others bore the clear hallmark of eastern Europe or points further east. He crafted six different melodies for his multi-dubbed choir (one of them a careful reversal of its predecessor), before Eno engineered another transition to the opening section. But rather than allowing the full four-line sequence to appear, he repeated the first two lines – with the result that 'Warszawa' was left to sway on that unresolved F. If this was minimalism, it was certainly not repetition: in 'Warszawa', there was literally no place like home.

[141] ART DECADE (Bowie)

Recorded October–November 1976; *Low* LP.

Bowie explained the pun in the title as a comment on the sterility of the art scene in late seventies West Berlin, isolated from the outside world. In fact, Berlin had been undergoing an artistic renaissance since the late sixties, with communes being formed in warehouses and lofts. By 1977, a group known as the Junge (or Neue) Wilde were consciously rekindling the fire of the expressionist movement. They opened the Galerie am Moritzplatz a few weeks after *Low* was released to showcase this eruption of creativity.

'Art Decade' was based around a gorgeously melancholy chord progression similar to Brian Wilson's instrumental title track from the Beach Boys' *Pet Sounds* album. Around this theme – carried forward, under Eno's supervision, on cello, synthesised strings, vibes and treated guitar – emerged the sounds of abstraction: some evoking visual impressions, such as the toy orchestra slowly awakening in the opening bars; others more fleeting and imprecise. Each repetition began in E♭ and then modulated graciously down and up the twelve-tone scale to arrive at a natural E, where the 'strings' remained while other textures swayed back and forth between E and F♯. The finished piece reinforced the opinion of Peter Baumann, from the German ambient band Tangerine Dream, that 'no other instrument can get such a warm sound as some synthesizers. But it's a new, different kind of warmth and intimacy.'

[142] WEEPING WALL (Bowie)

Recorded October–November 1976; *Low* LP.

The minimalist composer Steve Reich built several of his most significant sixties and seventies pieces around the raindrops-on-a-river impressions created by melodic percussive instruments such as the marimba, vibes and xylophone. In his most overt evocation of Reich's work* since 'Chant Of The Ever-Circling Skeletal Family' [104], Bowie replicated this effect with koto, xylophone and synthesiser. But whereas Reich would have been content to focus attention on his subtle variations of pattern, Bowie used his innovation as a backdrop to an unsettling blend of synthesised strings, a chorale of real and artificial voices, and a howling guitar that pulled naggingly at the melody of the traditional folk song, 'Scarborough Fair'. If the strings and voices represented order, then the guitar was a representation of anarchy, constantly trying to break free before being dragged back. Gradually, a mass of computerised voices – Bowie's among them – rose to the surface, as if echoing the guitar's struggle, before it too fell to earth. Whether the weeping wall of the title was in its traditional location of Jerusalem, or (as Bowie hinted) in Berlin, the sense of imprisonment and frustrated energy was palpable.

* For Robert Fripp's interpretation of the same idea, listen to King Crimson's 'Larks Tongues In Aspic (Part 1)'.

Berlin

Bowie's first visit to West Berlin was in October 1969, in the company of Kenneth Pitt. He saw the infamous wall that enclosed the 'free' sectors of the city, and caught a voyeur's glimpse of the nightlife portrayed in the musical *Cabaret*. The night after he returned to London, he and Angie watched a BBC TV documentary about Christopher Isherwood, the author of the thirties stories on which *Cabaret* was based. Angie would later declare Isherwood her favourite writer; Bowie was equally entranced, his enjoyment of *Goodbye To Berlin* enhanced by the uneasy decadence he had witnessed with his own eyes. He returned briefly in 1973, and again in 1976, before deciding after his concert at the city's Deutschlandhalle that this should become his refuge from the chilling liberation of Los Angeles. 'I have to put myself in those situations to produce any reasonably good writing,' he insisted later, 'forcing myself to live according to the restrictions of that city.'

The city that one commentator dubbed 'the twentieth century's dystopia: a city of expressionistic anguish' had, by the mid-seventies, become 'unsettlingly foreign, a place where alien cultures and customs were evident at every turn'. Bowie spent much of his leisure time in Kreuzberg, a milieu of aliens (economic migrants from Turkey, labourers from Africa and Asia who had been expelled when the East no longer required their services) and artists; punks and radicals; drugs and prostitution. It was an ideal venue for a man who wanted to feel a hint of danger, and did not wish to travel far for his kicks. Addicts and teenage whores gravitated towards the Zoo Station, inspiring an early-eighties movie (*Christiane F*) for which Bowie provided the soundtrack. The modern expressionist painters exhibited at their newly opened gallery and filled the cafés and gay bars with radical chatter: Bowie soon crossed paths with their most prominent figure, Salome, an artist and punk musician. Among the paintings Salome was displaying during Bowie's residence in Berlin was his *Fuck* series of canvases, which might have been designed to appeal to the singer: they featured naked, masked balloon-creatures in homosexual poses, against vivid blood-red sheets.

Red was the colour of another group of extremists adrift in West Germany: the Rote Armee Fraktion (RAF/Red Army Faction, commonly known as the Baader–Meinhof Group). This was an anti-capitalist terrorist cell, determined to exile American influence from West Germany, bring down former Nazis who still occupied positions of privilege, and pledge solidarity with the oppressed peoples of the world, especially the Palestine liberation movement. Its roots lay in the late-sixties protests of students and other activists, met with violence by police in West Berlin. Founder member Gudrun Ensslin declared: 'This fascist state means to kill us all . . . This is the Auschwitz generation, and there's no arguing with them.' Ensslin, Baader, Meinhof and others were arrested, and either escaped from prison or went on the run before they could be sentenced. Their crusade was joined by groups of mental-health patients who, like the radical psychiatrists of Britain, believed that the repressive state was the cause of their inability to exist within the system; and, unlike their UK counterparts, took up arms alongside the Red Army Faction.

Bowie's time in Berlin saw the battle between terrorists and the state reach a bloody climax known as the Deutscher Herbst (German autumn), which involved the kidnapping and killing of a prominent German industrialist; the hijacking of a Lufthansa jet in Majorca, the pilot of which was killed (alongside three of the hijackers); and the suicide* in their cells of all the leading RAF figures. At the same time, violence framed the city from another direction, as the East German government built their third and most impregnable wall around West Berlin, sparking another bout of suicides among the effectively imprisoned residents. Doctors diagnosed a widespread epidemic of *Mauerkrankheit* (or wall-sickness). Every few months, meanwhile, an inhabitant of the East would attempt to scale the wall, and fall victim to the mines that littered the border area.

Little wonder, then, that Bowie recalled later that West Berlin was 'an ambiguous place', where it was hard 'to distinguish between the ghosts and the living'. It was, he said, the city that foretold the future of Europe; and, more oppressively, 'a macrocosm of my own state of mind': an isolated outpost amidst a sea of oppression, perhaps. Yet it was here that he was able to complete two records, plan a third, and regain the sense of identity that he had virtually destroyed in Los Angeles. The Bowie who left Berlin for New York in 1979 was, physically, mentally and morally, almost unrecognisable as the haunted, addicted figure who had arrived there three years earlier.

* Many supporters refused to believe that their icons had killed themselves after the Lufthansa hijacking failed to bring about their release, preferring to believe that they must have been murdered by the state.

[143] SUBTERRANEANS (Bowie)

Recorded December 1975 & September 1976; *Low* LP.

Soon after the *Low* sessions had finished, Brian Eno revealed the methodology behind 'Warszawa' [140] and 'Subterraneans': 'Instead of having a lot of singing and an instrumental, there's a lot of instrumental and a tiny bit of singing . . . it's not words: it's phonetics. It's not lyrics, you see. He's just using very nice-sounding words that aren't actually* in any language.' He also hinted that 'Subterraneans' had been retrieved from Bowie's abortive attempt to supply soundtrack music for *The Man Who Fell To Earth*. Bowie had previously promised that the film soundtrack would feature electronic music 'without vocals that you'd recognise'. The track's title was a nod to Jack Kerouac, Bowie's favourite author as a teenager, whose novel *The Subterraneans* recounted an affair with an African-American woman (a subject with which Bowie enjoyed some familiarity). More substantial was the clue provided by the music itself, and in particular Bowie's superb multi-dubbed vocals: he must surely have been familiarising himself with the polyphonic writing of plainsong composers, as his lines were harmonised as if they derived from some long-suppressed setting of the Catholic mass.

The haunting quality of 'Subterraneans' (and, again, 'Warszawa') makes one regret that Bowie and Eno did not dare to create an entire album in this idiom. Even for an iconoclastic rock star, however, this might have been a risk too far. Instead we can cherish the still beauty of this piece, with its delicate textures of vibraphone, synthesised strings and echoed guitar, interrupted by an ominous bass guitar ascent that constantly threatened to stop short of resolution, but finally provided the F# note that the ear demanded. Subtle flickers of backwards guitar rekindled memories of rock's sonic experiments of 1966, by the Beatles and the Byrds – incongruous, in theory, for a piece so imbued with spirituality, but somehow perfect in context. Likewise Bowie's remarkable saxophone solo, his most elegant and directly emotional playing on any record, always opting for 'feel' rather than technical perfection.

* Bowie teased his audience by printing his near-lyrics, thereby inviting interpretation. I would love to believe that the 'share bride' line was actually a comment on the 1975 marriage between Cher and guitarist Gregg Allman.

Yet the album still had two last tricks to play. More than five minutes into the track, a strange croaking sound – like a grumbling bullfrog – could be heard beneath the chorale, debunking the spirituality of the piece. A few seconds later, 'Subterraneans' ended – not with comforting resolution, but with a hanging D from Bowie's voices, midway through that tantalising rise executed throughout by the bass guitar. It was completion and incompletion in the same moment: as unsettling, in its way, as the psychological dramas that this track seemed to have overcome.

Low LP

Brian Eno promised that *Low* would combine elements of 'recognisable Bowie' with 'the most exciting new concept' he'd come across in years. In retrospect, the format of the album – one side recognisable as 'rock', albeit hardly old-school; the other more ambient – came to appear almost inevitable, especially in the wake of a similar division of styles on *'Heroes'*. But in January 1977, when only the most dogged of 'Krautrock' aficionados had tracked down an import copy of *NEU! '75*, which operated on similar principles, *Low* was regarded as revolutionary. Like *Station To Station* before it, the album established Bowie as a recording artist whom it was impossible to second-guess. There seemed to be no obvious way of tracking his progression from *Hunky Dory* to *Low* in almost exactly five years: even now his willingness to risk losing his audience, and his reputation (many critics reacted badly to *Low*'s apparent lethargy), appears courageous.

His psychological turmoil aside, the crucial influences on *Low* were taken to be Brian Eno's resistance to traditional rock structures and sounds, and the mechanised, repetitive approach of much 'Krautrock'. Twenty-five years later, Bowie reflected that the German influence had been overemphasised: 'It's still a very organic, blues-driven sound . . . the actual rhythm section is not a metronome, electronic sound like the Germans were doing.' Indeed, what distinguished *Low* and Iggy Pop's *The Idiot* was precisely that amalgam of the darkest and most enticing elements of American and German musical cultures: the robotic, the escapist, the ethereal, the direct, all conveying a state of emotional dissonance, in which depression could be uplifting and boredom became transcendent.

[144] **SOME ARE** (Bowie/Eno)

[145] **ABDULMAJID** (Bowie)

[146] **ALL SAINTS** (Bowie/Eno)

> Recorded September–November 1976; *Low* extended CD [144/146]; *'Heroes'* extended CD [145].

Bowie's experiments with instrumental textures during the late seventies operated within a different sense of time than his 'rock'-oriented material of the same era. His songs on *Low*, *'Heroes'*, *Lodger* and *Scary Monsters* may have represented a decisive break from what had gone before, but they continued to demonstrate his subconscious desire for movement and progression in his career. Lyrically and musically, each set of recordings had a distinctive collective identity: they were recognisably the work of the same artist, but under the influence of different concepts and motives.

His instrumental work, with and without Brian Eno, was much more integrated – or, if you like, unadventurous. Bowie's giant leap was envisaging himself as an artist who could make music without words: once he had escaped the conventional borders of rock and pop, he was able to relax and play, without the almost addictive desire to create new sounds and styles. So his more ambient work was much more difficult to locate within a definite time frame: there was no stylistic or technological gulf between his earliest experiments on *Low*, and 'Crystal Japan' [179], recorded three years later during the *Scary Monsters* sessions.

'Some Are' and 'All Saints' were first released on the CD reissue of *Low*; 'Abdulmajid' (named, obviously after the event, for Bowie's second wife, Iman) appeared on the *'Heroes'* CD. Officially remixed in 1991, they may also have been augmented or completed at that time; while some sources insist that 'Some Are' actually pre-dated the Eno collaboration, and was written during the soundtrack sessions for *The Man Who Fell To Earth* in 1975.

'Some Are' differed from most of its contemporaries in having a set of lyrics (four lines of random images, emoted in a soft, intimate voice) and also a smooth texture that brought Bowie close to the troubled territory of New Age* music. Even at its least disturbing, however, Bowie's music introduced a little grit to the smooth surface of voice and synthesisers, in the form of an expanding hubbub of noise. 'Abdulmajid' followed a similar rise-and-fall melody to 'Crystal Japan', though in its 1991 presentation its gentle synthesiser tones were masked by a 'trance' rhythm that was obviously added long after the original recording date. 'All Saints' (its title borrowed from Kandinsky's turbulent canvases of 1911) represented a collage of sounds rather than a simple melody, with guitar power-chords and sustain suggesting the birth of a new genre, ambient R&B. Pleasant though all three compositions were, however, they added nothing substantial to Bowie's European canon.

Rock on the Titanic: Punk

Neither *Station To Station* nor *Low* topped the British album charts. But the records that did achieve that status in 1976 and 1977 included greatest hits compilations by Perry Como, Roy Orbison, Slim Whitman, Abba, the Beach Boys, the Stylistics, Bert Weedon, Glen Campbell, the Shadows, Frank Sinatra, Johnny Mathis, Connie Francis, Elvis Presley (in the aftermath of his death), the Supremes, Cliff Richard and Bread. This did not suggest a musical culture at ease with itself. The US charts, from which these retrospective compilations were barred, were dominated by the soft rock of Peter Frampton and Fleetwood Mac. Neither were the singles charts any more exhilarating: 1976 was the era of disco, easy listening, and singalong pop ditties that made the bubblegum hits of 1970 sound positively raw by comparison. You did not have to be on the dole or desperate for anarchy to find the likes of the Brotherhood of Man, David Soul or Showaddywaddy bland.

Rock was now something to be experienced in the arenas that David

* New Age is easy to recognise, virtually impossible to define: it exists on the mellow fringes of jazz, world music, classical music and ambient dance/trance. Originally linked with 'new age' spirituality in the late seventies, and then expanded into a marketing genre by the mid-eighties, it rapidly assumed a pejorative edge, as much for its attendant lifestyle as for its non-confrontational nature.

Bowie filled during his 1976 tour. As the Who's Pete Townshend recalled a decade later, 'That rather camp and glossy show-business side of rock was something that the audience wanted . . . The halls were getting bigger. So the staging had to be grander . . . and that did lead to theatrical pomposity.' By common consent, ticket prices were too high; rock stars were utterly distanced from their audiences, both in concert and in their everyday lives; the music of emotional and social liberation had become a form of alienation.

In two wonderful think-pieces in the *NME*, 'Is Rock 'n' Roll Ready For 1976?' (3/1/76) and 'The Titanic Sails At Dawn' (19/6/76), writer Mick Farren teased out the implications of this perilous divide between audience and artists. 'Is rock 'n' roll on an unalterable course to a neo-Las Vegas?' he asked in his first article. 'It sure looks like it.' Five months later, nothing had changed: 'Has rock 'n' roll become another mindless consumer product that plays footsie with jet set and royalty while the kids who make up its roots and energy queue up in the rain to watch it from 200 yards away? . . . It is time for the 70s generation to start producing their own ideas, and ease out the old farts who are still pushing tired ideas left over from the 60s.'

Farren exempted Bowie ('the only figure who seems to have the least interest in the social progress of rock 'n' roll') from criticism. Perhaps he had read Bowie's intuitive take on the inertia of modern pop culture, delivered to American journalist Lisa Robinson in February 1976: 'To cause an art movement, you have to set something up and then destroy it . . . the only thing to do is what the Dadaists, the surrealists did: complete amateurs who are pretentious as hell and just fuck it up the ass. Cause as much bad, ill feeling as possible, and then you've got a chance of having a movement. But you'll only create a movement when you have a rebellious cause, and you can't have a rebellious cause when you're the most well-loved person in the country.'

Taken alongside Farren's rhetoric, this was practically a blueprint for the punk-rock movement. Yet Bowie's instinct carried him further than that. In the wake of his early 1976 world tour, he effectively vanished for the remainder of the year – recording *The Idiot* and *Low*, in fact, but removed from the criticism that was hurled at other rock 'dinosaurs', such as the Rolling Stones and the Who. He reappeared on stage in early 1977, providing keyboards for Iggy Pop. As Iggy was acknowledged as one of the premier influences on punk, Bowie won street-level credibility by association. The sonic gulf between the two albums he released that year and the work of his peers simply reinforced his elite status amongst rock's elder statesmen.

'Punk was absolutely necessary,' Bowie declared in 1979, though as early as 1977 he had warned about the artistic dangers of group identity and uniformity: 'a set of people has the most devastating effect on one's chances of producing anything'. By then, anyone who had sampled the relentlessly conformist sound of most British punk, trapped between its stylistic barriers like a bobsleigh on the track, knew exactly what he meant. In his absence, he had sidestepped any accusations of irrelevance, and also the kind of creative misjudgement that, for example, caused Paul McCartney (only five years older than Bowie) to write a punk song, entitled 'Boil Crisis'.

Better still, few connections were drawn between Bowie's muddle-headed espousal of fascism as a form of social cleansing, and the Nazi paraphernalia displayed by many of the original wave of London punks. As journalist Norman Shrapnel noted in his end-of-the-decade survey, 'Germanic influences were plain, and anybody wanting to scare themselves with the more shuddering sort of 30s parallel had only to look at the decadent echoes . . . and at the black leather battalions, the storm-trooper uniforms, even the swastikas that broke out like a contagion.' Neither a dinosaur nor the inspiration for punk's most lamentable lapse in fashion, Bowie had continued to display his uncanny knack for remaining an outsider without losing touch with his audience. They, in turn, began to reflect his influence when they formed their own post-punk bands in the late seventies and early eighties, combining the scorched-earth philosophy of punk with the sonic experimentation of his 1976–80 work.

[147] BEAUTY AND THE BEAST (Bowie)

Recorded June–August 1977; *'Heroes'* LP.

Bowie's first twelve months back in Europe was a period of stunning creativity, which produced four albums (two solo, two by Iggy Pop). The last of them – reuniting the team of Bowie, Eno and Visconti – opened with an electronic growl, as if a computer had been awoken from a deep slumber. Then a piano hit the first two beats of every eight-beat bar (the rhythm tapped out on the edge of a cymbal); African percussion rattled menacingly; a guitar howled into life; the piano erupted to devour each beat; and the creator let out his own ominous groan, extended for five bars. If *Low* began in low profile, *'Heroes'* announced itself from the start as an uproarious celebration of man and machine – beauty and the beast, indeed, though the precise identity of each had still to be determined.

Another contrast: *Low* couldn't help but confess, even when it was without words; *'Heroes'* was a deliberate act of distancing Bowie from emotional disclosure, a show of bravado in the face of an unknown threat. Even when he sounded most open, the performance was under strict control – one calm Bowie (low voice) juxtaposed against one hysterical Bowie (high voice), to show off his range. This was a rambunctious display, then, as the singer tossed off lines from an adult nursery rhyme over a lumbering musical vehicle that was not funk, not rock, not disco, but some futuristic combination of them all. It represented minimalism par excellence: one chord to cover the verse and chorus; another (alternating between C major and C7) for the more halting middle section.

'I wanted to give a phrase a particular feeling,' Bowie explained in 1978. 'Each individual line I wanted to have a different atmosphere, so I would construct it in a Burroughs fashion.' Hence the distance; hence the spontaneous relief from the psychodramas of *Low*; hence the fact that 'Beauty And The Beast' was irresistibly obscure, but so cunningly assembled that it didn't matter for a second.

[148] JOE THE LION (Bowie)

Recorded June–August 1977; *'Heroes'* LP.

In 1974, performance artist Chris Burden had himself nailed to the roof of his Volkswagen Beetle in Venice, California. Such was the jolting shock inspired by his concept piece (called *Trans-Fixed*) that many people erroneously recalled having seen him driven around the city streets that day, when in reality his VW travelled no more than a few feet from his garage. His crucifixion maintained a theme that fuelled his work in the early seventies: risk and danger as a form of self-expression, entailing voyeuristic guilt from his audience. In that spirit, he was shot in the arm by his assistant in 1971; and in a 1974 piece named *White Light/White Heat*, after one of Bowie's favourite Lou Reed songs, spent 22 days lying on the floor of a New York gallery without eating. The fact that he remained out of sight throughout this latter performance, insisting that his audience take his pain on trust, merely added to the ambiguity.

Three years later, *Trans-Fixed* was transferred to Bowie's 'Joe The Lion', who expressed his (or Bowie's) pain in psychological terms. Whatever noise escaped from Burden's mouth as the nails pierced his flesh was surely matched when Joe/Bowie conjured up 'your *dreams* tonight' as a threat, not a delicious promise. Yet even self-mutilation wasn't enough to keep an audience amused. 'Thanks for hesitating,' Bowie muttered sarcastically, as if standing and watching the artist at work was the greatest sin of all.

'Joe' was also the name that Bowie used for the child that he and his wife had christened Zowie: 'Boy,' he shouted twice (emphasising the word IN BLOCK CAPITALS on the album insert). Was this a subliminal connection?

There were at least two levels of reality at work here, conscious and unconscious; most of us get up and go to sleep every day, avoiding the nagging of our creativity and our subconscious awareness. Bowie had been reading the work of Colin Wilson, whose constant reminder was: you could connect with the occult, with the potential of one's own psyche and artistry, if you would only WAKE UP.

But when you wake up, it's Monday, and the deadened cockney of Bowie's voice demonstrated that he could still remember the drudgery of daily life as a work-slave. Yet the alternative was to be an artist, and have nails driven through your hands. No wonder that 'Joe The Lion' began with an explosion of guitar noise across both channels, followed by a riff that seemed to be scurrying like a robot into dark corners in search of anyone hiding there. From there – bar the interlude of daily tedium – the track grew more and more intense, prompting one scream from Bowie that was every bit as agonised as John Lennon's wail for his parents on 'Mother' in 1970. This was a performance of utter conviction that – on the unconscious level, at the very least – found Bowie investigating the consequences of his chosen profession with a level of honesty so scathing that it took courage to continue.

[149] 'HEROES' (Bowie/Eno)

[150] 'HELDEN'

[151] 'HEROS'

Recorded June–August 1977; single A-side & 'Heroes' LP (UK [149]; Germany [150]; France [151]).

Courage requires heroes,* and not all 'heroes' are heroic – which was why Bowie chose to cloak his characters in a protective layer of irony, and inverted commas. Enough has been written elsewhere about the biographical inspiration for this song: Bowie watching out of the Hansa Studios window in West Berlin as two lovers met surreptitiously by the Wall, two lovers who may – or may not – have proved to be (married) record producer Tony Visconti and his lover Antonia Maass. Important though that incident must have been in personal terms, it diminishes the song to have it reduced to a factual account of an affair.

For Bowie clearly had more at stake than a romantic photograph (even if the snapshot of the tryst alongside the ultimate symbol of a divided planet was every bit as romanticised as his lovers in a doorway, or by the river's edge, in the 'Sweet Thing' medley [100]). He claimed as the album was released that the song was about the heroism of facing up to reality and staring it down. He was referring to political oppression, but that remark would have had a peculiarly personal resonance to the creator of *Low*. 'The *shame*,' he howled at one point, once again channelling the spirit of John Lennon[†] at his most agonised. There was certainly a discrepancy between the initial scenario of the song, which seemed to be nothing more edifying than a pick-up by a man trying to convince his soon-to-be-lover that one night of adultery was a heroic act; and the extent of Bowie's emotional

* Another 'Hero' was to be found on an album Bowie had certainly relished, *NEU!* '75. Sonically, however, that track exerted more influence on, arguably, 'Beauty And The Beast' [147] and, unmistakably, 'Red Sails' [168].
[†] Bowie certainly admired the *John Lennon/Plastic Ono Band* album, calling it 'very straight from the shoulder'; I'd wager that he listened to it often in 1976/77.

investment* in its later stages. Early in the song, Bowie was playful and intimate; later he sang as if his soul were on fire. 'People like watching people who make mistakes,' he had noted the previous year, 'but they prefer watching a man who survives his mistakes.' After the track was released, he preferred to distance himself from the song's emotional content, claiming he was trying to capture the heroism of the Turkish community living in the poorest quarters of West Berlin.

Eno's biographer David Sheppard described how this track was created: 'three oscillating VCS3 drones' from Eno, plus 'triumphal arcs of guitar [by Robert Fripp] filtered through Eno's extensive treatments . . . to freight the song with its towering opulence'. Structurally, '"Heroes"' was as simple as anything Bowie had written: it was based on a two-chord (D-G) progression, with a brief excursion to other familiar chords from the key of G. The combination of Eno's synthesisers and Fripp's guitars (three of them, apparently, all retained in the mix) created that strangest of contradictions, a peaceful cacophony of feedback and noise, with guitar notes sustained to infinity. The drums heightened and withdrew the drama, as required, occasionally skipping a backbeat to prove that some humanity was involved. But all the emotional weight of the song rested on Bowie, who successfully journeyed from seduction to existential despair as if it were the most hackneyed route of all. As, indeed, it may have been, for 'heroes' such as these.

For the first time since 'Space Oddity' [1], Bowie reached out beyond the English-speaking audience, recording single-length versions of '"Heroes"' in French and German. His vocal on the German edition, '"Helden"', was astonishingly intense; on the French '"Heros"', however, he sounded defeated, by the language as much as the despair.

[152] SONS OF THE SILENT AGE (Bowie)

Recorded June–August 1977; 'Heroes' LP.

Bowie arrived at the sessions for his second Visconti/Eno collaboration with this solitary song, which (perhaps inevitably) he intended as the

* Angus MacKinnon, in the *NME*, pronounced this 'Bowie's most moving performance in years'.

title track for his successor to *Low*. *'Heroes'* would have been a very different record had he continued in this direction, for 'Sons Of The Silent Age' revisited themes and sounds from the previous decade, rather than focusing single-mindedly on the contemporary. Although some of his references were personal – he provided his best vocal impression of Anthony Newley since 1967, while the robotic characters of his narrative belonged to some hybrid of *Diamond Dogs* and Fritz Lang's (silent-age) *Metropolis* – others had surprisingly obvious antecedents. Of these, the Beatles were the most recognisable, with the backing voices in the long melodic descent of the middle section evoking their 1968 recording 'Sexy Sadie', while Bowie's final vocal flourish echoed the closing bars of Paul McCartney's hit single 'Jet'. All of which explained, perhaps, the feeling of spiritual emptiness that pervaded the lyrics, as if everything in life were stale and repetitive – whether one was listening to music by Sam Therapy or King Dice (both existing only in Bowie's imagination). The song's chorus reflected that feeling, with its bored drift back and forth between G and F major chords. The only disruption to the mundane (however attractively expressed) was the initial saxophone-driven climb from the A to D major chords, omitting only C♯ along the way.

[153] BLACKOUT (Bowie)

Recorded June–August 1977; *'Heroes'* LP.

As 'Beauty And The Beast' [147] had already made clear, Bowie was determined on this record to keep autobiography at bay. 'I still incorporate a lot of [William] Burroughs' ideas,' he said, 'and I still purposely fracture everything, if it's making too much sense.' That has not prevented biographers from assuming that 'Blackout' was inspired by an incident in 1977 when Bowie was hospitalised, believing erroneously that he was suffering a heart attack. Equally intriguing, for those who wanted to conflate life and art, was the fact that this was the fourth consecutive song on *'Heroes'* that referred to drinking: by his own admission, alcohol was one of the pulls on Bowie's addictive personality during the late seventies. Yet searching for a definite meaning was not always a fulfilling pastime: when Bowie declaimed himself to be under Japanese influence, was he revealing the depth of his immersion in Japanese culture? Briefly assuming the persona of Yukio Mishima, the novelist and nationalist who died in a particularly gruesome ritual suicide in 1970? Or merely tossing off the kind of boast that comes easily to the lips of the wit and bon viveur when they're being faced with a disgraceful exit from a bar?

Then there were the musical references in this most cacophonous of performances, which began with what sounded like a large shipment of crates being dropped at enormous height from a dockside crane. Wasn't the introduction reminiscent of Paul McCartney's 'Beware My Love' (unlikely listening for Bowie and Eno, one would have thought)? Weren't the falsetto vocals at the end a pastiche of the Beatles? And in particular, didn't Bowie's ecstatic cry of 'woo-hoo' sound as if it belonged on John Lennon's 'I Am The Walrus'? (Maybe John Lennon was the one under Japanese influence . . .) If the Beatles references were too much, then how about the Velvet Underground, and the combination of thin, stabbing guitar and pounded piano in the style of 'White Light/White Heat'?

This is where speculation takes you. It was enough to label this a study of someone's psychological decay, and relish the glorious intensity of Bowie's performance – perhaps the most carefree he had sounded on record since 'Let's Spend The Night Together' [72] nearly five years earlier. An entire generation of British rock bands was certainly listening closely, as the insistent keyboard motif whining beneath Bowie's procession of different vocal personae recurred throughout records by the likes of Echo & the Bunnymen and The Teardrop Explodes.

[154] **V-2 SCHNEIDER** (Bowie)

Recorded June–August 1977; 'Heroes' LP

Conceptually simple and sly, 'V-2 Schneider' combined the names of a German weapon of mass destruction from the Second World War with the surname of a member of Kraftwerk. Though it was a far more disruptive piece than anything the German band would have attempted, its vocal chorus – evolving slowly from the synthetic to the human – added some flesh and blood to the robotic refrains of Kraftwerk songs such as 'Autobahn' and 'Trans-Europe Express'.

Before then, the horror of the V-2 rocket had been represented by howls of feedback (a homage, perhaps, to guitarist Michael Rother of NEU!) and white noise, supported cinematically by the rat-tat-tat of percussion. Guitars and saxophones maintained the assault over a falling chord sequence, before the vocal respite. But the track ended with another descending roar of sound, symbolising the murderous advantage held by machine over man. It was a sombre message for a phase of Bowie's career during which he was entirely dependent on machinery.

[155] SENSE OF DOUBT (Bowie)

Recorded June–August 1977; 'Heroes' LP.

Brian Eno remembered that this instrumental took shape under the influence of his *Oblique Strategies* cards. (Eno's cards; Bowie's and Eno's overdubs; Bowie's writing credit.) 'It was like a game,' he told Ian MacDonald. 'We took turns working on it; he'd do one overdub and I'd do the next. Effectively [my card] said, "Try to make everything as similar as possible" . . . and [Bowie's] said, "Emphasise differences".' That clash of concepts was effectively the whole of the piece: not only was 'Sense Of Doubt' as eerie as its title suggested; it was based around the contrast between a repeated four-note piano motif (echoed on synthesiser) and the constant variations that greeted it. Each repetition prompted a different set of chords as a synthesised fanfare, while across the barren landscape roamed a menagerie of noises and effects – some vaguely human, some purely mechanical, all ominous and unnerving. Before and after it all were washes of sound, as if nature itself had been conquered by the machine, and even the tides and winds survived solely at the whim of a computer.

[156] MOSS GARDEN (Bowie/Eno)

Recorded June–August 1977; 'Heroes' LP.

Eno's biographer, David Sheppard, suggested that Bowie's initial input into 'Moss Garden' was 'restricted to impressionistic scene-setting' – in this instance, a place of remembrance located in tranquil surroundings in Kyoto, Japan. Though the music that Eno created was appropriately restful, gently drifting between F♯ and C♯ with the hum of synthesised strings, it was not entirely idealistic: the world interrupted the reverie in the form of an aeroplane flying across the channels, a dog barking, the distant throb of a gong slowing and echoing. All these sounds were created electronically. Bowie then augmented the piece with an improvisation on the Japanese instrument, the koto, first tracing the downward spiral of a scale, before playing amidst the possibilities opened by the prevailing keys. Depending on your point of view, his contribution either reclaimed the 'Moss Garden' carefully for humanity, or subverted Eno's original concept of an entirely electronic soundscape.

The almost visual textures of this sequence of compositions were indebted to the innovations of the German band NEU!, although their debut album extended the range and impact of ambient sound to include the jarring assault of a pneumatic drill (on the track 'Negativland'). In particular, 'Leb Wohl' (from *NEU! '75*) anticipated both the mood and the construction of 'Moss Garden'. The list of instruments utilised by Bowie and Eno on *Low* and *'Heroes'* also bears comparison with NEU!'s work, as if the two British musicians had set themselves the task of assembling an album using the German band's tools.

[157] NEUKÖLN (Bowie/Eno)

Recorded June–August 1977; *'Heroes'* LP.

From Kyoto, Bowie's conceptual camera cut to a district of Berlin where, he explained later, 'the Turks are shackled in bad conditions. They're very much an isolated community. It's very sad.' In keeping with the shift from garden to city sprawl, this piece treated Eno's synthesised canvas, with its rain and church bells, more harshly. Sustained guitar feedback created a gently acerbic tone, before the picture was filled out with keyboards and saxophone. The latter was perhaps Bowie's most telling contribution to any of his instrumental collaborations with Eno: using pure emotion to fill the holes left in his rusty technique, he expressed the frustration of the Turkish immigrants with some deliberately harsh flurries of sound, before sounding the retreat with two elongated howls of despair.

[158] THE SECRET LIFE OF ARABIA (Bowie/Eno/Alomar)

Recorded June–August 1977; *'Heroes'* LP.

In an uncanny prediction of what awaited him on his next album project, Bowie turned imaginary tourist on this conceptually flawed and creatively hollow piece, which provided a bathetic climax to the *'Heroes'* LP. It also provided a template for the New Romantic movement of the early eighties, which took its inspiration from the surface appearance of Bowie's work rather than its content. The vocals were mannered to the point of distraction; it was certainly difficult to find a rational explanation for his decision to tackle the word 'Arabia' with a cockney accent worthy of Dick Van Dyke. Likewise the combination of Bo Diddley's signature R&B rhythm and 'ethnic' instrumentation was curious rather than enlightening. The most exhilarating element of this evocation of Hollywood desert-movie clichés was the hand-clapping, and even that was produced artificially – in keeping with the entirely fantastic, but never uplifting, nature of the song.

'Heroes' LP

Having neglected to promote *Low* (the title extending its influence from his mental state to his public profile), Bowie compensated with an energetic round of publicity interviews when its successor appeared just nine months later. Yet he was far from being the egomaniac who had boasted a couple of years earlier that he was incapable of giving a poor performance. Indeed, his comments seemed designed to undercut any expectations about his music, which he described as 'just a collection of stuff that I and Eno and Fripp had put together . . . I could have used any of the songs as the title, because there's no concept to the album.'

To prove that the public always distrusts modesty, *'Heroes'* marked a definite step downwards in terms of raw commercial appeal. *Low* had benefited from following not only *Station To Station* but the first Bowie 'hits' compilation, *ChangesOneBowie*. *'Heroes'* had to follow *Low*, with which he had signalled that he had no intention of being either a Ziggy Stardust clone or a disco icon. Sales of those two albums were remarkably consistent in Britain, a testament to the loyalty of Bowie's fans. But in America, *'Heroes'* ended a run of eight Top 20 LPs, to become his worst-selling collection of new material since (ironically) the highly commercial *Hunky Dory*. Stranger still, the title track – acclaimed for at least three decades as one of Bowie's greatest songs and performances – failed to touch the mainstream pop audience, peaking at no. 22 in Britain and entirely escaping the US Hot 100 chart. Bowie had effectively destroyed his chances on Top 40 radio in the States when 'TVC-15' [129] didn't reproduce the dance-floor groove of 'Golden Years' [127]. A succession of major British hits ('Sound And Vision' [136], 'Boys Keep Swinging' [171], 'Ashes To Ashes' [184], 'Fashion' [185]) passed American radio by. (It took a collaboration with Queen for Bowie to make a brief return to the US Top 30, after which 'Let's Dance' eradicated the radio producers' misgivings.) Even at its most accessible, this album assembled a barrage of sonic elements that were acutely confrontational. As the *NME*'s Angus MacKinnon noted insightfully, its verbal content was equally abrasive: 'instamatic lyric overflow, sense and sentence overcut at every opportunity . . . At first it's impossible to keep up with the phenomenally fast event horizon'.

So dazzling was the assault upon the senses, in fact, that it was easy to overlook a crucial difference between this album and its predecessor. On *Low*, Bowie for once made no attempt to intervene a fictional self (or even an artistic one) between singer and audience. The songs could be interpreted as overtly autobiographical, and Bowie has said nothing since to deflect that interpretation. With *'Heroes'*, however, he reverted to a method that had protected him from intense scrutiny on the *Diamond Dogs* album: using vocals of astonishing physical commitment to voice lyrics that were oblique and often (through the use of the cut-up technique) deliberately evasive. Throughout *Low*, Bowie had rarely been more honest, or sung with less attempt to convey his emotional extremes; here, the positions were exactly reversed.

The Art of Expressionism

The covers of *The Idiot* and *'Heroes'* were, quite consciously, posed – posed in such a way as to expose the artificiality of portraits that appeared spontaneous or natural. The Scottish performance artist Bruce McLean, who in 1972 staged a retrospective at London's Tate Gallery, 'just for one day', set out in the early seventies to mimic, exploit and subvert 'the pose'. With a group of friends, he formed Nice Style, 'the world's first pose band', as a satirical commentary on the pretensions of rock stars (and performance artists). Nice Style could have performed alongside the Moodies, the defiantly kitsch 'mythic, cartoon-like ambassadors of a pure pop sensibility', who emerged at the same time from the arty Chelsea milieu that also spawned Roxy Music. Allowed an art-school background, Bowie might have fitted alongside either ensemble: instead, as he recalled, 'I was just a hack painter who wanted to find a new medium to work in, frankly. And rock 'n' roll looked like a very good vehicle.'

For many years, after his disillusioning apprenticeship as an advertising visualiser, Bowie sacrificed his pretensions towards being an artist.* It was only when he stopped performing in 1975 that he allowed himself to dabble in art as well as the occult. By the end of that year, he had become quite the polymath, proudly declaring that he had been writing, painting, creating lithographs, printing silk-screens. 'I'm doing lots of sculptures as well,' he added, 'sort of polythene and essential, functional things around the house. Some 15-foot† things.' He was convinced that a major gallery – perhaps the Metropolitan Museum, why not? – was about to stage an exhibition of his work, something for which he had to wait another twenty years.

Transplanted to Berlin in 1976, Bowie explored the local art scene and the city's museums. He was already an aficionado of German expressionist cinema; now he searched out expressionist canvases wherever he could find them. He was particularly struck by the work of Erich Heckel, one of four architecture students in Dresden who, in 1905, formed a group called Die Brücke ('the bridge'). Heckel's early work has been lauded for its 'ecstatic expressiveness': it included *Roquairol*, the portrait that was mimicked on the cover of *The Idiot*. In the metropolitan paintings of George Grosz, Bowie found all the decadent turmoil of Berlin in the immediate aftermath of the First World War, the artist's explanations for his apocalyptic visions being strangely reminiscent of Bowie's account of America on the verge of catastrophe in 1972.

One painter above all entranced Bowie, to the extent that he intended to portray him in a biopic that was being planned (but never filmed) by director Clive Donner. Egon Schiele had died from influenza in 1915, at

---

* Few rock stars had dared to express themselves in the visual arts by the mid-seventies, the exceptions including John Lennon, who married a conceptual artist; Joni Mitchell, whose talent as a painter was exhibited on her album covers; and Bob Dylan, whose ability as a painter did not yet merit the description of 'talent'.

† Length is rarely a good measure of art. One can't help recalling the occasion when Bob Dylan was asked, 'What are your songs about?' 'Oh, some are about six minutes . . .'

the age of 25, three days after his wife (and four after he had painted her on her deathbed). In that brief lifespan, he had already declared that 'everything is dead while it lives', and he filled his canvases with bodies that appeared to be broken and decaying while they were still functionally alive. His subjects were pictured in contorted poses – their torsos twisted, or crouched uncomfortably just above the floor. (Bowie's pose on the cover of 'Heroes' was a generic blend of Schiele and Heckel iconography.) Art critic Erwin Mitsch noted that in Schiele's late self-portraits – one of which, from 1913, resembles Bowie at his most razor-edged and skeletal – 'Mime and theatrical gesture have been exaggerated to abnormal tensions which are no longer subject to the will and cannot be controlled by it.' No wonder Bowie was attracted by the challenge of portraying the artist on screen. He knew the pull of what Mitsch called 'an uncompromising disregard for himself, and a fanatic search for truth, unchecked by any other consideration'. Thwarted by the collapse of the film project, and as yet uncertain of his ability to match Schiele's efforts in oils, he preserved his vision of the artist's work, and on Broadway in 1980 found a way to combine it with his own.

[159] MADMAN (Bowie/Bolan)

[160] SLEEPING NEXT TO YOU (Bowie/Bolan)

Recorded by David Bowie & Marc Bolan, September 1977; unreleased.

Marc Bolan's status as Britain's leading pop idol did not survive the arrival of Ziggy Stardust, a creature altogether more enigmatic and alluring. By 1973, Bolan's popularity was undeniably waning: effectively a one-hit sensation in the USA, he achieved his final Top 10 success in the UK that summer. Though his self-confidence rarely wavered, his cloak of stardom quickly wore thin, although he retained a loyal following of committed fans. In a 1974 article tellingly titled 'Bolan: Is He On The Wane?', the first glam-rock superstar was finally prepared to admit that Bowie was his 'only rival', having previously dismissed him as a camp (in both senses of the word) follower.

Bowie and Bolan sat up for several days in Bowie's New York

hotel room in the summer of 1974, endlessly rerunning a print of *A Clockwork Orange* ('it reminded us of our childhoods', Bolan claimed). High on cocaine, they concocted gargantuan plans for a joint album and a movie project, about which Bolan crowed: 'David will write the screenplay, I will write the music. We'll both have small roles, and we'll both direct it.' Bowie could invent schemes like this at any moment of the day; his vaults must be full of improvised film treatments, as he continually announced that he had just written 'several' or 'twenty' screenplays. Sadly, Bolan took the drug-fuelled proposals to heart, and wasted more of his diminishing supply of credibility by boasting about them to the British media, long after Bowie had forgotten the conversation. Bolan was still hyping the movie collaboration three years later (under another emblematic headline, 'Boastful Bolan'): 'I hope it's going to be out in a year. All I can tell you is that it's about a future society and reflects our own feelings. We're also bringing out an album, doing a side each. What a combination it's going to be. The two greatest musical influences of the Seventies joined together!'

As before, this meant more to Bolan than to Bowie, although the two men did meet up in the spring of 1977 during Bowie's UK tour with Iggy Pop, and kicked around some musical ideas. At that point Bowie also agreed to take part in the final programme of Bolan's TV series, *Marc!*, a low-budget affair scheduled for late-afternoon children's viewing. The series allowed punk music a rare showcase on British television, but otherwise merely emphasised how far Bolan's status had declined since the days of 'T.Rexstasy' six years earlier.

Before the filming, Bowie and Bolan worked up some fragments from their earlier jam session, in the style of Bowie's collaborations with Iggy Pop. An album of such experiments might have been an interesting project, though the tapes of work in progress demonstrated how much Bolan's desperate desire to be the centre of attention was starting to rile his old friend/rival. Their joint TV performance lasted just 70 seconds, before Bolan slipped off the stage as he was about to sing, Bowie chortled at his misfortune, and technicians declared that they were out of time. As, sadly, was Bolan: he died in a car accident a week later, before the show was broadcast.

[161] **PEACE ON EARTH/LITTLE DRUMMER BOY** (Grossman/ Fraser/Kohan; Davis/Onorati/Simeone)

Recorded by David Bowie & Bing Crosby, September 1977; single A-side.

In the world of light entertainment, before rock's unilateral declaration of independence from the rituals of show business, it was common-place for pop stars to guest on television programmes alongside more middle-of-the-road performers. The David Bowie who adored Sinatra and Garland, Anthony Newley and Sammy Davis Jr did not baulk at the invitation to appear on Bing Crosby's 1977 Christmas TV special – especially when allowed the opportunity to perform '"Heroes"' [149] for Crosby's audience. In keeping with the festive spirit of the show, Bowie also agreed to join the aged Crosby (who would die less than five weeks later) in a duet, on what he informed Crosby was his son's favourite seasonal song, 'Little Drummer Boy'.

In fact, Bowie hated that song, and only agreed to participate when the show's musical directors hastily concocted an appropriate refrain for him to offer as a counterpoint: 'Peace On Earth' (not to be confused with the Christmas song of the same name, earlier recorded by Dean Martin). The televised performance was preceded by some excruciatingly staged dialogue, in which Crosby pretended to be a visiting Yank in a British home, and Bowie turned up expecting to be greeted by friends, rather than a vaguely familiar American. 'You're the guy who sings, right?' he said in his best London-styled accent. Their duet was very much in Crosby's style, not Bowie's; it suggested that all conceptions of Bowie as a tortured rock auteur needed to be treated with a degree of scepticism.

Another project from 1977 reinforced that impression. The Phila-delphia Orchestra recorded *Peter and the Wolf*, Prokofiev's eerily charming children's suite, in 1975, and then waited two years to secure a narrator. John Gielgud and Alec Guinness politely turned them down, but Bowie agreed to the task, ostensibly as a Christmas present for his son. Having recently met Bing Crosby with a cockney accent, he now read Prokofiev's script in an altogether more cultured and rootless tone, speaking slowly, enunciating clearly and sometimes teetering on the verge of patronising his pre-teenage audience. But if his rendition lacked the gravitas of those by trained actors, such as

Ralph Richardson, Peter Ustinov and Sean Connery, it was perfectly respectable – another landmark in the career of an all-round family entertainer, in fact.

Sound and Vision #3: *Just A Gigolo*

During the period when Bowie was passing himself off as a crooner and narrator, strenuous efforts were being made by actor Dennis Hopper to secure the film rights to William S. Burroughs' autobiographical novel *Junky*. Hopper was scheduled to direct, and was apparently keen to offer Bowie a leading role, but he was unable to secure sufficient funding. Numerous other movie projects were also under Bowie's consideration during this period, among them a self-penned screenplay about Hermann Goering's role in the Nazi party ('Friends remember him being particularly interested in anything to do with Hitler,' one observer noted); a bio-pic about the expressionist painter Egon Schiele, which had the unpromising working title of *Wally*; and Ingmar Bergman's *The Serpent's Egg*, another examination of the extremes of German culture. Bergman's was the only film brought to fruition, though without any involvement from Bowie, who had instead secured a leading role in a film set in his adopted home city of Berlin.

Just A Gigolo was directed by David Hemmings, an iconic actor in British film history, with no experience behind the camera except for some footage he'd shot, at Bowie's request, during the UK concerts on the *Station To Station* tour. Bowie was disappointed with the results, but still agreed to sign up for Hemmings' movie. The crucial factor in his decision was the fact that he would be appearing alongside one of his idols from the golden age of cinema, Marlene Dietrich; or so he supposed. Dietrich refused to travel to Germany, and insisted on shooting her sequences in Paris, so the two actors never met.

In retrospect, Bowie admitted that he had been unimpressed by the script, which required him to play a First World War veteran who haplessly becomes a member of a militarist cabal, but decided to trust that Hemmings' charm might translate itself into a watchable piece of cinema. He was mistaken: by 1980 he was saying, 'The film was a cack, a real cack. Everybody who was involved in that film – when they meet each other now, they look away!' His initial feelings of anger at having been duped so easily were replaced by embarrassment and ultimately acceptance: *Just A Gigolo* had not, as some reviewers advised, ended his film career, so he could afford to be merciful.

For his part, Hemmings believed that the editing of the initial German release had gone awry, and that the longer English-language version would save his reputation. The English cut did at least allow Bowie's voice to be heard: in the original, his lines were overdubbed by a German actor with a much more authoritative tone. On screen, he played as if he were in a drawing-room comedy, while his fellow thespians believed they were acting out a historical drama. But Bowie remained unsurpassed in the seventies for any director requiring a portrayal of someone who couldn't quite *connect*.

[162] REVOLUTIONARY SONG (Bowie/Fishman)

Recorded 1978; single A-side & *Just A Gigolo* film.

Bowie had been unable to secure the role of soundtrack composer for his first full-length film, *The Man Who Sold The World*. For *Just A Gigolo*, in contrast, he found himself obligated to provide one piece of music – a condition he satisfied with the least imaginable degree of effort. Musical director Jack Fishman was presented with a tape of Bowie singing a thirties-style marching tune, with 'la la la' vocals, over rudimentary piano, street violin, and ramshackle percussion. Realising that was all he was going to get, he proceeded to dress Bowie's skeleton up in fancy dress, creating a song (for which he, not Bowie, penned the lyrics) with the aid of musicians known as the Rebels, who added a suggestion of flamenco to the European stew. In retrospect, 'Revolutionary Song' was of interest only because it represented an initial stage in Bowie's creative process: had this task (or tune) piqued his curiosity in any way, he would surely have built around his initial fragment, removing the melodic similarities to the Rolling Stones' 'Mother's Little Helper' along the way.

Exit the Actor: *Stage* LP

After a year or more of compulsive hedonism in Berlin, David Bowie had arrived at a position of stasis, from where there was nothing to be gained by continuing with his experiments in psychological dismantling. He had, he told journalist Timothy White in late 1977, 'taken some realist attitudes to try and stabilize my own personality. My *real* personality. It must still be in there somewhere.' White's verdict was both reassuring and chilling: 'The celebrated chameleon is transformed into an ordinary sight. He could be swallowed up in a crowd. For perhaps the first time in his protean career, David Bowie is emptied out.'

What would fill the space? Bowie clearly did not trust his ability to withstand temptation. In January 1978, he told Michael Watts: 'I get scared stiff of the idea of touring again because of all kinds of experiences that one has . . . The testing of one's personality to the fullest: can you cope on a tour? When you're shouldering the responsibility of the whole thing, it's quite easy to break up. Either way, you close up or you let loose. My tendency goes either way.' As he spoke, he was preparing to reveal plans for a touring schedule that would last – with a long summer break to begin work on a new album – for almost nine months, and reach more than one million people. The old impulse to keep himself busy as a means of avoiding mental disintegration was hard to disobey.

Once he had completed *Just A Gigolo*, he took a safari holiday in Kenya with his son, and then joined his band in New York, where Carlos Alomar had been guiding the initial rehearsals. It was clear from the outset that this was not a tour on which Bowie was keen to stamp any personality. This, he insisted, was the 'real' David Bowie, from which every hint of image and persona had been excised: 'I think the only thing that's false about my stage presence at the moment is an actual knowledge of stagecraft, which I do utilise. But apart from that, there's no conscious attempt to portray anybody other than myself.' It was as if everything associated with David Bowie had vanished apart from songs, and he had employed David Jones to present them in public. There was a hint of Jones' own experience, from the years before Bowie, in the way that the tour was advertised. Bowie, or Jones, had sketched a representation of the pose from the cover of *'Heroes'*, in the style of Egon Schiele – its integrity spoiled only by the three little stars that had been drawn over his head, as if this were a teenage pop annual from the early sixties. It was a technique that Jones might have learned during his time in the advertising agency, half a lifetime earlier, but it seemed strangely anachronistic in 1978.

Bowie/Jones could certainly not be accused of selling himself cheaply at these lengthy shows, which were documented on the low-key, almost emotionless double album *Stage*. The performances began in glacial fashion with extracts from *Low* and *'Heroes'*, the ambient instrumentals being forced to masquerade as arena entertainment. After an intermission, the 'real' David Bowie delivered a suite of songs from *Ziggy Stardust*, rendered into tame nostalgia by the lack of Spiders and showmanship. Aside from a raucous Brecht/Weill medley [163], the show slipped into a comfortable, impeccably professional but rarely compelling selection of hits and anthems. There was none of the brash swagger of the *Ziggy* years; none of the psychodrama of 1974; none of the relentless momentum of the *Station To Station* tour. Just Bowie: straight, purposeful, uneventful.

When the tour was over, Bowie was living in Switzerland rather than Berlin, having won custody of his son from his emotionally distressed wife. He was, he proclaimed, 'learning to be happy . . . I'm even practising walking down the street'. He was writing a book of short stories, and planning an album that might be called *Despite Straight Lines*. He had revised his past one more time: his creative peak was *Diamond Dogs*, he declared, whereas *Young Americans*, the album he'd proclaimed at the time as his most honest, was now said to have come from his 'cynical period'. And he was learning to come to terms with the fact that, on the basis of his performance in *Just A Gigolo*, critics did not believe that he could act. Meanwhile, his record company were promoting his back catalogue, under the headline: 'And one man in his time plays many parts'. Which begged the question: what future was there for a David Bowie who could not – or did not want to – act?

[163] ALABAMA SONG (Brecht/Weill)

Recorded July 1978; single A-side.

During his stay in Berlin, Bowie had been introduced to the music of the German cabaret artiste Lotte Lenya, best remembered as an interpreter of songs by Kurt Weill and Berthold Brecht. 'Alabama Song' – a medley of two starkly different melodies, known individually as 'show me the way to the next whisky bar' and 'moon of Alabama' – was taken from the Brecht/Weill musical, *The Rise and Fall of the City of Mahagonny*. Although the medley had been introduced into the rock repertoire a decade earlier by the Doors, Bowie's phrasing and tempo were clearly guided by Lenya's 1956 recording.

There were several minor differences between the two arrangements: Lenya's 'pretty boy' became female in Bowie's rendition, for example lending a rather alarming tenor to the insistent call for 'a little girl'; Lenya's juxtaposition of spoken and singing voices in the final verse was replaced by Bowie crooning histrionically over a lush chorus. But those were textural changes alongside the startling shifts in rhythm that Bowie imposed on the song. While his vocal kept perfect time, the accompaniment was wildly chaotic, with drums, saxophone and guitar each obeying its own deliberately haphazard metronome. Meanwhile, Bowie displayed an equally bewildering set of vocal personae – Germanic or cockney, crooning or ranting – to demonstrate that there were more ways of invoking the spirit of chance in a song than simply taking a pair of scissors to a lyric sheet.

[164] FANTASTIC VOYAGE (Bowie/Eno)

Recorded September 1978–March 1979; *Lodger* LP.

Station To Station, *Low* and *'Heroes'* had all announced themselves with noise. The first sound heard on *Lodger* was the gentle tap of percussion – a hint that this was likely to be less intense than recent adventures. One of three songs recorded during these sessions with exactly the same chord sequences (one was jettisoned; the other became 'Boys Keep Swinging' [171]), 'Fantastic Voyage' based its metaphorical exploration of Life with a capital L around a subdued replay of the '"Heroes"' [149] drone, lightened with piano and (according to one account) multi-dubbed mandolins, though it's not easy to distinguish their exact contribution to the song. That was perhaps a hint that Bowie was all too consciously returning to the recent past, offering a hint of the emotional tumult of *Low* (with the line about depression) and also a defensive self-justification for his more outré political comments of recent times. His efforts to pass as a textbook liberal – outraged by nuclear missiles, appalled by the Holocaust – were sadly too obvious to pass as art. But his vocal mastery, particularly his ecstatic rise up the scale to a resounding 'will we?', compensated for these flaws. So excited was piano player Sean Mayes by the prospect of Bowie's second climb that he peaked too early, and was left to wait for his leader to join him at the top.

[165] AFRICAN NIGHT FLIGHT (Bowie/Eno)

Recorded September 1978–March 1979; *Lodger* LP.

There was autobiography on *Lodger*, just as there had been on *Low*, but it was comprised of picture postcards from exotic lands, not an account of a mind at the end of its tether. Bowie claimed to have spent six weeks in Kenya before he was inspired to write this song, in which everything imaginable was going on but nothing was actually happening. 'I took a straightforward safari and spent a few hours with the Masai tribe,' he explained late in 1978. 'It's predictable that it will surface in the future . . . [but] I wanted to understand what I was seeing and what I was dealing with before I was presumptuous enough to start recording it.' Instead, he wrote this bizarre pastiche of Gilbert & Sullivan – or, rather, Todd Rundgren's version of Gilbert & Sullivan (think 'Song Of The Viking' from *Something/Anything*), crossed with Paul McCartney's own entry in the 'Me?-I've-just-been-to-Africa' stakes, 'Mrs Roosevelt' (from *Band On The Run*, recorded in Nigeria).

So we were given African percussion and jungle noises and Eno's 'cricket menace' (the insect, not the sport) and a tribal chant and some Swahili lyrics (wrongly transcribed: they basically say, 'Thanks, hello'), and a dictionary's worth of internal rhymes. Vocals, keyboards and bass all entered on the seventh beat of a bar (to emphasise that we were dealing with an alien culture). Bowie's defence: 'I would have thought it was pretty transparent that it was me trying to relate to that particular culture. Not in my wildest dreams would I think I was trying to represent them.' Which begged the question of why his response to Africa needed a traveller's bag full of Swahili words and native chants. Eno extended this method with David Byrne on the 1981 album *My Life In The Bush Of Ghosts*. Compare this to the way in which the German band Can's *Ethnological Forgery Series* treated 'world' music, from Asia to New Orleans, with lack of authenticity evident in both the concept and the deliberately 'unreal' reproduction of these 'alien' music forms. Yet it was Bowie's influence that would prevail in the decade ahead, when the decorations of 'world music' would become a common embellishment to rock careers that were becoming jaded with repetition.

Midway through this perfectly listenable, image-crammed but ulti-mately lightweight song, something altogether stranger occurred. Bowie effectively declared himself tired of being David Bowie, and tired of having an audience with expectations of him. He had, he said, a 'lust for the free life'. After which the song* – and the album – suddenly seemed to make sense, even if the fact that he had recorded *Lodger* at all suggested that the 'free life' was still some distance away.

[166] MOVE ON (Bowie)

Recorded September 1978–March 1979; *Lodger* LP.

After his 'African Night Flight' [165], what else to do but 'Move On'? This song sounded perilously as if it were intended as the manifesto of *Lodger*, with its restless travelling between cultures and landscapes. But in his efforts to prove himself a citizen of the planet, Bowie descended into rampant generalisations about Africans and Russians, like an instant expert who'd learned everything from a documentary on TV. (Nothing quite so crass had been heard in the popular music canon since Paul Simon categorised all the animals 'At The Zoo' in 1968. But Simon had the excuse that he was joking.) It didn't help that the 'move on' refrain was so melodically unin-spired, an unworthy vehicle for a set of chord changes that Buddy Holly would have recognised. Bowie delivered his verdicts in a

---

* Several critics have assumed a connection between this song and Scott Walker's 'Nite Flights', the title track of a 1978 Walker Brothers album, covered by Bowie on 1993's *Black Tie White Noise*. Bowie and Eno were certainly struck by the album, Bowie later describing it as including 'quite the most lovely songs that I'd heard in years'. But there are no musical or lyrical resonances from Walker's song on 'African Night Flight'. If anything, Walker's contributions to the *Nite Flights* LP sounded as if they were indebted to Bowie's *'Heroes'*, and in turn inspired several of the perform-ances on *Scary Monsters*.

pompous and self-satisfied voice, before a final outburst of passion as he recognised the obvious: his unrelenting travelling was just a disguise for 'drifting' helplessly in the wind.

As a symptom of his creative frustration, he grasped desperately at his own past: the central section of the song was based around the chorus of 'All The Young Dudes' [62], but with the tape reversed, Carlos Alomar deciphering the 'new' chord sequence. Bowie and producer Tony Visconti actually sang the 'Dudes' refrain, and then ran their efforts backwards beneath the song. Other inspiration was taken from the mid-section of the fifties R&B standard 'Kansas City', while Buddy Holly's 'Peggy Sue' was the obvious parallel for the track's chattering rhythm accompaniment.

[167] YASSASSIN (Bowie)

Recorded September 1978–March 1979; *Lodger* LP.

'Turkish for: Long Live,' explained the lyric sheet for *Lodger* helpfully. More accurately, the Turkish translation is *'yasasin'* (pronounced *yashasin*), though perhaps it was unrealistic to expect a cultural tourist to master a foreign tongue so quickly.

Bowie intended the song as a tribute to the Turkish immigrants massed in the Berlin suburb of Kreuzberg. But his attempts to think himself into their mentality were simply patronising to both sides. In an effort to capture the simple-hearted nature of Turkish life, he resorted to archaic English: his narrator's love was 'afeared', like the heroine of a traditional folk ballad.* But there was no flesh to his Turks: they were merely symbols, and flat ones at that.

To counterfeit the music of Turkey, Bowie built 'Yassassin' around a simple switch between two adjacent chords (E7 and F7), while encouraging violinist Simon House to play in recognisable 'Eastern' scale progressions. Violin and vocal both escaped the 4/4 time signature in another bid for ethnic authenticity. The blend of American funk and Jamaican reggae in the backing, however, suggested that for

---

* For any students of British pop history, the narrator's claim that he was not 'a moody guy' inevitably brought to mind 'I'm A Moody Guy', the first hit by early sixties pop star Shane Fenton – better known in the seventies as Alvin (no relation to Ziggy) Stardust.

Bowie every foreign signifier was of equal value: his Turks might as well have been Caribbeans or African-Americans.

[168] RED SAILS (Bowie/Eno)

Recorded September 1978–March 1979; *Lodger* LP.

Feeling seasick? Not sure about the language? Wish you'd stayed home? You need (rev up the new-wave-by-numbers riff) . . . red sail action.

The usual luggage was on board: synthesised strings, feedback howl, Kraftwerkian rhythm, a rich chorale of David Bowie voices, Adrian Belew's deliberately askew guitar solos. Despite being required to perform without having heard the track before, Belew didn't feel seasick: 'The one particular song I remember where I lucked out was "Red Sails", cos I started the guitar feeding back and it was right in key.' Bowie recalled that he had described the sound of NEU! to Belew before he added his solo, and that the guitarist had captured the perfect tone without ever hearing a note of the German band's music.

And the trip? Destination random: even Bowie didn't know or care what he meant by the 'hinterland', to which his final chorus was devoted. This was the cultural tourist's vacation, with no conclusions, no stereotypes, only a constant party with guests he would never meet again.

[169] D.J. (Bowie/Eno/Alomar)

Recorded September 1978–March 1979; *Lodger* LP.

On its release in 1979, 'D.J.' was widely classified alongside Elvis Costello's altogether more obvious 'Radio Radio' as an assault on the banality and blinkered mentality of US Top 40 radio stations. Costello accused radio programmers of trying to drug their listeners; Bowie's DJ was also in search of anaesthesia, but with more at stake than the conservatism of American radio formats. His challenge was also existential: 'What do I know?' Like David Bowie (alias David Jones, or D.J.), he had people who believed in him, and felt trapped by the responsibility. Nothing was certain any more: even the rhythm was insecure, as the song began with a stray half-bar, synthesised violins circled around an invisible centre, and Bowie's vocal entered what felt like a beat too soon. It added to the feeling that pervaded the entire album, in fact: where exactly are we? It was a pertinent question for a cultural tourist, adrift in the debris of other people's lives. Suitably enough, the track was littered with references to familiar musical themes, borrowed from the Rolling Stones, Neil Young, the Beach Boys and, of course, Talking Heads, with Bowie deliberately mimicking David Byrne's vocal style in the opening lines.

Appropriately, then, it was Byrne who would succeed Bowie as the intelligent person's rock star of choice in the early eighties, collaborating extensively with Brian Eno, dabbling with 'ethnic' rhythms and motifs, and combining urban anxiety with compelling art-rock that was tinged with the sensibility of minimalism.

[170] LOOK BACK IN ANGER (Bowie/Eno)

Recorded September 1978–March 1979; *Lodger* LP.

In which our hero witnessed 'the Angel of Death, hanging about in cafés waiting for people to die'. His tale read like prose on the page, and the transformation into song forced Bowie into an exaggerated vocal persona that would soon be imitated by eighties New Romantic performers such as Spandau Ballet. The aural centre of the piece was the chorus, though lyrically it added nothing but bombast to the effect: even its chord sequence was identical to the verses. Meanwhile, Tony Visconti and Bowie added maudlin voices of complaint in a strangely Liverpudlian tone – another stray Beatles reference to follow all the vague allusions to the group on *'Heroes'*. Propulsive and impatient, the track spotlighted Bowie's guitar during an instrumental break of such speed and dexterity that it must have been recorded in a lower key and at a slower pace, and then artificially accelerated to fit.

[171] BOYS KEEP SWINGING (Bowie/Eno)

Recorded September 1978–March 1979; *Lodger* LP.

If 'Fantastic Voyage' [164] treated Bowie's favourite chord sequence of the *Lodger* sessions with sensitivity, 'Boys Keep Swinging' bumped it around like a dodgem car, particularly when Bowie and Eno suggested that the musicians should swap roles – leaving Carlos Alomar, as the wonderfully chaotic percussionist, to turn the beat around, and Dennis Davis on minimalist bass (subsequently repaired by Tony Visconti). It's difficult at this distance to separate the track from its remarkable promotional film. In isolation, 'Boys Keep Swinging' was a romp that either satirised – or, more worryingly, reinforced – the male gang mentality, which Bowie would have known well from his mid-sixties spell as a mod.* The chorus swaggered along to a single chord (unlike 'Fantastic Voyage', with its more melodic shifts), while one of the basses played the riff from Larry Williams' 1957 rock 'n' roll classic, 'Bony Maronie'. Then Adrian Belew contributed a guitar solo that sounded as if it had been flown in from another dimension: which, thanks to Bowie's involvement, it effectively had. He explained: 'What I do is, say, use four tracks for a recorded solo and then I cut them up, knock up a little four-point mixer clipping the solos in and out. I give myself arbitrary numbers of bars in which they can play within a particular area, and go backwards and forwards from one track to another. The effect is somewhat histrionic.' So was the entire performance, from original conception to ramshackle delivery.

[172] REPETITION (Bowie)

Recorded September 1978–March 1979; *Lodger* LP.

Repetition was the cornerstone of American minimalist music; and of disco and funk; and of the popular music that attempted to marry these diverse approaches to sound. Brian Eno had introduced Bowie to the New York band Talking Heads, whose skeletal reproduction of funk through the prism of art-school aesthetics was undoubtedly influenced by Bowie's work, with and without Iggy Pop. Bowie later acknowledged that elements of 'D.J.' were intended as a homage to Talking Heads leader David Byrne, but he didn't mention the more overt debt he owed on this track, with its clipped vocal and relentless use of simple two-chord motifs.

* Bowie promised that his Boys could never be cloned, though by 1979 the mod revival was doing exactly that to the more individual modernist tradition of the early sixties. And talking of cloning, this track began life as a tribute to an old friend, under the working title 'Louis Reed'.

The man who had rued his own behaviour towards women on 'Can You Hear Me' [108] and 'It's Gonna Be Me' [116] now focused unwaveringly on a fictional case of domestic violence. A powerless angel watching lives unfold, he intervened just once, asking so softly for the violence to cease that there was no danger the protagonists would listen. Eno's electronic treatment was equally subtle, and a powerful if grim performance was undermined only by the melodic similarity between the line that expressed the assailant's frustration, and the chorus of America's 1972 soft-rock hit, 'Horse With No Name'.

[173] RED MONEY (Bowie/Alomar)

Recorded September 1978–March 1979; *Lodger* LP.

An album rife with self-cannibalism and self-depletion ended with a symbolic demonstration of both traits. 'Red Money' was built on the backing track of 'Sister Midnight' [132] from Iggy Pop's *The Idiot*, and proclaimed the unsettling message: 'project cancelled'.* By sheer coincidence, Bowie's pronouncement was released just two weeks after the British general election in which Margaret Thatcher led the Conservative Party to a resounding victory. Just as the quatrains of Nostradamus have been interpreted as a prediction of every major historical event since his death in 1566, so it would be tempting to imagine that here Bowie was anticipating the polarisation of cultural values, the death of liberal consensus, and the gradual decline of British industry that were the consequences of Thatcherism. Such a reading of 'Red Money' would be ridiculous, of course. But as acute an observer as Bowie would have known that any sense of community was under threat: in his own family, in rock culture, and in the wider societies beyond. *Lodger* began with Bowie insisting plaintively that life was a valuable commodity, and concluded with the resolution that it was our responsibility to preserve everything that constituted that value. At the end of a decade dominated by strains of individualism, he had still not quite given up on the power of collectivism.

Whatever 'red money' represented in Bowie's personal symbolism

---

* The following phrase, 'tumbling centre', was presumably a rendering of W.B. Yeats' often-quoted line: 'the centre cannot hold'.

– Russian roubles or blood-stained lucre – it roused him from stridency to near-hysteria by the end of the song, as he bellowed the title like John Lennon reliving his childhood agonies at the start of the decade. The 'Sister Midnight' track was treated to sonic distractions, in an effort to disguise its origins: a tumult of electronic noise, a series of funk riffs, a set of vocal harmonies that revisited the most intense moments of 'Breaking Glass' [134], and a final flurry of backwards guitar, as if Bowie were trying to reverse direction. It was too late for second thoughts, however: project cancelled.

Lodger LP

By his own exacting standards, *Lodger* was Bowie's one serious failure of nerve during the 'long seventies'. Expectations had been raised – not necessarily by Bowie himself – that the album would complete a trilogy alongside *Low* and *'Heroes'*. Although he briefly tried to puncture this idea, suggesting that the set would be completed by an album entitled *Fame* (which would have been an intriguing title for *Scary Monsters*, in retrospect), he eventually allowed himself to be caught up in the hype surrounding a supposed 'Berlin' triptych of collaborations with Eno. The fact that only one of the three had been entirely recorded in Berlin was merely a minor distraction to the publicity campaign.

In fact, *Lodger* was made in Switzerland, Bowie's latest haven. Eno arrived bearing a copy of the Walker Brothers' *Nite Flights* album, and a concept: the pair would consolidate the aleatory theme of their previous experiments by fashioning a record with the deliberately contradictory title of *Planned Accidents*. Elements of *Lodger* enacted that scenario perfectly, notably the switching of instruments on 'Boys Keep Swinging' [171] and the way in which visiting guitarist Adrian Belew was plunged into action without the safety of having heard the tracks that he was being asked to decorate.

The missing ingredient was songwriting – or, to be accurate, songwriting that aroused its composer's enthusiasm. 'If I'm bored, then people can see it,' Bowie had admitted in 1974. 'I don't hide it very well. Everything I do, I get bored with eventually. It's knowing where to stop.' Much of *Lodger* sounded as if Bowie had arrived at the sessions knowing exactly where his *Planned Accidents* would stop, and had fleshed out pages of his travel diary to fill the spaces. *Lodger* was his first studio record since *Pin Ups* that didn't need to be made, as critics swiftly recognised. It was treated with disdain by many reviewers, a representative sample of accusations including 'a piece of self-plagiarism . . . his last eight or so albums cut up, played backwards and then reassembled'; 'the most enervating and enervated album Bowie's made . . . Bowie is miserably confused'; and 'frustrating but well-crafted . . . ordinary by Bowie's recent standards' – none of which I feel tempted to rebut. The final critic was right, however: *Lodger* was impeccably well-crafted, very listenable and more commercial than its predecessors. It also proved to be more influential, proving easier to imitate in the decade ahead than *Low* or *'Heroes'* (not least by Eno, when in the company of David Byrne).

Lodger was also the first record for which Bowie produced promotional videos that were as radical as the songs they supported (more of which later). And its rather alarming cover art, photographed by Brian Duffy, outstripped any of the music for boldness. After one album with a deliberately low-profile jacket, and another on which Bowie chose to mimic the subject of an expressionist painting, *Lodger* represented a deliberate step into a world in which Egon Schiele became the art director for a futuristic horror movie, directed perhaps by David Cronenberg. Bowie's body was depicted across the gatefold sleeve, prone like Schiele's *Portrait of Friederike Maria Beer*, distorted like the same artist's lacerating self-portraits. It was as if the turmoil of the previous records had been focused on to the artwork of *Lodger*, leaving the music itself unsettlingly free of emotion.

[174] I PRAY OLE (Bowie)

Recorded *c.* 1978–9 (& 1990?); *Lodger* extended CD.

Retrieved from a 1979 tape for the 1991 CD reissue of *Lodger*, 'I Pray Ole' gave every aural indication of having been completed, if not fully formed, closer to the latter rather than during the sessions for *Lodger*. The drum sound – bombastic and intrusive – was certainly redolent of the late 1980s; while the style of Bowie's vocals, which were strangely conventional, didn't match anything else from the *Lodger* era. The lyrics were minimal and mock-clever; the underlying chord sequence borrowed from Cream's late-sixties hard-rock anthem 'White Room';

and even the use of cacophony as a means of interrupting expectations sounded perfunctory.

[175] PIANO-LA (Bowie/Cale)

[176] VELVET COUCH (Bowie/Cale)

Recorded by John Cale & David Bowie, October 1979; unreleased.

It was perhaps inevitable that Bowie would eventually collaborate with John Cale, one of the few British musicians of their generation who could match (and even outstrip) his maverick spirit. Bowie revered Cale as an original member of the Velvet Underground; while the two men were linked by their respective friendships with Brian Eno. With hindsight, it's sad that their partnership does not seem to have survived beyond a single session in a New York studio, during a break in Cale's touring schedule with his uncompromising *Sabotage/Live* band; and a cameo appearance by Bowie (playing outrageous violin) at a Cale concert in the same city.

These two low-fidelity recordings of semi-improvised songs – named by a bootlegger, rather than by either of the participants – escaped from the session. Through the sonic gloom, it was just possible to hear Bowie singing a wordless melody over a mournful Cale piano melody ('Piano-La') that reflected both men's love of the Beach Boys; and a more structured piece in the style of Cale's *Vintage Violence* or Bowie's *Hunky Dory*, over which Bowie contributed almost indecipherable lyrics ('Velvet Couch'). Incomplete though they were, these fragments were enough to whet the appetite for a more formal collaboration.

Bowie might also have resumed his partnership with Cale's former colleague Lou Reed in 1979. They shared a meal in London that April to discuss the idea of Bowie producing what proved to be Reed's *Growing Up In Public* album, but the occasion ended in a fist-fight after Bowie insisted – rather hypocritically, one might feel – that Reed would first have to abandon his intake of alcohol and drugs.

[177] SPACE ODDITY (Bowie)

Recorded December 1979; single B-side.

A decade after 'Space Oddity' [1] had introduced Bowie to the perilous lure of stardom, he returned to the song for a decade-ending TV performance, shown in Britain on *Kenny Everett's New Year's Eve Show* and in the USA on *Dick Clark's Salute To The Seventies*. 'Having played it with just an acoustic guitar onstage early on,' he explained, 'I was always surprised at how powerful it was just as a song, without all the strings and synthesisers. I really wanted to do it as a three-piece song.' Those three 'pieces' – piano, bass and drums – mirrored John Lennon's instrumentation on his 1970 album *Plastic Ono Band*, which had already left its mark on Bowie's vocals on the *'Heroes'* album. Indeed, after a sparse opening that pitched his voice (an octave above the original record) against lush 12-string guitar, and ten seconds of silence where the launch-pad countdown had once been, Bowie produced an exact replica of the sound that Lennon and Phil Spector produced on 'Mother' – bass and drum locked together in brutal unison, and the most basic of chords stabbed out on heavily echoed piano. The pause before the guitar showcase in the centre of the song was marked out with the thud of a bass drum: the same effect introduced the middle section of 'Isolation' on the same Lennon album. This was design, not coincidence, and it raised a tantalising possibility: what if Bowie had chosen to record his next album in *Plastic Ono Band* style?

By stripping bare a myth originally assembled in 1969, Bowie was effectively sealing off the seventies as a source of anything more than memory, nostalgic or otherwise. 'Space Oddity' had been written as an antidote to the mindless idealism of the late-sixties counter-culture; it re-emerged in a (British) society governed by a conservative clique whose guiding ethos was the erasure of everything that bore the taint of the sixties – the era that Margaret Thatcher's party held responsible for moral and social chaos and decay. Hence the relevance of reintroducing a spartan musical style that, in Lennon's hands, had signalled the end of a dream. The oddity was no longer the individual ostracised from society but, in the Britain of Thatcher's government, the person who still dared to believe in the power of collective action and the ability of society to care for all of its members, however alienated they might be.

[178] PANIC IN DETROIT (Bowie)

Recorded December 1979; *Scary Monsters* extended CD.

Whereas his remake of 'Space Oddity' [177] appeared as the B-side of a single, a second revision of the past remained unheard for more than a decade. That was probably because the 1979 version of 'Panic In Detroit' [67] was nothing more than fun, illuminating nothing beyond the fact that Bowie no longer took the song remotely seriously. The evidence for the prosecution: a hysterically mannered vocal ('panic innnnnn Dee-Troit') in the style of a mad (cracked?) actor; a cameo from Tony Visconti as a computer obsessed with correct spelling; and an arrangement that was dismissively quick, weirdly echoed, and punctuated with slowed-down cymbal crashes. An album like this might have worked, as an Agent Orange-style destruction of his past images; but one track in isolation merely sounded like an aberration.

[179] CRYSTAL JAPAN (Bowie)

Recorded February–April 1980; single B-side.

This instrumental (used as a drinks commercial in Japan, in Bowie's most blatant acceptance of the advertising ethos) was recorded during the sessions for *Scary Monsters (And Super Creeps)* in 1980, and originally intended as the album's closing track (at which point it would have been titled 'Fuje Moto San'). It demonstrated that Bowie no longer needed Brian Eno to create electronic soundscapes, even if Eno's influence was unmistakable (alongside that of the British sonic pioneer of the early sixties, Joe Meek, who might have written the melody of 'Crystal Japan' for one of his instrumental combos, such as the Tornados). The most conventionally 'pretty' of Bowie's experiments with ambient music, it set a striking melody (with key changes signalled by a plummeting bass tone) against a drowsy hum. The 'alien' motif from the hit science-fiction movie *Close Encounters Of The Third Kind* made a cameo appearance in the piece, suggesting that Bowie's intentions here were not entirely serious.

[180] IT'S NO GAME (PART 1) (Bowie; trans. Miura)

[181] IT'S NO GAME (PART 2) (Bowie)

Recorded February–April 1980; *Scary Monsters* LP.

The *Scary Monsters* album began and ended with the noise of a tape*
being rewound and then spinning freely on its reel: an admission
that this was, in the end, merely an artefact, a barrier between artist
and audience rather than a bridge. It was, moreover, an artefact of
ambiguous purpose, commenting on its creator's past while being
constructed out of random pieces of that heritage.

Take, for example, 'It's No Game', which utilised the structure,
melody and several lines of lyrics from 'Tired Of My Life' [27], a song
that Bowie insisted he had begun to write as early as 1963. Certainly its
most chilling line, about notoriety and suicide, dated from 1970 rather
than 1980. His lyrical additions to the song, besides the title's insistence
that this was a serious business, really, were either accidental couplings
of phrases (the first verse) or banal assertions of liberal humanism (the
references to fascism and the Third World). As with 'Fantastic Voyage'
[164] on *Lodger*, it was difficult to avoid the feeling that Bowie was
altogether too anxious to prove his political credentials after the embarrassment of his remarks on Hitler and fascism in the mid-seventies.

So words were not the purpose of this song – offered at either end
of *Scary Monsters* in arrangements so contrasting in mood that they
were almost baffling.

'Part 1' presented the lyrics in emphatically spoken Japanese (by
actress Michi Hirota), while Bowie delivered half of each verse in a
voice that ranged between distraught and agonising. Three lines in, he
was already screaming like a man undergoing the extremes of torture,
as Robert Fripp's guitar played a howling, no-exit riff behind him.
The song ended with Fripp delivering an excruciatingly atonal guitar
loop, while Bowie roared 'Shut up!' with the last shreds of his vocal
cords. The effect was stunning, scarifying, relentless – the product, it
seemed, of a soul in torment.

* As a keen student of the three LPs by the German band NEU!, Bowie would
have remembered the second side of *NEU! 2* beginning with the click and hum of
a needle landing on a vinyl record.

Or was it just acting, like the staged emotion of Hirota's monologue? Thirty-five minutes later, 'Part 2' revised 'It's No Game' as a lesson in emotional withdrawal, with a vocal that sounded subdued and resigned, repetitive but non-confrontational guitar riffs, and booming drums to announce the sonic values of a new decade. Where 'Part 1' climaxed with the signals of insanity, 'Part 2' just ended, draining colour from everything around it. And then the tape ran off the reel, as if Bowie was saying, 'That's it. I have nothing left to offer you.' He trailed hints of that message across the entire album.

[182] UP THE HILL BACKWARDS (Bowie)

Recorded February–April 1980; *Scary Monsters* LP.

'Up the hill backwards': as clever a statement of creative emptiness as Bowie could have concocted in that enervated state. In the deliberately banal chorus of this song, that title carried no hint of burden. But the physical task it described was something between an ordeal and an impossibility (try walking upstairs backwards as a quick demonstration). So was the possibility of dancing in 7/8 time,* as demanded by the augmented Bo Diddley riff that opened the song. Another throwback to fifties rock 'n' roll came in the verse, the first line of which used the same chord sequence as Eddie Cochran's anthem of teenage frustration, 'Summertime Blues'. In the chorus, there was a jaded chant of 'yeah, yeah, yeah', as a sarcastic reference to the carefree exuberance of the Beatles' 'She Loves You' – a trick he had already pulled on 'Always Crashing In The Same Car' [137] three years earlier.

This was a song about difficulty, about the disappearance of inspiration, and about the vacuum that might await someone who decided to step away from the necessity to be productive. Bowie made no attempt to disguise the jerry-built nature of the piece: the time signatures didn't marry up, there were no neat links between the separate sections of the song, and the lyrics were vaguely apocalyptic fragments. The only time inspiration seemed to take control was when Bowie relinquished the reins, to allow Robert Fripp's typically oblique guitar technique to tackle and control the final return to the 7/8 time signature.

* To be exact: seven bars in 7/8, followed by one bar in 3/8.

[183] SCARY MONSTERS (AND SUPER CREEPS) (Bowie)

Recorded February–April 1980; *Scary Monsters* LP.

Tony Visconti's excellent autobiography, *Bowie, Bolan & the Brooklyn Boy*, provided a telling – but, to the layman, potentially bewildering – account of how the sonic picture of this track was created: 'I programmed a descending bass line and fed the snare drum into the trigger circuit of the keyboard . . . We made [the bass] pulsate by putting it into a Kepex gate and we had Dennis Davis's eighth-note kick drum pattern trigger the bass.' He also described how this song, and indeed much of the album, emerged from fragmentation into the semblance of unity: 'We'd go back to specific sections [of the mix], sometimes as short as a two-second tom-tom fill, rearrange the faders, add special effects and equalization changes. Then I would edit all the smaller, special pieces back into the main mix with razor blade cuts and splicing tape.' This was state-of-the-art studio trickery for 1980 (though probably an anachronism by 1983), aided by the involvement of a genuinely creative and musically proficient producer in Tony Visconti. It was also a modus operandi that Bowie could never have mastered on his own: like his earlier collaborators, from John Hutchinson through Mick Ronson to Brian Eno, Visconti had presented Bowie with a paintbox that contained colours he had never seen before, and encouraged him to experiment.

This was the technological apogee of analogue recording, soon to be erased from history by the new possibilities and constraints of digital sound. With its razor blades and drums bleeding across the tracks, it was a last connection with the amateur science that had freed the likes of the Beatles to capture psychedelic inspiration on tape more than a decade earlier. Yet it was also sufficiently removed from the chords and notes of traditional music-making to allow the artist – however creative – to hide behind the process from time to time, and let the studio (and its master controller from Brooklyn) do the work.

Both Visconti and Bowie deserved credit for ensuring that the title* track of the *Scary Monsters* album survived that ingenuity and

* Bowie insisted as the album was released that he had seen the phrase 'scary monsters and super heroes' on the back of a Kellogg's Corn Flakes packet. His story revived memories of John Lennon basing the Beatles' 'Good Morning, Good Morning' on a TV advert for Corn Flakes.

manipulation with its energy intact. Like 'Up The Hill Backwards', this was ostensibly a portrait of exhaustion, with a woman who (unlike the cast of *Low*) found rooms unbearably claustrophobic and a man (like Bowie and John Lennon before him) who was on the run from what the ex-Beatle called 'the freaks on the phone'. There was a hint of narrative to the tale of their love and abuse, and a tip of the hat to Blondie guitarist Jimmy Destri. All this was delivered by Bowie in his finest long-distance approximation of a cockney accent, with a clipped ennui that might have made this a perfect song for Johnny Cash to cover. More Bowies emerged from every dimension as the song progressed, one of them shouting the chorus like a killer on a bad phone line.

If Bowie in all his vocal incarnations represented the scary monsters, then perhaps the super creeps did their work via the medium of Robert Fripp's triumphantly atonal guitar solo – his mastery of the instrument and oblique approach to a melody combining to create many of the most remarkable moments of this album. Finally, Bowie took another opportunity to reference the pioneering dynamics of NEU!, echoing the neo-punk sound of their 1975 track 'After Eight' in a defiantly post-punk environment.

[184] ASHES TO ASHES (Bowie)

Recorded February–April 1980; *Scary Monsters* LP.

The cinematic quality of 'Space Oddity' [1] in 1969 was erased when Bowie returned to the song a decade later, and reduced a widescreen epic to a starkly lit black-and-white photograph [177]. The strangely alienated space explorer from the year of *Apollo 11* had been placed in the sonic landscape of John Lennon's *Plastic Ono Band* album, in which all nerves were jagged and exposed and all emotions stripped to the bone.

In that context, it made perfect sense for Major Tom, the space oddity himself and a key part of the Bowie brand since 1969, to reappear a few months later as a junkie – though Ground Control, in the style of government agencies everywhere, was still trying to pretend that everything with their intrepid explorer was fine, just fine. Nobody seemed quite sure whether he was up there or down here, though with heroin running through his veins he alternated sharply between the two locations.

Bowie had been blatant about his drug use, so it was predictable that his confession that Major Tom was now a junkie would be widely interpreted as a commentary on his own struggles with illegal substances. The songwriter was certainly prepared to concede the most anguished section of the song – in which he effectively demolished his past as being neither good, bad nor spontaneous – as a confession.* 'Those three particular lines represent a continuing, returning feeling of inadequacy over what I've done,' he told the *NME*'s Angus MacKinnon in 1980. 'I have a lot of reservations about what I've done, inasmuch as I don't feel much of it has any import at all.' For the ambivalent space hero to become an addict, then, dismissed Bowie's last decade as clinically as it pronounced the hollowness of America's space mission.

With the benefit of another decade's hindsight, Bowie was able to reflect that 'Ashes To Ashes' represented a unification of who he was with what he'd been: 'You have to accommodate your pasts within your persona. You have to understand why you went through them . . . You cannot just ignore them or put them out of your mind or pretend they didn't happen, or just say, "Oh, I was different then".' But by 1990 he was different from how he'd been in 1980, and able to gloss over the ambiguity that had inspired this song. As he reminded us, we all know about Major Tom; but how did we know, and how accurate was what we were told, by Ground Control or by Bowie himself?

For example: Bowie once insisted that the musical inspiration for 'Ashes To Ashes' had been Danny Kaye's lilting children's song 'Inchworm', the chord changes of which were incorporated into his composition. Except that they weren't: any resemblance was purely in Bowie's mind (which is not to say that it didn't exist, merely that it wasn't audible to the listener). Bowie didn't mention, however, that he had heard the traditional rhyme about the 'gypsies in the wood' – the source of the chant that closes 'Ashes To Ashes' – in Anthony Newley's 1961 West End musical *Stop The World, I Want To Get Off*. The tune reappeared throughout Newley's score, just as Major Tom

---

* One line of 'Ashes To Ashes' paraphrased a manifesto from a letter by Frank Kafka: 'A book must be an ice-axe to break the frozen seas inside us.'

had resurfaced in Bowie's career: once as tragic hero, then again as children's bogeyman.

Even the chorus was unreliable, its nursery-rhyme melody offering only the illusion of safety and comfort. 'Ashes To Ashes' was the title,* but first time through, Bowie sang 'ashes to ash'. Likewise, the next line was delivered once as 'fun to funky' and once as 'funk to funky'. Did these words symbolise anything, or were they simply there as sound? And why did a spoken voice echo Bowie's singing in the second verse but not in the first, where at the equivalent point it was clearly reciting something totally different from what was being sung, though it was incomprehensible? No wonder that none of the identities in the song were fixed, and Bowie's vocal tone changed with almost every line – breathless and gossipy, then shocked but not surprised, joyous, resigned, each choice appearing almost random. Why were musical distractions mixed to the front, and the core of the track buried beneath them? Why did what sounded like a colonel from a Spike Milligan radio script for *The Goons* appear between verses, and then apparently take over as narrator for the second? Why so many questions, and so few satisfying answers?

'For me, it's a story of corruption,' Bowie declared in a 1980 interview, before offering half a dozen entirely different interpretations in the next couple of minutes. 'Ashes To Ashes' was certainly a confrontation with the past, a confession about the present, and a sense of misgiving about the future. All of which confusion was blurred when the video for the song was premiered on *Top Of The Pops*, and the visuals pushed the words and music into the background. A song that reeked of the era's dominant social philosophy – the triumph of the selfish individual, the death of mutuality – was reduced to a fashion parade, in which form it left a lasting impact on the New Romantic movement about to sweep through British pop.

* Not at the beginning: the song's original working title was 'People Are Turning To Gold', as if King Midas rather than Major Tom might have been the protagonist.

[185] FASHION (Bowie)

Recorded February–April 1980; *Scary Monsters* LP.

'I've always hated him so,' wrote rock critic Richard Meltzer about Bowie, whom he described as 'the man most responsible for the willy-nilly return to mass conformity under the aegis of hip: fashion, if you will'. That was a scathing verdict, and a naïve one – as if every other 'star' (of whatever medium) hadn't twisted fashion into his/her own shape, and every teenage rebellion wasn't (in George Melly's memorable summary of the sixties revolution) a revolt into style. Bowie's crime was merely that he didn't attempt to hide the corollary between individual example, cult acceptance and mass imitation. After all, it had been the core of every youth subculture since the Second World War; my father's complaint that 'you all try to look different by looking the same' could have applied to teddy boys, punks, skins, hippies (his specific target) or mods.

So here was David Bowie in 1980, years after he'd assured the Ziggy clones that they were not alone, now addressing 'Fashion' as fascism:* a tyranny of taste, imposed by a goon squad (the secret policemen in Elvis Costello's song of that title) issuing strict-time ballroom instructions. As so often with Bowie, it was difficult to know how seriously to take his words. It was quite possible, for example, to detect some class snobbery in his verses about people from bad homes† dancing their way to conformity, while those from good homes chattered inanely. But I don't believe for a second that Bowie set out to insult the working and middle classes: that was simply a possible reading of his collision of language. As the song said, you could listen to him or not listen at all: it was all the same.

* 'The next religion might come from the world of fashion,' opined the novelist J.G. Ballard in 1970. Or indeed from rock 'n' roll: the death of Elvis Presley in 1977 provoked a gradual blurring of reality and myth that prompted cultural critics to ponder whether he might ultimately become the subject of religious frenzy. By 1992, the BBC's Religious Affairs correspondent could write a book, *Elvis People*, with a blurb that claimed: 'It poses a serious question: are we witnessing the birth of a new religious movement?' Presleyism may one day have to fight for spiritual space with Jacksonism, Lennonism, and of course Cobainianity.

† That phrase had been the title of an Astronettes song seven years earlier [94], while the 'beep beep' refrain came from the decade-old 'Rupert The Riley' [36], and from the Beatles before that.

Elements of the song suggested that Bowie had been impressed, consciously or otherwise, by the mechanical structure of the 1979 novelty hit 'Pop Muzik' by M. There were other parallels, perhaps; the nonsense syllables that filled the final choruses could have come from Talking Heads' 'Psycho Killer' (and before that from Otis Redding's 'Fa-Fa-Fa-Fa-Fa', or earlier still from Chris Kenner's 'Land Of 1000 Dances'); while Robert Fripp's acerbic guitar riff was in the nerve-jangling tradition of John Lennon's 'Cold Turkey', which described – but unlike 'Ashes To Ashes' didn't name – the life of a junkie. As Bowie's voice became increasingly fey by the end of the track, so Fripp's guitar provided rugged emotional balance. Other elements depended strictly on chance: the song had its origins as an impromptu chant called 'Jamaica', while the 'whup-whup' bleep that opened the track was a reference signal from a sequencer, which not only established an entirely misleading rhythm at the start but then fell into time as what producer Tony Visconti called 'a kind of reggae upstroke'.

Most obviously, 'Fashion' sounded like David Bowie, as the complex interlocking rhythms of 'Fame' [125] were blended with the basic chord sequence of 'Golden Years' [127]. On an album that frequently found Bowie singing as if at a peak of emotional distress, 'Fashion' was delivered in almost robotic style, with the barest variation of tone. As such, it was perfect for the dance floor – and a deliciously blank canvas for the promotional video, proving (as with 'Ashes To Ashes' [184]) that Bowie now found more satisfaction in that art form than in record-making.

[186] TEENAGE WILDLIFE (Bowie)

Recorded February–April 1980; *Scary Monsters* LP.

To quote from Nicholas Pegg's encyclopaedic *The Complete David Bowie*: 'the lyric is often glossed as an attack on the herd of Bowie imitators who rose to prominence at the end of the 1970s: Gary Numan believes he is one of the song's subjects, telling [Bowie biographer] David Buckley that he was "quite proud about it at the time".'

Reading #1: Though I don't believe that Bowie was sufficiently alarmed about the career of Gary Numan* to devote an entire song to deflating his ego, elements of 'Teenage Wildlife' can certainly be interpreted as a rather grumpy, middle-aged and ungracious assault on anyone who had the temerity to be (a) successful and (b) younger than Bowie. As such, it could be filed alongside Todd Rundgren's 'Determination' as an example of the syndrome identified by rock critic Robert Christgau (in relation to Stephen Stills), whereby 'when he was young old people were wrong and now that he's old young people are wrong'. In this reading, the isolated man in the corner could have been the uppity new waver, or Bowie himself, unfairly singled out for criticism because of his advanced years (he was 33, a dangerous age for Messiahs).

Reading #1:2: As above, except that the target would be one of Bowie's contemporaries, attempting to transform his image in order to conform with 'the new wave boys'.

Reading #2: Rock as self-criticism, in the tradition of the Chinese Cultural Revolution: or, as Paul Simon once asked himself, 'Who you fooling?' In other words, 'Teenage Wildlife' was a message to a man out of time, who was also running out of road but still trying to convince the world he was more than a familiar body in 'brand new drag'.

Reading #3: Five years earlier, 'Fame' [125] had been 'bully for you, chilly for me' – 'you' being Bowie's former manager, Tony Defries. In 1980, Defries was still collecting his royalties from Bowie's new music. It was not a coincidence that, after *Scary Monsters*, Bowie did not release another new album until that deal had expired. Those figures must have tortured him if he woke in the night. But now Bowie promised his target 'chilly receptions': chilly for you, chilly for me. As the song's original working title put it, 'It Happens Everyday'.

Reading #4: 'Teenage Wildlife' was a non-linear, no-winners commentary on fame, image and the meaning of life, from a man riven by cynicism. It was assembled (like so many of his songs) out

---

* Gary Numan is a prime example of how context and time alter the meaning of art. For anyone over the age of 15 when the preternaturally awkward and robotic singer emerged in 1979, Numan was a joke. He's now acclaimed as a formative influence on industrial metal and a dozen related genres.

of phrases* from his notebooks, and shaped into form by contempt for everything around him. The targets in this reading: himself, Gary Numan, Tony Defries, his audience, the whole sordid charade of 'teenage wildlife', which had once occupied his dreams and now represented a living nightmare. It was an exit strategy, in other words, that Samson might have recognised: I'm going, and you're all coming with me.

Hearing #1: Almost seven minutes long, 'Teenage Wildlife' was an epic exercise in bombast, worthy of Bruce Springsteen, Meat Loaf (one of Springsteen's imitators) or (one of Springsteen's role models) Phil Spector. Indeed, Spector would have commended the use of bells pealing deep in the mix, and recognised the vocal interjections once used by his wife, Ronnie, on Ronettes singles such as 'Baby I Love You'. (Bowie used a virtually identical turn of wordless phrase on another *Scary Monsters* song, 'Kingdom Come'.) For Spector, the creator of the so-called Wall of Sound, cacophony was intended to provide emotional catharsis, for him if not necessarily for the listener.

Hearing #2: Perhaps the strangest aspect of *Scary Monsters*, and this song in particular, was Bowie's dominant vocal persona – vastly exaggerated, deliberately grotesque, strained, pompous, yet strangely vulnerable in its tendency to crack into a falsetto croon at inappropriate moments. Clearly Bowie had not forgotten how to sing: Robert Christgau assumed it was self-parody, and it was certainly a rejection of all of the Bowie identities that had served him for the previous decade. Maybe he was still listening closely to Scott Walker's performances on *Nite Flights*. Or maybe he was infatuated by Meat Loaf, whose recent *Bat Out Of Hell* album had easily outsold all of Bowie's work to date.

Hearing #3: The master of cunning pastiche, Bowie offered one of his most obvious 'clues' on 'Teenage Wildlife', by mimicking the verse structure of '"Heroes"' [149] so blatantly that it can only have been deliberate. Note, also, the conversational mention of his given name:

---

* One phrase, 'midwives of history', took an elliptical route to Bowie's song. The title of a 1940 poem by the American writer Lionel Abel, it was based on a common misquotation from Karl Marx's *Das Kapital*, to the effect that it is violence that forces the birth of a new society from the belly of the old. The phrase was brought into general political discourse via an essay by Hannah Arendt; and is often repeated as 'war and violence are the midwives of history', something that neither Marx nor Arendt wrote.

the last such acknowledgement in his work had been the cheery, 'Hi, Dave' in 'Can't Help Thinking About Me' [A14] fourteen years before. Back then, he was indeed nothing more than teenage wildlife, ready to be hunted and mounted as a trophy on a businessman's wall. Both songs sounded like autobiography, and revealed both more and less about Bowie than they appeared to.

Hearing #4: 'There's two basses on this, and I hope you appreciate it,' John Lennon muttered as he thought he was waving his career goodbye, completing the last song on his 1975 album *Rock & Roll* before entering several years of retirement. David Bowie didn't bother to announce it, but this was the only *Scary Monsters* song on which he employed both his visiting lead guitarists, Chuck Hammer and Robert Fripp. Let *them* fight it out.

Hearing #5: The eighties would, some complained, be a decade of sonic excess – drums too loud, guitar solos too fast and showy, too much echo, too much noise, vocals (think of Spandau Ballet's Tony Hadley) pretentious and (ill-)mannered. 'Teenage Wildlife' was Bowie's final glimpse into the future: a parade of everything we would learn to hate in the years ahead. In which light, the opening line sounded like a sarcastic abrogation of responsibility: *you* created this world, now *you* can live in it.

[187] SCREAM LIKE A BABY (Bowie)

Recorded February–April 1980; *Scary Monsters* LP.

For a song that had begun life as 'I Am A Laser' [93], 'Scream Like A Baby' always betrayed a mortal lack of focus. With 'It's No Game' [180], Bowie had proved that he could retrieve long-forgotten song fragments and use them to construct something relevant to his contemporary life. 'Scream Like A Baby' demonstrated the flaws in this method: unwilling to amend the original, bombastic melody of the song he'd originally written for the Astronettes in 1973, he found himself drawn to compose a set of lyrics that were equally overwrought. The resulting tale of rebel misfits – terrorists, maybe, or political outcasts: it was difficult to care – would have been rejected by those arch mythologists the Clash as being too banal. When delivered in a preposterously self-important tone, across a backing that mixed hard-rock guitar with the percussion sound of Motown, circa 1964, the lyrics sounded like a parody of Bowie's clumsiest imitators. There was only one memorable moment, as the narrator declared himself ready to become part of society, only to find himself unable to spit out the final oppressive syllables of the phrase.*

[188] KINGDOM COME (Verlaine)

Recorded February–April 1980; *Scary Monsters* LP.

Television's *Marquee Moon* album, issued in 1977, belied any sense of punk as a restrictive genre. Its fractured, expansive landscape, full of brittle melodies and exploratory guitar lines, was genuinely fresh terrain for rock 'n' roll, at a moment when most artists preferred to retreat behind the comfortable old/new-wave barricades erected by the media. At the heart of Television was Tom Verlaine, a self-consciously arty lyricist, mannered vocalist and inspirational guitarist, whose instrumental interplay with fellow guitarist Richard Lloyd has rarely been rivalled on record. The compressed energy of *Marquee Moon* quickly dissipated, and Television imploded, but as Verlaine began what proved to be an anti-climactic solo career with a self-titled album in 1979, he was widely regarded as someone who would help to shape the decade ahead.

Hence Bowie's interest – which dated back to 1974 – in Verlaine's work, reinforced by the suggestion from his own guitarist, Carlos Alomar, that he should consider recording this song. It was an intriguing choice for both Alomar and Bowie,† especially in the context of a record that signalled its own troubled genesis. 'Kingdom Come' was a song of frustration, boredom, repetition: exactly the pitfalls that Bowie could no longer ignore. Consciously or otherwise, he reinforced his negativity by a subtle alteration to the original lyrics. Verlaine complained repeatedly that he would be breaking rocks (like

---

* 'There is no such thing as society,' Margaret Thatcher would declare seven years later, as if to explain Bowie's verbal blockage.
† Bowie briefly considered tackling Cream's 'I Feel Free' on this album, a song that he had performed live with the Spiders in 1972. He abandoned the idea after recording a backing track, perhaps realising that the song's title contradicted everything else on his record.

a life prisoner or an enchained Greek god) 'till the kingdom comes', with the hope expressed that salvation might eventually arrive. Bowie removed the hope until the very end of the song, by which time it sounded hollow: until then, he could foresee no destiny beyond the endless breaking of rocks, a Sisyphean fate for a man who had always regarded work as a justification for living and a defence against unwelcome psychological urges.

As usual when tackling outside material, Bowie performed 'Kingdom Come' in the same key as the original, though he left his trace on the arrangement, which was an unhappy cross between the classic Motown sound and the sterility of American AOR (the elephants' graveyard of rock's vain pretensions to a rebel spirit). The explosive boom of the percussion on this track alone could be used to demonstrate a decade of production overkill to come; likewise Bowie's vocal, delivered as if he had forgotten how to do anything with his voice except over-emote like the hammiest of actors.

[189] BECAUSE YOU'RE YOUNG (Bowie)

Recorded February–April 1980; *Scary Monsters* LP.

Bowie explained away this song in 1980 as a message to his son's generation. 'I can't write young,' he admitted.* Yet there was little in 'Because You're Young' that hinted at an adult's mature advice. For this was a song of emotional fracture and disunion, sparked perhaps by the aftermath of his own marital breakdown, but tending towards a broader view of a world in which, as Bob Dylan might have said, everything was broken.

Fragmentation had always been safe territory for Bowie, in lyrical, musical and philosophical terms. Now he no longer seemed to have conviction in his own ability to control that process, and use the pieces of the past to create a future. 'Because You're Young' lived in the shadow of younger talents, most notably Elvis Costello. The introduction of Bowie's record mirrored that of Costello's 'Watching The Detectives'; the stabbed chords on a cheap organ suggested Costello's

---

* His original demo for the song suggested that he didn't entirely believe this verdict: lyrically incomplete, it was titled defiantly 'Because I'm Young'.

keyboard player, Steve Naïve; the chorus, like Costello's knowing throwbacks on his *This Year's Model* and *Armed Forces* albums, was pure early sixties; even the off-the-cuff vocal interjections in the fade-out sounded as if they belonged on Costello's 'You Belong To Me' or 'Radio Radio'. (The working title for *Armed Forces* had been *Emotional Fascism*, incidentally, a title that could usefully have been borrowed by Bowie for *Scary Monsters*.) To complete Bowie's debts, the song's title recalled the Duane Eddy instrumental hit from 1960, 'Because They're Young'; and the track ended with some guitar licks that might have been transported wholesale from the Beatles' *Revolver* album.

Between these reference points, and the entirely predictable melodic structure of the song, there was barely room for Bowie to plant his own flag. Even his choice of guitar accomplice, Pete Townshend,* seemed to represent an abdication of creative power: the Who's leader neither challenged Bowie nor fired his synapses, probably because of the quantity of alcohol that, as Townshend later admitted, had been consumed during the session. Bowie was equally forthright about his predilections during this period: 'My problem was cocaine, and then I went from cocaine to alcohol, which is a natural course of events.' 'Because You're Young' confirmed what much of *Lodger* had suggested: it had become increasingly difficult for Bowie to find inspiration from the creative methods that had served him faithfully for the previous decade.

Scary Monsters (And Super Creeps) LP

Bowie insisted that the techniques of rock ran at least a decade behind their equivalents in fine art. Yet there was an uncanny parallel between this 1980 album and the judgement of historian Stephen Paul Miller on the post-1975 work of the pop-art pioneer Jasper Johns: 'The later paintings systematically generate an ambiguity of surfaces throughout their canvases.' Rock critic Charles Shaar Murray expressed a similar sentiment eloquently in his *NME* review of *Scary Monsters*, describing 'the latter-day Bowie

---

* Ironically, the song may have left an indelible mark on Townshend after all. Bowie invented the word 'psychodelicate'; more than a decade later, Townshend issued a concept album entitled *Psychoderelict*.

sound' as 'a grinding, dissonant, treacherous, chilling noise where standard rock tonalities are twisted until their messages are changed'.

All of those adjectives were justified for a record that dealt so nakedly in extremes – high emotions, wild passions, grating sheets of noise, sweeping judgements of self-criticism. No wonder that, a decade after its release, Bowie said that, 'Scary Monsters for me has always been some kind of purge. It was me eradicating the feelings within myself that I was uncomfortable with.' It was as if he had rounded up all the schemes and pretensions that had obsessed him during the previous ten years, exaggerated the most mannered elements of his music-making, summoned up and then dispatched his legendary 'characters', and then exposed the hollowness that was left when all illusions were dispelled and all artifice uncovered. It was a record that announced, in word and in deed, that its creator had reached the end of the road; that there was no more mileage to be gained from continuing this particular experiment in combining confrontational art and lavish entertainment. The contrasting arrangements of 'It's No Game' [180/181] that opened and closed Scary Monsters set out its emotional terrain perfectly: here be desperate screams and rigid control, each equally telling about the artist's sense of his identity. He now had to face the biggest dilemma of his entire career: how to continue without leaning on the props – the identities, concepts, and drugs – that had sustained and protected him for the previous decade. He would no longer be the Bowie of the seventies: but what else did he have to sell?

Sound and Vision #4: A New Career in a New Medium

The traditional set of skills required of a rock star – record-making, live performance, posing for photographs – expanded with the advent of the music video. During the late seventies, videos moved beyond their original remit as a convenient means of promoting a new record to emerge as an independent branch of the entertainment industry. The next decade would introduce the phenomenon of the video artist, for whom musical or performance skills mattered less than the ability to convey an image and a lifestyle within a four-minute clip. In 1979, however, only the most modern and far-sighted artists were coming to terms with the demands and potential of the format.

It seems obvious in retrospect that David Bowie would be a video pioneer: he believed in both art and entertainment, the twin poles of the director; he had the mime skills to accentuate and dramatise emotions; he knew how to advertise and brand himself; and he was schooled in the history of twentieth-century visual art. Video was an entirely fresh art form, which could rediscover the techniques of surrealism and Dada as if they were newly minted.

There had been a brief flowering of rock promotional films in the late sixties, allowing the likes of the Beatles and the Rolling Stones to spare themselves the chore of touring the world's TV studios when they issued a new record. Both groups had hired visually inventive directors to produce films for songs such as 'Strawberry Fields Forever' and 'We Love You'. But few of their contemporaries and successors had taken up the challenge. When Bowie invited photographer Mick Rock to shoot cheap but striking clips for singles such as 'John I'm Only Dancing' [63] and 'The Jean Genie' [65] in 1972, what was radical was Rock's lack of pedigree as a film director, not the visual content. Later Bowie clips, for 'Be My Wife' [138] and '"Heroes"' [149], were no more daring, paling alongside those prepared by (for example) Queen for 'Bohemian Rhapsody' several years earlier.

Bowie's leap into the future came in 1979 with David Mallet's video for 'Boys Keep Swinging' [171]. It began conventionally enough, with the singer miming an extravagant performance in a suit that his younger mod self would have relished in 1965. But then Bowie appeared as a trio of drag queens, ranging from a vamp to an aged actress. One by one they took centre stage, the first two routines ending as he angrily tore off his wig and smeared his lipstick across his face in a gesture* of total contempt. If his videos for 'D.J.' [169] and 'Look Back In Anger' [170] were less iconoclastic, they still allowed him to explore intimations of significance that were not necessarily present in the songs themselves.

Bowie must now have realised that he could express himself more adventurously with visuals than on record. Nothing on *Lodger*, for example, matched the daring, Dada-inspired performances of 'Boys Keep Swinging', 'TVC 15' [129] and 'The Man Who Sold The World' [26] that he staged for the US television show *Saturday Night Live* in December 1979. For 'Boys Keep Swinging', a cigarette-thin puppet was visually attached to his human head, and literally kept swinging as Bowie manipulated the controls. He

---

* This visual motif harked back to the Dali/Buñuel film *Un Chien Andalou*, and was reproduced by a genuine woman in the clip for Bowie's 1983 single, 'China Girl'.

was carried forward to sing 'The Man Who Sold The World' in a full-body manikin, its angular construction the offspring of the strange coupling of Dadaist Hugo Ball and new-wave performance artists Devo. His handlers, Klaus Nomi and Joey Arias, had been plucked from the milieu at Fiorucci, the New York fashion store that (according to commentator Eve Babitz) gathered 'the whole 20th century in one place'. Its dayglo, fluorescent colours and self-conscious hedonism resembled a decadent form of pop art that could only have arisen from fin-de-decade New York – achieving a gothic poignancy when AIDS began to ravage the community that gathered at its East 59th Street location (Nomi becoming one of the first such casualties). Bowie carried that spirit into his 1980 videos for 'Ashes To Ashes' [184], where he donned a Pierrot suit to be followed along a bleak English shore by London's equivalent of the Fiorucci kids and (of course) a giant bulldozer; and 'Fashion' [185], a mock-performance clip featuring similar robotic moves to those pioneered by Nomi and Devo. By the time that he offered spirited, if ragged, renditions of 'Life On Mars?' [52] and 'Ashes To Ashes' on *The Tonight Show* in 1980, it was a surprise that he chose not to embellish the songs with anything more visually dramatic than the expression on his face as he reached for the high notes. (He would never perform 'Life On Mars?' in its original key again, subtly lowering the pitch for his eighties tours – a decade of smoking and six years of cocaine having exacted their revenge on his throat.)

His video-making seems to have renewed Bowie's faith in the power of the visual, which had been jolted by his experience with *Just A Gigolo*. As he completed work on the *Scary Monsters* album in New York, he took what was arguably his bravest artistic decision of a risk-filled decade, accepting the lead role in a non-musical play, *The Elephant Man*. As a teenager, he had read about the plight of John Merrick in Frank Edwards' book, *Strange People*, and had watched the initial production of the play on Broadway. The role required him to become a man trapped in the misshapen ghastliness of his own body, but without (unlike John Hurt in David Lynch's contemporaneous movie based on the same story) the aid of appropriate make-up and costume. Here, at last, Bowie was able to reveal how much he had learned from Lindsay Kemp. On stage, through subtle movements that betrayed the intensity of his plight, he became one of the twisted, distorted figures he had admired in the work of Egon Schiele, his voice a half-blocked caricature of a 'normal' man, the enormity of his character's ordeal conveyed all the more dramatically for his conscious lack of theatricality. This was one of Bowie's finest performances – musical or otherwise – of the long seventies, and tellingly, perhaps, also the only one to which he contributed not an ounce of irony. He was simply himself, not the reflected shadow of his own past; and simultaneously *not* himself, but John Merrick. He could finally justify the title he had awarded himself in 1971: the Actor.

Afterword

I

It was the Actor who learned, on 8 December 1980, that his friend John Lennon had been murdered, a mile and a half from where Bowie had just left the stage of the Booth Theater. The killer, who had attended an earlier performance of *The Elephant Man*, later admitted that he had considered Bowie as a target, before opting to kill the emblematic figure of the sixties, rather than the seventies.

Security at the theatre was strengthened, and Bowie was able to fulfil his commitment to *The Elephant Man*, though he declined the offer to extend his run beyond early January. Then he flew home to Switzerland, the manic tumult of New York City having lost its charm. Lennon's death encouraged him into seclusion, removing any temptation to stage the world tour he had vaguely promised for 1981. And there was another equally compelling justification for retirement. As mentioned earlier, Bowie's 1975 settlement with Tony Defries ensured that his ex-manager would receive (in perpetuity) 16 per cent of Bowie's income from all his recording projects and acting engagements until 30 September 1982; and 5 per cent of his earnings from concert appearances. The 16 per cent share also applied to any songs that Bowie wrote before that deadline. So there was a clear incentive for him to refrain from composing or recording a hasty successor to *Scary Monsters* until his obligations were at an end.

Yet he was incapable of absolute silence. The same drive that had impelled him towards work as a defence against madness was now focused on protecting him from his addictive urges. He recorded a theme song for the film *Cat People*, and was persuaded to collaborate with rock band Queen on a recording session that produced a chart-topping single, 'Under Pressure'. Even when trying to avoid boosting Defries' earnings, he could not escape the commercial power of his self-created mythology. His fame also won him roles in the films *The Hunger* and *Merry Christmas Mr Lawrence*, which helped to erase memories of his unfortunate part in *Just A Gigolo*.

None of this activity threatened to harm his reputation, or widen his horizons. His most adventurous work during this strange interlude was also, in financial terms, the least rewarding. In September 1981, he transferred the skills he had acquired during *The Elephant Man* to British television, delivering a strikingly low-key performance as the star of the BBC's staging of Bertolt Brecht's musical drama *Baal*. The four Brecht/Weill songs from the drama were released as a single; and like 'Alabama Song' [163], they suggested that the post-*'Heroes'* Bowie was never more himself than when articulating other people's themes. His performances displayed staggering vocal control and extravagant theatricality; an almost arrogant self-confidence and sure-footedness; and total artistic certainty. These qualities would prove elusive in the decade ahead.

II

In March 1960, the performance artist Gustav Metzger issued a manifesto proclaiming the necessity of creating 'Auto-Destructive Art'. It was, he declared, the only valid response to a world in which the super-powers stockpiled nuclear weapons, the population of the West wallowed in consumerism, the Third World starved, and society exerted a 'disintegrative effect' on its citizens. Metzger defined auto-destruction as 'art which contains in itself an agent which automatically leads to its destruction within a period of time not to exceed twenty years'.

Auto-destruction entered the world of rock music via Pete Townshend of the Who, who studied under Metzger at Ealing College of Art and borrowed his teacher's rhetoric to justify destroying his guitar as the climax to the band's performances. By the late seventies, however, rock appeared to be enacting its own process of auto-destruction, true to Metzger's twenty-year deadline. The apparently seamless tradition of what would later be called 'classic rock' was splintering under the pressure of cocaine-fuelled decadence and the incursion of new musical genres (notably punk, disco and the first stirrings of hip-hop). In truth, there had been disruptive and transgressive elements at work throughout the history of rock: what had fragmented was rock culture's sense of certainty and identity, the 'great man' theory of its history that imagined the music progressing endlessly from Elvis Presley through Bob Dylan, the Beatles and the Rolling Stones to (in one common reading of the rock narrative) Bruce Springsteen and perhaps Bob Marley.

The eternal outsider of the seventies, David Bowie escaped inclusion in this tradition, not least because his continual shifts of style and sound evaded easy categorisation. In the aftermath of punk, when nothing was less fashionable than to admit a debt to the monoliths of the previous era, Bowie was one of the few veterans who could be acknowledged without loss of face. His mark was unmistakable on the gloomy art rock of Siouxsie & the Banshees, Joy Division and the Cure; on the synthetic landscapes of the New Romantics; on the continual reinvention and sexual ambiguity that fuelled the stardom of Madonna and Prince. So prevalent, indeed, was his influence in the music of the early eighties that his own creative absence was barely noticeable.

He would soon reappear in spectacular style, not as an innovator but as an institution. Bowie celebrated the expiry of his contractual obligations in late 1982 by beginning work on his first new album in three years. His choice of producer was significant: Tony Visconti, his collaborator on a series of sonically challenging records, was sidelined in favour of Nile Rodgers, writer/guitarist for the New York band Chic. Rodgers' trademarks were a sparse, slippery disco groove and a dazzling surface sheen. Both qualities were in evidence on *Let's Dance*, an impeccably crafted and effortlessly commercial record that duly became the best-selling album of Bowie's career. Throughout, his vocals were subtle and transparent, seeming to be devoid of artifice. So too was the epic world tour that followed, in which the once deathly cocaine addict of the mid-seventies was miraculously transformed into a paragon of vitality and well-being, the gleam of his refashioned teeth rivalled only by the bleached glow of his hair. Though his repertoire mixed new hits with old, and was ecstatically received, there was no hint in this revamped Bowie of the tortured, ambivalent artist of old. It was as if he had exiled his questing, experimental spirit as an uncomfortable relic of an age that he preferred to forget. The Bowie of *Let's Dance* (and the clumsily titled *Serious Moonlight* tour) questioned nothing, risked nothing, stood for nothing. He had finally become the all-round entertainer of Kenneth Pitt's dreams, his cabaret aspirations of 1968 expanded to fill the stadia of 1983.

Once again, Bowie was in perfect tune with the times: the mid-eighties was the era of Armani rock, when the mavericks of yesteryear refashioned themselves as show ponies for the world's most celebrated designers, and the rhetoric of rock rebellion became the sanitised language of mass entertainment. If Bowie retained enough dignity to sidestep the constant round of Prince's Trust concerts inhabited by the likes of Eric Clapton, Phil Collins and Mark Knopfler, he was still offering merely the palest shadow of his former iconoclasm. More worryingly, he had shed any sense of artistic integrity. As the decade unfolded, each creative misfire seemed to corrode his former glory. In 1969, some Beatles fans had chosen to believe that Paul McCartney had died in a car crash in 1966, and an impostor had been substituted in his place. Albums as bereft of inspiration as *Tonight* (bar 'Loving The Alien', perhaps) and *Never Let Me Down* suggested that the real Bowie had been stuffed into a closet after the completion of *Baal*, and supplanted by a stray replicant from the 1982 movie *Blade Runner*. The *faux* Bowie fumbled with the familiar symbolism of the genuine model, thereby concocting the preposterous *Glass Spider* tour (a triumph of effects over effectiveness) instead of the Spiders From Mars, and a succession of haircuts and costumes that alluded to the uncanny strangeness of the seventies Bowie without any of his mystery.

In commercial terms, Bowie had never been more successful; or, arguably, more influential, as critic Nicholas Pegg noted: 'The cutting-edge ensemble choreography which soon became *de rigueur* among stadium superstars like Prince, Madonna and Jacksons Michael and Janet (not to mention the relentless parade of synchro-dancing boy bands), owes a tremendous debt to *Glass Spider*.' But having banked his cheques, and basked in the knowledge that he was finally achieving the monetary security that had evaded him throughout the seventies, Bowie was left curiously unsatisfied. The result was Tin Machine, a much-maligned attempt to sublimate his identity within a four-piece hard-rock band, and rekindle a sense of personal connection with his music. Tin Machine's two studio records inspired some of the most effective vocal performances of his career, but his commitment to them was undermined when they were overshadowed by another blatant exercise in milking nostalgia for money: the 1990 *Sound + Vision* tour. Explained at the time as a last opportunity to hear Bowie performing his greatest hits (a promise that predictably was not kept), this mammoth venture in stadium rock seemed to denote that he would no longer pretend to be an innovator or an explorer: like the Rolling Stones, he would sell the memory of his rebellious youth until he or his audience ceased to care or breathe.

III

Tin Machine stopped working in February 1992. Two months later, Bowie appeared alongside Mick Ronson at the Freddie Mercury tribute concert in London, closing his performance not with 'Rock 'n' Roll Suicide', as Ziggy Stardust would have done, but with an impromptu recitation of the Lord's Prayer. It was perhaps the single most shocking moment of his career: utterly sincere, totally in keeping with the ethos of the occasion, completely at odds with the totemic clichés of the classic rock tradition. Sadly, none of that defiant individualism was apparent on the album that followed: *Black Tie/White Noise* reunited Bowie with Nile Rodgers, with predictably slick and unfulfilling results.

After ten years that had brought him unimaginable wealth but little artistic satisfaction, he was offered a glimmer of inspiration from an unlikely source. Hanif Kureishi invited him to provide the soundtrack for a BBC TV adaptation of his novel *The Buddha of Suburbia*, which was rooted in the south London culture from which Bowie had emerged, and the mercurial London milieu he had helped to create. Bowie duly delivered an assortment of incidental music, and a title song that brilliantly combined his own past with Kureishi's themes, evoking the full span of his seventies work. His commitment to the

TV series ended there, but he returned to the studio three months later to rework and extend several of his incidental pieces, emerging after less than a week with a completed album. Erroneously packaged as a soundtrack record for *The Buddha of Suburbia*, it mixed cut-up 'sound poetry' with explorations of ambient sound reminiscent of his late-seventies work, as if the mere sight of a rough cut of Kureishi's films had been sufficient* to remind him who he was, and why he had once been a creative icon.

That flash of insight shocked Bowie out of the torpor that had surrounded him for a decade. In spring 1994, he embarked on a complex and deliberately uncommercial recording project intended to fuel a series of albums. His choice of collaborator was Brian Eno, with whom he had last worked on *Lodger*. Eno's *Oblique Strategies* cards guided the creation of many hours of music, and Bowie employed a cut-up computer program for lyrical inspiration, ensuring that the methodology that had shaped their seventies liaisons was suitably revised for a new era of technology. He emerged with 1.*Outside: The Diary of Nathan Adler*, the first (and last) instalment of what he described as 'a non-linear Gothic Drama Hyper-cycle'.

Issued after *Low* and *'Heroes'*, in some fantasy late-seventies landscape that enabled access to mid-nineties computers and samplers, 1. *Outside* would have consolidated Bowie's reputation as rock's most fearless exponent of the avant-garde as a means of mass communication. Instead, like his four subsequent albums, it entranced his (remarkably large) core of followers without touching or influencing anyone beyond the faithful. So it was that some of his most adventurous (1.*Outside* and the 1997 rock/dance crossover *Earthling*) and proficient ('*hours . . .*', *Heathen* and *Reality*, issued between 1999 and 2003) records remain unheard by all but a small fraction of the global audience who had relished his seventies and early-eighties output. Ironically, Bowie did complete an album that might have reached out to that wider audience, but his record company refused to release

---

* Bowie wrote in the sleeve notes: 'My personal memory stock for this album was made up from an almighty plethora of influences and reminiscences from the 1970s.' He provided a list, many items on which seemed to date back to his early-sixties exploration of London with his elder brother. He also referenced both T. Rex and Marc Bolan, unfortunately giving his friend's name as 'Mark', which robbed his tribute of some of its poignancy.

it. *Toy* was scheduled to appear in 2001, but Virgin/EMI entangled Bowie in what he described as 'unbelievably complicated scheduling negotiations', and the record was lost. Several songs dripped on to the market as B-sides and bonus tracks, but it was only in spring 2011 that the entire record leaked on to internet fan forums. Eleven of its fourteen tracks had been written or (in the case of 'Liza Jane' [A2]) first recorded by Bowie between 1964 and 1971. He approached them now in the guise of a kindly uncle left in control of an unruly pack of children. He deliberately adopted a low, husky delivery for the entire record, not because his upper register had vanished (as the subsequent *Heathen* and *Reality* proved) but perhaps to designate both his distance from the past, and also his mature acceptance of his bewildering array of youthful incarnations. It was a dignified, elegantly constructed album, from a man who had survived the process of selling himself to the world, and lived to tell the tale.

In October 2003, the 56-year-old Bowie embarked on what was intended to be a solid year of touring, performing an anything but predictable mixture of material old and new. It was a punishing schedule, which took its toll on his voice, and then his health. A concert in Oslo during June 2004 was interrupted when a fan throw a lollipop at the stage, and hit Bowie in the eye. Five days later, in Prague, he was forced to leave the stage after suffering what was described officially as a trapped nerve. He completed one more show, in Germany, before being hospitalised for emergency heart surgery. Since then, his live appearances have been restricted to cameos, and even they dried up after he introduced comedian Ricky Gervais on stage at a New York festival in May 2007. His most recent appearance on record came the following year, as fleeting guest vocalist on Scarlett Johansson's debut album. He chivalrously described her as 'mystical and twice cool', and then stepped into an elegant, unannounced retirement.

IV

In vanishing from the stage, Bowie was only repeating his effective disengagement from society in the late seventies. He exited the culture and history of that decade when he left Berlin for the closeted life of an exile, protected by wealth and fame from the vicissitudes of politics, economics and social instability. He would continue to comment on the world around him, but necessarily as an outsider – concerned or even outraged, perhaps, but not actually affected. He inhabited a world of his own making, and made no attempt to sell that world to his audience. Indeed, it was constructed precisely to keep the outside at bay. Instead, like every entertainer of his stature, he sold his own celebrity, and never more successfully than when he was repeating the past, rather than trying to create a future. Meanwhile, the world continued to turn, unmoved by Bowie's inconsistent musical output, but still caught in the idealised shadow of his golden decade.

There was no shame in that fate: few if any of his peers, especially those who enjoyed his degree of success, have maintained any sense of vitality in their careers beyond ten or at most twenty years of creative innovation. (The possible exception to this rule is Bob Dylan, for whom innovation consists of wilfully defying expectations while retaining a gloriously enigmatic mystique.) In any case, innovation is hard to sustain when one's audience clearly prefers familiar pleasures. Albums such as 1.*Outside* and *Earthling* stand up alongside the peaks of Bowie's seventies catalogue as exercises in inventiveness and daring; what they lack is meaning, any sense that they are shaping the culture around them or engaging in a dialogue with other artists. When the world refuses to let you change, and your body tells you to stop, it is more dignified to remain silent than to fight against the inevitable.

Bowie could be forgiven for feeling disappointed in a culture that celebrated him as a mercurial figure in a constant state of reinventing himself, and then refused to let him continue that process beyond 1980. Yet he had already achieved more in the previous decade than anyone around him, and the wider world is still assimilating the bewildering twists and curves of his trajectory through that decade. Nearly forty years after he invented Ziggy Stardust, his subversive attitude towards the creation of fame can still provide the likes of Lady Gaga with a template to follow. There is a valid case, in fact, for awarding Bowie the dubious credit of being the inventor of modern celebrity culture, in which a nonentity can be thrust into the maelstrom of media attention by virtue of a single appearance on a reality TV series or a talent show. But there is a profound difference between Bowie's self-manufacturing as a superstar in the early seventies, and the culture of *The X Factor* and *Big Brother*. Bowie was using stardom as a vehicle to explore deeper personal and social issues; artifice and irony were his weapons. In the twenty-first century, celebrity is its own reward, and today's instant superstars are selling nothing more momentous than their own fame. Artifice has become reality; irony has lost its purpose. Communication is instant, and ceaseless; but nothing is being said. No wonder that David Bowie, who always had something to communicate, has chosen to follow Major Tom into isolated silence, a distant observer of a world that he had once illuminated and enriched.

Appendix: The Songs of David Bowie: 1963–1968

[A1] **I NEVER DREAMED** (Jones/Dodds)

> Recorded by the Kon-Rads, August 1963; unreleased.

Not content with performing pop hits such as 'Let's Dance', 'Do You Wanna Dance', 'Sheila' and 'Ginny Come Lately' for local audiences in south London, Bowie encouraged his colleagues in the Kon-Rads to seek out a recording contract. The Beatles' stunning success with self-composed material, bypassing the need for songs from professionals in London's 'Tin Pan Alley', suggested that the Kon-Rads should pursue a similar route. Bowie was eager to prove himself the creative fulcrum of the band, without the expertise to back up his naïve self-confidence.

In advance of what proved to be an ill-fated audition for Decca Records, the Kon-Rads recorded several versions of the song they had chosen as their most commercial asset. The tape survived in the archive of the band's drummer, David Hadfield. 'I Never Dreamed' was probably composed by Bowie with the assistance of guitarist Alan Dodds; Hadfield remembered that Bowie would present the Kon-Rads with fragmentary ideas for songs, which the more proficient Dodds would shape into acceptable form. 'If anything, David was a poet not a composer,' Hadfield said. 'He was always seeing a news item in the paper and wanting to write a song about it. For example, there was one about a plane crash.'

No such drama infiltrated the mundane teenage narrative of 'I Never Dreamed', which was indistinguishable from other beat groups eager to emulate the success of the Beatles. Only the cocky charm of Bowie's vocal, and a cockney swagger in his vowels, hinted at what was to come.

[A2] LIZA JANE (Conn)

Recorded by Davie Jones & the King Bees, May 1964; single A-side.

When entrepreneur Leslie Conn was introduced to Bowie's second band, the King Bees, he saw not only an energetic bunch of young men who might, perhaps, rival the Rolling Stones, but also a quick source of music publishing income. It was a tradition in the fifties for managers, agents, producers and publishers to be listed as composers of rock 'n' roll and pop songs, regardless of their creative input: the businessmen were assured of a potentially lucrative cut of the record's royalties, while the artists were usually too ignorant or intimidated to complain.

This plague was in decline by 1964, but Leslie Conn still argued that he deserved the meagre earnings from the King Bees' debut single because he had hammered the tyro efforts of Bowie and George Underwood into commercial shape. In fact, none of the would-be composers could claim much originality, as 'Liza Jane' was based on a tune passed down through both the folk and gospel/blues traditions (usually as 'Little Liza Jane'). Bowie could easily have heard earlier renditions by Lonnie Donegan, Nina Simone or Fats Domino, though his version owed more to white predecessors than black. It was clearly intended to rival the Rolling Stones (compare the guitar solo and wolf whistles to the Stones' 'Walking The Dog') and the Yardbirds, though without the finesse of either. At 17, Bowie hadn't learned how to roar without rasping, and his R&B vocal style was painfully rough, often indecipherable (the second verse evades transcription) and ultimately clumsy. Tackling the final verse a major third above the melody line was a vain attempt to fabricate extra excitement – and it failed to convince more than a few hundred record-buyers to invest in the King Bees' solitary release.

[A3] LOUIE LOUIE GO HOME (Revere/Lindsay)

Recorded by Davie Jones & the King Bees, May 1964; single B-side.

The successor to the Kingsmen's hit 'Louie Louie' by the slick US garage band Paul Revere & the Raiders wasn't issued in Britain, so the King Bees must have been sold this generic R&B romp by its Tin Pan Alley publisher. While the Raiders had aped a key feature of the Isley Brothers' 'Shout' – briefly softening the mood before a tempestuous finale – the King Bees' pedestrian cover never slackened its relentless plod. Bowie's inadequacy as a blues shouter was exposed even more nakedly than on 'Liza Jane' [A2], with an occasional London vowel escaping his mid-Atlantic growl.

[A4] I PITY THE FOOL (Malone)

Recorded by the Manish Boys, January 1965; single A-side; alternate take on *Early On* CD.

David Jones was introduced to the Manish Boys, an R&B band from Maidstone in Kent, as a recording artist who already had the offer of an American tour under his belt. This entirely imaginary promise was enough to convince the band (named after a Muddy Waters blues tune) to accept him as their frontman.

There being no perceived shame in British R&B bands covering songs by black American blues artists, the Manish Boys were happy to follow the example of their more successful peers, such as the Rolling Stones (who had recently reached no. 1 in Britain with 'Little Red Rooster') and the Animals. Originally recorded (and probably written, despite the credit on the record) by R&B veteran Bobby 'Blue' Bland in 1961, 'I Pity The Fool' hinged around the contradiction between the dismissive lyrics, and Bland's despairing vocals. Producer Shel Talmy recommended the song to Bowie, whose seasoned delivery, variation of attack and acute sense of timing displayed an admirable flowering of technique since his first single, and showed how swiftly he could step into character with unfamiliar material. The tightly controlled arrangement – with Bowie alternating between an elegant croon and a pleading cry an octave higher – created a sense of tension sustained by a typically pointed guitar solo from session musician Jimmy Page.

The near-identical alternative take differed only in the order that Bowie tackled the verses.

When 'I Pity The Fool' was released, Conn and Bowie reprised the 'long hair' scandal of November 1964 to some effect, with the co-operation of the BBC – all sides agreeing to pretend that the group would not be allowed on screen unless he cut his hair. An honourable compromise was reached, and the Manish Boys duly appeared on the quaintly named 'youth' show, *Gadzooks! It's All Happening*. But it wasn't, for the Manish Boys at least, and Bowie quickly abandoned the group. 'He was probably aiming higher than the rest of us,' keyboardist Bob Solly reflected. 'He was more ruthless. At the time, his departure seemed bloody-minded and disloyal. But I think he was a nice fellow who sometimes had to be nasty in order to get on. He had no other thought in his head than success. He was absolutely positive that he would succeed.'

[A5] TAKE MY TIP (Jones)

> Recorded by the Manish Boys, January 1965; single B-side; alternate take on *Early On* CD.

Bowie's unexpectedly sophisticated baptism as a songwriter on record is unlike anything else in his catalogue, owing more to jazz-inspired hipsters such as Jon Hendricks and Oscar Brown (and their British counterpart, Georgie Fame) than to the R&B standards in his early repertoire. The core of the song was simple: a two-chord vamp over which Bowie dropped slick Americanisms as if he'd melded the spirits of Jack Kerouac and Frank Sinatra. Only the errant vowel sound of 'act *tall*' took him out of his depth. The conspicuous blue note (C in the key of A) in the horn/vocal melody en route to the chorus suggested that Bowie had written the basics on saxophone, and asked the group to arrange it – perhaps supplying the three-semitone descent with which the song opened, and the more surprising three-chord slide that guided them back from B major towards the original F♯. Shel Talmy was sufficiently impressed to pass the song to Kenny Miller, whom he was grooming as a potential teen idol, and who duly became the first outsider to record Bowie's material. Fresh from a no. 1 single in similar vein with 'Yeah Yeah', Georgie Fame might have been a more profitable target.

[A6] YOU'VE GOT A HABIT OF LEAVING (Jones)

Recorded by Davy Jones (& the Lower Third), July 1965; single A-side.

Moving relentlessly on, Bowie swiftly assumed control of the Lower Third, as he had the Manish Boys. Though American R&B remained their primary source of inspiration, their role models were closer to home, in the form of two London bands with whom they shared a producer, the Kinks and the Who. The teen aggression and pop-art pretensions of the Who certainly left their mark on the sound of this record, which appeared – to the alarm of the Lower Third – as a 'Davy Jones' solo release. Meanwhile, the Kinks' trademark shift from the tonic chord to the major second ('You Really Got Me' being the most memorable example) was the root of this flagrant attempt at echoing Ray Davies' composing style. Lyrically minimal, harmonically banal, the song briefly established a hint of tension that dissipated with Bowie's maudlin admission, 'sometimes I cry'. The Who's influence was highlighted as he imitated Roger Daltrey's macho vocalising, before a briefly explosive guitar solo that was clearly intended to rival the 'auto-destruction' of that group's 'Anyway, Anyhow, Anywhere' (see [86]), after which the tune subsided painfully back into its undistinguished theme.

[A7] BABY LOVES THAT WAY (Jones)

Recorded by Davy Jones (& the Lower Third), July 1965; single B-side.

1965 was the year when the Detroit-based Motown label extended beyond a mod cult in Britain and entered the mainstream, leaving its mark on everyone from the Small Faces ('Whatcha Gonna Do About It') to the Rolling Stones (whose cover of Marvin Gaye's 'Hitch Hike' showed how difficult it was to reproduce the effervescence of the Motor City sound). In keeping with his freshly coiffeured mod aesthetic, Bowie channelled Gaye's peacock pride into this jaunty blend of Motown and the Kinks (the guitar solo had all the anarchy of a Dave Davies creation). The song opened with a stuttering variation on a D chord that anticipated the launch of 'The Jean Genie' [65], sold the chorus immediately like a soap commercial, and settled into a two-chord swagger in which the confusion of the narrative (who's actually in control?) was overpowered by the easy precision of Bowie's phrasing. Like the best of the Small Faces or their more obscure mod rivals, the Action, 'Baby Loves That Way' is a time capsule of London's mid-sixties clubland.

[A8] THAT'S WHERE MY HEART IS (Bowie)

Recorded *c.* October 1965; *Early On* CD.

David Jones became David Bowie for professional purposes in September 1965, but retained his given name for legal purposes (as he has ever since). It was Jones, therefore, who signed a one-year publishing deal with Sparta Music, to coincide with the Lower Third's move from Parlophone to Pye. The Sparta contract required him to emulate Lennon and McCartney by providing material that other artists – with, the publishers hoped, a higher commercial profile than Bowie himself – might be able to record.

He duly set out to prove himself a one-man hit factory, while borrowing shamelessly from all around him. 'It took me a long time to get it right,' said Bowie of his early songwriting efforts. 'I didn't know how to write a song, I wasn't particularly good at it. I forced myself to become a good songwriter, and I *became* a good songwriter. But I had no natural talents whatsoever. And the only way I could learn was to see how other people did it.' Five of the songs he wrote in late 1965 were retrieved from Shel Talmy's archive for an anthology of Bowie's early work, revealing that his ambitions extended far beyond the R&B/soul mood of his singles. Regardless of their style, what linked these songs was their clumsy sense of structure and melodic development.

'That's Where My Heart Is'* epitomised the best and worst of Bowie's calculations, mixing an amusing impression of P.J. Proby's histrionic baritone with a Burt Bacharach-style chorus apparently fashioned for the equally hysterical Gene Pitney, and a mock-religious 'middle eight' that served only to extend the song beyond 90 seconds. Straining in the upper register, however, Bowie hinted at how he would croon 'Wild Is The Wind' [131] a decade later.

* The title was probably borrowed from a contemporary single by the Dixie Cups, 'Gee The Moon Is Shining Bright', a theme also included in Bowie's lyric.

His earliest efforts at songwriting were crafted at home, where he discovered the joys of overdubbing for the first time: 'I borrowed someone else's tape recorder. I'd just record a basic track on one tape machine, then play that back through the speaker, sing to it and play guitar parts over it onto the other tape recorder, backwards and forwards until there was nothing left but tape hiss, with the idea of a melody for a song way in the background.' From there, he graduated to a demo studio 'that Bill Wyman used . . . because it was very, very cheap', before being encouraged by Talmy to work at his IBC Studio in central London. No matter where they were made, however, none of these demos provoked any interest from other artists.

[A9] **I Want My Baby Back** (Bowie)

Recorded *c*. October 1965; *Early On* CD.

Another borrowed title (from a macabre US hit by Jimmy Cross, covered in Britain by the Downliners Sect) adorned an attractively maudlin venture into the falsetto-led sound of contemporary hits by the Rockin' Berries ('He's In Town') and the Tokens. With its double-tracked vocals, and confident use of familiar chord progressions from the vocal group era of the 1950s, 'I Want My Baby Back' used many of the tricks employed by the Beatles on their *With The Beatles* LP in 1963. Even the surge from D minor to D major in the approach to the chorus had a Lennon–McCartney flavour. Sadly an almost incoherent middle section spread contagion on everything around it, dooming the song to obscurity.

[A10] **Bars Of The County Jail** (Bowie)

Recorded *c*. October 1965; *Early On* CD.

The popular taste for Western-themed story songs in 1959/60, such as Johnny Horton's 'Battle Of New Orleans' and Marty Robbins' 'El Paso', coincided with Hollywood's epic ventures into similar areas – not least *The Alamo*, the indirect source for Bowie's choice of pseudonym. 'Bars Of The County Jail' was (appropriately enough for a narrative that ended in a hanging) a doomed attempt at reviving that country-folk tradition. For a rank failure, though, it was not without interest: the rowdy cockney vocal chorus was a tentative step towards the multi-dubbed chorales of songs such as 'The Bewlay Brothers' [51]; the schoolroom-clever rhyme of 'gold'/'stoled' evidenced an early playfulness with language; and the mid-section switch from the dominant G♯ to an unexpected F♯6 ('wherever I *can*') presaged the more sophisticated melodic progressions of Bowie's debut album.

[A11] I'LL FOLLOW YOU (Bowie)

Recorded *c.* October 1965; *Early On* CD.

Built around an attractive slide down the minor scale, with a brief excursion into the major, 'I'll Follow You' lent an air of poignancy to a scenario that – like the Police's 'Every Breath You Take' many years later – came closer to stalking than romance. Each verse ended with a wordless harmony motif reminiscent of the Searchers' 1964 hit 'Some Day We're Gonna Love Again'. But the formulaic middle section, always Bowie's weakness in his early composing career, was merely filler, while the guitar solo – one flourish, then incoherence – confirmed that this demo was designed to sell the song, not the group.

[A12] GLAD I'VE GOT NOBODY (Bowie)

Recorded *c.* October 1965; *Early On* CD.

Bowie's continuing difficulty in turning melodic fragments into a coherent structure was acutely obvious on this generic pastiche of the British beat sound that had dominated UK pop in 1963 and 1964, but was now beginning to sound anachronistic. It opened like a maudlin retread of one of the Kinks' more lacklustre early singles, 'Everybody's Gonna Be Happy', and moved through a series of sections that bore no apparent lyrical or musical connection.

[A13] BABY THAT'S A PROMISE (Bowie)

Recorded c. October 1965; unreleased.

The most promising of these early demos sadly escaped Shel Talmy's archive excavations in the late eighties, and therefore wasn't included on the *Early On* CD. 'Baby That's A Promise' was clearly indebted to the Small Faces (friends of Bowie's on the London mod scene), and beyond them to the Motown sound. If this song – built around a similar two-chord transition to 'You've Got A Habit Of Leaving Me' [A6] – might have fitted into the repertoire of the Small Faces, Bowie's vocal performance was altogether less focused, flitting between the almost parodic excess of P.J. Proby and the smooth swagger of Marvin Gaye. This combination would find a more suitable home a decade later, on his *Station To Station* album.

The Lower Third performed 'Baby That's A Promise' at an audition for the BBC in late 1965, alongside covers of James Brown's 'Out Of Sight' and – reflecting Bowie's bravado, if nothing else – the novelty song 'Chim-Chim-Cheree' from the Julie Andrews musical *Mary Poppins*. The BBC's Talent Selection Group delivered a brutal verdict on Bowie's potential: 'A singer devoid of personality. Sings wrong notes and out of tune.' It would have been little compensation for Bowie to know that they had been equally damning about Paul McCartney three years earlier.

[A14] CAN'T HELP THINKING ABOUT ME (Bowie)

Recorded by David Bowie & the Lower Third, December 1965; single A-side.

I'm not very sure of myself when it comes to thinking about me. I try and leave 'me' alone . . . It's much more of a realism for me to think that this [points around room] is all me, that there's nothing else in here. It's all outside. I prefer that way of existence.

David Bowie, 1973

Part autobiography, part emblematic snapshot of the narcissistic mod psyche, 'Can't Help Thinking About Me' launched Bowie's enduring pseudonym with a wry reflection that he'd 'blackened the family

name'. Whatever the crime – his effeminate appearance, sexual misde-
meanours, or simply abandoning his identity as a Jones – his exile set
up an intriguing scenario that flitted back and forth between insecurity and swaggering self-confidence. The uncertainty captured by the
sustained 4th adaptation of the opening A major chord gave way to
a sense of freedom emphasised by Bowie's joyous romp through the
key of E,* only for the song to enter a cul-de-sac with the frustrating
circularity of the chorus (the banality of which probably damned its
commercial chances). Its brief appearance in the *Melody Maker* singles
chart was, according to his co-manager Kenneth Pitt, achieved by
bribery, belying the fact that its sales were meagre at best.

That was scant reward for a record that, despite its structural flaws,
was infused with energy and personality. Its lyrical ambiguities caught
all the indecision of adolescence, with Bowie pining nostalgically for his
childhood while remembering how he had hated school. His vanished
Eden was a fantasy, as conceded, perhaps, by the punning reference to
'Never-Never Land', where Peter Pan and the Lost Boys were presumably repaying their hire-purchase bills. The narrative was assembled
with some literary skill, launching the listener head-first into the heart
of the drama in the opening line, and spotlighting Bowie's vulnerable
humanity with his girlfriend's disarmingly casual greeting, 'Hi, Dave.'

This was also his first great vocal performance, rich in passion,
his soaring delivery of the simple line 'I'm guilty' proclaiming his
pride in having escaped from the conventions of his upbringing. Like
'The London Boys' [A21], written around the same time, 'Can't Help
Thinking About Me' leaves one regretting that Bowie wasn't commissioned to compose a concept album about teenage London life in 1965.

[A15] AND I SAY TO MYSELF (Bowie)

> Recorded by David Bowie & the Lower Third, December 1965; single
> B-side.

In less convincing style than 'Baby Loves That Way' [A7], 'And I Say To
Myself' signalled Bowie's debt to the Motown stable, while retaining

---

* Composing on guitar by instinct rather than musical awareness, he incorporated
some 'borrowed' chords that gave the song a modal and chromatic effect.

the outdated British beat influence of 'Glad I've Got Nobody' [A12]. The opening flourish of an octave-spanning a cappella vocal, swiftly undercut by its accompaniment,* was startling, but the song swiftly subsided into banality and predictability – the latter never more evident than when the chorus revisited the I-vi-IV-V chord progression of many 1950s vocal-group records, while the Lower Third chanted the title with all the enthusiasm of schoolboys enduring detention after school. By contrast, Bowie's vocal oozed self-confidence worthy of Motown star Marvin Gaye.

Anyone searching for biographical resonance might be intrigued by the reference to a 'playgirl', repeating the theme from 'Bars Of The County Jail' [A10] of a poor boy's doomed infatuation with a rich girl, and raising the possibility that Bowie's relationship with the aristo-cratic teenager Dana Gillespie† might have sparked a class-conscious sense of inferiority.

[A16] DO ANYTHING YOU SAY (Bowie)

Recorded March 1966; single A-side.

Commercial failure once more encouraged Bowie to jettison his band, and within two weeks of leaving the Lower Third, he was performing with yet another outfit, the Buzz. True to form, their name was absent from his next single.

Stepping back from the self-disclosure of 'Can't Help Thinking About Me' [A14], Bowie merged two mod influences on this soul pastiche, reprising the two-chord vamp of the Kinks' 'Tired Of Waiting For You' against a snappy, Motown-styled track. Not that the Detroit label would ever have countenanced the recurrent dissonance in the almost laughably lethargic backing vocals, or sapped the strength of a major chord (the G, as each verse neared its end) by withdrawing its root. All Bowie's vocal bravado (plus a bubbling piano motif after

* The bass offered an ominous A-B-C climb against the less decisive E♭-D♭-E of the vocal melody.

† The mention of 'playgirl' pre-dated the magazine of that name by several years, and was probably inspired by the Marvelettes' 1962 Motown hit, and mod anthem, 'Playboy'. Dana Gillespie, meanwhile, pursued her own recording career, re-emerging in Bowie's story in 1971 [47].

the chorus) was required to keep the frail structure afloat, his boast of returning in a thousand years striking an eerie note in the light of his later obsession with the Third Reich.

[A17] GOOD MORNING GIRL (Bowie)

Recorded March 1966; single B-side.

'Take My Tip' [A5] had already signalled Bowie's willingness to flirt with jazz changes, and 'Good Morning Girl', dominated by the switch-back ride between first and fourth chords in a Dorian G minor scale, was exquisitely tailored towards the cooler end of the mod club scene. Besides a contemporary nod to Georgie Fame and his jazz organ, Bowie offered homage to Sammy Davis Jr in the ease with which he scatted his way alongside the guitar solo and through the climactic rush towards the final seventh chord. Alongside such zestful exhibi-tionism, the dismissive playfulness of the lyric was almost irrelevant.

[A18] I DIG EVERYTHING (Bowie)

Recorded July 1966; single A-side.

For the first time, one of Bowie's flirtations with the jazz/soul hybrid was promoted as an A-side, though from its dominant Hammond organ to its hip drug references (there was even a 'connection', six months before the Rolling Stones devoted a song to this archetypal sixties figure), it was aimed at an elite audience of knowing mods rather than the pop mainstream. The title (with the inevitable suffix 'man') might have been uttered by any character in Kerouac's *On The Road*, and Bowie's imagery was unashamedly American. On 'Good Morning Girl' [A17] he'd already slipped across the Atlantic with a dime, and now he met a time-check girl and a garbage man while claiming to have the Village (New York's Greenwich of that ilk, presumably) at his feet. Yet the song also visited London's Trafalgar Square, suggesting that location was less important than peer-group identification. The Latin-flavoured percussion was redolent of New York's Cuban community, whose music briefly became a Bowie obsession when he moved to the city in 1974. Most impressive of all was his impeccably assured vocal, whether he was lazily laying out for the organ or squeezing extra syllables into a line in the Bob Dylan tradition. None of this came close to approximating a 1966 hit single, however.

[A19] I'M NOT LOSING SLEEP (Bowie)

> Recorded July 1966; single B-side.

In the unconvincingly carefree tradition of the country standard 'She Thinks I Still Care', Bowie devoted an entire song to declaring how little the adventures of his socially climbing ex were preying on his mind. The recurrent shift between the tonic and the minor 2nd chords symbolised surging ambition, assuming defiant proportions amidst the strident major chords of the chorus. The structure was a tribute to Motown's growing sophistication, while Bowie's vocal expressed the barely suppressed anger of contemporary American 'garage-punk'* songs by the likes of the Standells and the Shadows Of Knight. Only one element jarred: each verse closed with a theatrical swagger worthy of Anthony Newley, who might also have suggested the abrupt key changes of the 'middle eight' had he ever experimented with mid-sixties rock.

[A20] RUBBER BAND (Bowie)

> Recorded October 1966; single A-side. Re-recorded February 1967; *David Bowie* LP.

Little more than three months separated 'I Dig Everything' [A18] from 'Rubber Band', yet there was virtually nothing to connect the two songs except Bowie's name. Rarely can any recording artist have conceived such a complete demolition of his existing image. Gone were the mod sensibility, the grounding in club soul and cool jazz, the casual lapses into American slang, the frenetic attempts to cater for

---

* The term was coined in the early 1970s to describe an aggressive, R&B flavoured form of urban US 60s rock heavily influenced by the Rolling Stones and the Yardbirds. The 'punk' tag was then applied to artists such as the New York Dolls and Patti Smith, before becoming tied to the altogether more restrictive sound of young Britain circa 1976/77.

the sections of London's youth culture with whom Bowie felt most comfortable. They were succeeded by an Englishness located firmly within earshot of Bow Bells, a fashionable nostalgia for national culture before it was infiltrated by American influences,* and a concentration on fictional characters rather than episodes of real or fantasised autobiography.

Kenneth Pitt and Anthony Newley are often credited – or blamed – for this abrupt change of technique and image; Pitt for his knowledge of musical theatre, Newley as the musical cockney with his heart on his sleeve and a smile on his lips. Pitt was merely responding to Bowie's own affection for the stage, however, in seeking to enlarge his potential audience; and Newley's distinctive tone, so often assumed to be Bowie's primary influence during this period, is only audible on a handful of songs, most notoriously 'The Laughing Gnome' [A37].

More relevant to Bowie's creativity was perhaps his brief collaboration with orchestrator and composer Carl Davis, with whom he was encouraged to pen songs for a musical film. Davis wasn't credited for his contribution to any of the material Bowie wrote during those weeks, but it's difficult not to believe that he was formative in teaching the singer how to construct theatrical songs and edit his own work with rigorous discipline.

'Rubber Band' and 'Please Mr Gravedigger' [A22] were selected by Bowie to represent his new approach, and recorded alongside the older 'The London Boys' [A21] during a remarkably productive day at Oak Studios in London. The three songs won him a contract with Decca's newly coined subsidiary label, Deram, alongside an array of kitsch easy-listening ensembles but also songwriter Cat Stevens, whose own brand of character-led songs, such as 'Matthew And Son', proved to be more overtly commercial than Bowie's.

Because (like Pye a year earlier) Decca blanched at promoting the 'controversial' 'The London Boys', 'Rubber Band' was selected as Bowie's debut single in his new guise. Its title – like that of another Decca act, the Elastic Band – was a simple pun, extended by Bowie into an economically told tale of a First World War soldier who loses

* The success of the vintage clothes store I Was Lord Kitchener's Valet, which opened in London's Portobello Road in 1964 and had extended to five shops by 1966, exemplified this trend. Edwardian jackets became a virtual uniform for the likes of the Jimi Hendrix Experience, the Beatles and the Rolling Stones in 1966.

his love to the 'little chappy' (the coyness was endemic to this era of his career) conducting a brass band in the park.

Operating under financial constraints that the British Prime Minister in 1966, Harold Wilson, would have recognised, Bowie and his bassist/arranger Dek Fearnley hired two musicians to impersonate the brass band, alongside the members of the Buzz. Though he lacked the orchestral colours that the song required, Fearnley compensated with a dextrous arrangement that involved multiple changes of tempo and key.* Like an artist's signature, he offered a magnificently inventive bass guitar run under the opening bars, before letting a peripatetic tuba take over the bass's role. Having parped its way majestically through the entire song, accompanied by trumpet and an occasional flourish of oboe, the tuba gradually slowed to a halt, like an exhausted bandsman struggling under its weight on a scorching July afternoon.

Bowie's melody was equally pictorial: trapped in its circularity during the verse, then rising in a pitch of rapidly quelled emotion as he lamented the band's inability to stay in tune.† Most striking, in retrospect, was his vocal performance, which featured none of the jazzy 'swing' of his recent singles – or, for that matter, of Anthony Newley's approach to novelty tunes. Instead, his delivery was formal and precise, like an H.G. Wells hero (Kipps, say, or Mr Polly) of lower birth attempting not to disgrace himself in the presence of his betters. Yet as the key changed and he abandoned the lower register of the introductory verse, he exhibited a sense of desperation that hinted at the *Station To Station* and *'Heroes'* LPs a decade ahead. As if the two-octave expanse of the song wasn't enough, he let loose a series of whoops and cries that carried him far beyond the high G that he regarded as the summit of his range.

Four months later, 'Rubber Band' was re-recorded more 'profes-

* The mock-baroque introduction in Gm is interrupted by the insistent root of Am, where the track remains for two verses before a trumpet solo and verse in Bm, a final verse in C♯m, and a coda in E♭m. The rhythm is equally varied, toying with the constraints of the 4/4 time signature.

† One wonders what influence this song might have had on the Beatles, about to begin work on their *Sgt. Pepper* album when 'Rubber Band' was released. They reprised the 'out-of-tune' theme on 'With A Little Help From My Friends', while both the *Pepper* uniforms and the orchestral colouring of several songs on the LP reflected Bowie's Georgian theme.

sionally', with a less surreal tuba accompaniment, and at a markedly slower tempo, for Bowie's debut LP. 'I hope you break your baton,' he quipped as the song ended, replacing the repressed anger of the single with a theatrical wave to show that it had all been an act.

[A21] THE LONDON BOYS (Bowie)

Recorded October 1966; single B-side.

The most enduring of Bowie's pre-fame compositions was originally composed in the final months of 1965 – before, it should be noted, any of his British contemporaries had dared to explore social commentary in their songs. What isn't certain is how closely his original blueprint of the song resembled the record he made a full year later. The holy grail for those intrigued by Bowie's early career would certainly be the original recording of 'The London Boys', taped in November 1965 for Tony Hatch at Pye Records. 'It goes down very well in the stage act, and lots of fans said I should have released it,' Bowie said shortly afterwards, 'but Tony and I thought the words were a bit strong . . . we didn't think the lyrics were quite up many people's street.' 'Can't Help Thinking About Me' [A14] was released instead, and the 1965 tape of 'The London Boys' seems to have been lost in one of Pye's vault-clearing exercises.*

Almost a year later, Bowie was still anxious to commit 'The London Boys' to tape; indeed, it was with that purpose in mind that he visited Kenneth Pitt at his London apartment in September 1966, seeking assistance and funding. Under the expert guidance of Dek Fearnley, he emerged with a remarkably astute portrayal of teenage life, as redolent of the metropolitan perils of its era as the groundbreaking television drama *Cathy Come Home* (first screened on 16 November 1966, four weeks after Bowie's recording session). The song, Bowie claimed of its original incarnation, 'generally belittles the London night life scene'. That description might have applied more accurately to 'Join The Gang' [A27], as it underplayed the psychological insight and empathy of 'The London Boys'. The latter peeled away the heady glamour of

---

* Bowie wasn't targeted for special treatment; Pye also succeeded in destroying almost all of their sixties master tapes by the Kinks.

life in what Ray Davies of the Kinks called the 'Big Black Smoke'* to reveal the alienation and emptiness beneath. It presented a 17-year-old girl, tempted into using 'pills' (barbiturates† or 'speed', most likely) to feign a sense of ease on London's mod scene, and aware that she can never return home. Then the perspective shifted to the boys whose approval she craved, and whose pride Bowie revealed to be as hollow as her mask of security.

In Dek Fearnley's almost baroque arrangement, using the orchestral textures of 'Rubber Band' [A20] to much darker effect, the song climbed through a series of dramatic key changes, reached a peak of despair – and then subsided gravely into a reprise of its oboe-led opening motif, leaving the characters adrift in their confused isolation. It's impossible to imagine the Lower Third, Bowie's backing group in November 1965, negotiating the complex twists of the chord structure, or even attempting them on guitar. The arrangement gave every indication of having been concocted at a keyboard, with Bowie at Fearnley's side to ensure that his voice was equal to the modulations.

Perhaps because, as an outsider from distant Bromley, he could identify with both the newcomer and the initiates, Bowie delivered a masterful performance. Registering each subtle emotional shift with the precision of a trained actor, he moved from the sombre resignation of the opening lines to the dramatic pathos of the finale – negotiating the octave leap at the end of each verse ('*some*one cares . . .') with ease. Such was his commitment to the song, in fact, that it was tempting to wonder whether the central character, who hates her

---

* 'Big Black Smoke', issued on the B-side of 'Dead End Street' in November 1966, offered an equally jaundiced perspective on a young girl's prospects in Swinging London. There are clear thematic links between the two songs: had Ray Davies perhaps heard Bowie's original recording at Pye, or was the coincidence merely synchronicity?

† The writer Kenneth Leach worked in a Soho coffee bar at the time this song was written, and when Bowie was frequenting such clubs: he noted that 1966 was the year when amphetamines were starting to be superseded by LSD or cannabis. His London boys, he wrote, 'were either homosexual or experimenting with homosexuality. The average age was about 18–19. There were at this time only a few heterosexual girls, and a large number of "chickens", that is, very young, pretty boys who were acquired and used by the older ones . . . Use of amphetamines by kids in the club was closely related to the confusion about sexual identity. There was as much boasting about the number of pills consumed as about the number of sexual acts.'

job, takes too many pills and is desperate for a milieu to replace her family, was none other than Bowie himself.

'The London Boys' clearly evoked the mid-sixties era perfectly for Bowie, who in assembling his *Pin Ups* album of material from this era in 1973 toyed with the idea of re-recording the song in small segments as a method of linking the other tracks. Sadly, the plan – similar to the structure of Elvis Presley's 1971 album, *Elvis Country* – was never followed through. But Bowie did reprise 'The London Boys' for his unreleased album *Toy* at the turn of the century.

[A22] PLEASE MR GRAVEDIGGER (Bowie)

Recorded October 1966; unreleased. Re-recorded December 1966; *David Bowie* LP.

To judge by its companions, the lost recording of 'Mr Gravedigger' from the October 1966 session would probably have incorporated numerous key changes and some subtle touches from a tuba and oboe. Two months later, producer Gus Dudgeon stripped away all its musical elements bar Bowie's plaintive voice and a funereal church bell. This slice of Grand Guignol starred a germ-infested serial killer and the heartless gravedigger of the (elongated) title, both played by Bowie with a theatrical panache that suggested his ideal medium might have been radio drama.

[A23] UNCLE ARTHUR (Bowie)

Recorded November 1966; *David Bowie* LP.

As Bowie explained nearly seven years after he wrote this song, 'I envisage a scenario first, then the music.' His earliest composition to merit a comparison with Anthony Newley's cockney whimsicality, 'Uncle Arthur' was a Donald McGill seaside postcard brought to life. Its cartoon characters – smothering mum, inadequate son – deserved to be painted in exaggerated tones, and Bowie *performed* rather than sang this major-chord music-hall romp in the (recent) tradition of the Kinks' 'Dandy', sounding more like a stage-school graduate than an R&B-obsessed mod. An oboe offered a sixteenth-century English dance to set the scene. Then the lyric began with stage directions to heighten the theatricality, Bowie telegraphed the laughs with Newley-style vim (not just *lust*, he leered) and only the call-and-response chorus – reminiscent in its three-chord simplicity of the Who's 1966 hit 'Substitute' – hinted at his past or future.

[A24] SHE'S GOT MEDALS (Bowie)

Recorded November 1966; *David Bowie* LP.

Another woodwind fanfare – oboe and flute trilling to introduce the theme – led into this uneasy blend of West End musical, garage rock and confused sexual politics. The opening lines of each verse were built around the distinctive chord sequence behind the Byrds' arrange-ment of 'Hey Joe', over which Bowie recited the outré scenario as if he was Tommy Steele's understudy. Each line was crammed with syllables, anticipating the verbal rush of 'Hang Onto Yourself' [31] five years later, before the title offered the punchline, chorused with all the grace of a pub full of drunken builders. The major plot develop-ment was revealed in the middle section, which wandered around its chord changes* with the same ease that its hero(ine) altered her gender. Some commentators have found presages here of Bowie's later profession of bisexuality, but his vocal mannerisms suggested this was simply being played for fun.

[A25] THERE IS A HAPPY LAND (Bowie)

Recorded November 1966; *David Bowie* LP.

Bowie named novelist and journalist Keith Waterhouse as one of his favourite authors in a 1966 interview, and this song borrowed the title[†] of a 1958 novel that was added to the secondary school

---

* These basically followed – with occasional substitutions – the 'circle/cycle of fifths' found everywhere from Bach to the Beatles' 'Lovely Rita'.

[†] Bowie had clearly read the book: though he changed the characters' names, he retained the location of their illicit adventures, in the rhubarb fields. Coincidentally, the leading role in the 1961 BBC Radio adaptation of this story was played by another David Jones, the future star of the Monkees.

curriculum a decade later. The book's poignant evocation of childhood resilience and burgeoning sexual awareness endured long beyond Bowie's tribute. But the song, like the novel, was immersed in a world psychologically and physically separated from adulthood, and Bowie delivered it in a voice full of knowledge and disillusion.

Under the influence of psychedelic drugs, other rock performers were beginning to investigate childhood in 1966/67, usually invoking innocence as a golden state (John Lennon's 'She Said She Said' offering a totemic example). Bowie's lyric wanted to believe in that innocence, though his performance undercut his hope. But there was an unexpected coda: after a deliciously melancholy stroll through a modal set of chords, the door was opened to sunlight, and Bowie scat-sang a potential trumpet solo to the fade over sumptuous chords that bridged the chasm between happiness and regret.

[A26] WE ARE HUNGRY MEN (Bowie)

Recorded November 1966; *David Bowie* LP.

Another book, Harry Harrison's popular 1966 science-fiction novel *Make Room! Make Room!*, was a likely source for this ambitious but ultimately unwieldy blend of environmental doom and arch comedy. Certainly their scenarios were similar: a world in which overpopulation has drained its most precious natural resources. It was a timely concern, as scientists calculated that the world's population had doubled from two billion to four billion in the previous 35 years, a rate of growth they believed to be unsustainable.* To halt this rise, experts stressed the importance of birth control, and suggested enforcing limits on the size of families; otherwise war (sparked by shortages of resources) and famine would take their toll. To these drastic solutions, 'We Are Hungry Men' added another: cannibalism (or, in the central character's amendment, exophagy: eating those who don't belong to one's own tribe). This was unconventional territory for a budding pop star, which was presumably why Bowie gave the subject a comic treat-

---

* For a more formal reaction to the problem than Bowie's, see Paul R. Ehrlich's controversial 1968 book *The Population Bomb*, which aroused widespread alarm and argument. Ehrlich predicted that overpopulation would force the rationing of water and food in the USA by the end of the 1970s.

ment, with producer Gus Dudgeon offering vocal impersonations like a cut-price Peter Sellers.

Musical connections still being Bowie's weakness as a composer, the multi-sectioned nature of 'We Are Hungry Men' resembled an awkward rock opera. After the dissonant chaos of the opening monologue, Bowie's Messianic character declaimed a repetitive and restricted verse melody. The populace replied with a hovering (and, again, melodically compressed) sequence of major 9th chords in (appropriately enough) a different key, the droning organ acutely reminiscent of Pink Floyd's* early experiments with the rock idiom. The menacing unison vocals looked ahead to the eerie ambience of 'Sons Of The Silent Age' [152]. Yet the darkest moment was still to come: after Dudgeon's monologue in the style of Sellers' Dr Strangelove, Bowie launched into a recitative that veered close to Schoenberg's *Sprechgesang*,† while trumpets added anarchic, rootless blasts. The effect was both urgent and disquieting, evoking a situation plummeting out of control, and setting up the final, carnivorous punchline.

[A27] JOIN THE GANG (Bowie)

Recorded November 1966; *David Bowie* LP.

In the final weeks of 1966, Bowie obtained an imported copy of the Mothers Of Invention's first album, *Freak Out!*. Its blend of social satire, affectionate rock 'n' roll pastiche and Dadaist *bricolage* established its primary creator, Frank Zappa, as a maverick composer and commentator on contemporary culture. Bowie was shocked and electrified by the anarchic extravagance of tracks such as 'The Return Of The Son Of Monster Magnet', and set out to create something equally adventurous as a stage act with the Buzz, using an array of backing tapes and sound effects. A primitive precursor of the synthesiser was

---

* Bowie may have seen Pink Floyd's performances at London's psychedelic clubs, though their first record was not released until March 1967. His exposure to an acetate of the Velvet Underground's debut album is another probable influence, with Fearnley's organ mirroring the emblematic viola drone of John Cale.

† *Sprechgesang* is a style of voice projection pitched between conventional singing and recitation, first used by Schoenberg in 1912 in his pioneering atonal song cycle, *Pierrot Lunaire*.

purchased, but proved impossible to synchronise, and the experiment was soon abandoned. But Zappa's flamboyant use of sonic collage did prove to be an audible influence on the cacophonous finale to this recording, which also reflected a cynical attitude towards the rock aristocracy that matched Zappa's own.

Every sin of contemporary pop stardom came under fire: media hype, indulgence in drugs, arrogance towards one's audience, underground elitism. To reinforce his playful but pointed message, Bowie borrowed from the heroes of the day, using the drum pattern from the Rolling Stones' 'Get Off Of My Cloud' to open the track, and underpinning one verse with the unmistakable motif of the Spencer Davis Group's 1966 hit 'Gimme Some Lovin'. Musical contempt was signalled via a deliberate use of discord,* and by setting most of the song to a jaunty music-hall rhythm reinforced by barrelhouse piano in the style of Kinks' session keyboardist Nicky Hopkins. Amusing though the track was, however, one wonders whether it was inspired as much by feeling like an outsider as it was by genuine outrage; as Bowie would have found at London's hippest clubs, there was a sharp social divide between the era's most prestigious stars and a journeyman like him.

[A28] DID YOU EVER HAVE A DREAM (Bowie)

Recorded November 1966; single B-side.

Pure vaudeville, from its chord changes (a variation on the 1920s hit 'I Wish I Could Shimmy Like My Sister Kate', which Bowie would later perform briefly on American TV [123]) to its strummed banjo and honky-tonk piano, 'Did You Ever Have A Dream' owed something to the self-proclaimed 'good-time music' of one of his favourite US groups, the Lovin' Spoonful.† It was delivered by Bowie in a voice that exuded personality without a hint of self-mockery, and might conceivably have brought him a much-needed chart presence had it been favoured above the more Newley-flavoured 'Love You Till Tuesday' [A39].

* Bowie's character essayed an octave jump to a high E, and landed in a heap somewhere between D and E♭.
† Their major 1966 hit was 'Daydream'; their first LP included a song entitled 'Did You Ever Have To Make Up Your Mind'.

[A29] SELL ME A COAT (Bowie)

Recorded December 1966; *David Bowie* LP. Vocals re-recorded by Feathers, January 1969; *Love You Till Tuesday* film.

Bowie's efforts at rebranding himself as a mainstream entertainer didn't preclude his recognising trends within popular music. Reprising the first line from the recent Simon & Garfunkel folk-rock hit 'I Am A Rock' at the start of his own venture into similar terrain was either an artistic homage or a daring display of cheek. Building the song around a descent vaguely reminiscent of that used in the same duo's previous hit, 'Homeward Bound', proved how closely he had studied his role models. The sense of sadness it conveyed was quite delicious, and contrasted with the staccato determination of the chorus. Bowie's vocal was impeccably controlled, resisting the temptation to wallow in emotional dramatics, and aside from some familiar clumsiness in the middle section, 'Sell Me A Coat' was a classy exhibition of his versatility. Beginning and ending the song, the melancholy 'la la' vocal refrain, rising to the dominant note of the key and falling sadly away, was draped in an echo so delayed that it heightened the sense of alienation.

The effect of a vulnerable young man, collar turned up against the wind, was somewhat deflated when Bowie returned to the song with Feathers more than two years later, having elected to include it in his 1969 TV special. The similarity to Simon & Garfunkel was heightened by the addition of a vocal counterpoint (in the tradition of the duo's arrangement of 'Scarborough Fair/Canticle') and delicate use of three-part harmony. Meanwhile, Bowie adopted a harsher tone of voice than on the original recording, as if to distance himself from the emotional root of the song.

[A30] LITTLE BOMBARDIER (Bowie)

Recorded December 1966; *David Bowie* LP.

The annual banality of the Eurovision Song Contest attracted less attention in Britain in the mid-sixties than at any time since. Sandie Shaw's victory in 1967 with the relentlessly chirpy 'Puppet On A String' opened the competition to contemporary pop stars, and in retrospect it's surprising that there is no record of David Bowie attempting to write the British entry in 1968 or 1969.* 'Little Bombardier', with its waltz tempo and 'oom-pah' arrangement,† demonstrated that he could easily have concocted something with a suitably simplistic melody. Had he entered this song, more people might have noticed its similarity to the *Beatles For Sale* track 'Baby's In Black'. (The two of them even employed the same trick of soaring to the octave of the key signature at the start of the middle section.) Eurovision judges might have baulked, however, at allowing a lyric that hinted, however vaguely, at the paedophile tendencies of a man who was, in the parlance of the times, 'simple'.

[A31] SILLY BOY BLUE (Bowie)

Recorded December 1966; *David Bowie* LP.

As befitted a man who chose to end his 1966 stage shows with 'You'll Never Walk Alone' or 'What Kind Of Fool Am I', Bowie knew the power of a dramatic ballad. He made several attempts at Deram to tame the species, with limited commercial success. 'Silly Boy Blue' was the oldest example, having existed in some form around a year earlier as a chronicle of his mod leanings. By December 1966 he had revamped it as a token of his passion for Tibetan Buddhism. Despite never having travelled closer to Tibet than East Anglia, he littered his song with spiritual and geographical references that only those steeped in Buddhist lore‡ could understand. They were personal totems, rather than attempts at communication – a badge of belonging as exclusive as anything the mod sensibility could imagine. Former pop idol Billy Fury's decision to record the song

---

* Elton John and Bernie Taupin reached the last six in the 1969 competition, only to lose out to 'Boom-Bang-A-Bang'.

† Or, in this case, to be exact, 'oom-pah-pah'. Though we tend to associate the term with German folk/pop music, it refers specifically to the movement between tonic and dominant, usually performed on tuba, but here exhibited on accordion.

‡ A quick guide: Lhasa is the Tibetan capital; a chela is a religious disciple; Tibetans create statues out of yak butter to mark religious festivals; the overself is a universal spirit beyond the everyday. Online collections of Bowie's lyrics claim the second line refers to 'Botella [or, more amusingly, Bordello] lanes'; he actually sings 'Potala', the palace near Lhasa that the Dalai Lama occupied before the Chinese occupation of 1959.

in 1967 reflected the strength of its melody rather than its words, which Fury did his best to disguise.

That melody began at its height (the dominant E in A major), and gently ebbed and soared back home. Trumpet fanfares erupted over calming cello in the first verse, giving way to a percussive rhythm familiar to sixties pop fans from the Ronettes' 'Be My Baby'. A mid-section that carried Bowie to the peak of his vocal range fell away as he sang the word 'die', enabling the key to modulate discreetly to B. There it remained, but after a fade in which Bowie alluded to Dionne Warwick's improvised ending to her 1964 classic 'Walk On By', a Beach Boys-inspired harmony section provided an elegant coda, sliding back and forth between B and A and thereby resolving both of the song's active key signatures.

So attached was Bowie to the song that he reprised it twice for BBC Radio sessions, rewrote the lyrics for his 1969 TV special (though it wasn't filmed for the show) and revamped it for his unfinished album *Toy* thirty years later. 'Silly Boy Blue' also formed part of the sound-track for his 1968 mime piece, 'Jetsun And The Eagle'.

[A32] MAID OF BOND STREET (Bowie)

Recorded December 1966; *David Bowie* LP.

Besides reading like a 'poor little rich girl' digest of a screenplay that could have been called *The Loneliness of the Long Distance Model*, 'Maid Of Bond Street' (as in Joan of Arc, the Maid of Orleans) offered a snapshot of the 16-year-old Bowie. Who else could have played the supporting role of the envious boy desperate to become a star? Whether the song was based on a real-life crush who'd been out of his league as a trainee, or whether he was simply jumping on to the 'Eleanor Rigby'/*Cathy Come Home* bandwagon of urban loneliness, Bowie fashioned this vignette into a gorgeous miniature of social satire. The Rolling Stones would have treated the Maid with contempt (compare their ventures into similar territory, on the *Aftermath* LP); Paul McCartney would have turned her into soap opera (as on 'She's Leaving Home' from the *Pepper* LP, or his later single 'Another Day'). Bowie chose instead to highlight the gulf between image and reality, as if he was tearing down a poster he'd helped to design three years earlier.

His utterly assured vocal performance – lingering on some phrases, rushing others as if hurrying for a train – was supported by perhaps his most convincing marriage to date of melody and subject. The song began deceptively in E major, then walked tentatively up the scale, looking for assurance, before finding sanctuary among a familiar I-vi-IV-V chord sequence in C major. But the relief was short-lived, as the middle section left the maid hovering uncertainly between major E and D chords, unable to find security. As both boy and girl were exposed as victims of the Swinging London myth, Bowie steered the song into a four-chord sequence that clearly alluded to the climax of his earlier visit to those same streets, 'The London Boys' [A21]. The minor chords of that song were replaced here by their major equivalents, slamming the door shut on the characters' dreams.

[A33] COME AND BUY MY TOYS (Bowie)

Recorded December 1967; *David Bowie* LP.

Guitarist John Renbourn, about to form the folk-rock group Pentangle with Bert Jansch, provided the stylish finger-picked accompaniment for Bowie's attempt to mimic the ageless mystery of the English folk tradition. If there were hints of Wordsworth and Blake in his idealistic view of childhood (compare 'After All' [20]), they sounded borrowed – assembled piecemeal, perhaps, from images in a book of young people's verse. Another source provided Bowie's 'Cambric shirt', also to be found in Simon & Garfunkel's 'Scarborough Fair/ Canticle', which was released in Britain four weeks before this song was recorded. Renbourn was clearly under instructions to replicate Paul Simon's guitar technique, exploiting the potential of some familiar folk chord progressions, but he could do little to rescue the middle section from its melodic clumsiness.

[A34] BUNNY THING (Bowie)

[A35] YOUR FUNNY SMILE (Bowie)

> Recorded December 1966; unreleased.

Bowie made full use of Renbourn's services, also featuring him on 'Bunny Thing', which chronicler Kevin Cann describes as a recitation 'in the style of a beat poet, complete with an improvised musical section'. 'Your Funny Smile', meanwhile, was (in Cann's account) 'like an unpolished recording from David's spell with Pye Records'. Both songs were included in the initial track listing for Bowie's debut LP, but quickly deleted, and he has blocked subsequent attempts to release them.

[A36] OVER THE WALL WE GO (Bowie)

> Recorded December 1966; unreleased demo. Recorded by Oscar, January 1967; single A-side.

'I'll sing you a song, it's not very long, all coppers are bastards.' That, in its entirety, is the traditional cockney tune that was the source for this novelty song – and which also found its way around the world, in a multitude of different forms, all intended to tweak the nose of authority. In his original demo, Bowie turned the 'bastards' into the child-friendly 'nanas', and added a prison-escape scenario, complete with an impression of British heavyweight boxing champion Henry Cooper, some Goons-inspired dialogue, and a flash of Scouse. The song was picked up by Oscar Beuselinck, the singer-actor son of a music publisher, who persuaded Bowie to add backing vocals to his rendition. Oscar's cast of characters (but not Bowie's) included a dramatically camp 'poofta'. Despite its novelty appeal, and similarity to subsequent hits by the Scaffold, Oscar's record wasn't a hit, though he enjoyed more success in later years as a singer and comic actor under the name Paul Nicholas.

'Over The Wall We Go' – written in skeletal form by late 1965 – owed its appearance on record to music publisher David Platz, who signed Bowie to his Essex Music roster when his Sparta deal expired in autumn 1966. It was now in Bowie's financial interests to deliver as many commercially oriented songs as possible to Platz, who tirelessly attempted to interest recording artists famous and obscure in his material. At his most ambitious, Platz sent demos of songs such as 'Silly Boy Blue' [A31] to American bands who were quite capable of writing their own material, like the Jefferson Airplane. Over the next two or three years, a huge quantity of 'lost' Bowie compositions were presented to Platz in demo form, and presumably sent out to artists and managers on a speculative basis. Some of them have survived on scratchy acetate discs; others remain a mystery. Among the missing titles from Bowie's mid-to-late-sixties output are 'April's Tooth Of Gold', 'Lincoln House', 'Say Goodbye To Mr Mind', 'Something I Would Like To Be', 'Take It With Soul' and 'The Girl From Minnesota'.

[A37] THE LAUGHING GNOME (Bowie)

Recorded January / February 1967; single A-side.

Just as Les Paul deserved the credit for pioneering vari-speed and multi-track recording techniques, American comedian Ross Bagdasarian was the man who discovered the comic potential of speeding up the human voice to sound like a cute animal (or, indeed, a gnome). After premiering this trick on 'Witch Doctor' in 1958, he launched a trio of lovable sound effects named the Chipmunks, whose debut single established sales records that would only be broken by the Beatles. Britain had its singing pig puppets Pinky and Perky, while Lou Monte's 'Pepino The Teenage Mouse' established the scenario of a human being annoyed by a high-pitched interloper.

So the invasion of hysterical gnomes – playfully voiced by Bowie and producer Gus Dudgeon – was merely the continuation of a long tradition. The circulation of a rough mix demonstrated that many groan-worthy gags were considered for inclusion and discarded; the completed track included a sly reference to Mick Jagger's time as a student at the London School of Eco-gnom-ics, and also referenced another popular variety act of the era, the Singing Postman (whose mysterious catch-phrase, in Norfolk dialect, was 'Have you got a loight, boy?').

If Bowie had been auditioning for a career as a children's entertainer, 'The Laughing Gnome' ought to have guaranteed him a lifetime's employment; it's easy to imagine him becoming the puppet's sidekick in *The Basil Brush Show*, or joining the cast of BBC TV's perennial Friday afternoon romp, *Crackerjack*. Strangely, the single didn't catch the attention of the producers of BBC Radio's *Children's Favourites*, thereby robbing us of an alternative future in which Bowie became the British equivalent of Danny Kaye. Only when reissued in 1973 did it achieve the success it deserved, while prompting cynics to question how Bowie could be taken seriously as a rock star with skeletons this bony in his closet. An embarrassment for Ziggy Stardust and Aladdin Sane, however, was merely another feather in the cap for the versatile entertainer of 1967.

Bowie would revive the vari-speed vocal trick, to much eerier effect, on songs such as 'After All' [20], 'All The Madmen' [23] and 'The Bewlay Brothers' [51].

[A38] THE GOSPEL ACCORDING TO TONY DAY (Bowie)

> Recorded January/February 1967; single B-side.

Presumably to avoid typecasting, Bowie ensured that the B-side of 'The Laughing Gnome' could never be mistaken for a children's song. 'The Gospel According To Tony Day' was lugubrious and cynical, with a melody that barely stretched to five notes, sung low, then an octave higher, and with the minimum of variation. The eight-bar verse, with a two-bar interlude, returned dolefully to the progression at the heart of 'Good Morning Girl' [A17]. Behind Bowie, an equally jaded rock rhythm section – reminiscent of Phil Spector's arrangement of 'Zip-A-Dee-Doo-Dah' for Bob B. Soxx & the Blue Jeans – supported the surreal inclusion of oboe and bassoon, where a blues guitar might have seemed more obvious. If the much-loved English comedian Tony Hancock had made a rock record at the height of his mid-sixties depression, it might have sounded like this, complete with its sarcastic mockery of the clichés of R&B ('gotta, gotta') and psychedelia ('your mind, blow it').

[A39] LOVE YOU TILL TUESDAY (Bowie)

> Recorded January 1967; unreleased demo. Recorded February 1967;
> David Bowie LP. Re-recorded June 1967; single A-side. German vocals
> overdubbed, January 1969; unreleased.

For Bowie and Pitt, 'Love You Till Tuesday' appears to have been the most important song recorded for Deram. A late addition to the *David*

Bowie LP, it was rearranged as a single, and still regarded as his most commercial offering more than 18 months later, as its prime position in his 1969 television special demonstrated. It certainly bore signs of having been conceived as a stage-school audition piece,* exhibiting Bowie the comedic song-and-dance man, with a smile on his lips, a tear in his eye, and a nod towards every all-round entertainer from Sammy Davis Jr to Roy Castle.

Its theatrical bent was obvious: the coy, self-congratulatory laugh Bowie awarded himself when he rhymed 'branch' and 'romance', the almost audible wink that accompanied his cockney impersonation of the Man in the Moon, the octave leap in each verse, and the jokey aside[†] that ended the song. When Ivor Raymonde's orchestral arrangement for the single added a coda comprising a few bars of the 'Hearts And Flowers' melody from Alphons Czibulka's *Wintermärchen*, used in countless films to signify bathos, he was simply adding treacle to a bag of sugar.

Not that the finished record – especially the LP version[‡] – was without its charm. The melody galloped up and down the scale like an acrobat, a xylophone tinkled a merry theme, followed immediately by an optimistic climb from a string section, and the final progression from a C major chord to C diminished, A♭, B♭ and back to C neatly set up and immediately resolved a moment of drama. Like several of its Deram counterparts, however, 'Love You Till Tuesday' helped Bowie by not connecting with the public, as its success – as with 'Rubber Band' [A20] and 'The Laughing Gnome' [A37] – would have eradicated any possibility that he might become a rock star in the subsequent decade. 'I would have been doing stage musicals, I could almost guarantee it,' Bowie reflected 30 years later. 'I'm sure I would have been a right little trouper on the West End stage. I'd have written ten Laughing Gnomes, not just one!'

---

* It should be noted, however, that Bowie's original demo, featuring several layers of vocals, was more in keeping with Pete Townshend's blueprints for the Who from the same era.

† Bowie may have been inspired to add this by Eartha Kitt's similar finale to 'Apres Moi', on *Down To Eartha*, an album that also included a song he considered for his cabaret repertoire, 'The Day That The Circus Left Town'.

‡ The single added an orchestra, and an unnecessary modulation, sounding more like a Eurovision contender than a potential pop hit.

[A40] WHEN I LIVE MY DREAM (Bowie)

Recorded February 1967; *David Bowie* LP. Re-recorded June 1967;
Love You Till Tuesday film. German vocals overdubbed, January 1969;
unreleased.

Like Anthony Newley's show-stopping ballad, 'Once In A Lifetime',
Bowie's 'When I Live My Dream' was an emotional tour de force
designed to bring a West End audience to its feet. Unfortunately, it
lacked a theatrical vehicle for which it could provide a cathartic climax,
thereby curtailing another career avenue for its composer. Its lyrics
might sometimes have sounded as if they had been translated too
hastily from a continental language, but the universal power of its
central image, the frustrated man crying out for the chance to fulfil
his destiny, could have overcome any flaws.

Had the song become better known, of course, then critics might
have pointed out how indebted the middle section was to the corre-
sponding portion of the Righteous Brothers' 'You've Lost That Lovin'
Feelin', using the same I-IV-V chord progression. They might also
have carped at the almost desperate efforts of the arranger to modulate into a higher key for dramatic effect, and then find a coherent
way home – a battle that endured into the final bar. By accident or
design, Bowie marked the crucial moments of the song by moving
the melody away from the root of the chord: it opened at B♭, accen-
tuating the Fsus4 chord, and soared to its height at high G, against an
E♭ chord. He negotiated the (almost) two-octave range and complex
twists and turns of the key changes with ease, however, reinforcing
Kenneth Pitt's view that the stage was his most promising prospect.

Two days after the *David Bowie* LP was released, he re-recorded
'When I Live My Dream' at a slower tempo, with curt electric guitar
chords marking out the third beat of each bar, like many of the 'uptown
soul' records made in New York around this time. The track was
doubtless intended as a single, but instead languished at Decca until
Pitt retrieved it for *The David Bowie Show* in 1969 – at which time he
also persuaded Bowie to tape a German translation of this song and
'Love You Till Tuesday' [A39] in the vain hope they might be required
by a German TV station.

[A41] PUSSY CAT (unknown)

Recorded March 1967; unreleased.

Bowie chronicler Kevin Cann reckons that this song, recorded immediately after the completion of the Deram LP, was a cover of a non-charting 1964 single by the novelty pop crooner Jess Conrad, of 'This Pullover' infamy. If it was a non-original, then a more likely source might be a 1966 soul single by Chubby Checker, 'Hey You! Little Boo-Ga-Loo', of which it formed the B-side. Whatever the case, Cann (the only researcher to have heard the track) makes it sound less than appealing, calling it 'a true oddity . . . David's vocal deteriorates as he appears to tire of the song.'

[A42] LITTLE TOY SOLDIER (AKA SADIE'S SONG) (Bowie/Reed)

Recorded with the Riot Squad, March/April 1967; unreleased.

If, as the novelist F. Scott Fitzgerald contended, 'the test of a first-rate intelligence is the ability to hold two opposed ideas in the mind at the same time, and still retain the ability to function', then Bowie's Janus-headed enthusiasm for the furthest extremes of popular music in spring 1967 suggested the presence of genius. While concocting novelty song-and-dance tunes and romantic ballads, he was also searching for a way to incorporate sonic distortion and sexual experimentation into his repertoire.

In November 1966, Kenneth Pitt visited New York in search of new avenues for Bowie to explore. He returned in mid-December with, so Bowie recalled in 2002, 'two albums he had been given by someone . . . Not being his particular cup of tea, he gave them to me to see what I made of them.' One was *Virgin Fugs* by the Fugs, a shambling collective of beat poets and hippies whose anarchic approach to melody, performance and common decency did not directly influence Bowie's music.* The other record, Bowie explained, 'a demo with the signature Warhol scrawled on it, was shattering. Everything I both felt and didn't know about rock music was opened up to me on one unreleased disc. It was *The Velvet Underground & Nico* album.' He would claim in the

---

* Bowie later claimed, however, that he added the Fugs' 'Dirty Old Man' to his live repertoire, alongside songs from the Mothers Of Invention's *Freak Out!* LP.

early seventies to have known nothing about Lou Reed and the Velvet Underground until he met Reed in 1971. That was patently untrue, as in the early weeks of 1967 he composed a song incorporating an entire verse written by Reed. Known variously as 'Little Toy Soldier' and 'Sadie's Song', it was taped at a rehearsal with the Riot Squad at a north London public house in March, alongside 'Silly Boy Blue' [A31], 'Silver Tree-Top School For Boys' [A43] and another Reed composition from that Velvet Underground album, 'Waiting For The Man' [A44]. Three weeks later, three of those songs were also recorded at Decca, for private rather than commercial consumption.

It is certainly impossible to imagine Decca* contemplating the release of 'Little Toy Soldier', a darkly comic and suggestive tale of sado-masochism. The fact that it included a sizeable extract from the Velvet Underground's 'Venus In Furs', sung by Bowie in an impression of Reed's Long Island monotone to the accompaniment of whip-cracks and cackling laughter, merely added legal problems to the central issue of vulgarity. Subject aside, the track opened like one of John Entwistle's more mischievous excursions into black humour with the Who, and incorporated a Mothers Of Invention-inspired 'freak-out' featuring bomb blasts, aircraft engines, traffic, and a healthy bout of coughing. Even the GPO's Speaking Clock telephone service made a cameo appearance.

Although Bowie's interest in Reed's work was maintained into the seventies, his adventures in experimental music were effectively laid to rest for almost a decade after this session. It is intriguing to wonder what might have happened if he had continued to work with the Riot Squad beyond the release of his debut album. He would, after all, have made a worthy replacement for Syd Barrett when the mercurial singer-songwriter left Pink Floyd in 1968.

[A43] SILVER TREE-TOP SCHOOL FOR BOYS (Bowie)

Recorded with the Riot Squad, March 1967; unreleased demo.

Alumni of the independent school Lancing College in Sussex include cabinet ministers, generals, bishops, ambassadors and the novelist

---

* More than a year later, the company refused to allow the Rolling Stones to issue an album cover portraying graffiti around a lavatory.

Evelyn Waugh, whose work influenced 'Aladdin Sane' [70]. The school governors might be less willing to celebrate another distinction: rumours of a sixties drugs bust among pupils that apparently inspired Bowie to write 'Silver Tree-Top School For Boys'. The lyrics mixed a satirical response to the incident with imagery reminiscent of more utopian visions of childhood, from William Blake and Lewis Carroll.

Bowie's demo of the song is not in circulation, leaving rival versions by the Beatstalkers (arguably the stronger of the two) and the Slender Plenty as our only evidence of how it might have sounded. The Beatstalkers accentuated its similarity to contemporary material by the Kinks, complete with a descending bass-line reminiscent of their hit 'Sunny Afternoon', and an opening riff in the style of another English band who left their mark on Bowie, the Move. The slightly awkward chord sequence in the middle section undermined a melody that might otherwise have fitted on to *Hunky Dory*.

[A44] WAITING FOR THE MAN (Reed)

Recorded with the Riot Squad, March/April 1967; unreleased.

Bowie described this song as the 'linchpin' of the first Velvet Underground album, lauding its 'throbbing, sarcastic bass and guitar'. He incorporated it into his stage repertoire with the Riot Squad (and sporadically since then), later boasting that this was 'the first time that a Velvets song had been covered by anyone, anywhere in the world'. His attempt to replicate the Velvets' sonic propulsion in the studio was only marginally successful, however. Both his harmonica and saxophone detracted from the sleazy urban ambience he was essaying, while bassist Brian Prebble veered away too obviously from the relentless key notes of the original recording. Bowie's vocal was a passable re-creation of Lou Reed's sound, though his efforts at transcription weren't: one of Reed's lines emerged as 'a good friendly behind' in Bowie's mouth, anticipating his later excursions into sexual adventurism.

[A45] EVERYTHING IS YOU (Bowie)

Recorded April 1967; unreleased demo.

Bowie intended 'Everything Is You' as a gift for Manfred Mann, but could only persuade his friends the Beatstalkers to record it: in pop terms, the equivalent of aiming for an Aston Martin and coming home with a Morris Minor. Like many of his compositions written for outsiders, it suffered from an extreme discordance between music and lyrics, with an ultra-commercial (for 1967) melody linked to a lumberjack's lament that belonged alongside 'Bars Of The County Jail' [A10] rather than in the Top 40.

His skills as a pop confectionist were not in doubt, however, as 'Everything Is You' opened with a radio-friendly wordless harmony line over three basic rock 'n' roll chords in the tradition of Buddy Holly (whose 'Heartbeat' bears close comparison). Though Bowie delivered the song with the jaded air of the John Lennon of 'I Don't Want To Spoil The Party', it had a natural effervescence that might have made it ideal for a group such as the Tremeloes. Bowie also indulged himself with a series of short, rhymed lines in the middle section that were heavily influenced by Bob Dylan.

Also written and demoed around the same time was another Bowie pop concoction, 'A Summer Kind Of Love' [see A54].

[A46] GOING DOWN (Bowie)

Recorded *c.* May 1967; unreleased demo.

It was not surprising that none of David Platz's Essex Music clients elected to record this bizarre exercise in avant-garde pop, which was as chaotic as some of the final recordings by one of Bowie's heroes from this period, Pink Floyd frontman Syd Barrett. The surviving performance of the song stopped and restarted almost at random, with the most basic of melody lines and lyrics (little more than a repetition of the title) interrupted by Bowie stamping his feet, hitting the microphone with his hand, or rattling any percussion within his reach. If completed and crafted, it wouldn't have sounded out of place alongside the more melodic elements of the Who's 1967 album,

Sell Out, but in its existing form, it would probably have proved too unorthodox for even Frank Zappa to consider.

[A47] LET ME SLEEP BESIDE YOU (Bowie)

Recorded September 1967; *The World Of David Bowie* LP.

Between the completion of Bowie's first album and this conscious attempt to create a single that would steer him in a fresh direction, a recognisable culture of British 'rock' emerged from its uncomfortable gestation in the pop scene. It provided the soundtrack for the underground and counter-culture, two terms attempting to herd the era's multifarious retreats from 'straight' society into a homogeneous whole. Musically, it was oriented towards the album rather than the single; it favoured volume and aural assault over instantly appealing melody; it was unafraid to take its inspiration from blues, jazz, literature, folk and beyond; and it was not concerned to limit itself to two-minute teenage melodramas. It self-consciously aimed at a slightly older, grubbier, perhaps better-educated audience: sixth-formers and students, in other words, rather than the pubescents and pre-pubescents who dominated the pop audience.

For the next decade, Bowie would attempt to span the divide, with varying degrees of success and acceptance. 'Let Me Sleep Beside You' was a tentative step into the new world, and (not at all coincidentally) his first session with producer Tony Visconti,* who exerted a major influence over Bowie's lifestyle for the next three years. It signalled its intentions with a guitar signature from jazz-rock pioneer John McLaughlin, and eschewed all the novelty elements heard on previous Deram releases. But the song still worked its way around familiar chord changes, with a dominant-tonic-subdominant progression supporting the understated chorus. Double-tracked for the middle section, Bowie held two notes ('void' and 'hap-pen') in a way that would become a trademark of his seventies records, while his strident call of 'Would you?' anticipated the vocal persona that would stride out of the *Ziggy Stardust* era.

* 'What interested me in the first place was hearing his demos, which were incredible,' Visconti recalled. 'He played all the guitars, he played his own bass, he did his backing vocals.'

Ultimately, it was another 'rock' characteristic, its willingness to step across bourgeois moral boundaries, that would keep this song from being released in 1967. Bowie later joked that his mother had told him it was indecent, but that anti-Oedipal explanation disguised the record company's misgivings.

[A48] KARMA MAN (Bowie)

Recorded September 1967; *The World Of David Bowie* LP.

Tony Visconti's primary contribution to this charming piece of science fiction was to follow the example of producer George Martin, whose arrangements for the Beatles' 'Eleanor Rigby' had shown the potential of a string section as an active, almost aggressive vehicle, rather than (as was customary on pop records) lush decoration. Lyrically indebted to Ray Bradbury's story sequence *The Illustrated Man*, in which cinematic tattoos spell out the characters' fates, 'Karma Man' worked its way elegantly through an ambiguous series of changes,* with only the leap back to the opening D at the end of the chorus sounding abrupt. It was one of Bowie's most creative marriages of words and music to date, the anxious staccato of the verses giving way to the melancholy acceptance of the chorus, reflecting the narrator's isolation from his unseeing companions. The song might have fitted perfectly in an alternative world in which the self-conscious 'progression' of rock could still have been focused on the pop charts.

[A49] IN THE HEAT OF THE MORNING (Bowie)

Recorded December 1967; BBC Radio session. Re-recorded March / April 1968; *The World Of David Bowie* LP.

'In The Heat Of The Morning' represented a valiant attempt by Bowie to merge the epic ballad style of 'When I Live My Dream' [A40] with the more restrained approach of 'Let Me Sleep Beside You' [A47]. In

* The word is appropriate: the melody that ended the first chorus was repeated in the middle of the 'Changes' [48] refrain four years later. Note also in this song the unusual verse structure of four 4/4 bars followed by one in 2/4: instinctive rather than studied, as ever with Bowie.

its Decca rendition, which required markedly more studio time than anything he'd recorded to date, it incorporated elements of pop (the string accompaniment, and a passionate hookline, which sadly wasn't the title); progressive rock (Mick Wayne's guitar motif, and some prominent Hammond organ); and even soul (the repeated wordless vocal riff, like a late-night response to the R&B standard 'Land Of 1000 Dances'). If the words spilled into over-romanticism,* there was a passionate engagement in his vocal that cut through his verbosity. His range was stretched further than before, to a high A, and the force with which he declaimed the phrase 'like a little soldier' anticipated the central sound of the *Station To Station* album eight years hence.

Deram's refusal to accept either this song or 'London Bye Ta Ta' [A52] as a potential single betrayed the fact that their interest in Bowie as an artist was exhausted, regardless of what he offered them. Despite that, Kenneth Pitt recalled that he and Bowie were still assembling material for a second Deram album. Songs such as 'Angel Angel Grubby Face', 'Threepenny Joe' and 'The Reverend Raymond Brown' survive only on a tape loyally retained by Pitt. Their titles suggest that Bowie was continuing to stockpile 'character' songs in the mistaken belief that they held his commercial future.

[A50] EVEN A FOOL LEARNS TO LOVE (François/Thibault/ Revaux/Bowie)

Recorded *c.* February 1968; unreleased demo.

Bowie's publisher, Essex Music, offered him several opportunities in 1967/68 to widen his portfolio by providing English-language translations of songs in foreign tongues. There were Israeli folk tunes, Belgian pop,† and a proven hit in the form of Claude François' melan-

---

* Bowie first taped the song for BBC Radio in December 1967, with no sign of the rock instrumentation that would dominate the Decca recording, and some even more painful imagery that he later excised.

† Bowie's lyrics for 'Love Is Always' and 'Pancho' were issued in Belgium by the female singer Dee-Dee, the original co-composer of the tunes. 'Pancho', the tale of a biker whose tough exterior belies his love for his girl, was a particularly amusing offering, which required Bowie to incorporate the French endearment, 'chou-chou'. His lyric also echoed a phrase about highways and byways from the Hollies' 1965 single, 'Look Through Any Window'.

choly French ballad about romantic separation, 'Comme D'Habitude'. Although François' passionate rendition was released in Britain, Essex boss David Platz rightly considered that the haunting melody required a libretto with international potential. Bowie supplied him with 'Even A Fool Learns To Love' – a phrase that fitted the space left by 'Comme D'Habitude' very inexpertly. The same lack of feeling for poetic scansion was apparent throughout Bowie's lyric, which he recorded at home to the accompaniment of the François original. It was left to American singer-songwriter Paul Anka to supply a more evocative lyric, hinged around the simple theme of doing things his way. Bowie took his revenge with 'Life On Mars?' [52].

[A51] ERNIE JOHNSON (Bowie)

> Song cycle comprising TINY TIM, WHERE'S THE LOO, SEASON FOLK, JUST ONE MOMENT SIR, VARIOUS TIMES OF DAY (Early Morning, Noon Lunch-Time, Evening), ERNIE BOY, A SONG OF THE MORNING, UNTITLED TRACK ('If your Oxford bags are oh so thin'). Recorded spring 1968; unreleased demo.

The *Ernie Johnson* suite – 35 minutes of comic songs and dialogue, interleaved with moments of extreme poignancy – demonstrated the extent of Bowie's ambitions during his career hiatus of 1968. It also highlighted the difficulties he found in translating his most extravagant concepts into a format appropriate for a mass audience. It was one of the most intriguing and at the same time frustrating projects that he ever conceived, full of imagination but totally lacking in coherence and structure. Only the surviving lyric sheets, which reveal Bowie's belief that the song cycle was complete ('Voila, fini,' he wrote at the end), suggest that this wasn't a venture that he abandoned midway through its creation.

The scenario – one hesitates to call it a narrative – runs like this. For reasons unexplained, Ernie Johnson is staging a suicide party in his Bayswater flat (this west London location signifying a certain level of poverty in 1968). We meet one of the first arrivals, Tiny Tim; more guests turn up, fire questions at their host, and demand to know where they can spend a penny; Ernie remembers the women he's loved over the previous year; then he's mysteriously transported to a park, where he has a conversation with a tramp while pretending to be a TV interviewer; time passes; he wakes up in the morning, ready for the day of his suicide; and finally he visits a Carnaby Street boutique to buy a suitable tie for the occasion, being casually insulted by the oh-so-trendy staff in the process. And there the sequence ends, leaving this drama about a suicide party without a suicide or even much of a party.

Taken individually, however, the constituent parts of *Ernie Johnson* were striking. 'Tiny Tim' (subsequently considered by Kenneth Pitt as a contender for a second Deram album) was an arch, colloquial* portrait of a gay young man, voiced by a cynical admirer. Set to the rhythm and riff of the Drifters/Searchers hit 'Sweets For My Sweet', it mixed acoustic guitar and foot-stomping percussion, with Bowie adopting the campest of vocal personae.

'Where's The Loo' mingled two and sometimes three Bowie voices over acoustic guitar, playing a motif vaguely reminiscent of the one that powered 'Queen Bitch' three years later. The narrators were a series of fresh arrivals at the party, who bombarded their host with staccato questions – the overall impression being similar to Peter Cook and Dudley Moore chatting over a Syd Barrett track.

'Season Folk' marked an abrupt change of mood, as an ultra-romantic solo ballad portraying Ernie's regretful memories of 'Ann' (all household chores and comfortable familiarity), 'Nearly Jane' (who like so many Bowie heroines of the sixties left him feeling socially and intellectually inferior) and 'Jill' (a London dolly-bird with a handbag full of mind-changing pills).

Ernie met the tramp in 'Just One Moment Sir', a dialogue sequence that found the two cockney characters bonding over some racist chat about 'nig-nogs', while the tramp repeated a charming refrain about scratching his itches. In his role as television reporter, Ernie ended the conversation by insulting his subject, after which Bowie envisaged the tramp retreating with a barrage of insults and V-signs.

Next, he evoked 'Various Times Of Day'. 'Early Morning' featured two long lines of poetry, delivered to the accompaniment of eerie, alien, heavily echoed voices. 'Noon Lunch-Time' was a snapshot of

---

* Much of the language was reminiscent of the sixties gay slang known as palare/ polari, as heard regularly on the 'Julian & Sandy' sketches in BBC Radio's *Round The Horne* comedy show.

London in midsummer, with office workers filling the parks while traffic wardens searched for victims. Finally, 'Evening' unfolded as if the Beach Boys had been attempting a merger of their stoned 1967 sound with Bowie's *Low*, an unearthly vision of anticipation and expectancy being built out of sonic distortion and mock-doo-wop vocals.

'Ernie Boy' occupied more familiar territory, as a character song introduced by some poignant lines of dialogue from the star of the show: 'Suicide isn't something I've always wanted to do . . . I know who I am.' Backing vocals spelled out his name in each refrain, while Bowie delineated the grim details of Ernie's life: poverty, emotional dislocation, alienation from the world of Swinging London. Perhaps Ernie and Bowie weren't so different after all.

'A Song Of The Morning' (alias 'This Is My Day') boasted the eerie cheerfulness of the Who at their most macabre, as Ernie welcomed the dawn of his final day on the planet. Reminding himself that he must wear his most flamboyant tie at the evening's party, he was transported back to the fashionable boutique where he had found it, for the untitled finale – delivered by the salesman in what Bowie specified as 'a trendy, gear, freak-out type feel. Cool dad.' This was the moment when several of his themes and infatuations collided: the ruthlessness of advertising, the Kinks' brand of social satire, Syd Barrett's whimsicality, the cacophony of Zappa and the Velvet Underground, the barrenness of psychedelia, and a recognition of the fine details of contemporary fashion. The song, and the suite, ended with a melee of voices and noise, before a repeated tape loop – a throwback to the end of the Beatles' *Sgt. Pepper* album, and also a preview of the finale of his own *Diamond Dogs* LP [104] – left the listener, and Ernie, marooned in limbo.

Bowie committed the song cycle to tape, typed up and signed its lyrics, and then apparently forgot all about *Ernie Johnson*, aside from an occasional musical motif finding its way on to *Hunky Dory* and *Ziggy Stardust*. Even he must have realised that this was not the route to public acceptance. Dark though the scenario of a suicide party might have appeared, however, it was still arguably more commercial than the libretto of *Tommy*, Pete Townshend's 1968 rock opera about a deaf, dumb and blind boy who is abused by his uncle and his cousin.

[A52] LONDON BYE TA-TA (Bowie)

Recorded March / April 1968; *David Bowie Deluxe Edition* CD.

In the proud tradition of the Beatles' 'If I Needed Someone', several songs by the Byrds, and the 'remedy' section of the Who's mini-rock opera, 'A Quick One While He's Away', 'London Bye Ta-Ta' was written around guitar variations on a D major chord,* the first Bowie tune to betray its instrumental origins so blatantly. The Byrds' link may not have been accidental: Bowie's 'strange young town' recalled the 'rain grey town' in the American group's 'Eight Miles High'. If the dense blend of strings and rhythm section was reminiscent of Phil Spector's 'wall of sound', and there was a flash of Dylanesque surrealism in the lyrics, the track now seems to resemble nothing more than Bowie's future self. Certainly the 'I love her' section could have fitted into the mouth of a more romantically inclined Ziggy Stardust.

The conversational chorus, based around a phrase Bowie overheard from a Caribbean woman in south London, was commercial enough to suggest that the song had potential as a single. Bowie certainly thought so: when he rounded up the best of his Decca recordings for *The World Of David Bowie* LP, he omitted 'London Bye Ta-Ta', which he had just re-recorded [12] as a putative follow-up to 'Space Oddity' [1].

[A53] WHEN I'M FIVE (Bowie)

Recorded May 1968; BBC Radio session.

Nothing Bowie wrote in the year after his debut album was released came closer to reproducing the spirit of that album than 'When I'm Five'. It was clearly designed for *performance*, requiring the narrator to take on the persona of an inquisitive four-year-old without – an almost impossible task – slipping into coyness. He effectively sabotaged that hope with what was clearly intended to be the song's most poignant moment, as the narrator saw a picture of Jesus. Note also the refer-

* The chorus melody in D was then repeated exactly in the verse, in the new key of C major.

ence to 'Grandfather Jones', Bowie's only acknowledgement on record of his true identity;* and, on the May 1968 BBC rendition to which he mimed in his 1969 TV special, the absolute precision of his vocal.

Equally assured was the melodic construction, with no hint of the stumbling transitions that had dogged many earlier songs. Opening, like 'London Bye Ta-Ta' [A52], with some D major variants, it supported the narrator's four-year-old determination with major-chord transitions, before the strings added a more whimsical tone, pursuing a rising diatonic figure in G and then A, before leading elegantly back into the verse.

[A54] A SOCIAL KIND OF GIRL (Bowie)

Recorded c. April 1968; unreleased.

As a reflection, perhaps, of his reduced commercial prospects, 1968 was one of the most fallow periods of Bowie's creative life. 'A Summer Kind Of Love' [see A45] having failed to attract a buyer, he rewrote the lyrics, taping a multi-voiced rendition that sounded as if it had been tailored for the already waning teen sensations the Monkees (it is certainly easy to imagine Micky Dolenz recording the song). At a moment when the Beatles had abandoned the pure pop of their early fame, 'A Social Kind Of Girl' leaned heavily on the relationship between lead and backing vocals found on songs such as 'I'm A Loser', 'Help!' and 'Another Girl'. There were also hints of the chorus from a more recent hit by the Lovin' Spoonful, 'She Is Still A Mystery'. With the aid of an experienced co-writer or arranger, Bowie might have enjoyed a lucrative 1960s career as a composer of mainstream pop for artists unable to confect their own.

It's a sign of his artistic confusion during this period that at the same time he was writing pop tunes for the teenage market, Bowie was contemplating an entirely different approach to his career. Twice in 1968, he and Kenneth Pitt prepared elaborate set-lists for a cabaret act, with Pitt even scripting dialogue to link the songs. There was no hint here of Bowie's previous enthusiasms for rock 'n' roll, R&B, Frank Zappa or the Velvet Underground, beyond the suggestion that

* Unless, of course, you read autobiographical resonance into the title of 'D.J.' [169].

he might extend the sonic potential of his performances by using sound-effects tapes between songs.

The first set included two Anthony Newley songs, three from the repertoire of Sammy Davis Jr, jazzy swing tunes popularised in 1963 by Tony Bennett and Oscar Brown Jr (whose 'Dat Dere' would surely have required Bowie to perform in blackface), and a few nods towards the more sophisticated margins of pop, via hits borrowed from Gene Pitney, Dusty Springfield, Dionne Warwick and Bobby Hebb. Only Bowie's own 'I Dig Everything' [A18] (already two years old) hinted at a personal stamp. Six months later, the pair tried again, adding the Beatles' 'All You Need Is Love', 'Yellow Submarine' and 'When I'm Sixty-Four', Eartha Kitt's* 'The Day That The Circus Left Town' (which demanded to be sung in the guise of a child, like Bowie's own 'When I'm Five' [A53]), Bowie's translation of 'Comme d'Habitude' [A50], and several original songs, including 'The Laughing Gnome' [A37] (for which sound effects would surely have been a pre-requisite). He might conceivably have carried off either of these repertoires with a degree of panache, but even the mere attempt would probably have made it impossible for him to pursue a viable career in rock during the seventies.

[A55] CHING-A-LING (Bowie)

Recorded by Turquoise, October 1968; unreleased. Vocals overdubbed by Feathers, November 1968; *Love You Till Tuesday* film.

The folk/mime/poetry trio Turquoise – rapidly renamed Feathers to avoid confusion with an existing psychedelic-pop group of the same name – dragged Bowie out of seclusion after a long period in which he had effectively been estranged from the music business. The project also allowed Bowie to work with Hermione Farthingale, who had been his girlfriend since their shared cameo in a BBC TV drama entitled *The Pistol Shot* earlier in the year. They were joined briefly by guitarist Tony Hill, who soon opted for the more visceral landscape of the rock band High Tide. His replacement was John Hutchinson, who would become Bowie's musical collaborator for the next few months.

---

* In later years, Bowie would occasionally toy during rehearsals with Kitt's standard, 'An Old-Fashioned Girl', which had been adopted as an anthem by her gay following.

Each incarnation of the group played three gigs with Bowie; the latter also appeared in the TV special showcasing Bowie's talents that Kenneth Pitt produced in the early weeks of 1969. So did this song, which was every bit as coy and childish (not childlike, as Bowie might have hoped) as its title. Its folksy/folky feel was perhaps intended to mimic the deliberate naivety of the Incredible String Band, but instead might have served for an 'improving' BBC TV show aimed at the pre-school audience. As a vehicle for Turquoise-cum-Feathers, it was unflattering, placing too much responsibility on Hermione Farthingale's stilted, flimsy voice. Much more significant, in retrospect, were the wordless backing vocals offering a counterpoint to the inane chorus. Their melody reappeared on 'Saviour Machine' [24], and their approach (strangely reminiscent of the soldiers' choruses from Leni Riefenstahl's Nazi documentary, Triumph Of The Will) would find a more sympathetic home on 'Time'.

The main melody of 'Ching-A-Ling' was supposedly written when Bowie played an earlier demo tape backwards through his home recorder. Its country-rock-flavoured introduction was in the same vein as 'Darlin' Companion' by the Lovin' Spoonful, though the Americans would never have dragged a song through such a clumsy set of key changes as those concocted by Bowie in a desperate bid to grab the listener's attention.

In keeping with the trio's purportedly democratic nature, Hill's song 'Back To Where You've Never Been' was taped at the same session.

Acknowledgements

This book was the brainchild of discussions between myself, my tireless and insightful agent Rupert Heath, and my incredibly supportive editors at the Bodley Head, Will Sulkin and Jörg Hensgen. Many thanks to them, and to the rest of the Bodley Head team, Kay Peddle and Hannah Ross.

Thanks are also due to the continued generosity of Andrew Sclanders (www.beatbooks.com) and Clinton Heylin; the invaluable technical advice of Mick Downs and Jon Astley; and the various contributions of Johnny Rogan, Katherine Williams, John Reed and Mark Paytress. I gained much insight into the life and character of the young David Bowie from my previous interviews with George Underwood, David Hadfield (of the Kon-Rads), Bob Solly (of the Manish Boys) and Dana Gillespie. All opinions and judgements are mine alone, however, as are any factual or musicological errors.

Once again, my most heartfelt thanks go to my wife, Rachel Baylis, who has supported me throughout the long and sometimes painful gestation of this book, without losing her patience, her remarkable sense of humour or (even more remarkably, after endless exposure) her enjoyment of Bowie's music. Much love, as always, to her, Catrin, Becca and the elusive Fred.

Source Notes

Introduction

Page 1 'People look to me': Burroughs, p. 229 • **Page 5** 'It consisted': quoted Ariel, p. 2 • **Page 6** 'This is a mad planet': to P.S. Salvo, *Sounds*, 1/12/72 • **Page 6** 'abandon all nations': quoted *IT*, 9/67 • **Page 6** 'Collective nightmares': quoted *RS*, 18/2/71 • **Page 8** 'Declinism was an established': Beckett, p. 177 • **Page 9** 'We are passing': *RS*, 18/2/71 • **Page 10** 'Next day, all hell': Almond, p. 29 • **Page 12** 'The new alchemical dream': quoted Kaufman p. 6 • **Page 12** 'the narcissistic preoccupation': ibid., p. 7 • **Page 12** 'Our therapies become': quoted *NME*, 1/11/75 • **Page 13** 'In the 70s': to Timothy White, *Musician*, 7/90 • **Page 13** 'I change my mind': Burroughs, p. 229

The Making of David Bowie: 1947–1968

Page 17 'The past loads us': Conrad, p. 712 • **Page 19** 'absolutely mesmerized': to David Cavanagh, *Q*, 2/97 • **Page 22** 'a man, handsome': Gillman, p. 65 • **Page 23** 'It was Terry': Tremlett, pp. 19–20 • **Page 24** 'I tried passionately': to Timothy White, *Musician*, 7/90 • **Page 24** 'I spent my days': ibid. • **Page 24** 'He was a very charming': to author • **Page 26** 'He cried an awful lot': to Timothy White, *Crawdaddy*, 2/78 • **Page 27** 'People who break down': *IT* 4–17/7/69 • **Page 27** 'a biochemical, neurophysical': Laing/Esterson, 1970, p. 12 • **Page 27** 'a social event': ibid., p. 17 • **Page 27** 'each person does not occupy': ibid., p. 19 • **Page 28** 'we were leaving confusion': Kerouac, p. 111 • **Page 28** 'the one and only holy': ibid., p. 6 • **Page 28** 'you've got to stick to it': ibid., p. 7 • **Page 28** 'going like mad': ibid., p. 14 • **Page 28** 'the only people for me': ibid., p. 9 • **Page 29** 'It was diabolical': to Richard Cromelin, *Phonograph Record*, 1/72 • **Page 29** 'I've been in the media': to Bruno Stein, *NME*, 22/2/75 • **Page 30** 'creative imagination': Thomas, p. 42 • **Page 30** 'The basic purpose': Dunn, p. 339 • **Page 30** 'see us as bundles': quoted ibid., p. 6 • **Page 30** 'Find some common desire': Huxley, p. 77 • **Page 31** 'The techniques of persuasion': Dunn, p. 5 • **Page 31** 'His main contribution': to author • **Page 32** 'David wasn't really': to author • **Page 33** 'a handsome six-footer': press release • **Page 33** 'all it takes': press release • **Page 33** 'Anyone who has the courage': to Leslie Thomas, *Evening News & Star*, 2/11/64 • **Page 34** 'the spirit of extravagance': Sontag, pp. 283, 279, 281 • **Page 35** 'mixed up': Pitt to Steve Turner,

NME, 18/5/74 • **Page 36** 'long back and sides': *Kentish Times*, 20/8/65 • **Page 37** 'I'd like to get into cabaret': Radio London interview, 8/66 • **Page 37** 'Nobody at that time knew': to Steve Turner, *NME*, 18/5/74 • **Page 37** 'There must be a hole': quoted Bardsley, p. 98 • **Page 38** 'Never cared for his performances': *NME*, 29/11/75 • **Page 38** 'I was Anthony Newley': to C.S. Murray, *NME* 242/73 • **Page 40** 'To begin with': Tremlett, pp. 62–3 • **Page 41** 'fumblings about how to bring': MTV interview, 1990 • **Page 41** 'When I wanted David': to Steve Turner, *NME*, 18/5/74 • **Page 42** 'As far as I'm concerned': *MM*, 11/66 • **Page 42** 'I'd like to take a holiday': ibid. • **Page 42** '[Zen] climbs': Humphreys, p. 1 • **Page 42** 'Zen is not a new thing': ibid., p. 68 • **Page 43** 'One puts oneself': BBC Radio interview, 1993 • **Page 43** 'I was convinced': to David Cavanagh, *Q*, 2/97 • **Page 44** 'David Bowie has no great voice': *Disc*, 10/6/67 • **Page 45** 'I want to act': *MM*, 11/66 • **Page 45** 'I used to work': to Bruno Stein, *NME*, 22/2/75 • **Page 45** 'I was a terribly earnest': to George Tremlett, *Jackie*, 10/5/70 • **Page 46** 'About two weeks before': Burroughs, p. 236 • **Page 46** 'I decided that': to George Tremlett, *Jackie*, 10/5/70 • **Page 46** 'I knew we shared': to Angie Errigo, *NME*, 17/7/77 • **Page 47** 'Lindsay Kemp was a living': to Richard Cromelin, *Phonograph Record*, 1/72 • **Page 47** '[Genet] has come': *IT*, 28/11–11/12/66 • **Page 47** 'I enabled him to free': quoted Buckley, p. 42

The Songs of David Bowie: 1969–1980

Page 53 'Imagine the 1990 version': to Mary Finnigan, *IT*, 15–21/8/69 • **Page 53** 'I want it to be': ibid. • **Page 53** 'Some event is awaited': *IT*, 30/1–12/2/67 • **Page 54** 'If we die, we want people': TV interview, 1966 • **Page 54** 'the people running': *IT*, 18–31/7/69 • **Page 54** 'The publicity image': to Mary Finnigan, *IT*, 15–21/8/69 • **Page 55** 'It's only a pop song': to Kate Simpson, *Music Now*, 20/12/69 • **Page 55** 'The question for us': Peter Stansill, *IT*, 1–16/1/69 • **Page 56** 'a very special piece': Pitt, p. 130 • **Page 56** 'I wrote part of': to Spencer Leigh, Radio Merseyside, 1977 • **Page 56** '"Space Oddity" was a Bee Gees': Gillman, p. 160 • **Page 59** 'With a guitar and memories': quoted Buckley, p. 67 • **Page 59** 'was convincing in his act': *Croydon Advertiser*, 21/2/69 • **Page 59** 'Janine is named': tape of demo • **Page 59** 'It's how I *thought*': to Penny Valentine, *Disc*, 25/10/69 • **Page 62** 'I'm not at ease': Burroughs, *Live*, p. 232 • **Page 63** 'was an awful experience': to Cameron Crowe, *Playboy*, 9/76 • **Page 65** 'an "energy centre"': *IT*, 10–23/10/69 • **Page 65** 'The plan is to turn on': *IT*, 23/5–5/6/69 • **Page 65** 'I feel almost middle-aged': to Gordon Coxhill, *NME*, 15/11/69 • **Page 65** 'Everything the boy says': to Penny Valentine, *Disc*, 25/10/69 • **Page 66** 'I always felt I was': to Timothy White, *Musician*, 7/90 • **Page 66** 'I heard a Wagnerian orchestra': Visconti, p. 139 • **Page 66** 'Never have I been so flipped': quoted Cann, p. 155 • **Page 67** 'David's career would have turned': Tremlett, p. 53 • **Page 67** 'Here we are in Beckenham': to Mary Finnigan, *IT*, 15–21/8/69 • **Page 67** 'I run an Arts Lab': to Chris Welch, *MM*, 9/69 • **Page 67** 'materialistic and selfish': Tremlett, p. 106 • **Page 67** 'These people': to Kate Simpson, *Music Now*, 20/12/69 • **Page 68** 'I basically wanted': to P.S. Salvo, *Sounds*, 2/12/72 • **Page 69** 'in a completely catatonic state': Mary Finnigan to Gillman, p. 178 • **Page 69** 'a barbecue, exotic tea stall': *IT*, 15–21/8/69 • **Page 69** 'vile . . . mercenary pigs': Mary Finnigan to Gillman, p. 178 • **Page 69** 'We go out on an air': to Penny Valentine, *Disc*, 25/10/69 • **Page 72** 'about a boy whose girlfriend': ibid. • **Page 72** 'describes how I felt': Tremlett, p. 105 • **Page 73** 'We found that the mass': to Richard Cromelin, *Phonograph Record*, 1/72 • **Page 73** 'The money I'm making': quoted in *Croydon Advertiser*, 30/6/72 • **Page 73** 'I never plan ahead': to George Tremlett, *Jackie*, 10/5/70 • **Page 73** 'He's a good bloke': *IT*, 5–17/12/69 • **Page 75** 'I think a lot of people': to Raymond Telford, *MM*, 28/3/70 • **Page 75** 'wrote the middle bit': to Spencer Leigh, Radio Merseyside, 1977 • **Page 75** 'She's an American citizen': Tremlett, p. 101 • **Page 77** 'I don't

want to be one': to Gordon Coxhill, *NME*, 15/11/69 • **Page 78** 'I throw myself on the
mercy': ibid. • **Page 78** 'I'm determined to be': ibid. • **Page 78** 'It seems to me that': ibid.
• **Page 78** 'What the underground has got': to Miles, *IT*, 27/2/70 • **Page 78** 'It's not that
they *want*': to Kate Simpson, *Music Now*, 20/12/69 • **Page 78** 'All my songs are very
personal': to Raymond Telford, *MM*, 28/3/70 • **Page 79** 'I was in silver lamé': quoted
Hoskyns, pp. 22–3 • **Page 80** 'We had been playing [it] live': Visconti, p. 150 • **Page 80** 'A
lot of my compositions': to Raymond Telford, *MM*, 28/3/70 • **Page 81** 'I very much
doubt': to Richard Cromelin, *Phonograph Record*, 1/72 • **Page 81** 'is a man with legal
knowledge': to Steve Turner, *NME*, 18/5/74 • **Page 81** '[Defries] absolutely *believed*':
Gillman, p. 210 • **Page 82** 'We came up with outrageous': Buckley, p. 87 • **Page 83** 'It's a
shame': to Steve Peacock, *Sounds*, 16/9/72 • **Page 83** 'The tape will remain': ibid. • **Page 85**
'Instead of commanding': John Godwin, *Occult America*, p. 245 • **Page 85** 'a caste of "men
of earth"': quoted *Friends*, 22/11/69 • **Page 86** 'a passion of mine at the time': Buckley,
p. 87 • **Page 86** 'The seventies are exploding': quoted Doggett (2007), p. 317 • **Page 87** 'Mick
Ronson, Woody': Buckley, pp. 88–9 • **Page 87** 'The songs were written by all four': *Mojo*,
10/97 • **Page 88** 'The only thing that I didn't think': ibid. • **Page 88** 'I see it now': to P.S.
Salvo, *Sounds*, 2/12/72 • **Page 88** '"All The Madmen" was written': to Richard Cromelin,
Phonograph Record, 1/72 • **Page 89** 'Our alienation goes to the roots': Laing (1967), pp. 11–12
• **Page 92** 'David spontaneously did': to Mark Paytress, *RC*, 1/95 • **Page 92** 'I felt very
ephemeral': to Timothy White, *Musician*, 7/90 • **Page 93** 'The exterior landscapes': *Friends*,
30/10/70 • **Page 94** 'It was meant to be our *Sgt. Pepper*': to Mark Paytress, *RC*, 1/95 • **Page
94** 'It's been a waste of a year': to Penny Valentine, *Sounds*, 6/2/71 • **Page 94** 'There can't
be another': *Sounds*, 10/4/71 • **Page 94** 'His unhappy relationship': *RS*, 18/2/71 • **Page 94**
'was a parody of Gabriel': to Cameron Crowe, *Playboy*, 9/76 • **Page 95** 'I used to have
periods': to Richard Cromelin, *Phonograph Record*, 1/72 • **Page 96** 'a lot of people are in': to
Miles, *IT*, 27/2/70 • **Page 96** 'the first haunted song': press release • **Page 98** 'was about the
homo superior race': to P.S. Salvo, *Sounds*, 2/12/72 • **Page 99** 'have given birth': ibid. • **Page
100** 'a certain feverishness': Beckett, p. 376 • **Page 100** 'This country is crying out': to Kate
Simpson, *Music Now*, 20/12/69 • **Page 101** 'All of a sudden, these great songs': *RC*, 2/87 •
Page 102 'His other great inspiration': *MM*, 22/1/72 • **Page 102** 'According to Jung': BBC
Radio One interview, 1976 • **Page 103** 'I didn't believe it till I came here': to Richard
Cromelin, *Phonograph Record*, 1/72 • **Page 103** 'I think I've been in prison': to P.S. Salvo,
Sounds, 2/12/72 • **Page 103** 'I got very sharp': to Steve Turner, *Beat Instrumental*, 7/71 • **Page
105** 'The moon goddess was the goddess': Wilson, p. 82 • **Page 106** 'ravishing, almost
disconcertingly': *RS*, 1/4/71 • **Page 106** 'Freud maintained': Conrad, p. 658 • **Page 109** 'I
would try and get anyone': quoted Buckley, p. 92 • **Page 111** 'I believe that Rudi': to Peter
Jones, *RM David Bowie Special*, 1972 • **Page 112** 'Really I'm just a dress designer': ibid. • **Page
112** 'I believe in fantasy': *Cheltenham Chronicle*, 1971 • **Page 114** 'Dylan belongs in a very
personal way': John Coleman, *Friends*, 13/11/70 • **Page 115** 'How do you know I'm not':
quoted Doggett (2007), p. 180 • **Page 115** 'It laid out what I wanted to do': to Robert
Hilburn, *MM*, 2/76 • **Page 116** 'Kind of a skit on Neil Young': BBC Radio One interview,
1972 • **Page 118** 'It's time to be proud': *IT*, 24/4–7/5/70 • **Page 119** 'an amazing position':
Sounds, 1/1/72 • **Page 119** 'We were all green with envy': to Paul Du Noyer, *Mojo*, 7/02 •
Page 121 'If you want to know all about': quoted Doggett (1991), p. 49 • **Page 121** 'I'm just
picking up on what other people': to Steve Peacock, *Sounds*, 14/8/71 • **Page 122** 'All the
while he was studying': quoted Needs/Porter, p. 51 • **Page 122** 'one of the leaders': live
recording, 25/9/71 • **Page 124** 'the creative drive of the conscious': Wilson, p. 100 • **Page 125**
'Life is flow, and Zen': Humphreys, p. 154 • **Page 125** 'Satori is the world of perpetual now':
ibid., p. 100 • **Page 127** 'The only thing that emerges': Wilson, p. 659 • **Page 128** 'Sometimes
I don't feel': to Mick Rock, *RS*, 8/6/72 • **Page 130** 'I like "The Bewlay Brothers"': US radio
interview, 1972 • **Page 134** 'has very little to do with David Bowie': *IT*, 30/12/71–13/1/72 •
Page 134 'What I've been trying to do': to Penny Valentine, *Sounds*, 3/4/71 • **Page 136** 'My
sexual life is normal': to Don Short, *Daily Mirror*, 24/4/71 • **Page 136** 'I'm gay, and I always

have been': *MM*, 22/1/72 • **Page 136** 'What's happening, David?': to C.S. Murray, *NME*, 18/10/75 • **Page 137** 'Everyone is part man': to Royston Eldridge, *Sounds*, 3/4/71 • **Page 137** 'We get so much action': to Nick Kent, *Frendz*, 7/72 • **Page 137** 'the year of the transvestite': Judy Sims, *MM*, 13/5/72 • **Page 137** 'I'm gay, inasmuch as I wear': *MM*, 14/7/73 • **Page 137** 'Bowie is physically a man': *MM*, 17/2/73 • **Page 137** 'Just because you're gay': to Nick Kent, *NME*, 28/4/73 • **Page 138** 'It's true, I am a bisexual': to Cameron Crowe, *Playboy*, 9/76 • **Page 138** 'Positively not': to Chris Charlesworth, *MM*, 13/3/76 • **Page 138** 'I found I was able to get a lot': to Paul Du Noyer, *Mojo*, 7/02 • **Page 138** 'Even if Bowie's claim': Boy George/ Gorman, p. 94 • **Page 138** 'When Bowie came up': Shepherd/Wallis, p. 279 • **Page 138** 'Probably the lyrics are a little': BBC Radio One interview, 1972 • **Page 140** 'naturist photographer': in *Frendz*, 9/6/72 • **Page 144** 'Realism, honesty and all these things': to Timothy White, *Musician*, 7/90 • **Page 144** 'I think [rock] should be tarted up': to John Mendelsohn, *RS*, 1/4/71 • **Page 144** 'I really wanted to write musicals': to Paul Du Noyer, *Mojo*, 7/02 • **Page 144** 'violence and glamour': Cohn (1970), p. 99 • **Page 144** 'he was all things at once': ibid.,p. 94 • **Page 144** 'I mean to make an ending': ibid., p. 130 • **Page 145** 'Most people still want their idols': to Cameron Crowe, *Playboy*, 9/76 • **Page 145** '[Bolan] had a potential riot force': Jaynie, *IT*, 27/1–10/2/72 • **Page 145** 'a quite lovely piece of faux-deco': Bowie/Rock, p. 17 • **Page 145** 'I'm going to be huge': to Michael Watts, *MM*, 22/1/72 • **Page 149** 'I get worried about dying': to Mick Rock, *RS*, 8/6/72 • **Page 149** 'I'll always remember going out': *NME*, 28/10/78 • **Page 151** 'I'm continually aware': to Henry Edwards, *After Dark*, 10/72 • **Page 151** 'It's a continual fantasy': *RM*, 18/8/72 • **Page 151** 'now high in the US charts': press advert • **Page 151** 'hype himself as something': *Oz*, 7/72 • **Page 151** 'could have been the work': Steve Peacock, *Sounds*, 10/6/72 • **Page 151** 'suggests the ascent and decline': *MM*, 1/7/72 • **Page 152** 'I'm very much a conglomerate': to Mary Campbell, Associated Press, 9/72 • **Page 152** 'the entire evening seemed like a tribute': Alexander Stuart, *Plays & Players*, 11/72 • **Page 152** 'I'm not what I'm supposed to be': to Hubert Saal, *Newsweek*, 9/10/72 • **Page 154** 'One of the great strengths': to Tony Horkins, *International Musician*, 12/91 • **Page 154** 'I don't know anything about fag rock': to Mary Campbell, Associated Press, 9/72 • **Page 155** 'If you look at what's happened': *Sounds*, 1/7/72 • **Page 156** 'Nijinsky meets Woolworth's': to Jean Rook, *Daily Express*, 5/5/76 • **Page 156** 'I don't want to go on the road': *MM*, 16/6/73 • **Page 156** 'Rock is entertainment that suggests': *Let It Rock*, 6/73 • **Page 158** 'the only interesting person around': to Roy Hollingworth, *MM*, 24/6/72 • **Page 158** 'The people I was around at the time': quoted Doggett (1991),p. 81 • **Page 158** 'A Star Is Born!': *MM*, 15/7/72 • **Page 158** 'will soon become the greatest': Charles Webster, *RM*, 15/7/72 • **Page 158** 'He was always running around': quoted Doggett (1991), p. 80 • **Page 159** 'There's a lot of sexual ambiguity': ibid. • **Page 159** 'I don't know what he was up to': ibid., p. 84 • **Page 159** 'a collection of songs witty': C.S. Murray, *NME*, 16/12/72 • **Page 160** 'I can't think of a time': to Jarvis Cocker, *The Big Issue*, 8/12/97 • **Page 160** 'In England, David Bowie may become': *New Yorker*, 14/10/72 • **Page 160** 'I had flu that night': 1983 radio interview • **Page 163** 'He's a collector': 1973 interview • **Page 163** 'the energy of six English bands': quoted Needs/Porter, p. 53 • **Page 165** 'a vague feeling of impending catastrophe': Howard Bloom, *Circus*, 7/73 • **Page 165** 'face up to a future': to Lenny Kaye, *Cavalier*, 1/73 • **Page 166** 'Time flowed always at the same reliable': Conrad, p. 60 • **Page 168** 'The book dealt with London': to Howard Bloom, *Circus*, 7/73 • **Page 168** 'Nina, do you ever feel': Waugh, p. 162 • **Page 168** 'on a splintered tree stump': ibid., p. 186 • **Page 169** 'After seeing *A Clockwork Orange*': *RS*, 8/6/72 • **Page 169** 'I got most of the look': quoted Paytress (1998), p. 97 • **Page 170** 'the idea of conscious stylisation': quoted Luytens/Hislop, p. 12 • **Page 170** 'cosmic Clockwork Orange jumpsuits': Bowie/ Rock, p. 80 • **Page 170** 'impossibly silly "bunny" costume': ibid. • **Page 170** 'He had just unleashed': to Timothy White, *Musician*, 7/90 • **Page 171** 'He has an unusual face': interview, 6/73 • **Page 171** 'there are no rules': quoted Luytens/Hislop, p. 18 • **Page 172** 'Life is so boring': Angry Brigade Communiqué #7 • **Page 172** 'The next religion might come': *Friends*, 30/10/70 • **Page 173** 'The idea was to fuck the sound up': to Tony Horkins,

International Musician, 12/91 • **Page 174** 'They were mostly older producer': to Howard Bloom, *Circus*, 7/73 • **Page 175** 'a very cold person': to Timothy Ferris, *RS*, 9/11/72 • **Page 176** 'I don't think Aladdin is as clearly': to C.S. Murray, *NME*, 27/1/73 • **Page 176** 'my interpretation of what America': to Howard Bloom, *Circus*, 7/73 • **Page 176** 'Aladdin Sane was a schizophrenic': *Cracked Actor* TV documentary • **Page 176** 'I thought [Aladdin] would probably': to Kurt Loder, *RS*, 23/4/87 • **Page 177** 'a musical in one act': to Martin Hayman, *Sounds*, 4/8/73 • **Page 178** 'I feel as though I'm on a tightrope': to Mary Campbell, Associated Press, 9/72 • **Page 178** 'I'm not too sure when': *Fan Magazine*, 4/73 • **Page 178** 'David's retirement was first talked': 1987 interview • **Page 178** 'There was a time when what': quoted Buckley, p. 149 • **Page 178** 'You start on this trail': BBC Radio interview, 1993 • **Page 179** 'In the end it was almost': 1987 interview • **Page 179** 'His manager decided just before': to Peter Harry, *RM*, 13/4/74 • **Page 180** 'various activities that have very little': to C.S. Murray, *NME*, 7/7/73 • **Page 180** 'The star was created': to C.S. Murray, *NME*, 11/8/73 • **Page 180** 'Maybe I'm not into rock 'n' roll': to C.S. Murray, *NME*, 9/6/73 • **Page 187** 'I don't know whether I want to be': to C.S. Murray, *NME*, 11/8/73 • **Page 188** 'It sometimes looked as if the originality': Shrapnel, p. 84 • **Page 188** '[Bowie's] in show business': to Tony Stewart, *NME*, 9/3/74 • **Page 190** 'a composer, arranger, singer, dancer': press release • **Page 190** 'David Bowie has taken his best shot': to Rob Partridge, *MM*, 12/1/74 • **Page 190** 'I honestly can't remember Mick': to Chris Charlesworth, *MM*, 13/3/76 • **Page 191** 'I just gave up trying': to Ben Fisher, *Mojo*, 10/97 • **Page 195** 'I'm an awful pessimist': to C.S. Murray, *NME*, 11/8/73 • **Page 196** 'After what I've seen of this world': *Circus*, 1973 • **Page 196** 'If I ever wrote about it': ibid. • **Page 196** 'Mrs Orwell refused': Ben Edmonds, *Circus*, 27/4/76 • **Page 197** 'Rejected applicants inevitably': Spurling, p. 151 • **Page 200** 'mix your own linguistic virus': *IT*, 31/8–13/9/67 • **Page 200** 'Cut up everything in sight': *IT*, 28/4–12/5/67 • **Page 201** 'My thought forms are already fragmented': *RS*, 2/76 • **Page 204** 'a premeditated rewrite': *NME*, 2/2/74 • **Page 205** 'what was now happening': Orwell, p. 174 • **Page 205** '"We are the dead," he said': ibid., p. 252 • **Page 206** 'black-haired, black-moustachio'd': ibid., pp. 18–19 • **Page 206** 'little sandy-haired woman': ibid., p. 19 • **Page 207** 'a hideous, grinding screech': ibid., p. 14 • **Page 208** '"*You're* doing it to *me*, stop it"': to Robert Hilburn, *MM*, 14/9/74 • **Page 208** 'I started fiddling around': Buckley, p. 187 • **Page 209** one rock journalist: Charles Shaar Murray (*NME*) • **Page 211** 'we used the Keypex': to Ron Ross, *Circus*, 12/74 • **Page 211** 'conceptualises the vision': press release • **Page 212** 'I wanted to make a film': to Angus MacKinnon, *NME*, 13/9/80 • **Page 212** 'my usual basket': to Paul Du Noyer, *Mojo*, 7/02 • **Page 212** 'simplistic and murky': Ken Emerson, *RS*, 1/8/74 • **Page 212** 'Mick was silly': to Cameron Crowe, *Playboy*, 9/76 • **Page 213** 'Lulu's got this terrific voice': *Rock Magazine*, 6/74 • **Page 213** 'I set out on a very successful crusade': to Cameron Crowe, *Playboy*, 9/76 • **Page 214** 'White rock has lost its contact': *NME*, 22/2/75 • **Page 214** 'Any artist who will mean as much': *Circus*, 2/75 • **Page 214** 'Every British musician has a hidden desire': ibid. • **Page 214** 'It's only now that I've got the necessary': to Robert Hilburn, *MM*, 14/9/74 • **Page 215** 'the Pimpmobile Pyramid-Heel': Wolfe, pp. 206–7 • **Page 215** 'it was an attempt to turn': to Paul Du Noyer, *Mojo*, 7/02 • **Page 217** 'He seems to be kicking and screaming': *NME*, 26/10/74 • **Page 217** 'the crossroads of multiple and confused': quoted booklet of 2010 DVD • **Page 218** 'a non-singer of the Lou Reed school': quotes from *Milwaukee Journal*, 14/10/74; *New York Times*, 2/11/74; *Boston Globe*, 15/11/74; *Philadelphia Bulletin*, 25/11/74 • **Page 219** 'You'd give him something to eat': to Peter Harry, *RM*, 13/4/74 • **Page 219** 'almost ravaged, beyond belief': Lisa Robinson, *NME*, 28/12/74 • **Page 219** 'self-destruct time': Gillman, p. 382 • **Page 219** 'I nearly threw myself': to Al Rudis, *Sounds*, 10/4/76 • **Page 219** 'moving very strangely': Lisa Robinson, *NME*, 14/12/76 • **Page 226** 'endless numb beat': to Cameron Crowe, *Playboy*, 9/76 • **Page 226** 'It obviously threatened': quoted Kaufman, p. 133 • **Page 227** 'Really, I'm a one-track person': to Robert Hilburn, *MM*, 14/9/74 • **Page 227** 'Strong emotion': Huxley, p. 76 • **Page 227** 'Hitler induced the German masses': quoted Heller, p. 14 • **Page 227** 'It could be argued': ibid. • **Page 231** 'one of the occult arts': Brennan, p. 32 • **Page 233** 'I never really knew what he was': Peebles,

p. 66 • **Page 234** 'I wouldn't inflict fame': to Moby, *Mojo*, 7/02 • **Page 234** 'some Stevie Wonder middle eight': Peebles, p. 65 • **Page 235** 'There's no gratification': to C.S. Murray, *NME*, 11/8/73 • **Page 236** 'psychic vampires': Gillman, p. 399 • **Page 237** 'the definitive plastic soul': to Cameron Crowe, *Playboy*, 9/76 • **Page 237** 'Basically, I haven't liked a lot': ibid. • **Page 237** 'It wasn't a matter of liking them': ibid. • **Page 238** 'I think he's very much a 70s artist': to Timothy Ferris, *RS*, 9/11/72 • **Page 238** 'His frame was impossibly slight': Tevis, (1963). • **Page 238** 'poems from outer space': ibid. • **Page 239** 'very strange and different': Burroughs, *Live*, p. 421 • **Page 239** 'It required non-acting': to Chris Charlesworth, *MM*, 13/3/76 • **Page 239** 'unembodied . . . always at one remove': Laing (1965), p. 80 • **Page 240** 'I just wish Dave': quoted Pegg, p. 388 • **Page 240** 'I've had short flirtations': to Cameron Crowe, *Playboy*, 9/76 • **Page 240** 'old vacuum-cleaner nose': *RM*, 14/6/75 • **Page 240** 'David has an extreme personality': Gillman, p. 383 • **Page 240** 'I'd found a soulmate': to Paul Du Noyer, *Mojo*, 7/02 • **Page 241** 'Give cocaine to a man': quoted Durlacher, pp. 32–4 • **Page 241** 'A very Aryan, fascist-type': to Timothy White, *Crawdaddy*, 2/78 • **Page 241** 'can be very charming': ibid. • **Page 241** 'dramatically erratic behaviour': ibid. • **Page 241** 'Everywhere I looked': to Angus MacKinnon, *NME*, 13/9/80 • **Page 242** 'pulled me off the settee': *NME*, 14/1/78 • **Page 242** 'partly autobiographical': *RM*, 2/8/75 • **Page 242** 'I've decided to write': *RS*, 2/76 • **Page 243** 'All the references within the piece': to David Cavanagh, *Q*, 2/97 • **Page 246** 'when I felt very much at peace': to Robert Hilburn, *MM*, 2/76 • **Page 247** 'There were days of such psychological': to Angus MacKinnon, *NME*, 13/9/80 • **Page 248** 'He also asked to have': to Timothy White, *Crawdaddy*, 2/78 • **Page 248** 'I'd been pretty godless': ibid. • **Page 250** 'That was recorded very much': Buckley, p. 235 • **Page 251** 'has an original timbre': James Roos, *Miami Herald*, 18/11/72 • **Page 252** 'I really, honestly and truly': *RS*, 2/76 • **Page 252** 'I have serious problems': quoted Buckley, p. 234 • **Page 252** 'I was out of my mind totally': to Angus MacKinnon, *NME*, 13/9/80 • **Page 252** 'a miserable time to live through': to David Cavanagh, *Q*, 2/97 • **Page 253** '*Station To Station* is probably the first': to Ben Edmonds, *Circus*, 27/4/76 • **Page 253** 'This time I'm going to make some': to Chris Charlesworth, *MM*, 13/3/76 • **Page 254** 'I'm trying to get over': ibid. • **Page 254** 'a bunch of lights': to Adrian Deevoy, *Q*, 6/89 • **Page 254** 'Two superstars of their time': press release • **Page 255** 'I could have been Hitler in England': to Cameron Crowe, *Playboy*, 9/76 • **Page 256** 'the best way to fight an evil force': to Timothy White, *Crawdaddy*, 2/78 • **Page 256** 'did some good because': US radio interview, 1978 • **Page 256** 'an idiot's dream': ibid. • **Page 257** 'He'll never make it': to Tina Brown, *Sunday Times Magazine*, 7/75 • **Page 258** 'a cross between James Brown': to Lisa Robinson, *NME*, 9/10/76 • **Page 259** 'totally riveted and fettered': *NME*, 2/4/77 • **Page 259** 'He was getting into his King': to Mac Garry, *ZigZag*, 3/76 • **Page 260** 'He was, in my opinion': to Timothy White, *Crawdaddy*, 2/78 • **Page 261** 'People simply can't cope': to Allan Jones, *MM*, 29/10/77 • **Page 261** 'David works very fast': to Miles, *NME*, 27/11/76 • **Page 261** 'fucks with the fabric of time': Visconti, p. 235 • **Page 261** 'I heard that it could change': Buckley (1999), p. 270 • **Page 264** Bowie explained this song: BBC Radio interview, 2000 • **Page 265** 'I think the twentieth century': Ballard, p. 14 • **Page 265** 'to accept the perverse eroticism': Ballard, p. 9 • **Page 265** 'hands down, the most repulsive': Ballard, p. 12 • **Page 266** 'It could've been anybody': to Michael Watts, *MM*, 2/78 • **Page 266** 'It was genuinely anguished': ibid. • **Page 266** 'most narrative': ibid. • **Page 267** 'this metallic, metronomic beat': to Toby Goldstein, *NME*, 24/12/77 • **Page 269** 'Music carries its own message': *NME*, 13/9/80 • **Page 269** 'To make him sound like a boy': Buckley, p. 267 • **Page 271** 'no other instrument': to Angus MacKinnon, *NME*, 22/9/79 • **Page 272** 'I have to put myself': to C.S. Murray, *NME*, 12/11/77 • **Page 272** 'the twentieth century's dystopia': Conrad, p. 319 • **Page 272** 'unsettlingly foreign': Large, p. 466 • **Page 273** 'This fascist state': Varon, p. 39 • **Page 273** 'an ambiguous place': to Jonathan Mantle, *Vogue*, 9/78 • **Page 274** 'Instead of having a lot': to Miles, *NME*, 27/11/76 • **Page 274** 'without vocals that you'd recognise': to Chris Charlesworth, *MM*, 13/3/76 • **Page 275** 'recognisable Bowie': *NME*, 16/10/76 • **Page 275**

'It's still a very organic': to Paul Du Noyer, *Mojo*, 7/02 • **Page 278** 'That rather camp': *RS*, 5/11/87 • **Page 278** 'To cause an art movement': to Lisa Robinson, *NME*, 6/3/76 • **Page 279** 'Punk was absolutely necessary': to Jean Rook, *Daily Express*, 14/2/79• **Page 279** 'Germanic influences were plain': Shrapnel, p. 85 • **Page 280** 'I wanted to give a phrase': to Michael Watts, *MM*, 2/78 • **Page 282** 'very straight from the shoulder': to Adrian Deevoy, *Q*, 6/89 • **Page 283** 'Bowie's most moving performance': *NME*, 8/10/77 • **Page 283** 'People like watching people': to Chris Charlesworth, *MM*, 13/3/76 • **Page 283** 'three oscillating VCS3 drones': Sheppard, p. 256 • **Page 284** 'I still incorporate a lot': to Michael Watts, *MM*, 2/78 • **Page 286** 'It was like a game': quoted Sheppard, p. 255 • **Page 286** 'restricted to impressionistic': ibid. • **Page 287** 'the Turks are shackled': to Allan Jones, *MM*, 29/10/77 • **Page 288** 'just a collection of stuff': to C.S. Murray, *NME*, 12/11/77 • **Page 289** 'instamatic lyric overflow': *NME*, 8/10/77 • **Page 290** 'mythic, cartoon-like': Bracewell, p. 261 • **Page 290** 'I was just a hack painter': to Allan Jones, *MM*, 29/10/77 • **Page 290** 'I'm doing lots of sculptures': to Russell Harty, TV interview, 1975 • **Page 290** 'ecstatic expressiveness': Elger, p. 58 • **Page 291** 'everything is dead': quoted Mitsch, pp. 49–50 • **Page 291** 'Mime and theatrical gesture': ibid., p. 28 • **Page 291** 'an uncompromising disregard': ibid., p. 25 • **Page 291** 'only rival': to Tony Norman, *RM*, 20/7/74 • **Page 292** 'it reminded us of our childhoods': to Bob Hart, quoted *RM*, 20/7/74 • **Page 292** 'David will write the screenplay': ibid. • **Page 292** 'I hope it's going to be out': to Robin Smith, *RM*, 16/4/77 • **Page 294** 'Friends remember him': Steve Turner, *The Independent*, 1991 • **Page 294** 'The film was a cack': to Angus MacKinnon, *NME*, 13/9/80 • **Page 296** 'taken some realist attitudes': to Timothy White, *Crawdaddy*, 2/78 • **Page 296** 'The celebrated chameleon': ibid. • **Page 296** 'I get scared stiff': *MM*, 2/78 • **Page 296** 'I think the only thing': to Jonathan Mantle, *Vogue*, 9/78 • **Page 297** 'learning to be happy': to Jean Rook, *Daily Express*, 14/2/79 • **Page 297** 'cynical period': press conference, 2/79 • **Page 299** 'I took a straightforward safari': US radio interview, 1978 • **Page 299** 'I would have thought': to Angus MacKinnon, *NME*, 13/9/80 • **Page 302** 'The one particular song': to Philip Bradley, *International Musician*, 6/90 • **Page 304** 'What I do is, say': to Angus MacKinnon, *NME*, 13/9/80 • **Page 306** 'If I'm bored': to Robert Hilburn, *MM*, 14/9/74 • **Page 307** 'a piece of self-plagiarism': Jon Savage, *MM*, 27/5/79; Angus MacKinnon, *NME*, 26/5/79; Paul Yamada, *New York Rocker*, 7/79 • **Page 309** 'Having played it': to Angus MacKinnon, *NME*, 13/9/80 • **Page 313** 'I programmed a descending': Visconti, p. 283 • **Page 313** 'We'd go back': ibid., p. 286 • **Page 315** 'Those three particular lines': to Angus MacKinnon, *NME*, 13/9/80 • **Page 315** 'You have to accommodate': to Timothy White, *Musician*, 7/90 • **Page 316** 'For me, it's a story': to Angus MacKinnon, *NME*, 13/9/80 • **Page 317** 'I've always hated him so': Meltzer, p. 218 • **Page 317** 'The next religion might come': *Friends*, 30/10/70 • **Page 318** 'the lyric is often glossed': Pegg (2006), p. 216 • **Page 318** 'quite proud about it': Buckley, p. 331 • **Page 319** 'when he was young': Robert Christgau, *Consumer Guide to the 90s*, p. 66 • **Page 323** 'I can't write young': to Angus MacKinnon, *NME*, 13/9/80 • **Page 324** 'My problem was cocaine': to Tricia Jones, *i-D*, 5/87 • **Page 324** 'The later paintings': Stephen Paul Miller, p. 219 • **Page 325** 'a grinding, dissonant': *NME*, 20/9/80 • **Page 325** 'Scary Monsters for me': to Timothy White, *Musician*, 7/90

Afterword

Page 330 'a disintegrative effect': quoted Mellor, p. 32 • **Page 332** 'The cutting-edge ensemble': Pegg (2006), p. 480 • **Page 335** 'unbelievably complicated': quoted ibid. p. 360

Appendix

Page 338 'If anything, David was a poet': to author • **Page 341** 'He was probably aiming higher': to Mark Paytress, *RC*, 5/00 • **Page 343** 'It took me a long time': to Paul Du Noyer, *Mojo*, 7/02 • **Page 344** 'I borrowed someone else's': to Tony Horkins, *International Musician*, 12/91 • **Page 346** 'I'm not very sure of myself': to C.S. Murray, *NME*, 11/8/73 • **Page 353** 'It goes down very well': *MM*, 11/66 • **Page 354** 'were either homosexual': quoted Davenport-Hines, p.256 • **Page 355** 'I envisage a scenario': to Martin Hayman, *Sounds*, 4/8/73 • **Page 364** 'in the style of a beat poet': Cann, p. 106 • **Page 364** 'like an unpolished recording': ibid. • **Page 367** 'I would have been doing stage musicals': to David Cavanagh, *Q*, 2/97 • **Page 369** 'a true oddity': Cann, p. 106 • **Page 369** 'the test of a first-rate intelligence': F. Scott Fitzgerald, 'The Crack-Up' (1936) • **Page 369** 'two albums he had been given': *Mojo*, 7/02 • **Page 371** 'linchpin . . . throbbing, sarcastic': ibid. • **Page 373** 'What interested me in the first place': to Penny Valentine, *Sounds*, 9/12/72

Bibliography

Recommendations for Further Reading

Kevin Cann's illustrated chronology of Bowie's career in London, *Any Day Now*, is a stunning visual and factual delight. Equally striking is *Moonage Daydream*, which mixes tantalising commentary from Bowie with seminal photographs by Mick Rock.

Paul Trynka's recent Bowie biography, *Starman*, is impeccably researched and told, depending on interviews with almost every surviving significant figure in his subject's career. For critical insight allied to biography, read David Buckley's highly rewarding *Strange Fascination*; while Nicholas Pegg's encyclopaedia, *The Complete David Bowie*, not only lives up to its title but is immensely readable and thought-provoking throughout. The grandparents of Bowie biography, however, remain the Gillmans, for their madness-heavy account of Aladdin (In)Sane; George Tremlett, thanks to his access to the pre-Ziggy Bowie; and the ever-loyal Ken Pitt, Bowie's closest adviser in the years leading up to his fame. By necessity, Tony Visconti's auto-biography deals with other subjects besides Bowie, but his account of their collaborations over the course of 30 years is fascinating. Finally, Mark Paytress' study of the making of *Ziggy Stardust* is arguably the single most provocative text about Bowie's self-creation as a superstar.

Several websites contain rich resources of Bowie material, notably Bowie Wonderland, 5 Years, Bowiezone, The Ziggy Stardust Companion and Teenage Wildlife. Finally, anyone who has enjoyed reading this book should also look at Chris O'Leary's Pushing Ahead

Of The Dame blog, an ongoing (at the time of writing) and intriguing critique of Bowie's entire catalogue, which I have resisted the strong temptation to read for fear that it might unduly influence my own thinking. You, however, don't have that problem!

Almond, Marc: *Tainted Life* (London: Sidgwick & Jackson, 1999)

Altman, Dennis: *Homosexual: Oppression and Liberation* (London: Allen Lane, 1974)

Archer, Michael: *Art Since 1960* (London: Thames & Hudson, 1997)

Ariel, David: *Kabbalah: The Mystic Quest in Judaism* (Lanham: Rowman & Littlefield, 2006)

Ballard, J.G.: *Crash* (London: Jonathan Cape, 1973)

Barber, Richard: *The Holy Grail: Reason & Belief* (London: Allen Lane, 2004)

Bardsley, Garth: *Stop The World: The Biography of Anthony Newley* (London: Oberon Books, 2003)

Barker, Hugh, & Taylor, Yuval: *Faking It: The Quest for Authenticity in Popular Music* (London: Faber & Faber, 2007)

Barrett, David V.: *The New Believers: A Survey of Sects, Cults and Alternative Religions* (London: Cassell, 2001)

Beckett, Andy: *When the Lights Went Out: Britain in the Seventies* (London: Faber & Faber, 2009)

Bockris, Victor: *Lou Reed: The Biography* (London: Plexus, 1995)

Bourdon, David: *Warhol* (New York: Harry N. Abrams, 1989)

Bowie, Angela: *Free Spirit* (London: Mushroom Books, 1981)

Bowie, Angela, & Carr, Patrick: *Backstage Passes* (London: Orion, 1993)

Bowie, David, & Rock, Mick: *Moonage Daydream: The Life and Times of Ziggy Stardust* (New York: Universe, 2005)

Bowman, David: *Fa Fa Fa Fa Fa Fa: The Adventures of Talking Heads in the 20th Century* (London: Bloomsbury, 2001)

Boy George & Gorman, Paul: *Straight* (London: Century, 2005)

Bracewell, Michael: *Re-Make/Re-Model: Art, Pop Fashion & the Making of Roxy Music 1953–1972* (London: Faber & Faber, 2007)

Braun, Eric: *Frightening the Horses: Gay Icons of the Cinema* (London: Reynolds & Hearn, 2002)

Brennan, J.H.: *Occult Reich* (London: Futura, 1974)

Brinton, Crane: *Nietzsche* (New York: Harper & Row, 1965)

Buckley, David: *Strange Fascination – David Bowie: The Definitive Story* (London: Virgin, 2005)

Burroughs, William S.: *Burroughs Live 1960–1997: The Collected Interviews of William S. Burroughs* (Los Angeles: Semiotext(e), 2000)

Cann, Kevin: *Any Day Now: David Bowie, The London Years: 1947–1974* (London: Adelita, 2010)

Carducci, Joe: *Rock and the Pop Narcotic* (Los Angeles: 2.13.61, 1994)

Christgau, Robert: *Christgau's Consumer Guide* (New York: St Martin's Griffin, 2000)

Clarke, Gerald: *Get Happy: The Life of Judy Garland* (London: Little, Brown, 2000)

Clutterbuck, Richard: *Britain in Agony: The Growth of Political Violence* (London: Penguin, 1980)

Cohn, Nik: *I Am Still The Greatest Says Johnny Angelo* (London: Secker & Warburg, 1967; rewritten edn., London: Penguin, 1970)

Conrad, Peter: *Modern Times, Modern Places: Life & Art in the 20th Century* (London: Thames & Hudson, 1998)

Crowley, Aleister: *The Confessions of Aleister Crowley* (London: Jonathan Cape, 1969)

Crowley, Aleister: *White Stains* (London: Duckworth, 1973)

Davenport-Hines, Richard: *The Pursuit of Oblivion: A Global History of Narcotics 1500–2000* (London: Weidenfeld & Nicolson, 2001)

Davies, Steven Paul: *Out at the Movies: A History of Gay Cinema* (Harpenden: Kamera Books, 2008)

DeGroot, Gerald: *The Seventies Unplugged: A Kaleidoscopic Look at a Violent Decade* (London: Macmillan, 2010)

DeLillo, Don: *Great Jones Street* (New York: Houghton Mifflin, 1973)

Dick, Philip K.: *The World Jones Made* (London: Panther, 1970)

Doggett, Peter: *Lou Reed: Growing Up In Public* (London: Omnibus Press, 1991)

Doggett, Peter: *The Art and Music of John Lennon* (London: Omnibus Press, 2005)

Doggett, Peter: *There's A Riot Going On: Revolutionaries, Rock Stars and the Rise and Fall of the 60s Counter-Culture* (Edinburgh: Canongate, 2007)

Doggett, Peter: *You Never Give Me Your Money: The Battle for the Soul of the Beatles* (London: The Bodley Head, 2009)

Downing, David: *Future Rock* (London: Panther, 1976)

Drury, Nevill: *Magic & Witchcraft* (London: Thames & Hudson, 2003)

Dunn, S. Watson: *Advertising: Its Role in Modern Marketing* (New York: Holt, Rinehart & Winston, 1969)

Durlacher, Julian: *Agenda Cocaine* (London: Carlton Books, 2000)

Elger, Dietmar: *Expressionism: A Revolution in German Art* (Cologne: Taschen, 1998)

Ellison, Harlan: *The Beast That Shouted Love at the Heart of the World* (London: Pan, 1979)

Feinemann, Neil: *Nicholas Roeg* (Boston: Twayne Publishers, 1978)

Fiell, Charlotte & Peter: *Decorative Art 70s* (Cologn: Taschen, 2006)

Gale, Matthew: *Dada & Surrealism* (London: Phaidon, 1997)

Garber, Marjorie: *Vice Versa* (London: Hamish Hamilton, 1996)

Geiger, John: *Nothing Is True Everything Is Permitted: The Life of Brion Gysin* (New York: disinformation, 2005)

Gillman, Peter & Leni: *Alias David Bowie* (London: Hodder & Stoughton, 1986)

Godwin, John: *Occult America* (New York: Doubleday, 1972)

Groom, Chris: *Rockin' Croydon* (Purley: Wombat, 1998)

Hadleigh, Boze: *The Vinyl Closet: Gays in the Music World* (San Diego: Los Hombres Press, 1991)

Harrison, Ted: *Elvis People: The Cult of the King* (London: Fount, 1992)

Heinlein, Robert A.: *Starman Jones* (Sevenoaks: NEL, 1976)

Heller, Steven: *Iron Fists: Branding the 20th Century Totalitarian State* (London: Phaidon, 2008)

Hewitt, Paolo, & Hellier, John: *All Too Beautiful: Steve Marriott* (London: Helter Skelter, 2004)

Heylin, Clinton: *Babylon's Burning: From Punk to Grunge* (Edinburgh: Canongate, 2007)

Hilton, Christopher: *The Wall: The People's Story* (Stroud: Sutton Publishing, 2001)

Hopkins, David: *After Modern Art 1945–2000* (Oxford: OUP, 2000)

Horn, Adrian: *Juke Box Britain: Americanisation and Youth Culture 1945–60* (Manchester: Manchester University Press, 2009)

Hoskyns, Barney: *Glam! Bowie, Bolan and the Glitter Rock Revolution* (London: Faber & Faber, 1998)

Humphreys, Christmas: *Zen Buddhism* (London: Diamond Books, 1996 [1949])

Hunter, Ian: *Diary of a Rock 'n' Roll Star* (London: Panther, 1974)

Hutton, Ronald: *The Triumph of the Moon: A History of Modern Pagan Witchcraft* (Oxford: OUP, 1999)

Huxley, Aldous: *Brave New World Revisited* (London: Chatto & Windus, 1959)

Isherwood, Christopher: *The Berlin of Sally Bowles* (London: The Hogarth Press, 1975)

Izod, John: *The Films of Nicholas Roeg: Myth and Mind* (London: Macmillan, 1992)

Joselit, David: *American Art Since 1945* (London: Thames & Hudson, 2003)

Kaufman, Will: *American Culture in the 1970s* (Edinburgh: Edinburgh University Press, 2009)

Kent, Nick: *Apathy For The Devil: A 1970s Memoir* (London: Faber & Faber, 2010)

Kerouac, Jack: *On The Road* (New York: Buccaneer, 1957)

Laing, R.D.: *The Divided Self: An Existential Study in Sanity & Madness* (London: Pelican, 1965)

Laing, R.D.: *The Politics of Experience and the Bird of Paradise* (London: Penguin, 1967)

Laing, R.D., & Esterson, A.: *Sanity, Madness and the Family* (London: Pelican, 1970)

Lanza, Joseph: *Fragile Geometry: The Films, Philosophy & Misadventures of Nicholas Roeg* (New York: PAJ Publications, 1989)

Large, David Clay: *Berlin: A Modern History* (London: Allen Lane, 2001)

Lasch, Christopher: *The Culture of Narcissism* (New York: Norton, 1979)

Leech, Kenneth: *Youthquake: The Growth of a Counter-Culture Through Two Decades* (London: Sheldon Press, 1973)

Leroy, Dan: *The Greatest Music Never Sold* (New York: Backbeat, 2007)

Lulu: *I Don't Want To Fight* (London: TimeWarner, 2003)

Luytens, Dominic, & Hislop, Kirsty: *70s Style & Design* (London: Thames & Hudson, 2009)

MacDonald, Ian: *Revolution in the Head: The Beatles' Records and the Sixties* (London: Vintage, 2005)

Mailer, Norman: *A Fire on the Moon* (London: Weidenfeld & Nicolson, 1970)

Marcus, Greil: *In The Fascist Bathroom: Writings on Punk, 1977–1982* (London: Viking, 1993)

Marcus, Greil: *Lipstick Traces: A Secret History of the Twentieth Century* (London: Picador, 1997 [1989])

Mellor, David: *The Sixties Art Scene in London* (London: Phaidon, 1993)

Meltzer, Richard: *A Whore Just Like the Rest: The Music Writings of Richard Meltzer* (Cambridge: Da Capo Press, 2000)

Miller, James: *Almost Grown: The Rise of Rock* (London: Arrow Books, 2000)

Miller, Stephen Paul: *The Seventies Now: Culture as Surveillance* (Durham: Duke University Press, 1999)

Mitchell, Tim: *Sedition & Alchemy: A Biography of John Cale* (London: Peter Owen, 2003)

Mitsch, Erwin: *Egon Schiele* (London: Phaidon, 1994)

Morgan, Ted: *Literary Outlaw: The Life & Times of William S. Burroughs* (London: The Bodley Head, 1991)

Müller, Jürgen (ed.): *Movies of the 70s* (Cologne: Taschen, 2003)

Needs, Kris, & Porter, Dick: *Trash! The Complete New York Dolls* (London: Plexus, 2006)

Nietzsche, Friedrich: *Thus Spake Zarathustra* (London: Penguin, 1969)

Nuttall, Jeff: *Bomb Culture* (London: Paladin, 1970)

Oldham, Andrew Loog: *Stoned: A Memoir of London in the 1960s* (New York: St Martin's Press, 2000)

Orwell, George: *Nineteen Eighty-Four* (London: Penguin, 2000 [1949])

Ott, Frederick W.: *The Great German Films: From Before World War I to the Present* (Seacaucus: Citadel Press, 1986)

Ozaniec, Naomi: *The Illustrated Guide to the Tarot* (New Alresford: Godsfield, 1999)

Packard, Vince: *The Hidden Persuaders* (London: Longmans, 1957)

Padel, Ruth: *I'm A Man: Sex, Gods and Rock 'n' Roll* (London: Faber & Faber, 2000)

Parker, Peter: *Isherwood: A Life* (London: Picador, 2004)

Paytress, Mark: *Twentieth Century Boy: The Marc Bolan Story* (London: Sidgwick & Jackson, 1992)

Paytress, Mark: *Classic Rock Albums: Ziggy Stardust* (New York: Schirmer Books, 1998)

Pearson, Keith Ansell, & Large, Duncan (eds.): *The Nietzsche Reader* (Oxford: Blackwell, 2006)

Pedler, Dominic: *The Songwriting Secrets of the Beatles* (London: Omnibus Press, 2003)

Peebles, Andy: *The Lennon Tapes* (London: BBC Publications, 1981)

Peel, John, & Ravenscroft, Sheila: *Margrave of the Marshes* (London: Bantam Press, 2005)

Pegg, Nicholas: *The Complete David Bowie* (London: Reynolds & Hearn Ltd, 2000 & subsequent editions)

Peiry, Lucienne: *Art Brut: The Origins of Outsider Art* (Paris: Flammarion, 2001)

Pitt, Kenneth: *Bowie: The Pitt Report* (London: Design Music, 1983)

Prendergast, Mark: *The Ambient Century* (London: Bloomsbury, 2003)

Reynolds, Simon, & Press, Joy: *The Sex Revolts: Gender, Rebellion & Rock 'n' Roll* (London: Serpent's Tail, 1995)

Rhodes, Colin: *Outside Art: Spontaneous Alternatives* (London: Thames & Hudson, 2000)

Richie, Alexandra: *Faust's Metropolis: A History of Berlin* (London: HarperCollins, 1998)

Rodgers, Bruce: *The Queens' Vernacular: A Gay Lexicon* (San Francisco: Straight Arrow, 1972)

Rombes, Nicholas: *A Cultural Dictionary of Punk 1974–1982* (London: Continuum, 2009)

Rosen, Robert: *Nowhere Man: The Final Years of John Lennon* (London: Fusion Press, 2000)

Ross, Alex: *The Rest is Noise: Listening to the Twentieth Century* (London: Harper Perennial, 2009)

Rotten, Johnny: *No Irish, No Blacks, No Dogs* (London: Plexus, 1994)

Salwolke, Scott: *Nicholas Roeg Film by Film* (Jefferson: McFarland & Co., 1993)

Sandbrook, Dominic: *White Heat: A History of Britain in the Swinging Sixties* (London: Little, Brown, 2006)

Sandbrook, Dominic: *State of Emergency: The Way We Were: Britain, 1970–1974* (London: Allen Lane, 2010)

Savage, Jon: *England's Dreaming: Sex Pistols and Punk Rock* (London: Faber & Faber, 1991)

Schulman, Bruce J.: *The Seventies: The Great Shift in American Culture, Society and Politics* (Cambridge: Da Capo, 2002)

Shail, Robert (ed.): *Seventies British Cinema* (London: Palgrave Macmillan, 2008)

Shepherd, Simon, & Wallis, Mick: *Coming On Strong: Gay Politics & Culture* (London: Unwin Hyman, 1989)

Sheppard, David: *On Some Faraway Beach: The Life and Times of Brian Eno* (London: Orion, 2008)

Short, Robert: *The Age of Gold: Surrealistic Cinema* (London: Creation, 2003)

Shrapnel, Norman: *The Seventies: Britain's Inward March* (London: Constable, 1980)

Sinfield, Alan: *Literature, Politics and Culture in Postwar Britain* (London: Continuum, 2004)

Sontag, Susan: *Against Interpretation* (New York: Dell, 1967)

Sounes, Howard: *Seventies* (London: Simon & Schuster, 2006)

Spoto, Donald: *Blue Angel: The Life of Marlene Dietrich* (New York: Doubleday, 1992)

Spurling, Hilary: *The Girl From the Fiction Department: A Portrait of Sonia Orwell* (London: Hamish Hamilton, 2002)

Stevenson, Nick: *David Bowie: Fame, Sound & Vision* (Cambridge: Polity Press, 2006)

Tent, Pam: *Midnight at the Palace: My Life as a Fabulous Cockette* (Los Angeles: Alyson Books, 2004)

Tevis, Walter: *The Man Who Fell To Earth* (New York: Fawcett Publications, 1963; revised edn Boston: Gregg Press, 1978)

Thomas, Denis: *The Visible Persuaders* (London: Hutchinson, 1967)

Thompson, Dave: *Children of the Revolution: Gum Into Glam 1967–76* (London: privately published, 1987)

Thompson, Dave: *To Major Tom* (London: Sanctuary, 2002)

Tremlett, George: *David Bowie: Living on the Brink* (London: Century Books, 1996)

Trynka, Paul: *Iggy Pop: The Biography: Open Up & Bleed* (London: Sphere, 2007)

Trynka, Paul: *Starman: David Bowie, The Definitive Biography* (London: Sphere, 2011)

Valentine, Gary: *New York Rocker: My Life in the Blank Generation* (London: Sidgwick & Jackson, 2002)

Varon, Jeremy: *Bringing the War Home: The Weather Underground, the Red Army Faction, and Revolutionary Violence in the Sixties and Seventies* (Berkeley: University of California Press, 2004)

Visconti, Tony: *Bowie, Bolan & the Brooklyn Boy* (London: HarperCollins, 2007)

Waite, Geoff: *Nietzsche's Corps/e: Aesthetics, Politics, Prophecy, or The Spectacular Technoculture of Everyday Life* (Durham: Duke University Press, 1996)

Walker, Alexander: *National Heroes: British Cinema in the Seventies & Eighties* (London: Harrap, 1985)

Walker, Martin: *The National Front* (London: Fontana, 1977)

Waugh, Evelyn: *Vile Bodies* (London: Penguin, 1996 [1930])

Wheen, Francis: *Strange Days Indeed: The Golden Age of Paranoia* (London: Fourth Estate, 2009)

Willett, John: *The Theatre of the Weimar Republic* (New York: Holmes & Meier, 1988)

Wilson, Colin: *The Occult* (London: Granada, 1979 [1971])

Wolfe, Tom: *Mauve Gloves & Madmen, Clutter & Vine* (New York: Farrar, Strauss, & Giroux, 1976)

Wood, Ean: *Dietrich: A Biography* (London: Sanctuary, 2002)

Zanetta, Tony, & Edwards, Henry: *Stardust: The Life and Times of David Bowie* (London: Michael Joseph, 1986)

Among the periodicals consulted (with abbreviations used in the Source Notes) were: *After Dark, Beat Instrumental, The Big Issue, Billboard, Boston Globe, Boston Herald, Cash Box, Cavalier, Chicago Tribune, Circus, Crawdaddy, Creem, Daily Express, Daily Mirror, Dirt, Disc & Music Echo, Evening News & Star, Evening Standard, The Face, Fan Magazine, Frendz, Friends, Gay News, The Guardian, Hello!, i-D, Ikon, Ink, Interna-*

tional Musician, International Times (IT), Jackie, Jeremy, Let It Rock, Man, Myth & Magic, Melody Maker (MM), Miami Herald, Milwaukee Journal, Mirabelle, Mojo, Montreal Star, Music Business Review, Music Now!, Music Scene, Music Week, Musician, New Musical Express (NME), New Orleans Figaro, New York Rocker, New York Times, New Yorker, Newsweek, The Observer, Ottawa Citizen, Ottawa Journal, Oz, People Magazine, Philadelphia Bulletin, Phonograph Record, Playboy, Plays and Players, Q, Radio Times, RCD, Record Collector (RC), Record Mirror (RM), Record Retailer, Record World, Rock Magazine, Rock Scene, Rolling Stone (RS), Sounds, Suburban Press, Sunday Times, The Times, Toronto Globe Mail, Toronto Star, Uncut, Village Voice, Vogue, Washington Post, Windsor Star, The Word, ZigZag

Index

Numbers in square brackets [ ] refer to individual song entries.
Page numbers in bold refer to main entry for song or album.